ANDEAN CIVILIZATION

A TRIBUTE TO
MICHAEL E. MOSELEY

UCLA COTSEN INSTITUTE OF ARCHAEOLOGY PRESS

MONOGRAPHS

CONTRIBUTIONS IN FIELD RESEARCH AND CURRENT ISSUES IN ARCHAEOLOGICAL METHOD AND THEORY

ANDEAN CIVILIZATION

A TRIBUTE TO
MICHAEL E. MOSELEY

EDITED BY
JOYCE MARCUS AND PATRICK RYAN WILLIAMS

MONOGRAPH 63
COTSEN INSTITUTE OF ARCHAEOLOGY
UNIVERSITY OF CALIFORNIA, LOS ANGELES

THE COTSEN INSTITUTE OF ARCHAEOLOGY PRESS is the publishing unit of the Cotsen Institute of Archaeology at UCLA. The Cotsen Institute is a premier research organization dedicated to the creation, dissemination, and conservation of archaeological knowledge and heritage. It is home to both the Interdepartmental Archaeology Graduate Program and the UCLA/Getty Master's Program in the Conservation of Archaeological and Ethnographic Materials. The Cotsen Institute provides a forum for innovative faculty research, graduate education, and public programs at UCLA in an effort to positively impact the academic, local and global communities. Established in 1973, the Cotsen Institute is at the forefront of archaeological research, education, conservation and publication and is an active contributor to interdisciplinary research at UCLA.

The Cotsen Institute Press specializes in producing high-quality academic volumes in several different series, including *Monographs*, *World Heritage and Monuments*, *Cotsen Advanced Seminars*, and *Ideas, Debates and Perspectives*. The Press is committed to making the fruits of archaeological research accessible to professionals, scholars, students, and the general public. We are able to do this through the generosity of Lloyd E. Cotsen, longtime Institute volunteer and benefactor, who has provided an endowment that allows us to subsidize our publishing program and produce superb volumes at an affordable price. Publishing in nine different series, our award-winning archaeological publications receive critical acclaim in both the academic and popular communities.

THE COTSEN INSTITUTE OF ARCHAEOLOGY AT UCLA
Charles Stanish, Director
Elizabeth Klarich, Assistant Director
Shauna K. Mecartea, Executive Editor & Media Relations Officer
Eric C. Gardner, Publications Coordinator

EDITORIAL BOARD OF THE COTSEN INSTITUTE OF ARCHAEOLOGY
Jeanne E. Arnold, Christopher B. Donnan, Shauna K. Mecartea, John K. Papadopoulos, James Sackett, Charles Stanish, and Willeke Wendrich

EDITORIAL ADVISORY BOARD
Chapurukha Kusimba, Joyce Marcus, Colin Renfrew, and John Yellen

This book is set in 10-point Janson Text, with titles in 26-point AT Classic.
Edited by Marjorie Pannell
Proofread by Carol Leyba
Designed by William Morosi
Index by Robert and Cynthia Swanson

Library of Congress Cataloging-in-Publication Data
Andean civilization : a tribute to Michael E. Moseley / edited by Joyce Marcus and Patrick Ryan Williams.
    p. cm. -- (Monograph / Cotsen Institute of Archaeology ; 63)
Includes bibliographical references and index.
ISBN 978-1-931745-53-6 (pbk. : alk. paper) -- ISBN 978-1-931745-54-3 (cloth : alk. paper)
1. Andes Region--Civilization. 2. Andes Region--Antiquities. 3. Indians of South America--Andes Region--History. 4. Indians of South America--Andes Region--Antiquities.
5. Indians of South America--Andes Region--Social life and customs. I. Marcus, Joyce. II. Williams, P. Ryan (Patrick Ryan) III. Moseley, Michael Edward. IV. Title. V. Series.

F2229.A563 2009
980--dc22

2008054452

CONTENTS

LIST OF FIGURES

LIST OF TABLES

CHAPTER 1

MICHAEL E. MOSELEY AND THE FOUNDATIONS OF ANDEAN CIVILIZATION

JOYCE MARCUS AND CHARLES STANISH

THIS BOOK CAME INTO being for several reasons, foremost among them our desire to thank Michael E. Moseley for the impact he has had on our lives and for his unique contributions to our understanding of Andean societies. We also wish to demonstrate how an individual's research interests can create what is effectively an entirely new field of anthropological archaeology. These chapters are not just tied together by our affiliation and affection for Mike but constitute a coherent set of studies informed by Moseley's far-ranging intellect and by a set of questions that reflect the current state of Andean archaeology.

We consider ourselves very lucky to have been Moseley's students, and each of us has benefited from his special style of mentoring. As many readers already know, Moseley is passionate and enthusiastic about archaeology. Less well known is his enthusiasm for the projects of his students and his unfailing confidence in his students' abilities. In fact, Moseley usually has confidence in his students long before they do, and this is one of the reasons he continues to be such an effective mentor. He inspired us and keeps us going precisely because he has so much confidence in us.

For these and countless other gifts we thank you, Michael Moseley, and we hope you enjoy this book. Since we could not include contributions from all of your former students working on the north coast (at

Chan Chan and other projects) or the south coast (at Moquegua and beyond), a future volume compiling their contributions should come as no surprise.

THE EARLY YEARS

Michael Edward Moseley has been interested in the remote past for a long time. At age ten, while visiting a local museum in Wiesbaden, Germany, where his father was stationed as a U.S. Air Force medical officer, Mike showed great interest in many of the fossils on display. By age eleven he had seen his first arrowheads in a museum in Washington, D.C., and he knew then that the field of archaeology was for him.

When the Moseley family moved to California, Mike began volunteering at the San Bernardino County Museum in Redlands, California. Only thirteen, he was already digging with many older amateur archaeologists (some of this work is described in Chapter 22). His volunteer work took him to the California desert, and at some point during those hot excavations Mike recognized that he not only loved archaeological fieldwork but needed more training from professional archaeologists. Thus, by the time he was fourteen, Moseley's mother was driving him to an archaeological field school in Colorado. There Mike found himself digging at a Plains Pueblo site. By age fifteen he was working with the Museum of Northern Arizona in Flagstaff. Throughout his teenage years, Mike excavated in the Southwest every year, becoming a dedicated and experienced fieldworker. His passion for fieldwork, built over many years in his youth, continues unabated to this day.

Moseley's academic trajectory paralleled his deepening interest in field studies. After completing high school he enrolled for two years at the University of Redlands, where he minored in geology and majored in anthropology. Subsequently he transferred to the University of California at Berkeley, graduating in 1963. His adviser, J. Desmond Clark, steered Moseley to Harvard University, where Moseley received his doctorate in anthropology in 1968. He was offered a professional appointment at Harvard, which gave him the opportunity to start developing the models for which he became renowned.

ENGAGEMENT WITH PERU

The better part of Moseley's fieldwork has been conducted in the Andes, initially with small grants and small field crews and subsequently as leader and mentor to many students who have gone on to notable academic and research positions. Peru came into particular focus for Moseley during his graduate studies, when he wrote a paper for Gordon R. Willey's Anthropology 207 seminar. In that paper Moseley began looking at societies that sustained themselves with marine resources. Out of this initial survey of the literature he formulated his hypothesis concerning the Maritime Foundations of Andean Civilization, or the MFAC hypothesis. Simply stated, Moseley's hypothesis was that the initial rise of social complexity along the coast of Peru could be sustained by marine resources. According to Moseley, the MFAC hypothesis "was formulated as an inductive, ad hoc explanation for a corpus of information on early coastal sites that accumulated gradually." In developing this hypothesis, Moseley had been influenced by Max Uhle, who was the first to recognize that the shell mound people that dotted the Pacific coast predated later civilizations. Moseley was also influenced by Junius Bird's pioneering research in Patagonia, Chile, and at Huaca Prieta in the Chicama Valley of Peru.

Moseley then began to think about how the maritime model could be tested. He decided he was ready to conduct fieldwork in Peru to see if such a model could be supported with empirical research.

Arriving in Peru in 1966 for the first time, he set about conducting fieldwork on the central coast, investigating the very early societies that relied on marine resources. This work formed the empirical foundation of his Ph.D. dissertation, "Changing Subsistence Patterns: Late Preceramic Archaeology of the Central Peruvian Coast," which Moseley successfully defended in 1968. Together, that dissertation and his early fieldwork laid the groundwork for his 1975 pathbreaking book, *Maritime Foundations of Andean Civilization*, in which Moseley articulated the broad thesis that stable and localized resources could provide the subsistence base of a complex society. Those resources could be either grain agriculture or marine resources, which would be readily available to people living on the narrow strip of coast between the steep Andean foothills and the biorich Pacific Ocean. The book proved to be a watershed in Andean studies, redirecting subsequent studies along new paths. In modern scholarship its influence is equaled only by John Murra's thesis of vertical archipelago or zonal complementarity and María Rostworowski's model of specialization among coastal communities.

At the end of his first year of teaching at Harvard University, during which he offered courses on Andean prehistory and on method and theory in archaeology (the latter co-taught with Gordon Willey), Moseley spent the summer in Cambridge writing a grant proposal for a project at the great prehistoric metropolis of Chan Chan. This new field project in Peru would be a major departure from Moseley's previous focus on the Preceramic period. The size and monumentality of Chan Chan would have posed formidable challenges to any project director, but Moseley was up to the task and secured major grants to start a new project. Moseley focused on both the hinterland of Chan Chan as well as the central part of Chan Chan, which covers 6 km^2 and consists of ten large walled enclosures (*ciudadelas*), nine of which—Rivero, Velarde, Laberinto, Tschudi, Bandelier, Squier, Uhle, Chayhuac, and Gran Chimú—are rectangular in plan and range from 88,000 to 220,000 m^2 in area.

Moseley took many students to Chan Chan and gave them rare opportunities to develop their own projects and theses; some of the contributors to this book got their start in Andean archaeology at Chan Chan. Among the many students who worked with Moseley at Chan Chan and in the Moche Valley were Garth Bawden, Geoff Conrad, Kent Day, Richard Keatinge, Ulana Klymyshyn, Alan Kolata, James Kus, Paul Ossa,

Shelia Griffis Pozorski, Thomas Pozorski, John Topic, and Theresa Lange Topic.

By directing his attention to Chan Chan, Moseley planned to shed light on urbanism and the Kingdom of Chimor. Moseley focused special attention on how such a huge city grew in size through time, how it continued to feed its growing population, and most of all, how it organized its work force to construct a series of impressive architectural compounds and irrigation works. Moseley invited all the students he could to join him in tackling the challenges that such an immense city posed. The Chan Chan-Moche Valley Project began in 1969 and lasted until 1974, although many spinoff projects continued for years afterward.

MODEL BUILDING: THE KEY ROLE PLAYED BY NATURAL DISASTERS

Michael Moseley is known for the theoretical innovations he has introduced, and for his singular ability to combine data and theory. He virtually stood Andean archaeology on its head by demonstrating the long- and short-term influences of the natural environment on human culture and settlement choices in the Andes. The dynamic relationship of humans and the environment has long been a central concern for Moseley, and his models incorporate many kinds of natural phenomena that formerly had been overlooked in Andean archaeological reports. One phenomenon that exemplifies this approach is the occurrence of natural catastrophes. Using paleoclimatological and archaeological data, Moseley has shown the effects of El Niño on prehistoric agricultural constructions. He has similarly forced researchers to consider the effects of downcutting rivers and large-scale earth movements in understanding irrigation and settlement patterns. This attention to the natural environment has led to a much more rigorous research climate, one that allows a more nuanced understanding of the developing political economy in early Andean civilizations.

THE MOQUEGUA VALLEY OF SOUTHERN PERU

Moseley left Harvard University to take a position as curator of Middle and South American archaeology and anthropology at the Field Museum of Natural History in Chicago. Mike's colleague (and former student)

Robert Feldman joined Mike as a research associate and visiting curator at the Field Museum as well.

During that time, Mike met Robert Pritzker, a member of the Field Museum's board and a strong supporter of science and the arts. Pritzker was also a shareholder in a company that had a financial interest in the Southern Peru Copper Corporation (SPCC), based in Moquegua and Ilo on the south coast of Peru. The director of the mine's operation in Moquegua and Cuajone, Victor Barua, and his wife, Lucy, had asked Pritzker if he could help locate an archaeologist who would establish a research program in Moquegua. Pritzker put Mike in contact with Victor and Lucy, and with the addition of Dr. Fernando Cabieses, the Programa Contisuyo was born.

The sheer amount of work that has been and continues to be conducted under the auspices of Programa Contisuyo is amazing. Most of the valley, from 3200 meters above sea level to the coast, has been surveyed and published by a number of archaeologists, including Bruce Owen, Ryan Williams, Donna Nash, Paul Goldstein, Charles Stanish, Mark Aldenderfer, Antonio Ribeiro, Don Rice, and Bertha Vargas. Paul Goldstein has conducted continuous research at the site complex of Omo, first discovered by Mike and colleagues after viewing air photographs obtained by Robert Feldman.

Programa Contisuyo was a unique organization. Partially funded by SPCC and by private donors such as Pritzker, the Programa offered researchers from Peru, the United States, and at least half a dozen other countries the opportunity to work in the entire Department of Moquegua. Mike was always generous with his resources, particularly his beloved big blue Ford truck, and as a result, all kinds of research flourished.

It was around this time that the site of Cerro Baúl was first described in a scientific journal, *Gaceta Andina*, by Luis Lumbreras, Elías Mujica, and Rodolfo Vera. Entitled "Cerro Baúl: Un enclave Wari en territorio Tiwanaku," the article brought to light this incredible site in the southern Peruvian desert. Mike and Bob Feldman began work there, in collaboration with their Peruvian colleagues. Work at Cerro Baúl has continued to the present day and is directed by Donna Nash and Ryan Williams.

After a good stint at the Field Museum from 1976 to 1984, Mike left for warmer climes, taking a job at the University of Florida at Gainesville. Programa Contisuyo continued to operate with a younger generation of Mike's students at the helm, while Mike continued to provide intellectual direction for much of their work.

Moseley's continuous labor in the field is noteworthy and impressive. He continues to do fieldwork in Peru every year, and it is this fieldwork that has given him unparalleled knowledge of the coastline and some of the Pacific watershed valleys. From the north coast to the far south coast, Moseley's projects and excavations have made major contributions to understanding the pace and tempo of developments from the Preceramic period to the rise and fall of militaristic empires.

An example of Michael Moseley's influence is seen in a 2005 article by Moseley, Donna Nash, Ryan Williams, Ana Miranda, Mario Ruales, and Susan deFrance. The influence of that archaeological study is expected to extend well beyond the fields of urban studies, anthropology, and archaeology. It is a case study of the rise and fall of two expansionist empires that coexisted for a substantial period of time, apparently without either empire succeeding in dominating the other. The borders of the Wari and Tiwanaku empires almost met in the middle of the Moquegua Valley of Peru, not far from Cerro Baúl, the southernmost outpost of the Wari Empire and a spectacular site sitting atop a shaft of stone. This study shed new light on the founding and abandonment of this unique site, and on the Wari and Tiwanaku empires of Peru and Bolivia. Extensive excavations by Moseley and his colleagues have shown the sequence of key buildings and how each was ritually terminated. Ethnicity, imperial expansion, religious practices and beliefs, and activity areas (for feasting, termination rites, and so on) are all well documented archaeologically and iconographically. The investigators were even able to document the burning down of an ancient brewery. The consequences of imperial expansion are observable in the marks of abandonment and termination, the final darkness of another organized polity in ancient Peru.

A LOOK BACK, AND FORWARD

Moseley's work underscores the importance of in-depth knowledge of a geographic region and how sterile our theoretical frameworks would be without such detailed knowledge. Combining hard-won data with inductive insight, Moseley's work has challenged scholars working in other regions to implement a framework as broad, ambitious, and explanatory. Among the books Moseley has written, five stand out for their importance to all scholars working in the area, and more generally to archaeologists striving to construct a regional history

anywhere in the world: *Twenty-Four Architectural Plans of Chan Chan, Peru* (with Carol J. Mackey), *Chan Chan: Andean Desert City* (with Kent C. Day), *The Northern Dynasties: Kingship and Statecraft in Chimor* (with Alana Cordy-Collins), *The Maritime Foundations of Andean Civilization*, and *The Incas and Their Ancestors: The Archaeology of Peru*. These books show his exceptional ability to marry his field data to a theoretical framework. His particular strength lies in evaluating economic, environmental, and political factors and incorporating them into a framework to explain the evolution of Andean polities, from simple villages to empires.

Before Moseley entered the field of Andean prehistory, the Andes Mountains and natural environment were generally viewed as passive landscapes, a background against which cultural events played out. Moseley, in contrast, put the natural environment in the foreground. Moseley told us that mountains were being uplifted, rivers were downcutting, and shorelines were growing and expanding. In other words, the natural world, with its myriad changes and unpredictable catastrophes, had much more of an impact on sociocultural rises and falls than we formerly imagined. Along with cycles of warfare, economic competition, and conquests, we learned that natural disasters could have caused some of the regional abandonments, resettlements, and population movements detectable in the archaeological record. Moseley showed us that the hills are alive with the sound of earthquakes, floods, subductions, and uplifts. Today we recognize that human culture combines with natural processes to effect change, and such knowledge has made all the difference in how we view Andean prehistory.

From his first article, published in 1962 in the *Quarterly of the San Bernardino County Museum*, to his most recent work, published in the *Proceedings of the National Academy of Sciences*, Moseley has produced a marvelous body of work. But his publications are only part of his body of influence: his passion for the Andes has been passed on to colleagues and students. It is fair to say that Moseley's three early interests—subsistence, the Preceramic period, and the coast of Peru—have been among the enduring themes of his career.

In addition, Mike Moseley has probably trained more Andeanists than anyone else, inviting students from Harvard University, the Field Museum, the University of Chicago, and the University of Florida to Áspero, to Chan Chan, and to the Moquegua Valley. He has trained the next generation of Peruvian archaeologists at numerous academic institutions and in the bar of the Southern Peru Copper Corporation Country Club. He will forever be known as a great researcher and generous teacher, insightful in critiques, generous in praise, and dedicated to extending the horizon of current knowledge.

SELECTED BIBLIOGRAPHY OF MICHAEL E. MOSELEY

1962   Field Work at Guapiabit (Southern California). *Quarterly of the San Bernardino County Museum* 9(2):16–29. San Bernardino, CA.

1966   The Discovery and Definition of Basket Maker: 1890 to 1914. *The Masterkey* 40(4):140–154. Los Angeles.

1968   *Changing Subsistence Patterns: Late Preceramic Archaeology of the Central Peruvian Coast*. Unpublished doctoral dissertation, Department of Anthropology, Harvard University, Cambridge, MA.

1968   (with Christopher B. Donnan) The Use of Stone Flakes for Cleaning Fish. *American Antiquity* 33(4):502–503.

1968   Early Peruvian Fishhooks: Their Manufacture and Use. *The Masterkey* 42(3):104–111. Los Angeles.

1969   (with Thomas C. Patterson) Late Preceramic and Early Ceramic Cultures of the Central Coast of Peru. *Ñawpa Pacha* 6:115–133.

1969   (with Linda K. Barrett) Change in Preceramic Twined Textiles from the Central Peruvian Coast. *American Antiquity* 34(2):162–165.

1969   Assessing the Archaeological Significance of *Mahamaes*. *American Antiquity* 34(4):485–487.

1971   (with Warwick M. Bray) An Archaeological Sequence from the Vicinity of Buga, Colombia. *Ñawpa Pacha* 7–8:85–103.

1971   (with Paul P. Ossa) La Cumbre: A Preliminary Report on Research into the Early Lithic Occupation of the Moche Valley, Peru. *Ñawpa Pacha* 9:1–16.

1972   (with Carol J. Mackey) Peruvian Settlement Pattern Studies and Small Site Methodology. *American Antiquity* 37(1):67–81.

1972   (with Margaret Ann Hoyt) The Burr Frieze: A Rediscovery at Chan Chan. *Ñawpa Pacha* 7–8: 41–58.

1972   Subsistence and Demography: An Example of Interaction from Prehistoric Peru. *Southwestern Journal of Anthropology* 28(1):25–49.

1973   (with Stanley G. Stephens) Cotton Remains from Archaeological Sites in Central Coastal Peru. *Science* 180(4082):186–188.

1973   (with Gordon R. Willey) Aspero, Peru: A Reexamination of the Site and Its Implications. *American Antiquity* 38(4):452–468.

1973   (with Carol J. Mackey) Chan Chan, Peru's Ancient City of Kings. *National Geographic Magazine* 143(3):318–345.

1973   (with Luis Watanabe) The Adobe Sculptures of Huaca Los Reyes: Imposing Artwork from Coastal Peru. *Archaeology* 27(3):154–161.

1974   (with Carol J. Mackey) *Twenty-Four Architectural Plans of Chan Chan, Peru*. Peabody Museum Press, Harvard University, Cambridge, MA.

1974   Organization as Preadaptation to Irrigation: The Evolution of Early Water Management Systems in Coastal Peru. In *Irrigation's Impact on Society*, edited by Theodore E. Downing and McGuire Gibson, pp. 77–82. Anthropological Papers of the University of Arizona, no. 25. University of Arizona Press, Tucson.

1974   (with Stanley G. Stephens) Early Domesticated Cottons (*Gossypium barbadense* L.) from Archaeological Sites in Central Coast Peru. *American Antiquity* 39(1):110–122.

1975   *The Maritime Foundations of Andean Civilization*. Cummings Publishing Co., Menlo Park, CA.

1975   Prehistoric Principles of Labor Organization in the Moche Valley, Peru. *American Antiquity* 40:191–196.

1975   (with Charles Mansfield Hastings) The Adobes of Huaca del Sol and Huaca de la Luna. *American Antiquity* 40(2):196–203.

1975   (with Heather Lechtman) The Scoria at Chan Chan: Non-metallurgical Deposits. *Ñawpa Pacha* 10–12:135–170.

1975   Chan Chan: Andean Alternative of the Preindustrial City? *Science* 187(4173):219–225.

1975   Secrets of Peru's Ancient Walls. *Natural History* 84(1):34–41.

1976   (with Carol J. Mackey) The Chan Chan-Moche Valley Archaeological Project: The First Field Season. *National Geographic Society Research Reports*, pp. 317–324. Washington, DC.

1977   Waterways of Ancient Peru. *Field Museum of Natural History Bulletin* 48(3):10–15. Field Museum of Natural History, Chicago.

1977   (with Robert A. Feldman) Beginnings of Civilization along the Peruvian Coast. *Geoscience and Man*

18:271–276. Louisiana State University, Baton Rouge.

1978 *Pre-Agricultural Coastal Civilizations in Peru.* Carolina Biology Reader 90. Carolina Biological Supply Co., Burlington, NC.

1978 *Peru's Golden Treasures: An Essay on Five Ancient Styles.* Field Museum of Natural History, Chicago.

1978 The Evolution of Andean Civilization. In *Ancient Native Americans*, edited by Jesse D. Jennings, pp. 491–541. W. H. Freeman, San Francisco.

1978 An Empirical Approach to Prehistoric Agrarian Collapse: The Case of the Moche Valley, Peru. In *Social and Technological Management in Dry Lands: Past and Present, Indigenous and Imposed*, edited by Nancie L. Gonzalez, pp. 9–43. AAAS Selected Symposium Series, no. 10. Westview Press, Boulder, CO.

1979 (with Fred L. Nials, Eric E. Deeds, Shelia G. Pozorski, Thomas G. Pozorski, and Robert A. Feldman) El Niño: The Catastrophic Flooding of Coastal Peru. Part I. *Field Museum of Natural History Bulletin* 50(7):4–14. Field Museum of Natural History, Chicago.

1979 El Niño: The Catastrophic Flooding of Coastal Peru. Part II. *Field Museum of Natural History Bulletin* 50(8):4–10. Field Museum of Natural History, Chicago.

1981 (with Robert A. Feldman and Charles R. Ortloff) Living with Crisis: Human Perception of Process and Time. In *Biotic Crises in Ecological and Evolutionary Time*, edited by Matthew Nitecki, pp. 231–267. Academic Press, New York.

1982 (co-editor with Kent C. Day) *Chan Chan: Andean Desert City.* School of American Research and University of New Mexico Press, Albuquerque.

1982 (with Alan L. Kolata) Chan Chan: Cloistered City . . . the Home of God-Kings." *Early Man* 4(1):6–9. Evanston, IL.

1982 (with Robert A. Feldman) Vivir con crisis: Percepción humana de proceso y tiempo. *Revista del Museo Nacional* 46:267–287.

1982 Living with Crises: A Relentless Nature Stalked Chan Chan's Fortunes. *Early Man* 4(1):10–13.

1982 (with Charles R. Ortloff and Robert A. Feldman) Hydraulic Engineering Aspects of the Chimu Chicama-Moche Intervalley Canal. *American Antiquity* 47(3):572–595.

1982 (with Robert A. Feldman and Irene Pritzker) New Light on Peru's Past. *Field Museum of Natural History Bulletin* 53(1):3–11. Field Museum of Natural History, Chicago.

1982 Introduction: Human Exploitation and Organization on the North Andean Coast. In *Chan Chan: Andean Desert City*, edited by Michael E. Moseley and Kent C. Day, pp. 1–24. University of New Mexico Press, Albuquerque.

1982 (with Eric E. Deeds) The Land in Front of Chan Chan: Agrarian Expansion, Reform, and Collapse in the Moche Valley. In *Chan Chan: Andean Desert City*, edited by Michael E. Moseley and Kent C. Day, pp. 25–53. University of New Mexico Press, Albuquerque.

1983 (with Robert A. Feldman) The Northern Andes. In *Ancient South Americans*, edited by Jesse D. Jennings, pp. 139–178. W. H. Freeman, San Francisco.

1983 (with Robert A. Feldman, Charles R. Ortloff, and Alfredo Narvaez) Principles of Agrarian Collapse in the Cordillera Negra, Peru. *Annals of the Carnegie Museum* 52(13):299–327. Carnegie Museum of Natural History, Pittsburgh, PA.

1983 Patterns of Settlement and Preservation in the Viru and Moche Valleys. In *Prehistoric Settlement Patterns: Essays in Honor of Gordon R. Willey*, edited by Evon Z. Vogt and Richard M. Leventhal, pp. 423–442. University of New Mexico Press and Peabody Museum of Archaeology and Ethnology, Harvard University, Cambridge, MA.

1983 (with Charles R. Ortloff and Robert A. Feldman) The Chicama-Moche Intervalley Canal: Social Implications and Physical Paradigms. *American Antiquity* 48(2):375–389.

1983 Central Andean Civilization. In *Ancient South Americans*, edited by Jesse D. Jennings, pp. 179–240. W. H. Freeman, San Francisco.

1983 Desert Empire and Art: Chimor, Chimu, and Chancay. In *Art of the Andes, Pre-Columbian Sculpted and Painted Ceramics from the Arthur M. Sackler Collections*, edited by L. Katz, pp. 78–85. Arthur M. Sackler Foundation, Washington, DC.

1983 The Good Old Days Were Better: Agrarian Collapse and Tectonics. *American Anthropologist* 85(4): 773–799.

1983 (with John R. Topic) Chan Chan: A Case Study of Urban Change in Peru. *Ñawpa Pacha* 21:153–182.

1984 (with Robert A. Feldman) Hydrological Dynamics and the Evolution of Field Form and Use: Resolving the Knapp-Smith Controversy. *American Antiquity* 49(2):403–408.

1984 (with Patricia S. Essenpreis) Fort Ancient: Citadel or Coliseum? *Field Museum of Natural History Bulletin*

55(6):5–10, 20–26. Field Museum of Natural History, Chicago.

1985 Hydraulic Engineering and Historical Aspects of the Pre-Columbian Intravalley Canal Systems of the Moche Valley, Peru. *Journal of Field Archaeology* 12(1):77–98.

1985 The Exploration and Explanation of Early Monumental Architecture in the Andes. In *Early Ceremonial Architecture in the Andes*, edited by Christopher B. Donnan, pp. 29–58. Dumbarton Oaks, Washington, DC.

1987 Punctuated Equilibrium: Searching the Ancient Record for El Niño. *Quarterly Review of Archaeology* 8(3):7–10.

1988 Large Monuments and Precocious Formative Development. *Quarterly Review of Archaeology* 9:1–6.

1988 (with William J. Conklin) The Patterns of Art and Power in the Early Intermediate Period. In *Peruvian Prehistory*, edited by Richard W. Keatinge, pp. 145–163. Cambridge University Press, Cambridge.

1988 (with Robert A. Feldman) Fishing, Farming, and the Foundations of Andean Civilisation. In *The Archaeology of Prehistoric Coastlines*, edited by Geoff Bailey and John Parkington, pp. 125–134. Cambridge University Press, Cambridge.

1988 Hypothesis of Agrarian Collapse. *Yearbook of Science & Technology*, pp. 32–34. McGraw-Hill, New York.

1989 (with Christopher O. Clement) Agricultural Dynamics in the Andes. In *Ecology, Settlement and History in the Osmore Drainage, Peru*, edited by Don S. Rice, Charles Stanish, and Phillip R. Scarr, pp. 435–456. BAR International Series 545 (ii). British Archaeological Reports, Oxford.

1990 (with Christopher O. Clement) Patterned Agrarian Collapse at Carrizal, Peru. *Florida Journal of Anthropology* 14:47–55.

1990 (with Robert A. Feldman and Irene Pritzker) Nuevo luz sobre el pasado del Perú. In *Trabajos arqueológicos en Moquegua, Perú*, edited by Luis K. Watanabe, Michael E. Moseley, and Fernando Cabieses, vol. 1, pp. 215–226. Programa Contisuyo del Museo Peruano de Ciencias de la Salud and Southern Peru Copper Corporation, Lima.

1990 Fortificaciones prehispánicas y evolución de tácticas militares en el Valle de Moquegua. In *Trabajos arqueológicos en Moquegua, Perú*, edited by Luis K. Watanabe, Michael E. Moseley, and Fernando Cabieses, vol. 1, pp. 237–252. Programa Contisuyo del Museo Peruano de Ciencias de la Salud and Southern Peru Copper Corporation, Lima.

1990 (with Christopher O. Clement) Patrón de colapso agrario en Carrizal, Ilo, Peru. In *Trabajos arqueológicos en Moquegua, Perú*, edited by Luis K. Watanabe, Michael E. Moseley, and Fernando Cabieses, vol. 2, pp. 161–176. Programa Contisuyo del Museo Peruano de Ciencias de la Salud and Southern Peru Copper Corporation, Lima.

1990 (co-editor with Luis Watanabe and Fernando Cabieses) *Trabajos arqueológicos en Moquegua, Perú*, vols. 1 and 2. Programa Contisuyo del Museo Peruano de Ciencias de la Salud and Southern Peru Copper Corporation, Lima.

1991 (with Robert A. Feldman, Paul S. Goldstein, and Luis Watanabe) Colonies and Conquest: Tiahuanaco and Huari in Moquegua. In *Huari Administrative Structure: Prehistoric Monumental Architecture and State Government*, edited by William H. Isbell and Gordon F. McEwan, pp. 112–140. Dumbarton Oaks, Washington, DC.

1991 (with Christopher O. Clement) The Spring-Fed Irrigation System of Carrizal, Peru: A Case Study of the Hypothesis of Agrarian Collapse. *Journal of Field Archaeology* 18(4):425–443.

1991 Structure and History in the Dynastic Lore of Chimor. In *The Northern Dynasties: Kingship and Statecraft in Chimor*, edited by Michael E. Moseley and Alana Cordy-Collins, pp. 1–41. Dumbarton Oaks Research Library and Collection, Washington, DC.

1991 (co-edited with Alana Cordy-Collins) *The Northern Dynasties: Kingship and Statecraft in Chimor*. Dumbarton Oaks, Washington, DC.

1992 Maritime Foundations and Multilinear Evolution: Retrospect and Prospect. *Andean Past* 3:5–42.

1992 (with James B. Richardson III) Doomed by Natural Disaster. *Archaeology* 45(6):44–45.

1992 (with J. Tapia, Dennis Satterlee, and James B. Richardson III) Flood Events, El Niño Events, and Tectonic Events. In *Paleo-ENSO Records, International Symposium, Extended Abstracts*, edited by L. Ortlieb and J. Machare, pp. 207–212. OSTROM, Lima.

1992 (with David Wagner and James B. Richardson III) Space Shuttle Imagery of Recent Catastrophic Change along the Arid Andean Coast. In *Paleoshorelines and Prehistory: An Investigation of Method*, edited by Lucille Lewis Johnson and Melanie Stright, pp. 215–235. CRC Press, Boca Raton, FL.

1992   *The Incas and Their Ancestors: The Archaeology of Peru.* Thames and Hudson, London.

1994   (with Christopher O. Clement) New Light on the Horizon. *The Review of Archaeology* 15(2):26–41.

1994   (with David Keefer) Catastrophic Effects of Combined Seismic Landslide Generation and El Niño Flooding on Prehispanic and Modern Populations in Peru. *Geological Society of America, Annual Meeting Abstracts with Programs* 26(7):A342. Seattle, WA, USA, Oct. 24–27, 1994.

1997   Climate, Culture and Punctuated Change: New Data, New Challenges. *The Review of Archaeology* 18(1):19–28.

1997   (with David Keefer and Dennis R. Satterlee) Recognizing Seismic Input in Flood Sediments. *Geological Society of America, Abstracts* 28(7):118. Salt Lake City, UT, USA, Oct. 20–23, 1997.

1997   Catástrofes convergentes: Perspectivas geoarqueológicas sobre desastres naturales colaterales en los Andes Centrales. In *Historia y desastres en América Latina*, edited by V. García Acosta, pp. 59–76. La Red, Lima.

1998   (with David K. Keefer, Susan D. deFrance, James B. Richardson III, Dennis R. Satterlee, and A. Day-Lewis) Early Maritime Economy and El Niño Events at Quebrada Tacahuay, Peru. *Science* 281(5384):1833–1835.

1998   (with Christopher Clement, J. Tapia, and Dennis Satterlee) El colapso agrario de la subregión de Moquegua. In *Moquegua: Los primeros doce mil años*, edited by Karen Wise, pp. 9–16. Museo Contisuyo, Moquegua, Peru.

1998   Andean Coastal Adaptations: Uniformitarianism and Multilinear Evolution. In *Pacific Latin America in Prehistory*, edited by T. Michael Blake, pp. 171–180. Washington State University Press, Pullman.

1998   (with Karen Wise) Introducción. In *Moquegua: Los primeros doce mil años*, edited by Karen Wise, pp. 1–8. Museo Contisuyo, Moquegua, Peru.

1999   Convergent Catastrophe: Past Patterns and Future Implications of Collateral Natural Disasters in the Andes. In *The Angry Earth: Disasters in Anthropological Perspective*, edited by A. Oliver-Smith and S. Hoffman, pp. 59–71. Routledge, New York.

1999   (with Charles R. Ortloff and Robert A. Feldman) Preposterism: Oxymorons of Post-Modern Prehistory. *The Review of Archaeology* 20(1):1–11.

2000   Confronting Natural Disaster. In *Environmental Disaster and the Archaeology of Human Response*, edited by Garth Bawden and Richard Martin Reycraft, pp. 219–224. Maxwell Museum of Anthropology, Anthropology Papers, no. 7, Albuquerque, NM.

2000   (with Patrick Ryan Williams and Donna Nash) Empires of the Andes. *Discovering Archaeology* 2(2):68–73.

2001   (with Dennis R. Satterlee, David K. Keefer, and Jorge E. Tapia A.) The Miraflores El Niño Disaster: Convergent Catastrophes and Prehistoric Agrarian Change in Southern Peru. *Andean Past* 6:95–116.

2001   (with Daniel H. Sandweiss) Amplifying Importance of New Research in Peru. *Science* 294 (547): 1651–1652.

2001   *The Incas and Their Ancestors: The Archaeology of Peru*, rev. ed. Thames and Hudson, London.

2002   Modeling Protracted Drought, Collateral Natural Disaster, and Human Responses in the Andes. In *Catastrophe & Culture*, edited by Susanna Hoffman and Anthony Oliver-Smith, pp. 187–212. School of American Research, Santa Fe, NM.

2003   (with David K. Keefer and Susan D. deFrance) A 38,000-year Record of Floods and Debris Flows in the Ilo Region of Southern Peru and Its Relation to El Niño Events and Great Earthquakes. *Palaeogeography, Palaeoclimatology, Palaeoecology* 194:41–77.

2004   (with David K. Keefer) Southern Peruvian Desert Shattered by the Great 2001 Earthquake: Implications for Paleoseismic and Paleo-El Niño-Southern Oscillation Records. *Proceedings of the National Academy of Sciences* 101:10878–10883.

2005   (with Donna Nash, Patrick Ryan Williams, Susan D. deFrance, Ana Miranda, and Mario Ruales) Burning Down the Brewery: Establishing and Evacuating an Ancient Imperial Colony at Cerro Baúl, Peru. *Proceedings of the National Academy of Sciences* 102(48):17264–17271.

2005   (with Michael Heckenberger) From Village to Empire in South America. In *The Human Past*, edited by Chris Scarre, pp. 640–678. Thames and Hudson, London.

2006   Commentary on "Crucible of andean civilization the peruvian coast from 3000 to 1800 BC" by J. Haas and W. Creamer, *Current Anthropology* 47(5): 758-759.

2009   (with D. Sandweiss, R. Shady Solís, D. Keefer and C. Ortloff). Environmental change and economic development in coastal Peru between 5,800 and 3,600 years ago. *Proceedings of the National Academy of Science* 106(5):1359-1363.

CHAPTER 2

PREHISTORIC POPULATION DYNAMICS IN THE ANDES

RICHARD C. SUTTER

IN RECENT YEARS, A consensus has developed among most osteologists about the peopling of the New World. However, despite nearly a century of scholarly investigation by biological anthropologists, it could be argued that the population history of South America, and more specifically of the Andes, remains poorly understood. In this chapter, I examine current evidence on the peopling of the Andes and discuss how that topic relates to Michael Moseley's maritime hypothesis. In so doing I hope to shed light on prehistoric population dynamics and propose tentative explanations that future archaeological and bioarchaeological investigations can evaluate empirically.

MOLECULAR STUDIES RELATED TO THE PEOPLING OF SOUTH AMERICA

Although a number of molecular studies have examined variation among contemporary (Rothhammer and Silva 1992; Turbón et al. 1994; Merriwether et al. 1995; Lalueza-Fox et al. 1997; Moraga et al. 2000; Keyeux et al. 2002; Williams et al. 2002) and prehistoric South Americans (Rogan and Salvo 1990; Haydon 1993; Lalueza-Fox 1996; Demarchi et al. 2001; Shinoda et al. 2002; Shimada et al. 2003) there is little consensus regarding the timing and number of migrations that

occurred during the peopling of South America, especially the Andes. Although some authors have suggested that a single migration accounts for the peopling of South America (Merriwether et al. 1994, 1995; Bonatto and Salvano 1997a, b), others have argued that at least two migrations occurred (Turbón et al. 1994; Lalueza-Fox 1996; Lalueza-Fox et al. 1997; Moraga et al. 2000; Demarchi et al. 2001; Keyeux et al. 2002). This discrepancy is due in part to the nature of the data examined by molecular studies and in part to methodological problems that limit the ability to generalize from these results. Molecular studies examining nuclear DNA are usually limited to studies of living South Americans. Although contemporary variation among living South Americans provides us with some insight into prehistoric population dynamics, those data are affected because ethnohistorically known Andeans—the Inka, Aymara, and others—and even pre-Inka states such as the Tiwanaku (Blom 1999) often sent colonists to disparate locations. This problem is compounded by the decimation of prehistoric Andean populations by perihistoric epidemics (Rothhammer and Bianchi 1995). These factors limit our ability to use the nuclear DNA of living South Americans, because extant DNA variability may not accurately reflect that of ancient South Americans. Therefore, to understand prehistoric population dynamics and relations, molecular studies need to sample prehistoric remains.

Although a limited number of studies have been successful in isolating nuclear DNA from prehistoric remains of South Americans (see, e.g., Haydon 1993), these attempts are plagued by difficulties in finding and amplifying preserved ancient nuclear DNA. Nuclear DNA is fragile and, compared to mitochondrial DNA (mtDNA), relatively large and complex; further, there are few available copies to isolate. In the few instances in which nuclear DNA has been isolated from prehistoric human remains, the segments that were recovered were unpredictable. In other words, even when nuclear DNA is recoverable, there is no guarantee that each sample will represent the same segment of nuclear DNA. Until successful recovery and amplification techniques are developed for nuclear DNA, information derived from this line of evidence will be limited.

Because mtDNA is smaller and every cell has multiple copies of it, mtDNA has been the molecular material of choice for ancient DNA studies. However, studies employing mtDNA suffer from a number of problems. Methodologically, mtDNA is treated as a single genetic locus with multiple alleles (Williams et al. 2002). Given that mtDNA is treated as a single gene, attempts to reconstruct relations among both living and prehistoric populations using mtDNA do not take into account the evolutionary histories of nuclear genes.

Furthermore, analyses are compounded by the fact that mtDNA is inherited only through the maternal line. This greatly limits our ability to generalize population histories based on a single locus. Indeed, a recent investigation by Williams and colleagues (2002) that compared historically known village fissioning patterns of Yanomamo with phylogenies derived from both nuclear and mtDNA found that the mtDNA did not adequately represent the relatedness among the villages, while the tree diagram they produced using nuclear DNA did match the known relations among Yanomamo villages. An independent study by Matisoo-Smith (2002) that examined both modern and archaeological remains of *Rattus exulans* from the South Pacific also produced divergent pictures of the nature of colonization and appears to confirm the impressions derived from the study by Williams et al. The authors of both of these studies cite mtDNA's unilocus nature and uniparental inheritance—which effectively reduces the population size to one-fourth that of nuclear DNA studies—as reasons why mtDNA failed to perform as well. Indeed, Williams et al. (2002:255) question whether the methods developed for the analysis of multilocus nuclear DNA data are appropriate for the analysis of

single-locus mtDNA. Although ancient mtDNA studies of prehistoric Andeans may eventually provide us with greater resolution on prehistoric population dynamics, mtDNA studies must first overcome both susceptibility to sampling error and the methodological issues associated with estimating genetic relatedness based on a single genetic locus.

MORPHOLOGICAL STUDIES RELATED TO THE PEOPLING OF SOUTH AMERICA

Early osteological studies of prehistoric South Americans were largely descriptive rather than explanatory in nature. Aleč Hrdlička (1923) was the first to describe the physical characteristics of South American populations. After measuring a large series of crania he had collected from archaeological contexts at the Peruvian sites of Pachacamac and the Chicama Valley, Hrdlička claimed that prehistoric coastal Peruvian populations were characterized by medium stature and brachycephaly, whereas high-altitude populations were short and dolichocephalic. Hrdlička suggested that all Native Americans, including South Americans, were directly descended from Mongoloid populations. However, Hrdlička had little or no temporal or spatial control for most of the skulls in his collection. Many of the crania from each region were from unknown sites and looted contexts from multicomponent sites.

Following in the descriptive tradition of Hrdlička, others attempted to establish racial typologies for South American populations based on cranial shape and somatic type (Imbelloni 1938; Cooper 1942; Birdsell 1951). The goal in developing these typologies was to explain the origins of the observed phenotypic variability. Although it was widely believed that Native Americans strongly resembled Mongoloid populations, these investigators felt that the amount of biological variation that exists among New World populations could not have arisen from a single founding population. These anthropologists held that the proto-Mongoloids preceded subsequent migrations of Mongoloids. For example, José Imbelloni (1950) claimed that his Fuegides and Pampides racial types represented the earliest South American migrants, who were subsequently followed by migrations of the ancestors of Laguides, Amazonides, and Pueblo-Andides.

While acknowledging regional trends in Native American phenotypic data, Marshall Newman (1951) argued that the variation observed among Native Americans (and, by extension, South Americans) could have arisen from a single Mongoloid migration through genetic drift and environmental selection. For the Andes, Newman (1943) reported that craniometric data for the central Andean crania indicated two closely related altiplano cranial types—one in the north, one in the central Andes—and a third, more distantly related coastal group. Newman (1948) later argued that the differences he detected among the craniometric measures of coastal and highland populations became less evident through time. Based on independent craniometric analyses of collections from the Peruvian highlands and central coast, Mary Ericksen (1962) supported Newman's claim that craniometric variability among coastal and highland cranial series decreased through time. Ericksen suggested that this trend was due to the breakdown of breeding isolation of coastal populations following the introduction of agriculture to the coast by highland groups.

Christy Turner (1983, 1985) examined genetically influenced tooth and root trait frequencies for both Asian and New World populations. Based on analyses of his data, Turner suggested that modern New World populations were descended from three discrete migratory events, with the earliest population, the Paleoindians, having given rise to all Amerind-speaking North Americans and all Central and South Americans. His surveys of dental trait variability revealed that northeast Asians and all Native American populations exhibit a more complex pattern of tooth cusp and root number than Southeast Asians. Turner referred to populations exhibiting this increased complexity of dental traits as "sinodonts," whereas the simpler dental characteristics observed among Southeast Asians, Australians, and Pacific Rim populations he referred to as "sundadonty." Turner (1985, 1990) estimated that sinodont dental traits evolved in northeast Asia from preexisting, less elaborate sundadont tooth cusp and root traits approximately 20,000 years before the present. However, it is important to note that sinodonty and sundadonty represent two contrasting extremes for Asian dental morphology. Indeed, Asians and Asian-derived populations (i.e., Native Americans) exhibit a wide range of dental trait variation that varies between these two polar extremes for Asian dental morphology. Although this rigid dichotomy has been shown to be too static to characterize Native American dental trait variability (Powell 1993; Lahr and Haydenblit 1995; Haydenblit 1996; Sutter 1997, 2005; Powell and Neves

1998), it still serves as a useful way to characterize dental trait variability.

Although Turner's studies were without precedent in both size and scope, some have criticized Turner's conclusions, noting that his Paleoindian sample consisted of dentitions from both early and late Archaic remains (Powell 1995), and that his Paleoindian sample was distinct from subsequent samples he analyzed (Powell 1993). Further, Turner's South American sample analysis treated all dentitions, irrespective of their chronological or geographic placement, as a single sample. Because he has not yet published his South American data in detail, it is impossible to evaluate the validity of his conclusions for prehistoric South Americans.

Other recent craniometric and dental studies report that the Paleoindian remains are distinct from subsequent prehistoric Native Americans (Powell 1993). Others note both geographic and chronological trends indicating that proto-Mongoloid dental (i.e., sundadont) and craniometric morphology existed among Preceramic or aceramic populations of Baja California (González-José et al. 2003), Mesoamerica (Haydenblit 1996), and South America (Lahr 1995, 1996; Lahr and Haydenblit 1995; Sutter 1997, 2005; Powell and Neves 1998, 1999; Neves et al. 1999a–d, 2001; González-José et al. 2003, 2005; Sardi et al. 2005). This variability has caused many osteologists to posit two migratory events for the peopling of the Americas, an initial proto-Mongoloid colonization followed by a Mongoloid migration (Powell 1995, 2000; Powell and Neves 1998; Jantz and Owsley 1998a, b, 2001; Neves et al. 1999a–d, 2001; Steele and Powell 1999, 2002; Neves and Blum 2000).

Although many of these scholars have implied that the second migratory event constituted replacement of the preexisting proto-Mongoloid populations, Joseph Powell and Walter Neves (1999) correctly point out that many of the detected patterns may be due to the initial population structure of the colonists. Using the same traits and protocol adopted by Turner, I have previously argued (Sutter 1997, 2005) that the geographic and temporal trends for dental trait data among twelve prehistoric south-central Andean mortuary populations indicate there were at least two peopling events for the region: an early migration, represented by the Paleoindians and their descendants, followed by a more recent demographic expansion of food-producing populations. Based on a limited number of samples and currently available osteological and dental data from North and Central America, I suggested that the more recent demographic expansion initially had its source among prehistoric food-producing Central Americans, who then expanded south into South America and mixed with the preexisting foraging populations.

For this study, I report on epigenetic tooth cusp and root traits for forty-four prehistoric Andean mortuary samples. These data are examined in order to understand the factors responsible for the observed dental trait variability and to place these samples in a broader evolutionary context.

PREHISTORIC ANDEAN MORTUARY SAMPLE ANALYIS

Materials and Methods

The forty-four mortuary samples representing the dentitions of more than 2,500 skeletal and mummified remains were examined. All dental data were scored by me. These samples represent all chronological periods and both highland and coastal sites of the Andes (Figure 2.1, Table 2.1). The data collection for this study focused on mortuary samples from Peru and Chile, with excellent provenience and chronological control. For this study, all dentitions were visually inspected and scored for thirty-two morphological tooth cusp and root traits (Table 2.2) using standardized casts and descriptions (Turner et al. 1991). Nonmetric dental traits are highly heritable among living populations (Biggerstaff 1970, 1973; Portin and Alvesalo 1974; Escobar et al. 1976; Berry 1978; Harris and Bailit 1980; Scott 1980; Hassanali 1982; Nichol 1989) and have been used to reconstruct genetic relations among both prehistoric and living populations (Brewer-Carias et al. 1976; Green 1982; Turner 1983; Wijsman and Neves 1986; Sofaer et al. 1986; Haydenblit 1996; Donlon 2000). They have also been demonstrated to closely reflect those derived from molecular data among humans and other nonhuman primates (Braga 2001). Such traits have the advantage of being scorable for highly fragmented skeletal material.

Standard data analysis procedures were used to make results presented here comparable to those presented in other nonmetric dental trait studies. Dental trait frequencies for each mortuary sample were calculated using the "individual count" method (Turner and Scott 1977). In cases in which an individual exhibited asymmetry in the expression of a given trait, the greatest level of expression was used. This scoring procedure assumes that a single genotype is responsible for any given trait's expression, and that when asymmetry exists

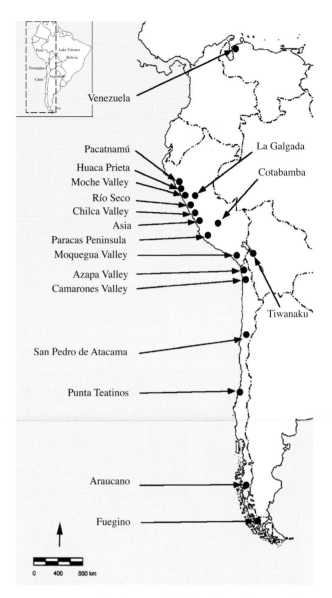

Figure 2.1. Geographic locations of the forty-four prehistoric Andean mortuary samples examined during this study.

among bilateral traits, the side exhibiting the maximum expression is closest to the true underlying genotype for the trait. The procedure also maximizes sample sizes; in cases where a given trait is observable for only one antimere but not the other, the observable side is counted as the maximum expression for that trait. This scoring procedure counts individuals for the calculation of trait frequencies.

For this study, all traits were included if observations could be made for all of the samples examined. Each mortuary sample's dental trait frequencies were used to calculate the average taxonomic distance (ATD; Sokal and Sneath 1963). This statistic was chosen because of its Euclidean properties and its use in another

Table 2.1. Forty-four prehistoric Andean mortuary samples examined by this study.

Sample	Cultural Affiliation	Location	Antiquity	Chronological Period	References	Collection Location[a]
Paleoindian[b]	Paleoindian	Throughout Andes	>8000 YBP	Paleoindian	Multiple (see note 2)	Multiple
Venezuela	Unknown	Altagracia, Venezuela	AD 1250?	Late Prehistoric	—	AMNH
Pacatnamú	Moche III – IV	Jequetepeque Valley, Peru	AD 300 – 500	Moche III – IV	Donnan and Cock 1986	INC, Trujillo, Peru
Huaca Prieta	Cotton Preceramic	Chicama Valley, Peru	3100 – 1800 BC	Cotton Preceramic	Bird and Hyslop 1985	AMNH
Cerro Oreja—Salinar	Salinar	Moche Valley, Peru	200 BC	Early Intermediate	Carcalén 1995	INC, Trujillo, Peru
Cerro Oreja—Gallinazo 1	Early Gallinazo	Moche Valley, Peru	200–100 BC	Early Intermediate	Carcalén 1995	INC, Trujillo, Peru
Cerro Oreja—Gallinazo 2	Middle Gallinazo	Moche Valley, Peru	100 – 1 BC	Early Intermediate	Carcalén 1995	INC, Trujillo, Peru
Cerro Oreja—Gallinazo 3	Late Gallinazo	Moche Valley, Peru	AD 1 – 200	Early Intermediate	Carcalén 1995	INC, Trujillo, Peru
Huaca de la Luna—Urban Sector	Moche	Moche Valley, Peru	AD 200–600	Early Intermediate	Tello et al. 2003	UN–Trujillo
Huaca de la Luna—Platforms	Moche	Moche Valley, Peru	AD 200 – 600	Early Intermediate	Montoya 1995; Tello 1995; Uceda 2001; Tufinio 1997	UN–Trujillo
Huaca de la Luna—Sacrifices	Moche	Moche Valley, Peru	AD 500	Early Intermediate	Bourget 1997; Verano 2001	UN–Trujillo
La Galgada	Cotton Preceramic	Tablachaca Valley, Peru	2850 – 1950 BC	Cotton Preceramic	Grieder and Bueno 1988	MNAAHP, Lima, Peru
Río Seco	Late Preceramic	Huaura, Peru	1800 – 1733 BC	Late Preceramic	Wendt 1964	CIZA, Lima, Peru
Paloma	Middle Preceramic	Chilca Valley, Peru	5700 – 2800 BC	Middle Preceramic	Engel 1980; Benfer 1984, 1986	CIZA, Lima, Peru
Chilca 1	Late Preceramic	Chilca Valley, Peru		Late Preceramic	Engel 1960,1966a,1981	CIZA, Lima, Peru
Asia	Late Preceramic	Mala Valley, Peru	3000 – 1262 BC	Late Preceramic	Engel 1957,1963	CIZA, Lima, Peru
Cotabamba	Killke	Cotabamba Valley, Peru	AD 1350	Late Intermediate Period	—	AMNH
Paracas 1	Paracas	Paracas Penninsula, Peru	300 BC	Early Horizon	Tello 1926	MNAAHP, Lima, Peru
Cabezas Largas	Paracas	Paracas Penninsula, Peru	300 BC	Early Horizon	Engel 1966b,1981	CIZA, Lima, Peru
Falda	Paracas	Paracas Penninsula, Peru	300 BC	Early Horizon	Engel 1966b,1981	CIZA, Lima, Peru
Tiwanaku[c]	Tiwanaku I – IV	Island of the Sun, Bolivia	500 BC – AD 1100	Tiwanaku I – IV	Bandelier 1910; Stanish and Bauer 2004:193–197	AMNH
La Yaral	Tumilaca & Chiribaya	Moquegua Valley, Peru	AD 950 – 1150	Middle Horizon/Late Intermediate	García 1988; Rice 1993	Centro Mallqui, Ilo, Peru
Ilo Preceramic	Late Preceamic	Moquegua Valley, Peru	3000 – 1500 BC	Late Preceramic	Sutter 1997, 2000	Centro Mallqui, Ilo, Peru
Chiribaya Alta	Chiribaya	Moquegua Valley, Peru	AD 950 – 1350	Middle Horizon/Late Intermediate	Buikstra 1989,1990,1995	Centro Mallqui, Ilo, Peru
San Gerónimo	Chiribaya	Moquegua Valley, Peru	AD 950 – 1350	Middle Horizon/Late Intermediate	Jessup 1990b	Centro Mallqui, Ilo, Peru
Azapa Chinchorro	Chinchorro	Azapa Valley, Chile	5000 – 2000 BC	Middle Preceramic	Sutter 1997, 2000	MSMA, Arica, Chile

Table 2.1. (Continued)

Sample	Cultural Affiliation	Location	Antiquity	Chronological Period	References	Collection Location[a]
Playa Miller-7 (Laucho)	Laucho	Azapa Valley, Chile	500 BC	Initial Period	Focacci 1974	MSMA, Arica, Chile
Alto Ramírez	Alto Ramírez	Azapa Valley, Chile	500 BC – AD 500	Initial Period – Early Horizon	Sutter 1997, 2000	MSMA, Arica, Chile
Azapa-140	Maitas–Chiribaya	Azapa Valley, Chile	AD 800 –1350	Middle Horizon/Late Intermediate	Muñoz and Focacci 1985	MSMA, Arica, Chile
Azapa-6	Cabuza	Azapa Valley, Chile	AD 900 –1350	Late Intermediate	Focacci 1993	MSMA, Arica, Chile
Azapa-71	Cabuza	Azapa Valley, Chile	AD 900 –1350	Late Intermediate	Focacci 1961, 1968	MSMA, Arica, Chile
Azapa-75	Tiwanaku/ Maitas–Chiribaya	Azapa Valley, Chile	AD 500 – 950	Middle Horizon/Late Intermediate	Muñoz and Focacci 1985	MSMA, Arica, Chile
Azapa-141	Cabuza	Azapa Valley, Chile	AD 900 – 1350	Late Intermediate	Focacci 1980; Espinoza et al. 1994	MSMA, Arica, Chile
Azapa-8	Gentilar	Azapa Valley, Chile	AD 1350	Late Intermediate	Focacci 1961	MSMA, Arica, Chile
Playa Miller-4	San Miguel Maitas Chiribaya	Azapa Valley, Chile	AD 1200	Late Intermediate	Focacci 1969; Espinoza et al. 1994	MSMA, Arica, Chile
Camarones Chinchorros	Chinchorro	Camarones Valley, Chile	3000 – 500 BC	Middle/Late Preceramic	Aufderheide et al. 1993	MSMA, Arica, Chile
Camarones-8	Gentilar	Camarones Valley, Chile	AD 1350	Late Intermediate	Muñoz 1989	MSMA, Arica, Chile
Camarones-9	Inka	Camarones Valley, Chile	AD 1400	Late Horizon	Muñoz 1989	MSMA, Arica, Chile
Toconao	Early Horizon	San Pedro de Atacama, Chile	500 BC	Early Horizon	Berenguer and Dauelsberg 1989	MPLP, San Pedro de Atacama, Chile
Coyo Oriente	Middle Horizon	San Pedro de Atacama, Chile	AD 500	Middle Horizon	Berenguer and Dauelsberg 1989	MPLP, San Pedro de Atacama, Chile
Casa Parroquial	"Tiwanaku"	San Pedro de Atacama, Chile	AD 500	Middle Horizon	—	MPLP, San Pedro de Atacama, Chile
Punta Teatinos	Late Preceramic	Coquimbo Bay, Chile	2000 – 1000 BC	Late Preceramic	Soto et al. 1975	MNHN, Santiago, Chile
Araucano	Aceramic	South Central Chile	Late Prehistoric	Aceramic	—	MNHN, Santiago, Chile
Fueguino	Aceramic	Southern Chile	Late Prehistoric	Aceramic	—	MNHN, Santiago, Chile

[a] Institutional abbreviations: AMNH, American Museum of Natural History; CIZA, Centro de Investigaciones de Zonas Áridas, Universidad Agraria Nacional–La Molina; INC, Instituto Nacional de Cultura; UN, Universidad Nacional de Trujillo; MNAAHP, Museo Nacional de Antropología, Arqueología e Historia del Perú; MSMA, Museo San Miguel de Azapa; MPLP, Museo Padre Le Paige; MNHN, Museo Nacional de Historia Natural.
[b] The South American Paleoindian sample consists of human remains that predate 8000 BC (calibrated radiocarbon years) from the following sites: Pampa de los Fósiles 13 (n = 2) (Chauchat and Dricot 1979; Chauchat 1988), Lauricocha (n = 6) (Bórmida 1966), Tres Ventanas (n = 2) (Engel 1977, 1982; Benyon and Siegel 1981; Vallejos 1982), Cueva Quiche (n=2) (Engel 1982), Pampa Santo Domingo (n = 2) (Engel 1982), Acha-2 and Acha-3 (n = 5) (Muñoz et al. 1993; Standen and Santoro 2003), Cerro Sota (n = 8) (Bird 1988), Palli Aike (n = 3) (Bird 1988), and Cañadón Leona (n = 4) (Bird 1988).
[c] The Tiwanaku sample consists of Upper Formative period (500 BC–AD 500) and Middle Horizon (AD 500–1100) individuals excavated by Bandelier (1910) from the sites Titi-Uayani (n = 28), Tiwanaku (n = 3), and Kea Kolla Chico (n = 26) (see also Stanish and Bauer 2004). Only those individuals associated with Tiwanaku and pre-Tiwanaku (Qeya) grave goods were included for this study.

Table 2.2. Dichotomized dental trait frequencies for forty-four prehistoric Andean mortuary samples.

Sample	UM3PCA	UM1 PARA	UP1R T	UI2PCA	UI1WING	LM3CA	LM2 RT	LM1 RT	LP1 TOME	ULP12 ODONT
Paleoindian	0/13	2/13	10/10	1/17	2/12	1/15	10/10	1/11	1/13	0/24
Venezuela	1/18	4/16	15/17	1/21	10/19	3/21	8/18	1/22	2/19	0/50
Huaca Prieta	4/30	1/25	19/26	0/39	9/38	2/33	23/26	0/28	0/15	0/55
Pacatnamú	6/20	2/20	12/16	2/26	11/22	1/21	10/16	1/16	2/21	1/42
Cerro Oreja—Salinar	0/10	5/16	9/9	0/19	7/9	0/13	7/10	0/16	0/10	2/100
Cerro Oreja—Gallinazo1	1/50	12/67	35/42	1/68	19/28	3/60	26/40	1/52	5/50	6/155
Cerro Oreja—Gallinazo2	4/35	5/41	32/36	1/45	22/26	1/46	18/24	2/42	3/40	2/119
Cerro Oreja—Gallinazo3	2/24	3/37	19/24	0/47	16/19	1/38	18/27	1/29	2/24	0/83
Moche—Urban sector	3/22	1/17	16/20	0/23	17/21	1/19	8/14	0/16	0/14	0/39
Moche—Platforms	4/25	0/28	17/17	1/34	13/29	4/38	14/54	0/35	0/32	2/55
Moche—Sacrifices	6/40	10/33	29/33	1/40	22/35	7/41	23/32	0/34	1/36	2/109
La Galgada	1/11	2/5	16/17	1/13	10/18	5/21	18/25	0/22	0/25	0/19
Río Seco	0/12	1/16	9/10	0/23	5/20	1/14	12/13	1/20	0/14	3/41
Paloma	5/50	0/23	31/36	3/76	19/60	3/61	33/54	5/56	0/49	1/53
Chilca 1	3/17	1/13	13/13	0/17	1/14	3/18	12/19	0/15	0/19	0/41
Asia	2/13	2/19	11/12	0/21	3/12	1/12	11/12	0/20	2/13	0/43
Paracas 1	8/36	1/28	24/30	1/41	18/43	3/18	4/8	2/12	2/15	1/58
Cabezas Largas	14/39	2/32	29/32	2/43	21/41	4/32	13/18	2/20	0/28	0/105
Falda	8/24	1/19	18/24	1/27	15/21	2/15	9/11	1/11	1/9	0/28
Cotabamba	6/42	5/37	12/24	1/42	26/36	1/26	11/16	2/24	0/17	0/96
Ilo Preceramic	3/10	0/8	10/11	0/11	0/9	1/14	9/11	0/11	2/13	2/37
Chiribaya Alta	21/123	9/130	112/130	8/150	66/139	12/121	86/110	5/135	9/115	2/372
San Gerónimo	9/41	1/43	36/44	6/50	23/42	9/43	27/42	0/45	2/43	1/140
La Yaral	7/42	5/45	29/42	4/47	31/48	6/43	25/38	3/44	1/37	1/146
Tiwanaku	8/42	4/23	26/36	3/50	25/38	2/22	15/18	1/14	0/23	0/58
Azapa Chinchorro	13/62	0/48	55/58	6/65	5/62	5/60	52/57	1/66	1/47	0/122
Playa Miller-7 (Laucho)	16/49	0/42	46/47	3/50	1/49	6/24	20/22	0/24	1/20	3/84
Alto Ramírez	11/59	0/44	48/51	4/60	12/59	9/44	31/33	0/41	2/39	0/124
Azapa-140 (Maitas-Chiribaya)	18/72	5/73	40/52	4/76	17/73	15/68	42/52	0/65	6/44	0/242
Azapa-6 (Cabuza)	9/39	4/35	24/30	2/42	8/38	5/33	18/24	0/27	4/23	0/85
Azapa-71 (Cabuza)	4/48	2/49	42/48	2/50	9/51	4/43	32/39	0/43	8/46	7/99
Azapa-75 (Tiwanaku/ Maitas-Chiribaya)	1/15	0/17	12/13	2/18	4/17	1/14	6/12	0/14	0/11	0/24
Azapa-141 (Cabuza)	1/12	2/17	6/10	0/16	4/15	0/10	5/7	0/14	1/9	0/45
Azapa-8 (Gentilar)	7/22	0/21	10/16	0/24	9/23	3/21	18/21	0/19	2/20	1/64

Table 2.2. (Continued)

Sample	UM3PCA	UM1 PARA	UP1R T	UI2PCA	UI1WING	LM3CA	LM2 RT	LM1 RT	LP1 TOME	ULP12 ODONT
Playa Miller-4 (San Miguel)	15/39	0/35	35/36	8/41	7/41	2/25	18/20	0/21	0/21	3/87
Camarones Chinchorros	2/17	0/11	15/15	0/19	2/19	2/13	7/10	0/12	0/11	0/21
Camarones-8	5/12	0/12	11/11	1/13	7/12	1/13	6/9	0/12	0/11	0/33
Camarones-9	1/17	0/21	10/15	0/21	9/19	1/17	10/10	1/18	1/13	0/40
Toconao	1/28	2/9	22/28	0/37	10/34	0/29	7/11	1/18	2/31	0/22
Coyo Oriente	17/134	2/75	71/85	6/137	36/124	5/71	17/27	0/14	3/73	2/223
Casa Parroquial	1/9	0/5	4/6	0/8	6/9	2/8	3/6	0/7	2/10	1/28
Punta Teatinos	22/82	0/40	63/65	0/93	18/75	18/84	31/61	0/75	0/69	3/149
Araucano	4/28	2/23	20/23	0/32	9/28	4/17	9/14	0/15	1/14	2/56
Fueguino	0/43	0/38	18/20	0/45	7/42	0/28	13/16	0/16	1/16	0/103

UM3PCA – Upper third molar – present/congenitally absent; UM1PARA – Upper first molar parastyle; UP1RT – Upper first premolar root number; UI2PCA – Upper second incisor – present/congenitally absent; UI1Wing – Upper first incisor winging; LM3CA – Lower third molar congenital absence; LM2RT – Lower second molar root number; LM1RT – Lower first molar root number; LP1TOME – Lower first premolar Tome's root; ULP12RT – Upper/lower first and second premolar odontome.

investigation by this author (Sutter 2007). The ATD is highly correlated with other measures that are commonly used in biodistance studies (Sokal and Sneath 1963; Constandse-Westermann 1972; Finnegan and Cooprider 1978; González-José et al. 2001). The matrix of ATD values was analyzed using Ward's hierarchical clustering procedures. Hierarchical clustering procedures produce easily interpretable visual representations (i.e., tree diagrams) of complex distance matrices (Aldenderfer and Blashfield 1984; Norusis 1994) (Table 2.3). Ward's clustering procedure forms clusters that minimize variance within each cluster while maximizing the variance among clusters.

Results

Inspection of the dental trait frequencies for the forty-four Andean mortuary samples examined here reveals that more complex root and tooth cusp traits (i.e., sinodonty) are observed at highest frequencies among northern Peruvian sites associated with food production. These traits are observed at lowest frequencies among Paleoindians, all Preceramic period samples, and most food-producing samples of the Southern Cone. I have previously reported (Sutter 2003; Sutter and Cadwell 2004) that when classified by discriminant functions analysis using Turner's previously published dental trait frequencies for both Asian and New World populations, the Andean Paleoindians, Preceramic period samples, and Chilean samples of the Southern Cone examined by

this study are classified as sundadonts (i.e., more similar to Southeast Asians' dental trait frequencies), whereas all Peruvian mortuary samples are classified as sinodonts (i.e., more similar to northeast Asians' and other Native Americans' dental trait frequencies). The results of this and the aforementioned investigations reveal that prehistoric south-central Andean populations do not strictly adhere to the sinodont/sundadont dichotomy as suggested by Turner (1985, 1990). As I have reported elsewhere (Sutter 1997, 2000, 2005, 2007), there are clear and statistically significant diachronic and geographic trends in dental trait frequencies among prehistoric Andean mortuary samples.

The hierarchical clustering diagram reveals clear chronological and temporal trends in tooth trait expression among the forty-four prehistoric Andean samples examined (Figure 2.2). In the cluster diagram, mortuary samples characterized by lower frequencies of tooth cusp and root traits are found in Cluster 1, while those samples characterized by higher frequencies of tooth cusp and root traits are found within Cluster 2. On closer inspection, the mortuary populations in Cluster 1 represent either Preceramic populations or populations from the Southern Cone of South America, or both. Of note, the Andean Paleoindian sample is also found in Cluster 1. In addition, with one exception, La Galgada, all the Peruvian Preceramic mortuary samples (i.e., Huaca Prieta, Chilca I, Paloma, Ilo Preceramic, and Río Seco) are also located in Cluster 1.

Table 2.3. Average taxonomic distance values between forty-four prehistoric Andean mortuary samples.

Sample	Paleoindian	Venezuela	Pacatnamú	Huaca Prieta	CO-Sal	CO-G1	CO-G2	CO-G3	HLL-US	HLL-Plats	HLL-Sacs	La Galgada	Río Seco	Paloma	Chilca I	Asia	Cotabamba	Paracas I	Cabezas Largas	Falda	Tiwanaku	La Yaral	Ilo PC	Ch Alt
Paleoindian																								
Venezuela	0.21																							
Pacatnamú	0.19	0.11																						
Huaca Prieta	0.13	0.16	0.11																					
CO-Sal – Cerro Oreja-Salinar	0.22	0.13	0.17	0.21																				
CO-G1 – Cerro Oreja-Gallinazo 1	0.20	0.10	0.11	0.16	0.09																			
CO-G2 – Cerro Oreja-Gallinazo 2	0.23	0.15	0.14	0.20	0.09	0.07																		
CO-G3 – Cerro Oreja-Gallinazo 3	0.24	0.14	0.13	0.19	0.11	0.06	0.04																	
HLL-US – Huaca de la Luna – Urban Sector	0.25	0.13	0.12	0.18	0.12	0.08	0.08	0.05																
HLL-Plats – Huaca de la Luna – Platforms	0.17	0.11	0.10	0.12	0.15	0.12	0.15	0.15	0.13															
HLL-Sacs – Huaca de la Luna – Sacrifices	0.18	0.10	0.11	0.15	0.09	0.08	0.10	0.11	0.11	0.12														
La Galgada	0.22	0.16	0.19	0.20	0.16	0.14	0.17	0.18	0.19	0.19	0.12													
Río Seco	0.07	0.18	0.16	0.08	0.19	0.17	0.20	0.20	0.21	0.14	0.16	0.21												
Paloma	0.16	0.13	0.11	0.09	0.19	0.13	0.17	0.17	0.16	0.09	0.15	0.17	0.12											
Chilca I	0.14	0.17	0.16	0.11	0.24	0.21	0.25	0.25	0.24	0.12	0.19	0.22	0.13	0.12										
Asia	0.08	0.18	0.14	0.09	0.20	0.16	0.19	0.20	0.21	0.14	0.15	0.19	0.07	0.12	0.12									
Cotabamba	0.25	0.16	0.12	0.17	0.17	0.12	0.13	0.11	0.11	0.18	0.14	0.21	0.21	0.18	0.25	0.21								
Paracas I	0.20	0.10	0.08	0.13	0.19	0.14	0.17	0.16	0.14	0.10	0.14	0.20	0.17	0.10	0.14	0.16	0.16							
Cabezas Largas	0.18	0.14	0.07	0.13	0.17	0.14	0.14	0.15	0.13	0.09	0.11	0.18	0.15	0.12	0.15	0.13	0.16	0.10						
Falda	0.22	0.17	0.10	0.17	0.17	0.12	0.10	0.11	0.12	0.15	0.12	0.18	0.19	0.16	0.23	0.17	0.12	0.14	0.10					
Tiwanaku	0.19	0.15	0.09	0.14	0.13	0.10	0.10	0.10	0.11	0.14	0.08	0.17	0.16	0.15	0.21	0.15	0.08	0.14	0.10	0.08				
La Yaral	0.21	0.11	0.07	0.14	0.14	0.08	0.11	0.09	0.08	0.12	0.09	0.17	0.17	0.13	0.20	0.17	0.07	0.11	0.10	0.09	0.06			
Ilo Preceramic	0.14	0.23	0.18	0.12	0.28	0.24	0.27	0.27	0.27	0.17	0.23	0.24	0.14	0.14	0.11	0.10	0.27	0.18	0.18	0.22	0.23	0.23		
Ch Alt – Chiribaya Alta	0.13	0.12	0.07	0.09	0.14	0.10	0.13	0.13	0.13	0.08	0.09	0.17	0.10	0.10	0.14	0.09	0.14	0.10	0.07	0.10	0.08	0.09	0.16	
San Gerónimo	0.19	0.11	0.07	0.12	0.16	0.11	0.13	0.12	0.11	0.08	0.10	0.18	0.16	0.12	0.16	0.15	0.14	0.09	0.07	0.10	0.10	0.07	0.19	0.07
Azapa Chinchorros	0.09	0.22	0.17	0.10	0.25	0.22	0.25	0.25	0.25	0.15	0.20	0.24	0.09	0.14	0.10	0.08	0.25	0.18	0.15	0.21	0.20	0.21	0.08	0.13

17

18

Table 2.3. (Continued)

Sample	Paleo-indian	Vene-zuela	Pacat-namú	Huaca Prieta	CO-Sal	CO-G1	CO-G2	CO-G3	HLL-US	HLL-Plats	HLL-Sacs	La Galgada	Rio Seco	Paloma	Chilca I	Asia	Cota-bamba	Paracas I	Cabezas Largas	Falda	Tiwa-naku	La Yaral	Ilo PC	Ch Alt
Playa Miller-7	0.14	0.24	0.20	0.14	0.29	0.25	0.28	0.28	0.28	0.18	0.22	0.25	0.14	0.17	0.11	0.11	0.28	0.20	0.17	0.23	0.23	0.23	0.08	0.16
Playa Miller-4	0.14	0.22	0.16	0.13	0.25	0.23	0.24	0.25	0.24	0.15	0.20	0.24	0.14	0.16	0.13	0.11	0.25	0.18	0.13	0.20	0.19	0.20	0.11	0.13
Alto Ramírez	0.09	0.20	0.16	0.10	0.23	0.20	0.22	0.23	0.23	0.14	0.17	0.22	0.08	0.14	0.11	0.07	0.23	0.17	0.13	0.18	0.17	0.18	0.11	0.11
Azapa-140	0.13	0.17	0.11	0.08	0.23	0.18	0.21	0.21	0.20	0.14	0.15	0.20	0.11	0.13	0.11	0.08	0.19	0.12	0.12	0.16	0.15	0.15	0.11	0.09
Azapa-6	0.13	0.15	0.11	0.08	0.22	0.17	0.21	0.21	0.20	0.13	0.15	0.20	0.11	0.12	0.10	0.08	0.19	0.11	0.12	0.17	0.15	0.15	0.10	0.09
Azapa-71	0.09	0.17	0.14	0.08	0.22	0.17	0.21	0.21	0.21	0.13	0.17	0.21	0.07	0.11	0.10	0.06	0.22	0.14	0.15	0.19	0.17	0.17	0.10	0.10
Azapa-75	0.17	0.13	0.13	0.11	0.20	0.16	0.21	0.20	0.18	0.08	0.17	0.21	0.14	0.08	0.09	0.15	0.21	0.11	0.14	0.21	0.18	0.16	0.16	0.12
Azapa-141	0.16	0.16	0.12	0.06	0.21	0.15	0.20	0.18	0.18	0.15	0.16	0.21	0.13	0.11	0.15	0.12	0.15	0.13	0.16	0.17	0.14	0.14	0.15	0.11
Azapa-8	0.18	0.19	0.10	0.09	0.22	0.17	0.19	0.18	0.18	0.15	0.16	0.22	0.14	0.15	0.17	0.12	0.15	0.14	0.11	0.12	0.12	0.12	0.15	0.10
Camarones Chinchorros	0.12	0.18	0.16	0.10	0.23	0.20	0.24	0.24	0.23	0.11	0.19	0.22	0.10	0.11	0.04	0.10	0.25	0.15	0.15	0.22	0.20	0.20	0.10	0.13
Camarones-8	0.21	0.16	0.10	0.16	0.17	0.15	0.15	0.15	0.13	0.09	0.13	0.20	0.18	0.15	0.18	0.16	0.19	0.13	0.06	0.12	0.13	0.13	0.20	0.10
Camarones-9	0.15	0.20	0.14	0.11	0.19	0.15	0.16	0.16	0.18	0.17	0.16	0.21	0.11	0.15	0.20	0.12	0.14	0.17	0.15	0.13	0.11	0.13	0.19	0.10
Casa Parroquial	0.25	0.12	0.12	0.18	0.18	0.12	0.15	0.12	0.11	0.14	0.14	0.21	0.21	0.16	0.22	0.21	0.13	0.11	0.16	0.14	0.14	0.09	0.25	0.14
Coyo Oriente	0.14	0.12	0.09	0.06	0.18	0.14	0.18	0.17	0.16	0.07	0.14	0.20	0.10	0.07	0.09	0.10	0.17	0.09	0.11	0.16	0.14	0.13	0.13	0.08
Toconao	0.14	0.11	0.11	0.08	0.17	0.13	0.18	0.17	0.17	0.12	0.13	0.18	0.11	0.10	0.12	0.11	0.16	0.12	0.14	0.18	0.14	0.13	0.16	0.10
Punta Teatinos	0.19	0.14	0.13	0.12	0.22	0.19	0.22	0.22	0.19	0.08	0.17	0.21	0.16	0.11	0.07	0.15	0.22	0.10	0.12	0.20	0.19	0.17	0.14	0.13
Araucano	0.15	0.11	0.10	0.09	0.18	0.14	0.18	0.18	0.16	0.08	0.12	0.18	0.11	0.09	0.09	0.11	0.18	0.09	0.11	0.16	0.14	0.12	0.14	0.08
Fuegino	0.09	0.18	0.16	0.08	0.21	0.18	0.22	0.21	0.22	0.13	0.18	0.23	0.06	0.11	0.11	0.08	0.22	0.16	0.16	0.21	0.18	0.18	0.12	0.11

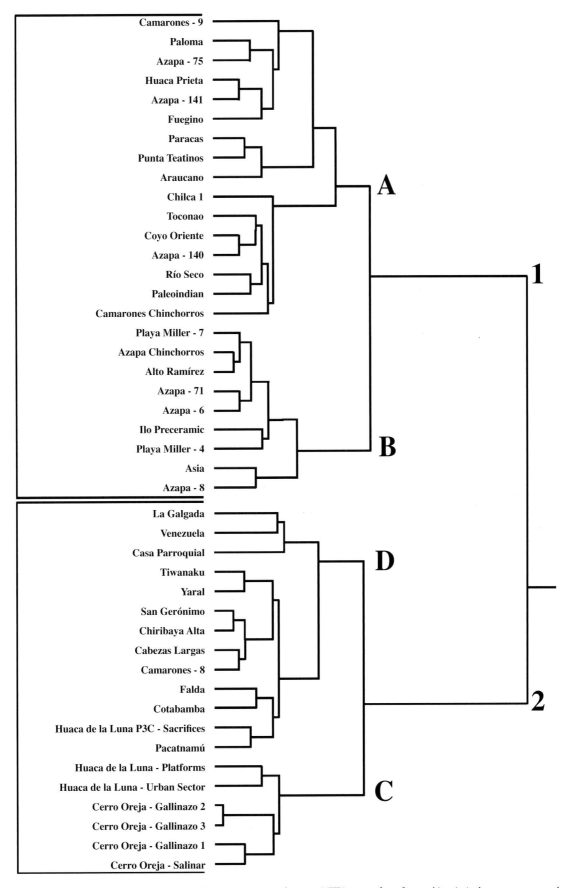

Figure 2.2. Hierarchical cluster diagram of the matrix of average taxonomic distances (ATD) among forty-four prehistoric Andean mortuary samples. The procedure resulted in two clusters, each containing two subclusters. The first cluster contains the Paleoindians and most Preceramic and Southern Cone samples, which are characterized by low frequencies of sinodont traits. The second cluster contains samples representing food-producing populations, primarily from Peru.

In contrast to samples found in Cluster 1, samples found in Cluster 2 are characterized by higher frequencies of sinodont tooth cusp and root traits. It is important to point out that all of the mortuary samples in Cluster 2 are associated with food production. Generally, the populations represented by the mortuary samples in Cluster 2 are from Peru. There are two notable exceptions to this tendency: the Middle Horizon Casa Parroquial sample from San Pedro de Atacama and the terminal Late Intermediate period mortuary sample from Camarones-8 are also both found in Cluster 2. These exceptions and their relations to other south-central Andean samples examined by this study deserve closer examination and are discussed in more detail below.

Because one of the goals of this study was to focus on the emergence of social complexity and biological relations among prehistoric south-central Andeans, cluster analysis was also performed on a subset of the data that included the Paleoindian sample and samples from the south-central Andean region. This is justified because clusters formed by Ward's clustering procedure are influenced by the globally optimal solution (Aldenderfer and Blashfield 1984). For this reason, the degree of relatedness among south-central Andeans may be obscured by examining only the globally optimal solution for all forty-four prehistoric Andean mortuary samples.

The resulting cluster diagram using only the Paleoindian and prehistoric south-central Andean samples produced two broad clusters (Figure 2.3). The first cluster has two subclusters, the first containing the Paleoindians, the Late Archaic Ilo Preceramic and Azapa Chinchorro samples, northern Chilean Formative period samples from Playa Miller-7, and Alto Ramírez, and the Late Intermediate period mortuary sample from Playa Miller-4. The second subcluster contains only northern Chilean samples. These include the Late Archaic Camarones Chinchorro sample, Formative period Toconao, and Middle Horizon Coyo Oriente samples from San Pedro de Atacama, Middle Horizon and Late Intermediate period inland samples from the Azapa Valley (Azapa-6, Azapa-71, Azapa-75, Azapa-140, Azapa-141), and the Late Horizon Camarones-9 samples.

The second cluster contains the Late Archaic/Middle Horizon Tiwanaku sample, all Late Intermediate period Moquegua Valley samples (i.e., Yaral, Chiribaya Alta, and San Gerónimo), the Middle Horizon Casa Parroquial sample from San Pedro de Atacama, Chile,

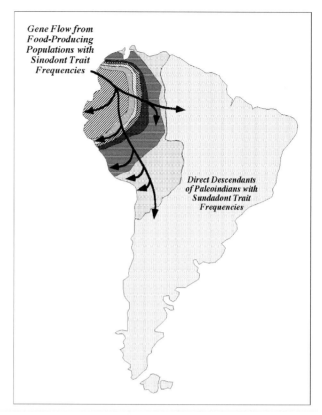

Figure 2.3. The hypothesized spread of sinodonty into South America via the Isthmus of Panama. Theoretically, this migratory event—best described as a demic expansion—was driven by the increased fertility of the preexisting sinodont Central American sinodont population. This demic expansion would have begun during the Boreal period and its impact would have been limited south of the Peruvian-Chilean border as a result of decreased agricultural productivity in the Atacama Desert.

and terminal Late Intermediate period Gentilar samples from northern Chile (Azapa-8, Camarones-8). The implications of these results are discussed below.

Discussion

Although there is considerable variability in the dental trait morphology among the forty-four prehistoric Andean mortuary samples reported here, there are clear chronological and directional trends indicating that the number and complexity of tooth cusps and roots increase through time (i.e., dental traits become more complex or sinodont-like) and are observed at their highest frequencies in the northern Andes. These tooth trait frequencies decrease among the mortuary samples reported here as one moves south. The broader implications of these results are that at least two migratory events occurred in the prehistoric Andes. While in situ microevolution may account for some of the observed differences in dental trait variability among prehistoric Andean populations, I have argued elsewhere (Sutter

1997, 2000, 2005, 2007) that this variability is probably the result of a second migration into South America (Figure 2.4).

According to this scenario, the first migration corresponds to the initial colonization of South America by the Paleoindians, while the second migration is represented by northern and central Andean populations that would have been characterized by relatively higher frequencies of increased tooth cusp and root number. Tentatively—based in part on the first appearance of sinodonty at La Galgada, and following observations made by Newman (1948) and Ericksen (1962)—I propose that the second wave followed a north-to-south route along the Andean highlands, and later proceeded from the highlands to the coastal valleys. Additional Andean samples with good chronological

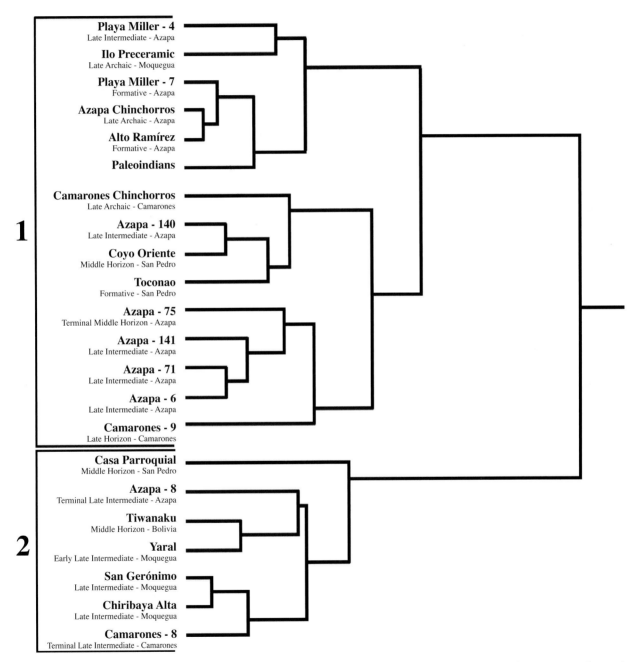

Figure 2.4. Hierarchical cluster diagram of the matrix of average taxonomic distances (ATD) among the Paleoindians and twenty-one south-central Andean mortuary populations. The first cluster contains mortuary samples from Tiwanaku, the Middle Horizon Casa Parroquial sample from San Pedro de Atacama, Late Intermediate period Chiribaya samples from the Moquegua Valley, and terminal Late Intermediate period samples from Azapa-8 and Camarones-8. The second cluster contains the Paleoindians, Ilo Preceramic sample from the Moquegua Valley, and all remaining samples from northern Chile.

control will have to be examined to test the validity of this proposed route. Indeed, Haas (2004) implies that this demographic expansion may have had its origins in the coastal valleys of northern Peru, while Lathrap (1970) proposed an Amazonian source for this influence. However, support exists for the Andean route by molecular studies (Demarchi et al. 2001; Keyeux et al. 2002).

Rather than indicating a large-scale migration resulting in population replacement, the second wave likely represents increased fertility among the earliest food-producing populations arriving in South America from the north from Mesoamerica via the Isthmus of Panama. According to this scenario, food-producing populations of Mesoamerica would have been characterized by higher frequencies of complex tooth cusp and root traits relative to the earlier South American populations that represent direct descendants of the Paleoindians. This economic shift resulted in both substantial and directional gene flow associated with these cultural changes and can best be described as a demic expansion (also referred to as "demic diffusion" or "wave of advance")—a well-established concept in molecular studies that other investigators have applied to explain observed genetic and morphological changes among prehistoric populations to the demic expansion of food-producing populations into Europe (i.e., the LBK expansion) (Sokal and Menozzi 1982; Sokal et al. 1991; Barbujani et al. 1994; Cavalli-Sforza et al. 1994; Jacobs 1994; Semino et al. 1996; Pinhasi and Pluciennik 2004). The higher fertility of intensive agriculturalists relative to that of both foragers and horticulturalists is well documented in the anthropological literature (Clark and Brandt 1984; Campbell and Wood 1988; Armelagos et al. 1991; Bentley et al. 1993a, b).

Indeed, in a study using the same forty-four prehistoric Andean mortuary samples reported here, I (2007) examined three competing models explaining the peopling of the Andes using the matrix method technique. These models include one that posits all prehistoric Andeans are directly descended from the Paleoindians, a second that posits complete replacement of the Paleoindians by a subsequent migration of populations characterized by sinodonty, and a third model showing demographic expansion of food-producing populations whose origins begin in the northern Andes and proceed south through time toward the Southern Cone. For the single migration model (i.e., Paleoindian origins from all prehistoric Andeans), two migrations with complete replacement of the Paleoindian model,

and demic expansion models, I (2007) showed that once geographic distance is controlled for, the demic expansion model is significantly related to the biodistances among the forty-four prehistoric Andean samples and best explains the observed patterns.

While the exact timing of the demic expansion into South America is difficult to estimate (given the relatively limited number of mortuary samples available for study), compelling evidence exists. Theoretically, this demic expansion would be closely related to the beginning of food production in the Formative period of different regions of South America. Accordingly, this expansion had its origins in northwestern South America, where the earliest evidence for agriculture is found (Pearsall 1992). The shift to food production and the hypothesized demic expansion likely corresponded with worldwide environmental changes during the Boreal period (4500–3500 BC). The Boreal period is characterized by highly variable precipitation and increased temperatures (Heusser 1983; Núñez 1983; Thompson et al. 1992). Archaeologically, this period is associated with the restricted distribution of important resources, and humans responded to these changes through the intensified exploitation of important resources and experimented with new forms of subsistence.

In South America, a number of plants were already being cultivated prior to the end of the Boreal period (Quilter and Stocker 1983; Quilter 1991; Pearsall 1992); however, a complete shift to food production had not occurred. Conditions during the subsequent Atlantic period (3500–1500 BC) are implicated in the increased productivity of C3 plants (Sage et al. 1995) such as maize, sedges, and other important New World cultigens (Street-Perrott et al. 1997). The Atlantic period is characterized by a decrease in temperature and an increase in humidity and atmospheric CO_2 levels. This period also marks the emergence of modern ocean levels, ocean currents, and the El Niño (ENSO) phenomenon (Thompson et al. 1992; Sandweiss et al. 1996, 1999). The increased productivity of these plants may have triggered the economic shift from simple supplemental cultivation of tropical domesticates to intensive agriculture.

The results reported here beg the question, what were the origins of these initial sinodont populations? I have previously proposed two possibilities. First, it is possible that sinodonty was already present among the initial colonists of the New World (Sutter 2005). Others report that North American Paleoindian dental (Powell

1993, 1995, 2000; Scott and Turner 1997; Powell and Neves 1998; Powell and Rose 1999) and craniometric morphology (Neves et al. 1996a,b; Jantz and Owsley 1998a, b; Neves et al. 1999a–d, 2001; Powell and Neves 1999; Powell and Rose 1999) is highly variable, but much less so among South American Paleoindians (Neves and Pucciarelli 1991; Munford et al. 1995; Neves et al. 1996a, b, 1999a–d, 2001; Powell and Neves 1998). Powell (1995) and Powell and Neves (1999) correctly point out that it is possible that microdifferentiation among the initial colonizers of the New World led to some local Paleoindian populations being characterized by sinodonty while others may have been characterized by sundadonty. If this were the case, then the initial colonizers of South America, characterized by a sundadont dental pattern, may have experienced a bottleneck as they passed through Central America to South America.

The second possibility is that the Paleoindians and their direct descendants—who would have been characterized by sundadonty and a "proto-Mongoloid" (Munford et al. 1995; Neves et al. 1996a; Brace et al. 2001; González-José et al. 2003, 2005) or "generalized Mongoloid" (Lahr 1995, 1996, 1997) morphology—are genetically and morphologically distinct from other Amerindians and northeast Asians who are characterized by sinodonty and Mongoloid craniometric morphology. Once again, this is not a novel proposition, as others also contend that the Amerindian samples reported by Turner (1983, 1985) and Greenberg et al. (1986) represent two or more genetically and morphologically distinct populations (Neves and Pucciarelli 1989; Powell 1993, 1995, 2000; Lahr 1995, 1996, 1997; Munford et al. 1995; Neves et al. 1996b; Powell and Neves 1998, 1999; Neves et al. 1999a, c, 2001; Steele and Powell 2002). As Lahr (1995:188) correctly points out, this scenario does not necessarily require a revision in dating the arrival of the Paleoindians and other Amerindians, nor does it preclude their arrival in two simultaneous but morphologically distinct colonizing populations.

Whichever of the two aforementioned models explains the origins of New World populations characterized by sinodonty or a Mongoloid craniofacial morphology, the data presented both here and by others (Lahr and Haydenblit 1995; Powell and Neves 1998; González-José et al. 2002) suggest that the earliest inhabitants of South America and their Preceramic period descendants would have been characterized by sundadonty and a proto-Mongoloid or generalized Mongoloid craniofacial morphology, while the subsequent demic expansion would have been associated with populations characterized by sinodonty and a Mongoloid craniofacial morphology. Based on trends in the currently available craniometric and dental data, the most likely source for the detected demic expansion was external to South America.

IMPLICATIONS FOR MOSELEY'S MARITIME HYPOTHESIS

Moseley (1975, 1992) has cogently argued that large, dense Preceramic populations of north and central coastal Peru were supported by essentially unlimited marine resources. He suggests that the reliance on marine resources would have permitted the emergence of craft specialization, and a need to organize large public works would have required organizational leaders. These factors, Moseley contends, made Preceramic coastal populations pre-adapted to sociopolitical complexity and the emergence of civilization. Although recent reports of Caral from the Supe Valley, Peru are claimed to contradict Moseley's maritime hypothesis (Haas 2004), investigators' impressions of the refuse from Caral indicate an almost exclusive reliance on marine resources, with the only cultigen being an economic plant, cotton (Haas 2004).

Data from my study suggest that the Preceramic mortuary populations associated with early monuments on the north and central coast of Peru represent direct descendants of the Paleoindians (see Figure 2.2). With the exception of La Galgada, an aceramic food-producing population of the northern sierra of Peru (Grieder and Bueno 1988), all other Preceramic mortuary populations examined in this study (Huaca Prieta, Río Seco, Paloma, Chilca I, Asia, Ilo Preceramic, Azapa Chinchorros, Camarones Chinchorros, Punta Teatinos, Araucanos, and Fueginos) also represent direct descendants of the Paleoindians.

Among the forty-four prehistoric samples I examined, the impact of the proposed demic expansion associated with the north-to-south spread of food production is first detected in the northern Peruvian sierra at La Galgada. Did food production and, hence, sinodonty appear first in the highlands and proceed west into the coastal valleys? Given the limited number of highland Preceramic mortuary populations available for study, it is unclear whether the appearance of sinodonty at La Galgada represents a real trend or an anomaly.

If this trend was the case, then terminal Preceramic coastal populations likely received substantial gene flow from in-migration of adjacent sierra populations from the east. This explanation receives some support from previous morphological studies that note gene flow among coastal populations (Newman 1948; Ericksen 1962; Turner cited in Benfer 1984). Indeed, both Ericksen (1962) and Newman (1948) suggest that these trends were due to an influx of highlanders into the coastal areas.

The results of my study neither support nor contradict Moseley's maritime hypothesis. However, insofar as some of the Preceramic samples I examined were from sites used by Moseley to support his hypothesis, it is unlikely that Late Preceramic north and central coastal populations represent direct ancestors to later agricultural populations of the region or—contrary to suggestions implied by Haas (2004)—to the subsequent development of complexity detected throughout the Peruvian Andes. Rather, the results presented here provide us with provocative new insights regarding population dynamics and possible external cultural influences at the close of the Preceramic period on the coast of Peru. Relative to neighboring food-producing populations to the east and north, the primarily maritime-based subsistence of Preceramic coastal populations would have been characterized by a lower rate of population growth. During the Cotton Preceramic-Early Horizon transition, populations of the northern and central coast would have received an influx of migrants from neighboring food-producing populations from the east and north that would have been characterized by higher frequencies of complex tooth and root traits. However, this influx does not represent a migration with population replacement. Instead, adjacent neighboring populations that gradually adopted food-production (and with which the coastal populations presumably would have had both exchange and breeding relations) would have had greater rates of population increase, thereby interbreeding with existing coastal populations and "drowning out" their genetic contributions. This model may account for the appearance of apparently "Amazonian" iconographic influence among coastal Cupisnique ceramics and clay friezes.

The proposed demographic expansion would have proceeded south into the southern highlands and coast of Peru as the economy shifted to food production during the Early Horizon. The population influx is apparent among the Early Horizon Cabezas Largas and Falda mortuary populations of the Paracas region.

Interestingly, Tello's Paracas sample is not located with other Peruvian food-producing populations but instead is located in Cluster 1A. This exception will require further consideration by subsequent studies that consider additional samples from the south-central coast of Peru.

IMPLICATIONS OF THE DEMIC EXPANSION FOR THE SOUTH-CENTRAL ANDES

If we focus on only those Peruvian samples from the south-central Andes, a number of important relationships can be ascertained that have important implications for understanding the population dynamics and the emergence of complex societies of the region. More specifically, a topic that has received considerable attention by investigators is the relationship between the Tiwanaku and other populations of the region. Questions remain regarding where and to what degree Tiwanaku colonists were responsible for spreading Tiwanaku material culture. While both archaeological and biodistance studies apparently confirm the presence of Tiwanaku colonists in the middle Moquegua Valley (Goldstein 1993; Blom et al. 1998; Blom 1999; Knudson 2004), others report that Tiwanaku's influence in the Azapa Valley, Chile (Sutter 1997, 2000; Sutter and Mertz 2004), the eastern valleys of Bolivia (Blom and Janusek 2001; O'Brien 2003), and San Pedro de Atacama (Stovel 2002; Knudson 2004) was primarily cultural and not biological.

Of related interest are the possible secondary population dispersals and cultural influences that resulted from the environmentally induced collapse of the Tiwanaku (Kolata 1993; Ortloff and Kolata 1993). The primary region of focus for these studies has been the Moquegua Valley, Peru (Owen 1993; Sutter 1997, 2000; Lozada 1998; Lozada and Buikstra 2002; Knudson 2004). Following the collapse of Tiwanaku's influence in the middle Moquegua Valley, there is an apparent dispersal of previous Tiwanaku colonists, with new settlements appearing both on the coast and along the upper tributaries to the Moquegua Valley and the simultaneous emergence of new, highly variable ceramic styles, including Tumilaca and Chiribaya (Bawden 1989, 1993; Goldstein 1993; Owen 1993). Although most scholars recognize a direct relationship between Tiwanaku and subsequent Tumilaca and Chiribaya ceramics (Goldstein 1985; Bawden 1989; Owen 1993), some scholars

(Lozada 1998; Lozada and Buikstra 2002) contend that Chiribaya represents a primarily coastal and Middle Horizon polity with roots in earlier coastal inhabitants. Others, however, argue (Owen 1993; Sutter 1997, 2000; Umire and Miranda 2001) that the coastal Chiribaya represent post-Tiwanaku-influence terminal Middle Horizon/early Late Intermediate period migrants from the middle Moquegua Valley. Based on his excavations and complete survey in the coastal Moquegua, Owen (1993, 2005) argues that this migration occurred during the collapse of the Tiwanaku polity's influence in the middle Moquegua Valley region.

Based on a number of radiocarbon dates from human skeletal materials, Lozada (1998:52) and Lozada and Buikstra (2002:54–57) argue that the coastal Chiribaya were contemporaneous with both the Tiwanaku and their colony in the middle Moquegua Valley. By logical extension, if the coastal Chiribaya were contemporaneous with the Middle Horizon Tiwanaku, then the coastal Chiribaya could not be related to the highland Tiwanaku or the Tiwanaku colonists from the mid-valley region. To support these claims, Lozada (1998) and Lozada and Buikstra (2002) present biodistance comparisons based on nonmetric cranial trait frequencies recorded for the coastal Chiribaya from Chiribaya Alta, San Gerónimo, and Algodonal, and compare these mortuary populations with a coastal Formative period mortuary sample from Roca Verde and with middle valley remains from La Yaral and Tiwanaku-affiliated remains from Chen Chen. Using a model-bound approach, these investigators report that all of the samples are significantly different from the middle valley Chen Chen sample, yet fail to exhibit significant distances among the remaining samples. Because of this, they argue, the coastal Chiribaya have both their cultural and genetic origins among the preceding Formative period coastal populations, as represented by the Roca Verde mortuary sample. However, a critical evaluation of both the chronology and biodistance analyses for the Moquegua Valley coastal Chiribaya reveals that Lozada's (1998) and Lozada and Buikstra's (2002) scenario for the coastal Chiribaya is problematic.

To begin with, Lozada's (1998) and Lozada and Buikstra's (2002) revised chronology for the coastal Chiribaya relies on radiocarbon dates from human skeletal remains associated with Chiribaya ceramics. These investigators report dates for the Chiribaya that range between AD 772 and AD 1113. Overlapping radiocarbon ranges from remains associated with different Chiribaya ceramic styles led the investigators

to argue that these ceramics were contemporaneous. However, the dates reported by Loazada (1998) and Lozada and Buikstra (2002) are centuries earlier than numerous dates reported for other Chiribaya contexts (Stanish and Rice 1989:8; Owen 1993:407–408, 2002, 2005) and contradict relative chronologies derived from both ceramic seriation and excavated stratified sequences (Jessup 1990a,b; Owen 1993; Umire and Miranda 2001). Further, Owen's (2002) investigation of the relationship between radiocarbon dates from both Chiribaya human remains and their associated wool textiles indicates that dates based on the human remains are on average more than 100 years earlier than those based on their associated textiles. Owen (2002) points to studies indicating the Chiribaya had a large marine component in their diet, leading him to suggest a dramatic carbon reservoir effect for dates from human remains. Indeed, the preponderance of dates for the coastal Chiribaya indicates that they existed between AD 900 and AD 1350 and represent a cultural phenomenon that postdates the Tiwanaku influence in the middle Moquegua Valley.

Perhaps even more problematic are both the data and biodistance analyses employed by Lozada (1998) and Lozada and Buikstra (2002). First, with the exception of Chen Chen, all other data were collected by the principal author of these studies. Notably, the Chen Chen sample—the only mortuary population Lozada did not record herself—exhibits significant differences from all other mortuary samples examined, yet none of the other sample comparisons produced statistically significant differences (Lozada 1998:103–107; Lozada and Buikstra 2002:97–98). According to the investigators, the data for Chen Chen—which were scored by Blom (1999)—are comparable to data from their study: in order to evaluate interobserver error between Lozada and Blom, the two evaluators scored a collection not used in Blom's or Lozada's studies. According to Lozada (1998:99) and Lozada and Buikstra (2002:94), traits were eliminated only in instances where Lozada and Blom's scores for the commonly scored collection were significantly different from one another (i.e., 90% disagreement). Traditionally, traits scored by different investigators are included in biodistance analyses only in instances where the traits are scored with 90% agreement between evaluators. The criteria employed for evaluating interobserver error cast serious doubt on the underlying cause for the significant differences reported between the Chen Chen sample and those scored by Lozada.

Lozada (1998) and Lozada and Buikstra (2002) have also called into question previous studies that explore the origins of the coastal Chiribaya (Sutter 1997, 2000) because these studies employed a parametric, model-free approach using the mean measure of divergence (MMD). However, the simple mean frequency difference formula used by Lozada (1998:101) and Lozada and Buikstra (2002:95) to estimate biological relatedness among their samples fails to take into account sample sizes. Indeed, the biodistance formula used by the authors causes traits with either very high or very low frequencies to be weighted disproportionately (Hallgrímsson et al. 2004:262). Because Lozada's (1998) data are not presented in full, it is not possible to fully evaluate to what degree the aforementioned problem might influence her results. However, inspection of the table of frequencies (Lozada 1998:Appendix B) indicates that 113 (35%) of 323 trait frequencies used for biodistance calculations were extreme (i.e., >0.9, <0.1). With more than one-third of the trait frequencies being extreme, any conclusions based on the significance of biodistance values from their study are equivocal. Further, although the alternative nonparametric, model-bound approach is proposed to be superior to the MMD (Lozada 1998:101; Blom 1999; Lozada and Buikstra 2002:95), a recent comparison of the two approaches found both that the MMD is a more conservative statistic and that its results are highly correlated with those derived using the bootstrap technique (Hallgrímsson et al. 2004:265).

The cluster diagram produced from biodistance results for the Paleoindian and twenty-one south-central Andean mortuary samples examined in my study indicate that the post-Tiwanaku-influence Moquegua Valley Chiribaya samples from La Yaral, Chiribaya Alta, and San Gerónimo are all located in the same sub-cluster as the Tiwanaku sample, along with the Middle Horizon San Pedro de Atacama Casa Parroquial sample and terminal Late Intermediate period Gentilar samples from Azapa-8 and Camarones-8 (see Figure 2.3). All of these samples would all have received contributions from the agriculturally driven demic expansion into the south-central Andes. Their close proximity in the cluster diagram implies recent common ancestry among these samples. It is also noteworthy that the earliest sample from the Moquegua Valley, the Ilo Preceramic mortuary sample, clusters with the Paleoindians and other Preceramic period and Southern Cone samples in a second cluster, suggesting these populations are directly descended from the Paleoindians.

If we consider temporal trends in these results as they relate to the question of relations among both Middle Horizon and post-Middle Horizon samples, the San Pedro de Atacama Casa Parroquial mortuary population is the Middle Horizon sample most similar to the Tiwanaku population. These results are provocative, given the nature of the Casa Parroquial sample: although not yet reported, the sample is composed of possible nonlocal individuals from a wealthy group tomb (Lautaro Núñez, pers. comm.). According to Núñez, individuals from this grave were interred with elaborate ceramics, textiles, and spectacular gold keros, snuff tubes suggesting strong material ties with the Tiwanaku Middle Horizon polity. The placement of the sample from Casa Parroquial with the Middle Horizon sample from the Tiwanaku Basin strongly suggests that these samples shared recent common ancestors. It is clear, based on the clustering of the San Pedro de Atacama Formative period Toconao and Middle Horizon Coyo Oriente samples with the Paleoindians and other northern Chilean samples of the second cluster, that these samples are not closely related to the Tiwanaku sample, contrary to the assertion of some investigators (Berenguer and Dauelsberg 1989; Oakland 1992). These results from the Middle Horizon Coyo Oriente sample are consistent with Knudson's (2004) examination of strontium isotopes of bones and teeth, which indicated that none of the individuals from Coyo Oriente had strontium signatures characteristic of the Lake Titicaca Basin. Although strontium isotopes cannot address common recent ancestry between the Tiwanaku and Coyo Oriente populations, the data can provide insights into where individuals may have been raised as children and where they lived as adults. All of the individuals from Coyo Oriente sampled by Knudson (2004) were raised on local diets, indicating their local origin.

Middle Horizon samples from the Azapa Valley are also found in the same cluster (although a different sub-cluster) as the Paleoindian sample, suggesting a direct ancestor-descendant relationship among these samples, with relatively little genetic contribution from Middle Horizon Lake Titicaca Basin populations. Indeed, Sutter and Mertz's (2004) study of nonmetric cranial trait variation among Azapa Valley samples also failed to report evidence for a nonlocal immigrant mortuary population.

Among post-Tiwanaku samples, the middle Moquegua Valley La Yaral sample is most similar to the Tiwanaku mortuary population, followed by the contemporaneous samples from Chiribaya Alta and San Gerónimo. Their placement within the same cluster with the Tiwanaku sample indicates an ancestor-descendant relationship among Middle Horizon Titicaca Basin populations and terminal Middle Horizon/early Late Intermediate period coastal Chiribaya. Indeed, Knudson's (2004) strontium isotope analysis indicated that one (25%) of four individuals sampled from El Yaral and four (33%) of twelve individuals from Chiribaya Alta (Knudson 2004:114–116) were raised at nonlocal, likely Titicaca Basin locations (i.e., ones with a different strontium signature). Interestingly, although they are supposed to be altiplano colonists, only four (16%) of twenty-five individuals interred at the middle valley Chen Chen site were found to be raised on nonlocal diets. However, Knudson's results clearly indicate that some Moquegua Valley Chiribaya individuals represent migrants who were raised in the adjacent highlands to the east. Although Knudson's data do not provide information regarding common recent ancestry among the coastal Chiribaya and preceding Middle Horizon middle valley Chen Chen colonists, they do make a strictly coastal origin model for the coastal Chiribaya untenable.

Unfortunately, the biodistance results presented by this study do not indicate at what point in the past the Tiwanaku and coastal Chiribaya samples shared a common ancestor. However, these results provide support for Owen's (1993, 2005) archaeologically based model for the origins of the Chiribaya. Owen contends that prior to the collapse of Tiwanaku's influence in the middle Moquegua Valley, the coastal valley was sparsely populated by Algodonal Early Ceramic peoples whose sites were smaller and fewer than those of the subsequent post-Tiwanaku occupation of the valley. Beginning around AD 900, Owen (1993, 2005) detects the appearance of both Chiribaya and Ilo-Tumilaca/Cabuza ceramic traditions on the coast, with a simultaneous and substantial increase in both site size and site number. These new ceramic traditions, Owen contends, are strikingly similar to those found in the middle Moquegua Valley that appeared in the vacuum created by the collapse of the Tiwanaku's influence. Based on the striking cultural similarities to the previous middle valley populations and the unmistakable differences from the preceding Algodonal Early Ceramic coastal inhabitants, Owen (1993) argues the coastal Chiribaya and Ilo-Tumilaca/Cabuza represent migrants from the middle Moquegua Valley. In light of both the archaeological data and the biodistance results presented here,

it appears that Lozada's (Lozada 1998; Lozada and Buikstra 2002) model for the origins of the Chiribaya is unlikely.

In northern Chile, with the exceptions of the terminal Late Intermediate period samples from Azapa-8 and Camarones-8, all the remaining Late Intermediate period samples cluster with the Paleoindians (see Figure 2.3). Two important conclusions can be drawn from these results. First, there is only a small genetic contribution from the Titicaca Basin detected among both terminal Middle Horizon and Late Intermediate period northern Chilean mortuary populations. Second, the demographic expansion detected in Peru had a limited impact beyond southern Peru until very late in prehistory. Both the Azapa-8 and Camarones-8 samples are terminal Late Intermediate period samples associated with Gentilar ceramics. Whereas Gentilar is relatively rare in the adjacent altiplano (Dauelsberg 1983), some have posited there may be some altiplano influence among the populations represented by these ceramic traditions (Dauelsberg 1983; Muñoz 1989:105; Schiappacasse et al. 1989). It is presently unclear whether the populations represented by the Azapa-8 and Camarones-8 Gentilar mortuary samples represent Late Intermediate period altiplano colonists or simply local coastal populations that received substantial gene flow following the collapse of the Middle Horizon Tiwanaku.

The only Late Horizon sample from the south-central Andes, Camarones-9, clusters with the first cluster. Although burials from Camarones-9 were interred with Inka ceramics (Muñoz 1989), it appears, based on the biodistance relations to other northern Chilean and Paleoindian samples, to be a population with locally indigenous ancestors.

As to why the demic expansion of sinodonty had relatively little impact south of the Peruvian-Chilean border until the terminal Late Intermediate period, I submit the following explanation. The demic expansion model requires differential reproductive rates between adjacent populations. Geographic data for Peru (ONERN 1976, 1984) indicate that, as a general trend, both coastal valley agricultural productivity and rainfall decrease as one proceeds from north to south along the west coast of Peru. This trend is exacerbated in the Atacama Desert of northern Chile. Indeed, as one proceeds from the Lluta to the Azapa, Camarones, and valleys farther south, the irrigable land, river discharge, and agricultural output all decrease (Rodríguez 1989:51–54), with less than 0.03% of the total land being agriculturally productive. In light of the substantial decrease in agricultural productivity in the south-central Andean region as one proceeds from north to south, the demographic differential that was driving the wave of gene flow detected in northern and central Peru would have also have been substantially decreased. Indeed, a number of both molecular (Demarchi et al. 2001; Lalueza-Fox 1996; Lalueza-Fox et al. 1997; Merriwether et al. 1994; Moraga et al. 2000; Turbón et al. 1994) and osteological studies (Lahr 1995, 1996; Lahr and Haydenblit 1995; González-José et al. 2001) support the notion that Southern Cone populations may represent descendants of the Paleoindians who received relatively little genetic contribution from food-producing northern and central Andean populations.

CONCLUSIONS

The dental trait data presented here provide insights into Michael Moseley's interests in the relationship among the environment, the emergence of social complexity among Preceramic coastal people, and population dynamics in the south-central Andes. Following the initial colonization of South America by the Paleoindians, a subsequent migratory event likely occurred in association with the climatic optimum as a result of increased fertility among Central American sinodonts who made the economic shift to food production. This event can be described as a demic expansion, or gene flow, resulting from increased fertility of the aforementioned food-producing populations.

The demic expansion proceeded from northeastern South America south during the Formative period in each adjacent region in the Peruvian and Bolivian Andes. The implication for Moseley's maritime hypothesis is that preexisting Cotton Preceramic coastal populations of the north and central coast of Peru received substantial gene flow from adjacent food-producing populations living to the north and east.

In the south-central Andes, the demic expansion would have been slowed by narrow valleys and the lesser precipitation that resulted in lower population size and fertility. Additional samples are needed to determine the precise time of arrival of sinodonty in the south-central Andes. The epigenetic dental traits provide us with compelling insights into population dynamics during and immediately following the Middle Horizon. Populations of the Titicaca Basin had relatively little impact in some coastal valleys, such as the

Azapa and Camarones valleys of northern Chile, but likely contributed colonists to the middle Moquegua Valley, and possibly had a limited presence at San Pedro de Atacama.

Following the collapse of the Tiwanaku's presence in the middle Moquegua Valley, their former colonists apparently dispersed and colonized the coastal Moquegua Valley, quickly establishing a new ethnic identity with the emergence of the Chiribaya and Ilo-Tumilaca/Cabuza cultural traditions. It is not until the terminal Late Intermediate period that populations associated with higher tooth cusp and root frequencies are detected among northern Chilean Gentilar coastal populations. However, the exact nature of relations among the Gentilar and Late Intermediate period altiplano señoríos is unclear.

The biocultural histories proposed here for both the Cotton Preceramic of coastal Perú, and Middle Horizon in the south-central Andes are not intended to be the final word. Rather, these scenarios are intended to provoke thoughtful scholarship and critical evaluation of the ideas presented by this chapter. Our current knowledge is limited by the relatively few mortuary samples that have been examined in this vast region. With additional mortuary samples with tight chronological control, rigorous analyses, and critical evaluation of the available biological and archaeological data, future investigations will certainly lead to revisions of the ideas presented by this chapter.

Acknowledgments

This research was made possible by the kindness of many people and institutions. I am greatly indebted to the following individuals: Dr. Jane E. Buikstra, Dr. Karen Wise, and Dr. Karen Rasmussen for collections from Moquegua, Perú; Dr. Iván Muñoz, Juan Chacama, Guillermo Focacci, Percy Dauelsberg, and Mariela Santos for facilitating my research in the Museo San Miguel de Azapa, of the Universidad de Tarapacá, Arica, Chile; Dra. Hilda Vidal Vidal, Dr. Claude Chauchat, and Dr. Alberto Bueno for facilitating my access to collections at the Museo Nacional de Antropología, Arqueología e Historia del Perú; Dra. Silvia Quevedo Kowasaki for facilitating my access to collections at the Museo Nacional de Historia Natural, Santiago, Chile; Dr. Lautaro Núñez and Dra. María Costa for facilitating my access to collections at the Museo Padre Le Paige, San Pedro de Atacama, Chile; Dra. Ana María Hoyle, José Carcelén, Dr. John Verano, Dr. Christopher Donnan for access to collections from

Cerro Oreja and Pacatnamú; Dr. Santiago Uceda for facilitating my research on collections from Huaca de la Luna; Dr. Robert Benfer, Jr., Dr. Frederic Engel, Dra. Miriam Vallejos for facilitating my access to materials at the Centro de Investigaciones de Zonas Áridas of the Universidad Nacional Agraria-La Molina, Lima, Perú; Dr. Ian Tattersall, Dr. Craig Morris, Dr. Kenneth Mowbray, and Gary Sawyer for facilitating my access to collections at the American Museum of Natural History. The following institutions and organizations provided logistical support: the Southern Peru Copper Corporation; Programa Contisuyu (now the Asociación Contisuyu); Centro Mallqui, Perú; Museo San Miguel de Azapa, Arica, Chile; Museo de Arqueología San Pedro de Atacama, Museo Nacional de Historia Natural, the Centro de Investigaciones de Zonas Áridas, Lima, Perú; Museo Nacional de Antropología, Arqueología e Historia del Perú, Museo de la Universidad Nacional de Trujillo, Perú; Museo del Sitio Huaca Arco Iris, Trujillo, Perú; and the American Museum of Natural History. This research was funded in part by a Fulbright Fellowship for my research in Chile during 1993–1994, NSF grant no. 9816958, and by Purdue Research Foundation Summer Faculty Research Grant for my research in Peru and Chile in 1998–2001.

REFERENCES

Aldenderfer, Mark S., and Roger K. Blashfield
1984   *Cluster Analysis*. Sage Publications, London.

Armelagos, George J., Alan H. Goodman, and Kenneth H. Jacobs
1991   The Origins of Agriculture: Population Growth during a Period of Declining Health. *Population and Environment* 13:9–22.

Aufderheide, Arthur C., Iván Muñoz, and Bernardo Arriaza
1993   Seven Chinchorro Mummies and the Prehistory of Northern Chile. *American Journal of Physical Anthropology* 91:189–202.

Bandelier, Adolph
1910   *The Islands of Titicaca and Koati*. The Hispanic Society of New York, New York.

Barbujani, Guido, Andrea Pilastro, Silvia De Domenico, and Colin Renfrew
1994   Genetic Variation in North Africa and Eurasia: Neolithic Demic Diffusion vs. Paleolithic Colonisation. *American Journal of Physical Anthropology* 95:137–154.

Bawden, Garth
1989   The Tumilaca Site and Post-Tiahuanaco Occupational Stratigraphy in the Moquegua Drainage. In *Ecology, Settlement, and History in the Osmore Drainage, Peru*, edited by Don S. Rice, Charles Stanish, and Phillip R. Scarr, pp. 287–302. BAR International Series 545(ii). British Archaeological Reports, Oxford, U.K.
1993   An Archaeological Study of Social Structure and Ethnic Replacement in Residential Architecture of the Tumilaca Valley. In *Domestic Architecture, Ethnicity, and Complementarity in the South-Central Andes*, edited by Mark S. Aldenderfer, pp. 42–54. University of Iowa Press, Iowa City.

Benfer, Robert A.
1984   The Challenges and Rewards of Sedentism: The Preceramic Village of Paloma, Peru. In *Paleopathology at the Origins of Agriculture*, edited by Mark N. Cohen, pp. 531–558. Academic Press, Orlando, FL.
1986   Holocene Coastal Adaptations: Changing Demography and Health at the Fog Oasis of Paloma, Peru 5000–7800 B. P. In *Andean Archaeology, Papers in Memory of Clifford Evans*, edited by Ramiro Matos Mendieta, Solveig A. Turpin, and Herbert H. J. Eling, Jr., pp. 45–64. Monograph 27, Institute of Archaeology, University of California, Los Angeles.

Bentley, Gillian R., Tony Goldberg, and Grazyna Jasienska
1993a   The Fertility of Agricultural and Non-Agricultural Traditional Societies. *Population Studies* 47:269–281.
1993b   Is the Fertility of Agriculturalists Higher than that of Nonagriculturalists? *Current Anthropology* 34:778–785.

Berenguer, José, and Percy Dauelsberg
1989   El Norte Grande en la Orbita de Tiwanaku. In *Culturas de Chile: Prehistoria desde sus orígenes hasta los albores de la conquista*, edited by Jorge Hidalgo, Virgilio Schiappacasse, Hans Niemeyer, Carlos Aldunate, and Iván Solimano, pp. 129–180. Andrés Bello, Santiago.

Berry, A. Caroline
1978   Anthropological and Family Studies on Minor Variants of the Dental Crown. In *Development, Function and Evolution of Teeth*, edited by Percy M. Butler and Kenneth A. Joysey, pp. 81–98. Academic Press, New York.

Benyon, Diane E., and Michael I. Siegel
1981   Ancient Human remains from Central Peru. *American Antiquity* 46:167–178.

Biggerstaff, Robert H.

1970   Morphological Variations for the Permanent Mandibular First Molars in Human Monozygotic and Dizygotic Twins. *Archives of Oral Biology* 15:721–730.

1973   Heritability of the Carabelli Cusp in Twins. *Journal of Dental Research* 52:40–44.

Bird, Junius B.

1988   *Travels and Archaeology in South Chile.* University of Iowa Press, Iowa City.

Bird, Junius B., and John Hyslop (eds.)

1985   *The Preceramic Excavations at the Huaca Prieta, Chicama Valley, Peru.* Anthropological Papers of the American Museum of Natural History, vol. 62, pt. 1. The American Museum of Natural History, New York.

Birdsell, Joseph B.

1951   The Problem of the Early Peopling of the Americas as Viewed from Asia. In *Papers on the Physical Anthropology of the American Indian,* edited by William S. Laughlin, pp. 1–68. The Viking Fund, New York.

Blom, Deborah E.

1999   *Tiwanaku Regional Interaction and Social Identity: A Bioarchaeological Approach.* Unpublished doctoral dissertation, Department of Anthropology, University of Chicago.

Blom, Deborah E., Benedikt Hallgrímsson, Linda Keng, María Cecilia Lozada, and Jane E. Buikstra

1998   Tiwanaku "Colonization": Bioarchaeological Implications for Migration in the Moquegua Valley, Peru. *World Archaeology* 30(2):238–261.

Blom, Deborah, and John Janusek

2001   Explaining Diversity: Migration and Trade in the Eastern Andean Valleys, Icla, Bolivia. Paper presented at the 66th Annual Meeting of the Society for American Archaeology, New Orleans, LA, USA.

Bonatto, Sandro, and Francisco Salzano

1997a   Single and Early Migration for the Peopling of the Americas Supported by Mitochondrial DNA Sequence Data. *Proceedings of the National Academy of Sciences* 94:1866–1871.

1997b   Diversity and Age of the Four Major mtDNA Haplogroups, and Their Implications for the Peopling of the New World. *American Journal of Human Genetics* 61:1413–1423.

Bórmida, Marcelo

1966   Los esqueletos de Lauricocha. *Acta Praehistorica* V–VII:1–34.

Bourget, Steve

1997   Las excavaciones en la Plaza 3A de la Huaca de la Luna. In *Investigaciones en la Huaca de la Luna 1995,* edited by Santiago Uceda, Elías Mujica, and R. Morales, pp. 51–59. Universidad Nacional de La Libertad–Trujillo, Trujillo.

Brace, C. Loring, A. Russell Nelson, Noriko Seguchi, Hiroaki Oe, Leslie Sering, Pan Qifeng, Li Yongyi, and Dashtseveg Tumen

2001   Old World Sources of the First New World Human Inhabitants: A Comparative Craniofacial View. *Proceedings of the National Academy of Sciences* 98(17):10017–10022.

Braga, José

2001   Cranial Discrete Variation in the Great Apes: New Prospects in Palaeoprimatology. In *Phylogeny of the Neogene Hominoid Primates of Eurasia,* edited by Louis de Bonis, George D. Koufos, and Peter Andrews, pp. 151–190. Hominoid Evolution and Climate Change in Europe, no. 2. Cambridge University Press, Cambridge.

Brewer-Carias, Charles A., Steven A. LeBlanc, and James V. Neel

1976   Genetic Structure of a Tribal Population, the Yanomama Indians. XIII. Dental Microdifferentiation. *American Journal of Physical Anthropology* 44:5–14.

Buikstra, Jane E.

1989   *Chiribaya: A Biocultural Approach to the Study of a Prehistoric Andean Polity.* National Science Foundation grant no. BSN 89 20769. Manuscript in the possession of the author.

1990   Sumario de la Investigación de Restos Humanos de Omo, Moquegua y San Gerónimo, Ilo. In *Trabajos arqueológicos en Moquegua Perú: Vol. 3,* edited by Luis K. Wantanabe, Michael E. Moseley, and Fernando Cabieses, pp. 59–68. Programa Contisuyo del Museo Peruano de Ciencias de la Salud, Southern Peru Copper Corporation, Moquegua, Peru.

1995   Tombs for the Living . . . or . . . for the Dead: The Osmore Ancestors. In *Tombs for the Living: Andean Mortuary Practices,* edited by Tom D. Dillehay, pp. 229–280. Dumbarton Oaks, Washington, DC.

Campbell, Kenneth L., and James W. Wood

1988   Fertility in Traditional Societies. In *Natural Human Fertility: Social and Biological Determinants,* edited by Peter Diggory, Malcolm Potts, and Sue Teper, pp. 39–69. Macmillan, London.

Carcelén, José

1995   *Proyecto de rescate arqueológico Chavimochic: Informe de entrega de obra. Tomo II, Volumen IV: Rescate arqueológico Flanco Norte y Arenales al oeste de Cerro Oreja. Canal Madr—II Etapa: Variante Cerro Oreja.* Instituto Nacional de Cultura, La Libertad, Trujillo.

Cavalli-Sforza, Luigi L., Paolo Menozzi, and Alberto Piazza

1994   *The History and Geography of Human Genes.* Princeton University Press, Princeton, NJ.

Chauchat, Claude

1988   Early Hunter-Gatherers on the Peruvian Coast. In *Peruvian Prehistory: An Overview of Pre-Inca and Inca Society,* edited by Richard W. Keatinge, pp. 41–66. Cambridge University Press, Cambridge.

Chauchat, Claude, and Jean M. Dricot

1979   Paléontologie humaine: Un nouveau type humain fossile en Amérique du Sud: l'Homme de Paiján (Pérou). *Comptes-Rendus des Scarces de L'Academie des Sciences, Sciences Naturelles* 289, Série D:387–389.

Clark, J. Desmond, and Steven A. Brandt (eds.)

1984   *From Hunters to Farmers: The Causes and Consequences of Food Production in Africa.* University of California Press, Berkeley.

Constandse-Westermann, Trinette S.

1972   *Coefficients of Biological Distance.* Anthropological Publications, Ooosterhout.

Cooper, John M.

1942   Areal and Temporal Aspects of South American Culture. *Primitive Man* 15:1–38.

Dauelsberg, Percy

1983   Investigaciones arqueológicas en la sierra de Arica. *Chungará* 11.

Demarchi, Dario A., Graciela M. Panzetta-Dutari, Sonia Colantonio, and Alberto J. Marcellino

2001   Absence of the 9-bp Deletion of Mitochondrial DNA in Pre-Hispanic Inhabitants of Argentina. *Human Biology* 71(4):575–582.

Donlon, Denise A.

2000   The Value of Infracranial Nonmetric Variation in Studies of Modern *Homo sapiens:* An Australian Focus. *American Journal of Physical Anthropology* 113(3):349–368.

Donnan, Christopher B., and Guillermo A. Cock (eds.)

1986   *The Pacatnamú Papers. Volume 1.* Museum of Cultural History, UCLA, Los Angeles.

Engel, Frédéric A.

1957   Sites et établissements sans céramique de la cote Perúvienne. *Journal de la Société des Américanistes* 46:67–155.

1960   Un group humain datant de 5000 ans à Paracas, Pérou. *Journal de la Société des Américanistes, Paris* 49:7–35.

1963   A Preceramic Settlement on the Central Coast of Perú. *Transactions of the American Philosophical Society* 53. Philadelphia.

1966a   *Geografía humana prehistórica y agricultura precolombina de la Quebrada de Chilca.* Universidad Agraria, Lima.

1966b   *Paracas: Cien siglos de cultura peruana.* Librería-Editorial Juan Mejía Baca, Lima.

1977   Early Holocene Funeral Bundles from the Central Andes. *Paleopathology Newsletter* 19:7–8.

1980   Paloma Village 613: A 6000 Year Old "Fog Oasis" Village in the Lower Central Andes of Peru. In *Prehistoric Andean Ecology,* vol. I, edited by Frederic A. Engel, pp. 103–135. Humanities Press, New York.

1981   *Prehistoric Andean Ecology,* vol. 2, *The Deep South.* Humanities Press, New York.

1982   *De las begonias al maíz: Vida y producción en el Perú antiguo.* Universidad Nacional Agraria, Lima.

Ericksen, Mary F.

1962   Undeformed Pre-Columbian Crania from the North Sierra of Peru. *American Journal of Physical Anthropology* 20:209–222.

Escobar, Victor, Michael Melnick, and P. Michael Conneally

1976   The Inheritance of Bilateral Rotation of Maxillary Central Incisors. *American Journal of Physical Anthropology* 45:109–116.

Espinoza, Gustavo, Teresa Cañipa, Leticia Latorre, Vikki Cassman, Richard C. Sutter, Guillermo Focacci, and Mariela B. Santos

1994   Registro *computacional de las colecciones arqueológicas Azapa* 6, Azapa 71a, Azapa 71b, Azapa 140, y Azapa 141. Departmento de Arqueología y Museología, Universidad de Tarapacá, Arica, Chile.

Finnegan, Michael, and Kevin B. Cooprider

1978   Empirical comparison of distance equations using discrete traits. *American Journal of Physical Anthropology* 49:39–46.

Focacci, Guillermo

1961   Excavaciones en San Miguel de Azapa. *Boletines del Museo Regional de Arica.* Universidad de Tarapacá, Arica, Chile.

1968   Boletas de Campo: Excavaciones en AZ-71. Field notes on file at the Museo San Miguel de Azapa, Universidad de Tarapacá, Arica, Chile.

1969 Boletas de Campo: Excavaciones en Playa Miller 4, 2 y 6. Field notes on file at the Museo San Miguel de Azapa, Universidad de Tarapacá, Arica, Chile.

1974 Excavaciones en Playa Miller 7. *Chungará* 3:23–74.

1980 Síntesis de la arqueología del extremo norte de Chile. *Chungará* 6:3–23.

Foccaci, Guillermo
1993 Excavaciones arqueológicas en el cementerio AZ-6 valle de Azapa. *Chungará* 24/25:69–124.

García, Manuel
1988 Excavaciones de dos viviendas Chiribaya en el Yaral, valle de Moquegua. Unpublished B.A. thesis, Universidad Católica "Santa María," Arequipa, Peru.

Goldstein, Paul S.
1985 Tiwanaku Ceramics of the Moquegua Valley, Peru. Master's thesis, Department of Anthropology, University of Chicago.

1993 Tiwanaku Temples and State Expansion: A Tiwanaku Sunken-Court Temple in Moquegua, Peru. *Latin American Antiquity* 4:22–47.

González-José, Rolando, Silvia Dahinten, and Miguel Hernández
2001 The Settlement of Patagonia: A Matrix Correlation Study. *Human Biology* 73(2):233–248.

González-José, Rolando, Antonio González-Martín, Miguel Hernández, Hector M. Pucciarelli, Marina Sardi, Alfonso Rosales, and Silvina Van der Molen
2003 Craniometric Evidence for Paleoindian Survival in Baja California. *Nature* 425:62–65.

González-José, Rolando, Clara García Moro, Silvia Dahinten, and Miguel Hernández
2002 Origin of Fueguian-Patagonians: An Approach to Population History and Structure Using R Matrix and Matrix Permutation Methods. *American Journal of Human Biology* 14(3): 308–320.

González-José, Rolando, Walter Neves, Marta M. Lahr, Silvia González, Hector Pucciarelli, Miguel Hernández Martínez, and Gonzalo Correal
2005 Late Pleistocene/Holocene Craniofacial Morphology in Mesoamerican Paleoindians: Implications for the Peopling of the New World. *American Journal of Physical Anthropology* 128(4):772–780.

Green, David L.
1982 Discrete Dental Variations and Biological Distances of Nubian Populations. *American Journal of Physical Anthropology* 58:75–79.

Greenberg, Joseph H., Christy G. Turner, and Steven L. Zegura
1986 The Settlement of the Americas: A Comparison of the Linguistic, Dental, and Genetic Evidence. *Current Anthropology* 27:477–497.

Grieder, Terence, and Alberto Bueno Mendoza (eds.)
1988 *La Galgada, Peru. A Preceramic Culture in Transition.* University of Texas Press, Austin.

Haas, Jonathan
2004 Mitayo: The Beginnings of Civilization in the Andes. Paper presented at the annual meeting of the Midwest Conference on Andean and Amazonian Archaeology and Ethnohistory. University of Illinois at Champaign-Urbana, Urbana.

Hallgrímsson, Benedikt, Barra Ó Donnabháin, G. Bragi Walters, David M. L. Cooper, Daníel Gudbjartsson, and Kari Stefánsson
2004 Composition of the Founding Population of Iceland: Biological Distance and Morphological Variation in Early Historic Atlantic Europe. *American Journal of Physical Anthropology* 124(3):257–274.

Harris, Edward F., and Howard L. Bailit
1980 The Metaconule: A Morphological and Familial Analysis of a Molar Cusp in Humans. *American Journal of Physical Anthropology* 53:349–358.

Hassanali, Jameela
1982 Incidence of Carabelli's Trait in Kenyan Africans and Africans. *American Journal of Physical Anthropology* 59:317–319.

Haydenblit, Rebecca
1996 Dental Variation Among Four Prehispanic Mexican Populations. *American Journal of Physical Anthropology* 100:225–246.

Haydon, Rex C.
1993 *Survey of Genetic Variation Among the Chiribaya of the Osmore Drainage Basin, Southern Perú.* Doctoral dissertation, Department of Anthropology, University of Chicago. University Microfilms International, Ann Arbor, MI.

Heusser, Calvin J.
1983 Quaternary Pollen Record from Laguna de Tagua Tagua, Chile. *Science* 219:1429–1432.

Hrdlička, Aleč
1923 The Origin and Antiquity of the American Indian. In *Annual Report of the Board of Regents of the Smithsonian Institution*, pp. 481–493. U.S. Governmental Printing Office, Washington, DC.

Imbelloni, José

1938   Tabla clasificatoria de los Indios, regiones biológicas y grupos raciales humanos de America. *Physis* 12:230–249.

1950   La tabla clasificatoria de los indios a los trece años de su publicación. *Runa* 3:200–210.

Jacobs, Kenneth

1994   Human Dento-Gnathic Metric Variation in Meso-lithic/Neolithic Ukraine: Possible Evidence of Demic Diffusion in the Dnieper Rapids Region. *American Journal of Physical Anthropology* 95:1–26.

Jessup, David

1990a   *Desarrollos generales en el Intermedio Tardío en el valle de Ilo, Perú.* Report submitted to the Instituto Nacional de Cultura, Lima.

1990b   Rescate arqueológico en el Museo de Sitio de San Gerónimo, Ilo. In *Trabajos arqueológicos en Moquegua, Perú*, vol. 3, edited by Luis K. Wantanabe, Michael E. Moseley, and Fernando Cabieses, pp. 151–165. Programa Contisuyo del Museo Peruano de Ciencias de la Salud, Southern Peru Copper Corporation, Moquegua, Peru.

Jantz, Richard L., and Douglas W. Owsley

1998a   Pathology, Taphonomy, and Cranial Morphometrics of the Spirit Cave Mummy. *Nevada Historical Society Quarterly* 40:62–84.

1998b   How Many Populations of Early North Americans Were There? *American Journal of Physical Anthropology Supplement* 26:128.

2001   Variation among Early American Crania. *American Journal of Physical Anthropology* 114:146–155.

Keyeux, Genoveva, Clemencia Rodas, Nancy Gelvez, and Dee Carter

2002   Possible Migration Routes into South America Deduced from Mitochondrial DNA Studies in Colombian Amerindian Populations. *Human Biology* 74(2):211–233.

Kolata, Alan L.

1993   *The Tiwanaku: Portrait of an Andean Society.* Blackwell, New York.

Knudson, Kelly J.

2004   *Tiwanaku Residential Mobility in the South Central Andes: Identifying Archaeological Human Migration Through Strontium Isotope Analysis.* Unpublished doctoral dissertation. Department of Anthropology, University of Wisconsin, Madison.

Lahr, Marta M.

1995   Patterns of Modern Human Diversification: Implications for Amerindian Origins. *Yearbook of Physical Anthropology* 38:163–198.

1996   *The Evolution of Modern Human Diversity: A Study of Cranial Variation.* Cambridge University Press, New York.

1997   History in the Bones. *Evolutionary Anthropology* 6:2–6.

Lahr, Marta M., and Rebecca Haydenblit

1995   Traces of Ancestral Morphology in Tierra del Fuego and Patagonia. *American Journal of Physical Anthropology Supplement* 20:128.

Lalueza-Fox, Carles

1996   Mitochondrial DNA Haplogroups in Four Tribes from Tierra del Fuego-Patagonia: Inferences about the Peopling of the Americas. *Human Biology* 68:855–871.

Lalueza-Fox, Carles, Alejandro Pérez-Pérez, Eva Prats, Luis Cornudella, and David Turbón

1997   Lack of Founding Amerindian Mitochondrial DNA Lineages in Extinct Aborigines from Tierra del Fuego-Patagonia. *Human Molecular Genetics* 6:41–46.

Lathrap, Donald W.

1970   *The Upper Amazon.* Thames and Hudson, Southampton, UK.

Lozada, María Cecilia

1998   *The Señorío of Chiribaya: A Bio-Archaeological Study in the Osmore Drainage of Southern Perú.* Unpublished doctoral dissertation, Department of Anthropology, University of Chicago.

Lozada, María Cecilia, and Jane E. Buikstra

2002   *El Señorío de Chiribaya en la costa sur del Perú.* Instituto de Estudios Peruanos, Lima, Peru.

Matisoo-Smith, Elizabeth

2002   Something Old, Something New: Do Genetic Studies of Contemporary Populations Reliably Represent Prehistoric Populations of Pacific *Rattus exulans*? *Human Biology* 74(3):489–496.

Merriwether, D. Andrew, Francisco Rothhammer, and Robert E. Ferrell

1994   Genetic Variation in the New World: Ancient Teeth, Bone, and Tissue as Sources of DNA. *Experientia* 50:592–601.

1995   Distribution of the Four Founding Lineage Haplotypes in Native Americans Suggests a Single Wave of Migration for the New World. *American Journal of Physical Anthropology* 98:411–430.

Montoya, Maria

1995   Excavaciones en la unidad 11 de la Plataforma I. In *Investigaciones en la Huaca de la Luna 1995*, edited by Santiago Uceda, Elías Mujica, and Ricardo Morales, pp. 29–38. Universidad Nacional de La Libertad, Trujillo, Peru.

Moraga, Mauricio L., Paola Rocco, Juan F. Miquel, Flavio Nervi, Elena Llop, Ranajit Chakraborty, Francisco Rothhammer, and Pilar Carvallo
2000 Mitochondrial DNA polymorphisms in Chilean Aboriginal Populations: Implications for the Peopling of the Southern Cone of the Continent. *American Journal of Physical Anthropology:* 113: 19–29.

Moseley, Michael E.
1975 *The Maritime Foundations of Andean Civilization.* Cummings Publishing Co., Menlo Park, CA.
1992 *The Incas and Their Ancestors.* Thames and Hudson, London.

Munford, Danusa, Maria do Carmo Zanini, and Walter A. Neves
1995 Human Cranial Variation iMuNew1996a, n South America: Implications for the Settlement of the New World. *Brazilian Journal of Genetics* 18:673–688.

Muñoz, Iván
1989 El período formativo en el Norte Grande (1.000 a.C. a 500 d.C.). In *Culturas de Chile: Prehistoria desde sus orígenes hasta los albores de la conquista,* edited by J. Hidalgo, V. Schiappacasse, H. Niemeyer, C. Aldunate and S. Iván, pp. 107–128. Andrés Bello, Santiago.

Muñoz, Iván, and Guillermo Focacci
1985 San Lorenzo: Testimonio de una comunidad de agricultores y pescadores postiwanaku en el valle de Azapa (Arica-Chile). *Chungará* 15:7–30.

Muñoz, Iván, Bernardo Arriaza, and Arthur C. Aufderheide
1993 *Acha-2 y los orígenes del poblamiento humano en Arica.* Ediciones Universidad de Tarapacá, Arica.

Neves, Walter A., and Max Blum
2000 The Buhl Burial: A Comment on Green et al. *American Antiquity* 65:191–193.

Neves, Walter A., and Hector M. Pucciarelli
1989 Extra-Continental Biological Relationships of Early South American Human Remains: A Multivariate Analysis. *Ciencia e Cultura* 4:566–575.
1991 Morphological Affinities of the First Americans: An Exploration Analysis Based on Early South American Human Remains. *Journal of Human Evolution* 21:261–273.

Neves, Walter A., Max Blum, and Joseph Powell
2001 Paleoindian Skeletal Remains from Santana do Riacho I, Minas Gerais, Brazil: Archaeological Background, Chronological Context and Comparative Cranial Morphology. *American Journal of Physical Anthropology Supplement* 31:112–113.

Neves, Walter A., Diogo Meyer, and Hector M. Pucciarelli
1996a Early Skeletal Remains and the Peopling of the Americas. *Revista de Antropología* 39:121–139.

Neves, Walter A., Danusa Munford, and Maria do Carmo Zanini
1996b Cranial Morphological Variation in the Colonization of the New World: Towards a Four Migration Model. *American Journal of Physical Anthropology Supplement* 22:176.

Neves, Walter A., Danusa Munford, Maria do Carmo Zanini, and Hector M. Pucciarelli
1999a Cranial Morphological Variation in South America and the Colonization of the New World: Towards a Four Migration Model? *Ciencia e Cultura* 51: 151–165.

Neves, Walter A., Joseph F. Powell, and Erik G. Ozolins
1999b Extra-Continental Morphological Affinities of Lapa Vermelha IV, Hominid 1: A Multivariate Analysis with Progress Numbers of Variables. *Homo* 50:263–282.
1999c Extra-Continental Morphological Affinities of Palli Aike, Southern Chile. *Interciencia* (Venezuela) 24:258–263.

Neves, Walter A., Joseph F. Powell, André Prous, Erik G. Ozolins, and Max Blum
1999d Lapa Vermelha IV Hominid 1: Morphological Affinities of the Earliest Known American. *Genetics and Molecular Biology* 22:461–469.

Newman, Marshall T.
1943 A Metric Study of Undeformed Indian Crania from Perú. *American Journal of Physical Anthropology* 1:21–45.
1948 A Summary of the Racial History of the Peruvian Area. *American Antiquity* 13:16–19.
1951 The Sequence of Indian Physical Types of South America. In *Papers on the Physical Anthropology of the American Indian,* edited by William S. Laughlin, pp. 69–97. The Viking Fund, New York.

Nichol, Christian R.
1989 Complex Segregation Analysis of Dental Morphological Variants. *American Journal of Physical Anthropology* 78:37–59.

Norusis, Marija J.
1994 *SPSS Professional Statistics 6.1.* SPSS, Chicago.

Núñez, Lautaro
1983 Paleoindian and Archaic Cultural Periods in the Arid and Semiarid Regions of Northern Chile. In *Advances in World Archaeology,* vol. 2, edited by Fred Wendorf and Angela E. Close, pp. 161–203. Academic Press, New York.

Oakland, Amy R.

1992   Textiles and Ethnicity: Tiwanaku in San Pedro de Atacama, North Chile. *Latin American Antiquity* 3:316–340.

O'Brien, Tyler G.

2003   *Cranial Microvariation in Prehistoric South Central Andean Populations: An Assessment of Morphology in the Cochabamba Collection, Bolivia.* Unpublished doctoral dissertation, Department of Anthropology, State University of New York at Binghamton.

ONERN (Oficina Nacional de Evaluación de Recursos Naturales)

1976   *Inventario, evaluación, y uso racional de los recursos naturales de la costa,* vol. II, *Informe y anexos.* ONERN, Lima.

1984   *Recursos hidráulicos del sur del Perú.* ONERN, Lima.

Ortloff, Charles R., and Alan L. Kolata

1993   Climate and Collapse: Agro-Ecological Perspectives on the Decline of the Tiwanaku State. *Journal of Archaeological Science* 20:195–221.

Owen, Bruce

1993   *A Model of Multiethnicity: State Collapse, Competition, and Social Complexity from Tiwanaku to Chiribaya in the Osmore Valley, Peru.* Unpublished doctoral dissertation, Department of Anthropology, University of California–Los Angeles, Los Angeles.

2002   Marine Carbon Reservoir Age Estimates for the Far South Coast of Perú. *Radiocarbon* 44(3):701–706.

2005   Distant Colonies and Explosive Collapse: The Two Stages of the Tiwanaku Diaspora in the Osmore Drainage. *Latin American Antiquity* 16(1):45–80.

Pearsall, Deborah M.

1992   The Origins of Plant Cultivation in South America. In *The Origins of Agriculture,* edited by C. Wesley Cowan and Patty J. Watson, pp. 173–206. Smithsonian Institution Press, Washington, DC.

Pinhasi, Ron, and Mark Pluciennik

2004   A Regional Biological Approach to the Spread of Farming in Europe: Anatolia, the Levant, South-Eastern Europe, and the Mediterranean. *Current Anthropology* 45S: S59–S82.

Portin, Peter, and Lassi Alvesalo

1974   The Inheritance of Shovel Shape in Maxillary Central Incisors. *American Journal of Physical Anthropology* 41:59–62.

Powell, Joseph F.

1993   Dental Evidence for the Peopling of the New World: Some Methodological Considerations. *Human Biology* 65:799–819.

1995   *Dental Variation and Biological Affinity among Middle Holocene Human Populations in North America.* dissertation, Department of Anthropology, Texas A&M University. Unpublished doctoral dissertation.

Powell, Joseph F.

2000   History, Population Structure, and Time: New Approaches for Understanding Biological Change in the Americas. *American Journal of Physical Anthropology Supplement* 30:253.

Powell, Joseph, and Walter Neves

1998   Dental Diversity of Early New World Populations: Taking a Bite out of the Tripartite Model. *American Journal of Physical Anthropology Supplement* 26:179–180.

1999   Craniofacial Morphology of the First Americans: Patterns and Process in the Peopling of the New World. *Yearbook of Physical Anthropology* 42:153–188.

Powell, Joseph F., and Jerome C. Rose

1999   Report on the Osteological Assessment of the "Kennewick Man" Skeleton (CENWW.97.Kennewick). In *Report on the Non-Destructive Examination, Description, and Analysis of the Human Remains from Columbia Park, Kennewick, Washington,* Department of Interior (editor). ParkNet - National Park Service, http://www.nps.gov/archeology/kennewick/powell_rose.htm

Quilter, Jeffrey

1991   Late Preceramic Peru. *Journal of World Prehistory* 5:413–432.

Quilter, Jeffrey, and Terrance Stocker

1983   Subsistence Economies and the Origins of Andean Complex Societies. *American Anthropologist* 85:542–562.

Rice, Don S.

1993   Late Intermediate Period Domestic Architecture and Residential Organization at La Yaral. In *Domestic Architecture, Ethnicity, and Complementarity in the South-Central Andes,* edited by Mark S. Aldenderfer, pp. 66–82. University of Iowa Press, Iowa City.

Rodríguez, Manuel

1989   *Geografía Agrícola de Chile.* Editorial Universitaria, Santiago.

Rogan, Peter K., and Joseph J. Salvo

1990   Molecular Genetics of Pre-Columbian South American Mummies. *Molecular Evolution* 122:223–234.

Rothhammer, Francisco, and Nestor Bianchi

1995   Origin and Distribution of B mtDNA Lineage in South America. *American Journal of Human Genetics* 56:1247–1248.

Rothhammer, Francisco, and Claudio Silva

1992 Gene Geography of South America: Testing Models of Population Displacement Based on Archaeological Evidence. *American Journal of Physical Anthropology* 89:441–446.

Sage, Rowan F., Jiri Santrucek, and David J. Grise

1995 Temperature Effects on the Photosynthetic Response of C3 Plants to Long-Term CO_2 Enrichment. *Vegetation* 121:67–69.

Sandweiss, Daniel H., Kirk A. Maasch, and David G. Anderson

1999 Transitions in the Mid-Holocene. *Science* 283:499–500.

Sandweiss, Daniel H., James B. Richardson, Elizabeth J. Reitz, Harold B. Rollins, and Kirk A. Maasch

1996 Geoarchaeological Evidence from Peru for a 5000 Years BP Onset of El Niño. *Science* 273:1531–1533.

Sardi, Marina L., Fernando Ramírez Rozzi, Rolando González-José, and Hector M. Pucciarelli

2005 South American Craniofacial Morphology: Diversity and Implications for Amerindian Evolution. *American Journal of Physical Anthropology* 128(4):747–756.

Schiappacasse, Virgilio, Victor Castro, and Hans Niemeyer

1989 Los desarrollos regionales en el Norte Grande (1.000 a 1.400 d.C.). In *Culturas de Chile: Prehistoria desde sus orígenes hasta los albores de la conquista*, edited by Jorge Hidalgo, Virgilio Schiappacasse, Hans Niemeyer, Carlos Aldunate, and Iván Solimano, pp. 181–220. Andrés Bello, Santiago.

Scott, G. Richard

1980 Population Variation of Carabelli's Trait. *Oral Biology* 52:63–78.

Scott, G. Richard, and Christy G. Turner

1997 *The Anthropology of Modern Human Teeth: Dental Morphology and Its Variation in Recent Human Populations.* Cambridge University Press, New York.

Semino, Ornella, Guisepe Passarino, Agnese Brega, Marc Fellous, and A. Silvana Santachiara-Benerecetti

1996 A View of the Neolithic Demic Diffusion in Europe Through Two Y Chromosome-specific Markers. *America Journal of Human Genetics* 59:964–968.

Shimada, Izumi, Ken-ichi Shinoda, Steve Bourget, Walter Alva, and Santiago Uceda

2003 MtDNA Analysis of Mochica Populations: Results and Implications. Paper presented at the Midwest Conference on Andean and Amazonian Archaeology and Ethnohistory, Feb. 23, Chicago, IL, USA.

Shinoda, Ken-ichi, Izumi Shimada, Walter Alva, and Santiago Uceda

2002 DNA Analysis of Moche and Sicán Populations: Results and Implications. Poster presented at the Sixty-Seventh Annual Meeting of the Society for American Archaeology, Mar. 21, 2002, Denver, CO, USA.

Sofaer, Jeffrey A., Patricia Smith, and Edith Kaye

1986 Affinities between Contemporary and Skeletal Jewish and Non-Jewish Groups Based on Tooth Morphology. *American Journal of Physical Anthropology* 70:265–275.

Sokal, Robert R., and Paolo Menozzi

1982 Spatial Autocorrelations of HLA Frequencies in Europe Support Demic Diffusion of Early Farmers. *American Naturalist* 119:1–17.

Sokal, Robert R., Neal L. Oden, and Chris Wilson

1991 Genetic Evidence for the Spread of Agriculture in Europe by Demic Diffusion. *Nature* 351:143–145.

Sokal, Robert R., and Peter H.A. Sneath

1963 *Principles of Numerical Taxonomy.* W. H. Freeman, San Francisco.

Soto, Patricia, Francisco Rothhammer, Carlos Valenzuela, Elena Llop, and Zuraiya Harb

1975 Aplicación de un método de distancia genética en la comparación de poblaciones prehispánicas de América. *Chungará* 5:73–79.

Standen, Vivien, and Calogero Santoro

2003 Patrón funerario arcaico temprano del sitio Acha-3 y su relación con Chinchorro: Cazadores, pescadores, y recolectores de la costa norte de Chile. *Latin American Antiquity* 15(1):89–109.

Stanish, Charles, and Brian S. Bauer

2004 *Archaeological Research on the Islands of the Sun and Moon, Lake Titicaca, Bolivia: Final Results from the Proyecto Tiksi Kjarka.* Cotsen Institute of Archaeology Press, Los Angeles.

Stanish, Charles, and Don Rice

1989 The Osmore Drainage, Peru: An Introduction to the Work of Programa Contisuyu. In *Ecology, Settlement and History in the Osmore Drainage*, pp. 1–14, edited by Don Rice, Charles Stanish, and P. Scarr. British Archaeological Reports International Series. Oxford.

Steele, D. Gentry, and Joseph F. Powell

1999 Peopling of the Americas: A Historical and Comparative Perspective. In *Who Were the First Americans?: Proceedings of the 58th Annual Biology Colloquium, Oregon State University*, edited by Robson Bonnichsen, pp. 91–120. Peopling of the Americas series. Corvallis, WA: Center for the Study of First Americans.

2002 Facing the Past: A View of the North American Human Fossil Record. In *The First Americans: The Pleistocene Colonization of the New World*, edited by Nina G. Jablonski, pp. 93–122. Memoirs of the California Academy of Sciences 27. San Francisco.

Street-Perrott, F. Alayne, Yongsong Huang, R. Alan Perrott, Geoffrey Eglinton, Philip Barker, Leila Ben Khelifa, Douglas D. Harkness, and Daniel O. Olago

1997 Impact of Lower Atmospheric Carbon Dioxide on Tropical Mountain Ecosystems. *Science* 278: 1422–1426.

Stovel, Emily M.

2002 *The Importance of being Atacameño: Political Identity and Mortuary Ceramics in Northern Chile*. Unpublished doctoral dissertation, Department of Anthropology, State University of New York at Binghamton.

Sutter, Richard C.

1997 *Dental Variation and Biocultural Affinities Among Prehistoric Populations from the Coastal Valleys of Moquegua, Perú, and Azapa, Chile*. Unpublished doctoral dissertation, Department of Anthropology, University of Missouri, Columbia.

2000 Prehistoric Genetic and Culture Change: A Bioarchaeological Search for Pre-Inka Altiplano Colonies in the Coastal Valleys of Moquegua, Peru, and Azapa, Chile. *Latin American Antiquity* 11:43–70.

2003 Prehistoric Human Migrations into the Andes as Indicated by Dentally Derived Biodistances. Paper presented at the 31st Annual Meeting of the Midwest Conference on Andean and Amazonian Archaeology and Ethnohistory, Field Museum, Chicago, IL, USA.

2005 The Prehistoric Peopling of South America as Inferred from Epigenetic Dental Traits. *Andean Past* 7:183–217.

2007 Nonmetric Dental Variation among Prehistoric Andeans. *American Journal of Physical Anthropology Supplement* 42:228.

Sutter, Richard C., and Lindsay Cadwell

2004 Genetically Influenced Tooth and Root Traits of Human Remains from La Galgada (3000–1000 BC), Peru: Results and Biological Implications. Paper presented at the 2004 Central States Anthropological Society Annual Meeting, Milwaukee, WI, USA, April 15, 2004.

Sutter, Richard C., and Lisa Mertz

2004 Nonmetric Cranial Trait Variation and Prehistoric Biocultural Change in the Azapa Valley, Chile. *American Journal of Physical Anthropology* 123: 130–145.

Tello, Juan

1926 Los descubrimientos del Museo de Arqueología Peruana en la península de Paracas. *XXII Congreso Internacional de Americanistas, Roma. Actas y memorias*, Vol. I, pp. 679–690. Rome.

Tello, Ricardo

1995 Excavaciones en la unidad 12 de la Plataforma I. In *Investigaciones en la Huaca de la Luna 1995*, edited by Santiago Uceda, Elías Mujica, and Ricardo Morales, pp. 29–38. Universidad Nacional de La Libertad, Trujillo.

Tello, Ricardo, José Armas, and Claude Chapdelaine

2003 Prácticas funerarias Moche en el complejo arqueológico Huacas del Sol y de la Luna. In *Moche: Hacia el final del milenio*, vol. 1, edited by Santiago Uceda and Elías Mujica, pp. 151–188. Pontificia Universidad Católica del Perú, Lima.

Thompson, Lonnie G., E. Moseley-Thompson, and Patrick A. Thompson

1992 Reconstructing Interannual Climate Variability from Tropical and Subtropical Ice-Core Records. In *El Niño: Historical and Paleoclimatic Aspects of the Southern Oscillation*, edited by Henry F. Diaz and Vera Markgraf, pp. 295–322. Cambridge University Press, Cambridge.

Tufinio, Moisés

1997 Excavaciones en Unidad 13, Frontis Norte de la Plataforma I de la Huaca de la Luna. In *Investigaciones en la Huaca de la Luna 1997*, edited by Santiago Uceda, Elías Mujica, and Ricardo Morales, pp. 33–40. Universidad Nacional de La Libertad, Trujillo.

Turbón, Daniel, Carles Lalueza, Alejandro Perez-Perez, Eva Prats, P. Moreno, and José Pons

1994 Absence of the 9 bp mtDNA Region V Deletion in Ancient Remains of Aborigines from Tierra del Fuego. *Ancient DNA Newsletter* 2:24–26.

Turner, Christy G.

1983 Dental Evidence for the Peopling of the Americas. In *Early Man in the New World*, edited by Richard Shutler, pp. 147–157. Sage Publications, Beverly Hills, CA.

1985 The Dental Search for Native American Origins. In *Out of Asia*, edited by Robert Kirk and Emöke

Szathmary, pp. 31–78. Journal of Pacific History, Inc., Canberra.

1990   Major Features of Sundadonty and Sinodonty, Including Suggestions about East Asian Micro-evolution, Population History, and Late Pleistocene Relationships with Australian Aboriginals. *American Journal of Physical Anthropology* 82:295–318.

Turner, Christy G., Christian R. Nichol, and G. Richard Scott

1991   Scoring Procedures for Key Morphological Traits of the Permanent Dentition: The Arizona State University Dental Anthropology System. In *Advances in Dental Anthropology*, edited by Mark A. Kelly and Clark S. Larsen, pp. 13–32. Wiley-Liss, New York.

Turner, Christy G., and G. Richard Scott

1977   Dentition of Easter Island. In *Orofacial Growth and Development*, edited by Albert A. Dahlberg and Thomas M. Graber, pp. 229–250. Mouton, Chicago.

Uceda, Santiago

2001   Investigations at Huaca de la Luna, Moche Valley: An Example of Moche Religious Architecture. In *Moche Art and Archaeology in Ancient Peru*, edited by Joanne Pillsbury, pp. 47–67. National Gallery of Art and Yale University Press, Washington, DC.

Umire, Adán, and Ana Miranda

2001   *Chiribaya de Ilo: Un aporte a su difusión.* Consejo Nacional de Ciencia y Tecnología, Arequipa, Perú.

Vallejos, Miriam

1982   Hombre preagrícola de las cuevas Tres Ventanas de Chilca, Perú: Textilería. *Zonas Áridas* 2:21–32.

Verano, John W.

2001   War and Death in the Moche World: Osteological Evidence and Visual Discourse. In *Moche Art and Archaeology in Ancient Peru*, edited by Joanne Pillsbury, pp. 111–126. Yale University Press, New Haven.

Wendt, W. E.

1964   Die präkeramische Siedlung am Río Seco, Peru. *Baessler-Archiv* 11:225–275.

Wijsman, Ellen M., and Walter A. Neves

1986   The Use of Nonmetric Variation in Estimating Human Population Admixture: A Test Case with Brazilian Blacks, Whites, and Mulattoes. *American Journal of Physical Anthropology* 70:395–405.

Williams, Sloan, Napoleon A. Chagnon, and Robert S. Spielman

2002   Nuclear and Mitochondrial Genetic Variation in the Yanomamö: A Test Case for Ancient DNA Studies of Prehistoric Populations. *American Journal of Physical Anthropology* 117:246–259.

CHAPTER 3

EARLY FISHING AND INLAND MONUMENTS

CHALLENGING THE MARITIME FOUNDATIONS OF ANDEAN CIVILIZATION?

DANIEL H. SANDWEISS

WHEN MICHAEL E. MOSELEY published *The Maritime Foundations of Andean Civilization* in 1975, many archaeologists found anathema the idea that complex society could arise on the economic basis of intensive fishing rather than (or along with) intensive agriculture. Reaction was rapid and intense (Osborn 1977; Raymond 1981; Wilson 1981). However, new research on early coastal complexes inspired by the book and the hypothesis (e.g., Quilter et al. 1991) supported the maritime hypothesis while calling attention to the often ignored agricultural component of the original formulation (Moseley 1978, 1992; Moseley and Feldman 1988; Quilter 1991). For a decade, as coastal Andean research turned to other issues, the MFAC debate lay dormant. Since the late 1990s, however, new work has brought two new challenges to the hypothesis.

In 1975, the standard sequence for the development of Andean coastal subsistence systems (Lanning 1963, 1967) had intensive fishing appearing only at the start of the Late Preceramic period, just before the onset of monument building and other indicators of Andean civilization. Moseley (1975) relied on this chronology in his formulation of the maritime hypothesis, with the consequent implication that discovery of the ocean about 5000 ^{14}C yr BP (5800 cal yr BP)[1] led rapidly to the other changes in the economy and social organization of the Late Preceramic period.

Over the intervening years, the antiquity of Andean maritime adaptations was pushed back to the Middle Preceramic period (e.g., Richardson 1973; Llagostera 1979; Stothert 1985, 1988, 1992; Benfer 1990; Sandweiss 1996a) and then to the Early Preceramic period, tentatively at first (Richardson 1978; Sandweiss et al. 1989) and then definitively (Keefer et al. 1998; Sandweiss et al. 1998; Sandweiss, Cano et al. 1999a; deFrance et al. 2001). If Moseley was right that seafood played a critical role in the rise of Andean civilization, and if ancient Peruvian coast-dwellers had sophisticated maritime subsistence systems in place as early as 13,000 cal yr BP, why didn't they develop complex societies sooner? In other words, does the seven-millennium delay between the onset of fishing lifeways and of complex coastal societies invalidate the maritime hypothesis?

A second challenge to the maritime hypothesis comes from the recent discovery of large stepped platforms and complex residential arrangements dating to the later Late Preceramic period inland at Caral in the Supe Valley and subsequently in neighboring valleys (Shady Solís et al. 2001; Shady Solís 2005; Haas et al. 2004) (see Figure 3.1 for the location of Caral and other sites mentioned in the text). These massive monuments were built far from the shore, in the middle valley, where irrigation agriculture was the only local means of intensifying production. Does this early inland florescence mean that fishing was an irrelevant sideline in the

Figure 3.1. Sites, settlements, and geographic features mentioned in the text.

creation of coastal Andean civilization? In other words, as some scholars asked in the media after the initial publication of the new work at Caral, "Is the maritime hypothesis dead?" (e.g., Fountain 2001; Pringle 2001).

In this chapter, I review the history of research on early maritime adaptations and on Late Preceramic coastal subsistence and monumentality. Although for at least two decades, most researchers in the central Andes have preferred to move beyond subsistence (e.g., Quilter 1992), economy remains basic if insufficient by itself to understand ancient society. Subsistence data are at the core of the maritime foundations hypothesis and are the focus of this chapter; social process must be treated elsewhere (e.g., Roscoe 2008). Given the available information, I argue that Moseley's maritime foundations hypothesis remains viable in the face of both of the recent challenges.

EARLY MARITIME ADAPTATIONS IN THE ANDES

Brief History of Discovery

Although Charles Barrington Brown (1926) was the first to recognize and report preceramic sites on the coast of South America, it was not until the 1930s and 1940s that such sites received widespread attention, as the result of Junius Bird's excavations in northern Chile (Bird 1943) and at the Late Preceramic site of Huaca Prieta in northern Peru (Bird et al. 1985). Bird found evidence for intensive fishing in both areas, but most attention focused on his characterization of the inhabitants of Huaca Prieta as America's first farmers (Bird 1948).

During the 1950s, Frédéric André Engel began research on preceramic coastal archaeology in Peru. He, too, found evidence of marine resource utilization but chose to focus on other issues, in particular the use of the lomas (fog meadow) resource zone. Engel was the first to acquire radiocarbon dates from multiple coastal sites (e.g., Engel 1957, 1980), though the significance of some of these dates went unrecognized for decades (e.g., Quebrada Jaguay 280, Buenavista).

In the 1960s, Edward Lanning was the first to give serious consideration to preceramic Andean maritime adaptations during his work on the central coast of Peru. At and around Ancón, Lanning studied a series of preceramic sites and produced the first detailed sequence for the coastal Preceramic epoch (Lanning 1963, 1967). Maritime adaptations played a role in

his reconstruction of events: he found no significant use of marine resources until after 5800 cal yr BP and an increasing importance of seafood thereafter. In his landmark text *Peru before the Incas*, Lanning (1967) used this sequence as a model for all of Peru. Unfortunately, as Richardson (1981) pointed out years later, Lanning failed to take into account the possible effects of postglacial eustatic rise in sea level on the preservation of archaeological sites. This phenomenon had been recognized long before the 1960s, and by that time the approximate chronology and magnitude of sea level change were understood (for the current standard sea level curve, see Fairbanks 1989). Because the continental shelf is relatively wide and shallow at Ancón, the shoreline there lay many kilometers to the west when people first arrived in the region, about 13,000 cal yr BP, and early maritime sites were probably located on this now submerged coast. The ocean reached its modern position only about 5800 cal yr BP—the same time that Lanning first found evidence for marine resource use.

Sites stand out on the desert coast of Peru and northern Chile. If Lanning had not found early maritime sites, then it was easy to think that none existed. Other archaeologists naturally followed Lanning's lead. Working in the same region in the late 1960s, Moseley (1968, 1975) excavated a number of Late Preceramic sites near Ancón. Confirming Lanning's observation that animal remains were predominantly marine, he placed these data in the broader context of the central coast Late Preceramic archaeological record. Noting that the first large coastal temples dated to this time and region, Moseley proposed the controversial maritime foundations of Andean civilization hypothesis, namely, that seafood and not just agriculture underwrote the first formation of Andean civilization. Implicit in this theory was the idea that temple building and other indicators of a more complex social organization dated to a time immediately after people began using marine resources, and that marine resources therefore had something to do with this transformation. However, even this initial formulation of the maritime foundations hypothesis acknowledged contemporary agriculture but noted that the most important crops were "industrial" plants, cotton and gourd. Later reconsiderations of the hypothesis placed greater emphasis on the complementary roles of fishing and farming (Moseley and Feldman 1988; Moseley 1992).

While Moseley was digging on the central coast, James B. Richardson III (1969, 1973, 1978) was working on the far northern coast of Peru, near the oil port of Talara, where the continental shelf is extraordinarily narrow. In the late 1960s and early 1970s, Richardson found Middle and even Early Preceramic period sites that contained abundant evidence of marine resource use, especially shells of edible mollusks. One of these shells, from the Amotape campsites, yielded a radio-carbon date of about 12,200 cal yr BP (Richardson 1978). During the Late Preceramic period, the Talara region was a relative backwater compared to the central coast of Peru, and in the 1970s there was no reason to believe this was not the case earlier. Why, then, would the earliest Talareños take advantage of seafood while the innovative inhabitants of the central coast ignored this easy and abundant source of nutrition? Something was wrong with this picture.

In 1981, Richardson published his answer to this question: Early and Middle Preceramic peoples on the central coast probably *were* using marine resources, but the sites containing evidence for this practice lay on dis-tant shorelines now drowned by a rising sea. The issue is preservation of entire landscapes and settlement pat-terns: where the continental shelf is narrow, as at Talara, the 60 m of sea level rise between 13,000 and 6000 cal yr BP (Early and Middle Preceramic periods) caused relatively little horizontal displacement of the shoreline, while in areas of wider shelf, the shoreline would have moved significant distances over this same period.

The ocean off western South America is so rich in biota that people probably made use of it up and down the coast from the moment they first arrived. As a test implication of this hypothesis, Richardson suggested that early maritime sites should be located and still preserved in those parts of the coast, like Talara, where the shelf is narrow and the shoreline moved only a short horizontal distance as sea level rose. Appropriate areas of narrow shelf included the far northern Peruvian coast near Talara and the Peruvian south coast from the Paracas Peninsula south through northern Chile. Agustín Llagostera (1979) had excavated a northern Chilean shell midden site at Quebrada de las Conchas (now called La Chimba 13) in the 1970s and got two dates almost 11,000 years old. This site now fit into the emerging picture. Even earlier dates (beginning about 13,250 cal yr BP) came from another Chilean site, Quereo, excavated by Chilean archaeologist Lautaro Núñez (Núñez et al. 1983), though the site is located near the modern shoreline and had scant evidence of marine resource use, with the site's inhabitants seem-ingly focused mostly on land animals.

In 1983, to test the sea level/settlement hypothesis, Richardson and I began excavations at the large shell midden known as the Ring Site (Figure 3.2), in southern Peru not far north of the Chilean border (Sandweiss et al. 1989). We found that the site's inhabitants had exploited a wide range of marine animals: fish, shellfish, sea urchins, sea mammals, and seabirds. In contrast, bones of terrestrial animals were few and represented mainly small rodents. The Ring Site people probably used plant foods, but no evidence survived. We acquired a basal date of 11,250 cal yr BP on shell (corrected for ΔR), but all the other dated materials, both shell and charcoal, had ages between about 10,000 and 5800 cal yr BP.

Also in the 1980s, Karen Stothert (1985, 1988, 1992) began publishing the results of her excavations at the Las Vegas site in southern Ecuador, several hundred kilometers north of Talara. Stothert found that Las Vegas had a mixed economy that included marine and terrestrial resources. Dates ranged from 11,400 to 7450 cal yr BP; a pre-Vegas occupation dated between about 12,950 and 11,400 cal yr BP, but subsistence remains were too scarce to shed light on diet. At the same time, Claude Chauchat's work at sites of the Paiján culture of northern Peru showed people with an inland adaptation who were in contact with the shoreline as far back as 12,250 cal yr BP (Chauchat 1988; Chauchat et al. 1992). The section of the Peruvian coast where the Paiján sites are concentrated has the widest continental shelf of any part of Peru or Chile (Richardson 1981). Consequently, more land was lost here to postglacial sea level rise than anywhere else along the central Andean coast. The Paiján sites are on the inland side of the modern coastal plain, and the shoreline 12,000 years ago lay many kilometers farther west. In light of the presence of marine shells and fish bone in these inland sites, the Paiján people must have had stations near the ocean where they stayed while fishing and gathering shellfish, or else they were in contact with permanent coastal populations (Wing 1992; see also Dillehay et al. 2003). Unfortunately, these sites are long submerged.

By the end of the 1980s, numerous Middle Pre-ceramic maritime sites dating between about 10,000 and 5800 years ago had been excavated along the Ecuadorian, Peruvian, and Chilean coasts (e.g., Richardson 1973; Llagostera 1979; Stothert 1985, 1988, 1992; Benfer 1990; Sandweiss 1996a, b). By that time, it was clear that South American maritime adaptations were far earlier than Lanning, Moseley, and others had believed in the 1960s and 1970s. Still, all of the well-dated maritime occupa-tions postdated the first settlement of South America.

Figure 3.2. Michael Moseley at the Ring Site excavation, 1987.

They had nothing to say about migration routes and could be classified as a peripheral development by those who saw the transition from terrestrial hunting and gathering to farming as the crucial transformation of Andean civilization. The early dates from Amotape and the Ring Site could be dismissed—shell is a difficult material to date, and neither date was supported by similar results from the same site (e.g., Lynch 1991). Even in the mid-1990s it was impossible to demonstrate definitive Early Preceramic, Terminal Pleistocene (pre-11,400 cal yr BP) maritime adaptations in South America.

Early Preceramic Maritime Adaptations: Quebradas Tacahuay and Jaguay

In the late 1990s, the simultaneous publication in *Science* of two well-dated, Early Preceramic, Terminal Pleistocene maritime-adapted sites finally demonstrated that the exploitation of the ocean is as old as any other subsistence system yet discovered in the central Andes. At Quebrada Tacahuay, David Keefer, Susan

deFrance, and their colleagues found a marvelously well-preserved logistical camp for processing seabirds (Keefer et al. 1998), while at Quebrada Jaguay 280, my colleagues and I excavated the base camp of early fishing people (Sandweiss et al. 1998). Detailed information on both sites is available elsewhere (e.g., Keefer et al. 1998; Sandweiss et al. 1998; Sandweiss, Keefer, and Richardson 1999; deFrance et al. 2001; deFrance and Umire 2004; deFrance 2005; Sandweiss 2005); here, I review the relevant highlights.

South of Ilo and the Ring Site, deFrance, Keefer, and colleagues found and excavated Terminal Pleistocene archaeological deposits exposed in profiles along the Quebrada Tacahuay and preserved by rapid sedimentation during El Niño-derived flooding. Charcoal dates range from around 12,000 to 12,900 cal yr BP (deFrance et al. 2001; deFrance and Umire A. 2004). The excavations produced a substantial vertebrate faunal assemblage emphasizing seabirds, with some fishes and mollusks. The marine species are typical of the Peru Current today.

No information is yet available on plant use. A substantial flood deposit overlies the Terminal Pleistocene archaeological deposits, suggesting ENSO-like (El Niño/Southern Oscillation) conditions shortly before 12,000 cal yr BP. Shortly after that event, a reoccupation dated to the Pleistocene/Holocene transition includes birds, marine and terrestrial animals, reptiles, fishes, and mollusks (deFrance and Umire A. 2004). In the Terminal Pleistocene/Paleoindian-age deposits, lithics are local, terrestrial fauna is absent, and, although hearths are present, there is no evidence for structures (deFrance et al. 2001; deFrance and Umire A. 2004) such as those found at Quebrada Jaguay (see below). The excavators characterize the site as a "specialized coastal extraction station" (a logistical field camp, sensu Binford 1980) for processing seabirds.

Frédéric Engel (1981) discovered Quebrada Jaguay 280 (QJ-280) in 1970, though he did not then recognize the site's significance. QJ-280 lies on the banks of an ephemeral stream to the west-northwest of Camaná, Peru. In 1992, I first visited the site in the company of Bernardino Ojeda, who had worked there with Engel and who had pointed out to me the single Terminal Pleistocene radiocarbon date of ca. 11,800 cal yr BP that Engel had recovered from one of his three test pits. Because these pits were still open, we could see clearly that the site contained abundant marine shells and no obvious remains of terrestrial organisms. This information led me to investigate QJ-280 in detail. We now know that it is an early fishing site occupied between about 13,000 and 8300 cal yr BP, based on a suite of forty-one charcoal dates (Sandweiss et al. 1998, unpublished data). The site has two major components, Terminal Pleistocene (13,000–11,400 cal yr BP) and Early Holocene (10,600–8000 cal yr BP), with the latter subdivided into EHI and EHII.

I carried out the initial excavations at QJ-280 in 1996. Work concentrated on two sectors (Sandweiss et al. 1998; Sandweiss, Cano et al. 1999). In Sector I, we found basal deposits dating to the Terminal Pleistocene cut by an Early Holocene, semisubterranean circular house with a central hearth (Figure 3.3). In Sector II, we

Figure 3.3. Quebrada Jaguay 280, Early Holocene house in Sector I. The house pit cuts Terminal Pleistocene deposits and was filled with shell midden after abandonment.

found that all deposits dated to the Terminal Pleistocene or the very start of the Early Holocene. During this first season we opened only 4.5 m² in Sector II, and although we discovered a small cluster of apparent postholes, it was impossible to know if they belonged to a structure. To determine whether or not these holes were part of Early Preceramic buildings, we returned to QJ-280 in 1999 and opened up more of Sector II. Postholes were abundant, and the presence of a post base in one of them confirmed our functional interpretation. The excavation area included the better part of one structure from the basal occupation. This building appears to have been rectangular, with interior hearths, but it was not cut into the ground as the Early Holocene semi-subterranean house in Sector I was (Figure 3.4). After multiple rebuildings, indicated by multiple postholes along the same axes, the floor deposits were indurated by a halite cement derived from seawater (C. Fred T. Andrus, pers. comm.). Off-site samples show that away from the site, induration was the result of clay formation from long-term decay processes, so it seems likely that the seawater used on the floor came from human activity rather than a natural event such as a tsunami. Molds in the indurated floor suggest that the building had a post frame with hanging panels, like traditional post-and-reed houses in the region today.

In the 1996 excavations in Sectors I and II and in test pits in Sectors III and IV, we found that virtually all animal remains came from the ocean. Most were fish remains (mainly of drum fish [Sciaenids]) and shells (more than 99% wedge clams [*Mesodesma donacium*]). Crustacean remains of indeterminate species or origin (fresh vs. salt water) were particularly abundant in the Early Holocene deposits, but terrestrial animal remains were rare and, as at the Ring Site, consisted of small rodents (McInnis 1999). Results from the 1999 excavations are consistent with the earlier finds (Elizabeth J. Reitz, pers. comm.).

Macrobotanical remains were not well preserved at QJ-280. We did recover a few domesticated gourd rind fragments (Erickson et al. 2005) and some cordage from Early Holocene contexts, and *Equisetum* spp. (horsetail)

Figure 3.4. Quebrada Jaguay 280, Terminal Pleistocene house in Sector II. The postholes from the initial occupation of the house are marked with dark balloons.

fragments and *Opuntia* spp. (prickly pear) seeds from the Terminal Pleistocene component (Asunción Cano, pers. comm.). Nor were microbotanical remains particularly informative: analysis of phytoliths from this sector showed generally impoverished and degraded samples, though a basal context produced a number of reed (*Phragmites* sp.) phytoliths that might be derived from building material (Dolores Piperno, pers. comm.).

QJ-280 lithics come predominantly from local sources, mainly exposed delta deposits several hundred meters above the site (Tanner 2001). During the Early Holocene, Quebrada Jaguay residents made greater use of sandstone available in the adjacent quebrada bed than they had in the Terminal Pleistocene. Throughout the occupation, petrified wood was also used as raw material; the nearest outcrop we have located is about 30 km up the quebrada. Obsidian is present in very small quantities but is restricted almost entirely to the Terminal Pleistocene component. All of the obsidian tested comes from the Alca source, some 155 km inland from Quebrada Jaguay (Sandweiss et al. 1998). Most of the lithic remains, regardless of raw material, are late-stage debitage. Finished artifacts, or fragments of artifacts, are extremely rare in the collection. The QJ-280 lithic assemblage is consistent with a domestic function for the site, as suggested by the presence of structures.

In general, the characteristics of QJ-280 during the Terminal Pleistocene suggest a seasonal residential base camp occupied most likely during the austral summer when the ephemeral Quebrada flows. QJ-280 is the only site known in the immediate region for the Terminal Pleistocene, despite full-coverage survey of the area between Quebrada La Chira and the Camaná River, from the shoreline inland to about 750 masl (QJ-280 is approximately in the center of this survey zone). During the winter, the Terminal Pleistocene population of QJ-280 may have traveled to the highlands, as suggested by the presence of obsidian and prickly pear seeds. However, it is also possible that the inhabitants acquired the obsidian and prickly pear during short forays inland or via trade and that they spent the winter in the nearby Camaná Valley, which is well watered by a large permanent stream.

Summarizing early economic adaptations on the south coast of Peru, we find evidence for both base camps and logistical field camps (although with sample sizes of one). The QJ-280 base camp was occupied repeatedly if not permanently, and the inhabitants invested in a standing structure to house their domestic activities. At both sites, people focused on particular marine taxa, indicating subsistence specialization. Quebrada Jaguay maintained contact with distant highland locales, though the nature of this contact requires continued investigation.

During the Early Holocene, I see a settling in of the coastal population in the Quebrada Jaguay region. Our survey found many sites of this time with faunal assemblages similar to QJ-280. Obsidian and prickly pear virtually drop out, suggesting that links to the highlands had been cut or diminished—either the coast-dwellers stopped trading with the highlands or they ceased moving inland to procure these higher-altitude resources. At the same time, increased use of lower-quality but immediately available sandstone supports a reduced radius of action. In general, the Early Holocene remains suggest that the site remained a seasonal residential base camp, as it had been during the Terminal Pleistocene. However, it seems likely that the inhabitants now spent part of the winter among the cobble quarries in the adjacent lomas zones (Figure 3.5), which flourish during that season, rather than in the highlands. They may also have used the nearest permanent river valleys (Camaná and Ocoña), but possible evidence has been buried or destroyed by millennia of alluviation and farming. During the Middle Holocene, the Quebrada Jaguay region seems to have been abandoned, as were many parts of the south-central Andes that lacked permanent water sources (see Sandweiss 2003 and references therein).

LATE PRECERAMIC MONUMENTS AND SUBSISTENCE

Brief History of the Maritime Foundations Debate

When Michael Moseley first published *The Maritime Foundations of Andean Civilization* in 1975, none of the Late Preceramic monumental centers had been excavated in detail; indeed, the Preceramic age of many was unknown or in doubt. Moseley did have the results of his excavations and those of Lanning and Patterson in middens at smaller sites in the Ancón-Chillón region just north of Lima, the work of Engel (e.g., 1957) at a variety of sites along the coast, most reported only as survey data (with the exception of Asia Unit 1 [Engel 1963] and to a lesser extent El Paraíso [Engel 1966], which were studied and reported in greater detail), Bird's work at Huaca Negra in the Virú Valley and Huaca Prieta in the Chicama Valley (see Bird et al. 1985), and a handful of

Figure 3.5. Ben Tanner and Marty Yates analyzing lithic raw materials in the cobble quarry above Quebrada Jaguay.

other reports. From these scattered data, Moseley (1975) was able to discern a clear pattern in the subsistence data, namely, that animal remains were overwhelmingly marine in origin. Following Engel and Lanning, he also noted the presence of domesticated plants in the assemblages, with the industrial plants—cotton and gourd—predominating. As Moseley pointed out, these two plants played an important role in fishing economies as raw material for floats and nets.

Although the original formulation of the maritime foundations hypothesis (Moseley 1975) focused on mollusks as the major source of animal food, Moseley (1978) quickly realized that small, schooling fishes (anchovies and sardines) had been far more important in the Late Preceramic coastal diet; the use of 1/2-inch screens in the midden excavations, a common practice at the time, had undoubtedly biased the sample in favor of mollusks.

Robert Feldman's (1980, 1983, 1985) work at Áspero in the 1970s established that site as the earliest of the ^{14}C-dated Late Preceramic monumental centers, and

he demonstrated, as Moseley (1975) had observed, that the animal portion of the diet was based on marine organisms. He also found a suite of domesticated plants typical of the period. Feldman's excavations included only the latest construction phases of the multiphase mounds he investigated.

Early reactions to the maritime foundations hypothesis (Osborn 1977; Raymond 1981; Wilson 1981) were based not on new data but rather on theoretical assumptions about food preference and the relative productivity of different subsistence systems. Scott Raymond (1981) did make a telling point about the poor preservation potential of tubers and their possible importance in the diet. Tubers are high in carbohydrates, and a diet based on marine organisms would have required a source of carbohydrates for nutritional balance.

By the early 1980s, it was clear that the maritime foundations debate could not be resolved in the absence of integrated, carefully recovered subsistence data from the monumental centers. In the years following the publication of the hypothesis, other projects at Late Preceramic sites such as La Galgada, 74 km inland and 1100 masl (Grieder et al. 1988), and Los Gavilanes, a smaller coastal site (Bonavia 1982), continued to find a subsistence system in accord with Moseley's hypothesis. In 1983, in an attempt to lay to rest the diet debate and move on to other concerns about Late Preceramic society (see, e.g., the articles in Sandweiss [ed.] 1992), Jeffrey Quilter excavated at El Paraíso (Figure 3.6) and organized a multidisciplinary team to analyze the subsistence remains (Quilter et al. 1991). Quilter's team found that the great majority of animal remains were marine, that cotton and gourds dominated the remains of domesticated plants, and that wild plant foods, especially fruits, were also important. Like all the other data sets, but with the advantage of a research design and team organized specifically around the question of Late Preceramic subsistence, the El Paraíso results largely supported the postulates of the maritime foundations hypothesis, with the caveat that the dates fell very late in the Late Preceramic period.

Late Preceramic Inland Monumentality in the Supe and Surrounding Valleys

In a retrospective article published in 1992, Moseley placed the maritime foundations hypothesis in historical context and restated it with greater emphasis on the importance of the synergy between fishing and farming in the coastal Late Preceramic period (see also Moseley 1978; Moseley and Feldman 1988). The issue then lay dormant until April 2001, when Ruth Shady Solís and colleagues published a seminal paper on the radiocarbon age of Caral (also known as Chupacigarro Grande), a Late Preceramic monumental site 23 km from the shore in the Supe Valley (Figure 3.7). Though Shady had begun field work six years earlier, and although the lack of pottery and the typology of other artifacts had convinced her from the start that the site was Late Preceramic in age, it was the long set of radiocarbon dates (ca. 3900–4600 cal yr BP) that persuaded the broader community that Caral was, indeed, preceramic. This chronological confirmation was necessary both because of the site's large size (it is the largest Late

Figure 3.6. Unit 1 at El Paraíso in the Chillón Valley.

Figure 3.7. Several of the large Late Preceramic mounds at Caral in the Supe Valley.

Preceramic site known in the Andes, with six major mounds and a host of other structures and deposits) and because of its inland location. Until that time, the only known inland but precordilleran Late Preceramic monumental site was La Galgada, which is both smaller and closer to the high Andes than Caral.

In the better-known valleys around Lima, the earliest monumental sites of similar size or location to Caral date to the subsequent Initial period; in 1975, Moseley interpreted these sites as evidence for the onset of irrigation agriculture in conjunction with the adoption of pottery making. As Grieder et al. (1988) had for La Galgada, Shady Solís (Shady Solís et al. 2001; Shady Solís 2005) postulated that Caral's location constituted strong circumstantial evidence for Late Preceramic irrigation agriculture.[2] Though that postulation is quite likely correct, Moseley and I noted in a response to the 2001 *Science* paper (Sandweiss and Moseley 2001) that cotton and gourd remained the dominant species in the inventory of domesticated plant remains and

that marine species contributed virtually all the animal portion of the diet. We also pointed out that the list of domesticated plants from Caral is comparable to that from other contemporary coastal Late Preceramic sites, including Huaca Prieta, Los Gavilanes, La Galgada, and Áspero. There is no evidence that agriculture played a qualitatively different role at Caral than at other Late Preceramic coastal sites—Caral did not have a high-protein staple plant in sufficient quantities to supplant fish in the diet.

Shady and her team found that although Caral was the largest Late Preceramic site in the Supe Valley, it was by no means the only monumental site of that age (Shady Solís et al. 2001; Shady Solís and Leyva [eds.] 2003; Shady Solís 2005). Recent work by Jonathan Haas and colleagues (2004) in the valleys just north of Supe identified and dated eleven other centers to the Late Preceramic period, all of which apparently relied on the ocean for the animal portion of their diet. Indeed, on the basis of their research and that of others, Haas and colleagues (2004:1022) succinctly restate Moseley's maritime foundations hypothesis: "the path of cultural evolution in the Andean region diverged [in the Late Preceramic period] from a relatively simple hunting and gathering society to a much more complex pattern of social and political organization with a mixed economy based on agriculture and marine exploitation."

CONCLUSIONS

Is the maritime foundations hypothesis dead, as some have stated? I argue that it is not. Why, then, did coastal civilization not arise much earlier, given that sophisticated maritime adaptations date to many millennia prior to the Late Preceramic period? The answer may be quite simple. First, it is necessary to recognize that the economy of the Late Preceramic period combined fishing and farming, with marine organisms providing protein and domesticated plants providing carbohydrates and raw materials (Moseley 1978, 1992; Moseley and Feldman 1988; see also Haas et al. 2004). Second, the maritime foundations hypothesis must be understood for what it is: a statement of the economic underpinnings of early complex society in coastal Peru, not an argument for specific social processes. The economic organization of fishing and farming, the exchange of products produced by each activity (and interzonal exchange on a broader scale; see, e.g., Shady Solís and Leyva [eds.] 2003; Shady Solís 2005), and the challenges posed by climatic events all undoubtedly offered opportunities for nascent political entrepreneurs (see, e.g., Sandweiss 1996b; Sandweiss, Maasch, and Anderson 1999; Roscoe 2008), but those issues cannot be fully addressed until we have resolved Late Preceramic coastal lifeways.

Plant domestication has been documented in coastal Ecuador at least since the start of the Holocene for cucurbits (Piperno and Stothert 2003), with maize appearing there several millennia before the Late Preceramic period (Piperno and Pearsall 1998; Stothert 1988; Pearsall et al. 2004). However, there is no record of cotton prior to that time. Cotton is necessary to intensify fishing production, given the likely limitations on the amount of suitable wild fibers available on the desert coast of Peru. Fishing intensification also requires suitable fish species as prey. We know from the archaeological record that during the Late Preceramic period, the fishes of choice were small schooling fishes (sardines and anchovies) caught with cotton nets. As Andrus et al. (2002) recently noted, the return of an El Niño-dominated climatic regime to the coast of Peru at about 5800 cal yr BP signified increased productivity for the coast north of Lima, with a shift to lower trophic level species such as sardines and anchovies. Thus, although both plant domestication and sophisticated fishing systems were in place on the coast for millennia prior to the Late Preceramic period, it is only then that the most important elements of these systems came together: cotton and small schooling fishes. The site of Áspero on the shore of the Supe Valley contains these elements and, based on current data, predates the site of Caral inland in the same valley (Sandweiss and Moseley 2001). The economic data from the latter site do not show any significant variation from other coastal Late Preceramic sites, so Caral's precocious growth and inland location cannot be explained as the result of subsistence innovation. I suggest that the establishment upvalley of Caral and other inland Late Preceramic centers is best explained as an attempt to increase the production of cotton and gourds, to support intensification of the net-fishing begun at Áspero and similar coastal sites. Once established, the subsequent history of Caral-class sites was built on maritime foundations but directed by social processes much harder to discern.

NOTES

1. Unless otherwise noted, all dates in this chapter are calendar years BP, calculated using Calib 5.0.1 (Stuiver and Reimer 1993 and updates). Calibrated ages younger than 11,000 cal yr BP were run using the Southern Hemisphere calibration data set (McCormac et al. 2004); older dates were run using the Northern Hemisphere data set (Reimer et al. 2004). For marine samples I used Hughen et al. (2004), with P. J. Reimer's Peru-Chile regional average marine reservoir correction of $\Delta R = 286 \pm 104$ (http://calib.qub.ac.uk/marine).

2. Dillehay et al. (2005) have recently demonstrated the construction of small canals to the north of Caral and dated somewhat earlier than that site.

REFERENCES

Andrus, C. Fred T., Douglas E. Crowe, Daniel H. Sandweiss, Elizabeth J. Reitz, and Christopher S. Romanek
2002   Otolith $\partial^{18}O$ Record of Mid-Holocene Sea Surface Temperatures in Peru. *Science* 295:1508–1511.
Barrington Brown, C.
1926   On Stone Implements from North-West Peru. *Man* 64:97–101.

Benfer, Robert A.
1990   The Preceramic Period Site of Paloma, Peru: Bio-indicators of Improving Adaptation to Sedentism. *Latin American Antiquity* 1:284–318.

Binford, Lewis
1980   Willow Smoke and Dogs' Tails: Hunter-Gatherer Settlement Systems and Archaeological Site Formation. *American Antiquity* 45:4–20.

Bird, Junius B.
1943   Excavations in Northern Chile. *Anthropological Papers of the American Museum of Natural History*, no. 38 (Pt. 4). New York.
1948   America's Oldest Farmers. *Natural History* 57(7): 296–303, 334–335.

Bird, Junius B., John Hyslop, and M. D. Skinner
1985   The Preceramic Excavations at Huaca Prieta, Chicama Valley, Peru. *Anthropological Papers of the American Museum of Natural History*, no. 62 (Pt. 1). New York.

Bonavia, Duccio
1982   *Los Gavilanes*. Lima: COFIDE.

Chauchat, Claude
1988   Early Hunter-Gatherers on the Peruvian Coast. In *Peruvian Archaeology*, edited by Richard W. Keatinge, pp. 41–66. Cambridge University Press, Cambridge.

Chauchat, Claude, Elizabeth Wing, Jean-Paul Lacombe, Pierre-Yves Demars, Santiago Uceda, and Carlos Deza
1992   Préhistoire de la Côte Nord du Pérou: Le Paijanien de Cupisnique. *Cahiers du Quaternaire* 18. CNRS-Editions, Paris.

deFrance, Susan D.
2005   Late Pleistocene Marine Birds from Southern Peru: Distinguishing Human Capture from El Niño-Induced Windfall. *Journal of Archaeological Science* 32:1131–1146.

deFrance, Susan D., David K. Keefer, James B. Richardson III, and Adán Umire A.
2001   Late Paleo-Indian Coastal Foragers: Specialized Extractive Behavior at Quebrada Tacahuay, Peru. *Latin American Antiquity* 12:413–426.

deFrance, Susan D., and Adán Umire A.
2004   Quebrada Tacahuay: Un sitio marítimo del Pleistoceno Tardío en la costa sur del Perú. *Chungará* 36:257–278.

Dillehay, Tom D., Jack Rossen, Greg Maggard, Kary Stackelbeck, and Patricia Netherly
2003   Localization and Possible Social Aggregation in the Late Pleistocene and Early Holocene on the North Coast of Perú. *Quaternary International* 109–110:3–11.

Dillehay, Tom D., Herbert H. Eling, Jr., and Jack Rossen
2005   Preceramic Irrigation Canals in the Peruvian Andes. *Proceedings of the National Academy of Sciences* 102:17241–17244.

Engel, Frédéric A.
1957   Sites et Etablissements sans Céramique de la Côte Peruvienne. *Journal de la Société des Américanistes* 46:67–155.
1963   Asia Unit 1. A Preceramic Settlement on the Central Coast of Peru. *Transactions of the American Philosophical Society* 53 (Pt. 3).
1966   Le Complexe Précéramique d'el Paraiso (Pérou). *Journal de la Société des Américanistes* 55(1):43–96.
1980   *Prehistoric Andean Ecology: Man Settlement and Environment in the Andes*. Humanities Press for Hunter College, New York.
1981   *Prehistoric Andean Ecology: Man Settlement and Environment in the Andes*, vol. 2, *The Deep South*. Humanities Press for Hunter College, New York.

Erickson, David L., Bruce D. Smith, Andrew C. Clark, Daniel H. Sandweiss, and Noreen Tuross
2005   An Asian Origin for a 10,000-year-old Domesticated Plant in the Americas. *Proceedings of the National Academy of Sciences* 102:18315–18320.

Fairbanks, Richard G.
1989   A 17,000-Year Glacio-Eustatic Sea Level Record: Influence of Glacial Melting Rates on the Younger Dryas Event and Deep-Ocean Circulation. *Nature* 342:637–642.

Feldman, Robert A.
1980   *Aspero, Peru: Architecture, Subsistence Economy, and Other Artifacts of a Preceramic Maritime Chiefdom*. Unpublished doctoral dissertation, Department of Anthropology, Harvard University.
1983   From Maritime Chiefdom to Agricultural State in Formative Coastal Peru. In *Civilization in the Ancient Americas: Essays in Honor of Gordon R. Willey*, edited by Richard Leventhal and Alan Kolata, pp. 289–310. University of New Mexico Press and Peabody Museum of Archaeology and Ethnology, Harvard University, Cambridge.
1985   Preceramic Corporate Architecture: Evidence for Development of Non-Egalitarian Social Systems in Peru. In *Early Ceremonial Architecture in the Andes*, edited by Christopher B. Donnan, pp. 71–92. Dumbarton Oaks, Washington, DC.

Fountain, Henry

2001   Archaeological Site in Peru is Called Oldest City in Americas. *New York Times*, April 27, 2001.

Grieder, Terence, Alberto Bueno M., C. Earle Smith, Jr., and Robert M. Malina

1988   *La Galgada, Peru A Preceramic Culture in Transition.* University of Texas Press, Austin.

Haas, Jonathan, Winifred Creamer, and Alvaro Ruiz

2004   Dating the Late Archaic Occupation of the Norte Chico Region in Peru. *Nature* 432:1020–1023.

Hughen, Konrad A., Mike G. L. Baillie, Edouard Bard, J. Warren Beck, Chanda J. H. Bertrand, Paul G. Blackwell, Caitlin E. Buck, George S. Burr, Kirsten B. Cutler, Paul E. Damon, Richard L. Edwards, Richard G. Fairbanks, Michael Friedrich, Thomas P. Guilderson, Bernd Kromer, Gerry Mccormac, Sturt Manning, Christopher Bronk Ramsey, Paula J. Reimer, Ron W. Reimer, Sabine Remmele, John R. Southon, Minze Stuiver, Sahra Talamo, F. W. Taylor, Johannes Van Der Plicht, and Constanze E. Weyhenmeyer

2004   Marine04 Marine Radiocarbon Age Calibration, 0–26 cal kyr BP. *Radiocarbon* 46:1059–1086.

Keefer, David K., Susan D. deFrance, Michael E. Moseley, James B. Richardson III, Dennis R. Satterlee, and Amy Day-Lewis

1998   Early Maritime Economy and El Niño Events at Quebrada Tacahuay, Peru. *Science* 281:1833–1835.

Lanning, Edward P.

1963   A Pre-Agricultural Occupation on the Central Coast of Peru. *American Antiquity* 28:360–371.

1967   *Peru Before the Incas.* Prentice-Hall, Englewood Cliffs, NJ.

Llagostera, Agustín

1979   9,700 Years of Maritime Subsistence on the Pacific: An Analysis by Means of Bioindicators. *American Antiquity* 44:309–324.

Lynch, Thomas F.

1991   Paleoindians in South America: A Discrete and Identifiable Cultural Stage? In *Clovis: Origins and Adaptations*, edited by R. Bonnichsen and K. Turnmire, pp. 255–259. Center for the Study of the First Americans, Corvallis, OR.

McCormac, F. Gerry, Alan G. Hogg, Paul G. Blackwell, Caitlin E. Buck, Thomas F. G. Higham, and Paula J. Reimer

2004   SHCa104 Southern Hemisphere Calibration 0–11.0 cal kyr BP. *Radiocarbon* 46:1087–1092.

McInnis, Heather

1999   Subsistence and Maritime Adaptations at Quebrada Jaguay, Camana, Peru: A Faunal Analysis. Unpublished master's thesis, Institute for Quaternary Studies, University of Maine, Orono.

Moseley, Michael E.

1968   *Changing Subsistence Patterns: Late Preceramic Archaeology of the Central Peruvian Coast.* Unpublished doctoral dissertation, Anthropology Department, Harvard University, Cambridge, MA.

1975   *The Maritime Foundations of Andean Civilization.* Cummings, Menlo Park, CA.

1978   *Pre-Agricultural Coastal Civilizations in Peru.* Carolina Biology Reader 90. Carolina Biological Supply Co., Burlington, NC.

1992   Maritime Foundations and Multilinear Evolution: Retrospect and Prospect. *Andean Past* 3:5–42.

Moseley, Michael E., and Robert A. Feldman

1988   Fishing, Farming, and the Foundations of Andean Civilization. In *The Archaeology of Prehistoric Coastlines*, edited by G. Bailey and J. Parkington, pp. 125–134. Cambridge University Press, Cambridge.

Núñez, Lautaro, Juan Varela, and Rodolfo Casamiquela

1983   *Ocupación Paleoindio en Quereo.* Universidad del Norte, Antofagasta, Chile.

Osborn, Alan J.

1977   Strandloopers, Mermaids, and other Fairy Tales: Ecological Determinants of Marine Resource Utilization. The Peruvian Case. In *For Theory Building in Archaeology*, edited by Lewis R. Binford, pp. 157–206. Academic Press, New York.

Pearsall, Deborah M., Karol Chandler-Ezell, and James A. Zeidler

2004   Maize in Ancient Ecuador: Results of Residue Analysis of Stone Tools from the Real Alto Site. *Journal of Archaeological Science* 31:423–442.

Piperno, Dolores R., and Deborah M. Pearsall

1998   *The Origins of Agriculture in the Lowland Neotropics.* Academic Press, San Diego.

Piperno, Dolores R., and Karen E. Stothert

2003   Phytolith Evidence for Early Holocene Cucurbita Domestication in Southwest Ecuador. *Science* 299:1054–1057.

Pringle, Heather

2001   The First Urban Center in the Americas. *Science* 292:621.

Quilter, Jeffrey

1991   Late Preceramic Peru. *Journal of World Prehistory* 5:387–438.

1992 To Fish in the Afternoon: Beyond Subsistence Economies in the Study of Early Andean Civilizations. *Andean Past* 3:111–125.

Quilter, Jeffrey, Bernardino Ojeda, Deborah Pearsall, Daniel Sandweiss, John Jones, and Elizabeth Wing
1991 The Subsistence Economy of El Paraíso, Peru. *Science* 251:277–283.

Raymond, J. Scott
1981 The Maritime Foundations of Andean Civilization: A Reconsideration of the Evidence. *American Antiquity* 46:806–821.

Reimer, Paula J., Mike G. L. Baillie, Edouard Bard, Alex Bayliss, J. Warren Beck, Chanda J. H. Bertrand, Paul G. Blackwell, Caitlin E. Buck, George S. Burr, Kirsten B. Cutler, Paul E. Damon, and R. Lawrence Edwards
2004 IntCal04 Terrestrial Radiocarbon Age Calibration, 0–26 cal kyr BP. *Radiocarbon* 46:1029–1058.

Richardson III, James B.
1969 *The Preceramic Sequence and Pleistocene and Post-Pleistocene Climatic Change in Northwestern Peru.* Unpublished doctoral dissertation, Anthropology Department, University of Illinois, Urbana-Champaign.
1973 The Preceramic Sequence and the Pleistocene and Post-Pleistocene Climate of Northwest Peru. In *Human Variation*, edited by Donald W. Lathrap and Jody Douglas, pp. 73–89. University of Illinois Press, Urbana.
1978 Early Man on the Peruvian North Coast, Early Maritime Exploitation and Pleistocene and Holocene Environment. In *Early Man in America from a Circum-Pacific Perspective*, edited by A. L. Bryan, pp. 274–289. Occasional Papers no. 1 of the Department of Anthropology, University of Alberta, Edmonton.
1981 Modeling the Development of Early Complex Economies on the Coast of Peru: A Preliminary Statement. *Annals of Carnegie Museum* 50:139–150.

Roscoe, Paul B.
2008 Catastrophe and the Emergence of Political Complexity: A Social Anthropological Model. In *El Niño, Catastrophism, and Culture Change in Ancient America*, edited by Daniel H. Sandweiss and Jeffrey Quilter, pp. 77–100. Dumbarton Oaks, Washington, DC.

Sandweiss, Daniel H.
1996a Mid-Holocene Cultural Interaction on the North Coast of Peru and Ecuador. *Latin American Antiquity* 7:41–50.

1996b The Development of Fishing Specialization on the Central Andean Coast. In *Prehistoric Fishing Strategies*, edited by Mark Plew, pp. 41–63. Boise State University, ID.
2003 Terminal Pleistocene Through Mid-Holocene Archaeological Sites as Paleoclimatic Archives for the Peruvian Coast. *Palaeogeography, Palaeoclimatology, Palaeoecology* 194:23–40.
2005 Early Maritime Adaptations in Western South America. *The Mammoth Trumpet* 20(4):14–20, 21(1):14–17.

Sandweiss, Daniel H. (ed.)
1992 *Andean Past 3*. Cornell University Latin American Studies Program, Ithaca, NY.

Sandweiss, Daniel H., and Michael E. Moseley
2001 Amplifying Importance of New Research in Peru. *Science* 294:1651–1652.

Sandweiss, Daniel H., James B. Richardson III, Elizabeth J. Reitz, Jeffrey T. Hsu, and Robert A. Feldman
1989 Early Maritime Adaptations in the Andes: Preliminary Studies at the Ring Site, Peru. In *Ecology, Settlement, and History in the Osmore Drainage, Peru*, edited by Don S. Rice, Charles Stanish, and Phillip R. Scarr. BAR International Series 545 (i):35–84. British Archaeological Reports, Oxford.

Sandweiss, Daniel H., Heather McInnis, Richard L. Burger, Asunción Cano, Bernardino Ojeda, Rolando Paredes, María del Carmen Sandweiss, and Michael Glascock
1998 Quebrada Jaguay: Early Maritime Adaptations in South America. *Science* 281:1830–1832.

Sandweiss, Daniel H., Asunción Cano, Bernardino Ojeda, and José Roque
1999 Pescadores paleoíndios del Perú. In *Investigación y Ciencia*, October 1999, no. 277:55–61.

Sandweiss, Daniel H., David K. Keefer, and James B. Richardson III
1999 First Americans and the Sea. *Discovering Archaeology* 1(1):59–65.

Sandweiss, Daniel H., Kirk A. Maasch, and David G. Anderson
1999 Climate and Culture: Transitions in the Mid-Holocene. *Science* 283: 499–500.

Shady Solís, Ruth
2005 *La civilización de Caral-Supe: 5000 años de identidad cultural en el Perú*. Instituto Nacional de Cultura, Proyecto Especial Arqueológico Caral-Supe, Lima.

Shady Solís, Ruth and Carlos Leyva (eds.)
2003 *La ciudad sagrada de Caral-Supe: Los orígenes de la civilización andina y la formación del Estado pristino*

en el antiguo Perú. Instituto Nacional de Cultura, Proyecto Especial Arqueológico Caral-Supe, Lima.

Shady Solís, Ruth, Jonathan Haas, and Winifred Creamer

2001   Dating Caral, a Preceramic Site in the Supe Valley on the Central Coast of Peru. *Science* 292:723–726.

Stothert, Karen E.

1985   The Preceramic Las Vegas Culture of Coastal Ecuador. *American Antiquity* 50:613–637.

1988   La prehistoria temprana de la península de Santa Elena, Ecuador: Cultura Las Vegas. *Miscelánea Antropológica Ecuatoriana, Serie Monográfica* 10. Guayaquil.

1992   Early Economies of Coastal Ecuador and the Foundations of Andean Civilization. *Andean Past* 3:43–54.

Stuiver, Minze, and Paula J. Reimer

1993   An Extended 14C Data Base and Revised CALIB 3.0 14C Age Calibration Program. *Radiocarbon* 35:215–230.

Tanner, Benjamin R.

2001   Lithic Analysis of Chipped Stone Artifacts Recovered from Quebrada Jaguay, Peru. Unpubished master's thesis, Institute for Quaternary and Climate Studies, University of Maine, Orono.

Wilson, David J.

1981   Of Maize and Men: A Critique of the Maritime Hypothesis of State Origins on the Coast of Peru. *American Anthropologist* 83:93–120.

Wing, Elizabeth S.

1992   Les restes de vertébrés. In Préhistoire de la Côte Nord du Pérou: Le Paijanien de Cupisnique. *Cahiers du Quaternaire* 18:42–47. CNRS-Editions, Paris.

CHAPTER 4

QUEBRADA TACAHUAY AND EARLY MARITIME FOUNDATIONS ON PERU'S FAR SOUTHERN COAST

SUSAN D. DEFRANCE

QUEBRADA TACAHUAY REPRESENTS ONE of the oldest expressions of maritime adaptations in the Americas, with initial deposits dating to the Late Pleistocene and minor reoccupation of the site during the Early and Middle Holocene (deFrance 2002; deFrance and Umire 2004; deFrance et al. 1998, 1999, 2001; Keefer et al. 1998, 2003). Representing an ancient specialized activity site dating to more than 10,500 (rcyr BP) and focused on the exploitation of marine avifauna, the oldest contexts of human use at Quebrada Tacahuay are also intriguing because of the nature of their preservation, discovery, and archaeological investigations. Although many areas of the Andean littoral may have been occupied during the Late Pleistocene, only those relatively few sites located on land surfaces where the coastal shelf is very narrow survived rising sea level at the end of the Ice Age (Richardson 1998). In addition, preservation of the oldest anthropogenic deposits at Quebrada Tacahuay is the result of burial by a massive debris flow that was triggered by an El Niño Southern Oscillation (ENSO) paleoclimatic event (deFrance and Keefer 2005; Keefer et al. 1998, 2003). Subsequent flood events, as well as natural accumulations of aeolian sands, further sealed the deposits.

Although minor human reoccupation of the area occurred, the deposits were unknown until exposed in the mid-1990s during construction of a coastal highway connecting the southern Peruvian cities of Ilo and Ite. Survey of the region identified the deeply buried occupation within a series of road cut and water main profiles. Researchers conducted archaeological and geological investigations of the site in 1996, 1997, 1998, and 2001, with the last field season being the most extensive (deFrance 2002; deFrance et al. 1998, 1999, 2001; Keefer et al. 1998).

The 1997 and 1998 field seasons recovered unequivocal evidence of subsistence specialization in the use of marine resources, particularly marine birds and lesser quantities of shellfish and fish, as well as the production and use of tools made with stone from local coastal sources (deFrance et al. 2001; Keefer et al. 1998). However, the nature of these investigations was very limited because the archaeological deposits were buried under 2–3 m of sediment. The 1997 and 1998 field seasons consisted primarily of collecting volumetric samples of exposed cultural material and geological sediments, and very limited spatial excavation in the traditional archaeological sense. The objective of the 2001 field season was to move beyond the realm of subsistence and to recover data that would increase our understanding of the range of social phenomena associated with these early coastal inhabitants.

While documenting the existence of early maritime adaptations is a useful endeavor, much remains unknown about the cultural dynamics of these early populations. For example, did activities other than food processing and preparation occur at the site? Did the site hold evidence of structures or other cultural refuse that would elucidate the nature of coastal settlement and littoral adaptation? To address these questions, the 2001 field season activities focused on excavating large blocks to expose areas that might contain features (e.g., post molds from structures, human burials, non-food-processing contexts) and possibly new types of cultural material (e.g., nonlithic material or stone tools made of material from distant sources, additional bone tools other than the single worked mammal rib found in 1998) that would help characterize the range of site activities and behaviors.

Whereas previous investigations had primarily studied the stratigraphic units in profile view only, the 2001 methodology resulted in excellent horizontal exposure of the contacts between cultural and geological units. These large-scale excavations were successful in exposing two discrete cultural deposits (Unit 4c3 and Unit 5B) postdating the earliest occupation that were visible only in very limited fashion in the road cuts and water line profiles. The excavation of the Late Pleistocene occupation was also successful in exposing horizontal areas of occupation with dense subsistence and lithic refuse, as well as five discrete hearth features, some of which were buried and overlain with cultural material, indicating reuse of the site rather than a single-use episode. Large spatial excavations also exposed discrete geological strata (e.g., water-laid deposits and volcanic tephra) below the human occupation that were difficult to see in profile only. However, no new feature types or activity areas were identified in the oldest deposits, which supports the view that the site was largely an extractive locale where a limited range of activities took place, with the population residing elsewhere (deFrance et al. 2001, in press). Although no new types of features or activity areas were identified, the ability to excavate features in their entirety rather than from profiles was productive, particularly in regard to the recovery of archaeobotanical remains, especially fuel woods, and in understanding the depositional history of the site, as well as the recovery of additional subsistence remains. In this chapter I discuss the methods and results of the 2001 field season, how Quebrada Tacahuay broadens our understanding of some of the earliest inhabitants of the central Andean littoral, and research questions that can be addressed with the excavation of other early sites.

SITE SETTING AND ENVIRONMENTAL HISTORY

Quebrada Tacahuay (17.8° S latitude, 71.1° W longitude) is located approximately 30 km south of Ilo, Peru, on the distal end of a broad alluvial fan (Figure 4.1). Today, the deeply incised quebrada channel that drains the prominent fan is characterized by diverse Quaternary deposits, including course-grained flood and debris flow deposits with lenses of aeolian sands and volcanic tephra (Keefer et al. 2003:43). At the time the site was occupied it was approximately 0.7–0.9 km farther from the shoreline, and the quebrada channel was significantly shallower. Today the site is 0.3–0.4 km inland on a terrace overlooking a semilunate sandy and rocky shoreline that is bracketed by the rocky headlands of Punta Icuy to the north and Punta Picata to the south. With sea level 60–70 m lower when this site was first occupied (Bard et al. 1996) the bay habitat would have been significantly more protected, making it an appealing location for human exploitation.

Today the coastal climate is hyperarid, with rainfall averaging less than 5 mm per year (McCreary and Koretsky 1966, cited in Satterlee 1993). Sediments and deposits indicate that similar hyperarid climatic conditions have prevailed since the end of the Pleistocene (i.e., as manifested by lack of vegetation, little soil development, few organic inclusions, and desiccation cracks in-filled with aeolian sands) (Keefer et al. 2003:69). The nearest rivers to Quebrada Tacahuay are the Ilo, to the north, and the Locumba and the Sama to the south. These rivers have their source on the western slope of the high Andes, where their flow originates in lakes and in precipitation that mostly occurs from December to March. In their lower courses, these rivers traverse the hyperarid coastal desert. Flow diminishes throughout the year after the end of the highland rainy season, and before the completion of a recent irrigation project, the surface channel of the lower Ilo River was dry for most of the year below an altitude of approximately 1200 masl. However, aquifers that also have their source in the Andes provide water to a series of coastal springs that emerge in the foothills of the coastal cordillera at the interior margin of the coastal plain. In the prehistoric past, the main channel of the Ilo would have been seasonally dry, with water available only during the austral spring, when highland rainfall and snowmelt recharged the system. Although the water available in coastal springs was also tied to highland rainfall

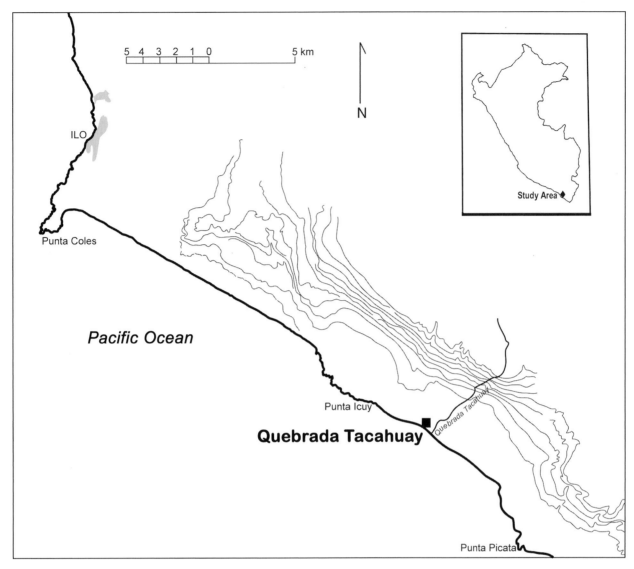

Figure 4.1. Site location of Quebrada Tacahuay in southern Peru.

patterns, a study of modern discharge patterns indicates that some springs generate water throughout the year, while others are seasonally dry (Clement and Moseley 1991).

At Quebrada Tacahuay, evidence for a coastal spring includes the presence of the main channel, paleochannels within the sedimentary sequence, and water-lain silts within the geological stratum containing the Late Pleistocene occupation materials (Keefer et al. 1998, 2003). These silts also suggest pluvial runoff, possibly as a result of minor El Niño activity. In the absence of a major tributary and with an inadequate supply of rainfall for human survival, the lack of fresh water might have been a significant limiting factor in human settlement if the spring did not generate water throughout the year (deFrance in press). The presence of potable

water probably attracted inhabitants to this area even though it was some distance from the coast at the time of earliest occupation. Unfortunately, we have no data on whether the Tacahuay spring was seasonal or not.

The only circumstance under which significant amounts of precipitation fall on the Andean coastal plain is associated with El Niño events. The typically torrential rainfall produced by El Niño events on this arid landscape generates severe flooding and the transport of huge amounts of sediment across the landscape. On a global scale, the Pleistocene antiquity of El Niño dates to more than 100,000 years ago (Tudhope et al. 2001). A synthesis of El Niño flood event frequency based on geological survey, sediment analyses, and historical and modern records for the Ilo region, including the deposits at Quebrada Tacahuay, indicates that El Niño events have been producing floods and debris flows there with variable frequencies during the Holocene and Late Pleistocene, with the oldest dated deposit being about 38,000 years old (Keefer et al. 2003); older, undated deposits of similar character suggest that El Niño has been affecting this region far longer than that. Differing frequencies of the dated sedimentary deposits suggest a period of high El Niño activity in the Early Holocene, followed by a mid-Holocene weakening or hiatus in activity and the subsequent resumption of moderate to high activity in the Late Holocene, after about 4600 rcyr BP (Keefer et al. 2003). These data underscore the differing intensity of events associated with El Niño, from small-scale perturbations to catastrophic Mega-Niños.

At Quebrada Tacahuay, two massive debris flow deposits dating to the Late Pleistocene and Early Holocene are greater in scale than the most severe recent ENSO events (i.e., those of 1982–1983, 1992–1993, and 1997–1998). One of these, Unit 7, was inferred to have been produced by an El Niño event that occurred shortly after a high-magnitude earthquake that destabilized large amounts of sediment (Keefer et al. 2003:70). The mid-Holocene hiatus in El Niño activity present at Quebrada Tacahuay has been documented in other areas of the Andes in association with human settlement and is also corroborated by paleoclimatic evidence from geographic regions outside the Andes (see Keefer et al. 2003 for a review). Although the modern periodicity of El Niño activity appears to have emerged within the last 5,000 years, El Niños have far greater antiquity.

At Quebrada Tacahuay the Upper Series of strata (Units 1–9) as defined by Keefer et al. (1998, 2003) is of archaeological relevance, with deposits that date from approximately 4500 rcyr BP to the Pleistocene and contain evidence of human occupation (Units 4c3 within Unit 4, 5, and 8).[1] Keefer completed the characterization of the geological history of sedimentation in collaboration with the archaeological investigations using the exposed road cut and water main profiles during the 1996, 1997, and 1998 field seasons, as well as with an assessment of the area following the June 23, 2001, earthquake.

A massive ENSO-induced debris flow (Unit 7) buried the earliest human occupation (Unit 8) under as much as a meter of sediment. Radiocarbon assays from archaeological contexts above and below the debris flow bracket this event sometime between 10,290 and 10,090 rcyr BP (deFrance et al. 2001). Sediment analysis indicates that the debris flow was viscous slurry characterized by a large sediment load moving relatively slowly and in laminar fashion, rather than a rapidly moving, turbulent liquid flow (deFrance and Keefer 2005). Consequently, the debris flow sealed the initial anthropogenic deposit instead of scouring it. Some avian skeletal material on the surface was pushed down into the base of the debris flow, while those elements already covered with wind-blown sands were protected.

A second, thinner debris flow (Unit 6) is interpreted as having been deposited relatively quickly after Unit 7, based on the radiocarbon dates that bracket the two units (Keefer et al. 2003). Minor human occupation occurs in Units 4 (Unit 4c3) and 5. Additional sheet-flood and debris flow deposits accumulated at the site and further sealed and buried the earliest anthropogenic deposit under 2–3 m of sediment (Keefer et al. 1998, 2003). After the deposition of Unit 1 more than 4500 rcyr ago, the quebrada downcut its channel several meters to its present elevation. Subsequently, no further sedimentation was deposited across the site.

ARCHAEOLOGICAL INVESTIGATIONS

Previous Studies

In 1996, shortly after construction of the coastal highway, Michael Moseley, David Keefer, and Dennis Satterlee identified the recently exposed archaeological deposits at Quebrada Tacahuay while examining land surfaces and geological deposits in the region. A single radiocarbon date from a hearth eroding from one of the water main profiles revealed the antiquity (10,770 rcyr BP) of an anthropogenic deposit of butchered and processed marine birds within an aeolian sand lens (8–40 cm in depth). Archaeologists conducted limited research at the site in both 1997 and 1998 (Keefer 1998; deFrance et al. 2001). The focus of these projects was to identify the nature of the early human use of the site, particularly the nature of subsistence activities. These investigations primarily entailed collecting volumetric samples from along the exposed road cut and water main profiles; minimal horizontal excavations conducted in 1998 revealed the presence of well-preserved avifauna and lithic refuse (Keefer 1998; deFrance et al. 2001).[2] Small hearths were identified and partially excavated from profiles; however, the 1998 horizontal excavations did not reveal any in situ features. The collection and analysis of fine-screened (1/16-inch, 1.8-mm mesh) volumetric samples in both 1997 and 1998 and the limited spatial excavations were successful in recovering abundant faunal refuse, a variety of unifacial lithic tools, and large quantities of debitage, as well as carbonized plant remains appropriate for radiocarbon dating. These data sets provided incontrovertible evidence for a specialized maritime economy focused on the exploitation and processing (i.e., butchering, cooking, consumption) of numerous cormorants and boobies, with lesser use of several species of finfish and limited use of marine shellfish. Faunal remains also included some seal or sea lion remains, indicating either active hunting or scavenging of marine mammals. Coastal stone sources provided chalcedony for the production of expedient cutting and scraping stone tools. The site's inhabitants did not consume any terrestrial resources of dietary consequence, nor did they obtain any material (e.g., stone, other raw materials) from other elevations or habitats. The site is interpreted as a specialized maritime extractive and processing locale that was preserved owing to its burial by the catastrophic if fortuitous paleoclimatic events (deFrance and Keefer 2005; Keefer et al. 1998, 2003; deFrance et al. 2001).

Despite having established the pattern of faunal exploitation, the predominant technology, and the chronological placement of the site's deposits, little else was known about the nature of the site occupation and the earliest coastal inhabitants. The excavations had recovered cultural materials but, being limited, had not defined the context of their use and behaviors other than faunal processing and preparation. The nature of coastal residence was also unknown. Did the inhabitants reside at this locale for any duration, only seasonally, or was it a single-use site where a large quantity of birds and some other fauna had been dispatched, processed, and consumed?

The 2001 Excavations

The 2001 season consisted of the excavation of four 5 × 5-m square blocks in areas where previous investigations had recovered abundant cultural material from Unit 8 deposits exposed in various profiles (Figure 4.2). To reach Unit 8, we excavated 2–3 m of largely sterile overburden using picks and shovels. Although excavation with heavy machinery might have expedited this process, we elected to use hand excavation in order to document the changes in geological strata.[3] Hand excavation also ensured that other ephemeral cultural deposits (in Units 4c3 and 5B) more deeply embedded in noncultural levels would be identified and not destroyed if they were encountered. Once intact

cultural deposits were identified, the block was subdivided into 1-m squares. As in previous seasons, all the material was screened with 1/16-inch (1.8-mm) mesh, and we saved it to be sorted in the field lab.

The excavation of the four blocks had varying degrees of success in locating unique cultural materials. Block 1 (see Figure 4.2) was placed in an area along the small profile designated 1A where previous excavations recovered a large quantity of lithic debitage and some tools in Unit 8. Following the excavation of Unit 1 in Block 1 we uncovered a very thin scatter (5 cm maximum depth) of marine mussel shell (*Choromytilus choros*) at the contact between Units 1 and 2. This scatter had not been identified previously in any of the profiles or excavations. There was no cultural material with the scatter. Although the shell lens was not dated directly, the dates of Units 1 and 2 place the deposit sometime between 4500 ± 60 and 7920 ± 80 BC. Once we exposed Unit 8 deposits we found only a small quantity of subsistence remains and lithic debris. A southern extension of the excavation (0.85 × 2 m to the profile edge) in the area of Profile 1A recovered some additional stone artifacts, but not a discernible workshop area. If a workshop with more defined features existed in this area, it was apparently destroyed when site sediments were removed with the construction of the water main. Within Block 1 and the extension, the Unit 8 deposits contained a variety of faunal remains, predominantly cormorant and booby remains, but also several elements of pelican and a small number of marine mammal elements, either seal or sea lion.

Block 2 was located northeast of Profile 1 near where the first hearth was sampled and where we excavated a 2 × 1.5-m context in 1998 (see Figure 4.2). At the surface of Unit 4 we uncovered a thin, amorphous scatter (maximum dimensions 1.54 m east-west × 1.45 m north-south) of mussel shell (*Choromytilus choros*) and charcoal along the east wall. The lens did not contain any cultural material or faunal remains other than the shell. This cultural deposit is also present in Profile 4; however, the shell lens is not found across the site and was encountered only in this excavation. A single AMS date on charcoal produced a date of 9010 ± 40 rcyr BP (Table 4.1). Once Unit 8 deposits were unearthed in Block 2, we found a thin scatter of cultural material, but no cultural features or concentrations of refuse. However, once we excavated Unit 8 and exposed the silt lens (Unit 8C) and the sterile Pleistocene deposits of Unit 9, we uncovered the remnant of a small stream channel running roughly east to west through the block

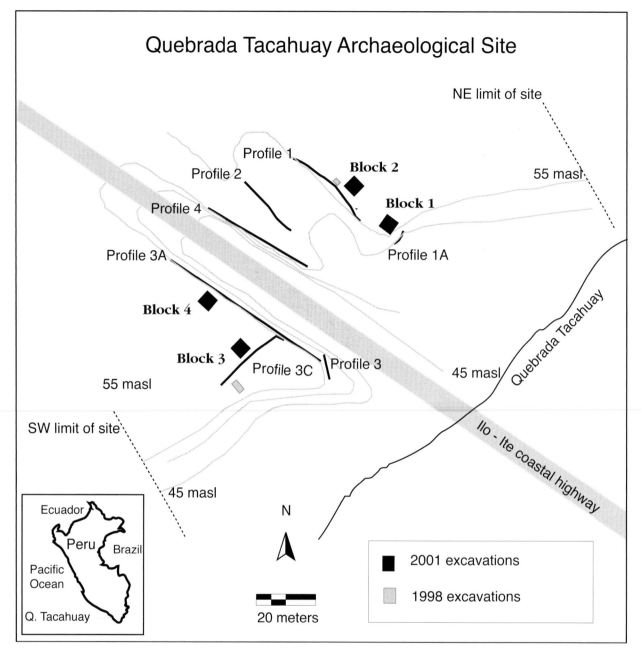

Figure 4.2. Site map of Quebrada Tacahuay indicating location of 2001 and previous excavations. (Map by P. R. Williams.)

(Figure 4.3). Water-lain sediments indicate that the channel carried either spring or pluvial water prior to the accumulation of the aeolian sands in Unit 8.

Block 3 proved to be the most productive in regard to cultural materials. This block and Block 4 were located on the coastal (south and west) side of the highway (see Figure 4.2). Block 3, adjacent to Profile 3C, contained very well-preserved archaeological deposits of both Unit 5 and Unit 8. Unit 5, an aeolian sand with silt, was unearthed below Unit 3 (Unit 4 deposits do not

occur in this area of the site). In road cut profile view, Unit 5 is homogeneous; however, in excavation, the stratum consists of two distinct sand lenses, an upper level of dense sterile sand approximately 8–10 cm deep (Unit 5A) and a second layer of less compact sand with gravel and cultural material (Unit 5B) approximately 16–18 cm deep. Unit 5B contains abundant remains of land snails, *Scutalus* sp.; however, these small snails are considered a nonfood species found in association with human-generated garbage. In Andean desert habitats

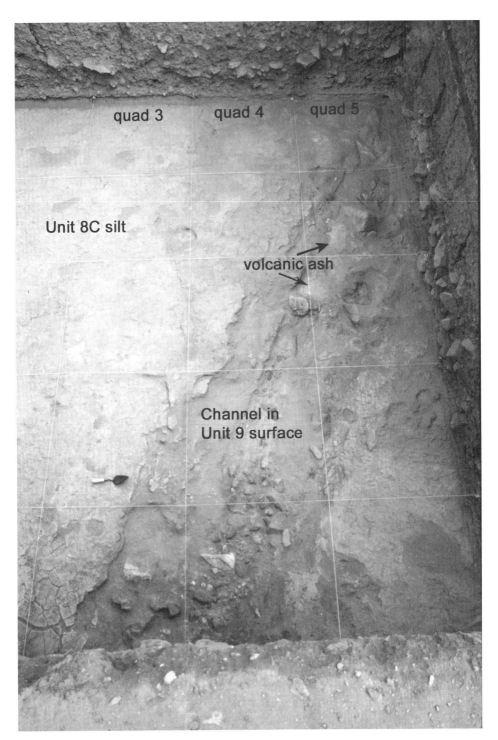

Figure 4.3. Remnant channel in Block 2, Unit 9 surface.

many terrestrial snails remain dormant until there is sufficient moisture to support the growth of the population (see Craig 1992). The abundance of land snails with human refuse suggests there was greater moisture at the time Unit 5B was deposited; however, we have no other data to corroborate this hypothesis. Once we reached the surface of Unit 5, the entire block was sectioned into 1-m quads. Cultural material recovered from Unit 5B includes chalcedony and basalt flakes, as well as a coastal block scraper. Also present are vertebrate and invertebrate subsistence remains. One archaeological feature, an amorphous hearth, was excavated along the north wall of the block (see Table 4.2). There was no evidence of surface preparation for the hearth.

Table 4.1. Radiocarbon dates from stratigraphic contexts at Quebrada Tacahuay.

Context (Profile or Block/Unit)[a]	¹⁴C yr BP	Calibrated 2-σ Ranges cal yr BP	Sample No. and Technique[b]	δ¹³C	Material
Block 2, Unit 4	9010 ± 40	10,230–10,150	172615AMS	−22.9	Charcoal
Block 3, Unit 5B	9850 ±150	11,950–10,970	159921Conv.	−25.6	Charcoal
Profile 3C, Unit 5B	10,050 ± 90	12,280–11,230	160707AMS	−22.2	Charcoal
Block 3, Unit 8B *bajo*	10,660 ± 80	12,960–12,340	160706AMS	−20.4	Charcoal
Profile 1A, Unit 8 (1998)	10,690 ± 60	12,960–12,380	172645AMS	−25.7	Charcoal

Note: All radiocarbon dates were calibrated using INTCAL98 (Stuiver et al. 1998) and are expressed as 2 sigma ranges. All dates have been corrected for isotopic fractionation.
[a] Profile refers to exposed roadcut or water line cut; Block refers to an excavation context; Unit refers to either a geological or an archaeological stratigraphic level.
[b] All dates run by Beta Analytic, Inc.

Following the excavation of Unit 5B we used picks and shovels to excavate the Unit 7 debris flow deposits. (Unit 6, a thinner ENSO-generated debris flow, was not found in this part of the site). Once Unit 8 deposits were exposed, we again established the 1-m grid system for the block. Although the sand matrix within Unit 8 remained uniform, we defined and excavated four discrete subunits of cultural material that were distinguished both by the degree of bone fragmentation or completeness and by their stratigraphic location and burial by the unit sands.

The layer of bone fragments found in the surface of Unit 8 and cemented into the base of Unit 7 was designated Unit 8A. These specimens had not been buried by wind-blown sands prior to the debris flow event. A deeper layer of buried bone elements, Unit 8B, included many complete skeletal elements some of which were partially articulated (e.g., ulnae and humeri, several cervical vertebrae, scapulae and coracoids, phalanges). Since Unit 8C was previously assigned to a sterile flood deposit within the Unit 8 sands (deFrance et al. 2001), Unit 8B was subdivided further. We designated subsequent levels of complete and fragmented bone as Unit 8B Level 2, and a deeper level of bone and cultural features largely buried by sand as Unit 8B *bajo* (lower).

Unit 8B contains five hearths: Features 2, 3, 4, 5, and 6 (Figure 4.4 and Table 4.2). Features 4 and 6 were buried by sands and occur at slightly deeper elevations than Features 2, 3, and 5; therefore, the contextual designation Unit 8B *bajo* was used to distinguish the stratigraphic location of Features 4 and 6. All of the features were partitioned and excavated in two halves to expose the feature profiles. As was the case with Feature 1 in Unit 5B, there was no surface preparation for the features; they are not defined by rocks or other material but rather consist of lenses of ash, charcoal, and burned and unburned bird bone. One of the more

compact hearths, Feature 5 consisted of a roughly circular, compact deposit with several strata, including a lens of dense burned botanical material (see Figure 4.4). The other hearths also contained varying amounts of bird bone, bony fish remains, some marine shell, and stone artifacts/chipped stones.

Since sands buried at least two of the features, they are stratigraphically slightly deeper than the other hearths. However, it was not known if this difference in depth translated to distinct depositional events separated temporally. The quantity and distribution of material across the site did not suggest a single episode when large numbers of birds were dispatched, processed, and consumed (i.e., an event analogous to Olsen-Chubbock for marine birds); however, the time depth involved was unknown. Efforts to radiocarbon date the subunits within Unit 8 were not successful.[4] Nevertheless, the accumulation and burial of some features by wind-blown sands indicates reuse of the site rather than a single depositional event.

Other than the hearths, the cultural materials are similar to those identified previously in Unit 8. Abundant marine bird remains and lithic material are common. Some scraping or cutting stone tools made of chalcedony are present. Some basalt and rosy quartz flakes are present, but we found no exotic lithic material.

Block 4 is located west of Profile 3A (south and west of the coastal highway). We believed this to be a high-probability area for the recovery of cultural material since we had recovered lithic tools from the adjacent profile. In contrast to the Unit 5 deposits in Block 3, Unit 5 sands in Block 4 did not contain cultural material. The Unit 8 deposits containing cultural material (Unit 8A) were extremely shallow. All of the cultural material was restricted to an 8- to 10-cm sand deposit with some fragmented bird bone and five fragments of marine mollusks. No other artifacts were found in this block.

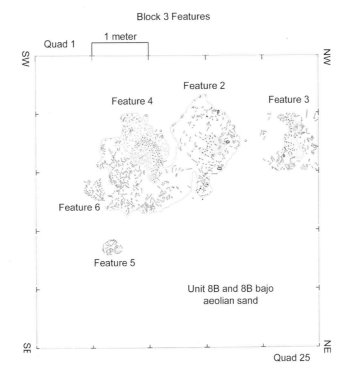

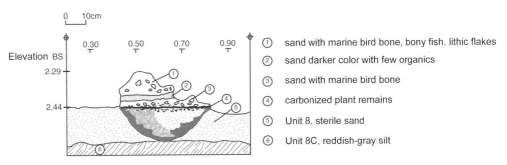

① sand with marine bird bone, bony fish, lithic flakes
② sand darker color with few organics
③ sand with marine bird bone
④ carbonized plant remains
⑤ Unit 8, sterile sand
⑥ Unit 8C, reddish-gray silt

Figure 4.4. Features present in Block 3, Units 8B and 8B *bajo*.

Although there was very little cultural material present, the geological deposits within Unit 8 included at least two red silt flood deposits (Unit 8C and Unit 8C1) that represent either pluvial sediments or very mild ENSO sediment flows. Unit 8 sands containing no cultural material separate the two minor flood events. Also present was a thin deposit of volcanic tephra present in Block 1 and elsewhere. This tephra is discontinuous across the site but visible in several profiles. Efforts to correlate the volcanic ash at Quebrada Tacahuay with a known Late Pleistocene volcanic eruption were not successful.[5]

In addition to the excavation of the four blocks, cultural deposits from a recently exposed profile were systematically investigated as part of the 2001 field season.

The 1997–1998 El Niño caused a washout of the coastal highway at Quebrada Icuy north of the site. The Peruvian Transportation Ministry removed deposits from Tacahuay for use as road fill in 1998 and again sometime between 1998 and 2000. These operations resulted in exposure of Profile 3C (parallel to Profile 3B, which was sampled in 1998) (see Figure 4.2). The profile exposed only the strata from the ground surface to the top of Unit 8. The majority of Unit 8 deposits remained covered. Although Unit 8 cultural deposits remained unexposed, the new profile provided excellent exposure of Unit 5. Faunal remains, chipped stone, and charcoal from Unit 5 were eroding from the deposit onto the surface of Unit 7.

We partitioned the best-preserved portion of the profile into fourteen 1-m sections. All of the cultural

Table 4.2. Description of features excavated in the 2001 field season.

Feature No.	Location	Unit	Quads	Dimensions	Depth Below Surface (BS) and Feature Depth	Function	
1	Block 3	5B	5, 10	1.92 m E-W × 0.92 m max. N-S	1.75 m BS, 12 cm — 5 strata	Hearth	charcoal, vertebrate fauna, marine bivalves, with *Scutalus* sp. terrestrial gastropods
2	Block 3	8B	3, 4, 8, 9, 13	1.76 m E-W × 1.12 m N-S	2.44 m BS, 18 cm — 7 strata	Hearth	charcoal, fragmented marine bird and marine fish elements, marine mollusks, and chalcedony tools and refuse, and a rosy quartz utilized flake.
3	Block 3	8B	10	0.71 m E-W × 0.36 m N-S	2.45 m BS, 4 cm — no internal strata	Hearth	charcoal, complete and fragmented marine bird elements, lithics
4	Block 3	8B *bajo*	7, 8, 12, 13	1.67 m E-W × 1.22 m N-S	2.44 m BS, 5 cm — 2 strata	Hearth	charcoal, complete and fragmented marine bird elements, marine bony fish elements, two chalcedony scrapers, several smaller flakes
5	Block 3	8B	17	0.26 m E-W × 0.37 m N-S	2.29 m BS, denser at 2.44 m BS, 29 cm — 4 strata	Hearth	dense carbonized botanicals, complete and fragmented marine bird elements
6	Block 3	8B *bajo*	11, 12	0.55 E-W × 1.5 m N-S	2.47 m BS, 20 cm — 2 strata	Hearth	small concentration with scatter of ash and charcoal, some marine bird elements

Note:
Feature 1 contained charcoal, vertebrate fauna, marine bivalves, with *Scutalus* sp. terrestrial gastropods, and a chalcedony coastal block scraper. Features 2–6 contained charcoal, ash, complete and fragmented marine bird and marine fish elements, and small quantities of marine mollusks. Features 2 and 4 also contained chalcedony lithic tools and refuse, and one rose quartz flake (Feature 2). Feature 5 was the most compact, with a dense mat of burned botanical material.

material on the surface of a 14-m section was recorded and collected. Loose fill on the slope of Unit 7 was collected and screened. Once the profile had been cleaned of loose material, small volumetric samples of the intact portion of Unit 5 were collected from nine 1-m sections. The volumes collected ranged from 3.0 to 6.0 liters. All of the material was fine-screened and collected for lab sorting. Profile 3C contained a fair quantity of cultural material, including chipped stone, marine shell, vertebrate faunal remains, and charcoal. *Scutalus* sp. shells are common throughout the profile. These data complement the findings from the excavation of Unit 5B in Block 3.

The 2001 Results

Five additional radiocarbon dates were generated from samples collected in 2001 (Table 4.1, Figure 4.5). One date was from the thin mussel shell deposit (Unit 4) uncovered in Block 2. Two dates were from Unit 5 cultural deposits, including one date from Feature 1 and one from Profile 3C. Two additional dates from Unit 8 deposits are within the time range of previous samples.[6]

When all of the radiocarbon dates from the cultural deposits are compared, it is evident that human use of the quebrada occurred during the Late Pleistocene and Early Holocene (Figure 4.5). Although we did not obtain a chronometric date from the thin mussel shell scatter present in Block 1, this appears to be a localized deposit (i.e., it is not found in any other area of the site). The shell scatter was deposited prior to Unit 1 (4559 rcyr BP), and therefore may be roughly contemporaneous with Unit 2 (7920 rcyr BP) and the only date from Unit 4c3 (7990 ± 80 rcyr BP) (see Keefer 2003 for a discussion of the relationship between Units 2 and 4).

The larger-scale excavations from 2001 support previous findings regarding maritime economy and subsistence. The site exhibits evidence of specialized extraction and processing of large numbers of marine birds and minor use of other coastal resources. The marine fauna identified from Unit 8 deposits in both Block 3 and from the southern extension of Block 1 is consistent with that found during the 1997 and 1998 field seasons (Table 4.3) (deFrance 2005). As was found during previous seasons, several avian elements (n =

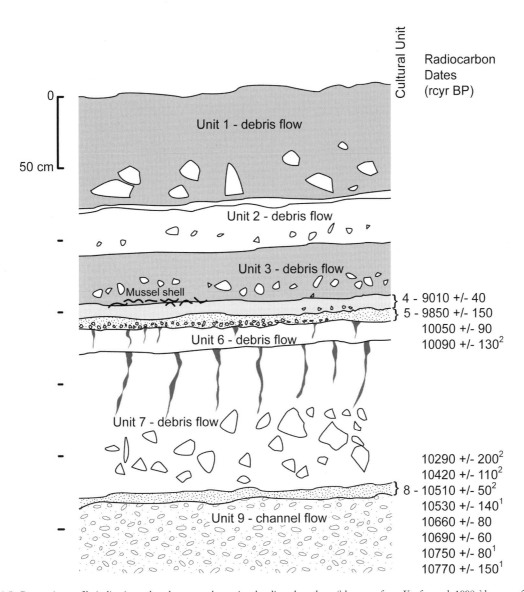

Figure 4.5. Composite profile indicating cultural strata and associated radiocarbon dates ([1]dates are from Keefer et al. 1998; [2]dates are from deFrance et al. 2001). All cultural materials (Units 4, 5, and 8) are within aeolian sand deposits. A choro mussel shell lens present in Unit 4c3 is not depicted in this profile.

191) and two marine mammal specimens bore evidence of butchering. There is no use of terrestrial resources that can be considered food items. The remains of small-sized reptiles (e.g., lizards and snakes) are present, but these are not considered to have been food refuse. Following the El Niño event that buried the Unit 8 deposits, human reoccupation of the area (Unit 5) was characterized by less use of marine birds, no use of marine mammals, and greater exploitation of marine finfish and shellfish (Tables 4.4 and 4.5). Shellfish use is more varied and includes taxa not consumed during the earliest use of the site (e.g., false abalone, limpet, chiton). All three of these are common on

rocky shorelines. Interestingly, the Unit 5 deposits also contain the remains of lorna (*Sciaena deliciosa*), which is also the most common bony fish in the deposits from Quebrada Jaguay, an early maritime site more than 200 km north of Tacahuay (Sandweiss et al. 1998; McGinnis 1999). The remains of one small canid, a probable fox, are the only evidence for a terrestrial mammal. Foxes are not a significant subsistence item in later time periods and the Tacahuay specimens do not contain butchering evidence; therefore, these remains are not interpreted as food refuse.

The lithic assemblage from the earliest occupation contains eight chalcedony unifacial cutting/scraping

Table 4.3. Fauna identified from Blocks 1 and 3, Unit 8.

Scientific Name	Common Name	NISP	MNI	Wt. (g)
Chiroptera	Bats	1	1	<0.1
Rodentia unidentified	Rodents	28	3	0.6
Arctocephalus sp.	Southern fur seal	5	1	42.6
Otaria cf. *flavescens*	Southern sea lion	1	1	25.9
Otariidae/Phocidae	Eared seals/sea lions	2	1	1.6
Pinnipedia	Seals, sea lions	2	0	1.6
Mammal unidentified (sm)	Unidentified small mammal	7	0	<0.1
Total Mammalia		**46**	**7**	**72.3**
Tinamidae cf. *Crypturellus* sp.	Tinamou	4	1	0.9
Pelecanus sp.	Pelican	83	5	55.8
Phalacrocorax sp.	Cormorant	2,023	28	1,818.3
Phalacrocorax bougainvillii	Guanay cormorant	346	40	—
Sula sp.	Booby	1,214	40	771.7
Phalacrocoracidae/Sulidae	Cormorant/booby	413	0	52.8
Calidris sp.	Sandpiper	5	2	0.2
Passeriformes	Songbirds	2	2	0.1
Passeriformes/Fringilliformes	Songbirds/finches	1		<0.1
Aves unidentified	Unidentified birds	n/c	0	2722.8
Total Aves		**4,091**	**118**	**5,422.6**
Lacertilia	Lizards	5	1	<0.1
Reptilia unidentified	Unidentified reptiles	1	0	<0.1
Total Reptilia		**6**	**1**	**0.0**
Tetrapoda unidentified (sm)	Unidentified small tetrapods	14	0	1.5
Clupeidae	Sardines, shad, herring	3	1	<0.1
Clupeidae/Engraulidae	Sardines, shad, herring/anchovies	7	0	<0.1
Engraulidae	Anchovy	1,507	31	1.3
Carangidae/Sciaenidae	Jack/drum	1	1	0.3
cf. *Mugil* sp.	cf. mullet	2	1	0.2
cf. Sciaenidae/Carangidae	cf. drum/jack	1	0	0.1
Osteichthyes unidentified	Unidentified bony fishes	1,497	{3}	18.0
Total Osteichthyes		**3,018**	**34**	**19.9**
Vertebrata unidentified	Unidentified vertebrates	n/c		1025.8
Total Vertebrata		**7,175**	**160**	**6,542.1**
Choromytilus chorus	Choro mussel	4	1	0.9
Mulinia cf. *edulis*	Clam taquillas	1	1	2.2
Semele cf. *corrugata*	Round clam	1	1	4.1
Veneridae	Venerid clam	1	1	1.0
Bivalvia unidentified	Unidentified bivalve	47	0	7.2
Total Bivalvia		**54**	**4**	**15.4**
Mollusca unidentified	Unidentified mollusks	269	0	6.4
Total Invertebrata		**323**	**4**	**21.8**
Sample Total		**7,498**	**164**	**6,563.9**

Table 4.4. Fauna identified from Block 3, Unit 5B.

Scientific Name	Common Name	NISP	MNI	Wt. (g)
Pseudalopex cf. *culpaeus*	Desert fox	18	1	3.1
Rodentia unidentified	Rodent	75	2	0.2
Mammal unidentified	Unidentified mammal	30		1.3
Total Mammalia		**123**	**3**	**4.6**
cf. Passeriformes	cf. songbirds	2	1	<0.1
Aves unidentified (medium-sized)	Unidentified birds	46	1	6.3
Total Aves		**48**	**2**	**6.3**
Lacertilia	Lizard	1	1	< 0.1
Serpentes	Snakes	1	1	< 0.1
Reptilia unidentified (cf. Lacertilia)	cf. lizard	123	1	0.5
Total Reptilia		**125**	**3**	**0.5**
Tetrapoda unidentified	Unidentified tetrapods	50	0	1.6
Sciaena deliciosa	Lorna	3	2	0.4
Osteichthyes unidentified	Unidentified bony fishes	25	1	0.8
Total Osteichthyes		**28**	**3**	**1.2**
Vertebrata unidentified (lg)		n/c		43.2
Total Vertebrata		**374**	**11**	**57.4**
Concholepas concholepas	False abalone	3	3	63.0
Fissurella sp.	Limpet	1	1	11.1
Gastropoda unidentified	Unidentified gastropod	5		1.6
Total Gastropoda		**9**	**4**	**75.7**
Choromytilus chorus	Choro mussel	19	2	44.2
Mytilidae	Mussel	1		0.2
Bivalvia unidentified	Unidentified bivalves	22		62.4
Total Bivalvia		**42**	**2**	**106.6**
Mollusca unidentified	Unidentified mollusks	204		111.7
Balanus sp.	Barnacles	15		0.2
Invertebrata unidentified		n/c		0.4
Total Invertebrata		**270**	**6**	**294.6**
Sample Total		**644**	**17**	**352.0**

Table 4.5. Fauna identified from Profile 3C, Unit 5.

Scientific Name	Common Name	NISP	MNI
Rodentia	Rodent	15	2
Mammal unidentified	Unidentified mammal	25	1
Total Mammalia		**40**	**3**
Phalacrocorax bougainvillii	Guanay cormorant	3	1
Aves unidentified	Unidentified birds	n/c	
Total Aves		**3**	**1**
Clupeidae	Shad, herring, sardines	4	2
Engraulidae/Clupeidae	Anchovy/shad, herring, sardine	1	0
Sciaena deliciosa	Lorna	1	1
cf. Sciaenidae	cf. drum	1	1
Osteichthyes unidentified	Unidentified bony fish	44	2
Total Osteichthyes		**51**	**6**
Total Vertebrata		**94**	**10**
Concholepas concholepas	False abalone	18	17
Total Gastropoda		**18**	**17**
Choromytilus chorus	Choro mussel	2	2
Total Bivalvia		**2**	**2**
Balanus sp.	Barnacles	2	0
Chiton *sensu latu*	Chiton	4	2
Mollusca unidentified	Unidentified mollusks	11	—
Total Invertebrata		**37**	**21**
Sample Total		**131**	**31**

tools (Figure 4.6). Also present are nonutilized rose quartz (n = 6) and basalt flakes (n = 4). We recovered two basalt cores and one basalt hammerstone. The Unit 8 deposits contain abundant debitage, primarily small chalcedony retouch, use, and thinning flakes (n = >900). The Unit 5 deposits contain utilized (n = 1) and nonutilized (n = 5) chalcedony flakes, as well as a small number of nonutilized basalt flakes (n = 2). The only tool present is the coastal block scraper from Feature 1 (Figure 4.6). Chalcedony debitage is also common in Unit 5 deposits (n = 243).

The only nonlithic artifact recovered in the 2001 season is a small, unfired clay ball approximately 2.5 cm in diameter found in Block 3, Unit 8B between Features 2 and 4, but not within either hearth. Spherical in shape, it is made of reddish sandy silt, probably the same material as Unit 8C. It is not notched or otherwise modified for use as a bola stone. And since it is unfired, it could not have been a net weight; therefore its function is not known.

DISCUSSION

The 2001 field season entailed excavation of 100 m² of site deposits and the collection of volumetric samples along a previously unstudied profile. These

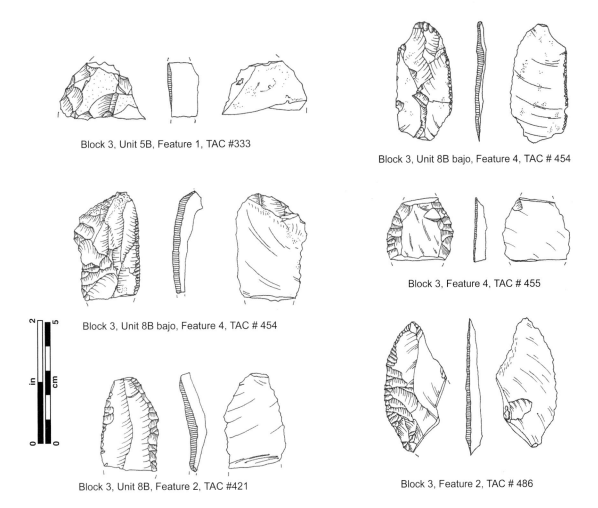

Block 3, Unit 5B, Feature 1, TAC #333

Block 3, Unit 8B bajo, Feature 4, TAC # 454

Block 3, Unit 8B bajo, Feature 4, TAC # 454

Block 3, Feature 4, TAC # 455

Block 3, Unit 8B, Feature 2, TAC #421

Block 3, Feature 2, TAC # 486

Figure 4.6. Examples of chalcedony lithic artifacts recovered during the 2001 field season.

investigations significantly expanded our understanding of site use and formation processes. They also confirmed previous interpretations of site economy and behavior focused on the acquisition of local foodstuffs and raw materials. Our investigations did not unearth any new types of features, nor did we recover material from other geographic regions or elevations. The material kit for this time period is exclusively utilitarian stone tools with the exception of one bone artifact (recovered in the 1998 field season) and the unusual clay ball from the most recent investigations.

Although these studies have defined the site economy, several aspects of behavior associated with the use of coastal resources during the Terminal Pleistocene remain unknown for this locale. The nature of both coastal residence and population movement for the people associated with Quebrada Tacahuay is not known. I argue that linear migration along the coast rather than population movement

to the interior makes better economic and adaptive sense, owing to the unavailability of water in many areas of the interior, particularly in the lower part of the Osmore drainage, and because of biological constraints on human adaptation to high-elevation settings (Aldenderfer 1998; deFrance in press). The degree of coastal specialization at Tacahuay does not suggest random or opportunistic use of coastal habitats. The economic and subsistence specialization support a model of coastal residence; however, without empirical data on coastal structures or residences, it is impossible to define the territorial pattern of land use. No post molds or evidence for structures were identified even with the large spatial area that was exposed during the 2001 season. Within the Tacahuay study region there are no exotic materials that indicate either population movement to other elevations or interactions with populations in other regions that resulted in the acquisition of raw materials.

If populations did not reside at Tacahuay, more permanent residence may have been at sites such as at the Ring Site (20 km north of Tacahuay; see Figure 4.1), or perhaps elsewhere along the coast, where deep refuse accumulated (deFrance in press). The Ring Site is a strong candidate since it has deposits dated to over 10,500 rcry BP and it has a long sequence of use through the Archaic period (Sandweiss et al. 1989). If movement to the interior was undertaken for subsistence reasons, I propose that it would not have been beyond the coastal cordillera or to elevations in excess of 1000 masl. A migration pattern that did not necessitate physiological adaptation to changes in elevation would have been biologically advantageous (deFrance in press).

Ten thousand years ago, the resources of the south-central Peruvian coast were bountiful. The coastal resources in the vicinity of Tacahuay are not subject to seasonal fluctuations in availability; therefore, there was no need to migrate to other areas in search of subsistence resources. In some areas of the south-central Andes, researchers have identified patterns of coastal-inland migration that included inland settlements with coastal refuse, as well as hunter-gatherers exploiting both the coast and low-elevation lomas (fog-dependent plant oases that form along low-elevation coastal hillslopes) (Núñez 1983, 1999; Llagostera 1989, 1992; Santoro 1993; Núñez et al. 1994). If water was a limited resource in coastal settings during the Late Pleistocene, people may also have devised storage methods that left no archaeological remains. With an active ENSO regime at the end of the Pleistocene, flexibility in subsistence strategies would have been advantageous; however, we have no evidence within the lower Osmore for a seasonal pattern of migration or for logistical stations that involved the exploitation of inland food resources such as terrestrial mammals.

Among the issues that remain to be addressed with investigations of other early coastal sites are the social contexts of settlement and foraging behavior. House floors, living areas, and nonfood domestic refuse could be used to address issues related to the social and gender organization of households. Trade and contact with people in other geographic areas (inland or other coastal areas) could be used to infer population movements and the social mechanisms for these interactions (i.e., to reduce risk, identify mates, obtain raw materials). In regard to environmental conditions, it is also evident that El Niño perturbations caused flooding during the period of initial human settlement along the Andean coast (Keefer et al. 1998, 2003); however, little is known of human reaction and adaptation to the changing environment at the end of the Ice Age.

The bioarchaeology of the earliest inhabitants is also an unstudied topic. Human remains from early sites have the potential to provide genetic and morphological data on the founding Andean populations, the chemical signatures of diet as well as information on ideological beliefs regarding the dead. Mortuary data would be particularly relevant to questions of both human origins and ideology. The social life, mortuary beliefs, and worldview of later complex coastal dwellers that possessed organized political structure have their origins with the first inhabitants of the Andean coast. Understanding the Late Pleistocene populations with archaeological data provides a foundation for interpreting coastal cultures through time. Goals of future research on early Andean littoral sites should address territoriality, residence patterns, and geographic variability in Late Pleistocene adaptations.

CONCLUSIONS

Archaeologists conducted three seasons of research at Quebrada Tacahuay. Small-scale investigations were completed in both 1997 and 1998. The 2001 field season was the most comprehensive, entailing the excavation of four 5 × 5-m blocks and the collection of volumetric samples from one profile. The goal of these large spatial excavations was to identify features and artifact types not previously identified that would expand our understanding of coastal behavior beyond subsistence and animal processing. These block excavations were successful in exposing three discrete pockets of cultural deposits in Units 2, 4, and 5 that are not uniform across the site. The Unit 5 deposits held the greatest variety of cultural refuse, including a small hearth, subsistence remains, and lithic tools, while the other two, more recent deposits yielded exclusively marine shell and charcoal. The Unit 5 subsistence remains are more varied than the older Unit 8 deposits; however, the economic focus continues to be maritime resources, with greater use of both finfish and shellfish. Volumetric samples of Unit 5 deposits from one profile produced well-preserved subsistence remains and some lithic tools, as well as abundant wood charcoal.

Of the four blocks, the Unit 8 deposits in Block 3 were the best preserved. Researchers excavated abundant marine bird refuse, lithic tools, and five hearths. The stratigraphic superposition of some features and the burial of others by aeolian sands indicate that the site was reused over some period of time rather than in a single-use episode. The temporal depth of site use for the earliest occupation is not known; however, the calibrated range of radiocarbon dates suggests the site was used intermittently over several centuries. The subsistence remains and stone artifacts support previous interpretations that the site was an extractive locale where marine birds and some other marine resources were processed, prepared, and consumed. The deposits contain no terrestrial fauna that is considered edible and no cultural material from other geographic locations. Although no new examples of features were uncovered, the excavations were successful in providing new data on site formation processes, particularly for sediments that immediately predate human use of the area. Within the Unit 8 deposits there are water-lain deposits, volcanic tephra, and sterile sands that accumulated prior to human occupation.

Future research should be directed at identifying the nature of coastal settlement, residence, and migration in southern Peru. At a broader level, research is also needed on the range of geographic variation in subsistence adaptations at the end of the Pleistocene and during the early Holocene. Research at Quebrada Tacahuay demonstrates that understanding dynamic landscapes and their role in both the burial and the preservation of cultural deposits helps elucidate some of the earliest maritime foundations.

Acknowledgments

Research was supported by FERCO, a Canaries Island Foundation created to honor Thor Heyerdahl's life and research, and by National Geographic Society grant no. 6963-01. I thank the following individuals who assisted with the 2001 field season: Adán Umire Alvarez, Ana Miranda, Erin Kennedy, Anna Wright, and our field crew. David Steadman identified some of the avian skeletal elements. Susan Duser assisted with the production of Figure 4.5. David Keefer read and commented on a draft version of the chapter. I owe special thanks to Michael Moseley for persuading me to join the field research at Tacahuay in 1997 and for his support throughout this project.

NOTES

1. Exclusive of the tens of meters of geological strata present in the main quebrada channel, more than 10 m of deeply stratified deposits (Units 1–22) were exposed at Tacahuay in road cut and water main profiles parallel to the channel; however, only the upper series contains evidence of human occupation (see Keefer et al. 2003).

2. In 1997 we studied volumetric samples (0.3–2 liters) from 22 linear areas (0.50–2 m long) along four profiles (Keefer et al. 1998). In 1998, volumetric samples (0.5–5 liters) were taken from forty-six linear areas along six profiles, and we completed the excavation of eight 1 × 1-m squares and one 2 × 1.5-m context (deFrance et al. 2001).

3. The decision not to use heavy machinery was not based on inexperience with this method. I had previously worked extensively with backhoe excavation in the removal of both urban overburden on eighteenth- and nineteenth-century sites in New Orleans and prehistoric sites in central Louisiana that were covered with alluvium; therefore, I was experienced with the technique. In addition to the desire to see the contacts between strata, hand excavation by a crew of laborers using picks and shovels was far more economical owing to the distance of the site from the nearest city, Ilo.

4. In an effort to discern if Unit 8 cultural material that derived from more deeply buried deposits was older, I submitted bird bone elements identified to taxon from four of the features for radiocarbon dating. Unfortunately, there was no collagen remaining in the skeletal elements, and they could not be radiocarbon dated.

5. The GISP2 (Greenland) ice core contains sulfate concentrations indicating considerable volcanism from approximately 12 to 12.5 k (calibrated age range; Zielinski et al. 1996) that corresponds to the calibrated time range of Quebrada Tacahuay. However, the tephra present at Tacahuay is not correlated with a specific event.

6. We obtained one anomalous C14 date on a presumably contaminated uncarbonized root fragment from Block 1, Unit 8C (the thin reddish gray water-lain silt deposits below the Unit 8 cultural material). Following the excavation of Unit 8 and the exposure of the thin silt lens, some small uncarbonized root fragments embedded in the silt were collected for AMS dating. The sample produced a date of 3170 ± 40 rcyr BP. Uncarbonized roots from Units 2 and 3 produced dates that were consistent with the stratigraphic sequence (Keefer et al. 1998); therefore, this anomalous sample was probably contaminated.

REFERENCES

Aldenderfer, Mark S.
1998   *Montane Foragers: Asana and the South-Central Andean Archaic.* University of Iowa Press, Iowa City.

Bard, Edouard, Bruno Hamelin, Maurice Arnold, Lucien Montaggioni, Guy Cabioch, Gérard Faure, and Francis Rougerie
1996   Deglacial Sea-Level Record from Tahiti Corals and the Timing of Global Meltwater Discharge. *Nature* 382:241.

Clement, Christopher O., and Michael E. Moseley
1991   The Spring-Fed Irrigation System of Carrizal, Peru: A Case Study of the Hypothesis of Agrarian Collapse. *Journal of Field Archaeology* 18(4):425–444.

Craig, Alan K.
1992   Archaeological Occurrences of Andean Land Snails. *Andean Past* 3:127–136.

deFrance, Susan D.
2002   Late Paleoindian use of Coastal Resources at Quebrada. Tacahuay: 2001 Field Season. Paper presented at the 21st Annual Meeting of the Northeastern Conference on Andean Archaeology and Ethnohistory, Pittsburgh, Pennsylvania.
2005   Late Pleistocene Marine Birds from Southern Peru: Distinguishing Human Capture from El Niño-Induced Windfall. *Journal of Archaeological Science* 32:1131–1146.
In press   Human Use of the Andean Littoral during the Late Pleistocene: Implications for Social and Economic Behavior. In *Flowing Through Time: Exploring Archaeology Through Humans and Their Aquatic Environment*, edited by Larry Steinbrenner. Proceedings of the 36th Annual Chac-Mool Conference, Calgary, Canada.

deFrance, Susan D., and David K. Keefer
2005   Burial and Site Integrity at Quebrada Tacahuay: A Late Pleistocene Forager Landscape from Coastal Southern Peru. *Journal of Field Archaeology* 30(4):385–399.

deFrance, Susan D., David K. Keefer, James B. Richardson III, and Adán Umire A.
2001   Late Paleo-Indian Coastal Foragers: Specialized Extractive Behavior at Quebrada Tacahuay, Peru. *Latin American Antiquity* 12:413–426.

deFrance, Susan D., Michael E. Moseley, and David K. Keefer
1998   An Early Maritime Adaptation on the Southern Coast of Peru: Preliminary Results from Quebrada Tacahuay. Paper presented at the 63rd Annual Meeting of the Society for American Archaeology, Seattle, WA.

deFrance, Susan D., and Adán Umire A.
2004   Quebrada Tacahuay: una ocupación marítima del Pleistoceno Tardío en el sur del Perú. *Chungará: Revista de Antropología Chilena* 36(2):257–278.

deFrance, Susan D., Adán Umire A., James B. Richardson, David K. Keefer, and Dennis R. Satterlee
1999   Quebrada Tacahuay, an Early Andean Maritime Occupation: Results from the 1998 Season. Paper presented at the 64th Annual Meeting of the Society for American Archaeology, Chicago, IL.

Keefer, David K., Susan D. deFrance, Michael E. Moseley, James B. Richardson III, Dennis R. Satterlee, and A. Day-Lewis
1998   Early Maritime Economy and El Niño Events at Quebrada Tacahuay. *Science* 281:1833–1835.

Keefer, David K., Michael E. Moseley, and Susan D. deFrance
2003   A 38000-Year Record of Floods and Debris Flows in the Ilo region of Southern Peru and Its Relation to El Niño Events and Great Earthquakes. *Palaeogeography, Palaeoclimatology, Palaeoecology* 194:41–77.

Llagostera, Agustín
1989   Caza y pesca marítima. In *Culturas de Chile, prehistoria desde sus orígenes hasta los albores de la Conquista*, edited by Jorge Hidalgo, Virgilio Schiappacasse, Hans Niemeyer, Carlos Aldunate del S., and Iván Solimano R., pp. 57–79. Editorial Andrés Bello, Santiago, Chile.
1992   Early Occupations and the Emergence of Fishermen on the Pacific Coast of South America. *Andean Past* 3:87–109.

McInnis, Heather E.
1999   Subsistence and Maritime Adaptations at Quebrada Jaguay, Camana, Peru: A Faunal Analysis. Master's thesis, Institute for Quaternary Studies, University of Maine, Orono.

Núñez, Lautaro
1983   PaleoIndian and Archaic Cultural Periods in the Arid and Semiarid Regions of Northern Chile. In *Advances in World Archaeology*, vol. 2, edited by Fred Wendorf and Angela Close, pp. 161–203. Academic Press, New York.
1999   Archaic Adaptation on the South-Central Andean Coast. In *Pacific Latin America in Prehistory: The Evolution of Archaic and Formative Cultures*, edited by T. Michael Blake, pp. 199–212. Washington State University Press, Pullman.

Núñez, Lautaro, Juan Varela, Rodolfo Casamiquela, and
    Carolina Villagrán
1994   Reconstrucción multidisciplinaria de la ocupación de
    Quereo, centro de Chile. *Latin American Antiquity*
    5(2):99–118.

Richardson, James B. III
1998   Looking in the Right Places: Pre-5000 B.P. Maritime
    Adaptations in Peru and the Changing Environment.
    Revista de Arqueología Americana 15:33–56.

Sandweiss, Daniel H., Heather McInnis, Richard L. Burger,
    Asunción Cano, Bernardino Ojeda, Rolando
    Paredes, María del Carmen Sandweiss, and Michael
    D. Glascock
1998   Quebrada Jaguay: Early South American Maritime
    Adaptations. *Science* 281:1830–1832.

Sandweiss, Daniel H., James B. Richardson III, Elizabeth J.
    Reitz, J. T. Hsu, and Robert A. Feldman
1989   Ring Site. In *Ecology, Settlement, and History in the
    Osmore Drainage, Peru*, edited by Don Rice, Charles
    Stanish, and Phillip R. Scarr, pp. 35–84. BAR
    International Series 545 (i). British Archaeological
    Reports, Oxford.

Santoro, Calogero
1993   Complementariedad ecológica en las sociedades
    arcaicas del área centro sur andina. In *Acha-2 y
    los orígenes del poblamiento humano en Arica*, edited
by Iván Muñoz, Bernardo Arriaza, and Arthur
    Aufderheide, pp. 133–150. Ediciones Universidad
    de Tarapacá, Santiago, Chile.

Satterlee, Dennis R.
1993   *Impact of a Fourteenth Century El Niño Flood on an
    Indigenous Population near Ilo*. Unpublished doc-
    toral dissertation, Department of Anthropology,
    University of Florida, Gainesville.

Stuiver, Minze, Paula J. Reimer, Edouard Bard, J. Warren
    Beck, G. S. Burr, Konrad A. Hughen, Bernd
    Kromer, Gerry McCormac, Johannes Van Der
    Plicht, and Marco Spurk
1998   INTCAL98 Radiocarbon Age Calibration 24,000-0
    cal BP. *Radiocarbon* 40:1041–1083.

Tudhope, Alexander W., Colin P. Chilcott, Malcolm T.
    McCulloch, Edward R. Cook, John Chappell,
    Robert M. Ellam, David W. Lea, Janice M. Lough,
    and Graham B. Shimmield
2001   Variability in the El Niño-Southern Oscillation
    Through a Glacial-Interglacial Cycle. *Science*
    291:1511–1517.

Zielinski, Gregory A., Paul A. Mayewski, L. David Meeker,
    S. Whitlow, and Mark S. Twickler
1996   An 110,000-Year Record of Explosive Volcanism
    from the GISP2 (Greenland) Ice Core. *Quaternary
    Research* 45:109–118.

CHAPTER 5

KEY RESEARCH THEMES IN THE SOUTH-CENTRAL ANDEAN ARCHAIC

MARK ALDENDERFER

A LTHOUGH THE STUDY OF the Archaic period (also known as the Preceramic) in the south-central Andes has a history spanning almost a century, beginning with the pioneering work of Uhle (1919, 1922), only relatively recently have archaeologists begun to acquire a more nuanced understanding of the variety and complexity of Archaic period adaptations across the region and how these adaptations influenced the course of subsequent social, political, and economic change. Chilean, Peruvian, Argentine, Bolivian, and foreign archaeologists have all contributed significantly to this effort.

In this chapter, I discuss how this understanding of the south-central Andean Archaic has been achieved, in relation to the following themes: the development of secure chronologies, the establishment of clear differences in the trajectory and pace of cultural development between the south-central Andean coast and the north-central coast of Peru, and the emergence of multidisciplinary research on human responses to Holocene climatic variability and change. It is fitting in a volume honoring Mike Moseley that two of these themes—the analysis of maritime adaptations, and paleoclimate and its effects on cultural process—have been major elements of his research program. Since sizable gaps remain in our knowledge of the Archaic period, however, I will mention these at the end of the chapter.

THE DEVELOPMENT OF SECURE CHRONOLOGIES

The earliest chronologies in the south-central Andes came from coastal contexts. Max Uhle and Ricardo Latcham began their research near Arica in 1908 (Willey 1998:xx), and in his synthesis of his research, Uhle (1922) proposed a "Paleolithic period" for the abundant lithic materials of the region. He also described the aceramic materials he recovered in primarily cultural terms—"*los Aborígenes de Arica*" (which became in later years the Chinchorro complex; Llagostera 1989). This fit well with the prevalent evolutionary schema of the times. Some years later, Junius Bird (1943) conducted a series of excavations at Quiani, Pichalo, Playa Miller, and Taltal that led him to define two major chronological periods stratigraphically, Arica 1 and Arica 2. The former was an aceramic culture based on fishing and shellfish collecting, the latter was fully agricultural and possessed ceramics. Arica 1 was divided into two subphases, Quiani 1 and 2 (or Pre-Pottery periods I and II), which were distinguished by "type fossils," in this case, shell fishhooks versus those made of composite materials. Such chronologies were common in the Andes at the time and were based primarily on projectile point form or tool reduction technologies. In some cases, such as the famous Ancón-Chillón sequence of north coastal Peru (Lanning 1963; Kaulicke 2000:418), tool forms

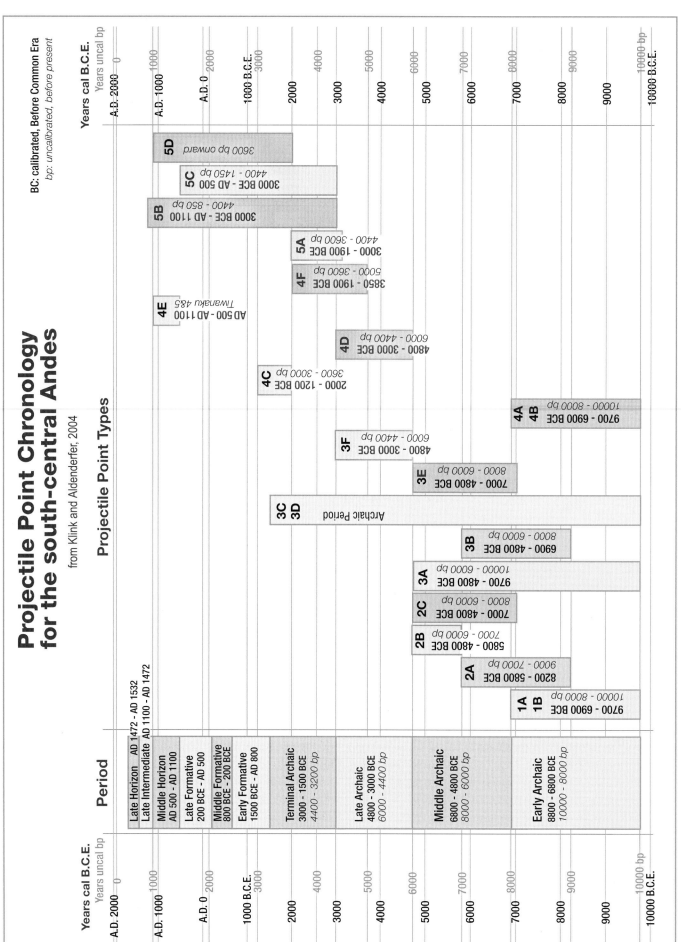

Figure 5.1. Types and time ranges for south-central Andean projectile points. (Courtesy of Nico Tripcevich, from Klink and Aldenderfer 2004. Reproduced by permission.)

from surface contexts were used as type fossils, as were points from excavated and stratified contexts.

The advent of radiocarbon dating in the 1950s revolutionized chronology building in archaeology, and the technique was quickly applied to the south-central Andes. And although many of the sequences generated by stratigraphic excavation were verified, it took some time before widely accepted phase names were adopted, simply because too few Archaic period sites had been excavated, and those that had were widely dispersed across the entire region. Archaeologists made do, then, with a periodization scheme of Early, Middle, and Late Archaic (or Preceramic) and, via radiocarbon dates, placed their sites (or levels within them) in the appropriate periods. Periods then became an intellectual shorthand not only for time but also for aspects of cultural processes within a generally evolutionary framework.

In some areas of the south-central Andes, specifically the highlands of extreme southern Peru and northern Chile, broadly compatible phase names and boundaries have been defined. In this instance, the phases are based on extensive excavation and testing at seven open-air sites and rockshelters in the Osmore and Río Chila drainages in Peru (Aldenderfer 1998:69–75, 2000, 2002) and at nine rockshelters in northern Chile (Santoro and Núñez 1987; Santoro 1989). In a series of extensive projects in the Río Ilave drainage (especially at the key site of Jiskairumoko), my students and I have defined another period, the Terminal Archaic, which is meant to mark a transition from a mobile foraging lifeway to one that was far more sedentary, with an economy based on camelid herding and intensive chenopod utilization (Craig and Aldenderfer 2002; Aldenderfer and Barreto 2004; Craig 2005). Although a number of coastal sites have recently been excavated (Schiappacasse and Niemeyer 1984; Sandweiss et al. 1989; Wise 1990, 2000; Muñoz et al. 1993; Rasmussen 1998; Lavallée et al. 2000), aside from the famous Chinchorro cultural complex and its mummified human remains (Arriaza 1995), few phase names have been developed, and the concept of cultural complexes is used as a substitute.

Projectile points have a long history of use as chronological markers in the south-central Andes, but until recently no comprehensive typology had been developed. Consequently, archaeologists were forced to compare points from the surface sites or excavations with better known sequences, such as that developed by John Rick (1980) at Pachamachay in the central Andes. This tactic tended to work reasonably well for the earliest time periods, but comparisons were forced and generally unsatisfactory for later time periods because of the regionalization of point style—that is, an increasing number of styles with limited geographic scope (Aldenderfer 1989). However, because of the increased volume of work, better reporting, and the widespread use of radiocarbon dating, Cindy Klink and I (2004) have developed a projectile point chronology for the south-central Andean highlands (Figure 5.1). It complements the Rick typology nicely and is able to capture local variability in the region in greater detail. Although it does not directly address the littoral, a review of the literature shows that many of our defined types appear in diverse contexts there. And although it is still tied closely to the period-based chronology, we hope to refine it in the future to associate styles as narrowly as possible with specific time ranges.

MARITIME ADAPTATIONS NORTH AND SOUTH

Looking back on the past from our current state of knowledge, it is unquestioned that the south-central Andean littoral during the Late Preceramic did not witness the same early and rapid rise toward social and political complexity as the north coast of Peru. However, as Moseley (1985:29–33) has noted, it was not until after the advent of radiocarbon dating that the early emergence of coastal complexity in the Late Preceramic on the north coast of Peru was finally recognized. The initial results of excavations at Áspero in 1941, for example, in which massive aceramic middens were found to be associated with masonry-faced monuments, were dismissed as aberrations simply because they did not fit then-prevalent notions of highland (i.e., Chavinoid) temporal priority. The dating programs during the 1960s and 1970s removed all doubt that the aceramic coastal mound complexes dated earlier than monumental architecture in the highlands. And although there continue to be debates about the social and political meaning of coastal complexity in the Late Preceramic—are these sites early states (Billman 2001), or some simpler form of persistent inequality (Haas and Creamer 2004)?—there is no question that these sites reflect a complexity orders of magnitude beyond the Middle Archaic foraging baseline identified by Quilter (1989) at Paloma.

A review of the state of knowledge of the south-central Andean littoral during the period of establishment of north coast temporal priority shows an acute awareness of the differences between the two regions. Out of necessity, Ravines (1972:174–182) focused his discussion of cultural sequences in the south-central Andes on projectile points, other material aspects of subsistence economy, and economic adaptations such as transhumance and settlement mobility appropriate for foragers. Farther south, in northern Chile, archaeologists discussed the spectacular Chinchorro complex with its artificially mummified human remains, but remained aware that this mortuary complex arose from a maritime foraging basis, with no evidence whatsoever of manifestations of cultural complexity (Alvarez 1969; Núñez 1969). And in their analysis of the Complejo Camarones, Schaedel and Munizaga (1957) described it as "el fenómeno de poblaciones marítimas con arquitectura" but made it clear the architectural remains at these sites were nothing like those found on the contemporary central coast of Peru (Llagostera 1989:70).

More recent research has confirmed these initial observations. In southern Peru, research at two Late Archaic village sites near Ilo, Carrizal and Kilómetro 4, has shown that although there is clear evidence of population aggregation and growth, there is no accompanying construction of large-scale public architecture or other obvious forms of early leadership strategies (Wise 1990, 2000). These patterns are reflected in northern Chile as well, where from 3000 to 1000 BC, while settlements aggregated and reflected a sedentarization process focused on marine resources, no evidence of complexity indicative of persistent leadership can be found (Núñez 1983). And although there are periodic attempts to make the Ring Site near Ilo into an expression of early monumental architecture (Sandweiss et al. 1989), the site could have been created by repeated reoccupation by maritime foragers and is far smaller than any of the north coast monumental centers.

The absence of complexity on the south-central Andean littoral has been demonstrated, but why this was the case is not entirely clear. Moseley (1975) defined for the north coast his maritime hypothesis, which asserts that early complexity arose within a context of environmental abundance—vast schools of anchoveta just offshore—and technological innovations—the industrial use of domesticated cotton for nets to capture the anchoveta. He argued that surpluses equivalent to those generated by agriculture could have been obtained, and these could have been used to support the activities

of emerging elites. His thesis has been challenged by those who believe that horticulture was more important than Moseley realized at least at some sites (Haas and Creamer 2001; Shady et al. 2001). But if the broad outlines of his hypothesis are true, just how this process was initiated remains a significant research question. Because a surplus can be generated does not mean that it must be. What is missing from Moseley's hypothesis is a sense of process—the context within which these surpluses were generated—and how were they used to create these impressive mound complexes.

What we know of the south-central Andean littoral can provide some insight into how to think about the cultural context of emerging complexity on the north coast. Environment did matter, apparently. The vast schools of anchoveta were in a sense a necessary condition for the emergence of complexity in the absence of intensive horticulture. No such schools of anchoveta or any other species approaching such densities existed along the southern littoral, and domesticated plants did not enter the diet in significant quantities in the south until well after the end of the Archaic (Quilter 1991). The correlation between abundance and complexity seems secure.

Out of necessity, archaeologists working on the south-central littoral focused on villages; on the north coast, most of the archaeology of the Late Archaic has focused on monuments. What is apparent in the south is that population densities were low throughout the Archaic, and although populations grew through time, they were never very large (Aldenderfer 1989). Most processual models of the emergence of complexity posit a scenario of regional packing leading to resource intensification, territory formation, and, frequently, the emergence of more complex political formations. On the southern littoral, populations were never large until well into the Formative, when domesticated plants, especially maize, formed the basis of the economy. This implies that Middle Archaic population levels must have been substantial along the north coast. The evidence from Paloma does suggest that at least some littoral groups there were essentially sedentary at that time, and it seems plausible to assert that if this is true, population densities sufficient to support the emergence of complexity could have been in place by the start of the Late Archaic. More systematic excavations in domestic contexts at these north coast mound complexes are urgently required before these assertions can be verified.

HUMAN RESPONSES TO CLIMATIC VARIABILITY DURING THE ARCHAIC

Although archaeologists of previous generations never ignored paleoclimatic reconstructions, they had few tools and fewer studies at their disposal to examine the effects of climate and climate change on the earliest inhabitants of the south-central Andes. Most early paleoclimatic reconstructions were concerned with making correlations between the well-defined glacial sequence of the Northern Hemisphere and the more poorly defined glacial epoch in the south (see, e.g., Núñez 1983:166–168). And, like their North American counterparts, South American archaeologists tended to be consumers of data developed by disciplines such as glaciology, palynology, paleoecology, and paleoclimatology rather than active participants in their creation (Lynch 1978:463–476). As the idea of multidisciplinary research gained greater hold in archaeology during the 1970s and 1980s, however, archaeologists increasingly became active participants in regional-scale as well as local paleoclimatic reconstructions (Lynch 1986, 1990), and by the start of the decade, Lynch (1990:199–200) could outline a set of pertinent questions about continent-wide paleoenvironmental conditions that required resolution. These included the following:

- Synchroneity of temperature and precipitation changes
- Movement of storm tracks and resultant changes in regional precipitation
- Extent and meaning of changes in gradients of snow line
- Correlation of glacial regimen with changes in lake levels and regional precipitation, evaporation, ablation, albedo, and vegetation
- Onset of ENSO (El Niño) phenomenon and its relation to central Andean climate and precipitation
- Extent and direction of changes in Amazonia (temperature, precipitation, vegetation, speciation) and their relation to happenings in the Andes and north coastal South America

The pace of paleoenvironmental research in the Andes quickened during the 1990s, and real progress was made in addressing each of Lynch's concerns. Not only did archaeologists benefit from the new data created, they also entered into close working relationships with natural scientists in a number of locations in the south-central Andes, and these partnerships have resulted in truly impressive reconstructions of both paleoenvironments and human responses to changes in them. Three research questions stand out as exemplars: the identification of ENSO events on the south-central Andean littoral, the resolution of the regional scale of the highland "Silencio Arqueológico," and reconstruction of the rise and fall of Lake Titicaca and its impact on the emergence of cultural complexity in the basin.

Although it is premature to say that the antiquity of El Niño has been established, we have a much better sense of how to define ENSO events and how they may have affected culture processes in the region. There is no question that ENSO events can be seen in the archaeological record from 5000 years BP to the modern era (Rollins et al. 1986; Sandweiss et al. 1996), and further, that these events had a significant impact on cultures across the Andes. What continues to be questioned is the antiquity and periodicity of these ENSO events and how they may have affected the earliest inhabitants of the region. Part of the problem is defining the regional scope of ENSO events. Although it is well known that ENSO events have effects across the Andes in both the highlands and the lowlands, recent studies have attempted to define more narrowly the scope of those effects. Sandweiss et al. (1996, 1997) argue that ENSO events on the littoral are most clearly seen north of 10° S latitude, and it is this area that the evidence for a 5000 BP onset is best observed. Others believe that the evidence offered by Sandweiss and colleagues for the date of the onset is equivocal at best (De Vries et al. 1997) or supports an inference that ENSO events have a much deeper antiquity (Wells and Noller 1997) extending far back into the Quaternary. Keefer et al. (1998) report they have good evidence for ENSO events in the Terminal Pleistocene at Quebrada Tacahuay, a finding that supports arguments of a greater age for the phenomenon.

What makes a more definitive understanding of ENSO events highly desirable is increasing evidence of significant, worldwide climatic change during the 8000–3000 BP window (Sandweiss et al. 1999). In the Andes on the central Andean littoral, early complex societies began to emerge shortly after 5000 BP, and there has been both acrimonious and enlightening debate about the importance or relevance of the onset of ENSO to this cultural process (Moseley 1975; Haas and Creamer 2001; Sandweiss and Moseley 2001; Shady et al. 2001). Although the south-central Andes did not witness a similar early appearance of cultural complexity, ENSO events may have had an influence on this failure as well. More research is urgently needed to resolve these debates.

A related mid-Holocene phenomenon is the so-called Silencio Arqueológico. The concept, if not the term, was developed by Chilean archaeologists during the 1970s and 1980s to describe what they saw as an abandonment of the south-central Andean highlands from roughly 8000 to 5000 BP, or much of the Middle Archaic (Núñez 1983; Santoro and Núñez 1987). The cause of this abandonment was the intense and persistent aridity of this time period. Although the direct evidence for abandonment came primarily from cave and rockshelter sites in the Salar de Atacama that showed no signs whatsoever of utilization, there also appeared to be a "hiatus" or less intense occupation of rockshelter sites in the western valleys of the Andes in northern Chile. This led archaeologists to extend the range of the abandonment into southern Peru as well. However, excavations at Asana in the Osmore drainage of southern Peru (Aldenderfer 1988, 1998) revealed a significant Middle Archaic occupation and led to serious debate about the geographic scope of the abandonment and the cultural and social meaning of the "silence."

Complicating this debate are startling claims by Betancourt et al. (2000) and Quade and Rich (2001), who have argued, based on evidence recovered from fossil rodent middens and wetland deposits, that the mid-Holocene was wetter than most other paleoclimatic reconstructions suggested. Given these data, it is hard to see how the abandonment could have been produced by environmental factors. However, the data obtained by Betancourt et al. are significantly at odds with paleoclimate reconstructions from the Lake Titicaca Basin (Baker, Rigsby et al. 2001; Baker, Seltzer et al. 2001) and data from the Salar de Atacama itself (Grosjean 2001; Núñez et al. 2002; Grosjean et al. 2003); these studies indicate regionwide aridity during this period. The character of the climate continues to be debated, but they have, along with an increased scope of archaeological research, caused the proponents of the silencio to define more narrowly its geographic scope "to the most arid regions of the central Andes" (Núñez et al. 2002:824), mostly south of 20° S latitude. Whatever the outcome of the debate, it is clear that a closer working arrangement of archaeologists and natural scientists has led to a far more nuanced understanding of the phenomenon.

Perhaps the best examples of the power of interdisciplinary research in the region come from the Lake Titicaca Basin, which has been the focus of archaeological and paleoclimatic research for more than two decades, best exemplified by the impressive multidisciplinary work by Kolata and his associates at Tiwanaku (Kolata 1996; Abbott et al. 1997; Binford et al. 1997). More recent paleoclimatic studies have created a far more detailed and accurate history of basin paleoclimatology which has had a significant impact on our understanding of Archaic period cultures.

The research my colleagues and I have done in the Río Ilave drainage demonstrates some of the insights we gained through this collaboration. The goal of our project was to create a detailed reconstruction of lake level rise and fall and combine this with the process of terrace formation along the Ilave in conjunction with regional survey and extensive excavation at a number of sites (Farabaugh et al. 2002; Rigsby et al. 2003; Rigsby et al. 2002). Prior to 9000 BP, the lake was near its Early Holocene high, but around 8000 BP it began to shrink in size and continued shrinking for the next 2000 years, reaching its historic low stand around 5500 BP. This corresponded to a period of intensive downcutting in the Ilave drainage. During this period the lake was highly saline, perhaps one-third the salinity of modern seawater, and thus it would not have been an attractive resource patch. Regional survey has confirmed the total absence of a Middle Archaic utilization of lake margins and has demonstrated conclusively that foragers used the interior at this time (Aldenderfer and Klink 1996). The lake rebounded rapidly, however, but did not reach a stable level until 4200 BP. The T2 terrace along the Ilave began to form during this time, and this had a major impact on settlement dynamics. This terrace would have been aggraded during the wet season, and this would have created new habitats for the growth of dense stands of both wild tubers and chenopods. During the Terminal Archaic, although site numbers decline, those sites present also increased in size and moved closer to the newly formed T2. I interpret this as a resource pull, and one that led relatively quickly to low-level food production using these species. Settlements became sedentary, and aggrandizers began to accumulate exotic goods such as gold and obsidian (Aldenderfer 2004; Aldenderfer and Barreto 2004; Craig 2005). While much remains to be done with these data, it is clear that we could not have examined the subtleties of culture process without a firmly established and reliable paleoclimate record.

WHAT WE STILL DON'T KNOW

Obviously, we have learned a great deal about the Archaic period over the past few decades, but there are still major geographic as well as conceptual lacunae worthy of discussion.

What happened on the eastern flanks of the Andes?
Although research over the past ten years has led to a significant improvement of our knowledge about later time periods on the eastern flanks of the Andes, especially the Late Intermediate period and Late Horizon, little of this research has translated into advances in knowledge of the Archaic period. What is interesting about this situation is that strong claims for a set of eastern flank and Amazon Basin influences on the Formative and later cultures of the high Andes have been made by archaeologists for decades (Lathrap 1971, 1977, 1985). At Chavín, iconographic representations illustrate lowland animals, such as the cayman and jaguar, and Lathrap has made other claims for the lowland origins of many of the architectural features of Late Preceramic and Formative period ceremonial sites both in the Andean highlands and on the Pacific coast (Lathrap 1985:254–255). What is striking is that these features simply appear de novo, from some ancient matrix. And this is the point: these features are surprising because we have no sense of what antecedent contacts between the Amazon Basin and the highlands during the Archaic may have been and what form they took. Improved knowledge of the Archaic would help to build a sounder explanatory framework for the "surprising" appearance of these traits. As pure speculation, I imagine the first contacts (if we do not consider actual migrants) took the form of the long-distance trade of feathers, drugs (various lowland hallucinogens such as *cebil*, which became popular in Middle Horizon times in the Titicaca Basin), and other prestige or status-related goods.

Elsewhere in the south-central Andes, some Chilean archaeologists and physical anthropologists have long argued for a trans-altiplano origin of Archaic period coastal peoples, specifically those of the so-called Chinchorro culture (Rivera and Rothhammer 1986; Rothhammer et al. 1986; Rothhammer and Silva 1992). In this case, the claims are based primarily on craniofacial measurements and on general parallels in aspects of ritual practice between the coastal cultures and those found in the Amazon Basin. Some sort of contact between the eastern flanks and the Pacific coast of Chile is certainly plausible, but the actual archaeological evidence for these claims is scant, to say the least. Testing a claim of contact requires archaeological data from the eastern flanks showing how a process of population movement or displacement might have occurred. Insight into this could be drawn from northwestern Argentina, where clear contacts between inhabitants of the salt puna and lowlanders has been documented (Mendoza 2002). Such a claim could also be bolstered by studies of ancient DNA. Although a number of DNA studies have been done on human remains from northern Chile (Moraga et al. 2000), none has yet demonstrated a convincing trans-altiplanic origin of these coastal peoples.

Where is the Bolivian Archaic?
It is not so much that the Archaic in Bolivia is unknown, rather that it is very poorly known, and there are puzzling aspects to our lack of knowledge about it. As Bolivian archaeologist Jorge Arellano (1992:309) has said, "Las investigaciones de este período en el área andina-altiplánica de Bolivia son probablemente las más atrasadas de Sudamérica." One of the iconic sites of early Andean archaeology, Viscachani, is found on the western Bolivian altiplano (Ibarra Grasso 1957; Patterson and Heizer 1965), and for years the site served as a basis of comparison with other Archaic period sites and materials as far away as northern Peru and the central Andes (Lanning and Hammel 1961; Ravines 1972). Typologies of bifaces and projectile points created from the collections recovered from the site gave insight into possible long-distance connections across the Andes, and stone tool reduction technologies likewise served as a point of departure for evolutionary schemes of cultural change. All of this was accomplished despite a major problem with the site: it had never been excavated, none of its components have been radiometrically dated, and consequently it floated in time, becoming early and late as other typologies that included time were created. Viscachani remains important, but it no longer has the luster it once had forty years ago.

Other areas of Bolivia have been integrated into better known regional sequences. Barfield (1961) described a number of sites in far western Bolivia near its borders with Chile and Argentina around two *salares*, Laguna Colorado and Laguna Hedionda. On the Chilean side, archaeologists such as Gustavo Le Paige (1958) had been studying the adjacent Salar de Atacama region for decades, and had created a relative cultural chronology based on stratigraphic excavations and typological comparisons. Extensive radiocarbon dating and paleoenvironmental reconstruction have validated much of the relative chronology and led to a number of important insights into cultural process and human response to climatic change and variability (Núñez et al. 2002).

One area of Bolivia that remains perplexing is the Titicaca Basin. The earliest radiocarbon evidence from the Bolivian side of the lake comes from the Island of the Sun, where Stanish and colleagues (2002) discovered an Archaic period occupation dating to 3780 ± 170 rcybp (4784–3690 cal BP, or 2700–1600 BC). They argue that the site could only have been accessed by watercraft at that time, but more recent bathymetric studies show that the site would in fact have been connected to the mainland (D'Agostino et al. 2002). However, this debate is not as important as the observation that the site would have been found near the lake margin, suggesting that the lake was seen as a major resource patch as early as the Late or Terminal Archaic. It is also clear that relatively little of this Archaic period lake margin has been lost to the major lake level rise that occurred sometime around 1500 BC (Klink and Aldenderfer 1996).

Archaeological surveys on the Bolivian side of the lake have yet to discover much more of an Archaic period occupation. Bandy (2001:87) reports that not a single Archaic period site was discovered during his survey of the Taraco Peninsula, which extends into Lake Winyamarca (the "little lake" to the southeast of the main body of water). He notes, however, that Winyamarca would have been dry for much of the Archaic period, and what became its margins saw intensive utilization only after the lake began to infill after 1500 BC. To the east, in the interior Tiwanaku Valley, Albarracín-Jordan and Mathews (1990:51–53) discovered only two Archaic period sites during their survey. Yet on the Peruvian side of the lake, in the Ilave drainage, I have documented the presence of hundreds of Archaic sites that range in date from the Early through Terminal Archaic periods (Aldenderfer and Klink 1996), and Cindy Klink (2004) has located dozens more deeper in the interior of the basin along the Río Huenque.

These differences are striking, and demand explanation. One could argue that at least in earlier surveys, Archaic period sites were not expected, and therefore were missed or overlooked. Another explanation is that postdepositional natural or cultural processes may have led to the destruction of the Archaic period record or modified it so substantially that it was not recognized. This seems implausible, given that similar disturbances have taken place on the Peruvian side of the lake. It may also be the case that much of the Bolivian side of the lake was simply not occupied during the Archaic, and that only after the lake began to fill did people move into it. This seems to be contradicted by the existence of Viscachani and the extensive Archaic occupation on the Peruvian side. One must also ask from where the Early Formative inhabitants of the lake came. In short, there are many more questions about the Bolivian Archaic than we have answers, and until they are resolved, we are poorly positioned to address questions of cultural process.

Process-related concerns

Where to begin? Although we have made impressive gains in our knowledge of the outlines of culture history in the south-central Andes, we have less control of many, if not most, aspects of culture process. Obviously, this situation will change as the volume of work done on the Archaic period increases, but this will take time.

At least from my perspective, the areas of greatest concern are the following:

1. The majority of archaeologists working in the region are confident that the primary route of the earliest migration of humans into the region was along the Pacific coast and thence into the highlands via the valleys of the western flanks. Research at Asana (Aldenderfer 1998), Quebrada Jaguay (Sandweiss et al. 1998), Quebrada Tacahuay (Keefer et al. 1998), and the Azapa Valley in northern Chile (Muñoz et al. 1993) has confirmed the general validity of this assertion.

However, some questions about this process still linger. The earliest styles of projectile points found in southern Peruvian and extreme northern Chilean highlands are stemmed forms, followed by spine-shouldered forms (Klink and Aldenderfer 2004). These forms generally date to ca. 10,000 rcybp. At Asana, for example, the earliest points are found in the Khituña phase, which dates between 10,100 and 8300 cal BP (Aldenderfer 1998:131, 2000:382). However, in the Chilean salt puna, including the Salar de Atacama region, the earliest point styles (so-called Tuina points) are small, ovoid bifaces, wholly different in form but essentially contemporaneous with or even earlier in time than the materials from Asana (Núñez 1992:288; Núñez et al. 2002). Given the extensive amount of research done by Núñez and his colleagues in the region, the differences appear to be real, and thus the situation raises a number of unresolved questions: Is this stylistic difference due to function, ethnicity, an earlier migration, or even a migration from a different direction?

2. We must obtain a better understanding of the variability in and trajectories of the development of low-level food production (sensu Smith 2001). The south-central Andes had a diverse set of food production trajectories, ranging from the pastoral and agropastoral economies of the altiplano, the farming of the western flanks valleys, and fishing on the Pacific littoral and the shores of Lake Titicaca. Mixed into the maritime economies at some point was cotton, which may have been used to create cloth used as a prestige or luxury good in trade between highlands and lowlands in addition to its obvious economic role (Aldenderfer 1999). To date, we have only hints as to how some of these food-producing economies emerged and became transformed through time. More effort needs to be directed at specific local circumstances, such as the emergence of the horticultural economies of the mid-valleys of the western flanks of the Andes. We know virtually nothing of how maize and other cultigens were introduced into the foraging economies of these peoples. But perhaps of greater interest is the need to document these trajectories in the Titicaca Basin. After all, this is the area in which complex societies first emerged in the south-central Andes, yet we have an extraordinarily incomplete understanding of how highland foraging economies became the complex agricultural economies of later prehistory. Developing this understanding will necessarily involve greater attention to plant domesticates, especially the tubers. This will be difficult, however, owing to preservation problems with the remains of these species. But since we know that tubers formed the basis of surplus production of the complex societies of the basin, we have to figure out just how this happened.

3. We all know that complex societies, including the archaic state of Tiwanaku, emerged on the altiplano. We remain in ignorance, however, of just how this happened, and indeed, we know next to nothing about *any* trajectory to complexity in the entire south-central Andes. This situation stands in sharp contrast to our extensive knowledge of other regions of the world that produced archaic states, such as Mesopotamia (Matthews 2003) and the Valley of Oaxaca (Marcus and Flannery 1996), to name just two regions. Instead, what we get are synthetic volumes on the origins of complex societies in which serious consideration of prehistory begins at ca. 1500 BC (Stanish 2003: Figure 5.1). In fact, 1500 BC is something of an iconic date in the south-central Andes. Complexity in some form simply seems to just *happen* around that time. For instance, Binford et

al. (1997:242) in their discussion of long-term changes in water levels of Lake Titicaca state, "Insufficient water inhibited intensive agriculture and the development of large, sedentary human populations." This statement asserts that sedentism could develop only with agriculture, and that agriculture sprang immediately and rapidly into existence at 1500 BC, when wetter climatic conditions appeared in the Titicaca Basin. Further, it implies that one need look for pathways to complexity no earlier than 1500 BC. However, as I have shown in a recent review of preludes to power in the Andean Late Preceramic (Aldenderfer 2004), although substantial evidence for persistent leadership (one form of early inequality and complexity) is not abundant, it is present in some parts of the south-central Andes, such as in the Río Ilave drainage, where aggrandizers obtained gold from the central Andes around 2500 BC. Although this form of leadership did not persist in the Ilave, it does provide clues for what we should be looking for in those areas of the basin in which substantial early complexity developed, such as around Chiripa in the southern basin and Pukara in the northern basin.

CONCLUSIONS

The good news is that after many years of neglect, the Archaic period has finally come into its own as a topic worthy of extensive study. This will certainly not be news to the Chileans or Argentines, who have been working on Archaic period topics for many decades. But it is heartening to see that Peruvian and Bolivian archaeologists and their foreign collaborators have been making impressive efforts in defining the Archaic in their respective nations. Full-coverage archaeological survey is now becoming the norm, and this means that open-air sites dating to the Archaic are being found throughout the region.

The bad news is not that we still have far to go with our understanding of the Archaic but that the archaeological record of the period is coming under increasing threat. Although sites of all time periods are destroyed by construction, agriculture, and development, those of the Archaic are particularly endangered. In the Titicaca Basin, for example, the advent of mechanized plowing is destroying huge numbers of open-air sites on the terraces surrounding the major rivers. Sites with architectural remains tend not to be plowed, simply because they provide a visible obstacle. So-called "dirt" sites offer no real resistance, and their contents are churned and mixed as mechanized plowing becomes the method of choice for turning the soil. In the western flank valleys, population growth has driven urban expansion along the slopes and terraces of the drainages. Although many parts of the south-central Andes have yet to experience these trends, these areas also tend to be the most isolated and most unlikely to have a substantial Archaic period record that can contribute new data that would help answer many of our most interesting and pressing research questions.

Of the many archaeologists who have contributed to the Archaic period renaissance in the south-central Andes, preeminent is Michael Moseley, who in the early 1980s created Programa Contisuyo. Although Moseley did not himself work on the Archaic, he persuaded others to do so, and he provided the critical infrastructure needed for success through his collaboration with Southern Peru Copper Corporation. Both Peruvian and North American archaeologists, including Karen Wise, Larry Kuznar, Karen Rasmussen, Nathan Craig, Cindy Klink, Adán Umire, Mary and Gladys Barreto, Phyllisa Eisentraut, Claudia Rumold, and myself, have benefited from his efforts. The result has been that the Osmore drainage, from coast to altiplano, has one of the best-understood Archaic records in the south-central Andes. For this and much more, it has been both a pleasure and honor to have known and worked with Mike over these past twenty years.

REFERENCES

Abbott, Mark, Michael W. Binford, Mark Brenner, and Kerry Kelts
1997   A 3500 14C Yr High-Resolution Record of Water-Level Changes in Lake Titicaca, Bolivia/Peru. *Quaternary Research* 47:169–180.

Albarracín-Jordan, Juan, and James Mathews
1990   *Asentamientos prehispánicos del Valle de Tiwanaku*, vol. 1. Producciones CIMA, La Paz, Bolivia.

Aldenderfer, Mark
1988   Middle Archaic Period Domestic Architecture from Southern Peru. *Science* 241:1828–1830.
1989   The Archaic Period in the South-Central Andes. *Journal of World Prehistory* 3:117–158.
1998   *Montane Foragers: Asana and the South-Central Andean Archaic*. University of Iowa Press, Iowa City.
1999   The Late Preceramic-Early Formative Transition on the South-Central Andean Littoral. In *Pacific Latin America in Prehistory: The Evolution of Archaic*

and Formative Cultures, edited by T. Michael Blake, pp. 213–221. Washington State University Press, Pullman.
2000   Cronología y conexiones: Evidencias precerámicas de Asana. In *El período Arcaico en el Perú: Hacia una definición de los orígenes*, edited by Peter Kaulicke, pp. 375–392. Boletín de Arqueología PUCP 3, 1999. Pontificia Universidad Católica del Perú, Lima.
2002   Explaining Changes in Settlement Dynamics across Transformations of Modes of Production: From Hunting to Herding in the South-Central Andes. In *Beyond Foraging and Collecting: Evolutionary Change in Hunter-Gatherer Settlement Systems*, edited by Ben Fitzhugh and Junko Habu, pp. 387–412. Kluwer Academic, New York.
2004   Preludes to Power in the Highland Late Preceramic Period. In *Foundations of Power in the Prehispanic Andes*, edited by Christina Conlee, Dennis Ogburn, and Kevin Vaughn. Archaeological Papers of the American Anthropological Association, Washington, DC.

Aldenderfer, Mark, and Mary Barreto
2004   Informe final: Excavaciones arqueológicas en Jiskairumoko, cuenca del Río Ilave, sub-región de Puno, Región "Jose Carlos Mariategui." Report submitted to the Instituto Nacional de Cultura, Lima.

Aldenderfer, Mark, and Cynthia J. Klink
1996   Archaic Period Settlement in the Lake Titicaca Basin: Results of a Recent Survey. Paper presented at the 36th Annual Meeting of the Institute of Andean Studies, Berkeley, CA, USA.

Alvarez, L.
1969   Un cementerio precerámico con momias de preparación complicada. *Rehue* 2:181–190.

Arellano, Jorge A.
1992   El desarrollo cultural prehispánico en el altiplano y valles interandinas de Bolivia. In *Prehistoria Sudamericana: Nuevas perspectivas*, edited by Betty J. Meggers, pp. 309–325. Taraxacum, Washington, DC.

Arriaza, Bernardo T.
1995   *Beyond Death: The Chinchorro Mummies of Ancient Chile*. Smithsonian Institution Press, Washington, DC.

Baker, Paul, Catherine A. Rigsby, Geoffrey O. Seltzer, Sherilyn Fritz, Tim K. Lowenstein, Niklas P. Bacher, and Carlos Veliz
2001   Tropical Climate Changes at Millennial and Orbital Timescales on the Bolivian Altiplano. *Nature* 409:698–701.

Baker, Paul A., Geoffrey Seltzer, Sherilyn Fritz, Robert
     Dunbar, M. Grove, Pedro Tapia, S. Cross, H. Rowe,
     and J. Broda
2001   The History of South American Precipitation for
        the Past 25,000 Years. *Science* 291:640–643.

Bandy, Matthew S.
2001   *Population and History in the Ancient Titicaca Basin.*
        Unpublished doctoral dissertation, Department of
        Anthropology, University of California, Berkeley.

Barfield, Lawrence
1961   Recent Discoveries in the Atacama Desert and
        Bolivian Altiplano. *American Antiquity* 27:93–100.

Betancourt, Julio, C. Latorre, Jason Rech, Jay Quade, and
     K. Rylander
2000   A 22,000-Year Record of Monsoonal Precipitation
        from Northern Chile's Atacama Desert. *Science*
        298:1542–1546.

Billman, Brian
2001   Understanding the Timing and Tempo of the
        Evolution of Political Centralization on the Central
        Andean Coastline and Beyond. In *From Leaders
        to Rulers*, edited by Jonathan Haas, pp. 177–204.
        Plenum Press, New York.

Binford, Michael, Alan Kolata, Mark Brenner, John Janusek,
     Matthew Seddon, Mark Abbott, and James Curtis
1997   Climate Variation and the Rise and Fall of an Andean
        Civilization. *Quaternary Research* 47:235–248.

Bird, Junius B.
1943   *Excavations in Northern Chile.* Anthropological
        Papers, American Museum of Natural History
        38(4). New York.

Craig, Nathan
2005   *The Formation of Early Settled Villages and the
        Emergence of Leadership: A Test of Three Theoretical
        Models in the Río Ilave, Lake Titicaca Basin, Southern
        Peru.* Unpublished doctoral dissertation, Department
        of Anthropology, University of California, Santa
        Barbara.

Craig, Nathan M., and Mark Aldenderfer
2002   Domestic Architecture from the Late Archaic
        South-Central Andean Site of Jiskairumoko. Paper
        presented at the 67th Annual Meeting of the Society
        for American Archaeology, Denver, CO, USA.

D'Agostino, Karin, Geoffrey O. Seltzer, Paul Baker, Sherilyn
     Fritz, and Robert Dunbar
2002   Late Quaternary Lowstands of Lake Titicaca:
        Evidence from High-Resolution Seismic Data.
        Palaeogeography, Palaeoclimatology, Palaeoecology
        179:97–111.

DeVries, Thomas J., L. Ortlieb, A. Diaz, L. Wells, and Claude
     Hillaire-Marcel
1997   Determining the Early History of El Niño. *Science*
        276:965–966.

Farabaugh, Renee L., Catherine A. Rigsby, Paul A. Baker, and
     Mark Aldenderfer
2002   Sedimentology and Geomorphology of the Río
        Ramis Valley (Peru). Presented at the annual
        meeting of the Geological Society of America,
        Denver, CO, USA, November.

Grosjean, Martin
2001   Mid-Holocene Climate in the South-Central Andes:
        Humid or Dry? *Science* 292:2391a.

Grosjean, Martin, Isabel Cartajena, M. Geyh, and Lautaro
     Núñez
2003   From Proxy Data to Paleoclimate Interpretation:
        The Mid-Holocene Paradox of the Atacama Desert,
        Northern Chile. *Palaeogeography, Palaeoclimatology,
        Palaeoecology* 194:247–258.

Haas, Jonathan, and Winifred Creamer
2001   Amplifying Importance of New Research in Peru.
        Science 294:1652–1653.
2004   Cultural Transformations in the Central Andean
        Late Archaic. In *Andean Archaeology*, edited by
        Helaine Silverman, pp. 35–50. Blackwell, Oxford.

Ibarra Grasso, Dick
1957   El Paleolítico inferior en América. *Cuadernos
        Americanos* 16:135–175. Mexico City.

Kaulicke, Peter
2000   Los estudios del período Arcaico en el Perú: Logros,
        problemas, y propuestas. In *El Período Arcaico en el
        Perú: Hacia una Definición de los Orígenes*, edited by
        Peter Kaulicke, pp. 417–436. Boletín de Arqueología
        PUCP 3, 1999. Pontificia Universidad Católica del
        Perú, Lima.

Keefer, David K., Susan D. deFrance, Michael E. Moseley,
     James B. Richardson III, Dennis Satterlee, and Amy
     Day-Lewis
1998   Early Maritime Economy and El Niño Events at
        Quebrada Tacahuay, Peru. *Science* 281:1833–1835.

Klink, Cynthia J.
2004   Archaic Period Research in the Río Huenque, Peru.
        In *Advances in the Archaeology of the Lake Titicaca
        Basin-I*, edited by Charles Stanish, Amanda Cohen,
        and Mark Aldenderfer, pp.13–24. Cotsen Institute of
        Archaeology, University of California, Los Angeles.

Klink, Cynthia J., and Mark Aldenderfer
1996   Archaic Period Settlement Patterns of the Peruvian
        Altiplano: A Comparison of Two Recent Surveys
        in the Southwestern Lake Titicaca Basin. Paper

presented at the 24th Annual Midwest Conference of Andean and Amazonian Archaeology and Ethnohistory, Beloit, WI, USA.

2004 A Projectile Point Chronology for the South-Central Andean Highlands. In *Advances in the Archaeology of the Lake Titicaca Basin-1*, edited by Charles Stanish, Amanda Cohen, and Mark Aldenderfer, pp. 25–54. Cotsen Institute of Archaeology, University of California, Los Angeles.

Kolata, Alan L. (ed.)

1996 *Tiwanaku and Its Hinterland: Archaeology and Paleo-ecology of an Andean Civilization*. Smithsonian Institution Press, Washington, DC.

Lanning, Edward P.

1963 A Pre-Agricultural Occupation on the Central Coast of Peru. *American Antiquity* 27:139–154.

Lanning, Edward P., and Eugene A. Hammel

1961 Early Lithic Industries of Western South America. *American Antiquity* 27:139–154.

Lathrap, Donald W.

1971 The Tropical Forest and the Cultural Context of Chavin. In *Dumbarton Oaks Conference on Chavin*, edited by Elizabeth Benson, pp. 73–100. Dumbarton Oaks, Washington, DC.

1977 Our Father the Cayman Our Mother the Gourd: Spinden Revisited, or a Unitary Model for the Emergence of Agriculture in the New World. In *Origins of Agriculture*, edited by Charles Reed, pp. 713–751. Mouton, The Hague.

1985 Jaws: The Control of Power in the Early Nuclear American Ceremonial Center. In *Early Ceremonial Architecture in the Andes*, edited by Christopher B. Donnan, pp. 241-267. Dumbarton Oaks, Washington, DC.

Lavallée, Danièle, Philippe Béarez, Alexandre Chavalier, Michèle Julien, Pierre Usselmann, and Michel Fontugne

2000 Paleoambiente y ocupación prehistorica del litoral extremo-sur del Perú. In *El período arcaico en el Perú: Hacia una definición de los orígenes*, edited by Peter Kaulicke, pp. 393–416. Boletín de Arqueología PUCP 3, 1999. Pontificia Universidad Católica del Perú, Lima.

Le Paige, Gustavo

1958 Antiguas culturas atacameñas en la cordillera chilena: Época paleolítica. *Revista Universitaria, Año 43, Anales de la Academia Chilena de Ciencias Naturales* 22:139–165. Santiago, Chile.

Llagostera M., Agustín

1989 Caza y pesca marítima (9000 a 1000 a.C.). In *Culturas de Chile: Prehistoria*, edited by Jorge Hidalgo L., Virgilio Schiappacasse F., Hans Niemeyer F., Carlos Aldunate del S., and Iván Solimano R., pp. 57–80. Editorial Andrés Bello, Santiago, Chile.

Lynch, Thomas F.

1978 The South American Paleoindians. In *Ancient Native Americans*, edited by Jesse D. Jennings, pp. 455–489. W. H. Freeman, San Francisco.

1986 Climate Change and Human Settlement around the Late-Glacial Laguna de Punta Negra, Northern Chile. *Geoarchaeology* 1:145–162.

1990 Quaternary Climate, Environment, and the Human Occupation of the South-Central Andes. *Geoarchaeology* 5:199–228.

Marcus, Joyce, and Kent V. Flannery

1996 *Zapotec Civilization: How Urban Society Evolved in Mexico's Oaxaca Valley*. Thames and Hudson, London.

Matthews, Roger

2003 *The Archaeology of Mesopotamia: Theories and Approaches*. Routledge, London.

Mendoza, Marcela

2002 *Band Mobility and Leadership among the Western Toba Hunter-Gatherers of Gran Chaco in Argentina*. Edwin Mellen Press, Lewiston, NY.

Moraga, Mauricio, Eugenio Aspillaga, Pilar Carvallo, and Francisco Rothhammer

2000 Analyses of Mitochondrial DNA Polymorphisms in Skeletal Remains and Extant Human Populations of Northern Chile. *Chungará* 32:263–264. Arica.

Moseley, Michael E.

1975 *The Maritime Foundations of Andean Civilization*. Cummings Publishing, Menlo Park, CA.

1985 The Exploration and Explanation of Early Monumental Architecture in the Andes. In *Early Ceremonial Architecture in the Andes*, edited by Christopher B. Donnan, pp. 29–57. Dumbarton Oaks, Washington, DC.

Muñoz, Iván, Bernardo Arriaza, and Arthur C. Aufderheide (eds.)

1993 *Acha 2 y los orígenes del poblamiento humano en Arica*. Ediciones Universidad de Tarapacá, Arica, Peru.

Núñez A., Lautaro

1969 Sobre los complejos culturales Chinchorro y faldas del Morro del norte de Chile. *Rehue* 2:111–142.

1983 Paleoindian and Archaic Cultural Periods in the Arid and Semiarid Regions of Northern Chile. *Advances in World Archaeology* 2:161–202. Academic Press, New York.

1992   Ocupación arcaica en la puna de Atacama: Secuencia, movilidad, y cambio. In *Prehistoria Sudamericana: Nuevas perspectivas*, edited by Betty J. Meggers, pp. 283–307. Taraxacum, Washington, DC.

Núñez A., Lautaro, Martin Grosjean, and Isabel Cartajena

2002   Human Occupations and Cultural Change in the Puna de Atacama, Chile. *Science* 298:821–824.

Patterson, Thomas C., and Robert Heizer

1965   A Preceramic Stone Tool Collection from Viscachani, Bolivia. *Ñawpa Pacha* 3:107–113.

Quade, Jay, and Jason Rech

2001   Mid-Holocene Climate in the South-Central Andes: Humid or Dry? Response. *Science* 292:2391a–2391b.

Quilter, Jeffrey

1989   *Life and Death at Paloma: Society and Mortuary Practices at a Preceramic Peruvian Village.* University of Iowa Press, Iowa City.

1991   Late Preceramic Peru. *Journal of World Prehistory* 5:387–438.

Rasmussen, Karen A.

1998   *Exploring the Origins of Coastal Sedentism in the South-Central Andes.* Unpublished doctoral dissertation, Department of Anthropology, University of California, Santa Barbara.

Ravines, Rogger

1972   Secuencia y cambios en los artefactos líticos del Sur del Peru. *Revista del Museo Nacional* 38:133–184. Lima.

Rick, John

1980   *Prehistoric Hunters of the High Andes.* Academic Press, New York.

Rigsby, Catherine A., Paul A. Baker, and Mark S. Aldenderfer

2003   Fluvial History of the Río Ilave Valley, Peru, and Its Relationship to Climate and Human History. *Palaeogeography, Palaeoclimatology, Palaeoecology* 194:165–185.

Rigsby, Catherine, Renee Farabaugh, and Paul Baker

2002   Quaternary Sedimentary and Geomorphic History of River Valleys in the Lake Titicaca Basin, Peru and Bolivia. *EOS Transactions*, AGU, 83(47), Fall Meeting Supplement, Abstract GC21B-0154.

Rollins, Harold B., James B. Richardson III, and Daniel H. Sandweiss

1986   The Birth of El Niño: Geoarchaeological Evidence and Implications. *Geoarchaeology* 1:3–15.

Rivera, Mario, and Francisco Rothhammer

1986   Evaluación biológica y cultural de poblaciones Chinchorro: Nuevos elementos para la hipótesis de contactos transaltiplánicos, cuenca Amazonas-Costa Pacífico. *Chungará* 16–17:295–306. Arica.

Rothhammer, Francisco, and Claudio Silva

1992   Gene Geography of South America: Testing Models of Populations Displacement Based on Archaeological Evidence. *American Journal of Physical Anthropology* 89:441–446.

Rothhammer, Francisco, Claudio Silva, Jose Cocilovo, and Silva Quevedo

1986   Una hipótesis provisional sobre el poblamiento de Chile basada en el análisis multivariado de medidas cranéometricas. *Chungará* 16-17:115–118. Arica.

Sandweiss, Daniel H., Kirk A. Maasch, and David G. Anderson

1999   Transitions in the Mid-Holocene. *Science* 283:499–500.

Sandweiss, Daniel H., and Michael E. Moseley

2001   Amplifying Importance of New Research in Peru. *Science* 294:1651–1652.

Sandweiss, Daniel H., James B. Richardson III, Elizabeth J. Reitz, J. Hsu, and Robert A. Feldman

1989   Early Maritime Adaptations in the Andes: Preliminary Studies at the Ring Site, Peru. In *Ecology, Settlement, and History in the Osmore Drainage, Peru*, edited by Don S. Rice, Charles Stanish, and Phillip Scarr, pp. 35–84. BAR International Series 545 (i). British Archaeological Reports, Oxford

Sandweiss, Daniel H., James B. Richardson III, Elizabeth J. Reitz, Harold B. Rollins, and Kirk A. Maasch

1996   Geoarchaeological Evidence from Peru for a 5000 Years B.P. onset of El Niño. *Science* 273:1531–1533.

1997   Determining the Early History of El Niño. *Science* 276:966–967.

Sandweiss, Daniel H., Heather McInnis, Richard L. Burger, Asunción Cano, Bernardino Ojeda, Rolando Paredes, María del Carmen Sandweiss, and Michael D. Glascock

1998   Quebrada Jaguay: Early South American Maritime Adaptations. *Science* 281:1830–1833.

Santoro, Calógero

1989   Antiguos cazadores de la puna (9000 a 6000 a.C.). In *Culturas de Chile: Prehistoria*, edited by Jorge Hidalgo L., Virgilio Schiappacasse F., Hans Niemeyer F., Carlos Aldunate del S., and Iván Solimano R., pp. 33–55. Editorial Andrés Bello, Santiago, Chile.

Santoro, Calógero, and Lautaro Núñez
1987   Hunters of the Dry Puna and the Salt Puna in
           Northern Chile. *Andean Past* 1:57–110.
Schaedel, Richard, and C. Munizaga
1957   *Arqueología Chilena.* Universidad de Chile, Santiago.
Schiappacasse, Virgilio, and Hans Niemeyer
1984   *Sitio Camarones 14. Descripción y análisis interpre-
           tativo de un sitio arcaico temprano de la Quebrada de
           Camarones.* Museo Nacional de Historia Natural,
           Publicación Ocasional 41. Santiago.
Shady Solís, Ruth, Jonathan Haas, and Winifred Creamer
2001   Dating Caral, a Preceramic Site in the Supe Valley
           on the Central Coast of Peru. *Science* 292:723–726.
Smith, Bruce D.
2001   Low Level Food Production. *Journal of Archaeological
           Research* 9:1–43.
Stanish, Charles
2003   *Ancient Titicaca: The Evolution of Complex Society in
           Southern Peru and Northern Bolivia.* University of
           California Press, Berkeley and Los Angeles.
Stanish, Charles, Richard L. Burger, Lisa M. Cipolla, Michael
           D. Glascock, and Esteban Quelima
2002   Evidence for Early Long-Distance Obsidian
           Exchange and Watercraft Use from the Southern
           Lake Titicaca Basin of Bolivia and Peru. *Latin
           American Antiquity* 13:444–454.

Uhle, Friedrich Maximilian
1919   La arqueología de Arica y Tacna. *Boletín de la
           Sociedad Ecuatoriana de Estudios Históricos Americanos*
           7–8. Quito, Ecuador.
1922   *Fundamentos étnicos y arqueología de Arica y Tacna.*
           Sociedad Ecuatoriana de Estudios Históricos
           Americanos, Quito, Ecuador.
Wells, Lisa E., and Jay S. Noller
1997   Determining the Early History of El Niño. *Science*
           276:966.
Willey, Gordon R.
1988   Junius Bouton Bird and American Archaeology. In
           *Travels and Archaeology in South Chile by Junius B.
           Bird*, edited by John Hyslop, pp. xiii–xxxi. University
           of Iowa Press, Iowa City.
Wise, Karen
1990   *Late Archaic Period Maritime Subsistence Strategies
           in the South-Central Andes.* Unpublished doc-
           toral dissertation, Department of Anthropology,
           Northwestern University, Evanston, IL.
2000   Kilómetro 4 y la ocupación del período arcaico en
           el área de Ilo, al sur del Perú. In *El Periodo Arcaico en
           el Perú: Hacia una definición de los orígenes*, edited by
           Peter Kaulicke, pp. 335–363. Boletín de Arqueología
           PUCP, no. 3, 1999. Pontificia Universidad Católica
           del Perú, Lima.

CHAPTER 6

TALKING DOGS AND NEW CLOTHES, OR THE MARITIME FOUNDATIONS HYPOTHESIS REVISITED

ROBERT A. FELDMAN

MICHAEL MOSELEY'S MARITIME FOUNDATIONS of Andean civilization hypothesis (referred to by Moseley as MFAC) for the origins of Andean complex society (Moseley 1975) generated a hostile response in some quarters when it was first presented, and continues to do so more than thirty years later. The late 1960s and early 1970s were a time when the search for universal cultural laws was the new wave in the discipline of archaeology. The idea that civilization could arise without being based on agriculture was something of a heresy because it ran counter to one of the old, accepted laws of archaeology: that an agricultural subsistence base was necessary for culture to move from the Stone Age toward civilization. The findings in the Fertile Crescent at Jericho, Jarmo, and other sites had shown this law to be true (hadn't they?), so why would it be different in Peru?

_____

Note: I have never been one to write long papers, and the present contribution is no exception. I do not intend it to be an exhaustive analysis of the topic but rather a personal statement, more like a call of "Hey! Take a look over here!" It is in the spirit of one of Moseley's favorite comparisons when disparaging someone's conclusions: they are like the emperor's new clothes: you might think they are something fancy, but there really is nothing there at all. It is a call to look at the archaeological data that exist without making preconceived judgments. I only hope that I might do the same.

Yet when Moseley looked at the Preceramic sites in Peru, the situation appeared to be different. The refuse middens he examined showed an abundance of fish and shellfish remains, with smaller amounts of marine mammal remains and even fewer land mammal remains. Maize, the iconic staple of New World civilization, was rare to absent. The most common cultivated plants (for there were cultivated plants in these Late Preceramic middens) were cotton and bottle gourds, "industrial" plants used for cordage, netting, and textiles and as containers, respectively.

This situation was acceptable so long as the Preceramic sites remained small fishing villages, but that was not to be the case. When Gordon Willey visited Peru in 1971, Moseley took him on a tour of coastal sites, stopping at Áspero, the scene of Willey's early excavations in Peru in 1941 (Willey and Corbett 1954). What had escaped notice in 1941 was clear in 1971: Áspero was dotted with mound constructions. A large looter's pit dug into one of the larger mounds showed internal wall and fill construction. Something was going on that did not fit with what was "known" at the time. Moseley and Willey's subsequent article in *American Antiquity* (1973) identified these mounds as evidence of "corporate labor." The identification of corporate labor at Áspero served to crystallize ideas that had been forming since the early 1960s.

Based on his excavations around Ancón and Chillón and on his work with Frédéric Engel, Edward Lanning

(1963, 1967) had proposed a succession of early hunting, fishing, and farming economies on the Peruvian coast. With the insight provided by Áspero, Moseley could tie together what had been isolated findings of larger-scale Preceramic and early Initial period architecture at sites such as El Paraíso (Engel 1966; Quilter 1985), Culebras (Lanning 1967), and Las Haldas (Matsuzawa 1974; Grieder 1975) into a coherent theory. That theory was the MFAC hypothesis, which proposed that the bounties of the Peruvian littoral zone provided a stable and sufficient subsistence base to support populations large enough and stable enough that labor could be devoted to nonsubsistence tasks, supporting social differentiation, monumental corporate constructions, and, ultimately, the origins of civilization in the Andes. The organizational structures that created the corporate constructions "pre-adapted" the societies for the eventual shift to building the irrigation canals needed for significant agricultural production on the desert coast of Peru (Moseley 1974), production that was necessary for the further development of the large prehistoric coastal empires.

It has been clear for quite some time that the subsistence patterns in coastal Peru prior to 2000 BC were more complex than presented in Moseley's original formulation of the maritime foundations hypothesis (see Burger 1985; Moseley 1985; Pozorski and Pozorski 1987; Quilter et al. 1991; Feldman 1992; Pearsall 2003). Humans are omnivores; they eat almost anything, animal and vegetal. To assume that a group has an exclusively marine diet is as likely to be wrong as to assume that it is exclusively agricultural. A variety of cultivated plants—including edible species, in addition to the industrial ones—are found at most Late Preceramic sites. Yet old ideas refuse to die, both the idea that agriculture was necessary for cultural development and the idea that the coastal Cotton Preceramic diet was based solely on maritime resources.

What, then, are the criticisms of the maritime foundations hypothesis? They can be loosely divided into four groups, which we can label environmental, dietary, regional, and typological. These categories, like most typologies of cultural phenomena viewed archaeologically, are not mutually exclusive, and the critics tend to include elements of two or more of them in their arguments.

Environmental criticisms argue that the maritime regime of the Peruvian coast was subject to periodic downturns associated with El Niño that would have limited the population to levels too low to have supported sedentary communities and corporate labor constructions. Dietary criticisms argue that the coastal Preceramic populations were consuming (and often producing) foods outside the maritime palette, such as maize or manioc.

Regional criticisms argue that the coastal Preceramic sites were not independent systems but instead were tied to interior settlements in other ecological zones, ranging up the valleys into the highlands. From sites in these other zones, the coastal population received significant amounts of nonmaritime foods or products (which are often seen as tied to significant political control).

Typological criticisms argue that, if the coastal sites were at a given level of political organization—if they were chiefdoms, for example—then they must have certain other features, such as an agricultural subsistence economy, most commonly seen as based on maize.

ENVIRONMENTAL CRITICISMS

An environmental criticism was put forward by Mary Parsons (1970) even before the maritime foundations hypothesis was crystallized in print. Others who followed included Osborn (1977a, b) and Lynch (1981). They argued that maritime resources could not be counted on to sustain a large population over more than a few generations. The reduction in anchoveta numbers with the El Niño warming of the coastal waters would result in starvation and population collapse, or so the argument went. This population bottleneck would prevent the establishment of large settlements and the rise of nonegalitarian social structures.

To counter the environmental criticisms, Moseley used a theoretical maximum population estimate from Osborn (pers. comm., cited in Moseley and Feldman 1988) of 6,626,772—a number well above any suggested Preceramic population level—to underscore the richness of the littoral. Moseley also used references to historical El Niños to show they also adversely affected irrigation agriculture by washing out canals and fields and disrupting societies. Indeed, the historical evidence indicates that El Niños probably had a greater impact on terrestrial resources than on marine resources.

Moseley also noted that the environmental arguments were usually theoretical analyses, "just so" stories that do not examine the archaeological record to see what actually took place. As such, they ignored the core of the maritime hypothesis, namely, that the conditions in Peru were unique. Rather than being the exception that proves the rule of the centrality of agriculture, however, he argued that the maritime adaptation of coastal Peru showed we needed to recognize that agriculture was not the cause of civilization but one of several pathways to the same end.

DIETARY CRITICISMS

Dietary criticisms posited that the maritime hypothesis was wrong in stating that fishing and shellfish collecting formed the primary subsistence base of the coastal Preceramic communities. David Wilson (1981) was one of those who argued that the true subsistence base was maize agriculture. His argument had a distinctly Mesoamerican slant and was based more on a priori typological assumptions than on any physical evidence: if coastal centers such as Áspero had monumental architecture indicative of developing social complexity, then they must have been supported by agriculture, which must have been maize-based. Scott Raymond (1981) made similar arguments but rested his agricultural alternative on tropical forest root crops such as manioc.

There are two points in these arguments that need examining. The first is whether or not the targeted food crop was present in the Preceramic. And if it was present, was it a significant source of food?

The best argument for the cultivation of maize during the Cotton Preceramic period was presented by Duccio Bonavia (1982), based on maize remains found in his excavations at Los Gavilanes (Huarmey North 1) and on analyses of that maize by Alexander Grobman (Bonavia and Grobman 1989; see also Bonavia 1982:157–180). They argued that the quantity and variety of maize plant parts found in storage pits that Bonavia associated with the Preceramic levels of Los Gavilanes could not be ignored. In a turnaround from the criticisms leveled at Moseley, Bonavia noted that the evidence for Preceramic maize "inicialmente no fueron aceptados por la mayoría de investigadores e inclusive fueron combatidas y no siempre de la manera más honesta" (Bonavia 1982:xix).

Some critics of Bonavia's proposition argued that the maize storage pits were intrusive and more recent than the Preceramic middens. The three identified occupational epochs at Los Gavilanes included increasing types and quantities of cultivated plants, beginning with *Canna* sp., *Arachis*, and *Inga*, the first two of which are not native to the coastal area. Maize was found in both Epoch 2 and Epoch 3. Interestingly, peppers and squash, which are usually the most common early cultivars, did not appear until Epoch 2, and beans did not appear until Epoch 3. Radiocarbon dates covered a wide range, from 4800 ± 500 BP to 2080 ± 130 BP, with most dates between 4000 BP and 3250 BP, which could overlap with the Initial ceramic period or even Early Horizon.

Maize is not common in other Preceramic contexts, which makes the quantity and variety of maize remains at Los Gavilanes even more unusual. Gordon Willey found maize cobs at Áspero, under a low plastered platform in his architectural cluster labeled Structure 2. The exact context of this sample remains unclear, however. The small room grouping where it was found was built on the upper layer of the midden and probably is late in the site's sequence. Furthermore, the maize appears to be of a morphologically later variety (see Robert Bird's argument below). My excavations at Áspero in 1973–1974 also found some maize in midden excavations. I was not able to rule out disturbance, either by human or animal action, and never felt secure that the maize at Áspero was Preceramic. However, it is entirely possible that I, too, was seeing what I chose to see, and I may have erred by saying that the emperor was naked when in reality he was clothed. The maize cobs I found were sent to Dr. Grobman for analysis, but I am unaware of any definitive results. Based on 35-mm color transparencies of the cobs that I took, Robert Bird (pers. comm.) felt that they were morphologically more recent than the context would suggest.

Robert Bird has been the strongest critic of Bonavia and Grobman. Bird (1978, 1990) argued, based on the morphology of early Peruvian maize from a number of sites, that the specimens Bonavia found at Los Gavilanes and that Willey and I found at Áspero were later than the Cotton Preceramic. He concluded that no maize had been found that could be *typologically* assigned to the Preceramic. Unfortunately, like so many arguments about the Peruvian Preceramic, it is based more on theory than on actual dated evidence.

Nevertheless, it is possible that the maize that has been found does belong with the Preceramic occupations. The interesting question then is, what does it mean? One of Moseley's favorite sayings is, "It's like the talking dog—people don't pay attention to what the dog says, or even care if they can understand it, they are simply amazed that it can talk at all."[1] In this case it's not that the maize has any identifiable significance or historical meaning, because for many (e.g., Wilson), the important fact is simply that it is there at all. Does the presence of some small quantity of maize in and of itself mean that the maritime foundations hypothesis is invalid, that the subsistence base of the coastal Cotton Preceramic sites was based on maize agriculture?

Some studies have attempted to answer the question of the importance of maize by examining skeletal remains. Study of isotopes in Early Horizon skeletal remains from Virú (Ericson et al. 1989) estimated that only 10%–20% of the dietary energy input came from maize, even at that "late" date. Data from the sierra (Burger and van der Merwe 1990) yielded a similar conclusion. Overall, these studies indicate that maize was, at best, of minor importance even well past the time when agriculture had become an important source of subsistence.

Even with careful attention to the recovery of plant remains in excavations, Pearsall (2003:213), referring mainly to Ecuador, wrote, "Documenting the trajectory of subsistence change during the Formative still eludes us, however. While the database has grown steadily, it is still difficult to answer this question: Is Formative subsistence agriculturally based, and if so, on what crops?" To attempt to answer this question, we need to look at a number of lines of evidence. Pearsall suggested the following criteria for identifying an agricultural subsistence base: "presence of domesticated plants, including productive carbohydrate sources; reduced reliance on wild plant resources; evidence that domesticates were important in diet and economy (ubiquitous occurrence, supporting isotope and health data in the case of maize, and presence of storage facilities and caches); and orientation of sites to agricultural lands" (Pearsall 2003:233). Before we address these questions, though, we need to look at other criticisms of the maritime foundations hypothesis.

REGIONAL CRITICISMS

Regional criticisms argue that the coast was not isolated from the upper valley and highland regions and that an active interchange took place between elevations. This interchange might range from simple exchange of food and agricultural products to complete political integration. In any case, the argument is that subsistence exchange took place, with the coastal populations receiving significant amounts of interior or highland agricultural produce. Proponents of a regional model

include Richard Burger, Terence Grieder, Tom and Shelia Pozorski, and Donald Lathrap.

Burger, from his highland perspective at Chavín de Huántar, has argued that the highlands and coast cannot be studied separate from each other (Burger 1985). He did not see significant amounts of foodstuffs being transported from one area to the other, however, primarily because of the lack of suitable pack animals at that time. He suggested that more portable commodities, such as salt and seaweed, were being transported up from the coast to meet dietary needs in an agriculturally based highlands.

Terence Grieder and Alberto Bueno (1985), working at La Galgada in the Tablachaca tributary of the Río Santa, almost up to the Callejón de Huaylas, associated irrigation canals with the later Preceramic and early Initial Period monumental architecture they excavated there. They noted the presence in burials of shells from the Pacific coast to the west and feathers from the tropical forest to the east, both clearly indicative of some form of long-distance exchange. Somewhat like Burger, they suggested it was not food that was going west to the coast, but cotton, grown in the irrigated fields near La Galgada. Interestingly, Shady (see below) also argues that cotton was an item of exchange between interior and coastal communities.

The Pozorskis worked up from the coastal zone of the Casma Valley into the upper valley region. In their excavations, they found remains of numerous varieties of cultivated food plants in Preceramic levels (Ugent, Pozorski, and Pozorski 1981, 1982, 1984; Pozorski and Pozorski 1987). The picture they developed is one of greater complexity in the range of plants eaten—and likely cultivated—in the Late Preceramic. These early sites were generally small, and while they do serve to show the range of plants cultivated in the Preceramic, they do not directly illuminate what was taking place in the coastal villages. Still, we need to stop and look to see what was there on the ground, as the Pozorskis have found good evidence of a variety of crops. Instead of jumping to conclusions, though, we need to develop a model or hypothesis to explain the data, rather than forcing the data into a preexisting model.

Throughout the occupation of Peru there were movements and contacts up and down the coast and up and down the valleys, between the coast and the upper elevations. It would be unrealistic to assume that food, as well as sumptuary goods and ideas, did not also move up and down the same elevation gradient. I think it is hardly coincidental that the greatest concentrations of early Peruvian monumental architecture are found in those coastal areas that have the easiest communication with highland areas, specifically with the Callejón de Huaylas: the Supe/Pativilca/Fortaleza multivalley complex, and the Casma/Nepeña multivalley complex. The explanation for this pattern will be found, I am confident, in a blending of influences, environments, and commodities that was possible in these areas, combined with access to stable and bountiful supplies of subsistence resources. The question remains as to where the "center of gravity" resided: were the innovative developments taking place on the coast, under a maritime regime, or in the highlands, under an agricultural regime, or perhaps somewhere in between? Resolution of these questions will depend on precise dating not only of monumental architecture but also of residential architecture and food remains, combined with isotopic and bioanthropological analyses of associated skeletal material.

A different sort of regional criticism was put forward by Donald Lathrap (1973, 1977, 1985), who argued that we should look to the high iconography of the early cultures to see where their origins were. The caymans, serpents, harpy eagles, and manioc of Chavín de Huántar were evidence to him of a tropical forest origin for Andean civilization. Yet the iconography we find in the early coastal Preceramic sites that is identifiable as to place is not from the tropical forest or from the highlands necessarily, but coastal, with crabs, serpents, and condors. If we look at later developments, as Moseley has pointed out, there were two overriding demographic and cultural centers of gravity in pre-Columbian Peru: the north coast and the southern highlands. Although the cultures of these centers share some basic iconography, such as the Staff God or Front-Faced Deity, some fundamental differences can be observed. In particular, we note the emphasis on marine iconography and symbolism in the classic north coast civilizations. In Moche art we see caballitos de totora, fishes and seabirds, conch shells and crab deities. The abundance of fish and seabird images in Chimu textiles and clay wall friezes is impossible to miss. When we look at the iconography of the southern demographic pole we see not seabirds but condors, eagles, and hawks; instead of sea fishes, we see lacustrine or riverine species; instead of seals, snails, and crabs, we see llamas and pumas; instead of rushes and fruits, we see potatoes and ulluco.

TYPOLOGICAL CRITICISMS

The recent article by Shady, Haas, and Creamer (2001) presented information on Shady's excavations at the site of Caral, in the Supe Valley. In that article, they identify Caral as dating to the Late Cotton Preceramic period (assigning it a 600-year time span between corrected dates of 2627 BC and 2020 BC), note the large number and large volume of monumental structures there, and claim that the site represents the earliest urban settlement in Peru. Haas and Creamer also argue that the inland location of Caral (some 23 km from the coast) and the presence of several species of cultivated plants negate the maritime hypothesis.

Before considering some of the arguments over the interpretation of Caral, I must digress with a bit of history.

The site Shady calls Caral was identified in print by Paul Kosok as the site of Chupacigarro Grande (Kosok 1965; see also Williams 1972). Kosok, a geographer working with archaeologist Richard Schaedel, incorrectly identified Chupacigarro Grande as dating to the Middle Horizon (ca. AD 750).[2] A distinguishing characteristic of Caral/Chupacigarro Grande is the presence of circular sunken plazas fronting some of the platform mounds.

In 1973 and 1974, as part of my doctoral dissertation research at Áspero, I did a quick surface survey of Chupacigarro Grande and fifteen other similar sites with circular sunken plazas (some identified by Kosok) in the Supe and adjacent Pativilca and Fortaleza valleys (Feldman 1980: Figures 2 and 28, pp. 98–102, and pp. 210–212; Feldman 1992). There were almost no artifacts to be found on the surface of these sites, but based on the finding of a few sherds of pottery identifiable as a thin neckless olla, I suggested that the sites dated to the Initial period (ca. 3500 BP). With the finding of the site of Piedra Parada, south of the Río Supe near the mouth of the Supe Valley, which has a circular sunken plaza, lacks pottery, and has twined cotton textiles, I hypothesized that the circular sunken plaza tradition began in Preceramic times, and that sites such as Chupacigarro Grande, while they could have started in the Late Preceramic, in the main dated to the Initial period (Feldman 1980:210–212).

Just prior to the time I was working at Áspero (but unknown to me until after I did my survey work), the Peruvian architect Carlos Williams (1972) identified two early ("Formative") architectural traditions: the U-shaped mound complex and the circular sunken plaza mound complex, and placed the Supe Valley sites, including Chupacigarro, within these traditions. Subsequently, Williams identified some thirty sites with mounds and circular plazas in the lower 40 km of the Supe Valley (Williams 1985).

With this historical background, it can be seen that the excavations at Caral serve to fill in much-needed detail relating to a number of very large early sites that obviously had great significance but that could not be securely placed in time. What is troubling about the recent work there are the generalizations and extrapolations some have made. The danger is that theoretical typological biases are driving the interpretation of the evidence, dressing the emperor in a suit of clothes drawn, as it were, from thin air.

A number of broad claims were made in the *Science* article on the dating of Caral by Shady, Haas, and Creamer (2001) and in the coverage that article received in the popular press. In a commentary letter published in *Science* in response to Shady, Haas, and Creamer, Sandweiss and Moseley (2001) made several points designed to bring discussion of Caral back into context: (1) that Caral is not the earliest Cotton Preceramic settlement with monumental architecture and/or domesticated plants, with Áspero, also in the Supe Valley, being a prime example; (2) that the protein component of the diet at Caral came from marine animals, and thus did not invalidate the maritime foundations hypothesis; and (3) that Caral is not the earliest site to suggest the use of irrigation agriculture in the Late Preceramic. Their letter did not address the issue of whether or not Caral was an urban settlement. Instead, it tried to show how Caral fit within a sequence of development that involved numerous Preceramic sites on both the Peruvian coast and in the Peruvian highlands.

In their response to Sandweiss and Moseley, Haas and Creamer (2001) noted that the monumental architecture at Áspero was of a much smaller scale than at Caral and thus could not be considered urban, and that the presence of cultivated plants at Áspero indicated that the maritime hypothesis was not correct. These responses, however, did not fully address the points Sandweiss and Moseley raised.

While it is undeniable that the architecture at Caral is much larger than that at Áspero, it needs to be noted that at least one mound at Áspero is more than 10 m high (not 4 m, as Haas and Creamer state [2001:1652]). Also, Áspero can only be considered a "tertiary residential center with minor public architecture," as

Haas and Creamer (ibid.) wrote, if it is contemporary with the inland sites. The radiocarbon dates from Áspero, however, put the initial levels of its corporate labor architecture earlier than Caral (Feldman 1980). Although Haas and Creamer argue that "it is premature to argue for the temporal priority of communal construction at the one fishing village [Áspero] in the entire [Supe Valley] system" (Haas and Creamer 2001:1652), they themselves argue for the priority of Caral not just in the Supe Valley, but on the entire central and northern Peruvian coast.

Haas and Creamer also rather cavalierly extrapolate from the excavation results at Caral to argue that the site was urban. A press release from the Field Museum (2001:1) said that Caral "was home to the earliest known urban settlement . . . in the New World." Likewise, a press release from Northern Illinois University (2001:1) quotes Creamer as saying, "This may actually be the birthplace of civilization in the Americas." Here, one suspects, the emperor is wearing clothes cut from an *a priori* typological construct of what is "urban," "civilization," and "the state."

Haas and Creamer subtly misrepresent the maritime hypothesis by saying that "at the core of MFAC is the idea that centralization, hierarchy, and social complexity arose in the context of the coastal fishing villages largely independent of *systematic* agriculture" (2001:1652–1653, emphasis added). The key word here is *systematic*, since what Moseley argued was that the coastal fishing villages were largely independent of *subsistence* agriculture. What the maritime hypothesis challenged, even in its original formulation, was the idea that "centralization, hierarchy, and social complexity" (to use Haas and Creamer's terms) required an agricultural subsistence base. The maritime hypothesis instead argued that population size and stability were the critical factors, and that there was more than a single path to those conditions.

Even in the earliest formulations of the hypothesis, Moseley (1975) distinguished between "industrial" plants, such as cotton, and food plants, such as beans and squash. He later modified his model by expanding the range of plants that were eaten, while retaining the perspective that the cultivated plants were minor components of the diet (Moseley 1992). Sandweiss and Moseley note that the subsistence remains found at Caral "indicate that even there, 23 km from the shore, seafood provided the entire animal component of the diet and cotton and gourds were among the most important crops. As Moseley presaged more than ten years ago [Moseley1992], Caral is fully consistent with MFAC" (2001:1652).

Haas and Creamer go on to argue incorrectly that "the cotton used in making the nets is also a domesticated crop. Because the nets are essential for exploiting the abundant anchovy populations on the coast, the maritime florescence discussed by Moseley is agriculture dependent from the beginning" (Haas and Creamer 2001:1653). In order to assert this argument, it is first necessary to disregard several thousand years of fishing that used nets and lines made of fibers other than cotton (such as at AS8, near Áspero, with one radiocarbon date of 6085 ± 180 BP [Feldman 1980:246]). It is then necessary to ignore the differences between floodwater farming and irrigation agriculture and between agriculture for producing raw materials and agriculture for subsistence.

It is interesting that Shady takes a somewhat different position than Haas does and recognizes that the bulk of the identifiable protein in the diet at Caral came from the sea. Shady argues that the area around Caral was under irrigation for the production of cotton, which was exchanged with the coastal peoples for fish and other seafood. Shady's position would not negate the maritime hypothesis, which argued that organized irrigation agriculture in Peru arose in the context of the patterns of labor organization that developed in coastal, maritime-based villages such as Áspero. Further, if Caral was dependent on marine protein, it would serve to reinforce the main postulate of the maritime hypothesis: that the extraordinarily rich marine protein production of coastal Peru supported large sedentary populations, which allowed for the construction of corporate labor projects such as earthen mounds, and that these organizational structures in turn facilitated the shift from floodwater farming to irrigation farming.

We can now return to Pearsall's (2003:233) criteria for determining an agricultural subsistence economy and apply them to Caral. We see productive domesticated plants such as squash, beans, and sweet potato (Shady et al. 2001:725) there, but most of these have a long history in Peru, extending back in time to sites few would call agricultural. We cannot as of now determine how important these plants were, but we can note that the major sources of animal protein were almost exclusively marine. Next, we do not have reported evidence for storage facilities. The strongest support for finding Caral agricultural come from its location—inland, where irrigation would be possible—but even here, Shady interprets the agriculture as directed to industrial crops (cotton) rather than

subsistence crops. Overall, the case for an agricultural subsistence base at Caral is weak.

Even if we were to grant that Caral was supported by agriculture, we still must answer the question of what that means in the grander picture of the development of Peruvian civilization. It should be noted that a classification or a typology is not an explanation. This might seem like a picky point, but labeling Caral as "urban" or "la ciudad más antigua de América" (Shady n.d.) or saying that it represents a "state level society" does little to advance our understanding of the processes that took place in third millennium BC Peru. What exactly does urban mean in the context of Peru, and especially third millennium BC Peru? If Caral was indeed urban, how did it get to that point? What was the connection between Caral and other, possibly earlier sites in the Supe region such as Áspero?

Further, what is the meaning of the great number of monumental sites with circular sunken plazas in Formative Peru? They spread over some 500 km of the coast and range in elevation from near sea level into and over the Andes. Were they contemporaneous—both within any one valley and across valleys—or sequential, or some degree of both? If at least some were contemporary, was there a hierarchy of sites, either within one valley or across valleys? Shady has argued that these sites are part of a Caral/Supe state, with an overriding ideology, social structure, and economy. I look forward to more results from her and her colleagues' work, as well as ongoing work by Alvaro Ruiz, Haas, and Creamer in the Pativilca Valley and Norte Chico region. These investigations hold the promise to clear up some of the chronological issues. Without proper regard for talking dogs and new clothes, however, the interpretive issues will remain.

NOTES

1. The original quotation from Samuel Johnson likened a woman preaching to a dog that could walk on its hind legs ("Sir, a woman's preaching is like a dog's walking on his hinder legs. It is not done well; but you are surprised to find it done at all." *Boswell: The Life of Johnson*, p. 116), but the saying has a wide distribution as a talking rather than walking dog.

2. Caral/Chupacigarro Grande does have secondary constructions that probably date to the Middle Horizon, but the primary occupation and the bulk of the visible monumental architecture have now been shown to date to the Late Preceramic and possibly Initial ceramic periods.

REFERENCES

Bird, Robert McK.

1978   Archaeological Maize from Peru. *Maize Genetics Cooperation Newsletter* 52:90–92.

1990   What Are the Chances of Finding Maize in Peru Dating before 1000 B.C.? Reply to Bonavia and Grobman. *American Antiquity* 55(4):828–840.

Bonavia, Duccio

1982   *Los Gavilanes.* Corporación Financiera de Desarrollo S.A., Lima.

Bonavia, Duccio, and Alexander Grobman

1989   Preceramic Maize in the Central Andes: A Necessary Clarification. *American Antiquity* 54(4):836–840.

Boswell, James

1791   *The Life of Samuel Johnson.* Edited by Christopher Hibbert. Penguin Books, New York, 1979.

Burger, Richard L.

1985   Concluding Remarks: Early Peruvian Civilization and Its Relation to the Chavín Horizon. In *Early Ceremonial Architecture in the Andes*, edited by Christopher B. Donnan, pp. 269–289. Dumbarton Oaks, Washington, DC.

Burger, Richard L., and Nikolaas J. van der Merwe

1990   Maize and the Origin of Highland Chavín Civilization. *American Anthropologist* 92(1):85–95.

Engel, Frédéric

1966   Le complexe précéramique d'El Paraiso (Perou). *Journal de la Société des Américanistes* 55:43–96.

Ericson, Jonathan E., Michael West, Charles H. Sullivan, and Harold W. Krueger

1989   The Development of Maize Agriculture in the Viru Valley, Peru. In *The Chemistry of Prehistoric Human Bone*, edited by T. Douglas Price, pp. 68–104. Cambridge University Press, Cambridge.

Feldman, Robert Alan

1980   *Áspero, Peru: Architecture, Subsistence Economy, and Other Artifacts of a Preceramic Maritime Chiefdom.* Unpublished doctoral dissertation, Department of Anthropology, Harvard University, Cambridge, MA.

1992   Preceramic Architectural and Subsistence Traditions. *Andean Past* 3:6786.

Field Museum

2001   Field Museum Anthropologists Establish Date and Importance of the Americas' Oldest City. Press release, April 26. Field Museum of Natural History, Chicago.

Grieder, Terence

1975   A Dated Sequence of Building and Pottery at Las Haldas. *Ñawpa Pacha* 13:99–112.

Grieder, Terence, and Alberto Bueno Mendoza

1985   Ceremonial Architecture at La Galgada. In *Early Ceremonial Architecture in the Andes*, edited by Christopher B. Donnan, pp. 93–110. Dumbarton Oaks, Washington, DC.

Haas, Jonathan, and Winifred Creamer

2001   Response. *Science* 294:1652–1653.

Kosok, Paul

1965   *Life, Land and Water in Ancient Peru.* Long Island University Press, Brooklyn, NY.

Lanning, Edward P.

1963   A Preagricultural Occupation on the Central Coast of Peru. *American Antiquity* 28:360–371.

1967   *Peru Before the Incas.* Prentice-Hall, Englewood Cliffs, NJ.

Lathrap, Donald W.

1973   Gifts of the Cayman: Some Thoughts on the Subsistence Basis of Chavín. In *Variation in Anthropology*, edited by Donald W. Lathrap and J. Douglas, pp. 91–105. Illinois Archaeological Survey, Urbana.

1977   Our Father the Cayman, Our Mother the Gourd: Spinden Revisited, or a Unitary Model for the Emergence of Agriculture in the New World. In *Origins of Agriculture*, edited by Charles A. Reed, pp. 713–751. Mouton, The Hague.

1985   Jaws: The Control of Power in the Early Nuclear American Ceremonial Center. In *Early Ceremonial Architecture in the Andes*, edited by Christopher B. Donnan, pp. 241–262. Dumbarton Oaks, Washington, DC.

Lynch, Thomas F.

1981   Zonal Complementarity in the Andes: A History of the Concept. In *Networks of the Past: Regional Interaction in Archaeology*, edited by P. D. Francis, F. J. Kense, and P. G. Duke, pp. 221–231. Proceedings of the 12th Annual Conference of the Archaeological Association of the University of Calgary, Alberta.

Matsuzawa, Shozo

1974   Excavations at Las Haldas on the Coast of Central Peru. *Proceedings of the Department of Humanities, College of General Education, University of Tokyo* 59:3–44. Cultural Anthropology, no. 2. Tokyo.

Moseley, Michael E.

1974   Organizational Preadaptation to Irrigation: The Evolution of Early Water-Management Systems in Coastal Peru. In *Irrigation's Impact on Society*, edited by Theodore E. Downing and McGuire Gibson.

Anthropological Papers of the University of Arizona 25:77–82.

1975 *The Maritime Foundations of Andean Civilization.* Cummings Publishing Co., Menlo Park, IL.

1985 The Exploration and Explanation of Early Monumental Architecture in the Andes. In *Early Ceremonial Architecture in the Andes*, edited by Christopher B. Donnan, pp. 29–58. Dumbarton Oaks, Washington, DC.

1992 Maritime Foundations and Multilinear Evolution: Retrospect and Prospect. *Andean Past* 3:5–42.

Moseley, Michael E., and Robert A. Feldman

1988 Fishing, Farming, and the Foundations of Andean Civilisation. In *The Archaeology of Prehistoric Coastlines*, edited by Geoff Bailey and John Parkington, pp. 125–134. Cambridge University Press, Cambridge.

Moseley, Michael E., and Gordon R. Willey

1973 Áspero, Peru: A Reexamination of the Site and Its Implications. *American Antiquity* 38:452–468.

NIU News

2001 Archaeologists Say Peru was Home to the Americas' Oldest Pyramids, Cities. Press release, April 26. Northern Illinois University Office of Public Affairs, DeKalb, IL.

Osborn, Alan J.

1977a Prehistoric Utilization of Marine Resources in Coastal Peru: How Much Do We Understand? Paper presented at the 76th Annual Meeting of the American Anthropological Association, Houston.

1977b Strandloopers, Mermaids and Other Fairy Tales: Ecological Determinants of Marine Resource Utilization—the Peruvian Case. In *For Theory Building in Archaeology*, edited by Lewis R. Binford, pp. 157–205. Academic Press, New York.

Parsons, Mary H.

1970 Preceramic Subsistence on the Peruvian Coast. *American Antiquity* 35(3):292–304.

Pearsall, Deborah M.

2003 Plant Food Resources of the Ecuadorian Formative: An Overview and Comparison to the Central Andes. In *Archaeology of Formative Ecuador*, edited by J. Scott Raymond and Richard L. Burger, pp. 213–257. Dumbarton Oaks, Washington, DC.

Pozorski, Shelia G., and Thomas G. Pozorski

1987 *Early Settlement and Subsistence in the Casma Valley, Peru.* University of Iowa Press, Iowa City.

Quilter, Jeffrey

1985 Architecture and Chronology at El Paraíso, Peru. *Journal of Field Archaeology* 12:279–297.

Quilter, Jeffrey, Bernardino Ojeda E., Deborah M. Pearsall, Daniel H. Sandweiss, John G. Jones, and Elizabeth S. Wing

1991 Subsistence Economy of El Paraíso, an Early Peruvian Site. *Science* 251(4991):277–283.

Raymond, Scott

1981 The Maritime Foundations of Andean Civilization: A Reconsideration of the Evidence. *American Antiquity* 46:806–821.

Sandweiss, Daniel H., and Michael E. Moseley

2001 Amplifying Importance of New Research in Peru. *Science* 294:1651–1652.

Shady Solís, Ruth

n.d. Caral. http://museoarqueologiasanmarcos.perucultural.org.pe/public.htm (retrieved October 4, 2004).

Shady Solís, Ruth, Jonathan Haas, and Winifred Creamer

2001 Dating Caral, a Preceramic Site in the Supe Valley on the Central Coast of Peru. *Science* 292:723–726.

Ugent, Donald, Shelia Pozorski, and Thomas Pozorski

1981 Prehistoric Remains of the Sweet Potato from the Casma Valley of Peru. *Phytologia* 49(5):401-415.

1982 Archaeological Potato Tuber Remains from the Casma Valley of Peru. *Economic Botany* 36(2): 182–192.

1984 New Evidence for Ancient Cultivation of *Canna edulis* in Peru. *Economic Botany* 38(4):417–432.

Willey, Gordon R., and John M. Corbett

1954 *Early Ancon and Early Supe Culture: Chavín Horizon Sites of the Central Peruvian Coast.* Columbia University Studies in Archaeology and Ethnology, no. 3. Columbia University, New York.

Williams, Carlos

1972 La difusión de los pozos ceremoniales en la costa peruana. *Apuntes Arqueológicos* 2:1–9. Lima.

1985 A Scheme for the Early Monumental Architecture of the Central Coast of Peru. In *Early Ceremonial Architecture in the Andes*, edited by Christopher B. Donnan, pp. 227–240. Dumbarton Oaks, Washington, DC.

Wilson, David

1981 Of Maize and Men: A Critique of the Maritime Hypothesis of State Origins on the Coast of Peru. *American Anthropologist* 83:93–120.

CHAPTER 7

CARAL-SUPE Y SU ENTORNO NATURAL Y SOCIAL EN LOS ORÍGENES DE LA CIVILIZACIÓN

RUTH SHADY SOLÍS

. . . y oyo a sus antiguos y en esta fe estan todos los indios que el dicho ídolo Guari pírco las chacras y saco las sequias y por estos le dan todo culto y veneración y le hacían ofrendas de día y de noche.

Pierre Duviols, 1986

PARA COMPRENDER EL DESARROLLO de Caral es necesario conocer las condiciones naturales y sociales del ámbito donde se formó la civilización más antigua de América, el mayor, a nivel del área nor-central del Perú, en el que ha sido identificado un conjunto de asentamientos del período Arcaico Tardío; y el inmediato, en el valle de Supe, en relación con los otros sitios pertenecientes al mismo período. Con este marco referencial, del área y del valle, adquieren significación y verdadera dimensión los resultados de la investigación en Caral, en los aspectos social, económico y político, que presentamos en este artículo.

Desde que iniciamos las investigaciones en el valle de Supe en 1994 y, posteriormente, a partir de 1996 las excavaciones en Caral,[1] éstas han continuado en forma ininterrumpida, con la metodología de excavaciones en área y de análisis multidisciplinario en gabinete. Se han hecho estudios del entorno y se han comparado los resultados de Caral con los de otros asentamientos del valle y del área en esa etapa del desarrollo.

Diversos aspectos del sistema social, modos de vida y cultura, inferidos a partir de los trabajos en Caral, y de su vinculación con otros asentamientos coetáneos, han venido siendo presentados desde 1997 en sucesivas publicaciones y a través de exposiciones y muestras museológicas (Shady 1997–2004). Estos resultados han sido enriquecidos con las investigaciones que simultáneamente hemos emprendido, con similar metodología, en otros cinco asentamientos del valle de Supe (Chupacigarro, Miraya, Lurihuasi, Allpacoto y Áspero), además de Vichama en el valle de Huaura; disponemos, así, de la información de cuatro asentamientos y contamos con mejor sustento para aproximarnos al conocimiento de la sociedad de Supe en los albores de la civilización.

LOS ORÍGENES DE LA CIVILIZACIÓN: NUESTROS PLANTEAMIENTOS

Los resultados obtenidos hasta la fecha nos permiten plantear que la sociedad de Supe vivió en asentamientos nucleados de diversos tamaños, distribuidos a lo largo del valle, desde el litoral hasta la terminación del valle medio; sustentados por una economía autosuficiente; cada uno con sus respectivas autoridades pero articulados en un sistema, que fomentó una dinámica esfera de interacción supralocal y contactos interregionales a larga distancia así como la formación de un gobierno centralizado.

Si bien los 20 asentamientos, que hemos reconocido en Supe del Arcaico Tardío, varían en cuanto a su extensión, número y tamaño o complejidad de sus componentes arquitectónicos (Shady, Dolorier, et al. 2000), comparten, por otro lado, características en la composición de las construcciones y en el diseño arquitectónico de algunas edificaciones. Todos los asentamientos tienen algún tipo de construcción pública, en particular un edificio anexado a una plaza circular hundida, en asociación con plataformas y conjuntos residenciales.

Es en base a los rasgos compartidos y a las diferencias entre los asentamientos que sustentamos: (1) La población del valle residía en asentamientos nucleados con su respectivo territorio de producción y su propio gobierno y autoridades. Esta forma de organización social y territorial, "pachaca", continuaría en el área a lo largo de la historia prehispánica. (2) Pero, asimismo, se constata que, alrededor de los 2600 a.C., los ocupantes de estos asentamientos se integraron en un sistema social organizado y jerarquizado, con una "zona central" en el valle medio inferior donde Caral habría sido el eje de irradiación social y cultural más destacado de la época.

A nivel del área norcentral, la zona de influencia directa de Caral comprendió el espacio entre el valle del río Santa por el norte y el valle del río Chillón por el sur, tanto en las regiones de costa como de sierra y selva andina. La información cultural y temporal disponible sugiere que la influencia del sistema social de Supe fue avanzando progresivamente, primero a las poblaciones de los valles inmediatos, del Pativilca, Fortaleza y Huaura; pero hacia los 2200 a.C. ya había alcanzado por el sur a los constructores del Paraíso en el valle del Chillón. Cabe señalar, sin embargo, que los asentamientos de esta zona (con excepción del Paraíso, que se construye al final del período) y de toda el área norcentral se diferencian de los Caral-Supe en cuanto a su menor extensión o tamaño, al menor número de componentes arquitectónicos, complejidad y volumen constructivo, además de los rasgos propios de los respectivos modos de vida y culturas de sus habitantes; lo primero indicaría un mayor desarrollo en "la zona central" de Caral, donde habría estado la sede más destacada del sistema social de Supe y de mayor prestigio en el área norcentral en los albores de la civilización.

Sobre la base de los hallazgos en los asentamientos del Arcaico Tardío del área de algunos elementos culturales compartidos ya se había reconocido que ellos participaron en una esfera de interacción, que fue denominada "tradición Kotosh" (Burger y Salazar 1980), pero no se tenían evidencias suficientes para evaluar la magnitud y relevancia que ésta había alcanzado.

Los resultados que se van obteniendo de las investigaciones en Caral indican, asimismo, que la sociedad de Supe produjo conocimientos avanzados en ciencia y tecnología; construyó las primeras ciudades planificadas del Nuevo Mundo y sentó las bases estructurales de lo que sería el sistema social y de gobierno en los Andes Centrales.

La antigüedad de este proceso, entre 2900 y 2000 a.C., está sustentada en los 73 fechados radiocarbónicos obtenidos en Caral, Chupacigarro, Miraya y Lurihuasi; y se refuerza al señalar, comparativamente, que los asentamientos del valle de Supe estuvieron habitados casi al mismo tiempo que las ciudades sumerias de Mesopotamia o cuando se construyó la pirámide de Sakara o las posteriores pirámides de Giza en Egipto. Pero a diferencia de las sociedades del Viejo Mundo, como Mesopotamia, Egipto e India, que tuvieron entre ellas relaciones de intercambio de bienes y conocimientos, que les permitieron aprovechar de las experiencias del conjunto, el proceso peruano se dio en total aislamiento no sólo de otras sociedades del viejo continente sino también del Nuevo Mundo, pues se adelantó en, por lo menos, 1500 años al de Mesoamérica, el otro centro de civilización prístina de América.

PUEBLOS Y CULTURAS DEL ÁREA NORCENTRAL Y SU MAYOR DESARROLLO

Aún cuando el poblamiento del territorio del Perú se produjo alrededor de los 12,000 años a.C. con actividades de apropiación de los recursos naturales en los diversos parajes de la costa y sierra de los Andes, como indican las evidencias arqueológicas de Lauricocha, Toquepala, Junín, en la sierra, o de Paiján, en los desiertos del litoral occidental, hubo distintos procesos culturales en relación con las condiciones naturales del medio habitado, que son muy diversas en los Andes Centrales. Alrededor de los 8000 años a.C. se habían conformado asentamientos sedentarios de pequeñas aglomeraciones, cuyas actividades de subsistencia ya incluían a la agricultura. Se ha identificado a cazadores-agricultores en las zonas altoandinas; agricultores-cazadores en los valles de la sierra; pescadores, recolectores de moluscos y agricultores en la costa, etc. (Shady 1995). Aparte de poseer modos de vida y culturas distintivos, estas poblaciones tenían diferentes ritmos de desarrollo. Hacia los 5000 años a.C. sólo en una parte del Perú, en el área norcentral, confluyeron condiciones sociales, culturales y naturales para el surgimiento de la civilización.

Los nueve valles de la vertiente occidental del área (Santa, Casma, Huarmey, Fortaleza, Pativilca, Supe,

Huaura, Chancay y Chillón), están geográficamente conectados entre si a través de la meseta altoandina de donde nacen sus respectivos ríos. La misma meseta los vincula también hacia el oriente con las cuencas del Marañón y el Huallaga, puertas de ingreso a la Amazonía. En esta área, así geográficamente articulada, que comprende regiones de costa, sierra y selva andina, han sido identificados asentamientos de variadas dimensiones con arquitectura pública y doméstica:

En la costa: El Paraíso en el valle del Chillón (Quilter et al. 1991), Río Seco en el litoral de Chancay (Wendt 1964), Bandurria en el litoral de Huaura (Fung 1988), Áspero en el litoral de Supe (Feldman 1980), Caral y otros en el valle de Supe (Shady 1997a, 2000a, b; Shady y Leyva 2003), Las Haldas en el litoral de Casma. En la sierra: La Galgada en el Tablachaca-Santa (Grieder et al. 1988), Huaricoto en el Callejón de Huaylas (Burger y Salazar-Burger 1980). En la selva andina: Kotosh en la cuenca del Huallaga (Izumi y Sono 1963; Izumi y Terada 1972) y Piruro en la cuenca del Marañón (Bonnier y Rozenberg 1988). La información arqueológica disponible permite inferir que ellos no eran exclusivamente santuarios o centros religiosos sino más bien asentamientos organizados con edificaciones residenciales y públicas, donde se realizaban actividades domésticas, económicas, administrativas, políticas, religiosas, sociales y culturales. La conjunción en estos asentamientos de unidades domésticas con edificios públicos para la realización de múltiples funciones revela autosuficiencia, cierta especialización laboral y un ordenamiento político. Ellos estuvieron sustentados en la producción de excedentes de sus habitantes, todo lo cual hizo posible, asimismo, su participación en las redes de interacción que se tendieron en el área entre regiones y entre cuencas. Compartieron productos, bienes manufacturados, elementos arquitectónicos, y conocimientos y participaron en determinadas ceremonias religiosas y ritos. La ubicación geográfica de Caral-Supe en el medio de esta área con producciones diversas, comunicada por el mar en la costa, por la meseta altoandina en la sierra y por los ríos de la Amazonía en la selva y articulada interregionalmente en dirección vertical en cortas distancias; así como su capacidad de acumulación de excedentes proveniente de una economía complementaria agrícola-pesquera, fueron estratégicas para las interacciones con poblaciones asentadas en zonas ecológicas diferentes, también con producciones excedentarias, poseedoras de experiencias adaptativas diversas así como de bienes distintivos.

Por todo lo indicado, consideramos que la creciente complejización social de Supe debe ser tratada en el marco de las condiciones naturales descritas para el área nor-central y de la situación social de las poblaciones que habitaban en las varias regiones y cuencas durante el Arcaico Tardío: en la región costeña; en la región adyacente de la sierra, en el Callejón de Huaylas y el Callejón de Conchucos; y en las vertientes orientales, en las cuencas del Marañón y del Huallaga (Figura 7.1a).

Entre estas sociedades, la de Supe pudo sintetizar en su beneficio los logros de experiencias adaptativas diferentes y supo aprovechar el excedente productivo del área. Los 20 asentamientos con arquitectura pública identificados a lo largo de 45 km en el valle de Supe, un valle de pequeña extensión, con escasas tierras y un río de régimen irregular, seco la mayor parte del año, difícilmente hubieran sido construidos sobre la base de la productividad obtenida únicamente por sus habitantes. La cuantiosa inversión de trabajo en obras monumentales y su permanente remodelación habrían sido sustentadas por la producción de las poblaciones de los otros valles del área, que las autoridades políticas del valle supieron captar. La extensión de los asentamientos principales de Supe, entre 40 y 80 ha frente a las 11 ó 13 ha de los asentamientos más extensos de los otros valles, expresa una marcada diferencia en cuanto a la capacidad de manejo económico e inversión de sus ocupantes.

ANTECEDENTES DE LA INVESTIGACIÓN

A pesar de su cercanía a Lima, la ciudad capital del Perú, y de conocerse que Supe contenía numerosos sitios arqueológicos, este valle no había sido suficientemente investigado, quizás porque se había asumido sin mayores evidencias que los espectaculares volúmenes arquitectónicos estaban afiliados culturalmente al período Formativo, del cual ya se tenía información proveniente de valles vecinos. Debido a su complejidad arquitectónica, estos sitios no habían sido correlacionados con los resultados obtenidos desde la década de los setenta en Áspero, en Puerto Supe, que ya era conocido en el medio arqueológico por su arquitectura y antigüedad desde las investigaciones de Feldman y los sugerentes planteamientos de Moseley (1975).

Previamente, en 1940, Kosok en un importante estudio sobre diversos valles de la costa había visitado el de Supe y descrito algunos aspectos de Caral, incluyendo una impactante foto aérea sobre un sector

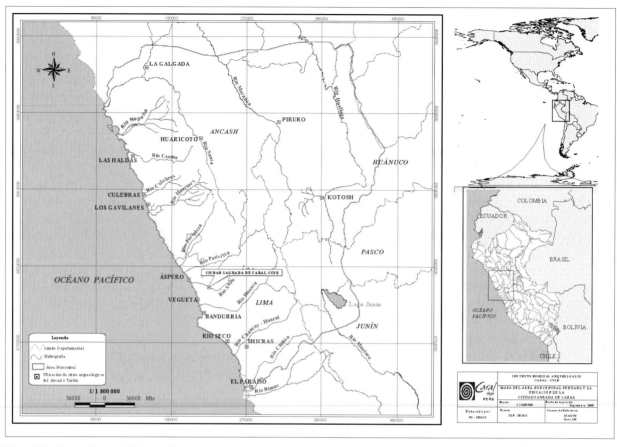

Figura 7.1a. Asentamientos del Arcaico Tardío en cuencas y regiones de costa, sierra y selva andina del área norcentral del Perú. (© Proyecto Especial Arqueológico Caral-Supe.)

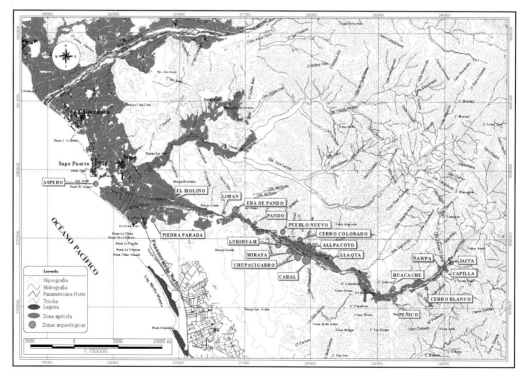

Figura 7.1b. Asentamientos del Arcaico Tardío identificados en el valle de Supe. (© Proyecto Especial Arqueológico Caral-Supe.)

de la ciudad. Cabe resaltar en este autor su plantea-miento pionero, no suficientemente valorado, acerca del destacado desarrollo alcanzado por las poblaciones costeñas (Kosok 1965:219). Por esos años, en 1941, Áspero fue reconocido por Willey y Corbett, quienes lo correlacionaron con los sitios Formativos de El Faro y Ancón (Willey y Corbett 1954:21–23); años después, en 1971, Willey y Moseley revisitaron Áspero, entre varios sitios de la costa, que por esos años ya habían sido identificados como pertenecientes al Arcaico Tardío, como Unidad I en el valle de Asia y Río Seco de León en Chancay. Esta información les permitió identificar los montículos con plataformas escalonadas, y sugerir que ellos podían pertenecer al Arcaico Tardío o Precerámico. Pero sólo a partir de las excavaciones de Feldman en ese mismo año en Áspero se obtuvo información sobre el contenido cultural y fechados para ubicar a este sitio en el período Arcaico Tardío del proceso cultural peruano. El autor atribuyó la arqui-tectura monumental de Aspero al trabajo corporativo de varias unidades domésticas, bajo la coordinación de un grupo dirigente; organización a la que caracterizó como jefatura corporativa. Sin embargo, no hubo una perspectiva del sitio como conjunto, no se excavaron las unidades domésticas y, tampoco, fue vinculado con los otros asentamientos del valle de Supe, que mostraban mayor extensión y complejidad arquitectónica (Feldman 1980, 1985, 1987, 1992). Por ello, en las tres décadas siguientes no destacó la importancia de Supe y del período Arcaico Tardío en la formación de la civiliza-ción, aún cuando hubo las sugerentes interpretaciones de Moseley sobre la importancia del recurso marino, que suscitó la polémica en torno al rol que habían tenido el recurso marino y la actividad pesquera frente a la actividad agrícola en el desarrollo civilizatorio andino (Moseley 1975; Raymond 1981; Wilson 1981).

Otras intervenciones aportaron información sobre algunos aspectos de la arqueología del valle de Supe, como los cateos y trincheras excavados en Caral por Engel (1987:82); el catastro de casi un centenar de sitios arqueológicos pertenecientes a diversos períodos, efec-tuado por Williams y Merino (1979) o los sugestivos estudios y sondeos realizados por Zechenter (1988) en Supe, al señalar las diferencias estacionales y de recursos naturales entre las ecozonas y sugerir un patrón de subsistencia complejo para los períodos Arcaico Tardío y Formativo, basado en la explotación de un conjunto diverso de recursos. Más recientemente, la prospección arqueológica conducida por nosotros a lo largo del valle bajo y medio de Supe en 1994–1995 (Shady 1995)

identificó los asentamientos pertenecientes al Arcaico Tardío, determinó sus características, parecidos y dife-rencias y planteó interpretaciones preliminares sobre el patrón de asentamiento y el sistema social. Pero ninguna de estas aproximaciones tuvo las evidencias contextua-lizadas para evaluar la importancia y significación de la sociedad de Supe y del período Arcaico Tardío en los orígenes de la civilización hasta que comenzamos las excavaciones en Caral en 1996 (Shady 1997a, b).

LA INVESTIGACIÓN ARQUEOLÓGICA EN SUPE Y LA ELECCIÓN DE CARAL

Si bien en 1994 iniciamos la investigación en el valle de Supe mediante una prospección arqueológica y dos años después habíamos identificado la recurrencia de determinados rasgos arquitectónicos en, por lo menos, 20 asentamientos, ubicados a lo largo del valle (Shady, Dolorier, et al. 2000; Shady y Leyva 2003:51–91), no teníamos indicadores arqueológicos para su afiliación cultural y temporal. Por eso, en 1996 decidimos efectuar excavaciones en uno de esos asentamientos y elegimos Caral, en base a cinco criterios: la ausencia de alfarería en la superficie del sitio, la extensión de éste, su diversidad arquitectónica con varios conjuntos domésticos y edificios públicos, la distribución ordenada de los edificios que indicaba una previa organización espacial y la monumentalidad de por lo menos siete construcciones elevadas de las 32 que se apreciaban en el sitio. Después de dos meses de trabajo en seis sectores diferentes del asentamiento tuvimos las evidencias arqueológicas suficientes para evaluar que estábamos en un sitio del Arcaico Tardío, a pesar de su complejidad arquitectónica (Shady 1997a, b); y que estos resultados cambiaban los conocimientos que hasta entonces se tenían sobre los orígenes de la civilización.

EL TERRITORIO HABITADO POR LA SOCIEDAD DE SUPE

El valle de Supe está en el centro del área norcentral del Perú, en las vertientes occidentales por donde dis-curre el río desde sus nacientes hasta su desembocadura en el Océano Pacífico, luego de un recorrido de 92 km de longitud. A lo largo de su curso, el río cambia abruptamente de dirección, primero va de noreste a suroeste desde sus nacientes hasta La Empedrada en el valle medio superior, desde allí enrumba al noroeste hasta el mar. El valle es estrecho, de 1.5 km de ancho, limitado por la cadena de cerros que lo encierra por sectores y está conformado por depósitos aluviales de arena, arcillas, limos, gravas y conglomerados. El río Supe tiene un régimen muy irregular con marcadas diferencias entre sus descargas, una máxima de 49,44 m³/seg (que en algunos años puede llegar a 60 m³/seg) y una media anual de 1,52 m³/seg; pero, en cambio, cuenta con permanente agua subterránea y con los ríos Pativilca y Fortaleza forma un sistema de valles interrelacionados.

Los asentamientos humanos del Arcaico Tardío se encuentran en la mitad inferior baja del valle de Supe, espacio donde se distinguen cuatro zonas: litoral y lomas; valle bajo; valle medio inferior y valle medio superior, cada una separada de las otras por condiciones geográficas y con sus respectivos recursos.

Asentamientos Humanos y Manejo del Valle de Supe Durante el Arcaico Tardío

A pesar de las condiciones del valle de Supe, escasas tierras y régimen irregular del río, hubo durante el Arcaico Tardío un mínimo de 20 asentamientos poblacionales, entre el litoral y los primeros 45 km. Todos estos sitios contienen conjuntos residenciales y también edificios públicos; y más del 50% posee alguna obra de arquitectura monumental (Figura 7.1b). En base al estudio comparativo de los asentamientos reconocidos mediante la prospección de superficie y de las excavaciones que venimos realizando en cuatro de ellos: Caral, Chupacigarro, Miraya y Lurihuasi, planteamos la siguiente forma de asentamiento y de organización social:

1. *Distribución de los asentamientos en el valle.* Los asentamientos identificados ocupan cuatro zonas ecológicas: uno en el *litoral* (1859,75 ha), Áspero; dos en el *valle bajo* (9214,5 ha), uno en la margen derecha, El Molino y uno en la margen izquierda, Piedra Parada; diez en el *valle medio inferior* (8472 ha), seis en la margen derecha, Limán, Era de Pando, Pando, Pueblo Nuevo, Cerro Colorado, e Allpacoto y cuatro en la margen izquierda, Lurihuasi, Miraya, Chupacigarro y Caral; cinco en el *valle medio superior* (7334,5 ha), cuatro en la margen izquierda, Peñico, Cerro Blanco, Capilla y Jaiva y uno en la margen derecha, Huacache. Como se puede apreciar, la zona del valle medio inferior, que no es la más extensa, concentra, sin embargo, el mayor número

de asentamientos, diez de un total de dieciocho. Es, además, interesante señalar un aparente ordenamiento en la ubicación de los asentamientos; están en número similar en ambas márgenes del río, nueve en la margen derecha y nueve en la margen izquierda; distribución que respondería a un patrón dual, como también se da en el interior de cada uno de los sitios que estamos excavando.

2. *Espacio ocupado.* Los asentamientos poblacionales fueron ubicados en las terrazas de los conos de deyección perpendiculares al valle; éste fue reservado para los campos de cultivo. Cada asentamiento incluía el espacio construido, en el cual ubicaban las viviendas y los edificios públicos, y la porción de tierras del fondo del valle y de las terrazas aluviales, demarcada por canales de riego principales. Es posible que la distribución del agua ya estuviera regulada.

3. *Extensión de los asentamientos.* Los asentamientos varían en tamaño: (a) de 80 a 55 ha: Era de Pando (79,74), Caral (66,0), y Pueblo Nuevo (55,01); (b) de 45 a 30 ha: Miraya (43,0), Lurihuasi (37,8), Chupacigarro (37,4), y Piedra Parada (33,5); (c) de 25 a 15 ha: Allpacoto (23,10), Peñico (22,05), y Áspero (15,0); (d) de 10 a 5 ha: Huacache (7,59), El Molino (6,96), y Jaiva (4,20); (e) de menos de 5 ha: Pando (1,95), Cerro Colorado (0,98), Cerro Blanco (0,80), Limán (0,48), y Capilla (0,16). De ellos, tres asentamientos destacan por su extensión: Era de Pando, Caral y Pueblo Nuevo, con el 46,07% del área total construida en el valle; le siguen en segundo lugar otros cuatro asentamientos: Miraya, Lurihuasi, Chupacigarro y Piedra Parada con el 34,82% de la superficie total construida. Estos dos grupos tienen el 80,89% del área construida. Es interesante que ambos se ubican mayormente en la zona media inferior. Los otros tres grupos ocupan el 13,80%, 4,30% y 1%, respectivamente. De la comparación se infiere que 11 asentamientos de los 18 tienen sólo un 19,11% del área construida. Estos resultados indican una distinción marcada entre los asentamientos; sugerimos que ella se debería a diferencias socioeconómicas, funcionales y de jerarquía social significativas entre los pobladores de las cinco clases de asentamientos (Tabla 7.1).

4. *Inversión de trabajo en las construcciones públicas.* El cálculo realizado sobre la cantidad y volumen de las estructuras de cada asentamiento permite hacer el siguiente ordenamiento: grupo 1: Pueblo Nuevo (28,99%), y Caral (27,31%); grupo 2: Miraya (12,85%), Era de Pando (8,54%), y Lurihuasi (7,04%); grupo 3: Allpacoto (3,76%), Peñico (3,12%), y El Molino (2,99%); grupo 4: Piedra Parada (1,67%), y Áspero

Tabla 7.1. Ordenamiento de los asentamientos por las hectáreas.

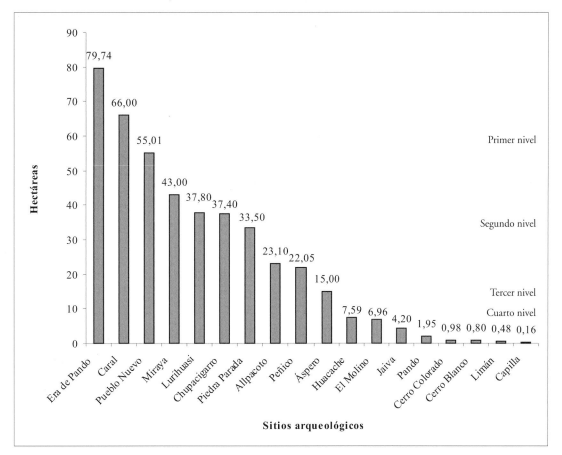

(1,64%); grupo 5: Chupacigarro (0,87%), y Huacache (0,57%); grupo 6: Cerro Blanco (0,30%), Cerro Colorado (0,12%), Jaiva (0,10%), Pando (0,07%), Limán (0,05%), y Capilla (0,001%). Esta información indica que el grupo 1 donde se encuentran Caral y Pueblo Nuevo concentra el 56,30% del total de fuerza de trabajo invertida. Le sigue el grupo 2, integrado por Miraya, Era de Pando y Lurihuasi, con una inversión de 28,43% del total, que representa la mitad del grupo anterior. El tercer y cuarto grupos, compuesto por cinco asentamientos, detentan el 13,18% del total. Es decir una cuarta parte del trabajo invertido en el primer grupo de asentamientos. Finalmente, la diferencia es muy notoria entre aquellos y los grupos quinto y sexto pues éstos, a pesar de estar integrados por ocho asentamientos, apenas exhiben el 2,08% del total de la fuerza de trabajo invertida. Es importante resaltar la concentración de más de la mitad del total de fuerza de trabajo invertida en sólo dos asentamientos: Pueblo Nuevo y Caral. El segundo grupo de asentamientos representa un poco más de la cuarta parte del total de la fuerza de trabajo invertida. Entre estos dos grupos

se hallan los cinco principales asentamientos del valle de Supe: Caral, Pueblo Nuevo, Miraya, Lurihuasi, e Era de Pando, de los cuales destacan Caral y Pueblo Nuevo, tanto por su extensión y complejidad como por la fuerza de trabajo invertida en sus construcciones. Es interesante que ambos se encuentran en el valle medio inferior, en la margen izquierda y derecha, respectivamente.

5. *Zona de ubicación*. Los indicadores señalan que los centros urbanos más extensos y complejos se encuentran concentrados en el valle medio inferior; ésta fue la zona central de mayor poder, bienestar y prestigio de la sociedad de Supe. A lo largo de unos 6 km de esta zona se encuentran siete asentamientos con arquitectura monumental, tres en la margen derecha: Pueblo Nuevo, Cerro Colorado y Allpacoto, y otros cuatro en la margen izquierda: Lurihuasi, Miraya, Chupacigarro y Caral. Esta habría sido "la zona capital", justamente ubicada en un espacio estratégico para la comunicación con los valles laterales vecinos. De los siete asentamientos, cuatro pertenecen a los grupos A y B de mayor extensión, así como a los grupos 1 y 2 de

mayor inversión de trabajo. Esta zona es intermedia entre la zona del valle bajo y el litoral, proveedora de los recursos de mar, y la del valle medio superior, al este, donde se encuentra la otra concentración de asentamientos pero de menor extensión y monumentalidad fue el centro del sistema. Los del valle medio inferior se articulan con la parte alta de los otros valles vecinos y, en particular con la meseta altiplánica desde donde se facilita la interacción con habitantes de otros valles, en la amplia extensión del área norcentral.

6. *Comunicación.* Las distancias entre los asentamientos ubicados en las diferentes zonas del valle es de 7,5 a 10 km y en el interior de una misma zona es de 2,6 a 4 km, a excepción de la "zona capital" en el valle medio inferior donde la distancia entre asentamientos es de 1 a 2,6 km.

7. *Seguridad.* El valle medio inferior está encerrado por la misma configuración morfológica de la cordillera y esto le da un espacio controlable. Lo separa del valle bajo la conjunción de los cerros que forman una garganta a la altura del sitio denominado Limán, pasada la cual se abre otra vez el valle y después nuevamente es cerrado por otra conjunción de cerros alrededor del sitio de Las Minas. Entre ambas gargantas se halla "la zona capital" con sus asentamientos.

8. *Vías o rutas de intercambio.* Los asentamientos más extensos están cerca de vías de acceso a los valles vecinos, en quebradas que van en dirección perpendicular al valle. Los centros urbanos de la "zona central", ubicados en la margen derecha, se vinculan a través de la quebrada de Allpacoto con los valles de Pativilca y Fortaleza; y aquellos de la margen izquierda, como Caral, Chupacigarro y Lurihuasi salen a diversas zonas ecológicas de los valles de Huaura y de Chancay. Igualmente, en el valle medio superior tienen ubicación estratégica los centros urbanos de Peñico, para la articulación de la sierra de Supe y su entorno colindante con el valle de Huaura, y el centro de Huacache, para la comunicación entre las dos zonas del valle medio de Supe con los poblados de la sierra de Pativilca y Fortaleza. Hacia la costa, Era de Pando articulaba a los asentamientos del litoral y los valles bajos de Supe, Pativilca y Fortaleza; mientras que Piedra Parada lo hace con el valle bajo y el litoral de los valles de Supe y Huaura. Esta selección del territorio en relación con rutas de tránsito indica la importancia del intercambio entre poblaciones asentadas en zonas ecológicas con recursos y bienes diferenciados.

9. *Jerarquización.* El patrón de asentamientos de Supe no muestra un sistema de asentamientos que haga suponer un ordenamiento jerarquizado lineal como ha sido descrito para otras áreas del mundo bajo un sistema político integrado (Wright y Johnson 1975), como se esperaría en un Estado territorial. En base a los indicadores mencionados para Supe se puede distinguir en el valle dos concentraciones de asentamientos, una principal, de primera categoría, ubicada en el valle medio inferior y otra menor, con asentamientos mayormente de cuarta categoría, en el valle medio superior. Pero, además de estas dos concentraciones hay algunos otros asentamientos de segunda importancia, distribuidos en el valle bajo; y uno de tercera en el litoral. Se hace evidente que no sólo hay variables políticas que explican este ordenamiento sino sociales, económicas y de mercado.

Por otro lado, los rasgos arquitectónicos recurrentes y compartidos por la mayoría de sitios, aún cuando sean a diferentes escalas indican que ellos tenían determinadas funciones similares. Los asentamientos serían unidades sociales autosuficientes y multifuncionales, donde se efectuaban actividades políticas, administrativas y religiosas. Aún cuando mantuvieron esta identidad y funciones, los asentamientos habrían sido integrados, en un período medio, a un sistema económico complementario conducido por un Estado prístino. Un modelo intermedio entre las ciudades-estado y el estado territorial. Este modelo de organización se extendería en el Perú prehispánico y perduraría aún durante el imperio Inca.

Los rasgos arquitectónicos similares a los del valle de Supe, que se encuentran en los asentamientos de los valles de Pativilca y Fortaleza, indican que las poblaciones de los tres valles estuvieron estrechamente articuladas, tanto en la zona del valle bajo como en las del valle medio; no obstante, como se ha indicado, el valle de Supe contiene los asentamientos más extensos y complejos, y debió ser el asiento principal del poder y de mayor prestigio. Estos tres valles habrían constituido el territorio donde tuvo su directa aplicación el sistema social y político de Supe. Sin embargo, la influencia de esta civilización se extendió también a toda el área norcentral ya señalada.

LA CIUDAD SAGRADA DE CARAL

Caral, ubicada a 184 km al norte de Lima y a 23 km desde el litoral, está asentada sobre una terraza aluvial desértica, en el valle medio inferior de Supe, a 350 msntm. En esta zona, el río pasa casi a nivel del valle con peces y camarones en la temporada de lluvias en la sierra; estaba contenido en ambas márgenes por el monte ribereño, un paisaje de bosque enmarañado y casi inexpugnable con gran variedad arbórea y arbustiva, como sauce, caña brava, carrizo, cola de caballo, etc. y animales como venados, roedores y aves, del cual quedan pequeños relictos. Esta zona cuenta, además, con los espacios cultivables del fondo del valle, de 1 a 1,5 km de ancho; con las terrazas aluviales, pobladas con guarangos y otras especies, también cultivables mediante irrigación; y con las tierras inundadas u "oconales", donde crecen totoras y juncos. Si bien el río está seco en la mayor parte del año, esta zona del valle dispone de una rica napa freática, aprovechada en las actividades domésticas como también en la irrigación de los campos cultivados.

El espacio construido de Caral se encuentra, sin embargo, en un ambiente desértico, por encima del valle, a unos 25 m, rodeado de cerros rocosos y dunas, aislado de los campos de cultivo de los cuales lo separa un denso bosque de guarangos.

ASPECTOS SOCIALES Y CULTURALES DE LA CIUDAD

Caral ocupa unas 66 hectares y comprende una zona nuclear, con 32 estructuras públicas, además de varios conjuntos residenciales, y una zona en la periferia, que limita con las terrazas de guarango y el fondo del valle, donde se construyeron varios conjuntos de viviendas (Figura 7.2). La disposición de las estructuras arquitectónicas indica un ordenamiento espacial de acuerdo a un diseño planificado de la ciudad antes de su construcción. En éste se tuvieron en cuenta criterios importantes de la organización social, como los estratos sociales jerarquizados y las divisiones simbólicas de los linajes: matrilineales-patrilineales, originarios-advenedizos, reflejadas en dos mitades: alta y baja, derecha e izquierda. A estos criterios se le sumaron otros, astronómicos, asociados, también, con determinadas deidades del panteón religioso; y funcionales: políticos, administrativos, económicos, ocupacionales, residenciales y de mercado.

Si bien, no hay murallas defensivas en torno a la ciudad, éstas fueron construidas en el interior de ella para separar algunos edificios o recintos de acceso muy privado.

En el espacio del núcleo, las edificaciones están distribuidas en dos grandes mitades: Caral alto, donde se pueden apreciar los volúmenes piramidales más destacados, uno de ellos con una plaza circular hundida; y Caral bajo, una mitad con estructuras públicas de menores dimensiones, entre las que destaca, sin embargo, un edificio que tiene anexada la más grande plaza circular hundida de la ciudad. Esta organización espacial responde a la división dual tradicional andina de Hanan y Hurin.

La Mitad Alta de Caral

En la mitad alta de la ciudad todas las construcciones han sido ubicadas alrededor de un gran espacio abierto o plaza, que tuvo también funciones públicas, de tipo político, económico y manufacturero. Se pueden distinguir dos grandes subespacios: uno, al oeste, conformado por los conjuntos piramidales, que hemos denominado la Pirámide Mayor y su plaza circular, la Pirámide Central, la Pirámide de la Cantera y la Pirámide Menor (Figura 7.2); el otro hacia el este constituido por la Pirámide de la Galería y la Pirámide de la Huanca, con un monolito hincado en el espacio entre ambas (Figura 7.2). Además de las estructuras mencionadas se encuentra en el lado sur de esta mitad alta, a todo lo largo de la terraza que la separa de la mitad baja, un extenso conjunto residencial distribuido en forma ordenada en varios subconjuntos (sector A). Pero, también, cada una de las estructuras piramidales están asociadas a dos o tres residencias, ubicadas en su entorno (Figura 7.3). Un mausoleo saqueado se halla hacia la periferia, al este de la mitad alta (Shady y Gonzales 2000; Shady y Leyva 2003:229–235).

Por su ubicación, tamaño, volumen constructivo y por la asociación con la plaza circular destaca la Pirámide Mayor como el principal edificio público de la ciudad (sector E).

La Mitad Baja de Caral

En este ámbito de la ciudad la distribución de las construcciones es diferente a la otra mitad pues éstas se encuentran alineadas en un eje este-oeste sobre una terraza baja, pero las fachadas de los edificios ya excavados están en dirección a la mitad alta. Los edificios, en general, son de menores dimensiones y no se encuentran estructuras piramidales altas ni medianas sólo pequeñas pero tiene un conjunto arquitectónico especial, el denominado Templo del Anfiteatro, justamente por estar conectado a la plaza circular hundida más grande de la ciudad (sector L). Esta mitad también contiene un conjunto residencial (sector NN2), algunas unidades domésticas al lado de cada edificio público, talleres (sector K) y un mausoleo saqueado en la periferia sur.

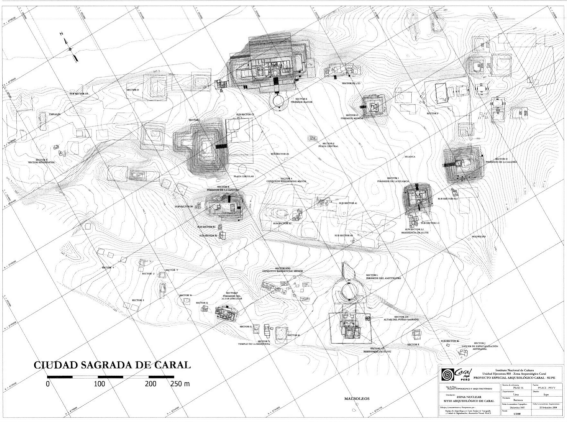

Figura 7.2. El espacio construido de Caral y su organización dual. (Foto por George Steinmetz.)

Figura 7.3. Dos unidades multifuncionales, vinculadas con los funcionarios de la "Pirámide de la Huanca." (© Proyecto Especial Arqueológico Caral-Supe.)

Concepción Arquitectónica de la Ciudad de Caral

Los 73 fechados radiocarbónicos indican que la ciudad estuvo funcionando a través de casi un milenio; y los edificios contienen, asimismo, las evidencias de esta prolongada ocupación con sucesivos períodos de construcción y remodelación. Se han distinguido grandes períodos de construcción y enterramiento de los edificios; pero, además, entre cada uno de estos períodos sucesivas fases de remodelación arquitectónica o de cambios menores, lo que hace un promedio de 20 a 25 fases constructivas por cada monumento o unidad doméstica. Cada período está diferenciado del anterior por algunos elementos del estilo y de la técnica constructiva, materiales y por el color de la pintura aplicada a las paredes. Se conservó, sin embargo, el diseño general, relacionado con la funcionalidad del edificio pero sobre todo con la memoria social que reforzaba la identidad cultural y le daba a la sociedad la percepción de continuidad y seguridad (Hodder y Cessford 2004). Sugerimos que las actividades relacionadas con los cambios mayores y con los cambios menores o remodelaciones estuvieron concordadas con ciclos astronómicos y con eventos sociales de gran significación.

Todas las edificaciones de la ciudad, por lo menos a partir del período Medio, alrededor de los 2600 a.C., hasta donde ha llegado nuestra investigación en la mayoría de edificaciones excavadas, muestran similares períodos constructivos y el mismo diseño, estilo, materiales y técnica arquitectónicos; por tanto, se puede inferir que estas obras debieron ser ejecutadas bajo un ordenamiento planificado, a cargo de autoridades, articuladas por un sistema político centralizado.

Han sido excavados los siguientes espacios construidos:

Los edificios públicos

En los períodos Medio y Tardío del largo funcionamiento de la ciudad se construyeron edificaciones piramidales de diverso tamaño, con determinada orientación estelar y bajo un similar diseño arquitectónico: un eje de ordenamiento interno, marcado por la escalera central, que conduce desde la base a la cima y la divide en dos cuerpos, cada uno de los cuales tiene una serie de terrazas superpuestas en forma escalonada, contenidas por muros de piedra. Hacia los lados del cuerpo principal se agregaron otros cuerpos o alas siguiendo un modelo escalonado, usando ángulos rectos y monolitos en las esquinas. Todos los edificios de la mitad alta presentan su fachada hacia el espacio abierto central.

Por la similitud en el diseño y en el estilo arquitectónico así como por el contexto de los materiales recuperados en los varios componentes excavados se ha inferido que estos edificios fueron construidos en los mismos períodos y que en sus ambientes se realizaron similares funciones múltiples: religiosas, políticas, económicas y administrativas. Sin embargo, las diferencias que ellos muestran entre si, en cuanto a ubicación dentro de la ciudad, extensión y volumen, cantidad de componentes y contextos especiales, podrían indicar distinciones de poder entre sus autoridades o gestores así como otras de índole social, que todavía no logramos probar. Estamos trabajando con la hipótesis que estos edificios sirvieron como un calendario urbano, vinculado con la celebración de fiestas, marcadas en relación con determinados astros, identificados con deidades del panteón supano y coordinado también con la conducción de las actividades laborales.

En las construcciones más destacadas utilizaron la piedra; otros edificios tuvieron recintos con paredes de palos y cañas entrabadas, construidas sobre las terrazas contenidas con muros de piedra. En el período Tardío se generalizó el uso de bloques de piedra cortados, entrabados con mortero de arcilla y "pachillas" o piedras de menores dimensiones. Las paredes llevaron, por igual, enlucidos de arcilla y pintura de color blanco, amarillo ocre, amarillo, rojo o blanco, según los períodos constructivos de la ciudad.

Las plazas públicas

En la ciudad se realizaron concentraciones públicas con diferentes participantes y con fines distintos en diversas clases de espacios: dos abiertos y otros dos construidos formalmente. Los dos espacios abiertos se encuentran en la mitad alta de la ciudad en asociación con los dos subconjuntos de edificios públicos, uno al oeste, el más grande, adonde confluyen todas las fachadas de los edificios (Figura 7.2); y otro al este, en relación con los dos edificios vinculados con un monolito, denominado "Huanca" (Figura 7.2). Ambos espacios muestran huellas de los postes de tiendas temporales y sirvieron para la instalación de ferias en algunos períodos del calendario festivo. Estas reuniones habrían sido masivas y acudirían grupos de comerciantes y peregrinos desde diferentes lugares del área norcentral.

En cambio, las plazas construidas están en cada una de las mitades de la ciudad y forman parte de la estructura arquitectónica más destacada de ellas: la Pirámide Mayor en la mitad alta y el Templo del Anfiteatro en la mitad baja. Tuvieron diferente uso, en concordancia con la función del edificio al que estaban asociadas.

La plaza circular de la Pirámide Mayor consiste en un espacio hundido, de 21,5 m de diámetro, delimitado por dos murallas circulares paralelas que formaron una plataforma circular elevada, a 3,0 m de altura del piso interno. Las escaleras de acceso están presididas cada una por dos grandes monolitos parados y uno central, de posición desconocida. La escalera norte de la plaza llega hasta la escalera central de la estructura piramidal (Figura 7.4) (Shady, Machacuay y Aramburu 2000).

La plaza circular hundida del Templo del Anfiteatro tiene dos escalinatas de acceso, ubicadas en el eje central, al que se alinea también el vano de ingreso al edificio piramidal. Se diferencia de la otra plaza por sus mayores dimensiones, 30 m de diámetro; carece de los monolitos pero en cambio se recuperó de ella, en el lado suroeste superior un conjunto de 32 flautas; en el lado Este un conjunto de 38 cornetas; y del centro de la plaza varias vasijas de mate, principalmente botellas pequeñas. Presenta, además, una gradería semicircular en la mitad superior (Figuras 7.5, 7.6).

Estas dos plazas comparten rasgos arquitectónicos, en la forma circular y hundida con dos escaleras de acceso alineadas en el eje del respectivo templo pero también muestran diferencias en cuanto a ubicación, dimensiones, algunos elementos formales y contextos. Se puede inferir que en ellas se realizaron actividades ceremoniales relacionadas con la de los edificios a los que estuvieron anexadas.

Las unidades residenciales multifuncionales

En la ciudad hay varios sectores residenciales, que contienen conglomerados de unidades domésticas; éstos varían en cuanto a ubicación, contexto ambiental, dimensiones, técnica y materiales constructivos; y, al igual que los edificios públicos muestran sucesivos cambios a través del tiempo. En el período antiguo las paredes tuvieron soportes de madera entretejidos con caña brava (*Gynerium sagitattum*), revestidos con argamasa de barro y arcilla, pintadas; en el período Tardío fueron construidas con piedras cortadas de granodiorita. En los lados externos de las viviendas se depositaron los desechos domésticos; en el lado posterior están las piedras quemadas y los hoyos donde se cocieron alimentos bajo la modalidad de "pachamanca" o de piedras calientes. Las unidades residenciales comparten una serie de componentes y en ellas se efectuaban actividades tanto domésticas como de manufactura, sociales y rituales.

Hemos distinguido las siguientes clases de unidades residenciales:

1. El Conjunto residencial Mayor, conglomerado de unidades domésticas, dispuesto en un ordenamiento espacial en la mitad alta de la ciudad, subdividido en subconjuntos, separados entre si por espacios abiertos, todavía no bien definidos. Las fachadas están dirigidas hacia los edificios públicos (sector A).

2. El Conjunto residencial Menor, de la mitad baja de la ciudad, acondicionado sobre una terraza aluvial al norte de los edificios públicos. El tamaño de las viviendas es comparativamente más reducido que en el conjunto residencial de la mitad alta de la ciudad, de la cual se diferencia también por las menores dimensiones del conglomerado. Esto permite interpretar que sus ocupantes constituían un grupo más reducido y tenían un estatus de menor jerarquía que los habitantes de la mitad alta (sector NN2).

3. El Conjunto residencial de la Periferia está conformado por varios subconjuntos o islotes ubicados a lo largo de la terraza que colinda con el valle. Las unidades domésticas son más pequeñas y su construcción se adecuó a la topografía del lugar. El material utilizado es muy similar al de los otros sectores. Por su ubicación y su menor tamaño y formalidad se puede interpretar que sus ocupantes pertenecieron al estrato social de menor estatus, quienes constituyeron la fuerza laboral más importante de la ciudad (sector X).

4. Las unidades residenciales de elite se encuentran en torno a cada uno de los edificios públicos con los cuales estuvieron vinculados y, aunque muestran un tamaño variado, en general son de mayores dimensiones que las unidades domésticas de los otros sectores. Por la ubicación, el tamaño, el material constructivo utilizado y el contenido, se ha interpretado que estas viviendas pertenecieron a un grupo social de mayor estatus, relacionado con el funcionamiento de los edificios piramidales.

TALLERES DE ESPECIALIZACIÓN ARTESANAL

Se han identificado dos en el extremo este de la mitad baja de la ciudad. Excavamos uno, conformado por tres recintos cuadrangulares. En los pisos se hallaron pequeñas oquedades selladas con una capa de arcilla, que contenían cuentas de crisocola, cuarzo lechoso, cristal de roca, *Spondylus* y opérculos. Junto a ellas se

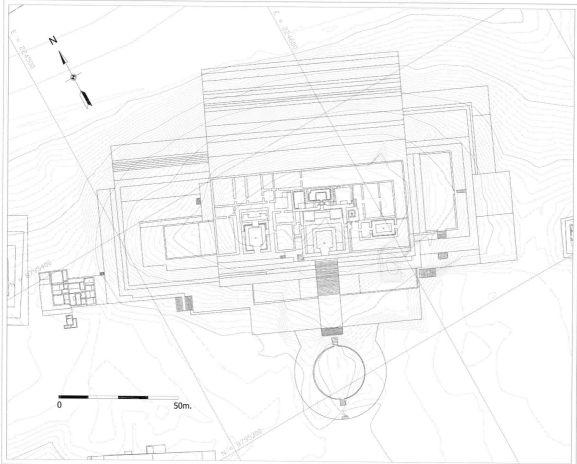

Figura 7.4. El complejo arquitectónico de la Pirámide Mayor y su plaza circular. (© Proyecto Especial Arqueológico Caral-Supe.)

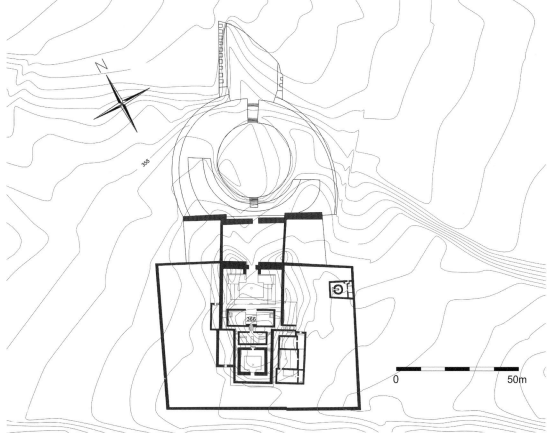

Figura 7.5. El complejo arquitectónico del "Templo del Anfiteatro." (Foto por by Walter Wust.)

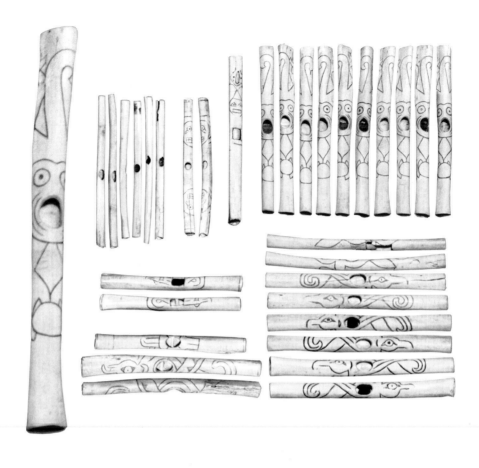

a.

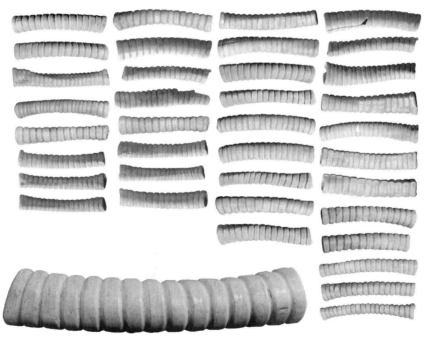

b.

Figura 7.6. Dos conjuntos musicales: a, flautas traversas; b, cornetas. (© Proyecto Especial Arqueológico Caral-Supe.)

encontraron desechos de talla así como herramientas de piedra y hueso. Estos recintos eran usados como talleres de producción artesanal para el suministro de artículos suntuarios (Figura 7.7).

SISTEMA ECONÓMICO DE LA SOCIEDAD DE SUPE

Se ha recuperado en Caral ingentes cantidades de pescados y moluscos no obstante su distancia al mar, entre 23 y 25 km. Predominan: anchovetas (*Engraulis ringens*), sardinas (*Sardinops sagax*), machas (*Mesodesma donacium*) y choros (*Choromytilus chorus*) (Shady 2000; Shady y Leyva 2003:107–122; Béarez y Miranda 2003:123–132). La ausencia de redes o instrumentos de pesca en la ciudad sugiere la adquisición de tales productos por medio del intercambio con poblaciones del litoral, como sus coetáneas de Bandurria y Áspero (Supe), donde se han encontrado anzuelos y redes, y con las cuales comparte elementos culturales.

Por otro lado, la abundante presencia en Caral de semillas de algodón (*Gossypium barbadense*) indica el especial énfasis que los habitantes del valle pusieron en ese cultivo, cuya fibra era demandada por los pobladores del litoral para la confección de las redes de pesca y de ropa. En el valle también cultivaron mates (*Lagenaria siceraria*), para la manufactura de los flotadores de las redes de pesca y de cuencos y vasos; y, fundamentalmente, plantas destinadas a su alimentación, como calabazas y zapallos (*Cucurbita* spp.), frijol (*Phaseolus vulgaris*), pallar (*Phaseolus lunatus*), achira (*Canna edulis*), camote (*Ipomoea batatas*), yuca (*Manihot esculenta*), pajuro (*Erythrina edulis*), maní (*Arachis hypogaea*), palta (*Persea americana*), guayaba (*Psidium guajava*), pacae (*Inga feuillei*), lúcuma (*Pouteria lucuma*) y ají (*Capsicum frutescens*). Se ha recuperado, asimismo, plantas como palillo (*Campomanesia lineatifolia*), achiote (*Bixa orellana*), huayruro (*Ormosia* sp.), tutumo (*Crescentia cujete*) y lloque (*Kageneckia lanceolata*), probablemente llegadas de otras zonas; así como junco (*Schoenoplectus* sp.) y otras, recogidas de las zonas pantanosas del valle (Shady 1999b, 2000b). El maíz (*Zea mays*) aparece sólo en el período tardío y en poca cantidad (Shady 2006).

La información sobre el patrón de asentamiento y las evidencias recuperadas de las excavaciones, en particular en las unidades domésticas, indican que la población de Supe residía en asentamientos nucleados, "pachacas", distribuidos tanto en el litoral como en el valle, con acceso a los recursos de uno de los mares más productivos del planeta, a las tierras del valle, mayormente llanas, de fácil riego con aguas del río y de los manantiales, a las zonas de humedales y lomas, que son todavía extensas y a la flora y fauna del monte ribereño. En esas condiciones se desarrolló una economía productiva, internamente complementaria, agrícola-pesquera, articulada por el intercambio.

Los agricultores del valle producían plantas alimenticias e industriales, como camote, zapallo, frijol o algodón, mates y maderos; en cambio, los asentamientos de pescadores del litoral extraían preferentemente anchovetas y sardinas, que deshidrataban en grandes cantidades, además de moluscos y algas, entre otros. La productividad de ambos sectores económicos, la disponibilidad de excedentes y la interdependencia entre sus componentes ocupacionales: del algodón, mates y madera los pescadores para la confección de sus embarcaciones, redes de pesca, flotadores y remos, y de la proteína del recurso marino los agricultores, fomentaron un intenso intercambio interno entre pescadores y agricultores y generaron una esfera económica supracomunal. Esta actividad conducida por las autoridades de los asentamientos o "pachacas" habría beneficiado económicamente a éstas.

El hilado y la manufactura de tejidos de algodón le agregaron un valor adicional en beneficio de los productores del valle. Por otro lado, al intercambio interno se adicionó un intercambio externo, para cubrir la demanda de las autoridades, actividad que creció y se extendió a otras áreas costeñas y a las regiones de sierra y selva del área norcentral, de donde los funcionarios de Caral adquirieron bienes como *Spondylus*, madera, caracoles, plantas medicinales, fibras vegetales, piedras semipreciosas, pigmentos, etc. La conexión alcanzó a grupos de lugares distantes, como la costa del extremo norte del país o Ecuador, para la adquisición del preciado *Spondylus*, con el cual manufacturaron objetos de valor simbólico.

Aquellas y estas actividades favorecieron la acumulación de riqueza, el incremento de prestigio y la formación de clases sociales; y le permitieron a la sociedad de Supe captar en su beneficio los excedentes producidos en el área, así como fortalecer el poder de sus autoridades, que habrían iniciado un proceso de integración política, bajo la forma de un gobierno centralizado.

Estos excedentes se invirtieron en:

1. Obras de infraestructura económica, como la construcción de reservorios, canales de riego y su mantenimiento.

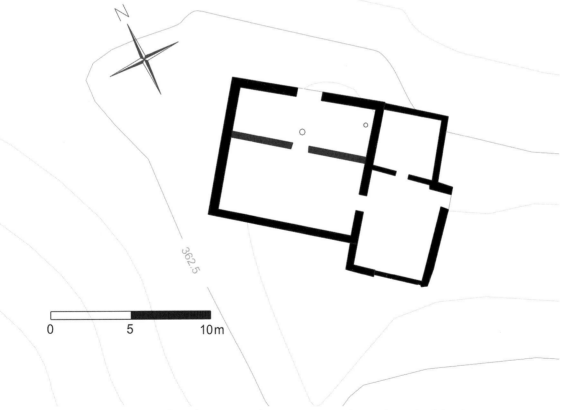

Figura 7.7. Recintos usados como talleres de producción artesanal. (© Proyecto Especial Arqueológico Caral-Supe.)

2. La construcción y permanente remodelación de los edificios públicos.
3. El mantenimiento de los funcionarios políticos, administrativos y religiosos.
4. El trabajo de especialistas dedicados a la producción de conocimientos en los campos de la astronomía, aritmética, geometría, medicina e agricultura y a su aplicación en la elaboración del calendario, en el diseño y construcción urbanos, en el acondicionamiento de los campos de cultivo y la administración de las aguas, etc.

RELACIONES SOCIALES DE PRODUCCIÓN

La comunidad o "pachaca" era la unidad básica de producción, y en el caso del valle, la encargada de habilitar periódicamente los canales de riego y de distribuir las tierras de cultivo, que eran de su propiedad entre las familias o ayllus, que la componían, para su cultivo y sustento. El trabajador pertenecía a una "pachaca" y a través de ella accedía al medio de producción. La "pachaca" congregaba a un número de unidades domésticas, linajes o ayllus, en torno a una porción de tierras regada por un sistema de canales, tenía sus propias autoridades y sus respectivos edificios públicos para fines multifuncionales, políticos, religiosos, económicos, administrativos, a la par que estaba articulada al sistema mayor del valle. El Estado integró a las "pachacas" de pescadores del litoral, de tejedores de juncos y esteras y de agricultores. Como hemos indicado, han sido identificados 20 asentamientos de "pachacas" a lo largo de los primeros 45 km del valle de Supe (Shady, Dolorier et al. 2000).

La Organización Sociopolítica y Política y la Formación del Estado

Los centros urbanos o "pachacas" contienen varios conjuntos de unidades residenciales y edificios públicos, cuyas diversas características son indicadores de las distinciones sociales al interior de cada asentamiento así como entre asentamientos. En las "pachacas" se realizaba un conjunto de actividades para garantizar el autosostenimiento como también de los especialistas y autoridades. Estos dirigían y controlaban a la fuerza de trabajo para la realización de todo tipo de actividad, en base a una ideología que justificaba la inversión y la distribución de la riqueza producida.

La recurrencia de determinados elementos arquitectónicos y formas culturales así como la distinción social al interior de cada asentamiento y entre el conjunto de ellos indican la integración de estas comunidades autosuficientes o "pachacas" a un sistema mayor que mantuvo, sin embargo, las autonomías de gobierno.

La presencia de determinadas estructuras arquitectónicas, como el edificio escalonado o ushnu, la plataforma con 13 cubículos, los recintos con hornacinas, entre otros, que aparecen en Caral, continuarán como símbolos del poder político y religioso a lo largo del proceso cultural andino hasta el imperio inca.

En varios edificios de la ciudad se han encontrado entierros humanos, mayormente de niños, todos vinculados con determinados rituales. Los objetos asociados a estos entierros indican diferencias de estatus, que en el caso de los niños, de menos de dos años, eran adscritos. Un diferente acceso a los bienes de consumo y de prestigio revela, asimismo, a una sociedad con desigual distribución de la riqueza.

La desigualdad social se hace también notoria en los resultados alcanzados por los estudios de paleopatología de los restos mortales de un individuo de 20 a 25 años. El cadáver había sido depositado junto con la capa de tierra y piedras al enterrarse un atrio de la Pirámide Mayor. El cuerpo estaba desnudo con los brazos extendidos y cruzados en la espalda y no llevaba ninguna ofrenda. Los estudios indican que tuvo una salud precaria en su infancia (espongiohiperortosis, cibra orbitalia e hipoplasia del esmalte, además de una patología oral profusa) derivada de una dieta hipoproteica asociada a anemia crónica; padeció de osteoartritis precoz de la columna dorsal baja y lumbar, patología asociada a trauma crónico por motivos laborales como la carga de peso excesivo por tiempo prolongado (transportando materiales para la construcción y remodelación de los templos o para el comercio a largas distancias), así como de osteocondritis dissecans, lesiones en las articulaciones metatarso falángicas de ambos pies, patología que se da en varones jóvenes que esfuerzan mucho sus pies; murió como consecuencia de un traumatismo cráneo-encefálico frontal. El hallazgo de falanges en nichos del templo enterrado corrobora la hipótesis de sacrificio de este individuo, perteneciente a la clase trabajadora de la estratificada sociedad de Supe (Lombardi y García 2004:1–16).

EL ROL DE LA RELIGIÓN

Para algunos se requiere constatar que hubo un ejército o fuerza militar para probar la existencia de la forma política estatal. Pero en el estado inicial de la formación estatal tal control de la población no fue necesario; la religión era el instrumento de cohesión y de coerción de la población, de gran efectividad (Shady 1999a,b).

La ideología prestigiada por el Estado de Supe habría actuado como el nexo de cohesión más importante de los grupos sociales o "pachacas" que se encontraban bajo la dominación del gobierno centralizado; ellos habrían compartido dioses generales y representaciones simbólicas de preceptos religiosos y cosmológicos. Como indican algunos documentos coloniales sobre el área, dioses como Huari habrían enseñado a los pobladores a preparar sus chacras, trazar sus canales, sembrar las plantas, mejorar sus cosechas y a poner sus hitos en defensa de sus pertenencias. Al sol, a la luna, a la tierra y al agua, simbolizados con determinadas formas, había que rendir culto, hacer ritos propiciatorios y cumplir con el calendario de ceremonias, asociado con los trabajos en los edificios públicos, en las tierras de los dioses, y de quienes eran sus intermediarios.

CONCLUSIONES

1. El temprano desarrollo de la civilización de Supe se debió a la creciente complejización de los sistemas sociales que se consolidaban en las varias regiones del área norcentral. Todos habían alcanzado a producir excedentes y a tener un nivel de organización que les permitía cierta especialización laboral, la construcción de edificios públicos y su participación en redes de intercambio interregional.

2. Las sociedades costeñas del área norcentral lograron significativos avances en el aprovechamiento de los recursos de la región alrededor de los 3000 a.C. Aplicaron nuevas tecnologías en la pesca, como las redes de algodón para la extracción masiva de anchovetas y sardinas, y en la agricultura, los canales de riego y la construcción de terrazas. Estas innovaciones incrementaron la productividad y fomentaron el intercambio de productos.

3. Los pescadores y agricultores de Supe a la par de su especialización laboral estuvieron integrados en un sistema económico complementario. Los pescadores dependían del algodón de los agricultores para la confección de las redes de pesca y los agricultores recibían a cambio pescado deshidratado (Shady 1997a).

4. El intercambio económico interno, local y regional primero, e interregional y a larga distancia después, benefició a los asentamientos ubicados en vías de comunicación y propició la acumulación desigual de riqueza y la formación de clases sociales.

5. La protección de los intereses de la clase enriquecida fomentó la integración de las comunidades o "pachacas" a un sistema político estatal. Su ámbito de manejo y control directo incluyó primero a las poblaciones de Supe, Pativilca y Fortaleza, pero su interacción y prestigio se extendieron por toda el área norcentral. Cuarenta y dos fechados radiocarbónicos han confirmado su antigüedad como la civilización más antigua del Perú y de América.

6. El sistema social de Supe se caracterizó por una división compleja del trabajo, con especialistas en actividades diversas a la de aquellos dedicados a la producción de bienes de subsistencia. Están los pescadores de anchovetas; los agricultores de algodón y mate; los artesanos; los constructores de las obras arquitectónicas; los artífices del calendario de actividades; las autoridades, etc.

7. El templo y las unidades domésticas de las autoridades fueron instituciones multifuncionales, para la conducción de las diversas actividades sociales, económicas, políticas, religiosas y para el ejercicio del poder sobre la población.

8. Caral fue el centro urbano donde residieron autoridades, especialistas, funcionarios, artesanos y servidores.

9. El valle medio inferior de Supe fue la sede donde se asentó el primer gobierno del sistema central, alrededor de los 2600 a.C. La cuantiosa inversión de trabajo en obras monumentales y su permanente remodelación fueron sustentadas por la productividad del área, que el Estado prístino captó. La desigual distribución de la riqueza está indicada por la jerarquía de unos asentamientos sobre otros; la distinción entre unidades domesticas; el tratamiento diferenciado en los entierros de niños y de adultos.

10. El Estado usó a la religión como instrumento de cohesión y control social. Ella garantizaba la reproducción de las condiciones materiales de vida pero ejercía también sanción y castigo.

11. Caral ha sido el modelo de organización social que desarrollaron otras sociedades en períodos posteriores en el territorio del Perú.

NOTA

1. Tomamos el nombre de Caral de la toponimia local, correspondiente al pueblo más cercano. Anteriormente, se conocía como Chupacigarro a éste y a otros tres asentamientos.

REFERENCIAS

Béarez, Philippe, y Luis Miranda
2003   Análisis arqueo-ictiológico del sector residencial del sitio arqueológico de Caral-Supe, costa central del Perú. En *La ciudad sagrada de Caral-Supe: Los orígenes de la civilización andina y la formación del estado prístino en el antiguo Perú*, editado por Ruth Shady y Carlos Leyva, pp. 123–132. PEACS/INC, Lima.

Bonnier, Elizabeth, y Catherine Rozenberg
1988   Del santuario al caserío: Acerca de la neolitización en la cordillera de los Andes Centrales. *Boletín del Instituto Francés de Estudios Andinos* 16(2):23–40. Lima.

Burger, Richard, y Lucy Salazar-Burger
1980   Ritual and Religion at Huaricoto. *Archaeology* 33(6):26–32.

Duviols, Pierre
1986   *Cultura andina y represión: Procesos y visitas de idolatrías y hechicerías en Cajatambo, siglo XVII.* CBC, Cusco.

Engel, Frédéric
1987   *De las begonias al maíz. Vida y producción en el antiguo Perú.* Centro de Investigaciones de Zonas Aridas (CIZA), Lima.

Feldman, Robert
1980   *Áspero, Peru: Architecture, Subsistence Economy and Other Artifacts of a Preceramic Maritime Chiefdom.* Unpublished doctoral dissertation, Department of Anthropology, Harvard University, Cambridge, MA.
1985   Preceramic Corporate Architecture: Evidence for the Development of Non-Egalitarian Social Systems in Peru. In *Early Ceremonial Architecture in the Andes*, edited by Christopher B. Donnan, pp. 71–92. Dumbarton Oaks Research Library and Collection, Washington, DC.
1987   Architectural Evidence for the Development of Nonegalitarian Social Systems in Coastal Peru. In *The Origins and Development of the Andean State*, edited by Jonathan Haas, Shelia Pozorski, and Tom Pozorski, pp. 9–14. Cambridge University Press, Cambridge.
1992   Preceramic Architecture and Subsistence Traditions. *Andean Past* 3:67–86.

Fung, Rosa
1988   The Late Preceramic and Initial Period. In *Peruvian Prehistory*, edited by Richard W. Keatinge, pp. 67–96. Cambridge University Press, Cambridge.

Grieder, T., A. Bueno, E. Smith, y R. Malina
1988   *La Galgada, Peru: A Preceramic Culture in Transition.* University of Texas Press, Austin.

Hodder, Ian, y Craig Cessford
2004   Daily Practice and Social Memory at Catalhöyük. *American Antiquity* 69(1):17–40.

Izumi, Seiichi, y Kazuo Terada
1972   *Andes 4. Excavations at Kotosh, Peru, 1963 and 1966.* University of Tokyo Press, Tokyo.

Izumi, Seiichi, y Toshihiko Sono
1963   *Andes 2. Excavations at Kotosh, Peru. University of Tokyo Expedition, 1960.* University of Tokyo Press, Tokyo.

Kosok, Paul
1965   *Life, Land and Water in Ancient Peru.* Long Island University Press, New York.

Lombardi, Guido, y Uriel García
2004   *Estudio del Esqueleto de la Pirámide Mayor de Caral.* Preprint. PEACS, Lima.

Moseley, Michael E.
1975   *The Maritime Foundations of Andean Civilization.* Cummings Publishing Co., Menlo Park, CA.

Quilter, Jeffrey, Bernardino Ojeda, Deborah Pearsall, Daniel Sandweiss, John Jones y Elizabeth S. Wing
1991   The Subsistence Economy of El Paraíso, an Early Peruvian Site. *Science* 251(4991):277–283.

Raymond, J. Scott
1981   The Maritime Foundations of Andean Civilization: A Reconsideration of the Evidence. *American Antiquity* 46(4):806–821.

Shady, Ruth
1995   La neolitización en los Andes Centrales y los orígenes del sedentarismo, la domesticación y la distinción social. *Saguntum* 28:49–61. Universidad de Valencia, España.
1997a   *La ciudad sagrada de Caral-Supe en los albores de la civilización en el Perú.* UNMSM, Lima.
1997b   Caral: La Cité Ensevelie. *Archéologie* 340:58–65. France.
1999a   La religión como forma de cohesión social y manejo político en los albores de la civilización en el Perú. *Boletín del Museo de Arqueología y Antropología* 2(9):13–15. UNMSM, Lima.
1999b   Los orígenes de la civilización y la formación del Estado en el Perú: Las evidencias arqueológicas de Caral-Supe (primera parte). *Boletín del Museo de Arqueología y Antropología* 2(12):2–4. UNMSM, Lima.

2000a Los orígenes de la civilización y la formación del Estado en el Perú: Las evidencias arqueológicas de Caral-Supe (segunda parte). *Boletín del Museo de Arqueología y Antropología* 3(2):2–7. UNMSM, Lima.

2000b Sustento socioeconómico del estado prístino de Supe-Perú: Las evidencias de Caral-Supe. *Arqueología y Sociedad* 13:49–66. Museo de Arqueología y Antropología, UNMSM, Lima.

2004 Caral-Supe, la civilización más antigua de Perú y de América. *Andean Archaeology III: North and South*, edited by William H. Isbell and Helaine Silverman. Plenum Press, New York.

Shady, Ruth, C. Dolorier, F. Montesinos y L. Casas

2000 Los orígenes de la civilización en el Perú: El área norcentral y el valle de Supe durante el Arcaico Tardío. *Arqueología y Sociedad* 13:13–48. MAA, UNMSM, Lima.

2006 Caral-Supe and the North-Central Area of Perú: The History of Maize in the Land Where Civilization Came into Being, en: J. E. Staller, R. H. Tykot y B. F. Benz (eds.), *Histories of Maize: Multidisciplinary Approaches to the Prehistory, Linguistics, Biogeography, Domestication, and Evolution of Maize*, 381–402, Elsevier, Amsterdam.

Shady, Ruth, y Miriam Gonzales

2000 Una tumba circular profanada de la ciudad sagrada de Caral-Supe. *Boletín del Museo de Arqueología y Antropología* 3(5):2–9. UNMSM, Lima.

Shady, Ruth, y Carlos Leyva (eds.)

2003 *La ciudad sagrada de Caral-Supe. Los orígenes de la civilización andina y la formación del estado prístino en el antiguo Perú.* PEACS/INC, Lima.

Shady, Ruth, M. Machacuay, y R. Aramburu

2000 La plaza circular del templo mayor de Caral: Su presencia en Supe y en el área norcentral del Perú. *Boletín del Museo de Arqueología y Antropología* 3(8):2–25. UNMSM, Lima.

Wendt, W. E.

1964 Die prakeramische Seidlung am Río Seco, Peru. *Baessler Archiv* 11(2):225–275.

Willey, Gordon R., y John M. Corbett

1954 *Early Ancon and Early Supe Culture: Chavín Horizon Sites of the Central Peruvian Coast.* Columbia University Press, New York.

Williams, Carlos, y Francisco Merino

1979 *Inventario, catastro y delimitación del patrimonio arqueológico del Valle de Supe.* INC, Lima.

Wilson, David

1981 Of Maize and Men: A Critique of the Maritime Hypothesis of State Origins on the Coast of Peru. *American Anthropologist* 83:93–120.

Wright, Henry T., y Gregory A. Johnson

1975 Population, Exchange and Early State Formation in Southwestern Iran. *American Anthropologist* 77:267–289.

Zechenter, Elzbieta

1988 *Subsistence Strategies in the Supe Valley of the Peruvian Central Coast during the Complex Preceramic and Initial Periods.* Unpublished doctoral dissertation, Department of Anthropology, University of California, Los Angeles.

CHAPTER 8

EARLY AGRICULTURE IN THE COASTAL OSMORE VALLEY, PERU

SYNCHRONOUS EVENTS AND MACROREGIONAL PROCESSES IN THE FORMATION OF ANDEAN CIVILIZATION

BRUCE D. OWEN

THE FIRST SOCIETIES TO build monumental architecture in South America depended on the rich marine resources of the Peruvian coast, but not exclusively. It was apparently the gradual addition of significant agricultural production to a mixed maritime and agricultural subsistence base that provided the resources for some Late Preceramic communities to build and operate large ritual facilities and to develop the social complexity necessary to organize those efforts, some as early as 2600 cal BC (Moseley 1975, 1992, 2001:112–113; Quilter 1991:397–401; Quilter et al. 1991; Burger 1995:28–33; Sandweiss and Moseley 2001; Shady Solís et al. 2001). Farming allowed settlement to expand inland, up the coastal river valleys. The commitment of valley dwellers to the farming side of an economy based on the exchange of agricultural crops and maritime catches underwrote the increasing number and scale of monumental centers in the Initial period, and roughly coincided with the widespread but variable adoption of ceramics, starting around 2000 cal BC (Pozorski and Pozorski 1988, 1990; Pearsall 1992; Burger 1995:58–60; Moseley 2001:131–134). Although the sociopolitical nature of these societies remains unclear (Haas 1982; Pozorski and Pozorski 1988, 2002; Quilter 1991:426–432; Burger 1995; Moseley 2001:114–115, 135–136), their works were impressive, and they laid the social, economic, and political foundations for the increasingly elaborate polities that

followed. Understanding the process through which coastal people committed to significant agricultural production is thus fundamental to understanding the development of social complexity in the Andes.

The end of the Initial period, marked by the abandonment of coastal platform mound centers, the appearance of new large architectural forms, and the expansion of the Chavín phenomenon with its monumental focus in the highlands (Burger 1995:60), was also accompanied by an agricultural change on the coast: the adoption of significant maize production (Quilter 1991:400; Burger 1995:209). Whether this shift in agricultural emphasis played a role in the dramatic changes in coastal society, was merely an incidental reflection of increasing contacts with the highlands, or was part of some other process remains to be assessed.

Explanations for the initial commitment to agriculture and the later refocusing on maize have involved both climate change and particularistic culture-historical approaches, and these approaches are not mutually exclusive (Quilter 1991:426–432; Burger 1995:57–58; Moseley 2001:131–132, 158). This chapter presents evidence from the far south coast of Peru that lends support to the important role played by large-scale environmental factors.

The far south coast of Peru and the northernmost coast of Chile provide a good testing ground for environmental and culture historical models because the region is geographically and culturally distant from the portions of the Peruvian coast that developed monumental architecture and early complex polities (Figure 8.1). The far south coast did not participate at all in the widespread exchanges of ideas and prestige goods indicated by the spread of platform mound architecture, Initial period and Early Horizon iconography, and portable objects in local or horizon styles associated with the coast to the north. Instead, it is characterized

by its own distinctive traditions, including Chinchorro mummification (Arriaza 1995; Wise 1995), later burial tumuli (Muñoz 1987; Owen 1993a, b; Goldstein 2000), and many other differences in material culture (Muñoz 1989; Núñez 1989, 1999). Nevertheless, the evidence described here indicates that people on the far south coast made the commitment to agriculture and subsequently shifted to an emphasis on maize at roughly the same times as their better known contemporaries

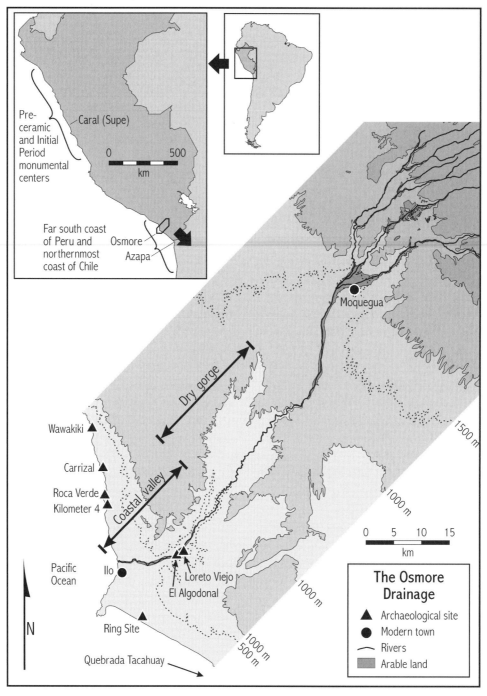

Figure 8.1. The Osmore Valley, the adjacent shoreline, and the macroregional context.

to the north. These synchronous events suggest that at least some factors encouraging these changes must have acted on a spatial scale large enough to encompass the separate interaction spheres of both the far south coast and the monument-building societies to the north. Such macroregional processes could have included broad environmental changes such as continental or even global climate trends; oceanographic changes along the Andean coast; or biological changes such as the evolution or introduction and spread of new varieties of plants, particularly maize.

THE COASTAL OSMORE VALLEY

The coastal Osmore Valley (Figures 8.1 and 8.2) comprises the coastal 25 km of the small drainage that originates in the highlands above modern Moquegua. Isolated from the major concentration of farmland near Moquegua by a narrow, dry, and largely uninhabitable stretch of the valley some 31 km long, the coastal valley

averages only 115 m wide in its upper portions, opening to about 300 m for the final 15 km to the sea. The amount of potentially arable land is paltry in comparison with the valleys both north and south of the mouth of the Osmore at the modern city of Ilo. The elevation of the valley floor ranges from sea level to about 325 masl. Rain is virtually unknown except in unusual El Niño years, although coastal fog frequently fills the valley and may be wet enough to dampen the ground. Land outside the valley bottom is barren desert, except for patches of desiccated lomas fog vegetation and a few small green areas near the shoreline that are watered by coastal springs. Even with the added water in the riverbed from the Pasto Grande canal project, completed in 1995, floodplain agriculture today requires irrigation using short canals and ditches. Prior to the completion of the Pasto Grande canal, water flowed in the coastal Osmore River (or Ilo River) for only a few days or weeks each year. Abundant archaeological remains suggest that the river flowed year-round at some periods in the past, and that some additional coastal springs existed

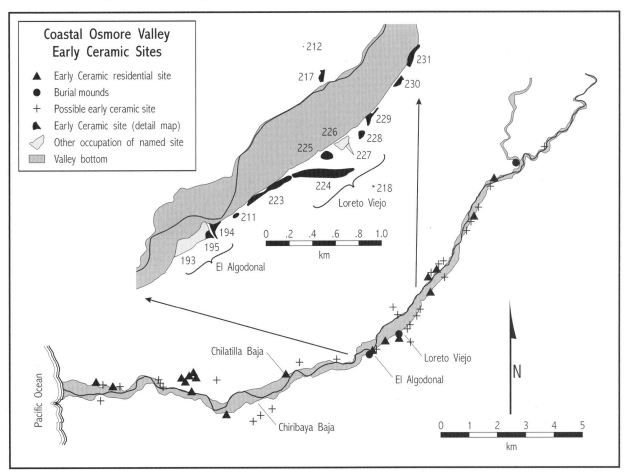

Figure 8.2. Early ceramic sites in the coastal Osmore Valley.

(Bawden 1989; Sandweiss et al. 1989; Stanish and Rice 1989; Wise 1989, 1997; Owen 1993a, b).

Archaic period sites such as Quebrada Tacahuay (Keefer et al. 1998), the Ring Site (Sandweiss et al. 1989), Kilometer 4 (Wise 1999), Carrizal (Wise 1997), and others both north and south of the mouth of the river attest to a very long prehistory of at least semi-sedentary foraging adaptations, with a heavy reliance on marine resources. No Archaic occupations have been recognized in the coastal valley, although they could have existed. Such early sites would be difficult to detect in the restricted spaces of the coastal valley, which have been heavily modified by later occupations, agriculture, talus slumping from the steep valley walls, and erosion by shifting meanders of the river.

Formative period occupations are known from coastal sites such as Carrizal (Bolaños 1987; Bawden 1989), Wawakiki (Bawden 1989), and Roca Verde (Del Aguila 1995), where the presence of early ceramics and a variety of burial practices have been documented. Dates, subsistence practices, and other matters remain sketchy. Within the valley, systematic pedestrian survey has located numerous Formative settlements (see Figure 8.2). Many of these have extensive, deep deposits and traces of eroded domestic terraces that suggest large or long-lasting permanent occupations, or perhaps seasonal occupations with considerable investment in permanent improvements (Owen 1993a). At least two have adjacent areas of burial tumuli similar to those known from the Azapa Valley and elsewhere (Muñoz 1987, 1989; Goldstein 2000). As elsewhere in the Andes, the early ceramics are generally restricted, neckless globular vessels with few or no handles, carinations, or distinguishable bases, with wiped or very incompletely pebble-burnished surfaces, and rare or no slip and paint. Many display soot or a crust of organic residues and were probably cooking vessels of a size appropriate to serve numerous people (Bolaños 1987; Bawden 1989; Owen 1993a, b).

Alcalde (1995) describes the stratigraphic sequence at one of these Formative period sites, identified as Site 173 in the valley survey and called Chilatilla Bajo in his report (Figure 8.2) (Owen 1993a:509, 539). Confirming the survey observations, Alcalde found strata with Late Intermediate period ceramics overlying strata containing Early Ceramic neckless ollas. He also reports that Formative period burials with "turbans" of colored yarns, reminiscent of the Azapa phase Early Ceramic tradition of northernmost Chile (Santoro 1980), were recovered from Chilatilla Bajo and Chiribaya Baja, farther downriver.

EL ALGODONAL AND LORETO VIEJO

This chapter is based on excavations and analyses of midden deposits from living surfaces and pit fills on several artificially leveled domestic terraces at two other early valley sites, El Algodonal and Loreto Viejo (see Figure 8.2). Although the occupation at El Algodonal appears to have begun in the Formative period, when early ceramics were already in use, Early Ceramic strata at Loreto Viejo overlay Preceramic ones in sometimes deep sequences on the same terraces.

El Algodonal is a multicomponent residential and mortuary site on a small elevated river terrace on the south side of the valley, about 12 km from the coast (Figures 8.2 and 8.3). The name El Algodonal refers to Sites 193, 194, and 195 in the survey numbering scheme. The area of interest here is the northeastern end of the site (Site 194), which is separated from the rest by a sharply eroded gully (see Figures 8.2 and 8.3). This steep, gravelly talus cone was initially explored because it contained a cemetery of Ilo-Tumilaca/Cabuza burials (Owen 1993a). Excavations revealed that the thick, inclined layers of gravel and rock into which the burials intruded had covered the remaining rear portions of much earlier, artificially leveled domestic terraces, at least one of which was protected at its back edge by a stone retaining wall. The front portions of the terraces were eroded away and damaged by looters' holes. The rear portions were buried deeply enough under the sloping talus surface to be preserved intact. A total of 12.4 m² on two different terrace levels was excavated by natural stratigraphic loci, revealing dense midden deposits compressed onto horizontal living surfaces, clusters of Early Ceramic sherds lying flat on the surfaces, shallow, bowl-shaped informal hearths, numerous pits originating at the floor level with distinctly different fills, and a large intact globular ceramic vessel set into the floor with a stone and mortar mouth constructed over it, closed by a thick unfired clay disk (Figure 8.4). This subfloor storage feature was completely empty except for a small cone of soil in the bottom that had filtered past one edge of the clay cover. Future analyses will consider the artifacts recovered and the differences between the pits; for present purposes, the deposits on and in these terraces are simply lumped together as representative of their Early Ceramic occupation (Owen 1993a:292–296, 1993b).

Just across the gully to the west is a convex, unterraced area with several protruding eroded wooden posts (see Figure 8.2, Site 195). Subsequent to the excavations described here, looters pitted this area and revealed it to be a burial tumulus composed of alternating thick layers of gravelly soil and uniform layers of reeds, essentially identical to burial mounds excavated at Loreto Viejo (see below; Owen 1993a, b) and well documented in the Azapa Valley Alto Ramírez culture (Focacci and Erices 1973; Focacci 1980; Muñoz 1987, 1989). This association of burial tumuli and Early Ceramic terraces recurs at Loreto Viejo (see Figure 8.2), suggesting that the people living on the terraces probably built the burial tumuli.

In 1990, the Early Ceramic terraces and Ilo-Tumilaca/Cabuza cemetery at El Algodonal were being eroded by a river meander that had already scoured away most of any talus slope that might have supported occupation farther upriver to the east. The subsequent construction of a road in this area has probably destroyed any traces that were left. Nevertheless, the 1990 survey did find early ceramics, midden, and a few eroded domestic terraces (see Figure 8.2, Sites 211 and 223) along the narrow remaining bits of talus slope. This material suggested that the Early Ceramic

occupation at El Algodonal may have been just the downriver end of a continuous band of residential terraces that would have stretched from at least the excavated eastern end of El Algodonal all the way to the Early Ceramic portion of what now appears to be the separate site of Loreto Viejo (see Figures 8.2 and 8.3). The name Loreto Viejo refers to Sites 224, 225, 226, 227, and 228. The whole area outlined in Figure 8.3 may not have been occupied at the same time, but all together it comprises an impressive expanse of early habitation debris some 1.5 km long. Buried and surface evidence from the eastern edge of Loreto Viejo at Sites 228 and 229, and at Sites 230 and 231 farther upriver, hint that the Early Ceramic residential terraces may have extended in patches or continuously considerably further yet.

The early terraces at Loreto Viejo are not deeply buried and are still faintly visible as a large number of horizontal corrugations in the steeply sloping valley wall. A total of 11.3 m² on three widely separated terraces were excavated by natural stratigraphic loci (Owen 1993a). One additional unit in the same sector of the site yielded little intact cultural material and is

Figure 8.3. South side of the coastal Osmore Valley, showing the early occupation from El Algodonal through Loreto Viejo.

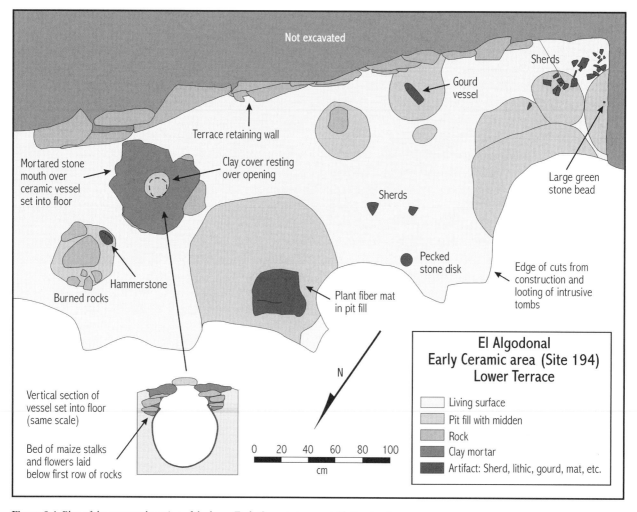

Figure 8.4. Plan of the excavated portion of the lower Early Ceramic terrace at El Algodonal.

excluded here. On the steeper slope where two of the excavation units were located, the front edges of the terraces have collapsed, leaving a strip 1–2 m wide of horizontal deposits and pits at the rear of each terrace, just a few centimeters below the current surface. No retaining walls were found in this part of Loreto Viejo, perhaps a result of the very small sample size. One of these terraces (Unit 2514) had at least 90 cm of superimposed horizontal strata with complexly crosscutting pits originating at different levels, suggesting a long occupation or repeated reuse of favored terraces. Unfortunately, this unit had to be abandoned before we reached the bottom of the cultural deposits. Another terrace (Units 2507 and 2510) had a similar sequence totaling about 60 cm from the original leveled subsoil surface to the highest intact cultural layer, with pits cut up to 50 cm deeper into the subsoil. The third excavated area (Units 2508 and 2513) was located on a more

gently inclined area formed by a slight knoll on the steep hillside. This area had only about 20 cm of horizontal cultural strata on top of nearly sterile leveling fill. The local topography is such that gravel moving down the slope passes around this natural protrusion rather than adding to cultural deposits left on top of it. This probably accounts for the shallow stratigraphy on the knoll, despite its attractive, more level and protected location. Many of the strata in these knoll units were relatively thick and exhibited extensive ash deposits and burned areas that had been cut by many small pits with distinctive fills, suggesting perhaps a cooking area or some other special function, in contrast to the other excavated terraces. As discussed later, radiocarbon dates, midden contents, and the absence of ceramics all suggest that the lowest levels in these units are much earlier than the ashy deposits above them, despite the shallowness of the sequence.

As at El Algodonal, the Loreto Viejo early terraces are close to a concentration of burial tumuli (see Figure 8.2, Site 225). Test excavations in two of the tumuli are described elsewhere (Owen 1993a, b).

SEPARATING PRECERAMIC FROM EARLY CERAMIC

Ceramics were scarce in the early occupations excavated at both El Algodonal and Loreto Viejo. Many loci had no ceramics at all, and few contained more than a handful of sherds. At El Algodonal, sherds were found sufficiently close to the artificially leveled sterile

subsoil that the entire sample was deemed to represent an Early Ceramic occupation, creatively dubbed the El Algodonal Early Ceramic. In previous work (Owen 1993a,b), I assumed the same about the Loreto Viejo excavations. This was incorrect.

Inspection of the Harris matrices in Figure 8.5 suggests that in the three Loreto Viejo early terrace excavations, ceramics are restricted to the upper strata. Table 8.1 shows that this stratigraphic pattern is statistically significant in two of the three cases, one with 5% confidence and the other with only 10% confidence. As expected, the stratigraphic distribution of ceramics at El Algodonal does not differ significantly from random.

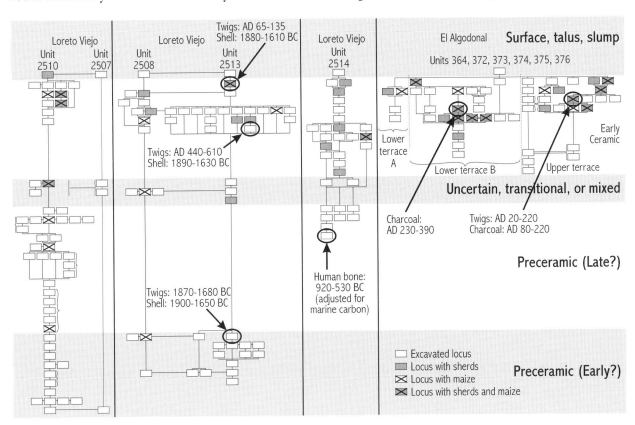

Figure 8.5. Harris matrices of Preceramic and Early Ceramic excavation units.

Table 8.1. Significance of stratigraphic distribution of ceramics and maize.

	Loreto Viejo Sites 2507, 2510	Loreto Viejo Sites 2508, 2513	Loreto Viejo Site 2514	El Algodonal Lower Terrace A	El Algodonal Lower Terrace B	El Algodonal Upper Terrace
Number of ranked sets of loci[a]	24	8	7	3	6	3
Ceramics[b]	<0.05	<0.10	Not sig.	Too few to test	Not sig.	Too few to test
Maize, all parts[b]	<0.05	<0.10	Not sig.	Too few to test	Not sig.	Too few to test

[a] Loci are lumped into minimal sets that can be stratigraphically ranked relative to the rest of the sequence. Each set is then assigned its rank based on stratigraphic order and is labeled with "present" or "absent" for sherds and maize. Loci that are stratigraphically related to others only from above, such as fill in a pit in subsoil, are excluded from all sets unless the locus above defines the penultimate set.
[b] Significance based on a nonparametric two-way Wilcoxon rank-sum test of stratigraphic rank of the sets by presence vs. absence. This tests the null hypothesis that sets with and without the specified item are randomly distributed among the stratigraphic ranks.

Based on the presence or absence of sherds in these Harris matrices, as well as field notes and drawings describing the strata, I have divided the Loreto Viejo sequences into Early Ceramic and Preceramic parts, as shown in Figure 8.5, separated by some loci that might be mixed, transitional, or difficult to categorize with certainty. The midden analyses described below confirm that the putatively Ceramic and Preceramic sets of loci differ dramatically in other ways, too.

The radiocarbon dates discussed below suggest that the Preceramic strata span a period of at least 1,000 years, and the Harris matrices in Figure 8.5 hint that maize may be rare or absent in the lower portions of the Loreto Viejo sequences. Again, this stratigraphic pattern is significant in two of the three Loreto Viejo excavations (Table 8.1). To accommodate these differences, I divided the Preceramic sequences into ad hoc "early" and "late" portions, as shown in Figure 8.5. This division is exploratory, rather than clearly indicated by the data. Although I present the proposed early and late Preceramic data here for comparison, the discussion and conclusions are based primarily on the entire lumped Preceramic sample.

DATING

Two radiocarbon dates on wood charcoal and one on mixed small twigs place the Early Ceramic occupation at El Algodonal around cal AD 20 to 390 (Table 8.2).[1] Two dates on small molle tree (*Schinus molle*) twigs from

Table 8.2. Radiocarbon dates of the Preceramic and Early Ceramic occupations of El Algodonal and Loreto Viejo.

Site and Provenience	Stratum Period	Context	Material	Lab. ID	¹⁴C Age[a]	δ¹³C (‰)	Cal AD/BC ±1σ[b]	Reference
El Algodonal 576-6-9	Early Ceramic	Midden on floor	Wood charcoal	Beta 51064	1750 ± 60	–29.2	AD 230–AD 390	Owen (1993a)
El Algodonal 375-8-1	Early Ceramic	Midden on floor	Wood charcoal	Beta 51062	1870 ± 50	–29.9	AD 80–AD 220	Owen (1993a)
El Algodonal 375-8-1	Early Ceramic	Midden on floor	Small twigs of various species	Beta 51063	1900 ± 60	–26.5	AD 20–AD 220	Owen (1993a)
Loreto Viejo 2513-5-4	Early Ceramic	Surface around hearth, stratigraphically late	Small twigs of *Schinus molle*	AA37163[c]	1895 ± 28[c]	–27.3	AD 65–AD 135	Owen (2002)
Loreto Viejo 2513-5-4	Early Ceramic (redeposited?)	Surface around hearth, stratigraphically late	*Choromytilus chorus* shell	AA37164	3936 ± 55	–0.8	1880 BC–1610 BC	Owen (2002)
Loreto Viejo 2513-14-33	Early Ceramic	Pit fill, stratigraphically intermediate	Small twigs of *Schinus molle*	AA40293[d]	1519 ± 31[d]	–25.7	AD 440–AD 610	Owen (2002)
Loreto Viejo 2513-14-33	Early Ceramic (redeposited?)	Pit fill, stratigraphically intermediate	*Choromytilus chorus* shell	AA40294	3951 ± 46	–0.1	1890 BC–1630 BC	Owen (2002)
Loreto Viejo 2513-11-18	Preceramic	Ashy surface, stratigraphically early	Small twigs of *Schinus molle*	AA37165	3439 ± 43	–26.7	1870 BC–1680 BC	Owen (2002)
Loreto Viejo 2513-11-18	Preceramic	Ashy surface, stratigraphically early	*Choromytilus chorus* shell	AA37166	3961 ± 47	–0.1	1900 BC–1650 BC	Owen (2002)
Loreto Viejo 2514-13-2	Preceramic	Extended face-down burial	Human rib	AA37149	2730 ± 41	–18.4	920 BC–530 BC	New

[a] Conventional radiocarbon age BP, including δ¹³C fractionation adjustment, no Southern Hemisphere correction. Data are as measured, prior to adjustments for the marine carbon reservoir age or partially marine diet, in the case of the human bone.

[b] 1-sigma ranges calibrated by OxCal v3.5 (Ramsey 2000), with no Southern Hemisphere correction. Terrestrial samples are based on atmospheric calibration curve from Stuiver et al. (1998). Marine samples are based on the marine calibration curve from Stuiver et al. (1998). ΔR = 171 ± 84 (Owen 2002). The calibrated date of the human bone sample is roughly adjusted for partial marine carbon content as determined experimentally for this valley (Owen 2002), by subtracting 103 years from the age and increasing the uncertainty to the square root of the sum of the squares of the laboratory estimate and 108 prior to calibration using the atmospheric calibration curve from Stuiver et al. (1998).

[c] Weighted mean of one measurement on each of two graphite targets prepared from the same sample (Bowman 1990:58).

[d] Weighted mean of two measurements on one graphite target and one measurement on a second target prepared from the same sample (Bowman 1990:58).

Early Ceramic strata at Loreto Viejo roughly agree, falling at cal AD 65–135 and cal AD 440–610.

Three radiocarbon dates on marine shell (*Choromytilus*) and one on small molle tree (*Schinus molle*) twigs place the beginning of the Preceramic occupation at Loreto Viejo around or before about 1900 to 1600 cal BC (see Table 8.2). These dates require some discussion.

The twig date and one of the shell dates come from the same stratum in the shallow Unit 2513, below the thick ashy layers. The conventional radiocarbon ages of these two samples are in gross agreement, but to make the shell date comparable to the terrestrial twig date it is necessary to calibrate both, taking the marine carbon reservoir effect into account for the shell. To do that accurately, it is necessary to know ΔR, the local adjustment to the apparent age of seawater. There are several estimates of ΔR that could be used, and no one of them is obviously preferable (Owen 2002). In Table 8.2, I have used 171 ± 84, which is derived by assuming that the two associated dates are identical. This is obviously circular, in that it forces the calibrated shell date to agree with the twig date. However, it is also probably correct. Two other estimates of ΔR from northern Chile, 136 ± 40 and 171 ± 34, are very similar and would also cause the shell and twig dates to agree closely. However, other samples from Late Intermediate period contexts in the coastal Osmore Valley suggest a ΔR of 362 ± 106. This difference could reflect changes in ΔR over time or across space, or perhaps is due to some

more complex issue not yet resolved. Using this ΔR of 362 ± 106, the one-sigma ranges of the three Loreto Viejo shell dates all fall within 1670–1380 cal BC. These dates are a bit more recent than the twig date, but still generally compatible. Additional dates would help, but the 1900–1600 cal BC range is a reasonable estimate with the information currently available.

All three shell dates are almost identical, and surprisingly early. The two in the upper strata, though, are associated with ceramics and with molle twigs that date to the same range as the Early Ceramic samples from El Algodonal. These two late twig dates are not even in stratigraphic order. This mess is explicable in light of the depositional history of the excavated area (Figure 8.6). The two agreeing, early dates are from a horizontal stratum just above the nearly sterile fill that roughly levels the area. The mismatched dates are from the fill of a pit that cuts through this earlier layer, and a horizontal layer that surrounds and immediately overlies the pit fill. The pit was apparently dug in Early Ceramic times, bringing up the much earlier shell from the layer that was dug through. Some of this early shell was incorporated into the pit fill and some into the surface deposits formed around and over the mouth of the pit. The same process of mixing and redeposition could account for the inverted order of the twig dates. Post hoc explanations of this kind are less than ideal, but the alternative of simply dismissing multiple agreeing dates is even less attractive. The dated materials had to

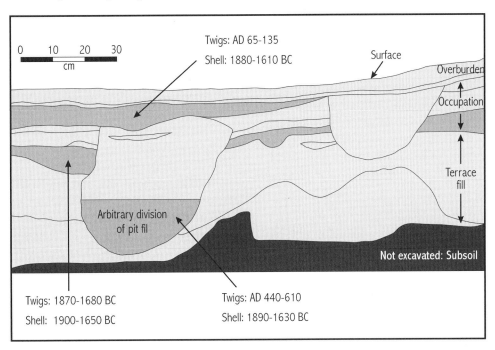

Figure 8.6. Profile of Loreto Viejo Unit 2513, showing stratigraphic context of the radiocarbon dates.

get onto the site somehow; they must be associated with some portion of the occupation.

Finally, the likelihood that the three shell samples all originated from the same area of a single early stratum raises the possibility that they are not independent, very closely agreeing dates at all but pieces of the same individual bivalve, distributed into three strata and dated three times by a phenomenal stroke of bad luck. However, the fact that one of the samples had a significantly different δ¹³C value than the other two suggests that at least two individual mollusks have been dated. The possibility that the two similar samples really represent a single dated organism cannot be discounted. This would reduce the number of roughly agreeing early dates for the Preceramic period to three.

Human bone from an evidently Preceramic burial was also dated (Owen 1993a). Dating human bone is problematic when the person may have eaten seafood, because an unknown fraction of the carbon in the bone should be adjusted for the marine carbon reservoir effect in the same way that shell dates are (Tauber 1983; Molto et al. 1997; Bayliss et al. 2004). This human bone was dated specifically to address that issue by comparing it to the date of an associated wool textile. Unfortunately, the wool textile sample did not produce a date. The human bone date can still be used for very rough chronological purposes, but only by applying a correction factor that has been determined empirically for burials in this valley, which greatly increases the error term. The result is a broad date range, from 920 cal BC to 530 cal BC. This rough date loosely brackets the adoption of ceramics to after 920–430 cal BC and before cal AD 20–220.

More dates are needed to better define these periods and to date directly the cultigens discussed in the next section. Despite the complexities discussed here, however, the available dates do grossly situate the Preceramic and Early Ceramic in time.

MIDDEN ANALYSIS METHODS

All the cultural strata excavated were either screened through 1/4-inch mesh or collected as flotation samples. This analysis describes only the material collected from the screens. Because of the large particle size of the gravel matrix and the density of plant material in many strata, the screened collections included many objects smaller than 1/4 inch, although these small items are certainly underrepresented. All the material

was identified to the degree of specificity possible and recorded by the author and by José Moya Y., Raúl Rosas H., and Gerardo Carpio D., working in the same room with constant cross-checking and comparison to a reference collection drawn mostly from the midden materials themselves to ensure consistency. Although none of us had training in paleoethnobotany, the extraordinary preservation made the identification of many macrobotanical remains obvious to anyone familiar with modern local crops and plants, and reference to descriptive publications such as Towle (1961), on hand in the field laboratory, helped resolve occasional doubts. Although we probably made more identification errors than specialists would have, the general patterning should be sound. Helberth Gamarra B. identified and recorded the marine shell. Items were recorded according to a detailed coding scheme that separated botanical materials by plant part as well as species, faunal materials by body part as well as species, textiles by material, color, structure, form, and so on. Items to be recorded together were weighed to the nearest 0.1 g. Below that, zero mass was recorded and a placeholder mass of 0.01 g was assigned during analysis. Many discrete items such as seeds were also counted, although counts are not used here.

The midden analysis is limited to loci that were screened (some small lenses were collected entirely as flotation samples) and that were determined to be unmixed samples of their periods, based on examination of field notes, profile and plan drawings, excavation photos, and Harris matrices. The complexity of the stratigraphy and the difficulty of discerning differences in the loose, gravelly soil made it likely that some loci as collected actually included portions of other natural strata that could pertain to a different period. These potentially mixed loci are excluded from the analysis, reducing the sample size but hopefully improving the clarity of the patterning.

Table 8.3 summarizes the sample for each period in terms of numbers of loci, area and volume excavated, the total mass of midden collected, and the total mass of plant material collected. No attempt has been made to estimate edible weight or caloric value from the recovered remains. The results should not be interpreted as direct indices of diet but rather as relative measures of changes in food production practices. Midden contents are quantified for analysis in several ways. Ubiquity is the percentage of loci in which the item was present. It indicates how widespread an item is, independent of the amounts found in each locus. The mass of the item

Table 8.3. Sample size and standardizing data.

Parameter Measured	Preceramic (Early?)	Preceramic (Late?)	Preceramic (Lumped)	Transitional, Mixed, Unknown	Early Ceramic
No. of loci	10	14	24	9	43
Total mass of midden collected (g)[a]	745.0	418.0	1163.0	576.2	10,433.5
Total mass of plant material (g)[a]	76.0	277.0	353.0	77.3	6040.4
Screened volume (liters)	240.0	374.5	614.5	438.0	2814.5
Excavated area (m²)	9.00	6.75	11.25	11.25	23.60

[a] Collections from screened soil. This analysis excludes material from flotation samples, nonartifactual materials such as unworked stones, and soil samples.

in a locus divided by the total mass of midden material in the locus (item mass/total mass) is an indicator of the relative magnitude of the item's contribution to the total midden sample. Unfortunately, standardizing by total midden mass introduces a bias when the analysis spans the Preceramic and Early Ceramic periods, because any food item is automatically a smaller percentage of midden mass in loci that contain heavy ceramics. A more stable alternative, also presented here, is to divide the mass of the item by the mass of all plant material in the locus (item mass/botanical mass). Even when the item in question is not botanical, such as shell or textiles, this approach still produces a measure or index that is standardized against a gross indicator of the amount of human activity represented by the locus.

While it is tempting to standardize by the volume of soil from the locus that was passed through 1/4-inch screens (item mass/screened volume), such an approach is problematic because strata deposited by different processes had very different proportions of artifacts per volume, or artifact density. Lenses of midden compressed onto floors have very high artifact densities, whereas pit fills often include more gravel and have much lower artifact densities. Unless there were enough loci to get a reasonable sample size while limiting analyses to a single type of context, any patterns in amounts standardized by volume will be strongly affected by the mix of depositional processes in the sample of loci. The effect of a different mix of deposition types in the two sample sets being compared could overwhelm any variation due to human behavior. Nevertheless, amounts standardized by volume are shown in the graphs, and the results generally agree with the other measures.

Tables 8.4 and 8.5 and the discussion in the next section present and analyze the data in multiple ways. Trends that show up in just one of the quantification schemes are worth noting but should be taken with a grain of salt. Trends that recur in multiple quantification schemes are more robust.

In Tables 8.4 and 8.5, the contents of the lumped Preceramic sample are compared to the Early Ceramic sample using statistical tests of significance. The ubiquity or percent presence measure summarizes presence/absence data by locus, so significance is evaluated with a chi-square test of counts of loci in a 2-by-2 matrix of Preceramic versus Early Ceramic by present versus absent. The mass data, standardized by total midden mass, by mass of plant material only, and by volume of soil screened, are compared using a nonparametric Wilcoxon rank-sum test (Gibbons 1993). This test, also called the Mann-Whitney-Wilcoxon test, gives meaningful results even for samples that are small, are not normally distributed, contain numerous zero values, or are divided into comparison sets that are of very different sizes. It is less sensitive than parametric tests such as t tests but more robust, in that it can correctly be used on archaeological data where parametric tests are inappropriate, and it is less prone to indicate spurious significant differences in typical archaeological data that suffer from one or more of the above problems.

RESULTS: PRECERAMIC AND EARLY CERAMIC MIDDEN CONTENTS

The contents of the Preceramic and Early Ceramic midden samples are summarized in Table 8.4. This table also separates out the ad hoc "early" Preceramic and "late" Preceramic samples and summarizes the contents of the loci that are transitional, mixed, or could not be confidently assigned to either the Preceramic or the Early Ceramic period. These samples are smaller, less clearly defined by the data, and, not surprisingly, did not produce very consistent results. They are included here for comparison, but statistical analysis is limited to the lumped Preceramic and Early Ceramic samples.

Table 8.5 shows the same data for only the earliest well-dated loci. The first pair of columns describes the

Table 8.4. Contents of Preceramic and Early Ceramic midden.

Material	Species or Type	Part or Subtype	Preceramic (Lumped) Loci	Preceramic (Lumped) Mass (g)	Preceramic (Early?) Loci	Preceramic (Early?) Mass (g)[b]	Preceramic (Late?) Loci	Preceramic (Late?) Mass (g)	Transitional, Mixed, Unknown Loci	Transitional, Mixed, Unknown Mass (g)	Early Ceramic Loci	Early Ceramic Mass (g)	Preceramic vs. Early Ceramic Difference Sig.?[a] Ubiq.	/All	/Plant
Entire midden sample (standardizing variables)															
Ceramic	All		24	1163.0	10	745.0	14	418.0	9	576.2	43	10433.5	n/a	<0.01	n/a
Plant	All species	All parts	24	353.0	10	76.0	14	277.0	9	77.3	40	6040.4	<0.01	<0.01	<0.01
	Achira (*Canna*)	All parts (root, stalk, leaf)	8	5.1	2	0.2	6	4.9	1	0.0	19	66.9		<0.01	<0.01
	Ají pepper (*Capsicum*)	All parts									4	0.3			
		Fruit									3	0.2			
		Stem (peduncle)									1	0.1			
	Algae	All parts	3	0.4	2	0.2	1	0.2	1	0.3	4	5.4			
	Bean (*Phaseolus vulgaris*)	All parts	11	8.1	7	7.0	4	1.1	5	5.9	28	102.1	<0.05	<0.10	<0.10
		Seed	8	5.2	6	4.4	2	0.8	4	3.2	20	15.3	<0.05	<0.05	<0.10
		Pod	6	2.8	3	2.5	3	0.3	5	2.6	22	80.6			
		Stem (peduncle)	1	0.1	1	0.1			1	0.1	10	6.2			
	Lima bean (*Phaseolus lunatus*)	All parts	7	14.2	6	13.7	1	0.5	2	4.3	9	7.6			
		Seed	3	7.4	2	6.9	1	0.5	2	2.7	4	3.2			
		Pod	5	6.6	5	6.6			1	1.6	5	4.4			
		Stem (peduncle)	1	0.2	1	0.2									
	Cactus	All parts (needle, etc.)									3	1.1			
	Cane	All parts (root, stalk)	3	1.8	1	0.8	2	1.0	2	3.2	26	449.4	<0.01	<0.01	<0.01
	Cotton (*Gossypium*)	All parts	17	18.5	7	8.9	10	9.6	6	3.9	35	116.2	<0.01	<0.01	<0.05
		Seed	5	6.3	4	6.2	1	0.1	3	1.4	25	72.4	<0.01	<0.01	<0.05
		Boll	11	9.6	4	0.7	7	8.9	5	1.0	22	23.7			
		Stem (peduncle)	1	0.2	1	0.2			2	0.6	5	1.2			
	Gourd (*Lagenaria*)	All parts	3	0.4	2	0.3	1	0.1	2	0.4	19	46.6	<0.01	<0.01	<0.01
		Seed	2	0.4	1	0.3	1	0.1	1	0.3	15	5.7	<0.05	<0.05	<0.05
		Shell	1	0.0	1	0.0			1	0.1	15	40.9	<0.01	<0.01	<0.01
	Grass, unidentified	All parts	20	53.2	9	6.9	11	46.3	7	8.5	39	472.1	<0.05	<0.05	<0.05
	Maize (*Zea mays*)	All parts	4	1.4	1	0.1	3	1.3	2	1.6	19	1528.0	<0.01	<0.01	<0.01
		Cob ± kernels							1	1.2	12	1287.1	<0.05	<0.05	<0.05
		Kernel coat									3	1.4			
		Kernel	2	0.5	1	0.1	1	0.4	2	0.4	8	206.4	<0.01	<0.01	<0.01
		Efflorescence									6	1.0			
		Stalk	3	0.9			3	0.9			14	32.1	<0.10	<0.10	<0.10
	Quinoa (*Chenopodium*)	All parts	1	0.2			1	0.2	1	0.1	6	9.2		<0.10	<0.10
		Seed	1	0.2			1	0.2	1	0.1	3	0.1			
		Efflorescence & seeds					1	0.2			4	9.1			
	Squash (*Cucurbita*)	All parts (seed)	1	0.2	1	0.2					3	0.6			
	Tree, guava (*Psidium guajava*)	All parts (fruit)									1	1.1			
	Tree, leguminous	All parts	1	0.1	1	0.1	1	0.1			6	1.0			
		Seed									6	1.0	<0.10	<0.10	<0.10
		Pod	1	0.1	1	0.1	1	0.1			6	1.0			

Midden Contents			Preceramic (Lumped)		Preceramic (Early?)		Preceramic (Late?)		Transitional, Mixed, Unknown		Early Ceramic		Preceramic vs. Early Ceramic: Difference Sig.?[a]		
Material	Species or Type	Part or Subtype	Loci	Mass (g)	Loci	Mass (g)[b]	Loci	Mass (g)	Loci	Mass (g)	Loci	Mass (g)	Ubiq.	/All	/Plant
	Tree, lúcuma (*Lucuma bifera*)	All parts (seed)	1	0.1			1	0.1			1	0.2			
	Tree, molle (*Schinus molle*)	All parts (seeds ± stems)									2	0.3			
	Tree, pacay (*Inga*)	All parts	5	9.7	1	0.1	4	9.6			17	44.6	<0.05	<0.05	<0.05
		Seed	1	1.0			1	1.0			11	15.9		<0.05	<0.05
		Pod	5	8.7	1	0.1	4	8.6			13	28.1			
	Tuber (mostly yuca, *Manihot*)	All parts	10	35.1	4	1.5	6	33.6	6	2.0	29	274.4	<.05	<0.10	<0.10
		Tuber skin	7	13.2	2	0.5	5	12.7	5	1.9	26	72.4	<.05	<0.10	<0.10
		Root (tuber)	8	21.9	3	1.0	5	20.9	1	0.1	17	202.0			
Animal	All species		8	10.0	1	4.8	7	5.2	6	5.5	25	50.3	<0.10	<0.10	<0.10
	Large mammal (most or all Camelidae)		2	4.8	1	1.1	1	3.7	2	4.0	15	28.9	<0.05	<.05	<0.05
	Cuy (*Cavia porcellus*)		1	1.4	1	1.4									
	Small rodent (mouse?)										4	7.4			
	Bird		5	1.0	1	0.9	4	0.1	3	0.1	17	4.5			
Feces	All species		13	55.2	4	2.5	9	52.7	4	3.0	25	925.1	<0.10	<0.10	
	Camelid		6	3.3	1	0.3	5	3.0	3	1.3	21	688.7	<0.10		
	Cuy (*Cavia porcellus*)								1	1.2	9	19.5	<0.05	<0.05	<0.05
	Dog		5	3.8			5	3.8			4	2.1			
Fish	All species	Bones, scales, whole	11	19.7	6	13.8	5	5.9	5	6.4	32	139.9	<0.05		
Shellfish	All species		17	665.3	10	616.8	7	48.5	7	440.2	32	296.6		<0.05	<0.05
	Choromytilus (mussel)		14	525.8	8	481.0	6	44.8	6	350.8	26	218.1		<0.10	
	Oliva (olive shell)								1	1.9	4	6.4			
	Tegula (marine snail)								1	0.1	3	2.8			
Crayfish	All (Parastacidae; shell fragments)		11	5.6	5	4.9	6	0.7	6	8.8	24	54.8			
Charcoal	All		19	35.9	10	22.7	9	13.2	8	26.5	39	537.9		<0.10	
Lithic	All (flaked and a bead)		1	6.8			1	6.8			4	4.4			
Textile	All types (mostly string, yarn, cordage)		13	4.9	5	0.4	8	4.5	6	0.7	26	23.0			
	Vegetal fiber other than cotton	Plain	1	0.1			1	0.1			7	1.7			
	Cotton	Plain	11	1.5	4	0.3	7	1.1	5	0.5	24	11.4	<0.05	<0.05	<0.05
	Wool and cotton together	Plain									7	1.8			
	Wool	Plain	5	3.3	1	0.1	4	3.2	4	0.2	19	5.7	<0.10		
	Wool	Dyed							1	0.0	8	2.3			
Other artifact	All materials		6	1.9	2	0.2	4	1.7	1	0.8	18	151.2	<0.05	<0.05	<0.05
	Botanical, not wood		5	1.6	2	0.2	3	1.4	1	0.8	13	100.6	<0.05	<0.05	<0.05
	Wood		1	0.3			1	0.3			11	32.7			
	Bone										2	0.8			
	Shell										1	1.9			
	Compound materials										3	15.2			

Note: Miscellaneous and minor categories are not broken out in detail lines but are included in totals on summary lines such as "all species" and "all parts."

[a] Significance of the difference in ubiquity (percent presence) is from a chi-square test of a two-by-two table of Preceramic by present vs. absent. The significance of the difference of mass in each locus as a fraction of all midden mass in the locus is from a nonparametric two-way Wilcoxon rank-sum test. The significance of the difference of mass in each locus divided by mass of plant material in the locus is from a nonparametric two-way Wilcoxon rank-sum test.

[b] Items too small to weigh in the field lab (<0.10 g) are assigned a placeholder mass of 0.01 g.

Table 8.5. Contents of well-dated earliest midden loci.

Material	Species or Type	Part or Subtype	LV2513-11-18 Only (Two Early Dates) Loci	Mass (g)[a]	LV2513-11-18 and Below Loci	Mass (g)
Entire midden sample (standardizing variables)			1	347.1	4	377.6
Ceramic	All					
Plant	All species	All parts	1	29.9	4	33.1
	Achira (*Canna*)	All parts (root, stalk, leaf)				
	Ají pepper (*Capsicum*)	All parts				
		Fruit				
		Stem (peduncle)				
	Algae	All parts	1	0.2	1	0.2
	Bean (*Phaseolus vulgaris*)	All parts	1	3.7	2	3.8
		Seed	1	2.7	1	2.7
		Pod	1	1.0	1	1.0
		Stem (peduncle)			1	0.1
	Lima bean (*Phaseolus lunatus*)	All parts	1	5.9	1	5.9
		Seed	1	1.8	1	1.8
		Pod	1	3.9	1	3.9
		Stem (peduncle)	1	0.2	1	0.2
	Cactus	All parts (needle, etc.)				
	Cane	All parts (root, stalk)	1	0.8	1	0.8
	Cotton (*Gossypium*)	All parts	1	5.7	2	6.2
		Seed	1	5.4	2	5.9
		Boll	1	0.1	1	0.1
		Stem (peduncle)	1	0.2	1	0.2
	Gourd (*Lagenaria*)	All parts	1	0.3	2	0.3
		Seed	1	0.3	1	0.3
		Shell			1	0.0
	Grass, unidentified	All parts	1	0.8	4	1.3
	Maize (*Zea mays*)	All parts				
		Cob ± kernels				
		Kernel coat				
		Kernel				
		Efflorescence				
		Stalk				
	Quinoa (*Chenopodium*)	All parts				
		Seed				
		Efflorescence and seeds				
	Squash (*Cucurbita*)	All parts (seed)				
	Tree, guava (*Psidium guajava*)	All parts (fruit)				
	Tree, leguminous	All parts				
		Seed				
		Pod				
	Tree, lúcuma (*Lucuma bifera*)	All parts (seed)				
	Tree, molle (*Schinus molle*)	All parts (seeds ± stems)				
	Tree, pacay (*Inga*)	All parts				
		Seed				
		Pod				
	Tuber (prob. yuca, *Manihot*)	All parts			1	0.6
		Tuber skin				
		Root (tuber)			1	0.6
Animal	All species		1	4.8	1	4.8

Midden Contents			LV2513-11-18 Only (Two Early Dates)		LV2513-11-18 and Below	
Material	Species or Type	Part or Subtype	Loci	Mass (g)[a]	Loci	Mass (g)
	Large mammal (most or all Camelidae)		1	1.1	1	1.1
	Cuy (*Cavia porcellus*)		1	1.4	1	1.4
	Small rodent (mouse?)					
	Bird		1	0.9	1	0.9
Feces	All species		1	1.4	2	1.7
	Camelid				1	0.3
	Cuy (*Cavia porcellus*)					
	Dog					
Fish	All species	Bones, scales, whole	1	7.2	2	11.9
Shellfish	All species		1	297.6	4	307.1
	Choromytilus (mussel)		1	188.0	3	194.7
	Oliva (olive shell)					
	Tegula (marine snail)					
Crayfish	All (Parastacidae; shell fragments)		1	2.6	2	4.8
Charcoal	All		1	3.4	4	13.9
Lithic	All (flaked and a bead)					
Textile	All types (mostly string, yarn, cordage)		1	0.2	2	0.2
	Vegetal fiber other than cotton	Plain				
	Cotton	Plain	1	0.2	2	0.2
	Wool and cotton together	Plain				
	Wool	Plain				
	Wool	Dyed				
Other artifact	All materials					
	Botanical, not wood					
	Wood					
	Bone					
	Shell					
	Compound materials					

[a] Items too small to weigh in the field lab (< 0.10 g) are assigned a placeholder mass of 0.01 g.

midden recovered from the single stratigraphic locus that produced the two early dates on shell and twigs. The next two columns summarize the midden from that locus plus the limited amount of additional material from the three screened loci stratigraphically below it. A number of other small loci stratigraphically below the two radiocarbon dates were collected entirely as flotation samples and are not considered here.

Several agricultural crops were present in the very earliest, well-dated Preceramic midden at Loreto Viejo, including beans, lima beans, and a tuber that is probably yuca (*Manihot*), as well as the cotton and gourd expected in coastal sites from the late Archaic onward (Table 8.5). Maize was absent. In the lumped Preceramic samples (Table 8.4), these crops were joined by achira, quinoa, squash, and pacay, a tree product that may or may not have been tended. Maize also appeared in the lumped Preceramic sample. All of these foods were mostly concentrated in the tentatively identified upper Preceramic strata, as indicated by the ad hoc "early" and "late" Preceramic columns. Although this concentration suggests they may have been later additions to a more limited early crop mix, the samples are so small that it would be unwise to put much faith in this conclusion. The principal finding is that beans, lima beans, and a tuber that is probably yuca were in use by around 1900 to 1600 cal BC (see Table 8.2), and that the rest, if not already cultivated by then, came into use before the adoption of ceramics, very roughly bracketed between 920 cal BC and cal AD 220.

The earliest Preceramic midden also contained small traces of the consumption of birds, cuyes (*Cavia*), and camelids, the latter indicated not only by a tiny amount of bone but also by a little feces. Despite the apparent presence of camelids, cotton but not wool yarns were identified in the early midden. Fish bone and marine shellfish, especially *Choromytilus* mussels, suggest that these early farmers continued to depend on maritime resources, and they clearly indulged a taste for camarones, or river crayfish.

The lumped Preceramic midden is similar to the earliest loci in regard to animal bone, shellfish, and fish bone. A fair amount of feces of both camelids and dogs, especially in the ad hoc "late" Preceramic sample, suggests that both were routinely present before the adoption of ceramics and may have become more common over time.

The addition of some wool yarns, again concentrated in the ad hoc "late" Preceramic sample, also suggests that the role of camelids at Loreto Viejo may have increased during the Preceramic period.

Figures 8.7 and 8.8 graphically illustrate the temporal trends in the more common taxa in Table 8.4, quantified in three different ways: as ubiquity, as grams divided by all botanical mass, and as grams per 10 liters of soil. As in Table 8.4, data are presented for the ad hoc "early" and "late" Preceramic samples, as well as for the loci that are indeterminate, mixed, or transitional. These categories are shown as unfilled bars, and a quick

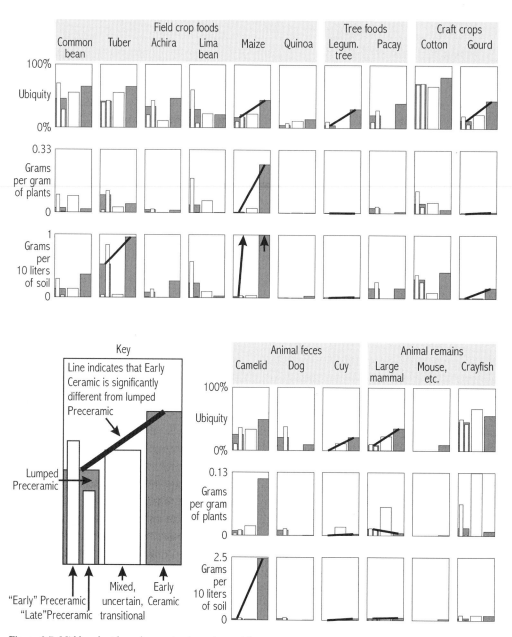

Figure 8.7. Midden chart key, plants, animal remains, and feces.

inspection shows that in many cases the behavior of these categories is erratic. These samples may simply be too small for real quantitative trends to be apparent. The lumped Preceramic and Early Ceramic loci are shown as filled bars. These are larger samples and generally show expectable trends. Differences between the Preceramic and Early Ceramic assemblages that are significant with at least 10% confidence are indicated with a trend line. Significance test results are also shown in Table 8.4.

Maize was a modest component of the Preceramic crop mix, probably mostly in the later part of the Preceramic. It is unfortunate that the ad hoc "early" and "late" Preceramic periods cannot be better dated at present, but this minor commitment to maize probably began after 920–530 cal BC.

The use of maize exploded around the time when ceramics were first adopted, sometime before cal AD 20–220. With the adoption of ceramics, maize became dramatically more ubiquitous, more predominant as a proportion of domestic refuse, and far more prevalent relative to volume of soil. The changes in all three ways of measuring maize shown in Table 8.4, as well as by

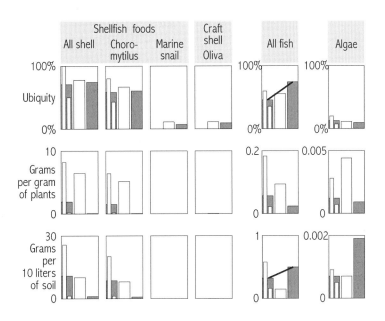

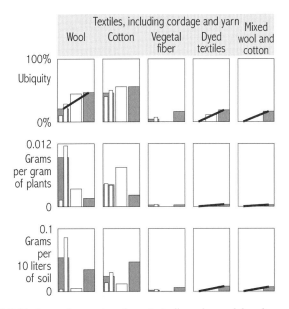

Figure 8.8. Marine products and textiles, principally cordage and threads.

grams per liter of soil, are statistically significant, with 1%, 5%, or 10% confidence, depending on which part of the maize plant is tallied. Figure 8.7 gives a visual impression of how sharp the quantitative increase was. Such a dramatic difference between the putatively Preceramic and Early Ceramic midden samples tends to confirm that they really are chronologically distinct, and that the analytical framework used here is generally sound.

Beans, tubers (mostly yuca), achira, and quinoa also may have become more common in the Early Ceramic period, although these trends are significant only for a single measure of tubers. It may be more correct to suggest only that they continued in consistent use. Lima beans may have declined in popularity in the Early Ceramic, but again, the trend is not significant. All of the ají pepper remains come from Early Ceramic loci, although because ají was never a large component of the midden, its absence from the small Preceramic sample does not necessarily mean that it was not in use before the Early Ceramic period.

The samples of tree fruits are also very small, but the trend seems to be toward a greater variety of products over time. Pacay, present in the Preceramic, continued in use. The pods and seeds of one or more leguminous trees such as algarrobo were present in the Preceramic refuse, but very rare. The seeds became significantly more common in the Early Ceramic by all three measures. Rare examples of guava and lúcuma fruits were added to the mix in the Early Ceramic, although their absence from the Preceramic midden could reflect nothing more than the small sample sizes. The berries and stems of the molle (*Schinus molle*) tree, which tend to be ubiquitous in Middle Horizon and Late Intermediate period contexts, are present but surprisingly scarce in the Preceramic and Early Ceramic midden sample.

Cotton continued to be important in the Early Ceramic period, and cotton seeds became significantly more common, even as the prevalence of the alternative fiber implied by wool yarns, camelid bone, and camelid dung was also rising. With the production of both cotton and wool increasing by some measures, perhaps it is not surprising that the Early Ceramic period also saw the first recovered examples of two-ply yarns combining one thread of each fiber. Dyed wool threads also first appeared in the Early Ceramic midden, including four loci with dark blue threads, three with red threads, and one with three green threads. Gourds, the other common craft or industrial crop, became significantly more common in the Early Ceramic period as well.

Consumption of camarones and marine algae (by all but one measure) appears to have both continued relatively unchanged into the Early Ceramic period. Cuy consumption may have gone up, since the amount of cuy feces in the Early Ceramic midden is significantly higher than in the Preceramic by all measures. Small rodent bones, not including remains of cuyes, may also have increased in the Early Ceramic period, although the trend is not significant. These patterns make sense in light of the apparently growing emphasis on agricultural production in the Early Ceramic period. Cuyes can be fed the unused parts of many crop plants, and small rodents may take advantage of larger amounts of stored food as production shifts away from gathered wild products and toward harvested agricultural ones. The consumption of camarones and algae would not be affected much by an increasing emphasis on agriculture, at least until irrigation began to affect the river level or alternative domesticated protein sources became important.

Marine shellfish, especially *Choromytilus* mussels, were ubiquitous in both Preceramic and Early Ceramic refuse. However, the amounts of marine shellfish relative to plant material and to volume of midden both declined, although none of the changes was statistically significant. At the same time, there was a statistically significant increase in the ubiquity of fish remains, as well as in their density by midden volume. Only relative to the exploding quantities of plant material does the growth in fish consumption seem to be damped out.

DISCUSSION

Inhabitants of the coastal Osmore Valley were committed agriculturalists by around 1750 cal BC, that is, by a date probably between roughly 1900 and 1600 cal BC, based on one-sigma error estimates. Assuming that the early dates at the terraced residential site of Loreto Viejo pertain to that permanent occupation rather than to some transitory early use of the spot, then the very location of the site some 13 km from the coast implies that its population must have relied in part on farming. Wild resources in such a tiny valley would have been limited, and people would presumably have chosen to settle there only if the general vicinity could have provided a reasonable fraction of their daily needs. The early dates are associated with limited traces of cultigens, including beans, lima beans, and a tuber that is probably yuca (*Manihot*), as well as cotton and gourd. Although there is always a chance that these associations are due to mixing or other sources of error, these particular strata were clearly defined, and multiple loci and numerous individual objects would have to have migrated across stratigraphic boundaries or become mixed to account for the data. Samples of the crops themselves are currently being exported for direct AMS radiocarbon dating. Although Núñez (1989, 1999) notes evidence of quinoa and maize agriculture in the northern Chilean inland valley of Tarapacá that is said to date to the fourth millennium cal BC, most of the Chilean late Archaic and Formative data that he and Muñoz (1989) reviewed paralleled the patterns and timing described here, with a tendency toward slightly earlier initial dates.

The shift toward inland, agricultural settlement appears to have occurred in the coastal Osmore Valley at roughly the same time as populations in the north, central, and south coast regions of Peru began making comparable shifts at the beginning of the Initial period. In this northern region, however, the commitment to agriculture was generally associated with the adoption of ceramics, although Pozorski and Pozorski (1990) note some variation in this regard, and the Supe Valley (Shady Solís et al. 2001) is a dramatic exception. Unlike most societies in the north, the people of the coastal Osmore farmed their beans, lima beans, yuca, achira, quinoa, squash, cotton, gourds, and even some maize for perhaps a millennium or more without the slightest traces of ceramics. As if the exceptions just noted were not sufficient to decouple agriculture from ceramics in Andean coastal prehistory, the coastal Osmore case adds to the evidence that committing to agriculture and adopting ceramics could be independent processes that occurred at different times. Even when the two changes seem contemporaneous, as in many Initial period societies, their independence in other cases means that each requires a separate explanation and that their contemporaneity is an interesting phenomenon that should be analyzed, rather than taken for granted.

Explaining the widespread commitment to inland farming at the beginning of the Initial period on the north, central, and south coast is fundamental to understanding the rise of the first societies in the New World that were complex enough to build monumental centers, since it was apparently the mixed economic base that made these developments possible. The explanations that have been proposed for this crucial process fall along a continuum of emphases that range from privileging climatic factors to downplaying such external influences and relying more on particularistic, sociopolitical processes (Quilter 1991:426–432; Burger 1995:57–58; Moseley 2001:131–132, 158). These factors and processes are not mutually exclusive. The early synchronous event in which the remote population of the coastal Osmore Valley and the monument-building societies of the north, central, and south coast all made the same shift toward inland agriculture at about the same time suggests that some large-scale, regional process influenced both portions of the coast in similar ways at the same time. No culture-historical explanation based on earlier social forms, emerging elites, power negotiations, or the like could have affected both the north, central, and south coast and the coastal Osmore Valley. If the synchrony is not a coincidence, the explanation will require a large-scale process such as regional climate change. Although there are other possibilities including possible changes in oceanographic parameters that might have affected maritime resources, ecological changes that could have affected agricultural potential, or perhaps even large-scale variations in tectonic processes such as coastal uplift climate is a tempting option.

Once again, the Supe Valley seems to be an exception (Shady Solís et al. 2001). If sites such as Caral were settled by farmers by 2600 cal BC, well before the move inland in other places, they would not have made this change under the same macroregional impulse that I postulate for everyone else. If the Supe Valley is the only exceptional case, the synchrony argument is still strong, because the many remaining temporal coincidences still have to be explained. If future research finds many more such exceptions, though, the foundation of the argument for macroregional causality will crumble.

As it happens, there is a documented macroregional climatological change at just the right time to explain the shift toward inland agriculture among the many coastal Andean societies that were not as precocious as that of the Supe Valley. Thompson et al. (2002) identify a dramatic, global climate desiccation anomaly between about 2500 and 1600 cal BC, while Weiss (2000), synthesizing a partially different mix of studies, finds a comparable severe dry period from about 2200 to 1900 cal BC. Coastal Andean populations that were geographically and culturally isolated from each other independently tended to commit to inland agriculture around the end of this drought period. This synchrony suggests that the improvement of climatic conditions for agriculture may have played a triggering or enabling, if not causal, role in the shift toward agriculture. That shift, in turn, led in some places to the mixed maritime and agrarian exchange-based economies that supported social complexity and monument building.

The Osmore material suggests one specific process that may have played a role in this development of economic and social complexity. Although the sample is small and the various measures do not paint a fully consistent picture regarding maritime resources, the data hint that while valley dwellers increased their commitment to agricultural crops, they may also have adjusted the marine component of their diet to include relatively less shellfish and more fish. If this finding proves correct here and elsewhere, it could imply changing emphases, technologies, and organizations of maritime production, probably driven by increasing demand. The actors could have been valley dwellers traveling to the sea to extract resources directly, or coastal maritime specialists producing for exchange. Fishing may offer more potential to increase output through investments in equipment, increasing labor inputs, and increasing collaboration and specialization in harvesting and processing than does shellfish gathering. The apparent shift from shellfish toward fish in the inland Osmore diets might reflect a logical response by maritime specialists who wished to increase output to serve a growing inland market with agricultural goods to exchange. This intensification of maritime production by shifting from individualized collecting to organized and capitalized fishing could have involved investments in capital and more complex labor organization, with the possibility for some groups and individuals to emerge as wealthier and more politically powerful than others.

Maize was a minor part of the Preceramic crop mix, apparently picking up in the later part of the Preceramic period, and dramatically dominating food refuse by the Early Ceramic period. Unfortunately, this process cannot yet be well dated, but it appears that after a long period of agriculture involving little or no maize, maize came into heavy use somewhere between 920 cal BC and cal AD 220. This is the same general pattern as is observed on the north, central, and south coast, where maize was rare or absent in Initial period agriculture, and was first generally adopted with the beginning of the Early Horizon, around 800–600 cal BC (Burger 1995).

Here the coastal Osmore material suggests, if very grossly, a second synchronous event. The similar pattern and the possible contemporaneity of the commitment to maize suggest that some single large-scale process may have influenced people in both the north, central, and south coast region and the coastal Osmore to increase their use of maize at around the same time. Explanations for the agricultural shift toward maize in the north have often involved influence from the highlands, paralleling the spread of Chavín iconography by means of trade, military incursions, population movements, ideological appeal, or other mechanisms (Burger 1995).

If future work shows the dates to agree reasonably well, no such culture-specific explanations will be able to account for the roughly simultaneous adoption of maize in the distant Osmore Valley. Moseley (1997) tentatively links dry periods suggested by low water levels in Lake Titicaca with the collapse of the Initial period U-shaped temple tradition around 1000–900 cal BC, and with the spread of Chavín Janabarriu phase iconography around 400–200 cal BC. With the current poor dating of the commitment to maize, either of these periods, or the trends leading into and out of them, might possibly have nudged widely separated populations to independently commit to maize. Better dates will be needed to connect a particular climatic shift to the adoption of maize.

The mechanism that would link such a climatic cause to the agricultural effect is not clear. The initial commitment to agriculture is credible as a generalized response to climatic change, and would have varied in specifics according to the local circumstances wherever it occurred. The shift to a significant emphasis on maize, however, involves the same, single species in every geographically isolated case. It is not obvious how the broad effects of climate change might bring about such a specific and uniform response in many different places. In this case, the macroregional causal factor might more likely be connected to the plant species itself, as would be the case with the development through human intervention, mutation, or hybridization of a variety of maize that was significantly more suitable for cultivation on the coast. The appearance of a new variety with a higher tolerance for salty coastal valley soils, for example, might account for the roughly contemporaneous shift toward maize among coastal farmers.

CONCLUSION

The midden data from Loreto Viejo and El Algodonal document the subsistence economy of the earliest agriculturalists known on the far south coast of Peru and its development over time. The associated dates indicate that people committed to inland agriculture on the far south coast at about the same time as did better known societies to the north. The roughly synchronized shift toward farming in coastal valleys in such widely separated places supports the view that climatic factors, specifically the amelioration of a long dry period, enabled, triggered, or perhaps caused the move toward inland farming both in the far south and on the rest of the Peruvian coast.

Although the commitment to inland agriculture did not presage further dramatic changes in the Osmore drainage, it was instrumental in the development of social complexity to the north. The trend among inland Osmore farmers toward consuming more fish and less shellfish hints that maritime specialists producing for exchange may have intensified production of the resource that responded best to greater capital investment and more complex labor organization. Such a change in maritime production practices toward potentially more capital intensive and coordinated operations in response to increasing demand from inland farmers may have been one mechanism through which the commitment to agriculture and the expansion of an economy based on exchange between farmers and fishers fostered social inequality and concentration of wealth among maritime specialists.

As at Caral, coastal Osmore farmers depended on agriculture for perhaps a millennium without using ceramics. The commitment to agriculture and the adoption of ceramics are not necessarily related, and each must be explained independently.

Like the farmers on the north, central, and south coast, the inhabitants of Loreto Viejo and El Algodonal initially planted little or no maize, but then adopted it as an important part of their diet sometime in the later portion of the first millennium BC or the beginning of the modern era. The dating is very rough, but this second, possibly synchronous event again suggests a macroregional process, in this case perhaps involving an evolutionary change in the maize plant itself.

When ecological changes are invoked as explanations in archaeology, it is often destructive processes that come to mind. Climate-related shifts and disasters are hypothesized to have done in the Initial period temple builders (Burger 1995), the Moche capital (Chapdelaine 2000; Moseley 2001), the Tiwanaku state (Kolata and Ortloff 1996), the Chiribaya (Reycraft 2000), and various Near Eastern societies (Weiss 2000), among many others (Bawden and Reycraft 2000; Moseley 1987). While Moseley (1997) and Binford et al. (1997) touch on the positive side of some climate variations, the emphasis is on desiccation, deluge, destruction, and decline. If the improving climate after 2000 cal BC did in fact lead people all along the coast of Peru to commit to agriculture, then this is one climate change that generously broadcast the seeds of complex and accomplished societies.

Acknowledgments

The field and laboratory work described here were conducted under the aegis of the Programa Contisuyo (now the Asociación Contisuyo), through which the Southern Peru Copper Corporation provided generous logistical support. Permissions for the fieldwork and export of radiocarbon samples were granted by the Instituto Nacional de Cultura of Peru. Funding was provided by NSF grants nos. 8903227 and 9982152, a DOE Fulbright-Hays dissertation research abroad grant, the Wenner-Gren Foundation, the UCLA Latin American Center, the UCLA Friends of Archaeology, a UCLA Chancellor's Dissertation Year Fellowship, and a personal donation from Guy Pinneo. Gerardo "Felipe" Carpio D., José Moya Y., and Raúl Rosas H. were the core of the field and laboratory team, which included over two dozen others at various times. Michael Moseley first encouraged me to work in the Ilo area. This research would have been impossible without the groundwork laid by Programa Contisuyo and other investigators before me, to whom I owe a debt of gratitude. Responsibility for any errors is solely my own.

NOTE

1. All calibrated date ranges are quoted at the 1σ confidence level, calibrated by OxCal v3.5 (Ramsey 2000) using Stuiver et al.'s (1998) atmospheric calibration curve, with no Southern Hemisphere correction or phase modeling. $\delta^{13}C$ corrections are included in conventional BP and calibrated AD dates.

REFERENCES

Alcalde Gonzales, Javier I.
1995   Ocupación humana en el período temprano en el Valle de Ilo: Chilatilla Bajo, Ilo Peru. *Actas del XIII*

Congreso Nacional de Arqueología Chilena, vol. 2, *Comunicaciones, Hombre y Desierto* 9(II):165–173.

Arriaza, Bernardo
1995   Chinchorro Bioarchaeology: Chronology and Mummy Seriation. *Latin American Antiquity* 6(1):35–55.

Bawden, Garth
1989   Pre-Incaic Cultural Ecology of the Ilo Region. In *Ecology, Settlement and History in the Osmore Drainage, Peru*, edited by Don S. Rice, Charles Stanish, and Phillip R. Scarr, pp. 183–205. BAR International Series 545 (i). British Archaeological Reports, Oxford.

Bawden, Garth, and Richard Martin Reycraft (eds.)
2000   *Environmental Disaster and the Archaeology of Human Response*. Maxwell Museum of Anthropology Anthropological Papers, no. 7. Albuquerque, New Mexico.

Bayliss, A., E. Shepherd Popescu, N. Beavan-Athfield, C. Bronk Ramsey, G. T. Cook, and A. Locker
2004   The Potential Significance of Dietary Offsets for the Interpretation of Radiocarbon Dates: An Archaeologically Significant Example from Medieval Norwich. *Journal of Archaeological Science* 31:563–575.

Binford, Michael W., Alan L. Kolata, Mark Brenner, John W. Janusek, Matthew T. Seddon, Mark Abbott, and Jason H. Curtis
1997   Climate Variation and the Rise and Fall of an Andean Civilization. *Quaternary Research* 47:235–248.

Bolaños B., Aldo
1987   Carrizal: Nueva fase temprana en el valle de Ilo. *Gaceta Arqueológica Andina* 14:18–22.

Bowman, Sheridan
1990   *Radiocarbon Dating*. University of California Press, Berkeley and Los Angeles.

Bronk Ramsey, Christopher
2000   *OxCal Program v3.5*. University of Oxford Radiocarbon Accelerator Unit, Oxford.

Burger, Richard
1995   *Chavín and the Origins of Andean Civilization*. Thames and Hudson, London.

Chapdelaine, Claude
2000   Struggling for Survival: The Urban Class of the Moche Site, North Coast of Peru. In *Environmental Disaster and the Archaeology of Human Response*, edited by Garth Bawden and Richard Martin Reycraft, pp. 121–142. Maxwell Museum of Anthropology Anthropological Papers, no. 7. Albuquerque, New Mexico.

Del Aguila Chávez, Carlos R.
1995   Roca Verde: Evidencia funeraria temprana en el litoral de Ilo (extremo sur del Perú). *Actas del XIII Congreso Nacional de Arqueología Chilena*, vol. 2, *Comunicaciones, Hombre y Desierto* 9(II):1–11.

Focacci, Guillermo
1980   Síntesis de la arqueología del extremo norte de Chile. *Chungará* 6:3–23.

Focacci, Guillermo, and Sergio Erices
1973   Excavaciones en túmulos de San Miguel de Azapa (Arica, Chile). In *Actas del VI Congreso de Arqueología Chilena*. Boletín de Prehistoria, special issue, 1972–1973, Santiago.

Gibbons, Jean D.
1993   *Nonparametric Statistics: An Introduction*. Quantitative Applications in the Social Sciences, Paper Series 90. Sage Publications, Newbury Park, California.

Goldstein, Paul S.
2000   Exotic Goods and Everyday Chiefs: Long Distance Exchange and Indigenous Sociopolitical Development in the South Central Andes. *Latin American Antiquity* 11(4):1–27.

Haas, Jonathan
1982   *The Evolution of the Prehistoric State*. Columbia University Press, New York.

Keefer, David K., Susan D. deFrance, Michael E. Moseley, James B. Richardson III, Dennis R. Satterlee, and Amy Day-Lewis
1998   Early Maritime Economy and El Niño Events at Quebrada Tacahuay, Peru. *Science* 281:1833–1835.

Kolata, Alan L., and Charles R. Ortloff
1996   Agroecological Perspectives on the Decline of the Tiwanaku State. In *Tiwanaku and Its Hinterland, Archaeology and Paleoecology of an Andean Civilization*, vol. 1, *Agroecology*, edited by Alan Kolata, pp. 181–201. Smithsonian Institution Press, Washington, DC.

Molto, J. Eldon, Joe D. Stewart, and Paula J. Reimer
1997   Problems in Radiocarbon Dating Human Remains from Arid Coastal Areas: An Example from the Cape Region of Baja California. *American Antiquity* 62(3):489–507.

Moseley, Michael E.
1975   *The Maritime Foundations of Andean Civilization*. Cummings Archaeology Series. Cummings Publishing Co., Menlo Park, CA.
1987   Punctuated Equilibrium: Searching the Ancient Record for El Niño. *The Quarterly Review of Archaeology* 8(3):7–10.

1992   Maritime Foundations and Multilinear Evolution: Retrospect and Prospect. *Andean Past* 3:5–42.

1997   Climate, Culture, and Punctuated Change: New Data, New Challenges. *The Review of Archaeology* 18(1):19–27.

2001   *The Incas and Their Ancestors: The Archaeology of Peru,* rev. ed. Thames and Hudson, London.

Muñoz Ovalle, Iván

1987   Enterramientos en túmulos en el Valle de Azapa: Nuevas evidencias para definir la fase Alto Ramírez en el extremo norte de Chile. *Chungará* 19:93–127.

1989   El Período Formativo en el Norte Grande (1.000 a.C. a 500 d.C.). In *Culturas de Chile: Prehistoria desde sus orígenes hasta los albores de la Conquista,* edited by Jorge Hidalgo L., Virgilio Schiappacasse F., Hans Niemeyer F., Carlos Aldunate del S., and Iván Solimano R., pp. 107–128. Editorial Andrés Bello, Santiago.

Núñez, Lautaro

1989   Hacia la producción de alimentos y la vida sedentaria (5.000 a.C. a 900 d.C.). In *Culturas de Chile: Prehistoria desde sus orígenes hasta los albores de la Conquista,* edited by Jorge Hidalgo L., Virgilio Schiappacasse F., Hans Niemeyer F., Carlos Aldunate del S., and Iván Solimano R., pp. 81–105. Editorial Andrés Bello, Santiago.

1999   Archaic Adaptation on the South-Central Andean Coast. In *Pacific Latin America in Prehistory: The Evolution of Archaic and Formative Cultures,* edited by Michael Blake, pp. 199–211. Washington State University Press, Pullman.

Owen, Bruce D.

1993b   Early Ceramic Settlement in the Coastal Osmore Valley, Peru: Preliminary Report. Paper presented at the 33rd Annual Meeting of the Institute of Andean Studies, Berkeley, CA, USA.

1993a   *A Model of Multiethnicity: State Collapse, Competition, and Social Complexity from Tiwanaku to Chiribaya in the Osmore Valley, Peru.* Unpublished doctoral dissertation, Department of Anthropology, University of California, Los Angeles.

2002   Marine Carbon Reservoir Age Estimates for the Far South Coast of Peru. *Radiocarbon* 44(3):701–708.

Pearsall, Deborah M.

1992   The Origins of Plant Cultivation in South America. In *The Origins of Agriculture,* edited by C. Wesley Cowan and Patty Jo Watson, pp. 173–206. Smithsonian Institution, Washington, DC.

Pozorski, Shelia, and Thomas Pozorski

1988   Late Preceramic through Early Horizon Subsistence in the Casma Valley. In *Economic Prehistory of the Central Andes,* edited by Elizabeth Wing and Jane Wheeler, pp. 95–98. BAR International Series 427. British Archaeological Reports, Oxford.

1990   Reexamining the Critical Preceramic/Ceramic Period Transition: New Data from Coastal Peru. *American Anthropologist* 92:481–491.

2002   The Sechin Alto Complex and Its Place within Casma Valley Initial Period Development. In *Andean Archaeology I: Variations in Sociopolitical Organization,* edited by William H. Isbell and Helaine Silverman, pp. 21–52. Kluwer Academic, New York.

Quilter, Jeffrey

1991   Late Preceramic Peru. *Journal of World Prehistory* 5(4):387–438.

Quilter, Jeffrey, Bernardino Ojeda E., Deborah M. Pearsall, Daniel H. Sandweiss, John G. Jones, and Elizabeth S. Wing

1991   Subsistence Economy of El Paraíso, an Early Peruvian Site. *Science* 251:277–283.

Reycraft, Richard Martin

2000   Long-term Human Response to El Niño in South Coastal Peru circa A.D. 1400. In *Environmental Disaster and the Archaeology of Human Response,* edited by Garth Bawden and Richard Martin Reycraft, pp. 99–120. Maxwell Museum of Anthropology Anthropological Papers, no. 7. Albuquerque, New Mexico.

Sandweiss, Daniel, and Michael E. Moseley

2001   Amplifying Importance of New Research in Peru. *Science* 294(5547):1651–1652.

Sandweiss, Daniel H., James B. Richardson III, Elizabeth J. Reitz, Jeffrey T. Hsu, and Robert A. Feldman

1989   Early Maritime Adaptations in the Andes: Preliminary Studies at the Ring Site, Peru. In *Ecology, Settlement and History in the Osmore Drainage, Peru,* edited by Don S. Rice, Charles Stanish, and Phillip R. Scarr. BAR International Series 545(i):35–84. British Archaeological Reports, Oxford.

Santoro, Calógero

1980   Estratigrafía y secuencia cultural funeraria fases: Azapa, Alto Ramírez y Tiwanaku (Arica-Chile). *Chungará* 6:24–45.

Shady Solís, Ruth, Jonathan Haas, and Winifred Creamer

2001   Dating Caral, a Preceramic Site in the Supe Valley on the Central Coast of Peru. *Science* 292(5517): 723–726.

Stanish, Charles, and Don S. Rice
1989   The Osmore Drainage, Peru: An Introduction to the Work of Programa Contisuyo. In *Ecology, Settlement and History in the Osmore Drainage, Peru*, edited by Don S. Rice, Charles Stanish, and Phillip R. Scarr. BAR International Series 545(i):1–4. British Archaeological Reports, Oxford.

Stuiver, Minze, Paula Reimer, and Tom Braziunas
1998   High-Precision Radiocarbon Age Calibration for Terrestrial and Marine Samples. *Radiocarbon* 40(3):1127–1151.

Tauber, Henrik
1983 ^{14}C Dating of Human Beings in Relation to Dietary Habits. In *PACT 8, Proceedings of the First International Symposium ^{14}C and Archaeology*, edited by W. K. Mook and H. T. Waterbolk, pp. 365–375. Council of Europe, Strasbourg, France.

Thompson, Lonnie G., Ellen Mosley-Thompson, Mary E. Davis, Keith A. Henderson, Henry H. Brecher, Victor S. Zagorodnov, Tracy A. Mashiotta, Ping-Nan Lin, Vladimir N. Mikhalenko, Douglas R. Hardy, and Jürg Beer
2002   Kilimanjaro Ice Core Records: Evidence of Holocene Climate Change in Tropical Africa. *Science* 298:589–593.

Towle, Margaret A.
1961   *The Ethnobotany of Pre-Columbian Peru*. Viking Fund Publications in Anthropology 30. Wenner-Gren Foundation for Anthropological Research, New York.

Weiss, Harvey
2000   Beyond the Younger Dryas: Collapse as Adaptation to Abrupt Climate Change in Ancient West Asia and the Eastern Mediterranean. In *Environmental Disaster and the Archaeology of Human Response*, edited by Garth Bawden and Richard Martin Reycraft, pp. 75–98. Maxwell Museum of Anthropology Anthropological Papers, no. 7. Albuquerque, New Mexico.

Wise, Karen
1989   Archaic Period Research in the Lower Osmore Region. In *Ecology, Settlement and History in the Osmore Drainage, Peru*, edited by Don S. Rice, Charles Stanish, and Phillip R. Scarr. BAR International Series 545(i):85–99. British Archaeological Reports, Oxford.

1995   La ocupación Chinchorro en Villa del Mar, Ilo, Perú. *Gaceta Arqueológica Andina* 24:135–149.

1997   The Late Archaic Period Occupation at Carrizal, Perú. *Contributions in Science* 467:1–16.

1999   Kilómetro 4 y la ocupación del período arcaico en el área de Ilo, al sur del Perú. *Boletín de Arqueología PUCP* 3:335–363.

CHAPTER 9

THE TIWANAKU OCCUPATION OF THE NORTHERN TITICACA BASIN

CHARLES STANISH

THE TALKING DOG

In the earliest days of Programa Contisuyo in the early 1980s, Michael Moseley and a crew of graduate students drove out to the newly discovered site complex of Omo in Moquegua. While we, the graduate students, started to argue about this canal or that tomb or some broken kero on the ground, Mike admonished us with his now famous critique: "It's like the talking dog—it doesn't matter what it says, it's the fact that it talks at all."[1] Mike once again had got the major point, namely, that this massive settlement represented the largest known Tiwanaku site outside the Titicaca Basin. Never before had a Tiwanaku colony of this size and preservation been found, and we graduate students were bogged down in trivial details. Mike taught us that the details of the huge site of Omo could wait a while but that the implications of this major find were worth savoring and required some deep reflection. A truly monumental discovery like this one offered an opportunity to look beyond the details and think about the big picture, as Mike has always done. It was a time to reflect on what this discovery meant for Andean cultural history in particular, and for understanding the process of archaic state expansion in general.

Mike has inspired many of us to think big, and this chapter is written in his honor, in remembrance of the spirit Mike created that day.

From 1998 to 2005, members of the Programa Collasuyu in Puno—a program modeled on Mike's Programa Contisuyo—conducted a comprehensive full-regional-coverage survey of the northern Titicaca Basin (Figures 9.1 and 9.2). We discovered more than 1,300 sites in an area of approximately 1,000 km^2. The survey covered the entire river drainage of Huancané-Putina from Lake Titicaca up to the town of Putina and east to the cordillera. We also covered the entire shoreline of Lake Arapa and the large pampa from Taraco to the edge of Lake Titicaca in the south. This survey covered all ecological zones in the northern Titicaca Basin, including the richest agricultural land in the entire Titicaca region. It is an area crisscrossed with raised fields, canals, and other agricultural features, indicating how important the region was for farming and pasture.

Of the more than 1,300 sites discovered during the survey, at least 280 had Tiwanaku-style or Tiwanaku-contemporary artifacts.[2] There are many implications of these data for understanding the nature of Tiwanaku expansion. A very dense population of Tiwanaku settlement is evident. However, the locations of those settlements differ substantially from settlement locations in the Juli-Pomata region (Stanish et al. 1997), the Tiwanaku Valley (Albarracín-Jordan 1990, 1996a, b; Albarracín-Jordan and Mathews 1990), the Katari region (Janusek and Kolata 2003), the Island of the Sun (Bauer and Stanish 2001; Stanish and Bauer 2004), and the Huatta area (Lémuz 2001).

The full implication of these settlement data for understanding Tiwanaku expansion into the northern Titicaca Basin is the theme of this chapter.

TIWANAKU: AN EVOLVING MODEL OF AN ARCHAIC STATE

The discovery of Omo was one of many watersheds for Tiwanaku studies that have occurred since the early 1980s. Along with the publication of Cerro Baúl by Luis Lumbreras and his colleagues, the existence of Omo indicated that Moquegua was home to the two great Middle Horizon states. Thanks to the subsequent work of many members of Programa Contisuyo (including Mike's students), we have learned a significant amount about the Tiwanaku occupation of Moquegua. Paul Goldstein's book (2005) synthesizes many of these finds. Likewise, the work of Bertha Vargas at Chen Chen and others has shown us how strong the Tiwanaku state was in the western coastal valleys. The work of Moseley, Donna Nash, and Ryan Williams, following the pioneering work of Robert Feldman, has brought to life the Wari occupation at Cerro Baúl, Tiwanaku's counterpart in the Moquegua Valley.

In an earlier publication (Stanish 2002), I described how our model of Tiwanaku has shifted over the last hundred years. Ephraim Squier's and Wendell Bennett's view of Tiwanaku as a largely depopulated ceremonial center was countered by Arturo Posnansky's (1945, 1957) view of Tiwanaku as an urban metropolis so grand that it influenced cultures as far away as the American Southwest. Carlos Ponce (1990, 1991, 1992, 1993) took up the "big state" model, which was ultimately attacked by many members of the Bolivian academy as being too close to the conservative political ideologies of the small but powerful urban elite who ran the country. By the 1980s the two polar views of Tiwanaku had been formalized into a series of models that coalesced around Ponce's state model (see Kolata 1993), on one side, with David Browman's (1978, 1980, 1981, 1984) decentralized model on the other (see Albarracín-Jordan 1996a for another decentralized state model).

It was against that backdrop that the Moquegua Valley Middle Horizon settlements were found. As I described in the 2002 publication, the discovery of the Omo complex strongly supported the Ponce model.

Subsequent work at Lukurmata and data from regional surveys also supported the state model. In the former case, the site was shown to be at least 1.5 km² in extent, with a massive Tiwanaku occupation that covered an earlier Upper Formative one. In the latter case, the settlement data from the southern and southwestern Titicaca Basin indicated that Tiwanaku politically absorbed earlier Upper Formative cultures, characteristic of a classic expansionist state.

The state model was largely supported until work in the northwestern Titicaca Basin (see Figures 9.1 and 9.2) indicated there were large areas there with little Tiwanaku settlement. The distinct nature of the settlement patterns in the north forced some of us to develop a new model of Tiwanaku. This model is outlined in three of my publications (Stanish 2001, 2002, 2003). Essentially, Tiwanaku maintained control of a contiguous territory to the south of the Ilave and Escoma rivers. North of these rivers in the Titicaca Basin, however, Tiwanaku maintained a string of colonies in

Figure 9.1. South America.

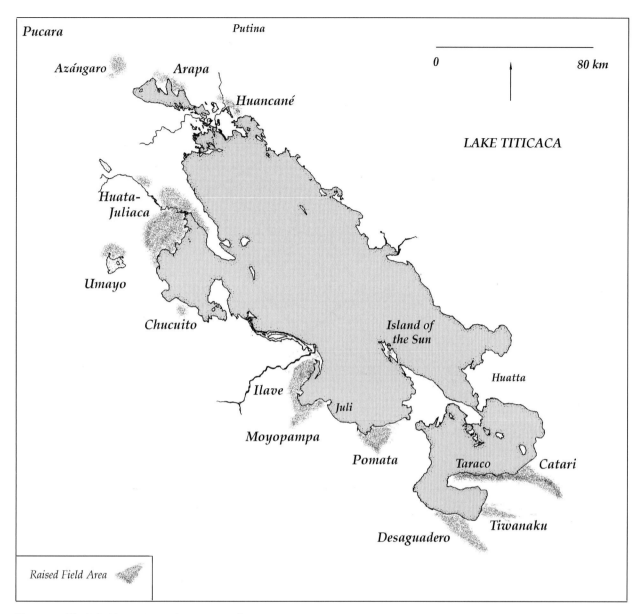

Figure 9.2. The Lake Titicaca Basin, showing areas of interest.

agriculturally rich areas near the lake and along the historically known road system. Outside the Titicaca Basin, Tiwanaku maintained at least four colonies—in the Arequipa area, Moquegua, Cochabamba, and in Larecaja (Figure 9.3). Local groups not incorporated into the Tiwanaku state were found throughout the region. In the northern Titicaca Basin, I called this culture "Late Huaña" (see below) and dated it to approximately AD 700–1000, contemporary with the Tiwanaku occupation (Figure 9.4).[3] Late Huaña peoples might have lived in areas away from direct Tiwanaku control, while Tiwanaku controlled small enclaves in key areas along the lake edge.

THE POST-PUCARA AND PRE-LATE INTERMEDIATE PERIODS IN THE NORTHERN TITICACA BASIN

For years, Titicaca Basin archaeologists sought to fit the northern lake area into the chronology developed for the south by Bennett and Ponce. They likewise tried to make it consistent with the Horizon framework used throughout the rest of the Andes, based on a master sequence from Ica. In 1956, John Rowe proposed a cultural historical sequence for Puno that was consistent with the Ica sequence and the southern Titicaca Basin data: Qaluyu, Pucara, "Bolivian

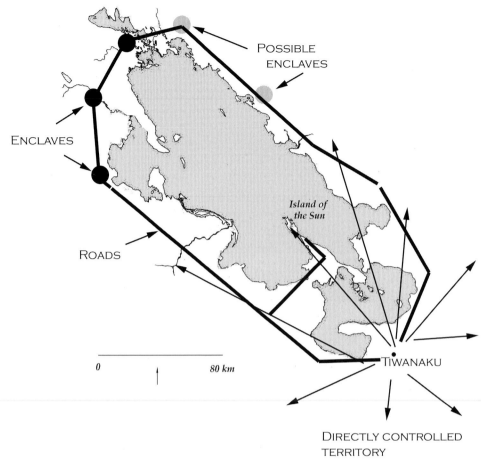

Figure 9.3. Tiwanaku political geography.

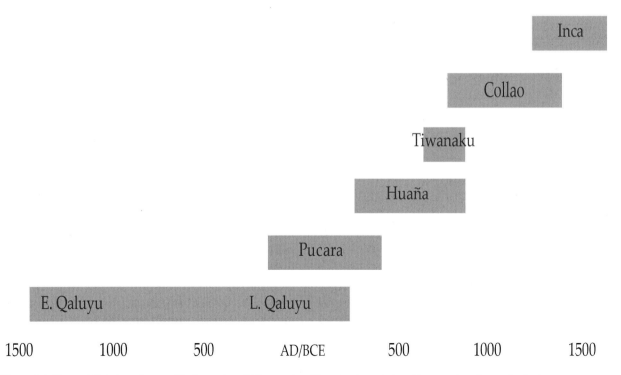

Figure 9.4. The modified chronology used in the northern Titicaca region. Note that the periods and/or ceramic styles overlap in time.

Tiahuanaco," Collao (local Late Intermediate period), and Inca (Rowe 1956:138). The Tiwanaku period was the Middle Horizon, while Qaluyu and Pucara seemed to fit comfortably within the Early Horizon and Early Intermediate periods. This was a very reasonable proposition at the time that Rowe offered it. However, one of the major conceptual impediments is the insistence by some archaeologists (even today) on fitting Titicaca Basin chronology into the master Ica sequence as first outlined by Rowe for the region more than fifty years ago.

One of the most enigmatic periods in the northern Titicaca Basin is that from the end of the Pucara culture, ca. AD 300 (Mujica 1978, 1987; Paredes 1985), to the Late Intermediate period, ca. AD 1000–1450. This time span covers the Tiwanaku or Middle Horizon period in the Ica sequence. The horizon chronology assumes that a Horizon style, such as Tiwanaku, will spread very quickly over a landscape. This is not the case in the Titicaca Basin. Tiwanaku Classic pottery was most likely manufactured as early as the early sixth century AD at Tiwanaku itself (Janusek 2003; Goldstein 2005). Excavation data indicate that Tiwanaku reached the Island of the Sun around the late seventh century (Seddon 1998) and the Isla Esteves a bit later. The precise timing of Tiwanaku expansion in the far north of the Titicaca region, around Tiwanaku, is unclear. Based on the dates for the Islands of the Sun and Esteves and the assumption that the spread was relatively smooth, it is not unreasonable to assume that Tiwanaku did not reach the Arapa-Taraco area until the very late seventh century or even the early eighth century AD.

Complicating this cultural historical reconstruction is the timing of the Pucara collapse. There is a small but excellent literature on the timing of the cessation of Pucara pottery manufacture and the main site's ceasing to exist as a major political power (Klarich 2005). The consensus date is around the end of the third or early fourth century AD for the end of Pucara influence. Recent carbon dates from Taraco indicate post-Pucara occupations at the site between AD 130 and AD 350.[4] This time period, unfortunately, is characterized by large margins of error and bimodal distributions of the calibrated dates. As a result, it is equally likely that the end of Pucara at Taraco, at least in the test excavation that we conducted, was as early as the middle of the second century or as late as the middle of the fourth century. These data, therefore, do not contradict the consensus date of around AD 300, but neither do they help to pinpoint a terminal date any better.

There is no question that the Pucara occupation ended at Taraco by the middle of the fourth century AD, and probably much earlier. This most likely represents a terminal date for Pucara in the northern basin as a whole, although it is possible that Pucara pottery manufacture could have continued into the fifth century. Given that Tiwanaku did not enter the northern basin until the seventh or eighth century, we have possibly a 200- to 300-year gap between the end of Pucara and the beginning of the Tiwanaku period.

For years, this gap was problematic for Titicaca Basin archaeologists. Luis Lumbreras and Hernán Amat (1968) sensibly argued for a hiatus in major human settlement, or at least major pottery manufacture, at this time. Others argued that Tiwanaku was earlier and Pucara a bit later, thereby eliminating the gap. Work over the years has not adequately resolved this issue. The problem of the "gap" between Pucara and Tiwanaku remained a major issue for investigative research in this region.

The Huaña Culture

In a 2003 publication I argued that there was no gap in human settlement between the end of Pucara and the beginning of the Tiwanaku occupation. I reached this conclusion on both theoretical and empirical grounds. In the first instance, it was theoretically improbable that such a rich area as that found from Lake Arapa to Huancané would be abandoned in the absence of a huge political or military force, neither of which existed in the Andes at that time (Arkush and Stanish 2005). Empirically, we consistently found pottery that fit a seriation between Pucara and Tiwanaku. We likewise found numerous sites with substantial Qaluyu, Pucara, Collao, and Inca, but which did not have Tiwanaku. Rather than argue for site abandonment, I think it is more likely that the ceramic chronology, based on the Ica sequence, was wrong. This meant that the "Middle Horizon" was a useless concept. The pre-Tiwanaku/post-Pucara styles were yet to be defined. Based on these inferences, I argued for a new culture that must have existed between Pucara and Tiwanaku. After consulting Aymara intellectuals, we applied the name "Huaña" to that culture, because that Aymara term referred to a drought or severe environmental stress, which seemed an appropriate description for that time (Bertonio 1612:Bk. I, 427, Bk. II, 147).

Based on my observations of the nature of Tiwanaku settlement patterns north of the Ilave and Suches rivers, I likewise argued that there existed a culture that was contemporaneous with Tiwanaku but was not incorporated into its political orbit, and this new culture dated to ca. AD 700–1000.[5] I named the period prior to Tiwanaku influence (between AD 300 and 700) the "Early Huaña," and the later period, contemporary with Tiwanaku, the "Late Huaña" period. These two periods were based on numerous empirical observations from our ongoing survey, plus ongoing excavations by various researchers (e.g., Edmundo de la Vega and Cecilia Chávez at Esteves Island near Puno).

THE NORTHERN TITICACA BASIN SURVEY PROGRAM

In 1998, members of the Programa Collasuyu, including Cecilia Chávez, Adán Umire, Aimée Plourde, José Núñez, and Edmundo de la Vega, began systematic survey of the Huancané and Putina regions in the northern Titicaca Basin (Figure 9.5). The first two seasons, 1998 and 1999, involved reconnaissance only. We toured a number of valleys in the north, from the

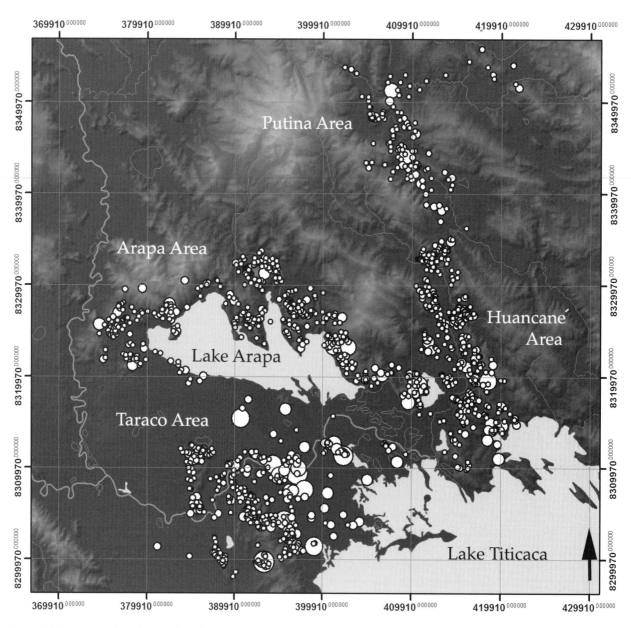

Figure 9.5. Survey areas from the 1999 through 2004 seasons. Each dot represents a site or site cluster. The size of the dot is roughly proportional to the size of the site.

Conima area in the east to the Juliaca-Ayabacas River in the northwest. After two years of large-site reconnaissance (Stanish et al. 2005), we decided to concentrate on the Huancané-Putina river valley first, then cover the area around Lake Arapa.

The decision to work in this region was based on several factors. First, we believed that the role of exchange from the eastern slopes of the Andes was critical in the development of the Middle Formative to Tiwanaku periods in the Titicaca region. In particular, maize, coca, and feline pelts were considered very important in the cultures for politically motivated feasting and other social events. Likewise, ethnohistorical and archaeological evidence, particularly the Garci Diez *Visita* and the Toledo *Tasa* (1975), indicated that gold, copper, lapis, and other ores and textiles were important commodities exchanged in the region as well.

The Putina river valley was selected as the most likely route for access to the eastern slopes. Three major roads all converge on Putina before crossing the Cordillera Real near Macusani. In 1999, Lawrence Coben and I conducted a brief reconnaissance in the Carabaya region, following the newly opened road to the hydroelectric plant at San Gabán (Coben and Stanish 2005). Although we did not discover any pre-Late Intermediate period[6] pottery or other diagnostics in the region during this brief survey, we did discover a vast settlement system dating to the local Late Intermediate period, known as Collao, and an equally impressive set of Inca roads and tambos. These data indicate that Late Intermediate period peoples had established trade networks in the forested areas, possibly based on patterns established by their ancestors some centuries before.

The Putina area was surveyed first. We then finished the Huancané region and moved west. The Lake Arapa area and Taraco were known to be regions rich in carved stelae and other Formative period artifacts (Chávez 1975; Chávez and Chávez 1975). We know that it was a major center of Formative period settlement. Analysis of the environmental data indicated that this area was also the richest agricultural zone in the Titicaca Basin. Huge areas of raised fields were evident on the aerial photographs. Canals and artificial cochas dotted the landscape, indicating intensive use of the entire region. This area was therefore an ideal zone in which to examine the full range of complex political development in the history of the Titicaca Basin.

The survey was executed as a classic full-scale regional coverage survey with teams of archaeologists separated by no more than 25 m (see Stanish et al. 1997 for a discussion of the methodology used in this survey). The Huancané-Putina section of the survey was conducted from 2001 to 2002. With the assistance of an NSF grant, work was completed in the lower Huancané region and around the entire Lake Arapa-Taraco area from 2003 to 2005.

All sites were recorded from the Early Archaic (Cipolla 2005) to the Early Colonial period. At the time of this publication, we have recorded 1,306 sites in approximately 1,000 km², with new ones added periodically as analysis and additional survey are completed. The distribution of all sites from all time periods is presented in Figure 9.5.

The Tiwanaku/Late Huaña Settlement Pattern

Well-defined ceramic markers easily identify the Tiwanaku presence in the region. Surface representation of diagnostics in the region is quite good, as seen in Figure 9.6. As with the Inca, virtually all Tiwanaku pottery outside of its core territory in the Titicaca Basin is locally manufactured. With a few exceptions (Islands of the Sun and Moon, Isla Esteves), the Tiwanaku state anticipated Inca policies of exporting a restricted set of pottery forms and iconographic representations into areas where they had influence. The pottery is locally manufactured, but it followed fairly strict canons of style.

Analysis of the artifact assemblages from the sites provides a means to define two kinds of sites that date to the period from ca. AD 700 to AD 1000: (1) sites with a substantial percentage of the decorated assemblage and diagnostic plainware assemblage composed of Tiwanaku pottery (Figures 9.7–9.11) and a small percentage identified as the contemporary Late Huaña (Figure 9.12) or other pottery styles (112 sites); and (2) sites with a small percentage of the decorated assemblage and diagnostic plainware assemblage composed of Tiwanaku pottery and a larger percentage identified as Late Huaña during this Tiwanaku/Late Huaña period (169 sites). I interpret the first category as sites that have been incorporated into Tiwanaku's political orbit. The second category is interpreted as sites maintaining exchange relationships with Tiwanaku-affiliated sites but displaying no evidence for direct political affiliation. This interpretation works well for sites up the Huancané-Putina River, where there were no Tiwanaku potsherds at all. In the lower valley sites, the presence of a few (always less than five) sherds in the surface collection, plus the presence of Late Huaña pottery, was sufficient to assign a non-Tiwanaku affiliation to

Surface diagnostics from site TA-731 near
Taraco, Lake Titicaca

Figure 9.6. Surface diagnostics found on survey. This quality is typical for the northern Titicaca Basin.

the site. It is possible that some of these sites could be in Category 1 and that the surface representation was poor. However, we usually had very large collections selected from the hundreds or thousands of sherds on the surface. The patterns are fairly robust between the upper reaches of the Putina Valley and the lake area. For sites near the lake, however, assignment to the autonomous Late Huaña category or to the Tiwanaku-affiliated category was more problematic. It was complicated by the fact that ethnography and history teach us that settlements such as these have fluid relationships with political entities like Tiwanaku. It is likely that many of the larger settlements assigned to either of the two categories would have cycled through periods of allegiance to the Tiwanaku state followed by some kind of autonomy. As my colleague Joyce Marcus (pers. comm., 2006) notes, the apparent dichotomy therefore is more of a continuum, with settlements oscillating between autonomy and affiliation, semi-autonomy, and even short-term incorporation. The existence of a large quantity of Tiwanaku pottery on the site simply means that at one point in its life cycle, the settlement and its people actively participated in events that marked a strong affiliation with Tiwanaku, particularly feasting and trading.

Given these caveats, the settlement patterns are quite instructive (Figures 9.13–9.15). The Tiwanaku occupation is very high in the region, higher in fact than in the Juli-Pomata area near Tiwanaku's core and roughly similar to that of the Tiwanaku Valley itself (see Albarracín-Jordan and Mathews 1990). Yet the Tiwanaku occupation is restricted to the edges of Lakes Titicaca and Arapa and the pampas near the rivers and road. There is no Tiwanaku site north of the lower end of the river in the Huancané-Putina Valley. This leaves several hundred square kilometers of rich farmland and pastureland outside Tiwanaku's immediate reach but clearly settled by contemporary Late Huaña peoples. There are contemporary Late Huaña settlements in this area, however, indicating that Tiwanaku peoples near the lake were in contact with the settlements upriver.

Tiwanaku Colonies

In one remarkable case (Figures 9.16–9.19) near Huancané, there is a small Tiwanaku "enclave" or colonial area (the main site is Hu-310) with a canal that draws water from an independent set of *pukios*, or springs. The entire small valley has a set of raised fields, elevated canals or aqueducts, a reservoir, and a few Tiwanaku sites. Just 3 km to the south is a contemporary site complex with its own raised fields, canals, and so forth. Figure 9.14 illustrates how the entire river valley of Putina and lower Huancané did not have any Tiwanaku sites, only local Middle Horizon ones, with an occasional Tiwanaku piece. This single exception proves the rule: the site

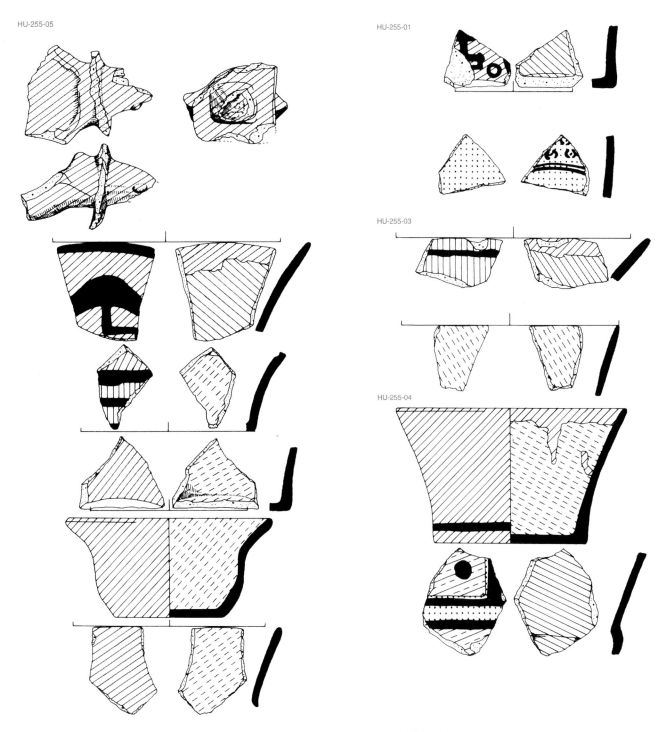

Figure 9.7. Tiwanaku pottery from the survey area.

Figure 9.8. Tiwanaku pottery from the survey area.

HU-280(R)01

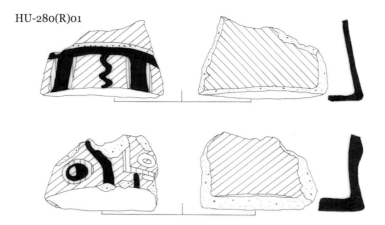

Figure 9.9. Tiwanaku pottery from the survey area.

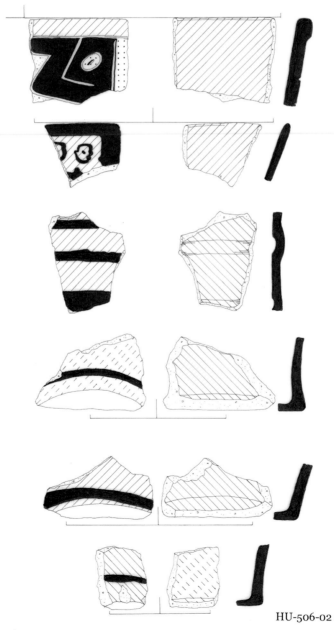

HU-506-02

Figure 9.10. Tiwanaku pottery from the survey area.

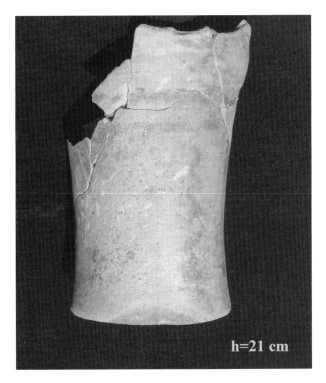

Figure 9.11. Tiwanaku pottery from the survey area.

TA-885.05
h=16 cm

Figure 9.12. Huaña pottery from the survey area.

complex around Hu-310 draws water from an independent source. In other words, like the Wari at Cerro Baúl in Moquegua, the Tiwanaku in the northern Titicaca Basin established enclaves in territory populated by complex polities outside their control. As at Cerro Baúl, excavations have revealed some interaction between the two peoples. But the two groups maintained a substantial cultural distance from each other.

Another large Tiwanaku site that is located among smaller Tiwanaku and Late Huaña sites is one located on a low hill in the Taraco pampa. The site, AR-1413, is in the middle of a relatively sparse and now largely unoccupied plain (Figures 9.20–9.23). At the top of the hill is a large set of structures characterized by open plazas (Figure 9.21). The walls are quite thick (Figure 9.23) and appear to be large, high external walls to enclose internal structures. There is little surface evidence of internal walls, but it is likely that perishable reed wall structures characterized the plaza areas.

CONCLUSIONS

The survey data indicate an intensive but restricted settlement of the northern Titicaca Basin by the Tiwanaku state. The Tiwanaku peoples moved into the northern

Titicaca region and established a number of settlements along the rivers and roads and near the raised field areas. Alongside the Tiwanaku settlement was a local culture known as Late Huaña. Late Huaña sites are found throughout the survey region. In particular, there are no Tiwanaku sites located in the higher reaches of the Putina River, whereas there are a number of Late Huaña sites in the area around Putina, indicating the existence of contemporary, non-Tiwanaku peoples in the northern Titicaca Basin.

The highly fluid and dynamic period from ca. AD 300 to 1000 in the northern Titicaca Basin was characterized by a series of new cultures that developed in the wake of Pucara collapse. It appears to be a classic case of chiefly cycling, as described by Joyce Marcus (1998). For several centuries, independent polities developed along this rich lakeshore and along the rivers. The Tiwanaku state moved into the region around the eighth century AD. We do not know the precise mechanisms by which this process of state expansion took place. What we can deduce from the settlement data from the Northern Titicaca Basin Survey was that the power (and the ability to incorporate people and polities) of Tiwanaku was limited in scope. The Tiwanaku state, like its counterpart of Wari to the north, was not a small version of the Inca state. Rather, the Tiwanaku state had the power to control many places, but it had to select the areas where it could establish a presence. The Tiwanaku established a small enclave in a marginal agricultural area near Huancané, focused on the site of HU-310, while contemporary and apparently autonomous groups lived close by. The Tiwanaku exercised much greater control along the Ramis River between lakes Arapa and Titicaca. Perhaps Tiwanaku established trade posts as permanent settlements. The intermingling of the Late Huaña and Tiwanaku sites suggests some kinds of interaction. Paul Goldstein (2005) suggests that in Moquegua, the Tiwanaku colonists maintained their identity by isolating themselves from the indigenous populations. Perhaps the Tiwanaku peoples in the Huancané region indeed avoided contact with their neighbors and maintained a "Cerro Baúl" model, with minimal interaction between two groups that were pursuing similar but independent goals in the same valley. Future research, particularly large-scale horizontal exposures and large excavations at Tiwanaku and Late Huaña sites, will help us understand this complex process of archaic state formation.

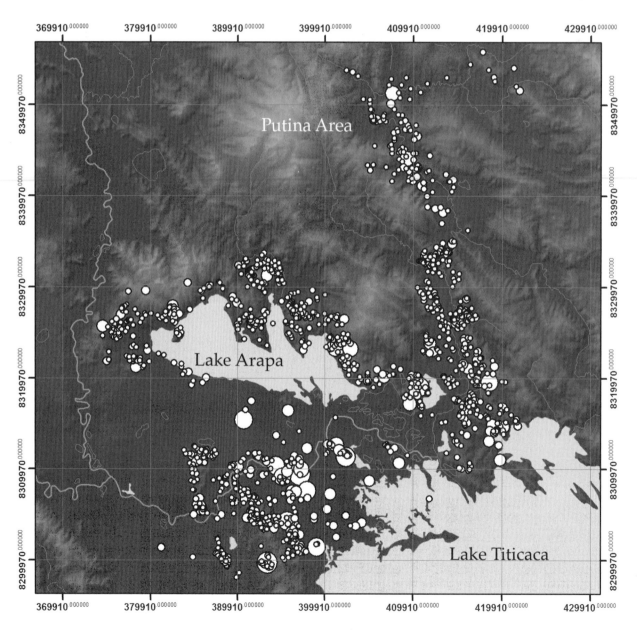

Figure 9.13. All sites in the survey areas. Each dot represents a site or site cluster. The size of the dot is roughly proportional to the size of the site.

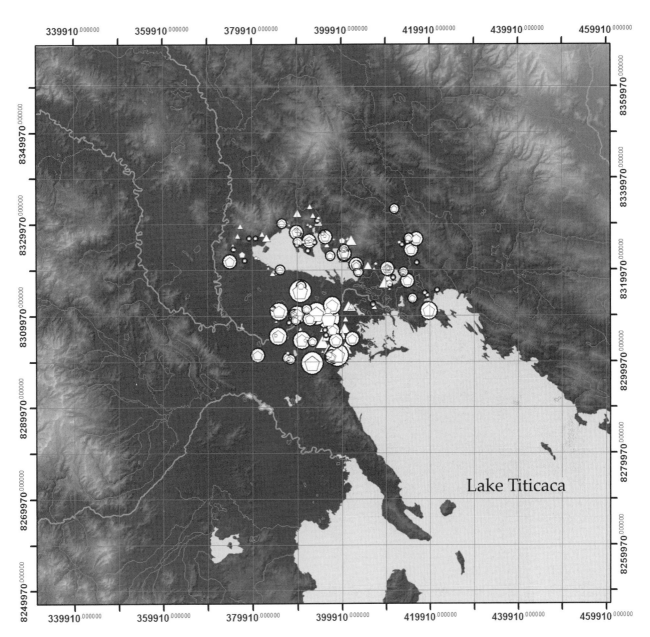

Figure 9.14. Tiwanaku sites in the survey areas. Note the clustering of sites around the lakes, rivers, and roads.

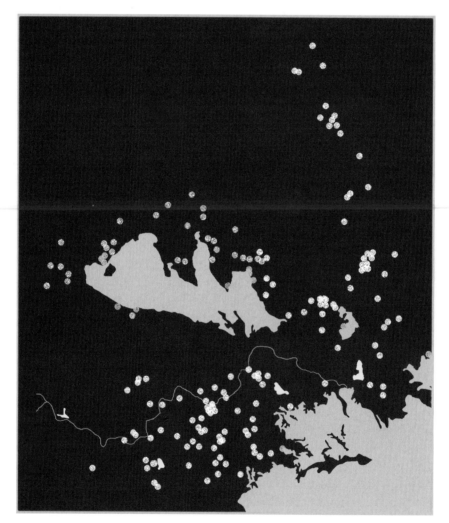

Figure 9.15. Late Huaña sites in the survey areas. Compare with Figure 9.14. Note the broader distribution of these sites throughout the survey area.

Figure 9.16. Tiwanaku enclave near Huancané.

Figure 9.17. Site HU-310 in the Tiwanaku enclave.

Figure 9.18. Agricultural features in the Tiwanaku enclave.

Figure 9.19. Site HU-310, from above.

Figure 9.20. Site AR-1413 from the north, distant view.

Figure 9.21. Site AR-1413 from the north, close-up view.

Figure 9.22. Surface of site AR-1413 with insert showing wall location.

Figure 9.23. Wall detail of site AR-1413.

NOTES

1. See Robert Feldman's Chapter 6 in this book for a more detailed discussion of the "talking dog" in Moseley's unique way of thinking.

2. The survey is ongoing. At the time this chapter was submitted, we had 1306 sites in an intensively covered area of 966 km^2, with an additional 114 km^2 of large-site reconnaissance. These figures will continue to increase over the next few years.

3. The Early Huaña period in the northern Titicaca Basin would correspond to that time from the collapse of Pucara, around AD 300, to the first Tiwanaku settlement, around AD 700. Recent excavations by Cecilia Chávez, Abigail Levine, and myself at the site of Taraco confirm that Early Huaña maintained a complex center. Chávez in particular has discovered an adobe pyramid with a ramp and steps. Early Huaña culture is poorly known, but future work promises to help us define this settlement and time period with much greater precision.

4. Three carbon dates taken from a level directly above the terminal Pucara occupation date a major fill episode (Cecilia Chávez, pers. com., 2004). This meter-thick level provided carbon from throughout the fill episode. All three dates are statistically identical. The calibrated dates using OxCal 3.10 are as follows:
1. AA66238, 14c age: 1805±37; wood, 120 AD (95.4%) 340 AD.
2. AA66239, 14c age: 1811±38; wood, 120 AD (93.4%) 330 AD.
3. AA66240, 14c age: 1781±37; wood, 130 AD (95.4%) 350 AD.

5. The complexities of just the space-time systematics in the northern Titicaca Basin emphasize the need to abandon the Ica master sequence for this region and instead create one more appropriate for understanding the cultural history (Stanish 2003). More stratigraphic and extensive excavations will be needed.

6. The Ica sequence terminology for the Late Intermediate and Late Horizon works for the circum-Titicaca Basin and is retained here.

REFERENCES

Albarracín-Jordan, Juan
1990   Prehispanic Dynamics of Settlement in the Lower Tiwanaku Valley, Bolivia. In *Tiwanaku and Its Hinterland: Third Preliminary Report of the Proyecto Wila Jawira*, edited by Alan Kolata and O. Rivera, pp. 276–296. La Paz.
1996a   *Tiwanaku: Arqueología regional y dinámica segmentaria.* Editores Plural, La Paz.
1996b   Tiwanaku Settlement System: The Integration of Nested Hierarchies in the Lower Tiwanaku Valley. *Latin American Antiquity* 7(3):183–210.

Albarracin-Jordan, Juan, and J. Mathews
1990   *Asentamientos prehispánicos del Valle de Tiwanaku*, vol. 1. Producciones CIMA, La Paz.

Arkush, Elizabeth, and Charles Stanish
2005   Interpreting Conflict in the Ancient Andes: Implications for the Archaeology of Warfare. *Current Anthropology* 46(1):3–28.

Bauer, Brian, and Charles Stanish
2001   *Ritual and Pilgrimage in the Ancient Andes: The Islands of the Sun and the Moon.* University of Texas Press, Austin.

Bertonio, Ludovico
1956   [1612] *Vocabulario de la lengua Aymará.* Juli. Facsimile edition, La Paz.

Browman, David
1978   Toward the Development of the Tiahuanaco (Tiwanaku) State. In *Advances in Andean Archaeology*, edited by D. Browman, pp. 327–349. Mouton, The Hague.
1980   Tiwanaku Expansion and Altiplano Economic Patterns. *Estudios Arqueológicos* 5:107–120.
1981   New Light on Andean Tiwanaku. *American Scientist* 69(4):408–419.
1984   Tiwanaku: Development of Interzonal Trade and Economic Expansion in the Altiplano. In *Social and Economic Organization in the Prehispanic Andes*, edited by David L. Browman, Richard L. Burger, and M. A. Rivera, pp. 117–142. BAR International Series194. British Archaeological Reports, Oxford.

Chávez, Sergio
1975   The Arapa and Thunderbolt Stelae: A Case of Stylistic Identity with Implications for Pucara Influences in the Area of Tiahuanaco. *Ñawpa Pacha* 13:3–26.

Chávez, Sergio, and Karen Chávez
1975   A Carved Stela from Taraco, Puno, Peru, and the Definition of an Early Style of Stone Sculpture from the Altiplano of Peru and Bolivia. *Ñawpa Pacha* 13:45–83.

Cipolla, Lisa M.
2005   Preceramic Period Settlement Patterns in the Huancané-Putina River Valley, Northern Titicaca Basin, Peru. In *Advances in Titicaca Basin Archaeology-I*, edited by Charles Stanish, Amanda Cohen, and Mark Aldenderfer, pp. 55–63. Cotsen Institute of Archaeology, University of California, Los Angeles.

Coben, Lawrence S., and Charles Stanish
2005   Archaeological Reconnaissance in the Carabaya Region, Peru. In *Advances in Titicaca Basin Archaeology-I*, edited by Charles Stanish, Amanda Cohen, and Mark Aldenderfer, pp. 243–266. Cotsen Institute of Archaeology, University of California, Los Angeles.

Goldstein, Paul
2005   *Andean Diaspora: The Tiwanaku Colonies and the Origins of South American Empire*. University Press of Florida, Gainesville.

Janusek, John
2003   Vessels, Time, and Society. In *Tiwanaku and Its Hinterland. II. Urban and Rural Archaeology*, edited by Alan Kolata, pp. 30–91. Smithsonian Institution Press, Washington, DC.

Janusek, John, and Alan Kolata
2003   Prehispanic Rural History in the Katari Valley. In *Tiwanaku and Its Hinterland. II. Urban and Rural Archaeology*, edited by Alan Kolata, pp. 129–174. Smithsonian Institution Press, Washington, DC.

Klarich, Elizabeth
2005   *From the Mundane to the Monumental: Defining Early Leadership Strategies at Late Formative Pukara, Peru.* Unpublished doctoral dissertation, Department of Anthropology, University of California, Santa Barbara.

Kolata, Alan
1993   *The Tiwanaku*. Blackwell, Cambridge.

Lémuz, Carlos
2001   *Patrones de asentamiento arqueológico en la peninsula de Huatta, Bolivia*. Licenciatura de Arqueología, Universidad Mayor de San Andrés, La Paz.

Lumbreras, Luis, and Hernán Amat
1968   Secuencia arqueológica del altiplano occidental del Titicaca. In *37th International Congress of Americanists, Buenos Aires, 1968: Actas y memorias*, vol. II, pp. 75–106.

Marcus, Joyce
1998   The Peaks and Valleys of Ancient States: An Extension of the Dynamic Model. In *Archaic States*, edited by Gary M. Feinman and Joyce Marcus, pp. 59–94. School of American Research, Santa Fe, NM.

Mujica, Elías
1978   Nueva hipótesis sobre el desarrollo temprano del altiplano del Titicaca y de sus áreas de interacción. *Arte y Arqueología* 5–6:285–308.
1987   Cusipata: Una fase pre-Pukara en la cuenca norte de Titicaca. *Gaceta Arqueológica Andina* 13:22–28.

Paredes, Rolando
1985   Excavaciones arqueológicas en Pukara-Puno. Master's thesis, Universidad de Cuzco, Peru.

Ponce Sanginés, Carlos
1990   *El templete semisubterraneo de Tiwanaku*. Editorial Juventud, La Paz.
1991   El urbanismo de Tiwanaku. *Pumapunku: Nueva Época* 1:7–27.
1992   El modelo integrador del estado prehispánico de Tiwanaku. *Enfoques* 16:26–27.

1993   La cerámica de la época I (aldeana de Tiwanaku). *Pumapunku* (n.s.) 4:48-49.

Posnansky, Arturo
1945   *Tihuanaco: The Cradle of American Man*, vols. I and II. Translated by J. F. Shearer. J. J. Augustin, New York.
1957   *Tihuanaco: The Cradle of American Man*, vols. III and IV. Translated by J. F. Shearer. J. J. Augustin, New York.

Rowe, John H.
1956   Archaeological Explorations in Southern Peru, 1954–1955. *American Antiquity* 22(2):135–150.

Seddon, Mathew
1998   *Ritual, Power, and the Formation of a Complex Society: The Island of the Sun and the Tiwanaku State.* Unpublished doctoral dissertation, Department of Anthropology, University of Chicago.

Stanish, Charles
2001   Formación estatal temprana en la cuenca del lago Titicaca, Andes surcentrales. *Boletín de Arqueología PUCP* 5:189–221. Pontificia Universidad Católica del Perú, Lima.
2002   Tiwanaku Political Economy. In *Andean Archaeology I: Variations in Socio-political Organization*, edited by Wiliam H. Isbell and Helaine Silverman, pp. 169–198. Kluwer Academic, New York.
2003   *Ancient Titicaca: The Evolution of Social Power in the Titicaca Basin of Peru and Bolivia*. University of California Press, Berkeley and Los Angeles.

Stanish, Charles, and Brian Bauer, eds.
2004   *Archaeological Research on the Islands of the Sun and Moon, Lake Titicaca, Bolivia: Final Results from the Proyecto Tiksi Kjarka*. Monograph no. 52. Cotsen Institute of Archaeology, University of California, Los Angeles.

Stanish, Charles, Edmundo de la Vega, Linda Steadman, C. Chávez Justo, Kirk Frye, L. Onofre Mamani, Matthew Seddon, and P. Calisaya Chuquimia
1997   *Archaeological Survey in the Juli-Desaguadero Region of Lake Titicaca Basin, Southern Peru*. Fieldiana: Anthropology, n.s., no. 29. Field Museum of Natural History, Chicago.

Stanish, Charles, Amanda Cohen, Edmundo de la Vega, Elizabeth Arkush, Cecilia Chávez, Aimée Plourde, and Carol Schultz
2005   Archaeological Reconnaissance in the Northern Titicaca Basin. In *Advances in Titicaca Basin Archaeology-I*, edited by Charles Stanish, Amanda Cohen, and Mark Aldenderfer, pp. 289–316. Cotsen Institute of Archaeology, University of California, Los Angeles.

Toledo, Francisco de
1975   *Tasa de la visita general de Francisco de Toledo*. Universidad Nacional Mayor de San Marcos, Lima.

CHAPTER 10

THE MOCHE USE OF NUMBERS
AND NUMBER SETS

CHRISTOPHER B. DONNAN

THREE HIGH-STATUS MOCHE TOMBS were
recently excavated at the site of Dos Cabezas.
Careful observation of the types, numbers,
and locations of objects in these tombs indicates
that the Moche were deliberately clustering objects
in sets of five, ten, twenty, and forty. The tombs also
include some objects that appear to have been deliberately made using these numbers. This evidence for
the deliberate and repetitive use of specific numbers
implies that the Moche considered these numbers
to be significant, perhaps carrying some symbolic
importance, and that they also appreciated how the
numbers could be combined and divided into sets.

The site of Dos Cabezas is located in the lower part
of the Jequetepeque Valley, immediately south of where
the Jequetepeque River flows into the Pacific Ocean
(Figure 10.1). Extending over an area of approximately
1 km², the site consists of pyramids, palaces, and
domestic structures that reflect a rich and complex pre-
Columbian occupation (Donnan 2001, 2003, 2007). On
the south part of the site there is a truncated pyramid
called Huaca Dos Cabezas (Figure 10.2).[1] It would
have been the most impressive architectural feature
at the site during the Moche occupation, and it still is
today. The three tombs that are the focus of this study
were located at the southwest corner of the pyramid,
approximately 9 m above its base (Figure 10.3).

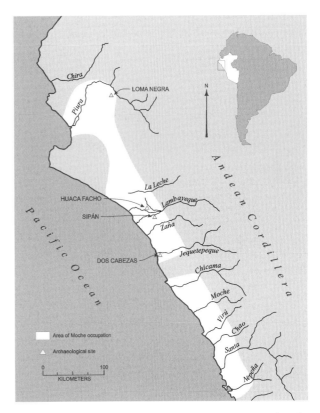

Figure 10.1. Map of the north coast of Peru showing the area of Moche
occupation.

165

Figure 10.2. Huaca Dos Cabezas as viewed from the northwest.

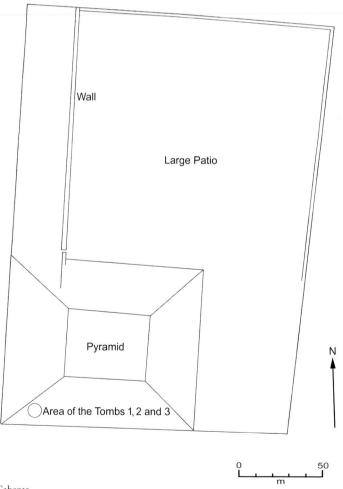

Figure 10.3. Plan of Huaca Dos Cabezas.

Each of the three tombs consisted of a rectangular burial chamber with a small compartment adjacent to one end (Figure 10.4). All three burial chambers, and their associated compartments, were positioned along a north-south axis and had been created by removing adobes from the solid adobe matrix of the pyramid. The compartments were meant to be miniature versions of the full-size tombs.[2]

Compartment 1

Of the three tombs and their adjacent compartments, Compartment 1 was the first to be excavated. Its upper part was filled with dirt and chunks of broken adobes, but on its floor there were clusters of ofrendas near the north and south sides (Figure 10.5). Ofrendas are small, crudely made ceramic vessels resembling cooking ollas or jars (Figure 10.6). They are unpainted, unburnished, and have an orange to buff color. They

are seldom found in Moche burials, and when they are, their number and position appear to be random. In this instance, however, there were twenty ofrendas—ten at the south side of the compartment and ten more at the north side. Those at the north side had been arranged in two clusters of five. Alongside the ofrendas at the south side of the compartment was a double-chambered whistling bottle. There was also a small copper figure, wrapped in a bundle of decomposed textiles, near the center of the chamber.

The ofrendas in this compartment suggested that the Moche may have deliberately placed them in sets of five and ten. It was also possible, however, that the sets of five and ten were a random occurrence and not the result of any conscious effort to cluster objects in this way. Clearly, this find alone was insufficient evidence on which the issue could be resolved.

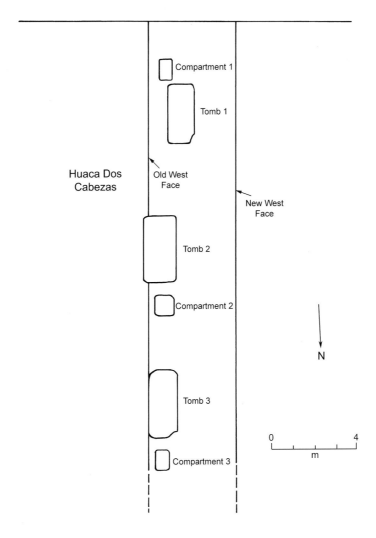

Figure 10.4. Plan of Tombs 1, 2, and 3 and their compartments.

Figure 10.5. Plan of Compartment 1.

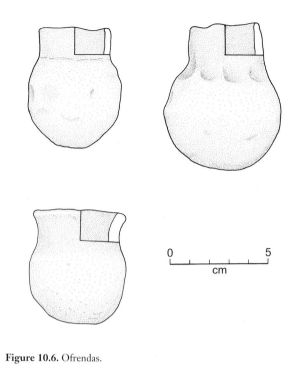

Figure 10.6. Ofrendas.

Tomb 1

Tomb 1 was located approximately 20 cm north of Compartment 1 (Figure 10.4). Two layers of nearly whole adobes sealed the upper part of the burial chamber. Beneath these, most of the chamber was filled with dirt and chunks of broken adobes. In this fill, approximately 70 cm below the upper edge of the chamber, were a small painted jar, a llama skull, the remains of a textile, and two clusters of five ofrendas, one near the northeast corner of the burial chamber and one near the northwest corner (Figure 10.7). This supported the idea that the Moche were deliberately creating sets of five and ten ofrendas, but to be certain of this more evidence was needed.

The floor of the burial chamber was approximately 140 cm below its upper edge. The bodies of two individuals were on the floor: a male approximately twenty-one years of age lying north-south in an extended position and a female approximately fifteen years of age lying crosswise at his feet (Figure 10.8). The only artifacts associated with the female were two spindle whorls in front of her left hand.

The male had been buried in a large funerary bundle, wearing a gold nose ornament and a cylindrical head-dress covered with platelets of gilded copper. Many other objects were in the bundle with him, including two copper nose ornaments, a spear thrower, and a large copper chisel.

Outside the funerary bundle, surrounding the man's head and torso, were three ceramic dippers, three stirrup spout bottles, and the skull and lower legs of a llama. There was also a cluster of twenty ofrendas that had been arranged in two groups of ten each. With these ofrendas, it seemed certain that the Moche had deliberately counted ofrendas in sets of five, ten, and twenty, and had placed these sets in clusters in Compartment 1 and Tomb 1. But was the use of these numbers restricted to the quantity and placement of ofrendas? The answer to this question was to come with the excavation of Tomb 2.

Tomb 2

Tomb 2 was much more elaborate than Tomb 1 and contained a much greater quantity and quality of associated objects. Its burial chamber was located approximately 285 cm north of Tomb 1 (Figure 10.4). Above the burial chamber were the bodies of a woman approximately fifteen years of age and a llama; neither had any evidence of textile or cane encasing them

(Figure 10.9). They were on a layer of adobes that had been placed without any noticeable pattern. Beneath that layer of adobes, however, was a layer that was well ordered. It consisted of forty adobes, carefully positioned, with twenty at the north end separated by a space from twenty at the south end (Figure 10.10). Each set of twenty was arranged in four rows, with five adobes in each. Here was ample indication that the Moche were creating sets of five, ten, twenty, and even forty, and that they appreciated how these sets could be divided into subsets of these numbers.

The layer of forty adobes rested directly on top of wood beams that formed the roof of the burial chamber. Although the beams were completely decomposed, their size and form could be reconstructed by the impressions that they left in the soil around them. Ten large beams extended north-south, and beneath them were four transverse beams that extended east-west (Figure 10.11).

Beneath the roof beams, the burial chamber had originally been an open space, devoid of fill. It contained the body of only one individual, an adult male eighteen to twenty years of age, who was buried in a

Figure 10.7. Plan of the upper level of Tomb 1.

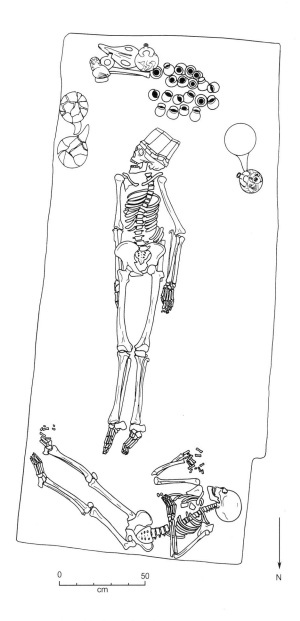

Figure 10.8. Plan of the floor of Tomb 1.

large funerary bundle that had been placed near the center of the floor (Figure 10.12).

There were many objects wrapped inside the funerary bundle. Among these were a large copper bowl, a pair of tweezers, tumi knives, spear throwers and spear points, shields, war clubs, headdresses, gold and silver nose ornaments, and a remarkable gold and copper burial mask. A full inventory and description of these objects is beyond the scope of this report, but suffice it to say, this was one of the richest Moche burials ever excavated by archaeologists.

What is germane to this study are the instances when objects or sets of objects seemed to reflect the deliberate use of five, ten, twenty, and forty. One occurrence of this was a necklace that was worn by the principal individual at the time he was buried. It consisted of forty quartz crystal beads, each of which was biconically drilled and polished so it was transparent. The beads varied in size from 1.16 to 2.02 cm in diameter. Some were extremely round, smooth, and well polished, while others were less well polished and had somewhat irregular surfaces. Although they were not well matched, and may even

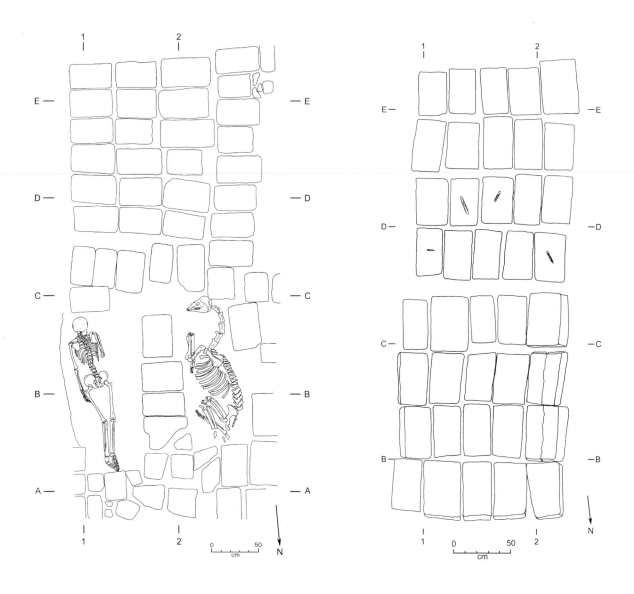

Figure 10.9. Plan of the layer above Tomb 2.

Figure 10.10. Plan of the adobes above Tomb 2.

have been produced by two or more different individuals, they had been assembled into a necklace of forty beads.

The individual had five gold objects in his mouth.[3] Four of these were nose ornaments, while the fifth was a piece of thin gold foil. All appear to have been deliberately folded or misshapen. It is curious that the four nose ornaments, each of which was beautifully crafted of sheet gold, were put together with a rather unimpressive piece of gold foil. This suggests that making a set of five objects was more important than having all the objects be similar. Among the many objects of gilded copper inside the funerary bundle were two nearly identical headdress ornaments, each made in the form of ten plumes (Figure 10.13).

Many objects had been placed in the corners of the burial chamber. In the southeast corner were a llama skull, a parrot skeleton, and three stirrup spout bottles, along with a cluster of five ofrendas (Figure 10.14). In the southwest corner were two jars, one olla, and two stirrup spout bottles, along with another cluster of five ofrendas (Figure 10.15).

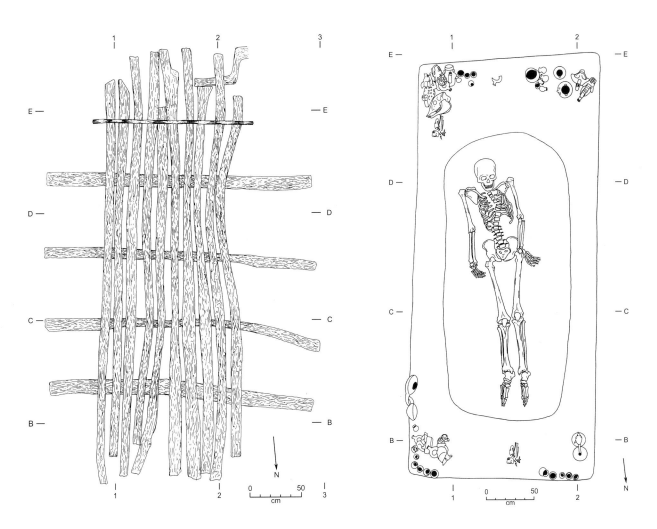

Figure 10.11. Plan of the roof beams of Tomb 2.

Figure 10.12. Plan of the floor of Tomb 2.

Figure 10.13. A gilded copper headdress ornament from Tomb 2.

In the northwest corner were a double-chambered whistling bottle and a cluster of five ofrendas (Figure 10.16) and in the northeast corner there were two dippers, one ofrenda, and two stirrup spout bottles, along with a cluster of five ofrendas (Figure 10.17).[4]

It should be noted that each of the four corners of the burial chamber had one cluster of five ofrendas. In addition, three of the four corners (southeast, southwest, and northeast) had five additional objects, making a total of ten. In the southwest and northeast corners the five additional objects were all ceramic vessels, implying that the clustered ofrendas were seen as one set of five and the other ceramic vessels were seen as another set of five. In the southeast corner, the cluster of ofrendas again made one set of five, while the other set of five consisted of three ceramic vessels, a llama skull, and a parrot skeleton. If the intent of the people who selected and placed these objects in the southeast corner was indeed to create two groups of five, it indicates that the llama head and parrot were seen as appropriate surrogates for ceramic vessels.

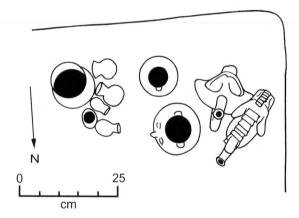

Figure 10.15. Plan of the southwest corner of Tomb 2.

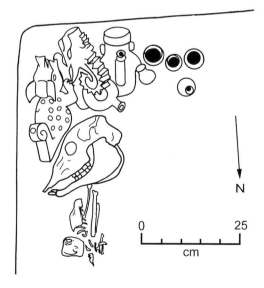

Figure 10.14. Plan of the southeast corner of Tomb 2.

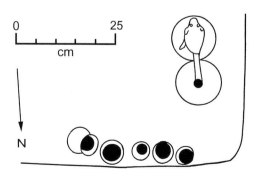

Figure 10.16. Plan of the northwest corner of Tomb 2.

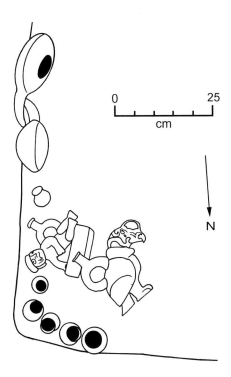

Figure 10.17. Plan of the northeast corner of Tomb 2.

Compartment 2

Compartment 2 was located approximately 38 cm north of Tomb 2 (see Figure 10.4). Within the sand and dirt fill of the compartment were various layers of objects. In the upper layer were three llama skulls, three lower legs of llamas, and twenty ofrendas (Figure 10.18). The ofrendas were arranged in two groups of ten, one forming a line along the south side of the compartment, the other forming a line near the north side. Below this upper level of objects were four ceramic bottles and various metal objects (Figure 10.19), and beneath these were three headdresses. On the floor of the compartment (Figure 10.20) was a copper figure, wrapped in textiles, similar to the one found in Compartment 1 (see Figure 10.5). Inside the textile wrappings and surrounding the copper figure were miniature versions of many of the objects that had been found in the funerary bundle of the principal individual in Tomb 2.

Tomb 3

The burial chamber of Tomb 3 was located approximately 240 cm north of Compartment 2 (see Figure 10.4). Above the burial chamber was a young adolescent, presumably a female, who was lying on a layer of adobes that rested on the roof beams. The adobes had collapsed into the burial chamber when the roof fell in, and were so broken and out of position that their

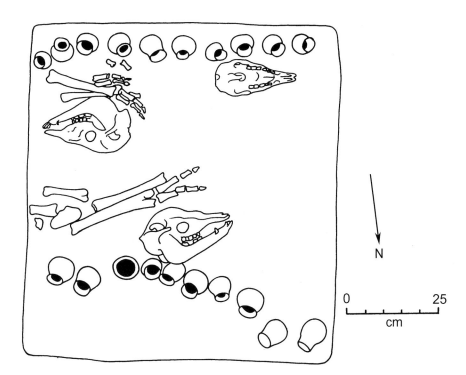

Figure 10.18. Plan of the upper layer of Compartment 2.

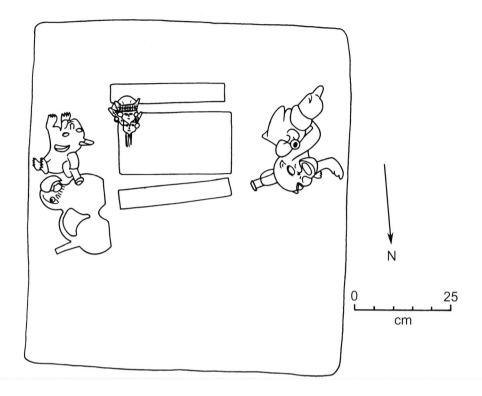

Figure 10.19. Plan of the middle layer of Compartment 2.

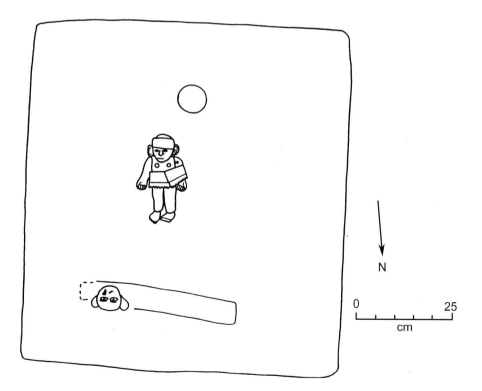

Figure 10.20. Plan of the floor of Compartment 2.

original placement could not be reconstructed (Figure 10.21). Therefore it is not possible to determine if they had been arranged in sets like the adobes above the roof of Tomb 2 (see Figure 10.10).

The roof of Tomb 3 was different from the roof of Tomb 2 since all of the beams extended east-west. Nevertheless, there were ten beams, just as there were ten beams extending north-south in the roof of Tomb 2. This suggests that this number of beams was deliberately used in both cases.

Beneath the roof beams the burial chamber had been partially filled with dirt and broken adobes, and partially left open. There were two individuals on the floor of the burial chamber, an adult male between eighteen and twenty-two years of age and a child approximately nine years of age (Figure 10.22). The child appeared to have been without any wrapping or associated objects, but the adult was buried in a large funerary bundle. Wrapped inside the funerary bundle were numerous metal objects, including headdresses, nose ornaments,

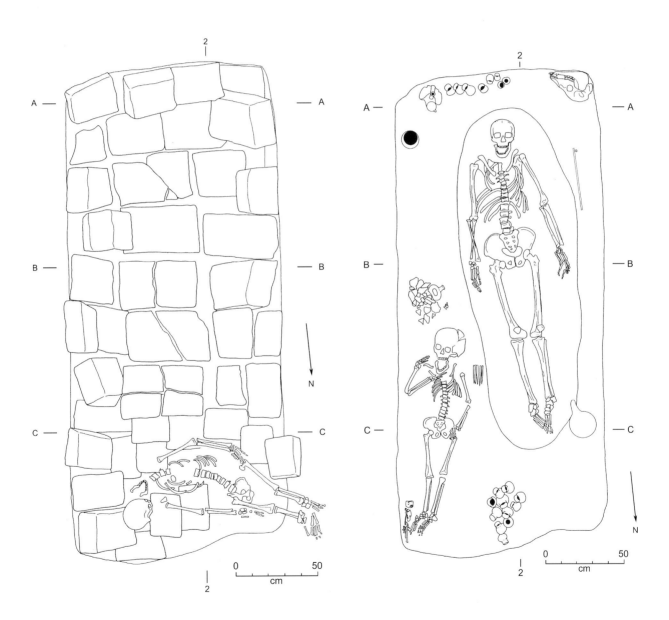

Figure 10.21. Plan of the layer above Tomb 3.

Figure 10.22. Plan of the floor of Tomb 3.

ingots, and a banner. None of these, however, were clustered in sets of five, ten, twenty, or forty, nor did they utilize number sets like some of the objects in Tomb 2. There were, for example, nine nose ornaments with this individual, two of which were in the mouth. Also in the mouth were two ingots, thus making a set of four objects rather than five.

There was a llama skull in the southwest corner of the burial chamber, and a parrot skeleton near the northeast corner. There were also two clusters of ofrendas, but the cluster near the north end of the burial chamber contained eleven, while the cluster near the south contained eight (Figure 10.22). This seemed curious since the ofrendas in Tombs 1 and 2, as well as the ofrendas in their associated compartments, were consistently in sets of five, ten, and twenty.

Other objects on the floor of the burial chamber included a dipper along the west wall, a small gourd bowl near the southeast corner, another stirrup spout bottle near the east wall, a spear thrower near the southwest side of the funerary bundle, and spear

points near the northeast side of the funerary bundle (Figure 10.22).

Compartment 3

Compartment 3 was approximately 70 cm north of Tomb 3 (see Figure 10.4). Its upper part was filled with dirt and chunks of adobe. On its floor were two sets of ofrendas: one set of ten near the south wall and the other set of ten near the north wall (Figure 10.23). Also on the floor were a llama skull and a copper figure wrapped in textiles. The latter was very similar in size and form to the copper figures found in Compartments 1 and 2.

The three tombs and their associated compartments at Dos Cabezas provide ample evidence for the deliberate grouping of objects into sets of five, ten, twenty, and forty. They also suggest that the Moche appreciated how sets could be divided into subsets—ten divided into two sets of five, twenty divided into two sets of ten or four sets of five, and forty divided into two sets of twenty or eight sets of five. These numbers and number sets were most frequently expressed with ofrendas, perhaps because numerous ofrendas were put into the tombs and compartments, while other kinds of objects were often represented by three examples or fewer. In Tomb 2, additional sets of five were made by combining different forms of ceramic vessels, and in one instance perhaps by combining ceramic vessels with faunal remains. The numbers and number sets were also expressed in the adobes above the roof of Tomb 2, the roof beams of Tombs 2 and 3, and finally in Tomb 2 by the number of objects in the mouth of the principal individual, his necklace of crystal beads, and his plume-like headdress ornaments.

ADDITIONAL MOCHE EXAMPLES

Other than at Dos Cabezas, there are only three places where the deliberate use of numbers and number sets by the Moche has been observed: Sipán, Loma Negra, and Huaca Facho[5] (see Figure 10.1). Sipán is an archaeological site in the upper Lambayeque Valley where Walter Alva excavated three royal Moche tombs between 1987 and 2000 (Alva 1988, 1990, 1994; Alva and Donnan 1993). In these tombs, the use of numbers and number sets was most evident in Sipán Tomb 3 (the Old Lord of Sipán), where there were six necklaces, each consisting of ten large gold or silver beads. The consistent use of ten beads in these necklaces was

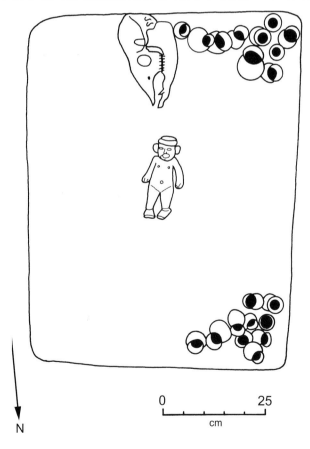

0   25
cm
N

Figure 10.23. Plan of the floor of Compartment 3.

noted in an early publication about the tombs (Alva and Donnan 1993:195), but at the time we were not aware of the deliberate use of numbers and number sets by the Moche, nor did we have an appreciation of how often other objects in the tomb were clustered in sets of ten. There were also ten gilded copper backflaps decorated with lizards, and ten silver backflaps without decoration (Alva and Donnan 1993:205). These may have been conceptualized by the Moche as a set of twenty, divided into two sets of ten. We now realize that there were also ten silver and ten gold bells decorated with the Decapitator (Alva and Donnan 1993:205)—again possibly seen as a set of twenty divided into two sets of ten. And finally, there were twenty large spherical bells made of gilded copper (Alva and Donnan 1993:184), and ten gilded copper discs with hollow spheres around their circumference (Alva and Donnan 1993:193–195).

Sipán Tomb 2 (the Bird Priest) contained two necklaces of gilded copper, but each necklace consisted of nine beads. There were no objects recovered from this tomb that were in sets of five, ten, twenty, or forty. In this respect, it is similar to Tomb 3 at Dos Cabezas, which had multiple objects that could have been clustered in sets of five and ten, but there was a conspicuous absence of the use of these numbers.

Sipán Tomb 1 (the Lord of Sipán) contained four necklaces, only one of which consisted of ten beads (Alva and Donnan 1993:93). One of the others consisted of twelve beads, and another of sixteen beads. But the most spectacular necklace in the tomb consisted of twenty beads, strung in two rows of ten, with each row made up of five gold beads and five silver beads (Figure 10.24). It seems likely that the composition of this necklace involved the deliberate use of five, ten, and twenty, as well as the division of ten into sets of five and the division of twenty into sets of five and ten.

Although there were many ceramic vessels in the three royal tombs of Sipán, there were no ofrendas. Moreover, although there were multiples of certain vessel forms, there appears to have been no attempt to cluster the ceramics in number sets. Furthermore, none of the three Sipán tombs exhibits the use of numbers or number sets in their roof beams or adobes above the roofs.

It is curious that the use of five, ten, and twenty is completely absent in Sipán Tomb 2, is only partially present in Sipán Tomb 1, yet is so prevalent in Sipán Tomb 3. This may be because Sipán Tomb 3 is older than Sipán Tombs 1 and 2, perhaps dating to a time when the use of the numbers and number sets was more prevalent than it was later. It should be noted, however, that the ceramics in Sipán Tomb 3 were very different from those in Sipán Tombs 1 and 2 and have a striking similarity to ceramics that have been excavated from Moche burials in the lower Jequetepeque Valley, where Dos Cabezas is located (Donnan and McClelland 1997). This suggests that Sipán Tomb 3 was more closely affiliated to the Jequetepeque tradition than were either Sipán Tomb 1 or Sipán Tomb 2, and the frequent use of numbers and number sets in Sipán Tomb 3 may have been due to this closer affiliation.

At both Dos Cabezas and Sipán the deliberate use of numbers and number sets can only be observed in the tombs discussed above; although tombs of lesser rank have been found at both sites, they have no evidence of it. The tombs where it has been found are among the richest Moche tombs ever excavated by archaeologists. Perhaps the use of these numbers and number sets was restricted to the upper echelon of Moche society.

Another place where the Moche use of numbers and number sets has been noted is the site of Loma Negra, in the upper Piura Valley (see Figure 10.1). Unfortunately, the material at Loma Negra was looted by grave robbers in the 1960s, and there is very little information about its original context. Hundreds of objects of sheet metal were found, including numerous nose ornaments, ear ornaments, headdresses, and objects that are thought to have been used to decorate clothing and architecture. Anne-Louise Schaffer studied a large sample of Loma Negra metal objects and noted that circular and rectangular forms were often simply divided with lines into four, six, eight, or sixteen sections (Schaffer 1988:11). She also found, however, that the crescent-shaped nose ornaments consistently have a linear sequence of ten figures, such as snails or birds, that extend from one end to the other. As she states, "the ten segments are not formed by any easy geometrical manipulation. Some significance should therefore be placed on this unexpected—but consistent—appearance of the number ten on these nose ornaments, something beyond playing with lines and shapes" (Schaffer 1988:12).

It appears that the Loma Negra metal objects were looted from high-status burials, again suggesting that the use of the numbers and number sets by the Moche may have been restricted to the elite of Moche society.

One other place where the use of numbers and number sets by the Moche has been noted is at Huaca Facho (Donnan 1972). Located in the Lambayeque

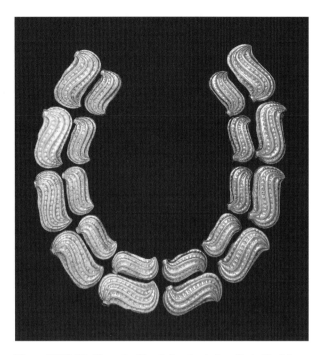

Figure 10.24. Necklace of gold and silver beads from Sipán Tomb 1.

Valley (see Figure 10.1), this temple had a façade with horizontal rows of niches (Figure 10.25). There were ten niches in the center of the façade, flanked on each side by two horizontal rows of five niches.[6]

It is curious that, to date, the use of numbers and number sets in Moche burials has been observed only at Dos Cabezas, Sipán, and Loma Negra. No Moche burials from other sites exhibit any attempt to cluster objects in this way. And with the exception of its use in the architecture at Huaca Facho, the Moche use of numbers and number sets has not been observed in Moche architecture or Moche iconography. Why it has such a limited distribution remains an enigma.

OTHER OCCURRENCES IN THE ANDEAN AREA

The use of five, ten, twenty, and forty has been noted in other contexts in the Andean area. Although no

convincing evidence of it prior to the Moche has been reported, there is ample evidence from later periods. Anita Cook (1992), in her analysis of two caches of Huari stone figurines found at Pikillacta, demonstrated that each cache consisted of forty figurines. Furthermore, twenty of the figurines in one of the caches matched twenty figurines in the other cache, thus dividing each set of forty into two sets of twenty—one set of matching figurines and one set of nonmatching figurines.

Barbara Wolf, working with Anita Cook and Bill Isbell on the Conchopata project in Ayacucho, excavated a shoebox-sized offering pit that contained as many as two hundred deliberately smashed miniature Conchopata urns, both decorated and plain, along with bones of llamas and guinea pigs (Wolf, pers. comm. 2003). The decorated urns were generally at the top of the pit, with the undecorated ones below. There was a total of forty decorated urns, each painted with three feline and three avian profile heads. Twenty of the decorated urns had the heads facing left and the other twenty had the heads facing right.[7]

Sue Bergh, in her detailed analysis of Middle Horizon tapestry tunics, found that there were two number systems that seem to underlie their composition. The most prominent system was based on two and its doubling to four, eight, sixteen, thirty-two, etc. But there was a secondary system, based on five and its doubling to ten, twenty, forty, etc. (Bergh 1999: n.77 on p. 155, n. 94 on p. 165, and n. 101 on pp. 168–169).

At the Huari site of Azángaro, the Central Sector of architecture was organized into forty rows of rooms, divided into banks of twenty (Anders 1991:170).

After the Middle Horizon, there are other occurrences of these numbers and number sets. Axe-monies that have been found in northern Peru and Ecuador were often tied into packets that were bound together with string. The number of axe-monies per packet is almost invariably five, ten, fifteen, or twenty (Holm 1978:351; Ubelaker 1981:100–101; Hosler et. al. 1990:20, 54; Mayer 1992:52–54).[8] It was observed that the repetitive use of these numbers in compiling the

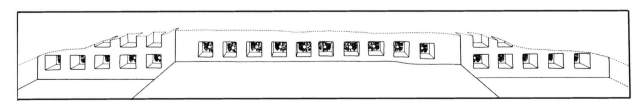

Figure 10.25. Niches in the façade of the temple at Huaca Facho.

packets indicates the use of numbers and fractions or multiples of numbers (Hosler et al. 1990:54).

Peter Eeckhout, who has been excavating Late Intermediate Period and Late Horizon material at Pachacamac, found an offering containing nearly one thousand espingo (*Nectandra* sp.) seeds, which had been strung together in long strands and then wrapped in textiles. Some of the strands were broken, but those that were complete repeatedly contained forty seeds (Eeckhout 2006).

The many occurrences of the use of five, ten, twenty, and forty in the Andean area indicate that these numbers had an important and lasting symbolic meaning to the native people. Although that meaning may have changed through time and space, it continued to be an important and fundamental way of both perceiving the world and organizing it in a meaningful way. The use of these numbers and number sets by the Moche is the earliest known occurrence in the Andean area.

NOTES

1. The central section of this pyramid was removed during a large-scale looting operation in the early Colonial period, leaving the summit with two humps or heads; hence the name Dos Cabezas (two heads).

2. These are the only Moche tombs known to have miniature tombs adjacent to them. They are very unusual because the principal individual in each tomb was extremely tall, among the tallest individuals ever reported from ancient America (Donnan 2001, 2003, 2007).

3. The Moche often placed metal objects in the mouth of the deceased before they were buried, most often a copper ingot or part of a broken copper implement (Donnan 1995:147).

4. There were only two other objects on the floor of the tomb. One, located near the center of the south wall, was a cluster of three ceramic fragments, including a stirrup spout that had been part of a vessel that was not found in the tomb (Figure 10.12). The other, located near the center of the north wall, was a parrot skeleton.

5. The site of Huaca Facho is sometimes called Mayanga (Bonavia 1985).

6. The upper row of five niches on each side was partially destroyed by erosion.

7. On average, the miniature urns were about 2 inches tall and 3 inches in diameter, but there were definitely smaller and larger ones. Because the urns were smashed, and the undecorated urns have not been reconstructed, it is not clear

how many of them were in the cache, nor whether there were sets of distinct sizes.

8. Two bundles were found to contain eighteen, but it has been suggested that either "someone was shortchanged, or that these packets may have originally contained twenty but have lost the outermost leaf from each surface" (Hosler et al. 1990:54).

REFERENCES

Alva, Walter
1988   Discovering the New World's Richest Unlooted Tomb. *National Geographic* 174(4):510–549.
1990   New Tomb of Royal Splendor. *National Geographic* 177(6):2–15.
1994   *Sipán*. Colección Culturas y Artes del Perú, Lima.

Alva, Walter, and Christopher B. Donnan
1993   *Royal Tombs of Sipán*. Fowler Museum of Cultural History, University of California, Los Angeles.

Anders, Martha
1991   Structure and Function at the Planned Site of Azángaro: Cautionary Notes for the Model of Huari as a Centralized Secular State. In *Huari Administrative Structure: Prehistoric Monumental Architecture and State Government*, edited by William H. Isbell and Gordon F. McEwan, pp. 165–198. Dumbarton Oaks Research Library and Collection, Washington, DC.

Bergh, Sue
1999   *Pattern and Paradigm in Middle Horizon Tapestry Tunics*. University Microfilms, Ann Arbor, MI.

Bonavia, Duccio
1985   *Mural Painting in Ancient Peru*. University of Indiana Press, Bloomington.

Cook, Anita
1992   The Stone Ancestors: Idioms of Imperial Attire and Rank among Huari Figurines. *Latin American Antiquity* 3:341–364.

Donnan, Christopher B.
1972   Moche Huari Murals from Northern Peru. *Archaeology* 25(2):85–95.
1995   Moche Funerary Practice. In *Graves for the Living*, edited by T. Dillehay. Center for Pre-Columbian Studies, Dumbarton Oaks, Washington, DC.
2001   Moche Burials Uncovered. *National Geographic*, March, pp. 58–73.
2003   Tumbas con entierros en miniatura: Un nuevo tipo funerario Moche. In *Moche: Hacia el final del milenio*, edited by Santiago Uceda and Elías Mujica, vol. 1,

pp. 43–78. Universidad Nacional de Trujillo and Pontificia Universidad Católica del Perú, Fondo Editorial. Lima.

2007   *Moche Tombs at Dos Cabezas*. The Cotsen Institute of Archaeology, University of California, Los Angeles.

Donnan, Christopher B., and Donna McClelland

1997   Moche Burials at Pacatnamu. In *The Pacatnamu Papers*, vol. 2, *The Moche Occupation*, edited by Christopher B. Donnan and Guillermo Cock, pp. 17–188. Fowler Museum of Cultural History, University of California, Los Angeles.

Eeckhout, Peter

2006   Semillas sagradas: El ishpingo (*Nectandra* sp.) en Pachacamac, costa central del Perú. In *Change in the Andes: Origins of Social Complexity, Pastoralism, and Agriculture*. Acts of the XIVth UISPP Congress, University of Liège, Belgium, September 2–8, 2001, edited by Le Secrétariat du Congrès, pp. 201–210. British Archaeological Reports, International Series 1524. Hadrian Books Ltd., Oxford, England.

Holm, Olaf

1978   Hachas monedas del Ecuador. In *Actas y trabajos del 3 Congreso Peruano: El hombre y la cultura andina*, edited by Ramiro Matos M., vol. 1, pp. 347–361. Lima.

Hosler, Dorothy, Heather Lechtman, and Olaf Holm

1990   *Axe-Monies and Their Relatives*. Dumbarton Oaks Studies in Pre-Columbian Art and Archaeology, no. 30. Dumbarton Oaks Research Library and Collection, Washington, DC.

Mayer, Eugen F.

1992   *Armas y herramientas de metal prehispánicas en Ecuador*. Materialen zur allgemeinen und vergleichenden Archaologie 38. Verlag C. H. Beck, Munich.

Schaffer, Anne-Louise

1988   Structure in the Loma Negra Metalwork. Paper presented at a meeting of the International Congress of Americanists, Amsterdam, July 1988.

Ubelaker, Douglas

1981   *The Ayalan Cemetery: A Late Integration Burial Site on the South Coast of Ecuador*. Smithsonian Contributions to Anthropology 29. Smithsonian Institution Press, Washington, DC.

CHAPTER 11

CURATED CORPSES AND SCATTERED SKELETONS

NEW DATA AND NEW QUESTIONS CONCERNING THE MOCHE DEAD

ALANA CORDY-COLLINS

The dead are difficult subjects. What's most remarkable about them is their constancy. They will be dead *in just this way* a thousand years from now.

Cunningham 1990:251–252; italics mine

ONE DOUBTS THAT NOVELIST Michael Cunningham had the Moche in mind when he wrote the above lines. As previous research has proposed, and as this essay will detail, some Moche individuals have been dead in at least two ways, others in perhaps three or more. These Moche were curated in locales that may never have been intended to be permanent resting places. Such deceased remained in their initial repositories only long enough for their bodies to desiccate from the elements, after which they were wholly or partially disinterred, to be deposited in the tombs of the newly and important dead.

CURATED CORPSES

In 1988 a crucial discovery was made concerning Moche funerary practices that called attention to special treatment of their important dead. A study of the occupants of the major royal tomb at Sipán in the Lambayeque Valley revealed that the three women interred there had died earlier—perhaps much earlier—than the other occupants (Alva and Donnan 1993; Verano 1997). Although in addition to the main occupant, the Sipán Lord, the tomb held a child, two adult males, and three adult females, only the female skeletons were partially disarticulated. The misaligned bones were primarily in

the upper body, particularly in the thoracic cavity. Soft tissue desiccation in the dry coastal environment and subsequent movement of the body from one location to another can result in this pattern (see Nelson 1998:203). Thus, it was argued that the Moche had curated the bodies of these women, with the apparent intent—certainly the result—of employing them as offerings in a later, important burial ritual.

Although the Sipán evidence was convincing, in 1988 it was the only known example of such a treatment. Furthermore, of the three royal tombs excavated there to date, only one included curated human bodies. That tomb is the most opulent one ever excavated by archaeologists, and it seemed possible that its curated females represented a special, very high-status yet isolated occurrence.

San José de Moro

In 1991 and 1992, however, excavations at the terminal Moche site of San José de Moro on the north side of the Jequetepeque Valley uncovered additional cases of human body curation (Cordy-Collins 1991, 1992). All were recovered from three large, high-status chamber tombs, along with the principal occupants, other individuals, and a vast amount of grave goods.

Of the four curated bodies recovered in 1991, one, an elite child 5–7 years of age,[1] was the tomb's principal occupant; unfortunately, because of its youth, it could not be sexed. The child's skeleton did, however, reveal a similar pattern of vertebral (cervical and thoracic) skewing to its right side, along with several of the right ribs (Figure 11.1). The tarsals, metatarsals, and foot phalanges were likewise disorganized. Both hands—all carpals, metacarpals, and phalanges—were entirely absent. In the same tomb lay a 14- to 16-year-old female,[2] interred at a right angle to the feet of the elite child, alongside a slightly younger individual of indeterminate sex (Figure 11.2). The disarray of this female's bones was again in the upper body region. The vertebrae and ribs were displaced laterally in both directions, and most cervical vertebrae were in the thoracic region. Some hand bones were loose behind the lumbar vertebrae, the sternum had slumped over the left rib cage and halfway down it, and the mandible was dislocated from the cranium and rotated 180 degrees from normal; a

few teeth were lodged inside the cranium. The adjacent juvenile was in correct anatomical alignment.

Also in 1991, the tomb of a priestess[3] yielded five individuals, three of whom exhibited mild to pronounced skeletal disarticulation (Donnan and Castillo 1992, 1994). A juvenile of indeterminate sex lay on its right side at the foot of the tomb (Figure 11.3).[4] Its mandible was disarticulated and lay beside the left forearm, which lacked all hand bones. Its right arm was represented only by the radius, with the humerus, ulna, and entire hand missing. An adult female flanked the priestess on each side. The one to her east[5] (proper right) side exhibited disarticulation of the cervical and thoracic vertebrae, and the sternum had slipped out of position (Figure 11.4). The female to the west showed more disarray.[6] The cervical and most of the thoracic vertebrae were missing, along with all left and most right ribs. Both hands were absent (Figure 11.4).

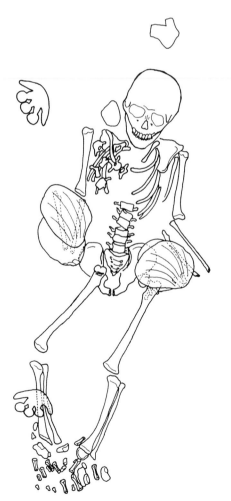

Figure 11.1. Elite child burial (MU 30 E7), San José de Moro, Jequetepeque Valley. (Courtesy Christopher B. Donnan and Luis Jaime Castillo B.)

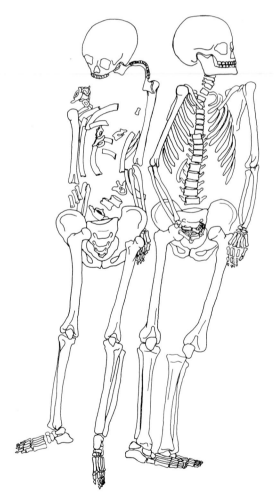

Figure 11.2. Curated 14- to 16-year-old female (left, MU 30 E5) from the tomb of the elite child, San José de Moro, Jequetepeque Valley. (Courtesy Christopher B. Donnan and Luis Jaime Castillo B.)

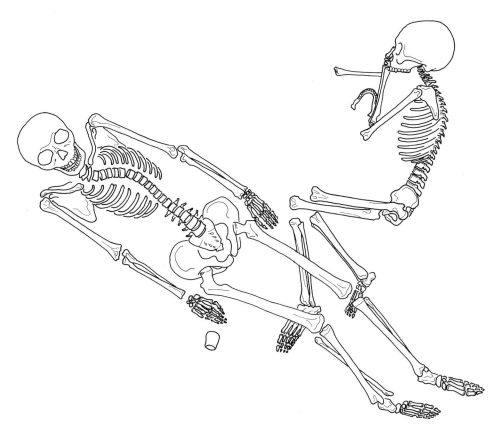

Figure 11.3. Curated juvenile (MU 41 E3) at the north end of the tomb of a Moche priestess, San José de Moro, Jequetepeque Valley. (Courtesy Christopher B. Donnan and Luis Jaime Castillo B.)

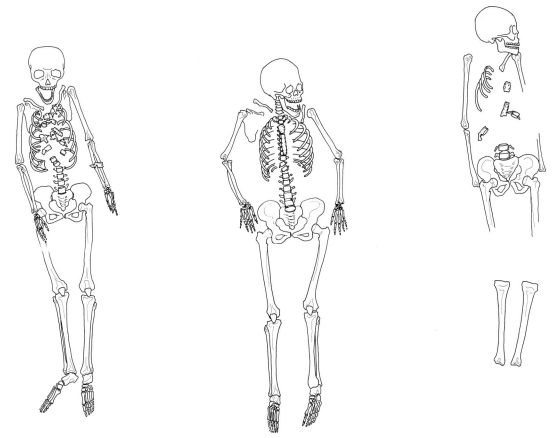

Figure 11.4. Pair of curated females to the left and right of a priestess (MU 41, E5, E6), San José de Moro, Jequetepeque Valley. (Courtesy Christopher B. Donnan and Luis Jaime Castillo B.)

In the following field season, 1992, a curated female was recovered from the tomb of another priestess.[7] The evidence for curation in this case is subtle. The adult female flanking the priestess is represented by a complete skeleton, the only anomaly being the position of the head (Figure 11.5). Andrew Nelson has shown that this posture, with the mandible resting on the thorax, can occur when an enshrouded body is lowered into a tomb feet first (Nelson 1998:200).

Dos Cabezas

In 1994, excavations at an early Moche site in the Jequetepeque Valley, Dos Cabezas, encountered additional evidence for reinterment of the curated deceased (Cordy-Collins 1994). Here, an elaborate tomb (Tomb B) dating to the early Moche period had been constructed on the southwest portion of the main pyramid (Donnan 2007; Donnan and Cock 1995). The tomb yielded four human interments, aligned around its periphery. Three of these were adult males, all of whose bones were in the correct anatomical position.[8] The fourth individual, a female of about 40 years,[9] exhibited specific positional anomalies (Figure 11.6). The cranium rested on its left side, and all vertebrae were twisted out of position. Likewise, all ribs were askew. Two significant misalignments were the right humerus rotated 180 degrees so that the proximal end rested near the right proximal ulna and radius, and the coccyx moved upward to lie by the left forearm. Although the position of head, spine, and ribs conceivably could be attributed to earth settlement, it would be physically impossible for the other misalignments to have occurred without human intervention. Following the scenario postulated for Sipán and San José de Moro, it seems likely that this female had died some time prior to construction of the tomb, her body had

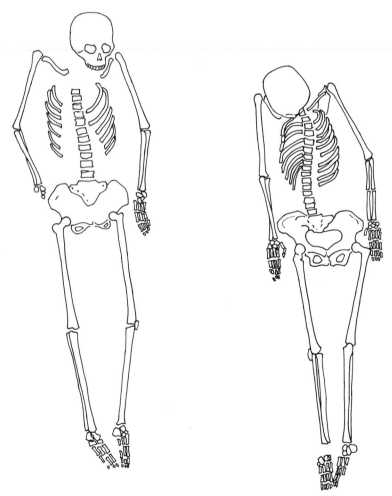

Figure 11.5. Curated adult female (right, MU 103 E8) to the west of a Moche priestess (MU 103 E5), San José de Moro, Jequetepeque Valley. (Courtesy Christopher B. Donnan and Luis Jaime Castillo B.)

been shrouded in textile and perhaps encased in a cane coffin, and she had been temporarily buried (curated) to await ultimate interment. When that moment came, she had been transported to the tomb locale and, during transport, desiccated flesh and space within the shroud or coffin had allowed many of her upper body bones to move out of their anatomical position.

SCATTERED SKELETONS

Although isolated instances of partial human skeletal material included in the graves of complete individuals were known in the literature (Donnan and Mackey 1978; Hecker and Hecker 1992 reporting H. Ubbelohde-Doering's 1937–1938 analyses), it was not

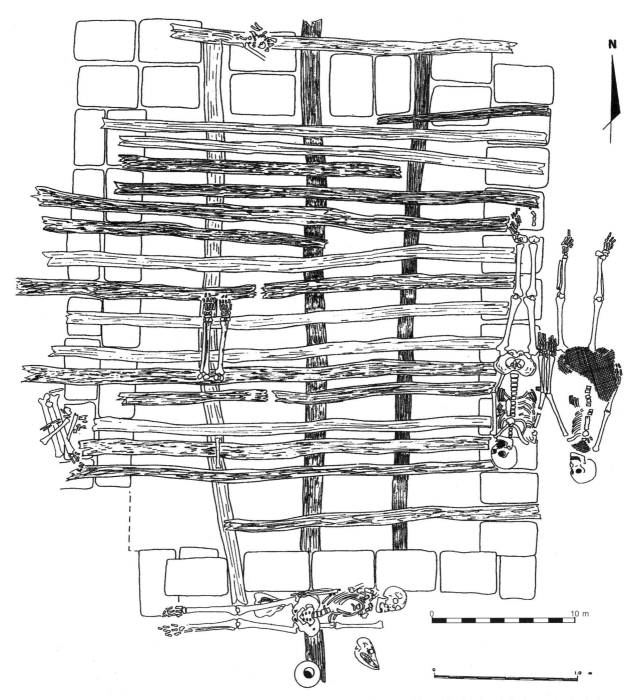

Figure 11.6. Superior view of Tomb B at Dos Cabezas, Jequetepeque Valley. Curated 40-year-old or older female and three partial individuals, two juveniles and an adult female (along with noncurated males on the east side). (Courtesy Christopher B. Donnan.)

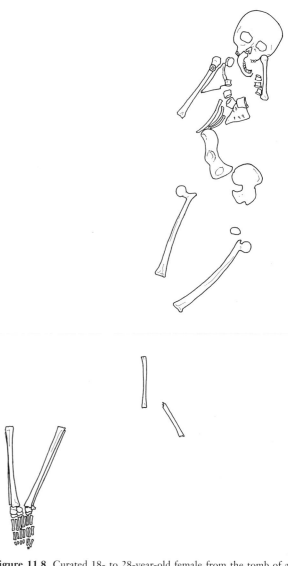

Figure 11.7. Curated and scattered 16- to 25-year-old female from the tomb of a priestess (MU 103 E7), San José de Moro, Jequetepeque Valley. (Courtesy Christopher B. Donnan and Luis Jaime Castillo B.)

until systematic osteological studies began in Moche cemeteries during the early 1980s that much attention was paid to the phenomenon.

San José de Moro

During the 1992 field season, five cases of extreme skeletal disarticulation and bone absence were encountered. They are considered here separately from the phenomenon of curation (Cordy-Collins 1992). All were in the tomb of the second priestess. Two were located at the north end at the level of the priestess, while two more may have been part of the closing ceremonies for the tomb because they were encountered above the level of the primary interment (the priestess). The uppermost of the latter two, age 16–25 years (Figure 11.7),[10] was represented only by her cranium (which was disarticulated from the mandible), the left scapula and ulna, two lumbar vertebrae, the sacrum, both femora, the right tibia, and the navicular. Furthermore, the left femur was

Figure 11.8. Curated 18- to 28-year-old female from the tomb of a priestess (MU 103 E6), San José de Moro, Jequetepeque Valley. (Courtesy Christopher B. Donnan and Luis Jaime Castillo B.)

inverted, with its posterior side up (the right femur was in the normal position), and the navicular of the right foot was lodged inside the maxilla. The second female, age 18–28 years, was encountered several centimeters below the first (Figure 11.8).[11] Her skeletal position anomalies included inversion of both femora, posterior side up. Although the left innominate was more or less in the correct position, the right was inverted at an oblique angle. Most vertebrae were bunched in the upper thorax region. The right humerus was in situ, but the proximal end of the left one projected upward into the maxillary area, while the distal end pointed almost straight downward. The right and left tibiae, fibulae, and tarsals-phalanges were located several centimeters to the northwest of the main bones. Remains of a cane pallet or coffin were evident beneath the body. It seems likely that this woman had originally been interred in a cane support or wrapping and that the foot end of it had degraded sufficiently so that, as it was lowered into the priestess' tomb, the weight of the enshrouded body allowed the postfemoral bones to slide out. The further disorganization of the bones inside the burial bundle (and loss of others) could have resulted from manipulating it into its final location.

The three partial bodies on the tomb floor also appear to be young females, but only two were complete enough for conclusive sexing (Figure 11.9). The remains of one, aged 17–19,[12] consisted of the cranium, both scapulae, the right clavicle, several thoracic vertebrae and ribs, and all arm and hand bones. The right arm was raised and separated from the body, the left was extended outward and down. The lower right leg overlay the right upper arm of the second female. The rest of the skeleton was absent. Less of the second female, aged 18–20 years,[13] was present, and the bones were more scattered. The cranium was complete and articulated with the cervical and some thoracic vertebrae. Several ribs and the left scapula also were present. The right humerus, ulna, radius, and hand were articulated but were located southeast of the body. No right scapula was found. The left radius and hand were articulated, but the humerus lay to the south and was inverted 180 degrees. The third occurrence is documented only by an incomplete cranium. However, several features (light mastoid processes and supraorbital tori, as well as sharp supraorbital margins) and incomplete eruption of the third molars argue for a female, aged 18–30 years. Additional scattered human

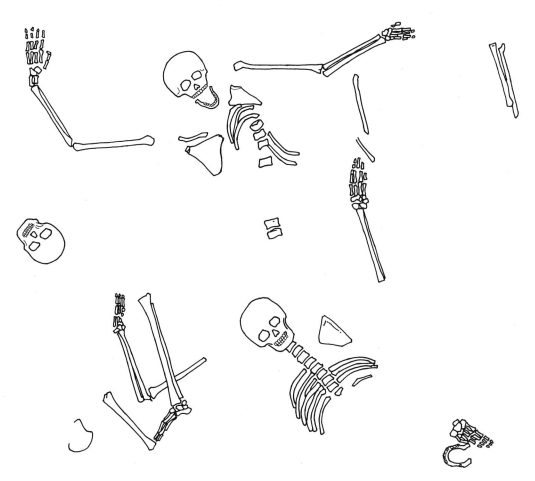

Figure 11.9. Scattered skeletal remains of a 17- to 19-year-old female (top, MU 103 E9), an 18- to 20-year-old female (bottom, MU 103 E10), the cranium of a probable 18- to 30-year-old female (left, MU 103 no no.), and additional human skeletal material, San José de Moro, Jequetepeque Valley. (Courtesy Christopher B. Donnan and Luis Jaime Castillo B.)

bones include a pair of radii and ulnae located to the west of the southernmost female, and an additional mandible and right hand located northwest of the northernmost female.

Dos Cabezas

Another intriguing aspect of Tomb B was the inclusion of two to four partial human bodies. Three clusters of skeletal material were laid on top of the tomb chamber over the roof beams (Figures 11.6, 11.10), and additional human bone was scattered beneath the beams throughout the sandy fill. On the west margin of the tomb lay the partial remains of an adult more than 25 years old.[14] This individual's bones included the radii and the right ulna as well as the postfemorals, except for the right patella and left foot. The gracility of the bone suggests it was a female. Over the westernmost of the longitudinal roof beams lay an incomplete juvenile between 14 and 16 years of age, represented by the left and right patellae, tibiae, tarsals-phalanges, and the left fibula, all in correct anatomical position (see Figure 11.6).[15] At the north end of the tomb, mixed with the bones of a parrot, were the partial remains of an adult

female of about 40 years old.[16] Only the cranium, manubrium, right clavicle, scapulae (right intact), humeri (proximal left intact), and six thoracic vertebrae were present (see Figures 11.6, 11.10). Inside the chamber, beneath the beams and mixed into the fill, were the remains of a juvenile, 10–15 years of age, represented by a partial cranium, the twelve thoracic vertebrae, and all arm and hand bones.[17] The two clusters of juvenile remains—the articulated lower long bones placed above the beams and the scattered bone inside the tomb—could be those of a single individual. Similarly, the two clusters of adult bones (on the west and north) also may have belonged to a single individual. In both the juvenile and adult instances, there is no repetition of specific bones, while there is sufficient overlap in age.

DISCUSSION

Curation

The cases I have described show that curating the remains of deceased individuals was a pattern among

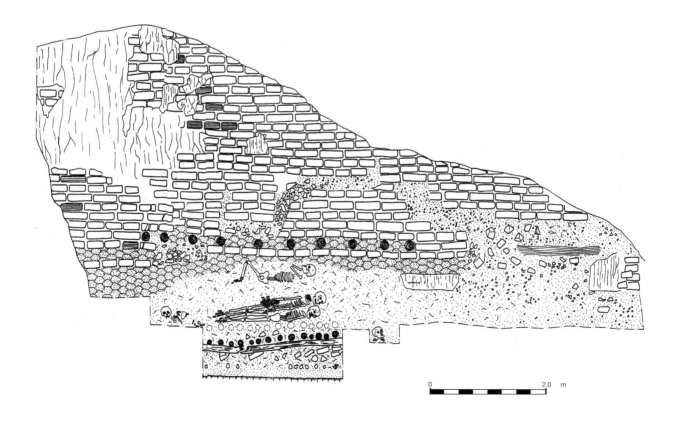

Figure 11.10. Profile view of Tomb B at Dos Cabezas, Jequetepeque Valley. (Courtesy Christopher B. Donnan.)

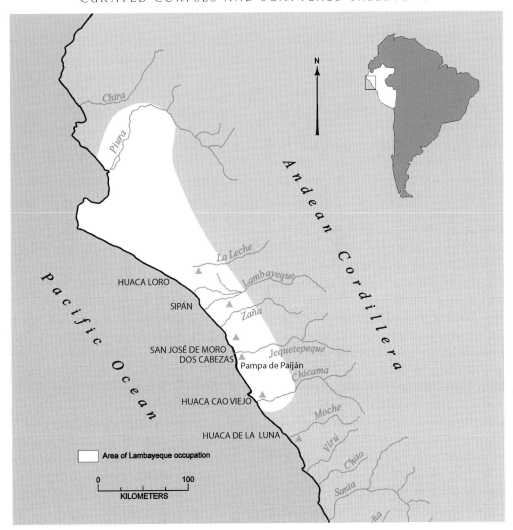

Figure 11.11. Map illustrating locales discussed in the text. (Courtesy Donald McClelland.)

the Moche from the third through the eighth centuries CE, particularly among the Moche Norteños (those living north of the Pampa de Paiján) (Figure 11.11).[18,19] Moreover, it appears that the Moche practice was continued into post-Moche times in the north. Three Lambayeque curated burials have been reported by Andrew Nelson at San José de Moro (1998:193), and Izumi Shimada et al. (2004) have reported contemporaneous cases from their excavations at the site of Huaca Loro at the Batán Grande complex in the Lambayeque Valley. As yet, however, no cases *as such* have been noted among the later Chimu.

Nonetheless, there are some points worth making in regard to this lack of Chimu evidence. First, the existence of human curations was unrecognized on the north coast prior to 1988, and second, the systematic practice of detailed examinations of human skeletal remains by field osteologists began only in the early

1980s. Thus, it is quite possible that other instances of curation have been excavated but not noted as such. A third point concerns the manner of entombing the kings of Chimor. Each lord apparently was interred in a vast mortuary complex within his palace precinct (see Conrad 1982). All these tombs were looted following the Spanish conquest, but one of the burial precincts, Las Avispas, has been examined in some detail (Pozorski 1979). Systematic collection of the disturbed human bone left scattered in the wake of the looting revealed the presence of more than 300 young female skeletons. It has been assumed that all young women were sacrificed at the time of the ruler's death and placed in prepared square-cut tombs surrounding the large central T-shaped tomb of the lord himself (Conrad 1982:103). However, because the original burial positions of the women's bones are unknown, and in light of what is now known about Moche and Lambayeque human curation practices, it is worth reconsidering the evidence. Although demographic figures are unavailable for Chimor at that moment in time, it would seem that removing more than 300 females of prime reproductive age from the population in one fell swoop would have had serious repercussions. A more plausible explanation is that some (if not all) of these individuals were already dead, safely curated, and awaiting reinterment with a Chimu lord. It is believed that each Chimu lord (of a total of nine or ten) was buried in his own funerary platform. The archaeological evidence suggests that each was not buried alone but rather surrounded by cells designed to contain other bodies. If the pattern observed at Avispas prevailed in the other platforms, we are faced with daunting numbers. If we are conservative and assume a life span of fifty years for each Chimu lord, and if we postulate that only a third the number of offering women found at Avispas was placed in each of the other royal funerary platforms, we still reach a figure of about 1,000 young women artificially removed from Chimu society. And if we consider the postulated dual concurrent rule (Kolata 1990), although the overall figure doesn't grow, the time period during which the interments would have taken place shrinks, and the impact on the society increases. Curation interments provide a reasonable alternative.

In 1995 an extremely pertinent archaeological discovery was made in the Moche Valley at the site of Huaca de la Luna (Uceda 1997b). A small but very detailed temple model with figurines was excavated that dates stylistically to Chimu times. It shows the elaborate enactment of a ceremony in which a deceased person is carried in a funeral bier. Most significant for the present study, at the rear of the temple, sequestered in a corridor, are two figurines shrouded as mummy bundles, or *fardos*. Upon unwrapping, the mummies were found to be female. A third figurine fardo, found in the fill of the tomb (but presumably originally part of the model), has been identified as a male (Uceda 1997b:157). If this model accurately portrays a funeral ceremony enacted on behalf of a member of the Chimu elite, it certainly suggests that curations existed in that society. Although various interpretations of the scene may be offered, a very plausible one is that a venerated male ancestor is being feasted and feted, attended by curated women, and that a "new" human offering is being added to his sepulcher.

The Curation Questions

It appears that curation of human bodies was practiced on the north coast of Peru in prehistoric times; the natural question is, why was it done? In an attempt to understand the phenomenon, it is useful to distinguish among curated bodies of single individuals found in simple tombs, curated bodies located in elaborate chamber tombs, and fragmentary scattered skeletal material found in some of the chamber tombs. Andrew Nelson has investigated curation of single individuals at San José de Moro and reports that males, females, and juveniles of indeterminate sex were all curated. He suggests that a prolonged period of funeral ritual may have created the circumstance (Nelson 1998:204–205). It should be noted that no individual found in one of these simple tombs was of elite status. Elites were buried in the chamber tombs—constructions of considerable effort—where they were accompanied by quantities of sumptuary goods, including human interments, some curated and others not. Scattered skeletal material belonging to males, females, and juveniles of indeterminate sex has also been found in most of the chamber tombs, including those excavated south of the Pampa de Paiján. To date, the only females found in correct anatomical position are the two priestesses from San José de Moro.[20] In contrast, all the males in the chamber tombs are properly articulated.[21]

Although future research may alter the picture we now have of exclusively female curations in chamber tombs, the frequency of female curation suggests the elevated position of some women in Moche society. The clear message is that certain women were of sufficient status and esteem that they would be conserved after death to bring prestige to the tomb of newly dead elites, both male and female. This message is important because it is not reflected in the art. Even through late Moche times, when women of status do appear in the art (Cordy-Collins 2001a, b), human representation is overwhelmingly male.[22]

While this remarkable north coast practice of (re)-interring the previously dead along with the newly dead is undeniable, researchers are still left with a plethora of questions. Who were these curated individuals in their societies? Who among the newly dead qualified to be entombed with a formerly dead individual? From what contexts were the curated bodies drawn? Although we cannot answer these questions as fully as we might like, some data are clear: All the curated persons so far identified as to sex were female, and they were always destined for the burials of nobility, a nobility that at least in one place and time (San José de Moro, ca. 750 CE) included women and children. The locale of their curation, prior to chamber tomb interment, is an intriguing question. One wonders if some of the empty tombs encountered, such as at Dos Cabezas, Huaca Cao Viejo, and Huaca de la Luna, might not have been the original curation loci (initial burial sites) for these women and children.

Data supporting that possibility come from excavations at Dos Cabezas in 2000 that revealed an apparently intact tomb (Tomb A) in the same area as Tomb B containing the curated bodies discussed above (Donnan 2007; Donnan and Cock 2001: Figure 13). Tomb A was constructed in a manner similar to three tombs (without curated bodies) located previously in the same area (Tombs 1, 2, and 3).[23] The roof beams were intact and a requisite miniature copper figure was in situ (Donnan 2007: Figures 2.2, 2.3, 2.9, 2.11; Donnan and Cock 2001: Figure 10),[24] although the burial did lack the traditional accompanying human offering. Moreover, it was discovered that bricks from a lower corner of Tomb A had been removed and that a painted mat—originally enshrouding the body or covering the tomb floor—had been dragged through the opened corner. An adult male body lay inside the tomb in a state of "segmental articulation" (Nelson 1998:203). This is to say that, although parts of the body were anatomically articulated, these articulated portions were not in their correct anatomical relationships vis-à-vis each other (Figure 11.12). Furthermore, the cranium had been carefully rearticulated with its mandible and positioned to face north. The right radius was the only missing bone. This segmental articulation suggests that the individual had been removed from his tomb after having been dead a relatively brief time: not long enough for his flesh to have sufficiently desiccated to allow the muscles and ligaments to divest completely from the bones, but sufficient time to allow the body to come apart at points of least resistance—perhaps less than a generation—when his tomb was opened. Another relevant feature of this burial is that there were *no* grave goods (other than the mat) inside the tomb. In attempting to understand this situation, it is important to realize that the pyramid into which this and the other tombs had been constructed *was occupied* by the Moche at the time the deceased were interred inside all these tombs (Donnan and Cock 2001). This condition would have made it difficult for a tomb to be ransacked without those living there being aware of it. The only reasonable conclusion to be drawn is that the disturbance of this adult male's tomb was sanctioned.[25] What was taken from it is unknown (other than the right radius, which may have been an accidental loss when the body was

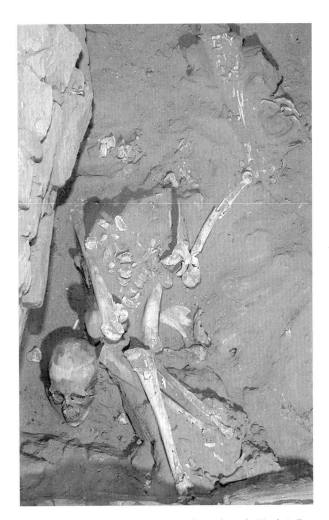

Figure 11.12. Ransacked burial of an adult Moche male, Tomb A, Dos Cabezas, Jequetepeque Valley. (Courtesy Christopher B. Donnan.)

removed and replaced), but lack of an attendant human offering, contemporary or curated, suggests that it was precisely an accompanying interment that was sought. One might question why this (presumed) primary body was only disarticulated and not reused in another burial elsewhere. It might be because (at least adult) males were not appropriate for curation. It should be recalled that the three intact tombs from this cemetery each contained the body of a young female (Donnan 2007; Donnan and Cock 2001).[26] It is worth mentioning that those tombs contained an array of grave goods, and worth reiterating that this ransacked tomb contained none. Could this absence suggest that curated humans were not the only "artifacts" sought or selected for reinterment with a newer burial?

Although we are able to address the practice of reinterment in Moche Norteño society in a limited way, we are left with numerous unanswered (and perhaps unanswerable) questions. How were those to be reinterred selected and by whom? Was it a reciprocal honor; that is, was the inclusion of a previously deceased individual with a newly deceased person an activity that increased the status of only the newly dead or of the formerly dead as well? What sorts of records or markers existed that allowed the living to locate the (temporary) resting places of the nonliving? Were only females curated/ reinterred, and were they ever reinterred more than once; can the scattered skeletal parts found in some tombs be accounted for as tertiary (or even more repeated) reburial?[27] What ends did reinterment serve? Were the formerly dead simply "wealth," artifacts that added prestige to the newly dead and their family, or did they function as liaisons between the newly dead and the world of the dead, a world with which they had already connected? Was it an early form of the very common ancestor worship in the form of mummy veneration so widely practiced into the eighteenth century in Peru (Doyle 1988)? Or were they, as one reviewer of this chapter has suggested, intended to act as servants in the afterlife for the elite newly dead?

Scattered Skeletons

Finally, one more situation may be relevant. At Dos Cabezas, excavations near the tombs mentioned above revealed the remains of a room burned in a bonfire.[28] It contained the burials of two males (one an adult, the other a juvenile), but, more significant for this discussion, it contained a scatter of camelid and human bones. The former were partially articulated and warped by the conflagration, indicating that they had been burned in the room while still fresh. The human bones, however, were disarticulated, dry when they burned, and clearly do not represent the remains of any entire individuals (Cordy-Collins 1997; Donnan and Cock 1996). That these scattered human bones were part of an offering is clear. Their source is unknown, but it is reasonable to suggest that they also were exhumed, formerly curated material that had been removed from their previous resting places expressly for inclusion in this new context. Their incompleteness suggests that they represent at least secondary and possibly tertiary or quaternary interments. A later, somewhat smaller-scale enactment of this Dos Cabezas occurrence was discovered at nearby Pacatnamu in a transitional late Moche-Lambayeque context (Cordy-Collins 1997). Certainly the disarticulated human body parts that were included—presumably as offerings in the graves discussed in this chapter—suggest that older graves were resources for the acquisition of the partial skeletons.

Relic Recovery

As the evidence of curation and reinterment mounts, it forces us to reconsider what burial meant to the Moche and their descendants. Our modern view, that a dead body is consigned to the earth in perpetuity, increasingly seems a very simplistic and inappropriately applied model for the ancient people of the Peruvian north coast.

Acknowledgments

I extend my sincere appreciation to Christopher Donnan, Guillermo Cock, and Luis Jaime Castillo for allowing me to use their unpublished field illustrations. I am also deeply grateful for the comments and suggestions made by colleagues who read earlier drafts of this chapter. Special thanks go to Paul Johnson for the eleventh-hour artwork. A slightly different form of this chapter was presented as "Scattered Skeletons and Curated Corpses: Cases of Tricky Taphonomy" at the 2005 Latin American Paleopathology Association annual meeting, Río de Janeiro, Brazil.

NOTES

1. Field address MU 30 E7.
2. Field address MU 30 E5.
3. Field address MU 41 E1.
4. Field address MU 41 E3.
5. Field address MU 41 E5.
6. Field address MU 41 E6.
7. Field address MU 103 E1.
8. The knees of A50 T1 B1 were raised in moderate flexion.
9. Field address A50 T1 B3.
10. Field address MU 103 E7
11. Field address MU 103 E6.
12. Field address MU 103 E9.
13. Field address MU 103 E10.
14. Field address A50 T1 B5.
15. Field address A50 T1 B6.
16. Field address A50 T1 F2.
17. Field address A50 T1 F1.
18. Régulo Franco, César Gálvez, and Segundo Vásquez (1998) report a single chamber tomb at Huaca Cao Viejo in the Chicama Valley, south of the Pampa de Paiján, that had been ransacked in antiquity. The skeletal remains of at least five individuals were recovered during the excavation, but none was complete. Because a principal interment could not be identified ("la total ausencia del cadaver del personaje

principal," Franco et al. 1998:16) and no curated body was encountered, this tomb is not in the same category as those at Sipán, San José de Moro, and Dos Cabezas.

19. Santiago Uceda reports a chamber tomb at Huaca de la Luna in the Moche Valley, south of the Chicama, where eleven individuals were found, only one of which was in a semiarticulated posture (although she lacked several bones) on the tomb margin (1997a:181–183).

20. It is possible that some of the juveniles whose bones are too young to sex were female.

21. The main occupant in one of the three chamber tombs excavated at San José de Moro in 1991 (MU 26 E3) was male. Likewise, his flanking burials were also male. Both were decapitated (Castillo and Donnan 1992:102); the head of the eastern male (MU 26 E5) was placed ca. 30 cm south of his shoulders, and the head of the western male (MU 26 E6) was absent from the tomb. The rest of both bodies was present and in correct anatomical position.

22. It might be argued that the famous erotic pottery features females as much as it does males. However, as Christopher Donnan has pointed out, none of the sexual activity portrayed "would lead to insemination and subsequent childbirth" (1978:177). In most cases we don't know that one of the human pair is a female; even though it is accoutred like a female, it could be a *berdache*. The famous Zuni berdache, We'wah, seems to have completely fooled Washington, DC society during his/her months living there and wearing female clothing (Roscoe 1991).

23. Field addresses: A52 T1 B1, A53 T1 B2, and A54 T1 B3.

24. Field address A53 T2 B1.

25. Tomb B may have been selectively looted in antiquity; no primary burial was found within the tomb. As mentioned in the text, as well as the four complete and the two to three partial individuals around the tomb margin there were the scattered skeletal parts of an individual inside the chamber. Inside also were the broken remains of fine ceramic ware (see Donnan 2007: Figures 3.14, 3.16; Donnan and Cock 1995, 2001).

26. The body on top of Tomb 3 was too young to sex (10–11 years), but the presence of a spindle whorl as the deceased's sole grave offering argues that the individual was female. In Moche Norteño graves where spindle whorls are present and the skeleton can be sexed, there is a 100% concordance between that artifact and a female interment.

27. To date, no male reinterments have been reported, but since we cannot reliably determine the sex of individuals below the age of puberty from the skeleton, we cannot say with certainty that male children were not curated/reinterred.

28. Field address A51.

REFERENCES

Alva, Walter, and Christopher B. Donnan
1993   *The Royal Tombs of Sipán.* Fowler Museum of Cultural History, University of California, Los Angeles.

Castillo Butters, Luis Jaime, and Christopher B. Donnan
1992   *Primer informe parcial y solicitud de permiso para excavación arqueológica Proyecto San José de Moro, primera temporada de excavaciones (Junio–Agosto de 1991).*

Conrad, Geoffrey W.
1982   The Burial Platforms of Chan Chan: Some Social and Political Implications. In *Chan Chan: Andean Desert City,* edited by Michael E. Moseley and Kent C. Day, pp. 87–117. University of New Mexico Press, Albuquerque.

Cordy-Collins, Alana
1991   Unpublished osteological field and laboratory notes, San José de Moro, 1991.
1992   Unpublished osteological field and laboratory notes, San José de Moro, 1992.
1994   Unpublished osteological field and laboratory notes, Dos Cabezas, 1994.
1997   The Offering Room Complex. In *The Pacatnamú Papers,* vol. 2, edited by Christopher B. Donnan and Guillermo A. Cock, pp. 283–298. Fowler Museum of Cultural History, University of California, Los Angeles.
2001a   Blood and the Moon Priestess. In *Ritual Sacrifice in Ancient Peru,* edited by Elizabeth P. Benson and Anita Cook, pp. 35–54. University of Texas Press, Austin.
2001b   Labretted Ladies: Foreign Women in Northern Moche and Lambayeque Art. In *Moche Art and Archaeology in Ancient Peru,* edited by Joanne Pillsbury, pp. 247–258. Yale University Press, New Haven, CT.

Cunningham, Michael
1990   *A Home at the End of the World.* Picador, New York.

Donnan, Christopher B.
1978   *Moche Art of Peru.* Museum of Cultural History, University of California, Los Angeles.
2001   Moche Burials Uncovered. *National Geographic Magazine* 199(3):58–73.
2007   *Moche Tombs at Dos Cabezas.* Cotsen Institute of Archaeology at UCLA, Monograph 59. Los Angeles.

Donnan, Christopher B., and Luis Jaime Castillo Butters
1992   Finding the Tomb of a Moche Priestess. *Archaeology* 45(6):38–42.

194 ANDEAN CIVILIZATION

1994 Excavaciones de tumbas de sacerdotisas Moche en San José de Moro, Jequetepeque. In *Moche: Propuestas y perspectivas*, edited by Santiago Uceda C. and Elías Mujica B., pp. 415–424. Universidad Nacional de La Libertad, Trujillo; Instituto Francés de Estudios Andinos.

Donnan, Christopher B., and Guillermo A. Cock
1995 Primer informe parcial: Proyecto Dos Cabezas. Primera temporada de excavaciones. Report submitted to the Peruvian Instituto Nacional de Cultura, Lima.
1996 Segunda informe parcial: Proyecto Dos Cabezas. Segunda temporada de excavaciones. Report submitted to the Peruvian Instituto Nacional de Cultura, Lima.
2001 Séptima informe parcial: Proyecto Dos Cabezas. Séptima temporada de excavaciones. Report submitted to the Peruvian Instituto Nacional de Cultura, Lima.

Donnan, Christopher B., and Carol J. Mackey
1978 *Ancient Burial Patterns of the Moche Valley, Peru.* University of Texas Press, Austin.

Doyle, Mary Eileen
1988 *The Ancestor Cult and Burial Ritual in Seventeenth and Eighteenth-Century Central Peru.* Doctoral dissertation, Department of History, University of California, Los Angeles. University Microfilms International, Ann Arbor, MI.

Franco, Régulo, César Gálvez, and Segundo Vásquez
1998 Desentierro ritual de una tumba Moche: Huaca Cao Viejo. *Revista Arqueológica Sian* 3(6):9–18.

Hecker, Giesela, and Wolfgang Hecker
1992 Huesos humanos como ofrendas mortuarias y uso repetido de vasijas: Detalles sobre la tradición funeraria prehispánica de la región costeña norperuana. *Baessler-Archiv*, Neue Folge, Band XL: 171–195.

Kolata, Alan L.
1990 The Urban Concept of Chan Chan. In *The Northern Dynasties: Kingship and Statecraft in Chimor*, edited by Michael E. Moseley and Alana Cordy-Collins, pp. 107–144. Dumbarton Oaks, Washington, DC.

Nelson, Andrew J.
1998 Wandering Bones, Archaeology, Forensic Science, and Moche Burial Practices. *International Journal of Osteology* 8:191–212.

Pozorski, Thomas
1979 The Las Avispas Burial Platform at Chan Chan, Peru. *Annals of the Carnegie Museum* 48. Carnegie Museum of Natural History, Pittsburgh.

Roscoe, Will
1991 *The Zuni Man-Woman.* University of New Mexico Press, Albuquerque.

Shimada, Izumi, Ken-ichi Shinoda, Julie Farnum, Robert Cornuci, and Hirokatsu Watanabe
2004 An Integrated Analysis of Pre-Hispanic Mortuary Practices: A Middle Sicán Case Study. *Current Anthropology* 45(3):369–402.

Uceda Castillo, Santiago
1997a El poder y la muerte en la sociedad Moche. In *Investigaciones en la Huaca de la Luna 1995. Proyecto Arqueológico Huacas del Sol y de la Luna*, edited by Santiago Uceda, Elías Mujica, and R. Morales, pp. 177–188. Facultad de Ciencias Sociales, Universidad Nacional de La Libertad, Trujillo.
1997b Esculturas en miniatura y una maqueta en madera. In *Investigaciones en la Huaca de la Luna 1995. Proyecto Arqueológico Huacas del Sol y de la Luna*, edited by Santiago Uceda, Elías Mujica, and R. Morales, pp. 151–170. Facultad de Ciencias Sociales, Universidad Nacional de La Libertad, Trujillo.

Verano, John W.
1997 Human Skeletal Remains from Tomb 1, Sipán (Lambayeque River Valley, Peru) and Their Social Implications. *Antiquity* 71(273):670–682.

CHAPTER 12

EXPLORATION OF PUNCTUATED EQUILIBRIUM AND CULTURE CHANGE IN THE ARCHAEOLOGY OF ANDEAN ETHNOGENESIS

GARTH BAWDEN AND RICHARD REYCRAFT

SOME OF MICHAEL MOSELEY'S most innovative work has concerned extreme environmental anomalies and their dynamic effects on past human societies in the Andes. In 1987 Moseley employed the concept of punctuated equilibrium as an explanatory model of environmental-cultural interaction in this physically volatile region. Simply stated, this model examines episodes of rapid stylistic change in the archaeological record in relation to extreme climatic fluctuations. Moseley viewed episodes of rapid stylistic change as representing major disruptions in political and subsistence systems brought about by widespread and prolonged environmental catastrophe. He used multiple lines of corroborating evidence, including data obtained from geoarchaeological survey, glacial ice cores, historical records, recent El Niños, and references in Andean myths. The punctuated equilibrium model permitted discussion of the Andean environment in a multifaceted sociocultural context, thereby avoiding recourse to simplistic models of environmental determinism. It also produced clear evidence for the temporal synchronization of major culture change and past environmental disasters. In the time that has elapsed since the model first appeared, environmental stress has become an accepted factor in studies of sociocultural change. This has been one of Michael Moseley's greatest contributions to Andean archaeology.

Moseley argued that disruptions of great magnitude cause significant change in the social order and, in extreme instances, lead to its complete overthrow. In the case of ancient Andean societies, such cataclysmic events are marked by major changes in the archaeological record. Moreover, their devastating impact was memorialized in myths and oral histories that were recorded in early Colonial period chronicles. Andean scholars have long recognized that the material record reveals long periods of ceramic continuity interrupted by relatively short-lived "horizons." However, Moseley rejected the position that these breaks reflected demographic realignment by migrating populations and asserted that more often than not, they represented major disruptions in political and subsistence systems initiated by widespread and prolonged environmental catastrophe.

In the Andes, the evidence of events of potentially catastrophic climatic disruption comes from the Quelccaya ice cores, supplemented by lake core data and local geomorphological observations. The records that have been used most fruitfully by Moseley (1992, 1999), Kolata (2000), and Shimada and his colleagues (1991) are reliable from the middle of the first millennium AD. They demonstrate a number of associated pluvials and severe droughts, two of which are among the most severe of such episodes ever known and represent the focus of this chapter.

The first of these episodes occurred toward the end of the sixth century AD, bringing extreme environmental and sociocultural disruption to large areas of the Andes. We focus here on its impact on the north coast of Peru. In this region, Moseley and his successors have uncovered evidence of pervasive sand movement and soil erosion in the archaeological record. This major disruption corresponds to the transition between the Middle and Late Moche phases of the north coast occupational sequence, a time when significant sociocultural changes were occurring in the region. Our second example comes from the fourteenth century AD. Heavy oxygen isotope ratio data from the Quelccaya glacier (Thompson et al. 1985) indicates that this episode also brought pan-Andean environmental disaster. Here we focus on the effects of related disruption on the far south coast of Peru. Dennis Satterlee (1993), working with Moseley, has confirmed many of the accompanying geophysical effects of this major disruptive phase. His research indicates that an extreme El Niño event affected the Ilo region around AD 1350, bringing torrential rains to the usually hyperarid area and deeply burying large segments of many Classic phase Chiribaya settlements in thick layers of flood-borne mud and boulders. The resulting impact on human occupation was manifested in changes in settlement form and in the ways in which people signaled their cultural identity.

In a study like ours, which accepts that great physical disaster played a major role in affecting the course of human history in the Andes, we must be careful not to revert to a simplistic acceptance of environmental determinism to explain changes in culture. Consequently, we stress that no matter the magnitude of environmental impact, active human agency remains central to shaping the course and outcome of the response. In this chapter we address the creative human dimension of the process, highlighting especially the various ways in which group affiliation and identity became active players in mediating changing social needs. We focus on the dynamic role played by ethnicity, which we define as shared recognition of group membership in a socially reproductive group. Within this context, ethnicity transcends any single determinant and changes through time according to circumstance and history. We also explore the relationship between ethnicity and political ideology, often used as a strategy to represent it as the shared foundation of group solidarity.

ETHNICITY AND ETHNIC IDENTIFICATION IN THE ARCHAEOLOGICAL RECORD

There is growing concern with the identification of ethnicity in archaeology, with various biological, material, and symbolic approaches being used to address its role and identification. However, all would agree that ethnicity is integrally concerned with the ways in which a human group asserts its shared membership and measures this against its counterparts either within the wider social entity or beyond. The strategies used to achieve conformity are neither uniform nor simple. Thus, we cannot merely equate style, culture, or physical affinity with ethnicity; it cuts across all of these. In this chapter we define ethnicity as the recognition of common membership by a social group both in the present and through time. Group members consciously share the same core values, interests, and goals and pass these on to their descendants in a self-referential and assertive manner. However, solidarity need not deny change, and the ethnic experience possesses great capacity to adjust in order to successfully negotiate historic circumstance while maintaining its core values.

On the surface, the self-ascriptive character of ethnicity, its particularity, and its capacity to change would appear to make its archaeological investigation difficult if not fruitless. After all, given the lack of any specific correlation of ethnicity with a particular type of material culture style (ceramic decoration, burial custom, etc.), there is little justification to ascribe ethnic significance to any individual or group of material signifiers purely on the basis of their formal characteristics—the basis of archaeological analysis. One way past this dilemma is through the study of social context. Ethnicity, in common with other social phenomena, does not exist in a vacuum. Rather, it is a manifestation of its location in time and space. Thus, if the context of social production can be identified, it follows that the related material artifacts can also be placed within their proper domains of meaning. Such a study requires reconstructing the historic trajectory that created the setting for ethnic construction, as well as the specific social arena within which it emerged.

ETHNOGENESIS AND THE POLITY

Ethnogenesis, or the formation of ethnic identity, is often a product of stress that accompanies the formation or collapse of large, complex, centralized social or political entities. At times of formation, hierarchical political, social, and economic institutions emerge to replace simple reliance on local kinship, community, ancestry, and sacred geography or place. These overarching institutions seek to establish a level of broad sociopolitical allegiance that cannot be achieved by narrowly focused integrative principles that promote local social affinity and intergroup differentiation. In response, threatened groups within the larger society seek to generate new ways of preserving their social identities.

Conversely, in the context of collapse, the wide suprastructural institutions that have often unified various regional groups for centuries are removed and local strategies reemerge. However, the passage of time and the restructuring of society that accompanies the life of a long-lasting polity prevent simple reversion to the situations existing prior to state formation. New forms of local ethnicity must be found out of the residual integrative structure of the collapsed state and whatever local strategies can be invented within the particular historic experiences of the group. It is this aspect of change that concerns us in this study. Specifically, we are interested in the way in which ethnicity played an active role in mediating the dramatic changes associated with two great episodes of prolonged and devastating environmental perturbation.

Ideology and Social Construction

We now turn to a particular mechanism through which ethnic identification is often asserted—ideology. In its most general guise, we define ideology as that specialized formulation of group experience that promotes the aspirations of its adherents in the wider social arena. Although it is usual to regard ideology chiefly as the means by which political power is consolidated and maintained within society, on a broader level it is active at all levels of social identity. Ideology is not in itself synonymous with ethnicity, for competing political groups often accept common ethnicity while affirming different ideologies. However, every ethnic group possesses a distinct and clearly defined set of qualities through which it asserts its distinctiveness and solidarity. Such formulations may incorporate the denominators of cultural exclusivity, religious belief, mythical associations, or a variety of other shared beliefs that are regarded as the exclusive legacy of the group. Together they form a specific complex of rules and beliefs that can confront the beliefs of other groups

in the political arena to assert group integrity and status. In this context, political ideology is a measure of ethnic identity.

During periods of stability, members of groups that espouse different values live in a state of complementary tension within the greater society. Although differing groups may well contest their differing views as the ideological agendas of political, corporate, or religious movements, this discourse need not affect the wider communal identity, which their adherents all share. In this dynamic process more dominant groups will have greater access to the resources (institutions, wealth, media) that can further their goals. The major exception to this situation is represented by the ruling authority, which asserts its dominant ideology (Abercrombie et al. 1980) with a vastly unequal utilization of the central institutions of political power. Through symbolic communication and participatory ceremony, its adherents seek to co-opt all members of the community into accepting the social order that it proclaims. In stable circumstances, where the existing social order is perceived as serving the common good, most people will accept the dominant ideology as an important general element of group identity. However, less dominant groups will still express their ethnic affirmation in attempts to gain more equal access. Individuals within such ethnic groups may switch affiliation if they perceive that the benefits will outweigh the costs.

History makes it abundantly clear that such periods of stability do not usually persist. In times of deprivation, the perceived contradiction between political discourse and the individual's lived reality can lead to fundamental challenge to the ruling order. If their circumstances remain unchanged, the deprived will inevitably reassess the existing order in the light of their own moral agendas and practical needs. With the disruption of central authority that results in political instability, local groups and local leaders will emerge to contain the crisis at their level. In more traditional societies, the leaders of large kin groups will have direct access to the corporate labor that is inherent in clan and moiety organization. Over time, the values and principles of contesting groups, newly formulated as tenets of assertive ideologies, consolidate into the conceptual foundations for exclusive group identity, resulting in irreparable divisions within society. What had been the basis for political contestation evolves into the basis for differentiated ethnicity.

The Symbolism of Social Action

Although symbols have been studied from various viewpoints, most scholars would agree that they include a wide range of conceptual, behavioral, and material forms whose meanings are rooted in the cognitive world models of their related cultures. Symbols codify people's experience, assert their particular values, ideologies, and stereotypes, and direct their relations with others. This quality makes symbols potent players in the affirmation of power at all levels of the social ladder and important forces for the negotiation and construction of group identity. Given the archaeological nature of our topic, we confine our discussion of symbolism to its material aspect.

A common cognitive origin ensures that symbols are understood throughout their community, while their potential for flexible interpretation allows subordinate groups to manipulate them in their own interests. This property becomes important in societies caught in a state of deep political and social turmoil such as that brought on by major environmental disruption. As contesting subgroups strive to assert their precedence or as new allegiances coalesce in response to social stress, symbolism becomes a powerful vehicle for reinforcing common awareness among their members and asserting their specific character and interests in the face of wider social pressures.

All symbolic systems are influenced to some extent by neighboring cultures through the continuous process of intercultural diffusion. This process is gradual and universal, and usually results in modification of meaning of the borrowed elements so that their original "foreignness" is forgotten. However, at times of stress, threatened groups may abruptly exchange discredited ideology for new foreign systems together with their symbols to enhance their political status or to reinforce group integrity by affiliating with potent transcendental beliefs. By its very nature, this form of adoption resists incorporation into the existing symbolic structure and may promote intrasocietal division and culture change.

Places also carry powerful symbolic meaning. The varied experiences that individuals draw from their particular historic and social locations converge in the places where social action occurs. Here they are actualized to effect stability or change. Elite architecture asserts symbolic force on behalf of dominant interests and includes forms associated with administrative, economic, and religious institutions together with the residences and burial places of the rulers. By contrast, architecture that falls largely under the control of commoners is almost entirely confined to their homes and, to a lesser degree, their burials. Household members, through daily practice, may reflexively manipulate ideas embedded in residential structure to effect change. By adjusting the symbolic content of their houses, people manipulate basic residential principles to strengthen their collective identity and assert social solidarity, the essence of ethnicity.

The Archaeological Search for Ethnicity

In addressing this problem, it is necessary first to understand what we mean by group identity in the material record. It is of course well understood these days that we cannot simply equate a particular "identity" of a group with the collection of material artifacts that make up its "archaeological culture." In fact, our two Andean examples incorporate several distinct symbolic sets. Each of these sets represents the material manifestation of a specific element of the group identity of the people who created them. Collectively they represent the ethnic identity of their makers.

At the deepest and least conscious level are formal elements that persist through long time periods and across the archaeological cultural phases established by archaeologists. These elements commonly include consistent ceramic shapes and decorative techniques and motifs, the basic elements used to create more ephemeral signifiers of identity. They represent in material form the deep cultural time-space experience of a people that has evolved in the *longue durée* as a culture.

At a more conscious level, there is no direct relationship between ethnicity and a specific category of material culture. Nevertheless, several investigations do suggest a relationship between certain aspects of material culture style and ethnic communication (Wobst 1977; Sackett 1982; Wiessner 1984; Boyd and Richerson 1987; Shennan 1989). These studies suggest the presence of at least three kinds of stylistic variation in cultural groups. Stylistic variation that actively signals ethnic communication has been termed *emblemic style* (Wiessner 1983). Emblemic artifacts, which are consciously manufactured as ethnic or social markers, must be capable of transmitting simple encoded messages from a distance (or, like projectile points deposited at kill locations, must be capable of being found and read by individuals over a large territory) (Wobst 1977; Wiessner 1983). *Isochrestic variation* represents generally unconscious stylistic variation that is set by enculturation and historical tradition (Sackett 1982; Boyd and Richerson 1987). This type of stylistic variation may carry considerable ethnic symbolism; however, because it reflects tradition and is used unconsciously, it may change more slowly and lag behind emblemic markers when ethnic changes occur in a society. The third kind of stylistic variation, *assertive style*, reflects the individual flare each artist consciously or unconsciously incorporates into his or her work (Wiessner 1983). Although assertive style may help identify a master craftsman in the archaeological record, the idiosyncratic variations in stylistic content employed by different artisans obfuscates ethnic identification.

Finally, symbols of political ideology constitute the most transient category of material symbolism. Rulers use these symbols to proclaim and support the sociopolitical order on which their power is based. Because the success and longevity of such ideological symbols depend on the success of their proponents in persuading their subjects of the benefits of their rule, they are most vulnerable to breakdown caused by historical contingency. A variety of different kinds of impact, both external and internal to society (war, attack, revolution, environmental collapse), can bring about the dramatic end of the dominant political order and equally abrupt elimination of its symbols.

Where, then, does this discussion leave us in the search for ethnicity in archaeology? We believe that we can circumvent the obvious problems associated with trying to correlate ethnic identity with material style and form by exploring the dynamics through which it comes into existence. We suggest that through the examination of the material remains of human groups in their spatial and temporal contexts, we can offer insight into the social contexts that encourage the construction of collective identity and the strategies employed to consolidate it. From this starting point, the physical (and archaeological) symbols of ethnogenesis find their logical place as players in the mechanisms of social production.

This archaeological strategy has three important requirements:

1. It must identify the full archaeological context of change within which ethnic formation occurred in a society. This requires knowledge of the particular history of the subject society, including both its internal development and external connections. It also requires knowledge of the circumstances that may have stimulated a section of society to reassess its relationship with the wider community at the time of ethnic formation.

2. It is necessary to determine that social change visible in the archaeological record was indeed caused by ethnogenesis. To do this we must identify cultural items that functioned as ethnic or social identifiers and distinguish them from material items employed by the dominant political ideology and the cultural baggage of background noise that represents isochrestic style. The archaeological record includes three components that are frequently confused by the researcher: the well-defined symbolism of a dominant political ideology, a wider set of material expressions of shared social identity, and the much broader array of material culture that represents the generally unconscious isochrestic stylistic tradition. Both political ideology and social identity actively employ material items as communication media. Stylistic attributes are specifically chosen because they convey pertinent emblemic information. To possess such excellent symbolic communication potential, these items must also be visible enough to pass along encoded information from a distance (Wobst 1977; Wiessner 1983).

The emblemic and visibility criteria eliminate several material culture categories from use as active ethnic or political symbols. For example, strictly domestic utensils seldom leave the confines of interior private space and thus should not encode messages intended for wide audiences. Likewise, interior clothing items, such as undergarments, are also seldom seen and are not apt to be employed as ethnic markers (Wobst 1977).

Other, more visible categories of material culture did likely assume emblemic status. Textiles were considered the primary indicator of ethnicity in the ancient Andean world and were also used as potent symbols of political ideology. This is especially true of hats and shirts, which would have been the most visible clothing items when seen from a distance. Ritually used ceramics were used for *chicha* (maize beer) preparation and food serving during large public ritual feasts. Vernacular domestic architecture, which is highly visible and geographically distinctive in many areas of the Andes, has previously been proposed as an ethnic marker (Stanish 1992; Aldenderfer and Stanish 1993). Monumental architecture is the most visible and the most powerful medium for a dominant political ideology in the ancient Andes. Finally, mortuary ritual and tomb design, although usually not observable from a distance, can act as a potent visual symbol of social cohesion, and as a component of mortuary ritual, tomb design may have been used emblematically in the society to enhance within-group solidarity, particularly in times of stress. Tomb design also appears to be geographically specific in some parts of the Andean region (Hyslop 1976; Stanish 1992; Reycraft 1998).

Although political ideology and social identity usually share a common cultural heritage and overlap in their symbolic content and perceived meaning within the wider community, they do represent ultimately complementary forms of social integration, and as such their distribution in space and over time will diverge.

3. To be sure that the archaeological changes do in fact represent a bounded social group, the wider extracultural archaeological record must be known. Thus, to study ethnic formation we must identify the component part of the process: the sociopolitical situation prior to ethnogenesis, the specific events that may have encouraged or caused it, its material expressions (as opposed to ideological symbolic modifications or technical changes), and the wider extragroup situation (this helps to recognize bounded units which measure their identity by symbolic or residential difference from their neighbors).

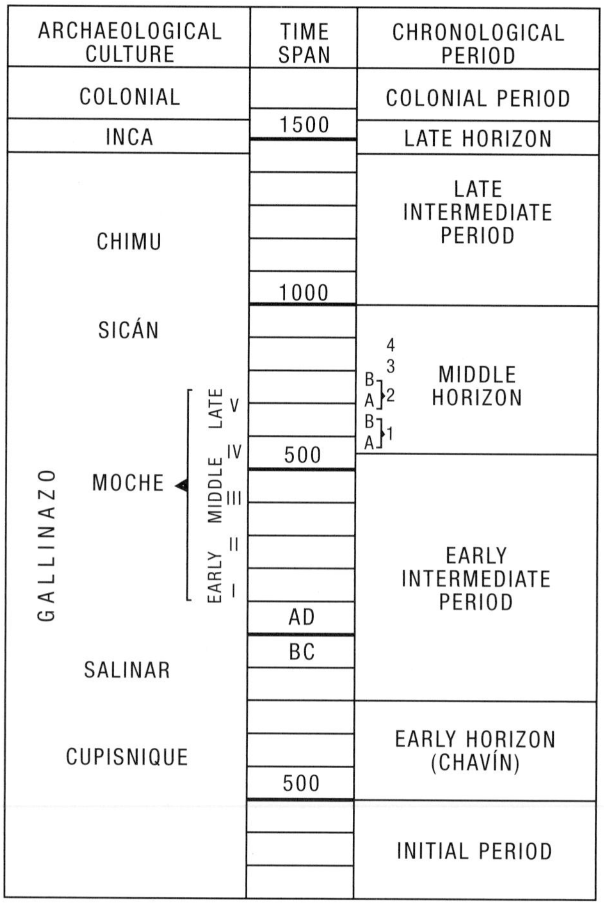

ARCHAEOLOGICAL CULTURE	TIME SPAN	CHRONOLOGICAL PERIOD
COLONIAL		COLONIAL PERIOD
INCA	1500	LATE HORIZON
CHIMU		LATE INTERMEDIATE PERIOD
SICÁN	1000	MIDDLE HORIZON
MOCHE	500	EARLY INTERMEDIATE PERIOD
SALINAR	AD / BC	
CUPISNIQUE	500	EARLY HORIZON (CHAVÍN)
		INITIAL PERIOD

Figure 12.1. Cultural chronology of the north coast of Peru.

THE NORTH COAST EXAMPLE

Moche society flourished along the Peruvian north coastal littoral from roughly AD 100 to at least the late eighth century AD. Following florescence in the Middle phase, major disruption breakdown occurred around AD 600 in the Late Moche period (Figure 12.1) in the face of catastrophic climatic disruption and external pressure. These events replaced a long period of stability with one of rapid change—the hallmarks of punctuated equilibrium. This dramatic disruption brought about profound political realignment, with local authorities struggling to rebuild the foundations of their power. However, they could not prevent the general collapse of Moche society that occurred around AD 750 in the context of demographic reorganization, settlement abandonment, the disappearance of state organization, and the breakdown of political and ideological structure. A further important outcome of this collapse was change in the material expression of group identity. Moche patterns of occupation, residential life,

and religious practice all gave way to new forms that heralded the Chimu and Sicán cultural phases as part of a process of ethnogenesis.

We examine this process in the three-stage format presented previously, first describing the sociopolitical situation existing before breakdown. This is the period (Middle period, Figure 12.1) when Moche civilization had fully consolidated and when it experienced its most successful and florescent phase. By examining this period of stability we can better understand the precise nature of the Moche social structure, and thus the strengths and weaknesses that shaped the subsequent leadership decisions in a time of crisis when prevailing authority was threatened. Second, we examine the developments of the period of crisis from AD 600 to 750. This is the relatively short period of a few generations during which Moche civilization experienced major, though geographically differential, disruption from external political and environmental disruptions. Finally, we discuss the period following AD 750, the later Middle Horizon period of Andean archaeological chronology, when Moche civilization as it had existed disappeared from the north coast region in the context of major sociopolitical change and ethnic transformation.

Pre-Collapse Situation (AD 300–600)

Middle Moche sociopolitical configuration was characterized by a number of small autonomous polities occupying north coastal river valleys of differing size and hydraulic capacity, sharing the same cultural forms and beliefs and—quite importantly—the same elite ideology (Bawden 2004). The only partial exception to this pattern involved the southernmost part of the region, where an extensive polity centered in the Moche Valley incorporated up to seven river valleys (Figure 12.2). Prior to the Moche conquest, these valleys had been dominated by the Gallinazo people, who adhered to a cultural form that shared the wider regional cultural heritage but who never adopted the Moche political system, its ideological symbolism, or its ethnic identity. In some valleys small Gallinazo polities persisted through much of the Moche period (Shimada 1994; Bawden 1996).

Each Middle Moche polity formed a sociopolitical and economic unit led by an elite group that wielded power largely through its success in manipulating traditional cultural and mythical principles through elaborate ritual. Their subjects were overwhelmingly agriculturalists living in small villages scattered along the edges of the river valleys and using small irrigation systems to water their fields. These people probably adhered to a social pattern in which local kin-related and largely self-sufficient communities were attached to their land by traditional principles of ancestral reverence and sacred place. Ethnic identity in such a society was strongly tied to local community and heritage. However, central power loosely integrated local allegiances in an internally contradictory sociopolitical system that always held the potential for tension between the aspirations of leaders and the needs of their subjects (Bawden 1996, 2001).

The Moche archaeological inventory supports this picture. Moche archaeological culture has commonly been confused with the symbolism of Moche ideology: codified elite iconography, monumental architecture, elaborate metallurgy, and jewelry. Specialist craftsmen who worked on behalf of the ruling elites created these fine materials and embellished them with the mythical and ritual imagery of the ruling political system. Production and distribution were tightly controlled, with the most elaborate items used in the central locations of power to enhance the status and authority of the rulers. However, other, less elaborate examples were distributed to lower-status groups to diffuse the concepts of official power through all strata of society and to tie them to the prevailing social order. These less elaborate symbols of elite rule accompany other material items that are devoid of elite ideological symbolism in the residential and burial places of the common population. These latter items should more properly be regarded as persisting isochrestic material features of the north coast cultural tradition than as markers of any particular archaeological "culture" or ideology. At this time of stability and general benefit, the common people were assimilating ideological aspects of the successful social order into their wider consciousness of group identity. We can assume that this successful, inclusive ideology became part of the shared reality of the north coast people and that its symbols became the signs of affiliation. Together with more basic forms, the two complementary symbolic categories form the material signifiers of a general Moche ethnicity.

Disruption

At the end of the Middle Moche period a well-documented series of droughts and El Niño episodes resulted in significant loss of agricultural land and destruction of the economic infrastructure (Shimada et al. 1991). This damage was accompanied by a period of internal social stress and political decline that affected all social groups and systems. Several themes mark this process. First, the record clearly shows loss of the strong ideological links that had previously united the various Moche polities. Instead, leaders confronted threats with strategies shaped by their local needs and decisions, leading to a range of different outcomes (Bawden 2001; Castillo 2001). Second, disruption permeated all social levels, leading to radical reorganization. Reconstitution was attained only with the creation of new institutions of power and new coercive strategies of community control. For elite and commoners alike, the resulting impact eroded the rationale for existing social roles and destroyed the traditional structural foundations of group identity that had given them meaning. Inevitably, traditional tenets of social identity were modified and their symbols rejected.

The Effects of Disruption

Although the effects of disruption were less severe in the northern areas, geographic and historic factors determined that the most severe impact fell on

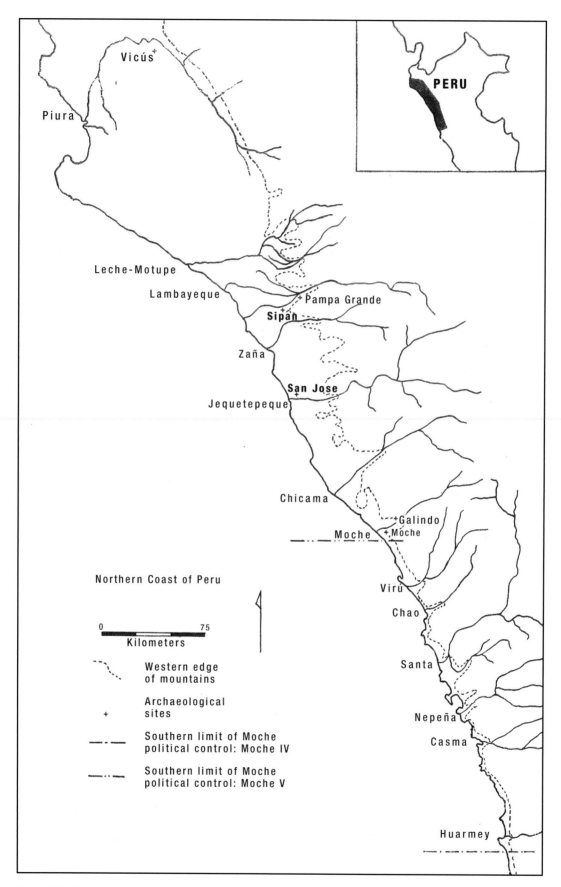

Figure 12.2. Map of the north coast region.

the Moche Valley, which in the previous period had controlled a domain extending south to Huarmey (see Figure 12.2). These extensive southern domains were abandoned and the Moche Valley itself was reduced to a small remnant, vulnerable to now-hostile neighbors. At this juncture it is impossible to know whether the breakdown was initiated by internal stresses or whether the well-documented series of major climatic disruptions in the late sixth century triggered the internal events. Certainly the various forces overlapped chronologically and became part of the same crisis faced by the leaders of the southern Moche polity. Their inability to successfully meet the challenges of these events at the outset led to breakdown in the long-lasting political system and its supporting ideology, alienation of the general populace from the structure of power, and rejection of its ideological symbols.

A key element in the southern response occurred in the conceptual realm, with rejection of the most important emblemic elements of the previously successful ideological system in the face of social disruption and political and economic breakdown (Bawden 2001; Castillo 2001). Most dramatic was abandonment of the largest architectural symbol of Middle Moche political ideology and power in the south—the great Huaca del Sol platform. However, this shift was accompanied by rejection of most other symbols of existing authority. Thus, the production of ceramic portraits of rulers, the ultimate symbols of individualizing government in the southern Middle Moche period, ceased, together with the wide range of representational symbolism that had also characterized the earlier time, indicating an end to the powerful rituals that had served to maintain social integration.

Equally dramatic was the breakup of the remnant Moche Valley polity into two successor ministates. A significant settlement maintaining some of the traditional Moche cultural forms remained at the site of the Huaca de la Luna (Chapdelaine 2000: Figure 2). However, concurrently, another new town of very different character, Galindo, was founded in the upper valley in a strategic location to control the best remaining agricultural land in the Moche Valley and its reduced and probably disillusioned and hostile population. Here most of the middle and upper valley population was clustered in a context of unprecedented social separation, with much of the population segregated in hillside *barriados*, separated from their rural ancestral places, and separated as well from the kin-related community organization that prevailed in

such settings (see Bawden 1982 and 2001 for a detailed presentation). Inevitably, this resettlement would have threatened the integrity of the local groups who formed the bulk of the population and alienated them from their leaders.

The nature of the new ideological system imposed by leaders in reaction to the rejection of its predecessor would doubtless have exacerbated this alienation. The founders of Galindo rejected the architectural forms and functions of their Middle Moche antecedents and replaced central platforms with innovative architectural forms that emphasized enclosure and social separation. The accompanying portable symbolism abandoned all traditional connection and instead linked leadership to pan-Andean concepts in an effort to free it from identification with the failures of the Middle Moche system. The new symbolic system was reserved for the exclusive centers of elite control and symbolism. Thus, both the physical centers of the new ideology and its portable symbols excluded commoners.

In response, commoners actively constructed their own innovative bases of social identity. This looked to the home as the focus for reconstitution of traditional identity through innovative in-house burial ritual, where interment in internal room platforms restored ancestral place to its kin in the autonomous social setting of the household (see Bawden 2001 for an explanation). At the same time all features of the modified elite ideology were rejected, with commoner burial goods consisting of simple undecorated ceramics and copper fragments of the pre-Moche north coast tradition. The internal social contradiction indicated by these changes culminated in the partial destruction and abandonment of Galindo in the mid-eighth century and the elimination of a "Moche" material identity. In the subsequent Chimu cultural phase, new demographic, architectural, and material symbolic forms emerge to replace this now-rejected complex.

Farther north, in the Jequetepeque Valley, history took a different course. Here, while major changes also occurred in the seventh and eighth centuries AD, they did not match changes in the south either in severity or in the degree of transformation they initiated. On the physical level, the climatic disruption that affected the entire north coast appears to have caused sand inundation in areas to the south of the river as it had in the Moche Valley, with accompanying loss of agricultural land (Shimada 1994:121–122). However, there was no accompanying loss of an extensive political and economic hinterland with the extreme disruption that this had inflicted in the southern state. Moreover, with the easier access to nearby highland resources provided by the topography and location of the Jequetepeque Valley, the material plight of its inhabitants was probably never as grave as that of the societies farther south.

Nevertheless, the rulers of Jequetepeque depended on the presence of their southern neighbors as ritual partners, both to conduct the ritual warfare that was a central part of their ceremonial of power and as participants in the wider shared political structure that supported all the Moche elites in a regionwide ideological system that sanctioned their positions and social order. The fall of the southern polity and the collapse of its conceptual foundations would have removed its rulers from this mutually supportive network, placing intolerable pressure on prevailing ideological practice and ultimately forcing its modification. Although transformation was not as severe as in the Moche Valley, significant change did occur (see Castillo 2001 for a full discussion). The appearance of new narrative scenes like the Burial Theme at this time, painted in the traditional style of Moche elite art and produced only in the Jequetepeque Valley, reveals this attempt to change the ideological focus from the earlier shared beliefs to new local myths and rituals of social integration.

In addition, to augment the power of its new ideology, leaders supplemented their new themes attached to traditional Moche media with elaborate foreign ceramic symbolism imported from the central coast, a region completely outside the Moche sphere. Here we see local rulers supplementing the traditional, though modified, structure that gave them the status of continuity with outside ideological symbols that brought meaning that transcended Moche social conception. Leaders here introduced new concepts augmented by foreign symbols of rank as a means to modify their ideological base and retain power, but attempted to do so within the overall context of existing Moche culture. Indeed, the archaeology of the period suggests they were able to achieve social change using the existing order rather than being forced to cling to power through radical transformation. However, the ideological changes that they initiated inevitably encouraged further innovation once the rigid control and codification that had characterized earlier symbolism and ritual had been loosened. Thus we find that the original foreign imports were later replicated in the valley and combined with more traditional Moche forms in the context of a decline in quality of elite craft. Thus, the process of cultural modification, once begun,

encouraged continued change into subsequent periods. This change steadily eroded traditional Moche forms of cultural identity, and by the so-called Transitional period of the later eighth century had progressed to the extent that it is difficult to talk of an integrated Moche cultural or ideological material inventory. Ethnogenesis was complete.

The far north coast took yet another course to sociocultural change and related ethnogenesis. In the Lambayeque Valley, although we see similarities to both of the examples discussed previously, the precise nature of response was determined by decisions that were again shaped by the peculiar geopolitical and historic circumstances in which local leaders found themselves. With the breakdown of the wider Moche elite network, disruption of the ritual process itself would have severely affected the basis of authority that had sustained the rulers of Sipán and other local Moche centers of the region. Local leaders addressed this challenge to their authority in a very different way than their southern counterparts. We noted that through much of its history, communities embracing the Moche political order coexisted on the north coast with others that retained allegiance to the older Gallinazo system. In the Late period, following the onset of the late sixth century crisis, Moche leaders incorporated these surviving Gallinazo populations into an expanded polity, established a new and elaborate capital at Pampa Grande in the upper valley using the newly conquered subjects as forced laborers to construct architectural edifices of unprecedented size, and significantly modified the traditional symbols of the revitalized political leadership (Shimada 1994).

These Lambayeque Valley developments with their major demographic and political innovations at first appear to herald an abrupt change with the past. However, closer examination reveals that they were intentionally undertaken within the context of persisting Moche tradition. Thus, some of the chief traditional institutions and symbols of authority remained as the focus of the transformed order. As was the case at San José de Moro in the Jequetepeque Valley, and in contrast to the Galindo transformations, the platform mound, the dominant architectural symbol of traditional Moche power and political ideology, was retained as the central focus of power at the new town of Pampa Grande. Indeed, this great structure and its subsidiaries stand at the center of the urban complex in a great walled precinct that arguably represents the greatest feat of construction ever accomplished by a Moche authority. Similarly, much of the Late period ceramic iconography of the valley remains solidly in the tradition of Moche material symbolism.

Lambayeque Valley rulers, like their southern counterparts, succeeded in their immediate intentions of halting the process of decline and reconstituting the supports of their political domains on new social and ideological principles. However, once initiated, this process carried with it long-term and probably unforeseen and unintended consequences. By initiating successful external conquest, the Lambayeque Moche leaders established new and broader managerial needs that could not be met by existing institutions. As Izumi Shimada describes (1994), the Gallinazo conquest and resettlement, combined with the managerial requirement of building a new city containing some of the largest structures ever built on the north coast, required a high degree of managerial specialization and institutional differentiation. Lambayeque leaders of the Late period instituted these necessary reforms, thereby creating greater political hierarchy and social complexity. Progressive merging of the previously distinct Gallinazo and Moche ethnicities in an urban city that removed both from their traditional rural contexts would have rather quickly stimulated the formation of new alignments and group affiliations at the site. Moreover, given this unprecedented level of internal social and ethnic differentiation, incorporating a resentful foreign population would have created significant internal tension, awaiting the next phase of weakness to emerge as a destructive force. This apparently happened in the later eighth century AD. Overt internal conflict at this time resulted in the burning of the central architecture of government, toppling of the political ideology at Pampa Grande, and rapid abandonment of much of the settlement.

Following the fall of Pampa Grande, artistic forms merged with those of the dominant highland Wari state at new centers of social integration such as Huaca La Mayanga (Donnan 1972) that echoed the settlement patterns of the Middle Moche period while clearly evoking very different symbolic messages. This new period of cultural reconstitution culminated in the so-called Early Sicán phase of Lambayeque Valley history, which also incorporated many Moche artistic and architectural modes and the belief systems that they expressed, but did so in the context of a very different ethnicity.

THE SOUTH COAST EXAMPLE
The Natural and Cultural Setting
Located at 17° S latitude, the lower Osmore drainage study area (Figure 12.3) is one of the southernmost and driest of the Peruvian drainages. Virtually no rainfall occurs below elevations of 2000–2500 masl during normal climatic conditions. Beginning around AD 700, several local ceramic traditions began to merge into a single archaeological culture, the Chiribaya. Between AD 1000 and 1360, the Chiribaya experienced a period of cultural florescence, population growth, and enhanced agricultural development. During this period, the presence of a two-tier settlement system, elaborate textiles and ceramics (Reycraft 1998; Lozada and Buikstra 2002), and elite burial paraphernalia (Umire and Miranda 2001; Lozada and Buikstra 2002) suggest the development of a complex society involving both elites and economic specialists. The primary settlement of this system was Chiribaya Alta (Figure 12.4), which has a disproportionate quantity of elite burials and elite residential structures. A 9-km-long irrigation canal carved into the rock face of the coastal valley wall clearly indicates the presence of large-scale corporate labor.

The Miraflores El Niño Event
Around AD 1360, an extreme El Niño event produced massive floods along the coastal valley and piedmont areas of the lower Osmore region. Evidence of this event includes a thick stratum of fossilized debris flows that covers many Chiribaya settlements. These debris flows contain encapsulated Chiribaya artifacts and structures that date to the AD 1000–1360 phase (Satterlee 1993; Reycraft 1998). The debris flows buried many Chiribaya sites with sediment accumulations between 1 and 10 m deep and destroyed the main valley irrigation canal. Approximately 77% of Chiribaya settlements, including Chiribaya Alta, were abandoned, and regional political unity disappeared. Post-disaster Chiribaya occupations in the lower Osmore were composed of small hamlets of farming and fishing folk, whose sites contain slight evidence of elite material culture.

Post-disaster Material Culture
A contemporary, neighboring culture, the Estuquiña, occupied the adjacent upper Osmore drainage (see Figure 12.3), a mountainous region that was not severely affected by the El Niño event. Prior to this event, Estuquiña and Chiribaya material culture had taken very different directions. For example, Estuquiña potters made their

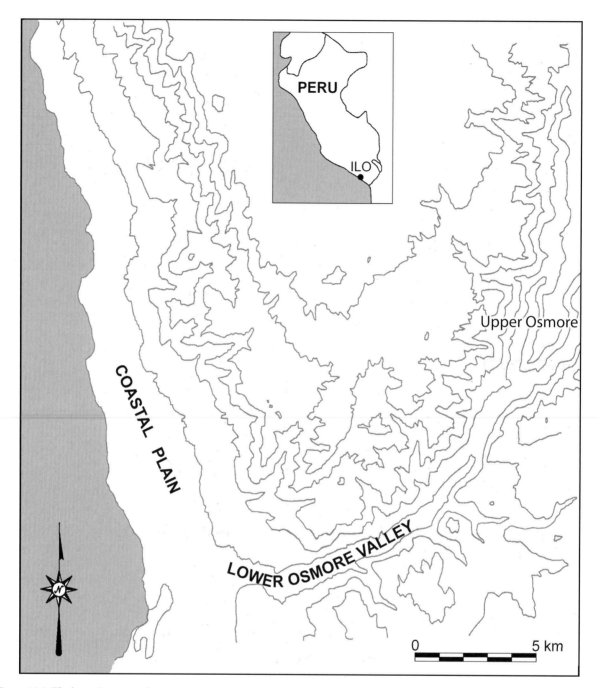

Figure 12.3. The lower Osmore study area

wares in distinctive vessel shapes (Lozada-Cerna 1987), which, in contrast to pre-disaster Chiribaya examples, were often simply embellished with red slips. After the AD 1360 event, Chiribaya potters began to introduce Estuquiña vessel shapes, rim angles, and rim protuberance types (Figure 12.5) into their vessels, especially bowls found in ritual contexts. Vessel decoration also changed dramatically after the event, as the Chiribaya fundamentally abandoned a 400-year-old elaborate, polychrome tradition in favor of red slip applications.

Similarly, Estuquiña textiles were largely decorated in natural hue combinations of black, gold, and tan over a coffee or brown base (Clark 1993), while pre-event Chiribaya textiles were often elaborately manufactured, with dyed purple, blue, red, and gold yarns over a coffee- or maroon-colored base cloth (Boytner 1992). In some cases the textile shapes also differed. For example, pre-event Chiribaya hats (Reycraft 1998) were tall, cylindrical, or square-shaped. Estuquiña hats were pillbox-shaped (Clark 1993).

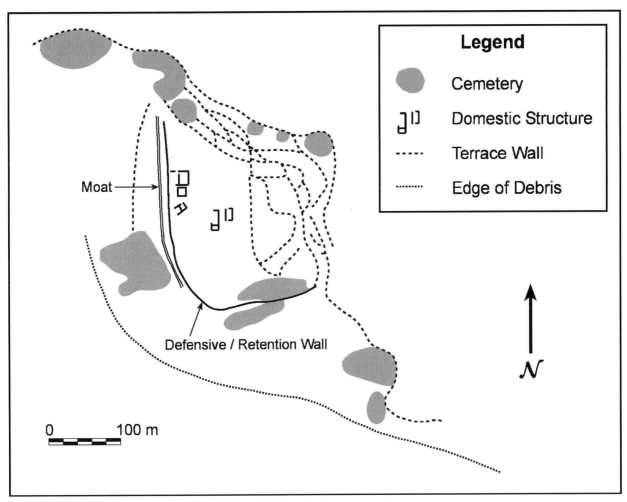

Figure 12.4. The Chiribaya Alta site.

After the disaster, Chiribaya weavers produced clothing with clear Estuquiña attributes. Post-disaster Chiribaya shirts and hats were predominantly decorated in natural hue combinations of black, gold, and tan or over a coffee or brown base (Figure 12.6). The weavers also copied Estuquiña textile forms, decorative motifs and manufacture techniques. For example, they produced pillbox-shaped hats with Estuquiña decorative motifs (Figure 12.7).

Although the ceramic and textile evidence suggests Estuquiña stylistic influence, the forms of the post-disaster Chiribaya domestic structures and tombs strongly indicate cultural continuity with the previous Chiribaya phase. During the Terminal phase, the Chiribaya constructed structures that were virtually identical to those of their Classic phase ancestors. Classic and Terminal phase Chiribaya tombs were also identical in design. No Estuquiña domestic structures and just a few Estuquiña-style tombs have been found

in the lower Osmore region. Thus, Estuquiña influence was most strongly felt in two kinds of Chiribaya material culture, visibly worn textiles and ritually used ceramics, which had the greatest potential to convey emblemic information reflecting ethnic identification.

In the south coast example, ethnogenesis appears to have accompanied the destruction of the economic and demographic foundations of society, together with the political order that had failed to prevent it. The ideological foundations of the Classic phase Chiribaya political elite were manifested in disproportionate quantities of elite burials and large residential structures at the prime site of Chiribaya Alta. Elite burials from this and other Classic phase Chiribaya sites contained the human remains of personal retainers, gold pectorals and ritual axes, intricately carved ritual drinking vessels, burial litters, ornate textiles, and warrior paraphernalia. This elite paraphernalia is not found at Terminal phase Chiribaya sites. With the destruction of

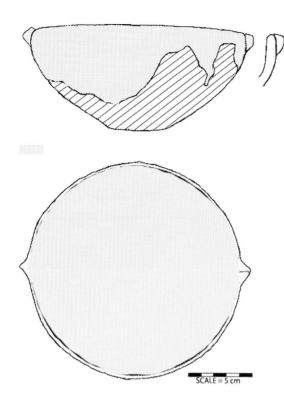

Figure 12.5. Post-disaster Chiribaya bowl.

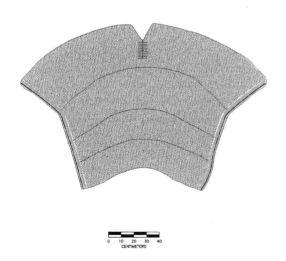

Figure 12.6. Post-disaster Chiribaya shirt.

Figure 12.7. Post-disaster Chiribaya hat.

the political elite, the leaders of local kin groups began to take charge and renegotiate the social foundations of Chiribaya society. The Terminal phase Chiribaya reached beyond weakened local social traditions to reconstruct group integrity in a new social context.

CONCLUSION

Moseley persuasively suggested that environmental calamity plays a major role in generating the changes in the archaeological record that we use to posit cultural disruption and transformation. In both the northern and southern coastal areas of Peru there is abundant evidence of the type of event that he posited, and there is also evidence that these events were accompanied by relatively rapid sociocultural change.

The research that we have presented further defines the relationships and clarifies the processes that characterize punctuated equilibrium. Ethnogenesis, or the formation of ethnic identity, is the outcome of historical circumstances that cause groups to coalesce around their own partisan values and interests, often asserting these values against others'. Consequently, to recognize and understand this process, it is necessary to know the specific historical and situational contexts within which it occurred. Ethnogenesis often occurs as a responsive coping mechanism prompted by profound change in the scale and structure of social integration such as that which accompanies the formation or collapse of complex sociopolitical systems. Thus, the hierarchical institutions of political, social, and economic control that accompanied Late Moche urban formation alienated the commoner population from traditional principles of group cohesion and from participation in the political order that actualized them in daily life. In response to such stress, people draw on deep cultural belief and circumstantial necessity to construct new foundations of group identity.

Although ethnic identity can evolve independently of political collapse, given a catastrophe of sufficient magnitude, both will change. This appears to have been the case in both the Moche and the Chiribaya cases. Although they existed at different levels of organizational complexity, both experienced processes of ethnic construction that involved concurrent removal of the pan-regional political networks that had relied on traditional principles of social identity for their legitimacy. In both of our examples, political collapse and ethnogenesis were part of the same process of social reconstruction, or in Moseley's term, punctuated equilibrium, with the extreme degree of environmental impact determining that change would be deep and pervasive rather than limited to a single social system.

REFERENCES

Abercrombie, Nicholas, Stephen Hill, and Bryan S. Turner
1980   *The Dominant Ideology Thesis*. Allen and Unwin, London.

Aldenderfer, Mark S., and Charles Stanish
1993   Domestic Architecture, Household Archaeology and the Past in the South-Central Andes. In *Domestic Architecture, Ethnicity, and Complementarity in the South-Central Andes*, edited by Mark S. Aldenderfer, pp. 1–12. University of Iowa Press, Iowa City.

Bawden, Garth
1982   Community Organization Reflected by the Household: A Study in Pre-Columbian Social Dynamics: *Journal of Field Archaeology* 9:165–183.
1996   The *Moche*. Blackwell Publishers, Oxford.
2001   The Symbols of Late Moche Social Transformation. In *Moche Art and Archaeology in Ancient Peru*, edited by J. Pillsbury, pp. 285–306. Yale University Press, New Haven.
2004   The Art of Moche Politics. In *Andean Archaeology*, edited by Helaine Silverman, pp. 116–129. Blackwell Publishing, Oxford.

Boyd, Robert, and Peter J. Richerson
1987   The Evolution of Ethnic Markers. *Cultural Anthropology* 2:65–79.

Boytner, R.
1992   Ilo-Tumilaca/Cabuza, Chiribaya, and Their Relationships with the Tiwanaku Culture as Can Be Seen in the Textiles from the Coastal Osmore Valley, Southern Peru. Master's thesis, Department of Archaeology, University of California, Los Angeles.

Castillo, Luis Jaime
2001   The Last of the Mochicas: A View from the Jequetepeque Valley. In *Moche Art and Archaeology in Ancient Peru*, edited by J. Pillsbury, pp. 307–332. Yale University Press, New Haven, CT.

Chapdelaine, Claude
2000   Struggling for Survival: The Urban Class of the Moche Site, North Coast of Peru. In *Environmental Disaster and the Archaeology of Human Response*, edited by Garth Bawden and Richard M. Reycraft, pp. 121–142. Maxwell Museum of Anthropology, Anthropological Papers, no. 7, Albuquerque, NM.

Clark, N. R.
1993   *The Estuquiña Textile Tradition: Cultural Patterning in the Late Prehistoric Fabrics of Moquegua, Far Southern Peru*. Unpublished doctoral dissertation, Department of Anthropology, Washington University, St. Louis, MO.

Donnan, Chistopher B.
1972   Moche-Huari Murals from Northern Peru. *Archaeology* 25(2):85–95.

Hyslop, John
1976   *An Archaeological Investigation of the Lupaqa Kingdom and Its Origins*. Unpublished doctoral dissertation, Columbia University, New York.

Kolata, Alan
2000   Environmental Thresholds and the "Natural History" of an Andean Civilization. In *Environmental Disasters and the Archaeology of Human Response*, edited by Garth Bawden and Richard M. Reycraft, pp. 163–178. Maxwell Museum of Anthropology, Anthropological Papers, no. 7, University of New Mexico Press, Albuquerque.

Lozada-Cerna, M.
1987   La cerámica del componente mortuorio de Estuquiña, Moquegua. Bachelor's thesis, Universidad Católica "Santa María," Arequipa.

Lozada, María C., and Jane E. Buikstra
2002   *El Señorio de Chiribaya en la costa sur del Perú*. Instituto de Estudios Peruanos, Lima.

Moseley, Michael E.
1992   *The Inca and Their Ancestors*. Thames and Hudson, London.
1999   Convergent Catastrophe: Past Patterns and Future Implications of Collateral Natural Disasters in the Andes. In *The Angry Earth, Disaster in Anthropological*

Perspective, edited by A. Oliver-Smith and S. Hoffman, pp. 59–72. Routledge, London.

Reycraft, Richard M.
1998   *The Terminal Chiribaya Project: The Archaeology of Human Response to Natural Disaster in South Coastal Peru*. Doctoral dissertation, University of New Mexico. University Microfilms, Ann Arbor, MI.

Sackett, J. R.
1982   Approaches to Style in Lithic Archaeology. *Journal of Anthropological Archaeology* 1:59–112

Satterlee, D.
1993   *Impact of a Fourteenth Century El Niño on an Indigenous Population near Ilo, Peru*. Doctoral dissertation. University of Florida, Gainesville. University Microfilms, Ann Arbor, MI.

Shennan, Stephen J.
1989   Introduction. In *Archaeological Approaches to Cultural Identity*, edited by Stephen J. Shennan. Unwin and Hyman Press, London.

Shimada, Izumi
1994   *Pampa Grande and the Mochica Culture*. University of Texas Press, Austin.

Shimada, Izumi, C. B. Schaaf, L. G. Thompson, and E. Mosley-Thompson
1991   Cultural Impacts of Severe Droughts in the Prehistoric Andes: Application of a 1500-Year Ice Core Precipitation Record. *World Archaeology* 22:247–270.

Stanish, Charles
1992   *Ancient Andean Political Economy*. University of Texas Press, Austin.

Thompson, L. G., E. Mosley-Thompson, J. F. Bolzan, and B. R. Koci
1985   A 1500-Year Tropical Ice Core Record of Climate: Potential Relations to Man in the Andes. *Science* 229:971–973.

Umire, Adán, and A. Miranda
2001   *Chiribaya de Ilo*. Consejo Nacional de Ciencia y Tecnología, Lima.

Wiessner, Pauline
1983   Style and Ethnicity in the Kalahari San Projectile Point. *American Antiquity* 48:253–276
1984   Reconsidering the Behavioral Basis for Style: A Case Study among the Kalahari San. In *Journal of Anthropological Anthropology* 3:190–234.

Wobst, Martin
1977   Stylistic Behavior and Information Exchange. In *For the Director: Papers in Honor of James B. Griffin*, edited by Charles E. Cleland. Anthropological Papers, no. 61. University of Michigan Museum of Anthropology, Ann Arbor.

CHAPTER 13

SETTLEMENT PATTERNS IN THE HUAMACHUCO AREA

JOHN R. TOPIC

AT TIMES WHEN I write about Huamachuco, I am referring to the Incaic province that stretched from the Chaupiyungas to the Marañón and from the Río Crisnejas in the north to the Tablachaca in the south (e.g., Topic 1992, 1998). Our survey of fortifications in the late 1970s covered the northwestern part of the province (Topic and Topic 1978, 1987). Currently we are studying Catequil, an oracle and the principal *huaca* of Huamachuco, whose shrine was located in the center of the province (Topic et al. 2002). In this chapter, I am concerned with a much smaller area around the modern town of Huamachuco.

The area under consideration is at the southern end of the Río Condebamba basin, extending from the Continental Divide in the west to the divide separating the Río Condebamba from the Marañón drainage (Figure 13.1). The major rivers are the Río Yamobamba in the west, the Río Grande de Huamachuco in the central part of the zone, and the Río Shiracmaca to the east. The Río Grande has its headwaters at Laguna Negra, on the slopes of Cerro Huaylillas, which is sometimes snow-capped in the winter months; an ancient road crosses this mountain, and the narrow survey track through here followed the road. The Marcahuamachuco Plateau is located between the Río Yamobamba and the Río Grande.

The major lake in the area, Laguna Sausagocha, is located in the northeastern part of the area, between the Río Shiracmaca and the tributaries of the Marañón (Figure 13.1).

Our work in Huamachuco spanned eight seasons, 1981–1984 and 1986–1989. The project was intended to combine intensive site survey with limited excavations. Unfortunately, in the second season it became clear that the countryside was not safe, and the focus changed to excavations at selected sites. Much of the area around Huamachuco still has not received intensive survey, and the dating of sites is largely based on surface collections of sherds that are rarely decorated.

Nevertheless, building on the work of McCown (1945) and Thatcher (1972), we were able to extend the list of known sites from 79 to 177. Of these, only 90 have been dated, and excavations have been conducted at only 13. This study is based on the 90 datable sites, which together have 122 datable occupations. These 122 occupations span all the ceramic periods and range in elevation from 2700 to 4100 masl. Although we made an effort to survey all altitudinal zones present in the area, the lower elevations are not as well represented as the middle and high zones. There is definitely a need for more survey work in the Huamachuco area, and this chapter is a very preliminary report on what is now quite an old data set.

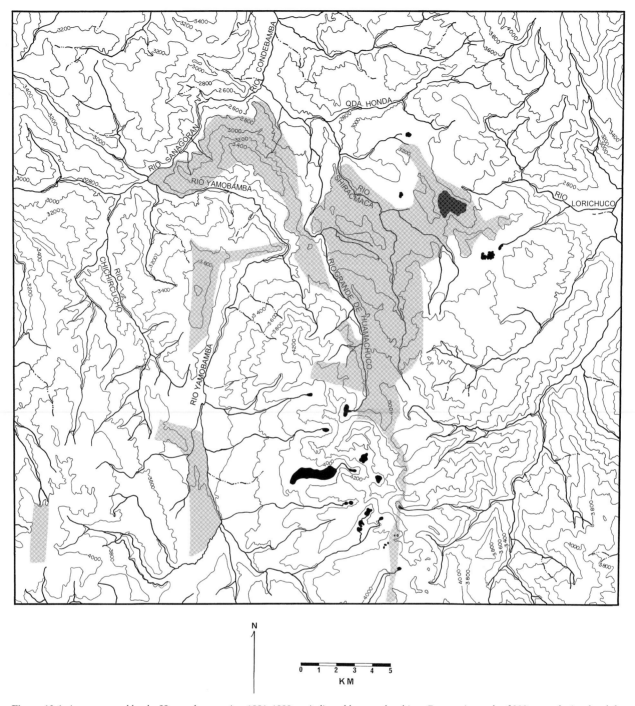

Figure 13.1. Areas surveyed by the Huamachuco project 1981–1989 are indicated by cross hatching. Contour intervals of 200 m are depicted and the names of significant rivers and streams are provided on this and subsequent figures. The lakes are shown in solid black.

Although the emphasis here is on the overall settlement patterns around Huamachuco rather than on the internal plans of individual sites, in the phase-by-phase descriptions I provide some information about individual sites. Three common building types are referred to: rectangular galleries, circular galleries, and curvilinear galleries. All of these are very long, narrow, above-ground masonry buildings. They are usually 2–3 m wide and more than 20 m long; at Marcahuamachuco there are several examples that are hundreds of meters in length. They are subdivided into a series of rooms so that on plans, they look like a row of small rectangular rooms joined end to end. The terms rectangular, circular, and curvilinear refer to the overall configuration of the buildings, not to the shape of the individual rooms. Figures 13.4 and 13.10 give some idea of how these buildings appear on maps. Most of these buildings are only one story tall, but during at least the Early Huamachuco, Amaru, and Late Huamachuco phases, multistoried galleries were built that were monumental in scale and constructed in a distinctive masonry style.

COLPA PHASE: ?–900 BC

Five sites have been tentatively placed in the Colpa phase, which we believe dates to the Initial period (Figure 13.2, Table 13.1). Only one of these sites has been excavated (PLd2-102). This site, which McCown (1945:263, Figure 12) called the Square Fort, appears to be domestic in nature and has no fortification features. It is almost square, but with rounded exterior corners, and measures about 16 m on a side. It is essentially a patio surrounded on three sides by long narrow rooms. The walls were probably constructed with *pirca* (unworked stone) foundations and adobe superstructure. The layout is quite formal and resembles the plans of Huari compounds in many respects, but this is not surprising, since Huari architecture was heavily influenced by Huamachuco (Topic 1991; Topic and Topic 2000).

Site 145 is a group of rockshelters within a large outcrop located high on the *jalca* (high altitude) south of Huamachuco. There are a few pictographs here, but since the site was probably occupied repeatedly, though sporadically, these cannot be dated.

Site 8, located on Cerro Mamorco, is poorly preserved. There are foundations of buildings and a possible small low mound.

Site 20, Cerro Huachac, is in many ways the most interesting site of this phase. It is located on a high, rugged, and barren spine surrounded on three sides by steep drop-offs. On the sole approach to the site, access is impeded first by an artificial trench and then by a wall about 4 m thick. There are three mounds inside the site, measuring 15 × 5 m × 2.5 m high, 15 × 15 m × 2 m high, and 10 × 30 × ca. 5 m high. This last mound seems to be constructed of rubble and dirt fill within rough retaining walls; it may have had a long curvilinear gallery running around its summit. Preservation of structures is poor at the site, but remains include at least two rectilinear galleries 20–30 m long with smaller internal divisions. Two sherds from this site have similarities to Pacopampa motifs, and it is on this basis that the site is dated. (Pacopampa is one of several ceramic phases defined at the site of Pacopampa; the phase dates to the Initial period.) However, there is also evidence for the manufacture of ground slate points at the site, and these suggest a date at the end of the Early Horizon in comparison with sites on the coast, such as Cerro Arena. The character of the site, which combines fortification features with a very isolated position, also is comparable with sites such as Chankillo in the Casma Valley, Quisque in the Nepeña Valley, and the fortresses of the Cayhuamarca phase in the Santa Valley, which we have interpreted as evidence for *tinku*, a ritualized, scheduled form of warfare (Topic and Topic 1997).

The type site for the phase is La Colpa (PLd2-11), a hill rising above prime farmland in the Yamobamba drainage. The hill is natural, but its contours have been modified by the addition of terraces and fill. No buildings are preserved, but sherds are numerous, and many are decorated or finely polished.

These few sites tell us little about the La Colpa phase settlement pattern. The sites are small, averaging just under 1 ha in area (see Table 13.9a). Most are located near arable land, indicating that farming was important. The combination of Cerro Mamorco, Cerro Huachac, and La Colpa, all in the lower Yamobamba drainage, may indicate that this area was a focus for the occupation. Site 145 was probably a temporary camping site. Cerro Huachac may be fortified, although it also has every appearance of being ceremonial in nature. Although architecture is poorly preserved, buildings at Sites 102 and 20 are clearly precursors to the buildings at Marcahuamachuco.

Table 13.1 Colpa phase sites with data on area, elevation (rounded to nearest 100 m), and other phases of occupation.

Site No.	Site Name	Area (m²)	Elevation (masl)	Other Occupations
8	Cerro Mamorco	9,900	3400	Santa Bárbara
11	La Colpa	12,000	3200	Sausagocha
20	Cerro Huachac	22,000	3300	
102		255	3300	
145		2,500	4100	Modern

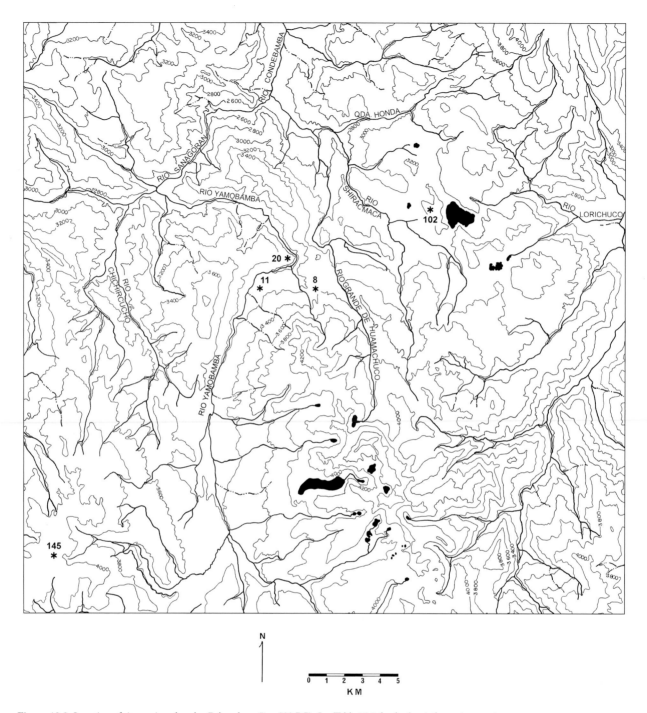

Figure 13.2. Location of sites assigned to the Colpa phase (? to 900 BC). See Table 13.1 for further information on sites.

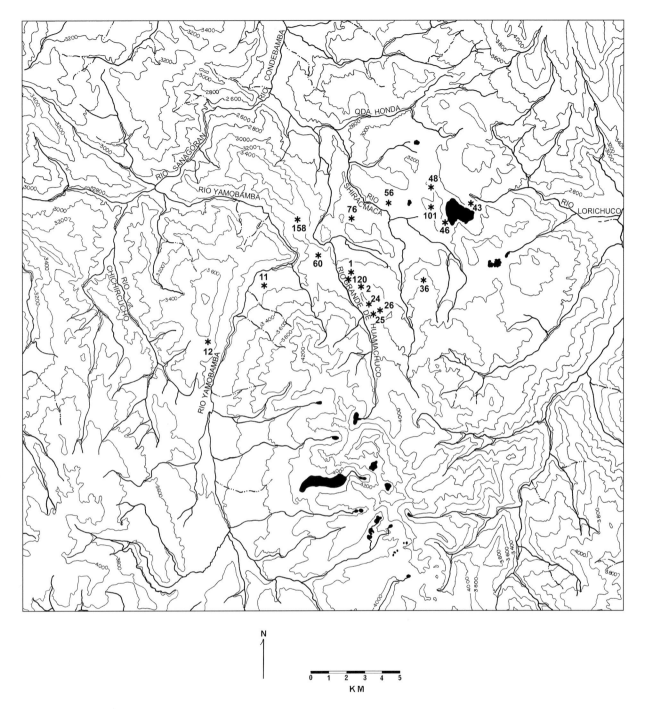

Figure 13.3. Location of sites assigned to the Sausagocha phase (900–200 BC). See Table 13.2 for further information on sites.

SAUSAGOCHA PHASE: 900–200 BC

We have placed seventeen sites in the Sausagocha phase, which we believe dates to the Early Horizon (Figure 13.3, Table 13.2). The ceramics from this phase, however, bear no Chavín iconography, and its absence suggests that the Huamachuco area was isolated from

events in surrounding regions during the Early Horizon (Topic and Topic 1985).

The distribution of settlement sizes (Figure 13.13b) suggests an emerging hierarchy of sites. Probably the most important site during this phase is Cerro Campana East (PLd2-43). This site, which is well described by McCown (1945:260–261, Figure 12), can certainly

Table 13.2 Sausagocha phase sites with data on area, elevation (rounded to nearest 100 m), and other phases of occupation.

Site No.	Site Name	Area (m²)	Elevation (masl)	Other Occupations
1	Sta. Bárbara	6,375	3400	Sta. Bárbara
2		9,141	3600	Amaru, Tuscan
11	La Colpa	12,000	3200	Colpa
12	Cerro Chico	8,000	3600	Tuscan
24		2,400	3600	Purpucala
25		120	3600	Purpucala
26		1,800	3600	Purpucala
36	Cerro El Toro	2,800	3600	Late Huamachuco, Tuscan, Sta. Bárbara
43	Cerro Campana East	50,000	3300	
46	Cerro Campana West	4,500	3200	Purpucala
48		1,050	3200	
56		17,500	3200	
60	Cerro Cacañan	17,100	3400	Tuscan
76		1,750	3200	Purpucala
101		195	3300	Purpucala
120		900	3400	
158	Canibamba	62,500	3200	Sta. Bárbara

be considered a village, if not a small town. Most of the architecture is rectangular in plan, and a common layout consists of a square or rectangular patio flanked on one or more sides by rectangular rooms. The two most interesting structures are two large square courts with rounded corners (McCown 1945: Figure 12e, f); their size and the more massive walls suggest that these are important structures and probably public in nature. I have speculated that these structures might be similar to the rooms with ritual hearths at sites like La Galgada (Topic 1998:117), but this speculation has not yet been confirmed by excavation.

Eight other sites probably represent hamlets. Many of these are poorly preserved so that little architecture is visible (Sites 1, 11, 56, and 158). In other cases there were multiple occupations, and it is difficult to confirm that the visible structures date to the Sausagocha phase. For example, Site 60 is a large mound on Cerro Cacañan and, although there are a few Sausagocha phase sherds, it is not clear that any part of the mound dates to that phase. Similarly, Site 2 has well-preserved architecture, but most of this probably dates to the Middle Horizon or Late Intermediate period. The two best examples of Sausagocha phase hamlets are Cerro Campana West (46) (McCown 1945: Figure 12) and Cerro Chico (12) (Figure 13.4). Much of the visible architecture at Cerro Campana West dates to the Purpucala phase, but excavations suggest that the site had a similar plan during the Sausagocha phase. Cerro Chico had only a small reoccupation during the Tuscan phase. Both sites

are on hills, and the architecture follows the contours of the hills. The basic plan consists of a series of small rectangular rooms joined into rows to form galleries that curve around the hillsides. The construction of rooms at different levels on the hill results in a concentric pattern of rooms and walls that enclose patio areas. The outer walls may have been useful for defense, and two trenches at Cerro Chico may also have been related to defense of the site.

A third group of sites (24, 25, 26, 48, 76 and 120) appears to represent households of varying sizes. Most of these sites consist of a circular patio surrounded or partially surrounded by small rooms. The plan of these sites is similar to the plans of Cerro Campana West and Cerro Chico but on a smaller scale. One site (76), however, is quite different and has at least three rectangular plazas and at least one 15-m-long narrow rectangular gallery. Another site (24) has a few conjoined rectangular rooms as well as a circular patio.

Although most Sausagocha phase sites appear to be primarily habitation sites, some may have served other purposes. Cerro Campana East (43) is larger and has a different plan from most of the other sites, and has the two special structures already mentioned; it may have served as a focus for much of the population in the Huamachuco area. The sites of La Colpa (11) and Cerro El Toro (36) have higher frequencies of decorated ceramics, and Cerro El Toro is also located on a very high hill, which has difficult access. Site 101 is a small mound with no evidence of domestic refuse, and the

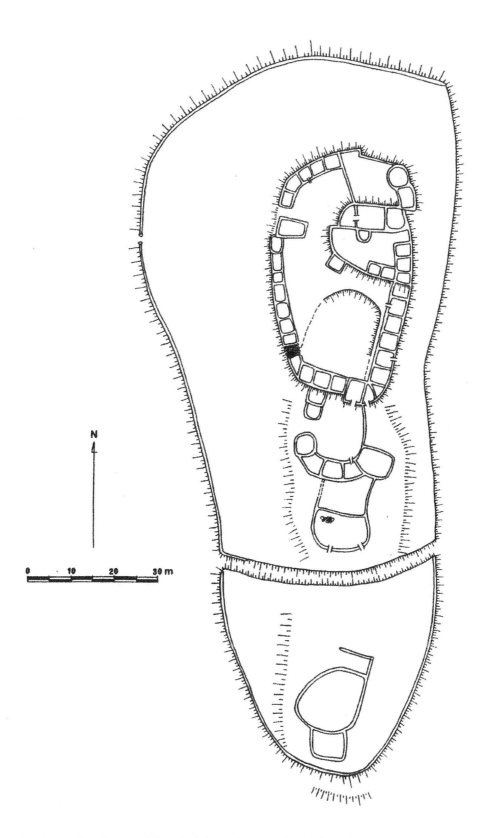

Figure 13.4. Plan of Cerro Chico (Site 12), a hilltop site dating to the Sausagocha and Tuscan phases.

Sausagocha phase occupation at Site 60 may also be associated with the beginning of the construction of the mound there.

The average size of Sausagocha phase sites (1.16 ha) is only slightly larger than the La Colpa phase average (see Table 13.9a). In fact, since some site areas are undoubtedly overestimated (especially those for Sites 60 and 158) due to later reoccupations, the average size of sites during the two phases is probably very similar. The Sausagocha phase sites, however, are much more clearly distributed into three size classes. Based on site areas, most of the population was living at relatively low elevations, around 3200 and 3300 masl (see Table 13.9b). This location probably reflects the importance of farming. Moreover, more than 25% of the Sausagocha phase site area clusters around Laguna Sausagocha itself, and this may reflect the importance of lacustrine and marsh resources. On the other hand, there is also a series of sites around 3600 masl (especially Sites 12, 24, 25, and 26) in areas where there is easy access to pasture. This site location probably reflects the increasing importance of herding (see Tables 13.9a and 13.9b).

PURPUCALA PHASE: 200 BC–AD 300

Thirty-three sites are dated to the Purpucala phase, which we believe dates to the first part of the Early Intermediate period (Figure 13.5, Table 13.3). In the future, it should be possible to divide Purpucala into early and late subphases. Ceramics characteristic of early Purpucala share many attributes with those of the Sausagocha phase and indicate continued isolation of the Huamachuco area. By the end of the Purpucala phase, however, there is clear ceramic influence from both the Recuay and Cajamarca styles.

Despite the increased number of sites in the Purpucala phase, the total site area is actually smaller than that occupied during the Sausagocha phase (see Table 13.9a). Also, the average site size declines dramatically. In part, these changes may be due to the shorter length of the Purpucala phase, resulting in lower total site area, and the tendency by some of our field assistants to define Purpucala phase sites more strictly, leading to more sites and a lower average size. In fact, when total site area is divided by the different durations of the phases, Sausagocha occupation averages 2.8 ha per century while Purpucala occupation averages 3.0 ha per century.

However, there does seem to be a real change in settlement pattern. First, there appears to be no site equivalent to Cerro Campana East; instead, there is a large increase in sites in the 0.4–0.8 ha range (see Figure 13.14a). Second, while the areas around Laguna Sausagocha and in the Río Grande de Huamachuco drainage, which were occupied earlier, continue to be a focus of occupation during the Purpucala phase, there is a significant development of sites in the Yamobamba drainage (Figure 13.5). It is difficult to say whether these new sites indicate population growth or simply movements into new territories, but despite the decrease in total site area I suspect that population growth was a factor.

The Purpucala phase settlements can be described in terms of site clusters. The Yamobamba sites are divided into two clusters. The first cluster (Group A in Figure 13.5), situated on Cerro Arena, is centered on two larger population concentrations (Sites 123 and 130). Both of these have the foundations of circular galleries preserved, and Site 130 also has rectangular and curvilinear galleries. There may have been a population on the order of thirty-five people at Site 123, and as many as 100 at Site 130. Sites 122 and 124 are smaller, three- to four-room affairs with possible corrals. Sites 132 and 133 are simple corrals. Site 125 is a small cave, and Site 126 consists only of two terrace walls.

The second Yamobamba cluster (Group B in Figure 13.5) is in the Candigurán area. Again, there is a series of corrals (Sites 134, 138, and 141), some of which have attached rooms. Sites 136, 137, 139, and 140 are larger and have circular, curvilinear, or rectangular galleries, as well as corral-like enclosures. Site 142 is the largest site of this phase. It is an exceptionally well-constructed site with quarried stone masonry and a defensive wall and dry moat flanking two sides. There are two circular galleries on the summit and at least two tiers of curvilinear galleries on the slopes. The architecture at this site is almost monumental in scale and is a clear antecedent to the later monumental architecture at Marcahuamachuco. Significantly, this site, and indeed all the Purpucala phase occupation in the Yamobamba area, is located near the main routes leading south to Santiago de Chuco and the Callejón de Huaylas and west toward the coast (see Figure 13.12).

Another site cluster consisting of Sites 3, 24, 25, and 26 is located near the Río Grande. Site 3 appears to be the focus of this cluster, although it is not exceptionally large. It has a short dry moat and defensive wall protecting it on the south. There is also a circular gallery

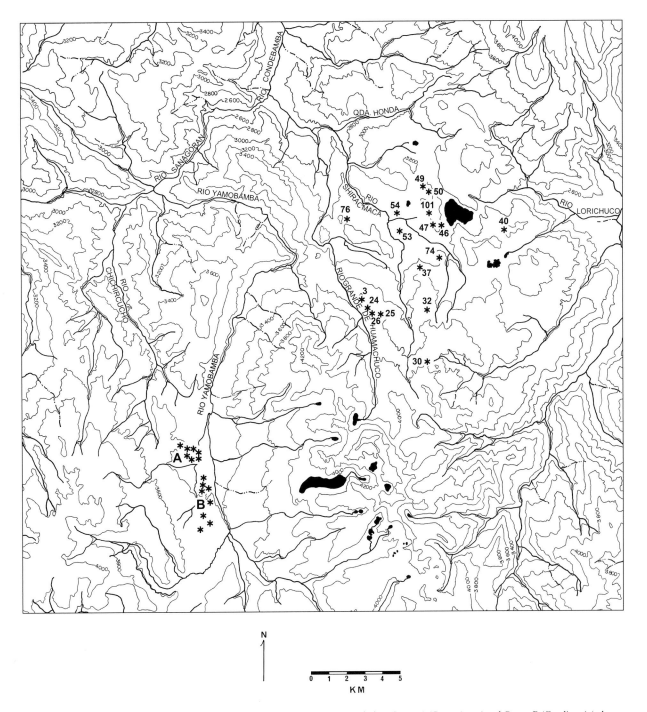

Figure 13.5. Location of sites assigned to the Purpucala phase (200 BC–AD 300), including Group A (Cerro Arena) and Group B (Candigurán) clusters. See Table 13.3 and the text for further information on sites.

on the summit, and a few rooms on the slopes of the hill. Sites 24, 25, and 26, which are probably small house groups, have already been mentioned in the section on the Sausagocha phase.

The Laguna Sausagocha area continued to be a focus of occupation. Sites 46, 49, and 50 are all located on small peaks that have been artificially leveled. There are

circular galleries around their summits and often curvilinear galleries on the lower slopes. Site 40 might also be part of this cluster; although poorly preserved, there is a large and dense sherd scatter and one small square mound. Site 101, described for the Sausagocha phase, is also a small square mound. Site 47 (McCown 1945: Figure 12) is probably the real focus for this area. It is,

Table 13.3 Purpucala phase sites with data on area, elevation (rounded to nearest 100 m), and other phases of occupation.

Site No.	Site Name	Area (m²)	Elevation (masl)	Other Occupations
3		3,200	3600	
24		2,400	3600	Sausagocha
25		120	3600	Sausagocha
26		1,800	3600	Sausagocha
30		720	3800	Early Huamachuco
32		1,210	3600	
37		6,072	3200	
40	Cerro Negro	15,000	3400	Early Huamachuco, Tuscan, Sta. Bárbara
46	Cerro Campana West	4,500	3200	Sausagocha
47		3,630	3200	
49		5,500	3200	
50		2,000	3200	
53		1,600	3200	
54		10,800	3200	
74		7,700	3300	
76		1,750	3200	Sausagocha
101		195	3300	Sausagocha
122	Cerro Arena 1	4,200	3500	
123	CerroArena 2	6,200	3500	
124	Cerro Arena 3	157	3500	
125	Cerro Arena 4	100	3400	
126	Cerro Arena 5	1,200	3400	
130	Cerro Arena 6	13,500	3400	
132	Cerro Arena 7	1,400	3300	
133	Cerro Arena 8	600	3300	
134	Candigurán 1	2,200	3400	
136	Candigurán 2	6,525	3400	
137	Candigurán 3	6,000	3400	
138	Candigurán 4	160	3400	
139	Candigurán 5	14,300	3400	
140	Candigurán 6	4,950	3500	
141	Candigurán 7	1,400	3500	
142	Candigurán 8	20,000	3600	

like Site 142, exceptionally well constructed and consists of rectangular galleries surrounding a trapezoidal patio (Topic and Topic 2000: Figure 8). Again, the architecture here verges on being monumental. There are many decorated sherds, including vessels with Recuay or Pashash influence. Site 47 may represent an elite household or the focus of public activities, which would have included the people living at Site 46.

The remaining sites seem not to relate to any site cluster. Site 54 has many decorated sherds, including some showing Cajamarca influence; the site is quite destroyed, but it appears to have had at least a circular gallery surrounding the summit of the hill. Site 53 now has only one 30-m-long rectangular gallery divided into five or six rooms. Site 37 had about fifteen rectangular

rooms, laid out in a row but not joined to form a gallery. These are surrounded by an oval enclosure. Site 74 is totally destroyed but has an extensive sherd scatter. Sites 30, 32, and 76 appear to be houses with corrals or patios.

The economy of the Purpucala phase was probably based on mixed farming and herding. Sites tended to cluster around three elevations (see Tables 13.9b and 13.9c: 3200 m, 3400 m, and 3600 masl), in contrast to the Sausagocha phase, when settlement clustered at 3200 masl. A large part of this change can be attributed to the growth of settlement in the Yamobamba area, and those settlements, with their numerous corral-like enclosures, reflect a continuing increase in the importance of herding. However, those sites also had access to farmlands as well as marshy areas along the Río Yamobamba. The Río Grande cluster also had access to both farming and herding lands, but was located above marshes. The Sausagocha cluster had access only to marshes and farmland, except for Site 40, which had access to all three resource zones.

The Purpucala phase, then, was probably characterized by population growth, continued diversification of the economic base, possibly increased warfare, perhaps the emergence of an elite, and, toward the end of the phase, increased interregional interaction.

EARLY HUAMACHUCO: AD 300–600

The nineteen sites of the Early Huamachuco phase (Figure 13.6, Table 13.4) fall into two classes, those with monumental architecture and those lacking monumental architecture. These two classes of sites overlap in size but appear to be distinct in terms of the functions they performed.

Several sites (38, 39, 40, 51, 131, 135) are quite large (Table 13.4: 0.5–6.3 ha), often with dense refuse, but are poorly preserved. It is likely there once were numerous buildings at these sites, and most have at least a few foundations remaining. There are no indications of monumental stone architecture, however, and it is possible that most of the structures were built primarily of adobe. The same is probably true for a series of much smaller sites (30, 42, 110, 111, 112) ranging in size from 100 m² to 900 m² (Table 13.4). These small sites often appear simply as leveled areas with stone retaining walls and a few sherds. These two sizes of sites without monumental architecture were probably primarily residential in nature and their populations were engaged in agriculture and herding.

The sites with monumental architecture fall into three size classes: 525–4,000 m², 5–20 ha, and ca. 240 ha. The largest of these sites, Marcahuamachuco, Cerro Sazón, Cerro Tuscan, and Cerro Amaru, are all within sight of each other and within about an hour's walk at a fast clip. The proximity and size of the sites suggest they performed different functions within a differentiated settlement system.

Marcahuamachuco is the largest site, has the best-preserved monumental architecture, and we have done a large amount of excavation at the site (for a map, see McCown 1945; Topic and Topic 2000; Theresa Lange Topic, Chapter 14, this volume). It covers the top of a high plateau 3.5 km long, but the whole area of the site was not occupied intensively, nor was the whole area occupied continuously. It appears that the earliest settlement was at the extreme northwest end of the plateau on Cerro Viejo. The occupation there probably started soon after AD 300. By AD 500, most of the occupation had shifted to the central and southeast areas of the plateau; excavations in these areas indicate that a variety of functions were represented.

Residence is most clearly indicated in the circular galleries on the central part of the plateau and in the curvilinear galleries, which most prominently border the steep cliff at the edge of the southeast end of the plateau. These galleries can be one to three stories tall and have abundant domestic refuse. There are seven clear examples of circular galleries, along with other associated architecture, in the central part of the plateau. The circular galleries are not perfectly round, but they do enclose a central patio in which small rectangular rooms are usually present. The curvilinear galleries form horseshoe-shaped loops with small rectangular structures located in the areas enclosed by the loops. Both the curvilinear and circular galleries are extremely long buildings, with the internal space divided into smaller rooms by frequent transverse walls; both were also built in segments, and the vertical joints of the segments are clearly visible.

The third class of building, which we have termed the "niched hall," is characterized by massive walls with a row of niches in one or more of the interior wall faces; the halls represent immense rectangular roofed volumes (Topic 1986). There are human bones incorporated in the thickness of the walls, probably representing secondary burials of defleshed bones. The niches were probably used primarily as places to leave renewable offerings, but occasionally a late burial is found in a niche. Niched halls are much wider than the galleries: Early Huamachuco phase niched halls have roofed areas of as much as 8 × 48 m, and the internal space is undivided. Ceramic collections from niched halls have higher proportions of spoons, cups, and decorated wares than found in the circular and curvilinear galleries. We have interpreted the niched halls as places where members of a lineage gathered to feast in honor of their ancestors, whose bones were buried in the walls (see also McEwan 1998). Most niched halls are located on the southeastern part of the plateau.

In addition to these three major classes of architecture, there are other types of buildings. The focal point of the site was probably a large architectural complex called the Castillo. The Castillo is similar to the circular galleries and may have had as many as five stories, with

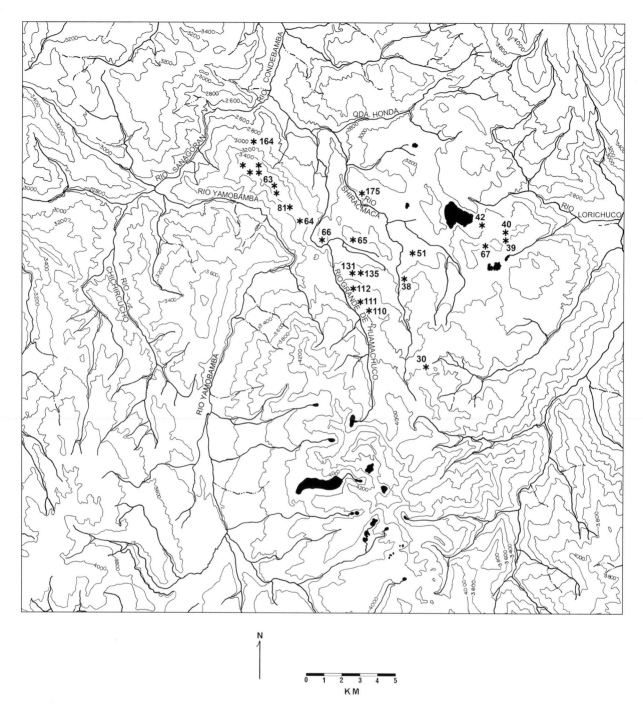

Figure 13.6. Location of sites assigned to the Early Huamachuco phase (AD 300–600). See Table 13.4 for further information on sites.

original entrances into the complex on the ground floor level. It is now almost completely filled with largely sterile rubble, to a depth of 9 m, which may have been used instead of scaffolding to facilitate construction, allowing heavy stones to be raised to the wall tops. The original intent may have been to remove the rubble fill once construction had been completed, but, for whatever reason, this was never done.

There are also at least three different types of burial structures at the site, including the niched halls, chulpa-like towers, and small, reenterable tombs that may have been used as temporary burial places until natural decomposition resulted in defleshed bones that could be incorporated into the walls of the niched halls (Topic and Topic 2000: Figure 5). In addition, there are numerous small rectangular buildings, at least two small circular

Table 13.4 Early Huamachuco phase sites with data on area, elevation (rounded to nearest 100 m), and other phases of occupation.

Site No.	Site Name	Area (m²)	Elevation (masl)	Other Occupations
30		720	3800	Purpucala
38		62,500	3200	
39		11,250	3400	
40	Cerro Negro	15,000	3400	Purpucala, Tuscan, Sta. Bárbara
42		900	3200	
51		8,000	3200	Modern
63	Marcahuamachuco	2,400,000	3500	Amaru, Late Huamachuco, Tuscan
64	Cerro Amaru	50,000	3400	Amaru, Late Huamachuco?
65	Cerro Sazón	200,000	3300	Amaru, Late Huamachuco?
66	Cerro Tuscan	120,000	3300	Amaru?, Late Huamachuco?
67		525	3400	
81	Las Huacas	2,400	3500	Amaru
110		255	3600	
111		100	3600	
112		875	3600	
131		6,000	3300	
135		5,500	3300	
164	Mallán	1,800	2800	Late Huamachuco
175	Pumabamba	3,864	3100	Late Huamachuco

structures that are possible storerooms, and large plaza areas. It is clear that a tremendous amount of construction took place at Marcahuamachuco during the Early Huamachuco phase, and construction continued through the Amaru and Late Huamachuco phases.

We originally interpreted Marcahuamachuco as the capital of an expansionist state (Topic and Topic 1986). However, we have reconsidered that interpretation, for a number of reasons. First, while Huamachuco influenced the architectural style at sites on the western side of the continental divide, the dating of this influence indicates a long trend, beginning before Marcahuamachuco and lasting into the Late Horizon. Although there is evidence for some forms of infrastructure that might be associated with a state—for example, roads—we have not been able to identify the large-scale public storage systems and other administrative structures that, in the Chimu and Inca cases, are associated with state operations (Topic 2003). The focus of activity at Marcahuamachuco seems to be lineage-based feasting in honor of the ancestors buried in the walls of the niched halls and other ritual activity in architecturally delimited public spaces (see Chapter 14, this volume). The domestic occupation in the circular and curvilinear galleries was related to those festivities and was probably seasonal rather than permanent; because of the lack of water on the plateau, major festivities may have been scheduled for the rainy season, with many fewer people in residence at other times of the year.

Cerro Sazón and Cerro Tuscan are intermediate in size and also have monumental architecture. Cerro Sazón was probably constructed about AD 400 and occupied through much of the Middle Horizon. It has some curvilinear galleries, but rectangular galleries associated with plazas and patios are more common (e.g., Topic and Topic 2000: Figure 9). Cerro Tuscan is located nearby, and the two sites may form a single site complex. Cerro Tuscan is much more poorly preserved than Cerro Sazón, but there are massive terraces, and human remains have been found at the site. Both sites seem to have evidence of domestic occupation; among the food remains recovered from Cerro Sazón were camelid bones and large quantities of carbonized maize. These sites are also closely associated with the north-south trunk route. At one point I interpreted Cerro Sazón as a tambo-like facility under the control of Marcahuamachuco (Topic 1991); while the function of the Cerro Sazón/Tuscan complex is not yet clear, it now seems more likely that the complex was the major settlement in the area at this time and possibly the political center for Huamachuco.

Cerro Amaru appears to be quite different in function; although most of the architecture is destroyed, the presence of offerings in three elaborate wells at the very top of the hill suggests that Cerro Amaru was a shrine related to water (Topic and Topic 1992). Interestingly, there are sizable maize storage facilities at Cerro Amaru for the support of cult activities (Topic and Chiswell 1992:226–229).

The group of small sites with monumental architecture probably performed a similar range of functions. Las Huacas is a shrine: although there are four artificial mounds at the site, the principal huaca was probably a natural stone outcrop which has been enclosed within a circular wall (Loten 1985:30–31). Pumabamba is a very formally planned site and exceptionally well built. It has monumental rectangular galleries surrounding a large rectangular patio. There are also some nonmonumental rooms forming a curvilinear gallery on the lower slope. It resembles Site 47, described for the Purpucala phase, and may have been either an elite residence or focus of community activities. Mallán, located in an area of spring-fed terraces below Marcahuamachuco, also may have been a focus of community activities related to agricultural production. It has a circular gallery and what appears to be a small niched hall. Site 67 is smaller and less well preserved, but has at least one well-built room and semicircular plazas.

The Early Huamachuco phase saw a dramatic increase in both total site area occupied and in the average size of sites, implying population growth (see Table 13.9a). Although a large part of this change can be accounted for by the presence of Marcahuamachuco, which was only seasonally occupied, and Cerro Amaru, a shrine, there are still three other settlements in the 3.2- to 25.6-ha size range; there were no sites in this range during the Purpucala phase (see Figure 13.14a). Certainly there was an aggregation of population during the Early Huamachuco phase, and much of it was concentrated around the location of the modern town of Huamachuco (Figure 13.6; see also Figure 13.11).

This population aggregation apparently caused some formerly well-occupied areas to be abandoned during the Early Huamachuco phase. This is especially noticeable in the areas immediately west of Laguna Sausagocha and in the Yamobamba area (Figure 13.6). It is difficult to understand why this would happen, but it might be related to changing subsistence strategies, since there is a growth in site area below 3400 masl and a decline in site area at 3600 masl (see Tables 13.9b and 13.9c).

Many Early Huamachuco phase sites appear to be related to roads (compare Figures 13.6 and 13.12). Sites 65, 66, and 175 are located near the Inca road leading north from Huamachuco, and this probably indicates that that route predates the Late Horizon by a considerable margin. Sites 131, 135, 110, 111, and 112 are located near a road leading south from Huamachuco up the Río Grande drainage. This road can still be traced on the ground but is not mentioned by Colonial documents; because there are a large number of steps on part of this route, it may not have been used often by Spanish horsemen. Several other sites (81, 64, and 164) are located on the access routes of Marcahuamachuco. We have not located Early Huamachuco phase sites along the southern route that is mentioned in documents, which went up the Río Yamobamba, but this area has not been well surveyed (compare Figures 13.1 and 13.6); there is a style of tenon heads and other stone carvings that is shared among Huamachuco, Santiago de Chuco, and Pashash (McCown 1945; Kroeber 1950; Schaedel 1952; Grieder 1978) that probably dates to this time period and suggests communication up the Río Yamobamba. The shrine of Catequil, located between Santiago de Chuco and Huamachuco, was occupied and functioning by this time period, though not necessarily as an oracle (Topic et al. 2002). It is notable that there is no evidence of direct Moche ceramic influence in the Huamachuco area.

AMARU PHASE: AD 600–800?

The dates for the Amaru phase are tentative. This is the time period during which Huari influence is felt in Huamachuco, and while it appears that Huari influence was probably restricted to Middle Horizon 1b and 2a, it is still difficult to date those phases absolutely. Partly because of this dating difficulty and partly because Huari influence was brief and present at only a few sites, it is also difficult to determine the settlement pattern precisely. We assume that many more sites than the eleven discussed here were actually occupied during this phase (Figure 13.7, Table 13.5). More specifically, it is probable that some sites classified as either Early Huamachuco or Late Huamachuco were also occupied during the Amaru phase.

A key event during the Amaru phase was the initiation of construction at Viracochapampa (61). This site has been viewed as an intrusive Huari center, and we agree that its construction relates to Huari influence in the area. However, we have also pointed out that the plan of Viracochapampa is based on specific types of buildings common in the Huamachuco area in the Early Huamachuco phase, and indeed earlier, and not present in Ayacucho until Middle Horizon 1B (Topic 1986, 1991; Topic and Topic 1986, 2000). Niched halls, one common element at Viracochapampa, occurred earlier at Marcahuamachuco, and rectangular galleries, which

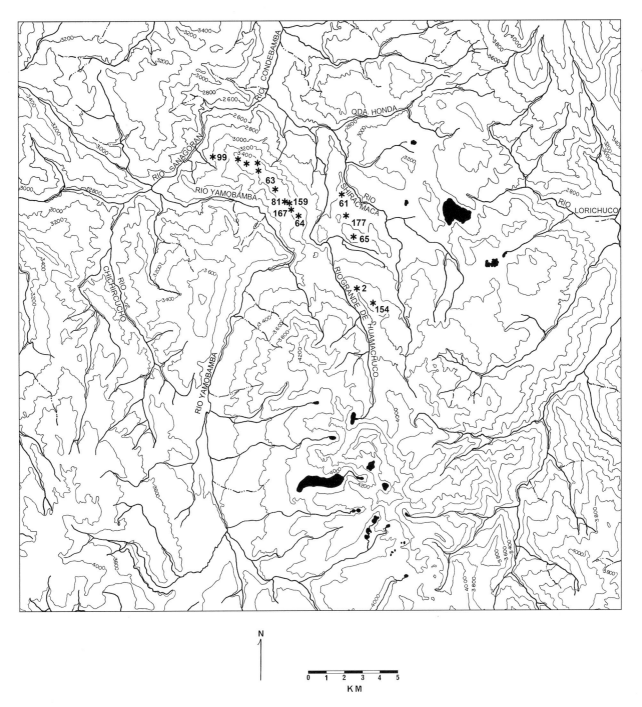

Figure 13.7. Location of sites assigned to the Amaru phase (AD 600–800?). See Table 13.5 for further information.

figure large in the Viracochapampa plan, occurred earlier at sites such as Cerro Sazón, Pumabamba, and Site 47; indeed, these rectangular galleries surrounding patios can be considered orthogonal variants of the circular and curvilinear galleries also common in the Huamachuco area. Niched halls and galleries are the main architectural components at Viracochapampa, and

the Huamachuco-derived gallery is the most recognizable element in "Huari" architecture throughout the central Andes (Topic and Topic 2000).

Construction at Viracochapampa was never completed, and thus we do not know what the final plan of the site was intended to be. Site 177 is the quarry area for the construction of Viracochapampa. There are

Table 13.5 Amaru phase sites with data on area, elevation (rounded to nearest 100 m), and other phases of occupation.

Site No.	Site Name	Area (m²)	Elevation (masl)	Other Occupations
2		9,141	3600	Sausagocha, Tuscan
61	Viracochapampa	324,875	3000	
63	Marcahuamachuco	2,400,000	3500	Early Huamachuco, Late Huamachuco, Tuscan
64	Cerro Amaru	50,000	3400	Early Huamachuco, Late Huamachuco?
65	Cerro Sazón	200,000	3300	Early Huamachuco, Late Huamachuco?
81	Las Huacas	2,400	3500	Early Huamachuco
99	Carbargón	5,400	3000	
154		10,625	3500	
159		2,000	3400	
167		1,500	3300	
177	La Cantera	2,400	3200	

no building remains there, but the size and number of quarry pits have permitted an estimate that construction activities at Viracochapampa lasted only five to twenty years (Topic 1991).

At least some of the labor required to build Viracochapampa was housed at the site itself (Topic 1991), but there is no evidence at Viracochapampa for the infrastructure (storage and feasting facilities) that would have been necessary to sponsor the construction. Cerro Sazón was contemporaneous and nearby. Although Huari ceramics are scarce at Cerro Sazón, they do occur in at least two buildings, one with evidence for the storage of meat and the other with probable evidence for chicha brewing (Topic 1991:158). This limited evidence may relate to the feasting of the workers. Significantly, the vast majority of ceramics in these buildings are local wares, suggesting strongly that local authorities, rather than agents of Huari, sponsored the construction. Viracochapampa has about the same number of niched halls as Marcahuamachuco, and Malcolm Horne (1989:36, 197) has calculated that it would have had, on completion, about 84% of the architectural area; it was probably meant to replace Marcahuamachuco as a center for lineage-based ancestor worship (Topic and Topic 2000; see also McEwan 1998).

Although it is clear from radiocarbon dates that Marcahuamachuco and Las Huacas continued to be occupied, there is no evidence of Huari ceramic influence at either site. Construction continued at both sites, and at Marcahuamachuco several monumental buildings were completed. The niched hall at Marcahuamachuco that is most similar in the proportions of its floor plan to the niched halls at Viracochapampa was constructed near the Castillo and had offerings, typical of the Middle Horizon, of sacrificed camelids and a cache

of 10 kg of *Spondylus* and small turquoise shell-shaped carvings, ritually broken, under its floor.

Huari ceramic influence is strongest at the shrine of Cerro Amaru (Thatcher 1972, 1975, 1977). However, Cerro Amaru began to decline in importance during the Amaru phase, while Marcahuamachuco continued to grow (Topic and Topic 1992, 2000).

There is one other site that we know of that is characterized by the Huari masonry style, typical of Viracochapampa (Topic 1991:163). This site, Carbargón (Site 99), is located north of Marcahuamachuco and appears to be a partially finished enclosure. If finished, Carbargón might have functioned similarly to Mallán, occupied at least during the Early and Late Huamachuco phases and possibly also during the Amaru phase. Both sites are associated with spring-fed agricultural terrace systems, but the terracing at Mallán is more extensive and more elaborate.

Site 154 was dated to the Amaru phase only because there are the partial foundations of what appears to be a rectangular enclosure. This site, like Carbargón, is dated on the basis of the architecture rather than the ceramics, which are scarce. In the same area Site 2 apparently continued the trend, already present in the Early Huamachuco phase, of population aggregation into larger settlements. Here there are three patio and room units, two more or less rectangular and one circular. The dating is based on radiocarbon evidence rather than ceramics.

Sites 159 and 167 are really aspects of a single site: there was once undoubtedly a small fortress at Site 159, but due to landslides, much of the artifactual evidence is found down the hill at Site 167. These artifacts are slingstones and projectile points; ceramics are very scarce. We have dated the sites to the Amaru phase on the basis of the obsidian projectile points, although these could just as easily fit into the Early Huamachuco or Late Huamachuco phase.

There is essentially very little change in the settlement pattern during the Amaru phase. There is a slight increase in site area (see Table 13.9a), largely accounted for by Viracochapampa which never really reached a functional stage. The major change may be that there is a decline in both the absolute area and the percentage by phase of the area occupied at 3200, 3300, and 3400 m elevation (see Tables 13.9b and 13.9c). This is accompanied by an increase in the area occupied below 3200 m. Both these trends, however, continue into the Late Huamachuco, and to some extent, the Tuscan phases. In fact, the occupation of areas below 3200 masl begins in the Early Huamachuco phase and increases continually through the Tuscan phase, if Viracochapampa is ignored. Thus, these are long-term trends, and Huari influence cannot be seen as resulting in any major change in the settlement pattern.

LATE HUAMACHUCO PHASE: AD 800?–1000

Although here we have placed only seven sites in the Late Huamachuco phase (Figure 13.8, Table 13.6), we believe that many of the Early Huamachuco phase sites and some of the Amaru phase sites continued to be occupied. The difficulty in dating results from the fact that there is very little change in the ceramic assemblage between Early Huamachuco and Late Huamachuco phases, an indication of the continuity of the local tradition during the brief period of Huari influence.

Still, excavated sites such as Cerro Sazón and Cerro Amaru have not produced carbon dates that fall within the phase. There is some architectural evidence, in particular two niched halls (Topic 1986), that suggests that parts of Cerro Sazón may have continued to be occupied during this phase, but much of the site was probably abandoned. Similarly, it appears that Cerro Amaru was largely, though not necessarily completely, abandoned. Thus, while these sites may still have been occupied, they were certainly not as large and did not fulfill the entire range of functions as in the two preceding phases.

The area occupied at Marcahuamachuco probably peaked during this phase. Curvilinear galleries saw a succession of reoccupations resulting in an accumulation of stratified floors and refuse, and there were also some new circular galleries built. Both radiocarbon evidence

and an architectural seriation indicate that niched halls also continued to be constructed. Continuity is also provided by the continued occupation of Mallán and Pumabamba.

The most significant change, then, seems to affect the sites in the middle size range: Cerro Amaru and Cerro Sazón.

The decline in importance of Cerro Amaru as a ritual site contrasts with the continued expansion of ritual activities at Marcahuamachuco. We have pointed to the differences in burial practices at the two sites as one possible factor in explaining these changes (Topic and Topic 1992, 2000). Although a mausoleum at Cerro Amaru contained one of the richest burials scientifically excavated in the Peruvian highlands (Topic and Topic 1984), the wall tombs at Marcahuamachuco have so few associated grave goods that Max Uhle speculated they might have been the tombs of slaves. Another way of characterizing the differences, however, is to consider the Cerro Amaru mausoleum to reflect an individualizing chiefdom, while the Marcahuamachuco niched halls represent community-oriented chiefdoms (Topic and Topic 1992, 2000).

The renewed emphasis on community autonomy and a form of ancestor veneration that emphasized the unity of lineage members, rather than the preeminence of their leaders, may also be related to the decline in importance of Cerro Sazón. In the previous phase, the leaders at Cerro Sazón may have been vying for regional political primacy and might even have sponsored the construction of Viracochapampa in order to replace Marcahuamachuco with a facility better located to serve their cause. We need further work to test these ideas, but this model would account for the continuity at the local level (Mallán and Pumabamba) as well as at a site emphasizing lineage membership and, also, the autonomy of individual lineages (Marcahuamachuco with its individual niched halls) joined in a loose cultural confederation.

The remaining sites with Late Huamachuco occupations continued to be occupied during the Tuscan phase, so while major political changes are evident during the Late Huamachuco phase, there was also a degree of continuity with earlier and later sites.

The site located high on Cerro El Toro (36) was reoccupied, and Site 88 was essentially an annex to it. If this site had been a shrine during the Sausagocha phase, its reoccupation at the same time that Cerro Amaru was abandoned may again be significant. Architecture at Cerro El Toro itself is largely destroyed, but at Site 88 there are six plaza groupings with quite small rooms

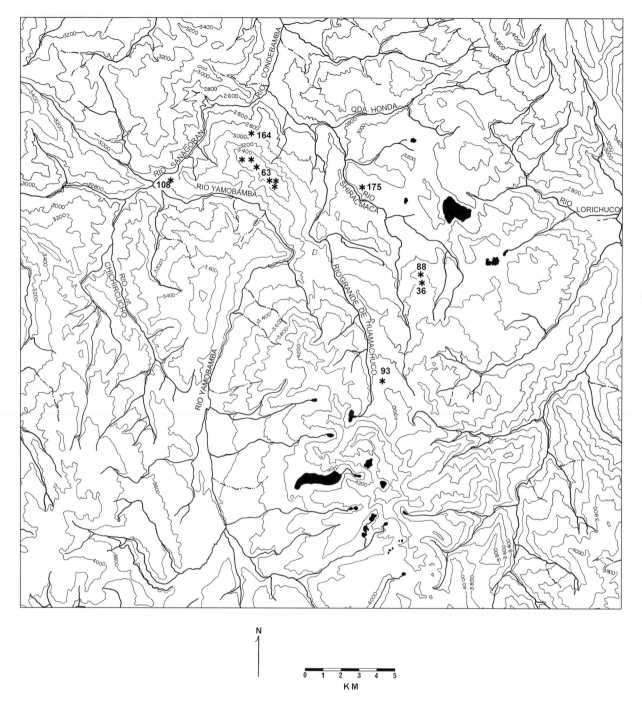

Figure 13.8. Location of sites assigned to the Late Huamachuco phase (AD 800?–1000). See Table 13.6 for further information.

Table 13.6 Late Huamachuco phase sites with data on area, elevation (rounded to nearest 100 m), and other phases of occupation.

Site No.	Site Name	Area (m²)	Elevation (masl)	Other Occupations
36	Cerro El Toro	2,880	3600	Sausagocha, Tuscan, Sta. Bárbara
63	Marcahuamachuco	2,400,000	3500	Early Huamachuco, Amaru, Tuscan
88		900	3500	Tuscan
93		1,500	4000	Tuscan
108	Vista Alegre	5,000	2700	Tuscan
164	Mallán	1,800	2800	Early Huamachuco
175	Pumabamba	3,864	3100	Early Huamachuco

(2 × 2 m or 2 × 3 m). These rooms are much smaller than normal domestic space, but without excavation we cannot determine whether they might have had some other function, such as storage.

The other two Late Huamachuco sites are probably related to domestic, herding, and agricultural activities. Site 93 is probably a house consisting of a patio and three rooms. It may be primarily related to herding activities, but its location along the road south may also have been important. Vista Alegre (108) has several leveled areas and terraces, as well as a dense ceramic scatter, but little preserved architecture. It is in an area ideal for the cultivation of fruits, maize, and other low-altitude crops.

In analyzing the distribution by elevation of these sites, it is best to use the actual areas (see Table 13.9b) rather than the percentages because many of the Early Huamachuco and Amaru phase settlements at 3200, 3300, and 3400 m elevation may have continued in use. From this perspective, it is significant that site areas actually increase in both the highest and lowest elevation ranges. This expansion reflects continued diversification of the economic base and, if middle elevation sites continued to be occupied, continued population growth.

On the broader regional level, it is noteworthy that the shrine of Catequil, the principal huaca of Huamachuco, was undergoing remodeling during this phase (Topic et al. 2002). The remodeling suggests that a change in ritual practice was widespread during this time period.

TUSCAN PHASE: AD 1000–1470

The Tuscan phase analysis highlights two changes. First, new ceramic styles appear that are easily distinguished from the Early and Late Huamachuco styles, allowing Tuscan phase sites to be readily identified. Second, there is no new monumental construction at Marcahuamachuco, so that if we discount the disproportionate influence of Marcahuamachuco on the sample, a return to a settlement pattern reminiscent of the Purpucala phase in terms of site size distributions is noticeable.

Although Marcahuamachuco was still occupied, we cannot date the construction of any monumental architecture there to this phase. The Tuscan phase occupation is sporadic and tends to occur within the shells of earlier buildings. Thus, the areas given for Marcahuamachuco in the analyses of size distributions exaggerate the importance of the site in the constructed Tuscan phase settlement system.

Three site clusters emerge during this phase (Figure 13.9). These three site clusters center around Cerro Grande (Site 16), Cerro Granadilla (Site 100), and Site 70, and probably specialized respectively in high-elevation herding and agriculture, low-elevation agriculture, and intermediate-level agriculture with some herding. This is not the settlement pattern one would expect if the economy were based on the vertical archipelago model; that model would predict large settlements at intermediate elevations, with satellites at higher and lower elevations.

Based on site area (Table 13.7), the Cerro Grande cluster was the most important. Cerro Grande (Figure 13.10) has monumental architecture in the form of a circular gallery crowning the summit that may have been constructed early in the Tuscan phase, or even late in the Late Huamachuco phase, because there is evidence of massive reconstruction. Cerro Chico (see Figure 13.4) has already been described; the Tuscan phase refuse here was light. Site 19 is a large settlement with a dense sherd scatter, with the remains of rooms, plazas and possible corrals. Walls are crudely constructed, however.

The Cerro Granadilla and Vista Alegre cluster has few architectural remains, but decorated ceramics are common.

Sites 40, 70, 71, and 73 form another cluster south of Laguna Sausagocha. Of these, Site 70 has the most impressive architecture, but it is not as well built as Cerro Grande. There is a circular patio at the top of the hill, and this is surrounded by several lower terraces on which were built rows of small square rooms. The other sites have few architectural remains, but possible corrals are still visible at Sites 71 and 73.

Of the other sites outside these clusters, Sites 2, 36, 60, 88, and 93 have already been mentioned. It is worth noting, however, that Site 60 had attained its full size and may be the largest artificial mound ever constructed in the Huamachuco area. Site 96 was simply a few sherds from one pot, but its location, along with Sites 104, 93, and 2, may be related to the use of the road that passes nearby. Similarly, Site 143 appears to be a windscreen, and may be a temporary stopping point near the road to the western slopes. Site 144 is a group of corrals.

It is useful to briefly eliminate Marcahuamachuco from the discussion, since it distorts all size distributions. If we eliminate the area of Marcahuamachuco (240 ha) from Table 13.9a, we have a total area of 28.44 ha for the remaining Tuscan phase settlement. Still

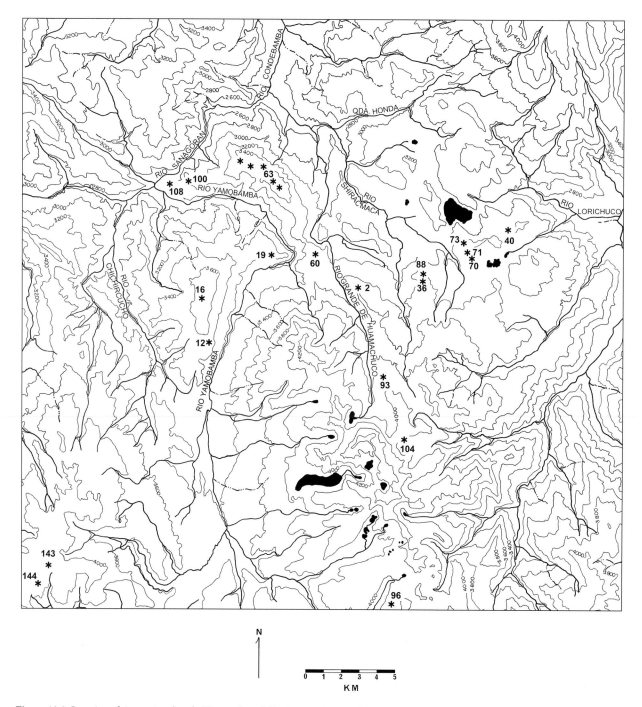

Figure 13.9. Location of sites assigned to the Tuscan phase (AD 1000–1470). See Table 13.7 for further information.

ignoring Marcahuamachuco, then, the average Tuscan phase site is about 1.5 ha in area. It is also useful to compare the Purpucala and Tuscan phases, since they represent the settlement patterns before and after the occupation of Marcahuamachuco. The total site area during the Tuscan phase was almost double the area occupied during the Purpucala phase, and the average site size was three times greater (see Table 13.9a). There

was a similar clustering of site areas into low, intermediate, and high elevations, but the range in elevation is larger (see Tables 13.9b and 13.9c). Both these comparisons indicate population growth from the Purpucala to the Tuscan phase. There is a similar pattern of sites clustered together, with one site in each cluster serving as a central place not because of its size, but because it has more elaborate architecture (see Figures 13.9

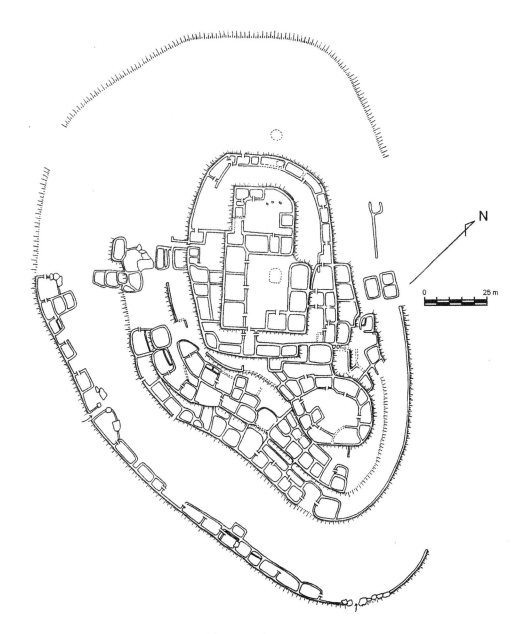

Figure 13.10. Plan of Cerro Grande (Site 16), a key site of the Tuscan phase.

and 13.10). This suggests a two-tiered site hierarchy, with each site cluster being an independent sociopolitical entity. On the other hand, Purpucala phase site clusters tended to be located in areas where they had access to several different resource zones, whereas the Tuscan phase clusters had access to only one or two. Thus, the Tuscan phase clusters may have been more economically specialized and might have needed to cooperate more than the Purpucala clusters. The need to cooperate might also have restrained any tendency toward armed conflict. Although Tuscan phase sites are often located on hills, there is little evidence that they were fortified.

Finally, it is worth noting that during the Tuscan phase the 3200 and 3300 m elevation areas were unpopulated or only very sparsely populated (see Table 13.9b).

SANTA BÁRBARA PHASE: AD 1470–1532

The Santa Barbara phase corresponds to the Inca domination of Huamachuco. Perhaps it is no coincidence that the main Inca sites are located around 3200 and 3300 m elevation (Figure 13.11, Table 13.8).

Table 13.7 Tuscan phase sites with data on area, elevation (rounded to nearest 100 m), and other phases of occupation.

Site No.	Site Name	Area (m²)	Elevation (masl)	Other Occupations
2		9,141	3600	Sausagocha, Amaru
12	Cerro Chico	8,000	3600	Sausagocha
16	Cerro Grande	31,400	3900	
19		56,700	3400	
36	Cerro El Toro	3,880	3600	Sausagocha, Late Huamachuco, Sta. Bárbara
40	Cerro Negro	15,000	3400	Purpucala, Early Huamachuco, Sta. Bárbara
60	Cerro Cacañan	17,100	3400	Sausagocha
63	Marcahuamachuco	2,400,000	3500	Early Huamachuco, Amaru, Late Huamachuco
70		12,000	3500	
71		5,280	3500	
73		400	3500	
88		900	3500	Late Huamachuco
93		1,500	4000	Late Huamachuco
96		9	4100	
100	Cerro Granadilla	48,000	3000	Sta. Bárbara?
104		40	4000	
108	Vista Alegre	5,000	2700	Late Huamachuco
143		59,800	4100	
144		11,200	4100	

Table 13.8 Santa Bárbara phase sites with data on area, elevation (rounded to nearest 100 m), and other phases of occupation.

Site No.	Site Name	Area (m²)	Elevation (masl)	Other Occupations
1	Sta. Bárbara	6,375	3400	Sausagocha
8	Cerro Mamorco	9,900	3400	Colpa
36	Cerro El Toro	2,880	3600	Sausagocha, Late Huamachuco, Tuscan
40	Cerro Negro	15,000	3400	Purpucala, Early Huamachuco, Tuscan
59		10,400	3300	
69		14,400	3500	
82	Las Colcas	720	3400	
157		250	4000	
158	Canibamba	62,500	3200	Sausagocha
179	Marcochuco	35,000	3300	
—	Huamachuco	250,000	3200	

Huamachuco itself was the main Inca center, but most of the evidence is now covered by the modern town (Topic and Topic 1993). What remains is a part of the Inca plaza, which must originally have been almost double its present size, and the probable remains of the *ushnu* underlying the chapel of San José. Finds of Inca ceramics are common in the town.

On the hill slopes surrounding Huamachuco are numerous Inca *colcas* (Figure 13:11: Sites 1, 8, 59, 82) (Topic and Chiswell 1992). We have estimated that there were once 215 colcas with average measurements of about 4 × 5 m. Slightly more than half of these have floors elevated on stone pillars (Site 1) and

were probably for storing a variety of goods in very dry environments. The other storerooms (Sites 8, 82, and 59) have earth floors and canals running under the floors. These were probably for tubers (Topic and Topic 1984:57–66; Topic and Chiswell 1992).

Other sites that were probably closely related to the Inca occupation are Sites 157, 158, and 179. Site 157 is located along the road; it is largely destroyed but appears to be a rectangular patio surrounded by rooms. We have only a very small sample of highly eroded sherds from the site, but they appear to be Late Horizon, and the site may be a *tambo*. Site 179 (Marcochuco) is probably a site housing *mitmaqkuna*. Documents tell of a *mitmaq*

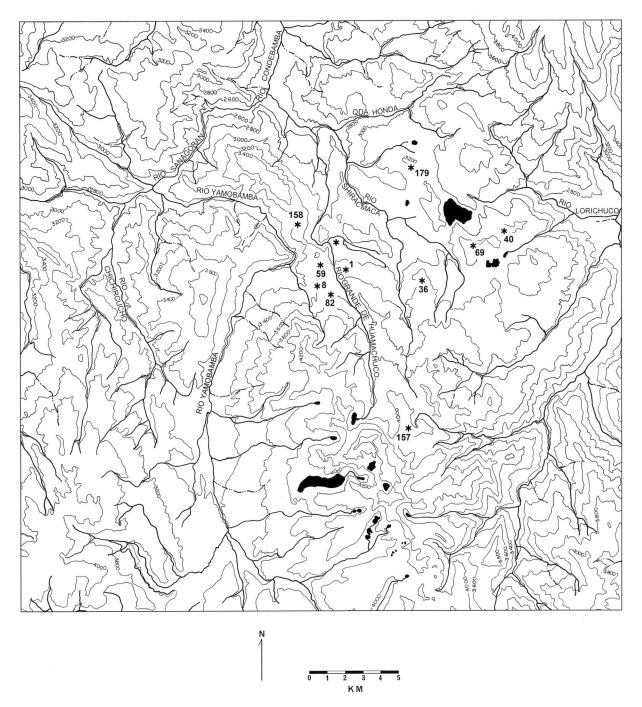

Figure 13.11. Location of sites assigned to the Santa Bárbara phase (AD 1470–1532). See Table 13.8 for further information.

settlement at a place called San Marcos de Chuco and, judging by the *tambos* served by these *mitmaqkuna*, the settlement should be in this general area (see, e.g., Topic and Topic 1993:36–37). The ceramics show heavy Inca influence but were probably locally made. Canibamba (Site 158) has been covered by a landslide, but ceramics with strong Inca influence have been recovered (Topic and Topic 1993).

The remaining sites represent the local population. Site 69 is a large, dense sherd scatter with few architectural remains. It undoubtedly housed much of the population formerly located at Sites 70, 71, and 73. Sites 36 and 40 continued to be occupied. Probably other Tuscan phase sites also continued to be occupied (see Figure 13.9). For example, Cerro Granadilla (Site 100) is located near the modern *caserío* of Llampa. Llampa

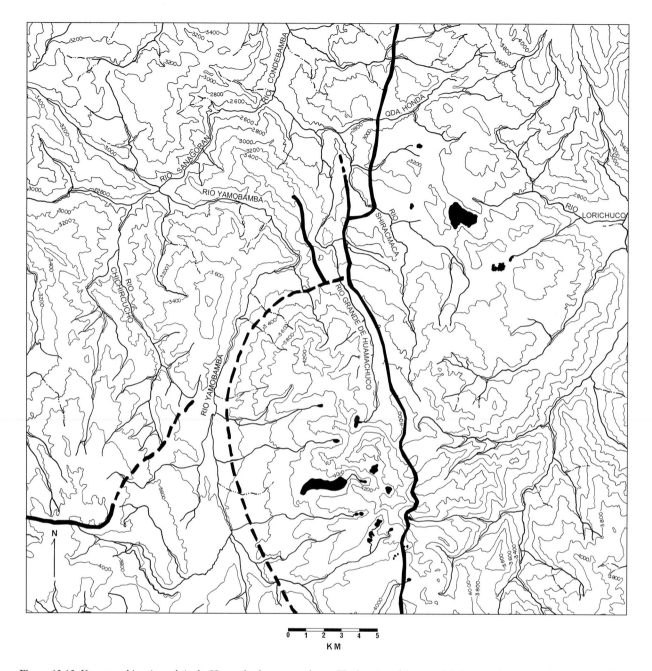

Figure 13.12. Known prehistoric roads in the Huamachucho area are shown. The location of these roads is based both on ground survey and colonial documentation. The dotted lines indicate the approximate locations of routes that are now destroyed. These routes were in use during the Santa Bárbara phase, but their initial use predates Incaic times.

was also the name of the highest ranked *waranga* and *pachaca* (autonomous lineage) in the Huamachuco area. The documentary sources generally describe a dispersed settlement pattern with the local population organized into four warangas (theoretically a group of 1,000 taxpaying households), each composed of a varying number of pachacas (a group of 100 taxpaying households) (Topic 1992, 1998; Topic and Topic 1993).

The most notable change in the site size distribution for this phase (see Figure 13.16b) reflects the presence of the Incaic administrative center at Huamachuco. This site corresponds in size to the second order sites, such as Cerro Sazón, during the Early Huamachuco and Amaru phases. There were no sites in this size range during the Late Huamachuco or Tuscan phases.

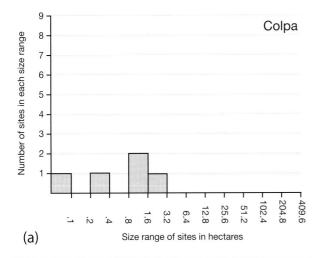

(a)

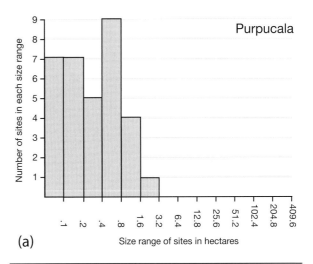

(a)

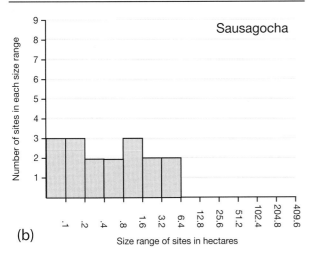

(b)

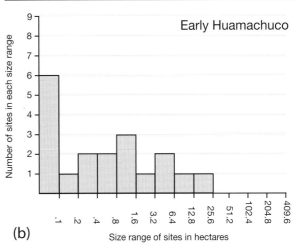

(b)

Figure 13.13. (a) Site size distributions for sites dating to the Colpa phase. (b) Site size distributions for sites dating to the Sausagocha phase.

Figure 13.14. (a) Site size distributions for sites dating to the Purpucala phase. (b) Site size distributions for sites dating to the Early Huamachuco phase.

SUMMARY

The data presented in this chapter support the following interpretations of long-term demographic, economic, and sociopolitical trends in the Huamachuco area.

Continual population growth. Continued population growth is best reflected in the gradual extension of occupation into both the low and high elevations (Tables 13.9b and 13.9c). The trend in total site area is less clear (Table 13.9a), largely because of distortions introduced by large, special-purpose sites such as Marcahuamachuco, Cerro Sazón, Cerro Amaru, and Viracochapampa. Although population growth appears to be continuous, we cannot yet specify the rate of growth at different times, nor can we suggest figures for population densities with any confidence.

Changes in subsistence strategies. Related to population growth, subsistence strategies change (see Tables 13.9b and 13.9c). The Colpa, Sausagocha, and Purpucala

phases all emphasize occupation in the 3200–3400 m elevations, and sites often have access to both marshes and farmland. Beginning in the Purpucala phase, there is a trend toward increasing use of the jalca for herding. Slightly later, beginning in the Early Huamachuco phase, there is a trend toward the increasing exploitation of low-altitude lands that were at times provided with terraced irrigation systems. Thus, there is evidence not only for the extension of subsistence activities into more marginal zones but also for the intensification of agricultural activities during the later phases. The vertical archipelago model may not explain the settlement pattern well at the level of the pachaca (for example, the site clusters of the Purpucala and Tuscan phases) within the Huamachuco Basin. The fact that some site clusters can be related to toponyms derived from pachaca and waranga names reflects the degree of territoriality that seems to be associated with these sociopolitical units.

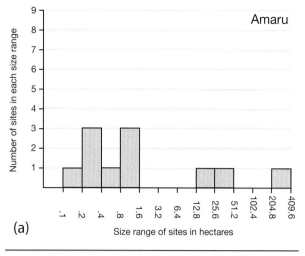

(a)

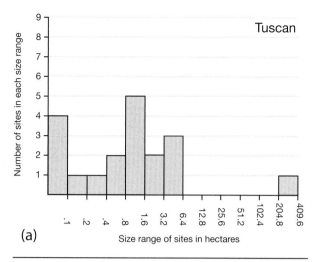

(a)

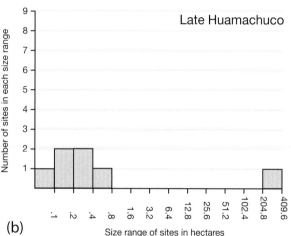

(b)

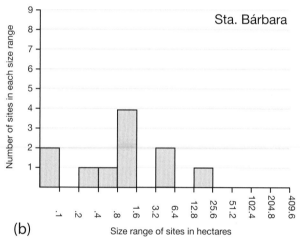

(b)

Figure 13.15. (a) Site size distributions for sites dating to the Amaru phase. (b) Site size distributions for sites dating to the Late Huamachuco phase.

Figure 13.16. (a) Site size distributions for sites dating to the Tuscan phase. (b) Site size distributions for sites dating to the Sta. Bárbara phase.

On the other hand, some members of each pachaca may have been dispersed among the site clusters, as may have been the case in the Cajamarca area (Remy 1992:62 ff.).

Changes in the size of sociopolitical units. When ceramics first appear in the Huamachuco area, there appears to have been only a rather small population which was largely isolated from developments in surrounding areas. The Colpa phase population probably lived in dispersed households with low archaeological visibility. The sites of this phase that we have discovered are probably not typical. Three seem to be ceremonial centers, while one seems to be a more elaborate household and suggests the beginnings of acquired status. During the Sausagocha phase, Cerro Campana East develops in an area of fairly dense population located around Laguna Sausagocha. There was probably public architecture at this site, and it may have functioned as the focus of one

or two pachaca-sized social units. La Colpa and Cerro El Toro may also have served as similar foci for more dispersed populations. The Purpucala phase witnessed the agglutination of population in the Yamobamba area to form another focus. By the end of this phase, architecture at two sites was almost monumental in scale, a true elite may have emerged, the size of sociopolitical units was probably intermediate between the pachaca and the waranga, and there was increasing contact with surrounding areas. Throughout these phases there is evidence for warfare, but it does not seem to have been particularly intense.

The Early Huamachuco phase witnessed the introduction of tension between two traditions. On the one hand, the tendency for an elite to differentiate themselves continued. The people buried in the mausoleum at Cerro Amaru were probably able to differentiate themselves in life by controlling the activities

Table 13.9a. Total site area and average size of sites by phase.

Phase	Total Area (ha)	Average Site Size (ha)
Colpa	4.67	0.93
Sausagocha	19.82	1.16
Purpucala	15.11	0.46
Early Huamachuco	288.97	15.21
Amaru	300.83	27.35
Late Huamachuco	241.59	34.51
Tuscan	268.44	14.12
Santa Bárbara	40.73	3.70

Table 13.9b. Area (× 1,000 m²) by phase and elevation (rounded to nearest 100 masl).

Phase	<3200	3200	3300	3400	3500	3600	>3600
Colpa	0	12.0	22.3	9.9	0	0	2.5
Sausagocha	0	99.3	50.2	24.4	0	24.3	0
Purpucala	0	35.8	9.9	59.0	16.9	28.7	0.7
Early Huamachuco	5.7	71.4	331.5	76.8	2402.4	1.2	0.7
Amaru	330.3	2.4	201.5	52.0	2413.0	9.1	0
Late Huamachuco	10.7	0	0	0	2400.9	2.9	1.5
Tuscan	53.0	0	0	88.8	2418.6	20.0	03.9
Santa Bárbara	0	312.5	45.4	32.0	14.4	2.9	0.2

Table 13.9c. Area (as percentage of total area by phase) and elevation (rounded to nearest 100 masl).

Phase	<3200	3200	3300	3400	3500	3600	>3600
Colpa		26	48	21			5
Sausagocha		50	25	12		12	
Purpucala		24	6	39	11	19	+
Early Huamachuco	+	2	11	3	83	+	+
Amaru	11	+	7	2	80	+	
Late Huamachuco	+				99	+	+
Tuscan	2			3	90	1	4
Santa Bárbara		77	11	8	4	1	+

at the shrine, which by the Amaru phase was possibly attracting pilgrims from as far away as Ayacucho. The Cerro Sazón/Cerro Tuscan complex may reflect increasing political centralization, which would also support the interpretation of an increasingly differentiated elite class. It is possible that these elites may have lived in compounds which took the form of rectangular galleries surrounding a central patio; we have these kinds of structures all the way back to the Colpa phase, as at Site 102.

On the other hand, Marcahuamachuco relates to a tradition of communal organization, which is reflected in another typical site plan: the circular and curvilinear galleries. These site plans promote high levels of interaction, since all the doors open out onto a central patio, and egalitarianism, since individual households are subsections of a single façade; in many respects, these sites are like Amazonian circular villages or the pueblos of the American Southwest. Again, we have these kinds of sites going back to the Colpa phase, for example at

Site 20. Marcahuamachuco combines the circular and curvilinear galleries with ancestral shrines, the niched halls, which were probably constructed and used by individual lineages or pachacas. At Marcahuamachuco, eventually about twenty different pachacas gathered to feast in honor of their ancestors. This gathering created a sense of shared identity, a cultural unity, without any overt implication of the dominance of one pachaca over another. It is quite possible that the score of pachacas maintaining facilities at Marcahuamachuco all lived within sight of the Marcahuamachuco plateau.

The tension between these traditions continued through the Amaru phase and possibly into the Late Huamachuco phase. But eventually the tension was resolved in favor of the more communal organization represented by Marcahuamachuco. Increased regional interaction correlated with the emergence of elites; interaction seems to decline during the Late Huamachuco phase. Elites benefit more than ordinary folk from interregional interaction, and the limited evidence that we have suggests that local elites at both Cerro Amaru and at Cerro Sazón promoted interaction with Huari. Conversely, at Marcahuamachuco there is little evidence for interregional interaction, while interaction between local groups was emphasized and facilitated.

Marcahuamachuco continued to be used in the Tuscan phase, but the lack of construction at the site suggests stagnation. By the Tuscan phase, the shrine of Catequil had gained at least regional importance; it would have served as a symbol of cultural identity for a larger area than Marcahuamachuco and may have undermined the importance of Marcahuamachuco. It was also now certainly functioning as an oracle (Topic et al. 2002).

I have here equated the site clusters of the Tuscan phase, and earlier phases, to the pachacas described in the early Colonial period. A much looser organization, at a level analogous to warangas, is suggested by the distribution of ceramic styles such as Huamachuco-on-White and Huamachuco Impressed; the distributions of these styles, however, do not coincide neatly with the locations of the Incaic warangas, nor do the distributions of these styles cover areas as large as those attributed to the Incaic warangas. I have argued, in fact, that much of the organization described in Colonial documents, including the equation of a Huamachuco ethnic group with the boundaries of the Incaic province, was created by the Inca (Topic 1998).

Acknowledgments

Work was supported by funding from the Social Sciences and Humanities Research Council of Canada and by Trent University, Peterborough, Ontario. Permission for the field research was granted by the CIRBM, Inc.

I thank Mike Moseley for guiding me into archaeology and teaching me how to look at sites. If I have looked and failed to see, the fault lies with me. I gratefully acknowledge the help and enthusiasm of the many Peruvian, Canadian, and American students and assistants who worked with the Huamachuco project and who gathered much of the information presented here. An earlier version of this chapter was presented at the symposium La Investigación Arqueológica en el Norte Peruano, held in Chiclayo, Peru, in November 1986. After the preparation of that paper, Malcolm Horne in 1989 wrote a thesis with much more detailed analysis than can be presented here; the interpretation given here, however, has evolved considerably from our views in the late 1980s.

REFERENCES

Grieder, Terence
1978   *The Art and Archaeology of Pashash*. University of Texas Press, Austin.

Horne, Malcolm Robert
1989   A Regional Analysis of Prehistoric Settlement Patterns in the Huamachuco Area, Peru. Master's thesis, Trent University, Peterborough, Ontario.

Kroeber, Alfred Louis
1950   A Local Style of Lifelike Sculptured Stone Heads in Ancient Peru. In *Beiträge Zur Gesellungs- und Völkerwissenschaft Professor Dr. Richard Thurnwald zu seinem achtzigsten Geburtstag gewidmet*, pp. 195–198. Verlag Gebr. Mann., Berlin.

Loten, H. Stanley
1985   Marcahuamachuco: Dynastic Architecture before the Inca. *Rotunda, A Publication of the Royal Ontario Museum, Toronto* 17(4):21–31.

McEwan, Gordon F.
1998   The Functions of Niched Halls in Wari Architecture. *Latin American Antiquity* 9(1):68–86.

McCown, Theodore D.
1945   Pre-Incaic Huamachuco: Survey and Excavations in the Region of Huamachuco and Cajabamba. In *University of California Publications in American Archaeology and Ethnology*, vol. 39, pp. 223–399. University of California Press, Berkeley and Los Angeles.

Remy, Pilar
1992   El documento. In *Las visitas a Cajamarca 1571–72/1578* (2 vols.), edited by María Rostworowski and Pilar Remy, vol. 1, pp. 37–109. Instituto de Estudios Peruanos, Lima.

Schaedel, Richard P.
1952   *An Analysis of Central Andean Stone Sculpture*. Unpublished doctoral dissertation, Yale University, New Haven, CT.

Thatcher, John P.
1972   *Continuity and Change in the Ceramics of Huamachuco, North Highlands, Peru*. Unpublished doctoral dissertation, University of Pennsylvania, Pittsburgh.
1975   Early Intermediate Period and Middle Horizon 1B Ceramic Assemblages of Huamachuco, North Highlands, Peru. *Ñawpa Pacha* 10–12 (1972–74): 109–127.
1977   A Middle Horizon 1B Cache from Huamachuco, North Highlands, Peru. *Ñawpa Pacha* 15:101–110.

Topic, John R.

1986   A Sequence of Monumental Architecture from Huamachuco. In *Perspectives on Andean Prehistory and Protohistory*, edited by Daniel H. Sandweiss and D. Peter Kvietok, pp. 63–83. Latin American Studies Program, Cornell University, Ithaca, NY.

1991   Huari and Huamachuco. In *Huari Administrative Structure: Prehistoric Monumental Architecture and State Government*, edited by William H. Isbell and Gordon F. McEwan, pp. 141–164. Dumbarton Oaks Research Library and Collection, Washington, DC.

1992   Las huacas de Huamachuco: Precisiones en torno a una imagen indígena de un paisaje andino. In *Fray Juan de San Pedro: La persecución del demonio: Crónica de los primeros agustinos en el norte del Perú*, edited by Teresa Van Ronzelen, Luis Millones, John R. Topic, José L. González, and Eric E. Deeds, pp. 41–99. Algazara y CAMEI, Málaga-México.

1998   Ethnogenesis in Huamachuco. *Andean Past* 5:109–127.

2003   From Stewards to Bureaucrats: Architecture and Information Control at Chan Chan, Peru. *Latin American Antiquity* 14(3):243–274.

Topic, John R., and Coreen Chiswell

1992   Inka Storage in Huamachuco. In *Inka Storage Systems*, edited by Terry Y. Levine, pp. 206–233. University of Oklahoma Press, Norman.

Topic, John R., and Theresa Lange Topic

1978   Prehistoric Fortification Systems of Northern Peru. *Current Anthropology* 19(3):618–619.

1985   Coast Highland Relations in Northern Peru: The Structure and Strategy of Interaction. Paper presented at the Sixteenth Annual Chacmool Conference on the Status, Structure, and Stratification: Current Archaeological Reconstructions, Calgary.

1986   El Horizonte Medio en Huamachuco. *Revista del Museo Nacional* 47:12–52.

1987   The Archaeological Investigation of Andean Militarism: Some Cautionary Observations. In *The Origins and Development of the Andean State*, edited by Jonathan Haas, Shelia Pozorski, and Thomas Pozorski, pp. 47–55. Cambridge University Press, Cambridge.

1992   The Rise and Decline of Cerro Amaru: An Andean Shrine during the Early Intermediate Period and Middle Horizon. In *Ancient Images, Ancient Thought: The Archaeology of Ideology*, edited by A. Sean Goldsmith, Sandra Garvie, David Selin, and Jeanette Smith, pp. 167–180. Proceedings of the Twenty-Third Annual Conference of the Archaeological Association of the University of Calgary.

1993   A Summary of the Inca Occupation of Huamachuco. In *Provincial Inca: Archaeological and Ethnohistorical Assessment of the Impact of the Inca State*, edited by Michael A. Malpass, pp. 17-43. University of Iowa Press, Iowa City.

1997   Hacia una comprensión conceptual de la guerra andina. In *Arqueología, antropología e historia en los Andes: Homenaje a María Rostworowski*, edited by Rafael Varón Gabai and Javier Flores, pp. 567–590. Instituto de Estudios Peruanos / Banco Central de Reserva del Perú, Lima.

2000   Hacia la comprensión del fenómeno Huari: Una perspectiva norteña. In *Huari y Tiwanaku: Modelos vs. evidencias*, edited by Peter Kaulicke and William H. Isbell. Boletín de Arqueología PUCP, no. 4, pp. 181–217. Lima.

Topic, John R., Theresa Lange Topic, and Alfredo Melly

2002   Catequil: The Archaeology, Ethnohistory and Ethnography of a Major Provincial Huaca. In *Andean Archaeology I: Variations in Sociopolitical Organization*, edited by William H. Isbell and Helaine Silverman, pp. 303–336. Kluwer Academic / Plenum Press, New York.

Topic, Theresa Lange, and John R. Topic

1984   *Huamachuco Archaeological Project: Preliminary Report on the Third Season, June–August 1983*. Trent University Occasional Papers in Anthropology, no. 1, Peterborough, Ontario.

CHAPTER 14

THE MEANING OF MONUMENTS AT MARCAHUAMACHUCO

THERESA LANGE TOPIC

THIS *HOMENAJE* PROVIDES AN excellent opportunity to celebrate the contribution of an archaeologist who has had a profound impact on Andean studies over the past forty years. Michael Moseley's diverse interests and his willingness to adapt to changes in the field have inspired all of us. I was fortunate to participate as an undergraduate in the Chan Chan-Moche Valley Project and to continue that association as a graduate student. Many of my warmest recollections of those stimulating years involve Moseley in the field. Whether visiting a new site on the north coast or striding through the enormous maze that was Chan Chan, he was a marvel to watch in action. His mind was fully engaged as he scanned the setting, analyzed the architecture, and hopped in and out of pits, reading the evidence and assembling the clues that would help him understand the site. Always, he was working with a model of the site as a dynamic setting for social action. His overview was expansive, and he sped up and down several levels of resolution, from the smallest to the largest. In Moseley's view there was an unbroken connection between the archaeological remains and lived human experience, and he had complete assurance that the meaning of the archaeological remains could be decoded. The awareness of and respect for this link is probably the most important thing that I learned from him.

This chapter is an exploration of a site very different from the coastal complexes on which Moseley trained his attention in the 1970s. Marcahuamachuco lies inland 100 km from Trujillo and 80 km south of Cajamarca, at an altitude of 3200 masl. Its overall scale is similar to Chan Chan's, with massive monumental construction dominating the scene, but the structures are of masonry, in contrast to the adobe of the coastal site. In this chapter I explore the reasons for the site's construction and use, and offer interpretations of the meanings the site conveyed to local people and to visitors during the centuries in which it was occupied.

Skepticism and self-reflection are hallmarks of all arenas of intellectual endeavor in the postmodern era, and archaeologists, like other scholars, frequently question the objectivity and neutrality of their enterprise. Many writers have reminded us that the work of interpreting archaeological data is not a straightforward process of discovering the past; we must acknowledge that we are also involved in creating histories (see Patterson 1986; Leone et al. 1987; Shanks and Tilley 1989; Trigger 1991); however well intentioned, we come to the analytical process with our own cultural and personal prejudices intact. When an archaeologist deals with questions close to the data—What building materials were used? What proportion of the diet came from the sea? What were the standard burial practices for the era?—the objectivity gap is not a crucial one. But as the archaeologist moves into areas of more profound social analysis of the prehistoric past, it is crucial that the likelihood of observer bias be taken seriously.

These preliminary comments are relevant in a discussion of prehistoric monumental architecture, because this is an arena in which Western biases about authority, hierarchy, and labor organization have had an especially distorting impact on the interpretation of the evidence. Andean monuments have largely been read through Western eyes and too often have been assigned values and meanings closer to the Western cultural and historical tradition than to those of the builders and users of the monuments. Here I attempt a rereading of Marcahuamachuco and its significance in a more Andean context.

ANDEAN MONUMENTS

In this chapter, a monument is defined as a structure designed and built to evoke feelings of awe in an observer. To say that a structure is monumental is to make a statement about scale, complexity, difficulty of construction, and elaborateness. A structure that is monumental lies beyond the ordinary; its existence, purpose, and function transcend the sphere of the quotidian.

In the central Andes, as in all other areas of the world in which prehistoric civilizations developed, monumental architecture is a remarkably visible and frequent reminder of past lifeways. These monuments have been a natural focus of archaeological attention from the earliest years of the discipline. In the early exploratory stage of archaeological research, investigators meticulously measured, mapped, and drew the *huacas*, mounds, temples, and great walls that are so prominent a part of the cultural landscape in Peru and Bolivia. The emphasis for many decades was on describing and dating the constructions. A sacred/secular or religious/public dichotomy in the presumed function of monumental structures appeared early (e.g., Squier 1973 [1877]:132–133) and continued unchallenged for many decades. The assertion that a structure had a religious function was considered a self-evident observation requiring no further explanation. "Mounds" and "temple-mounds," "temple and pyramid centers" constituted prima facie evidence for religious authority and priest-controlled societies (e.g., Willey 1948:12). Implicit evolutionary assumptions about the nature

of political authority underlay nearly all discussions of monumental construction (see Schaedel 1952).

In the 1970s and 1980s, in a move mirroring processualist trends in Americanist archaeology, Andeanists began to consider monumental constructions more carefully. The linkages between social institutions and the monuments they produced became a topic for investigation and explanation rather than assumption. This era yielded important new insights into monument construction. But the interpretive paradigms that prevailed at the time channeled analysis and explanation into two main lines.

The materialist approach tended to measure output in terms of energy expenditure. This interpretive framework saw monuments as outputs to which absolute values could be assigned: width, length, height, volume of fill. Following early experimental work like that of Erasmus (1965), these measurements could be converted into calculations of the number of man-days required for construction and the area from which labor must have been drawn. Many of us have worked within this framework (J. Topic 1991:160–161 for Viracochapampa, T. Topic 1982:272 for Huaca del Sol, T. Pozorski 1976: Appendix V for Caballo Muerto, R. Feldman 1983 for Áspero). This kind of approach allowed us to generate figures that facilitated comparisons between different times and places and to assign rank order in terms of physical attributes: "largest adobe huaca on the north coast" (Huaca del Sol, Hastings and Moseley 1975:196), "biggest Preceramic complex of monumental architecture yet documented in the continent" (El Paraíso, Moseley 1985:46). The materialist approach emphasized the sheer magnitude of human effort that went into monument building.

A second interpretive approach, essentially evolutionary, was closely linked to the materialist framework. Monuments were considered to be unambiguous indicators of the degree of political, economic, and administrative complexity that a particular prehistoric culture had achieved. A group could be positioned on the band-tribe-chiefdom-state spectrum of increasing complexity according to the size of monuments it constructed (see, e.g., Moseley 1975:113; Pozorski and Pozorski 1992:862–865).

Implicit in this approach was the conviction that there is a relatively straightforward correlation between the size of a project and the amount of planning, supervision, and organization required. A clear threshold was assumed to exist between voluntary labor and coerced labor, and large monuments constituted clear evidence that the threshold had been crossed and that coercive political authority had appeared on the scene. Andeanists have argued for the presence of the *mit'a* labor tax at increasingly earlier times in the prehistoric past as a means of explaining corporate labor investment in monumental architecture. But there has been little attempt to explore other models of labor recruitment and organization that stem from less hierarchical power relations.

Archaeologists through the 1960s and 1970s tended to focus on energy costs of monument construction and the levels of administrative complexity required for such projects to succeed, but interesting attempts to understand monuments as social space also began to appear. Donald Lathrap's (1985) remarkable evocation of Formative period ceremonial centers as places to capture and focus the power of the cosmos required the synthesis of interpretive strands from architecture, iconography, myth, and ritual. Richard Burger and Lucy Salazar-Burger (1980, 1991) presented persuasive explanations of how Formative ritual spaces were used, combining detailed archaeological investigation with ethnographic insights into ritual performance. Helaine Silverman (1990) drew a fascinating reconstruction of how Cahuachi served the Nazca population, using personal observation of modern religious pilgrimages to shed light on the archaeological evidence. Gary Urton (1990) has argued that modern inter-ayllu patterns of cooperation and competition in the Cuzco area can provide a model for task allocation within large groups. The recent work at Huaca de la Luna (Bourget 2001; Uceda 2001) provides fascinating detail on the use of one monument for the ritual sacrifice of captured warriors, and will require reconsideration of the situation of the monument in Moche social space.

These newer approaches to the interpretation of ritual spaces in general and monuments in particular have considerable explanatory power. They reflect a shift in perspective away from mechanical cost-benefit analyses and the conviction that ideology serves primarily to mask power imbalance. Replacing this essentially Western perspective is an increased willingness to examine monuments as integral parts of a wider cultural context, and a greater confidence in the ability of archaeology to understand monuments in their own terms.

MARCAHUAMACHUCO

This section explores the significance of Marcahuamachuco within the local cultural context during the time the site was occupied. The intent is to try to determine the meanings, memories, emotions, and knowledge evoked by the site in the mind of individuals who saw, heard, felt, built, maintained, and experienced the site. These diverse meanings cannot be understood merely by considering economics, administration, and labor organization; we must be willing to consider the realms of ritual, myth, cosmology, and kinship as well. The conclusions drawn from this exploration may not be testable in the traditional sense but should have a certain degree of plausibility.

Marcahuamachuco lies in the northern sierra of Peru, a few kilometers west of the modern town of Huamachuco. The earliest dates from the site cluster around AD 400, and construction ceased soon after AD 1000 (see John Topic, Chapter 13, this volume). Most construction at the site thus dates to the Middle Horizon. In eight field seasons between 1981 and 1989, the Huamachuco Archaeological Project conducted surveys, mapped the site, and carried out excavations in many different parts of the site. Although architectural preservation is generally quite good at the site, excavation was hampered by the enormous quantities of above-floor deposit, and poor organic preservation limited the kinds of materials that were recovered. Dating of individual structures and occupations was complicated by the simplicity and utilitarian nature of the ceramic style, which limits its usefulness in chronology construction. As the project unfolded, many preconceptions that project workers held about the site and the people who had built it had to be confronted and revised in response to anomalies in the archaeological record and increased awareness of local social traditions.

This chapter outlines several of the most important conclusions drawn from the research at Marcahuamachuco, without providing all of the background documentation.[1] The most important conclusions are as follows.

First, there was very little variability in domestic architecture or context at the site. Wherever excavations encountered hearths, grinding stones, and hearth-blackened sherds, it was in a context of either monumental or very big construction.[2] Domestic residence was in long, multistoried galleries that united many households under a common roof, behind a single massive and uniform façade. A household unit typically consisted of one or two ground-floor rooms and the upper-story space above. The open spaces onto which ground-floor doorways opened were an integral part of the household space; hearths occasionally occurred outside doorways, as did sun shades and other small structures.

Second, the Huamachuco polity most closely approximated a middle-range or chiefdom society, without a strong centralized authority. The evidence points to the presence in the southern Condebamba Basin of a number of lineages, each of which probably controlled land and other resources as a relatively autonomous corporate group. The lineages were undoubtedly ranked on the basis of size, power, productivity of resources controlled, and distance from supernatural ancestors. The relative rank and prestige of lineages vis-à-vis one another would certainly have been contested and shifting. There is no evidence at Marcahuamachuco of the kinds of markers that have been used elsewhere in the Andes as indicators of state-level complexity. There is no evidence of occupational specialization, centralized storage, or administrative architecture. There is no obvious evidence of differentiation in wealth or display in living quarters. Interpretation of status differences from burials is complicated by the frequency of secondary burial with no grave goods, as discussed later in the chapter.

Third, occupation of the site was probably seasonal. John Topic and I have estimated a maximum population for the site of 6,000, but there is insufficient arable land in the immediate vicinity to support so large a number year round; in addition, water resources at the site are very limited. It seems most likely that the number of people in residence in the domestic architecture at Marcahuamachuco fluctuated greatly, and that the population swelled at certain times of the year for major rituals and festivals. During much of the year many *huamachuquinos* were probably scattered about the valley and adjacent slopes in relatively small clusters of houses, near water, fields, and pastures.

Fourth, the Huamachuco area does not seem to have come under the political control of Huari in the Middle Horizon. Huari influence in the area is well documented in the early part of the Middle Horizon, most notably in the initiation of construction at Viracochapampa and in the presence of trade goods at Cerro Amaru (Topic 1991). Overall, however, the evidence points not to a military conquest or to economic domination but to the activities of traders and of religious pilgrims visiting the Cerro Amaru shrine (Topic and Topic 1992). There is considerable monumental construction at Marcahuamachuco in the Middle Horizon, but there is no a priori reason to attribute this phenomenon either to increasing centralization of indigenous authority within the Huamachuco polity or to Huari influence.

PHYSICAL CONTEXT

The site of Marcahuamachuco projects an exceptionally strong visual message. The individuals and groups who planned and built the various structures that make up the site were undoubtedly aware of the powerful effect they were creating. The site occupies the entire top of a southeast-northwest-trending plateau in the southern part of the Condebamba Valley (Figure 14.1). The plateau dominates the valley; it is an inescapable feature of the landscape, visible from up to 40 km away. The natural prominence of the plateau has been embellished by construction; the plateau edge is defined for most of its length by either a multistoried curvilinear gallery or a single tall masonry wall. In addition, the highest point on the plateau is accentuated by the construction of the Castillo, a massive, five-story-tall circular/spiral structure.

Viewed from any angle or distance in the valley, Marcahuamachuco sends clear messages of power, strength, and endurance. The site is also a visual statement of the relationship between humans and the earth: the colors, textures, and shapes of the built environment are a restatement of the natural environment. Marcahuamachuco as monument presents itself as a permanent part of the landscape, like the mountains themselves.

In terms of accessibility, the site is situated to serve the needs of the local population, not travelers. It is not on the north-south route that passes through the Condebamba Basin; today as in the past, one must go out of one's way to get to the site. The cliffs and steep slopes of the plateau also separate the site from the rest of the valley. Local people accustomed to the altitude can climb from the valley bottom to the plateau top in less than an hour. Still, it is a stiff climb that requires considerable effort.

Once the plateau top has been reached, the physical setting has a powerful impact. The air is thin and the wind blows continuously. Sounds carry from a great distance. Drums and flutes from fiestas in nearby hamlets below are clearly audible; a conch trumpet would probably be heard from 15 km away if the wind was right. Hawks hang motionless in the chasms beyond the plateau, riding the updrafts from the valley below. The night sky inspires awe as the Milky Way pivots over the site, with hundreds of thousands of intricate star patterns appearing extraordinarily bright and clear.

The horizon is distant, circular, and busy, consisting of a jagged perimeter of peaks. Several stand out for

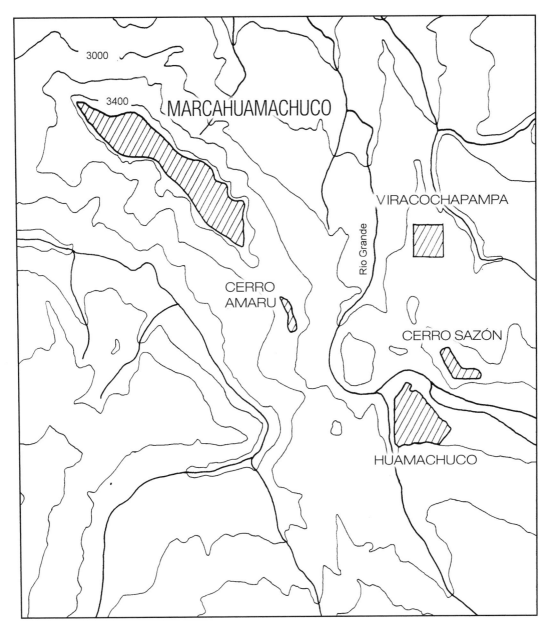

Figure 14.1. Map of the southern Condebamba Valley showing the location of Marcahuamachuco.

their unusual shape or color and are known to have figured prominently in prehispanic myth (San Pedro 1992 [1560], Topic 1992) and modern local folklore. The most noticeable feature on the horizon lies southeast of Marcahuamachuco. This is Cerro Huaylillas, the highest peak (4730 masl) in the vicinity and the most northerly in Peru to be snow-capped with any frequency. Visible beyond Huaylillas is Cerro Icchal, the peak on which the creator god of the huamachuquinos, Catequil, was considered to be present.

The daily cycle of day and night skies is even more spectacular here than at lower elevations. The sun rises very quickly, first casting a reddish glow on the highest peaks and gradually reaching down into lower canyons and slopes. Sunset is swift and extremely colorful, and from an open spot on the hilltop, the night sky is an overwhelming visual experience.

The extraordinary physical context of the plateau top produces a sense of a place that is out of the ordinary, transcending normal experience. In this setting the impact of ritual and ceremony would have been magnified, made more memorable, more profound. The physical landscape is palpable and present, and we can only begin to imagine the nonphysical landscape that lies over it, a spiritual landscape interweaving elements of myth, history, and cosmology that would have been discernible to every huamachuquino.

SPATIAL ORGANIZATION

The space on top of Marcahuamachuco made little sense to us in the first few seasons in the early 1980s as we looked for elite sectors, administrative structures, specialized storage complexes, a ceremonial precinct, and lower-class housing. Only gradually were the many contradictions resolved as we began to realize that in a very real sense, the entire site was ceremonial. Domestic residential zones were identified at the site, but the organizing principle was probably lineage affiliation, not class or occupation. Individual structures and complexes of buildings were dispersed on the plateau top, separated by surprising amounts of empty space. These open spaces served as buffers between individual structures and sectors. Their further significance became apparent only slowly, as we came to appreciate the concept of movement that explained patterns of doorways, gates, and vistas of natural and monumental phenomena.

Marcahuamachuco is best understood as an active stage set on which a series of performances was played out by groups of people continually moving, gathering, and dispersing. There is no close analogy in North American experience: a space or setting that combines elements of a very large family reunion, a state fair, and a papal mass in St. Peter's Square is perhaps an approximation. Complicating the interpretation is the fact that the pattern clearly evolved through time, moving toward greater centralization of spectacle, culminating in the construction of the Castillo in the center of the main ceremonial precinct.

A walk-through of the site begins in the northern sector, on Cerro de las Monjas (Figure 14.2). Here several circular galleries are located, all with considerable evidence of domestic occupation within. Each has a single principal entrance (the largest have one or two secondary entrances in addition). The principal entrance is not large or elaborate, but it leads directly into the interior patio. Excavation indicates domestic residence in the rooms around the patio, with hearths located sometimes inside rooms and sometimes outside rooms, and suggestions of food storage on the upper floor. Structures in the open patio itself are difficult to interpret; domestic refuse is found in them also, sometimes with a higher frequency of decorated or imported wares than in the gallery rooms proper. The patio rooms may have served as centers of entertainment or hospitality for the entire complex, not for preparing food and drink but for dispensing it (Beckwith 1990).

The circular galleries bespeak boundedness, separation, closed membership, and domesticity (Figure 14.3). We interpret them as the domestic and public space of specific lineages, used while the members were in residence at Marcahuamachuco.[3] The galleries vary considerably in area, volume, and elaborateness, suggesting that lineages were similarly varied in size and resources available to them.

The principal entrance of most circular galleries is oriented to the southeast, to the West Gate of Cerro del Castillo. Cerro del Castillo constitutes the southern half of the site and is considerably more built up than the northern half. The boundary walls and curvilinear galleries that define its limits are more massive than those in other sectors of the site. The West Gate is the principal entrance into Cerro del Castillo from the northern sector of the site (Figure 14.4). It is not an especially elaborate entrance, but it is massive and important.

To go from the circular galleries to the West Gate is a dramatic progression. One exits the safe enclosed space of the circular galleries onto a barren, windswept expanse of bedrock some 300 m wide. First one

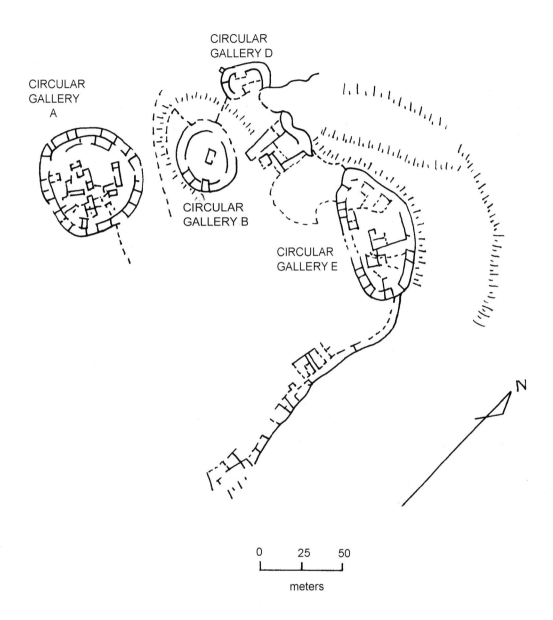

Figure 14.2. Plan of Cerro de las Monjas, Marcahuamachuco, with major circular galleries indicated.

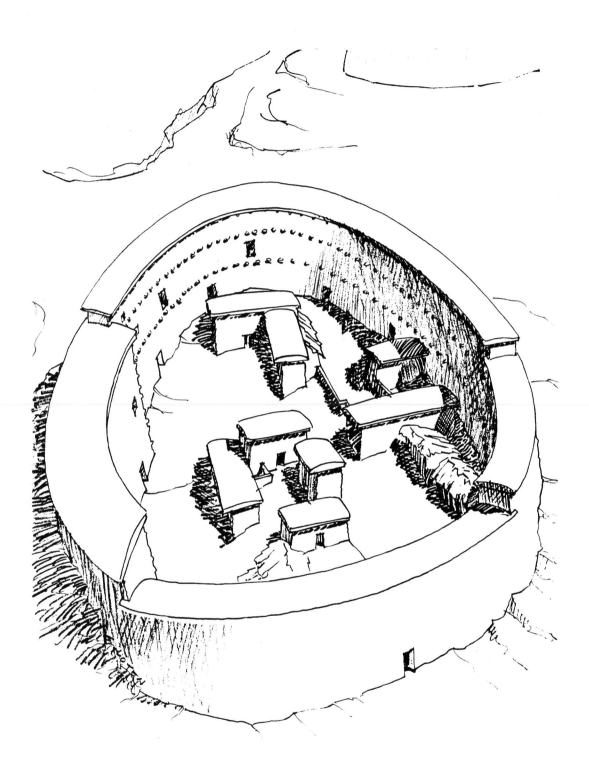

Figure 14.3. Drawing by Stan Loten of Circular Gallery A, Marcahuamachuco.

Figure 14.4. Drawing by Stan Loten of curvilinear gallery enclosing Cerro del Castillo with access through the West Gate. The view is southeast from Cerro de las Monjas.

Figure 14.5. View of the Castillo structure seen from road leading south from West Gate. Cerro Huaylillas is visible in the distance.

descends, then ascends, then passes through the gate no more than four abreast. Once inside the gate, more movement is necessary. One proceeds again a few hundred meters up a relatively steep slope; this is essentially vacant space. The eye is drawn to the horizon to the left and right, and to the long curvilinear galleries along the cliff edges. A sense of expectation rises as one nears the crest of the slope.

At the crest, both the Castillo and Cerro Huaylillas suddenly become visible, side by side on the horizon (Figure 14.5). In form, mass, and feel of rootedness and permanence, the Castillo is a restatement in the near distance of the peak visible behind it on the far horizon. The man-made and the natural have been aligned as a visual statement to the observer moving into the ceremonial core of the site.

Once one has reached the central part of Cerro del Castillo (Figure 14.6), there are two options. The individual or (more likely) group can go to a niched hall. There are ten or eleven of these dispersed around the Castillo Complex proper (Topic 1986). Some are rather small structures of a single story that simply provided a roofed space. Two of the examples, however, are quite sizable complexes, with a massive two-story roofed hall, a small patio or plaza in front, and smaller associated structures (Figure 14.7). These niched halls are gathering places where dozens (in the case of the small structures) or even hundreds (for the larger structures) can meet together.

Several lines of evidence have convinced us that each hall is built by a single lineage, to conduct rituals that honor lineage ancestors and reaffirm the solidarity of the group. Burials are rare at Marcahuamachuco, but human bone is frequently found in the walls of the niched halls,

often incorporated into the walls during construction (especially above lintels), and sometimes in rough niches in the walls. The bones were apparently placed without burial goods. No bones were found in undisturbed context, but judging by the size of wall openings and cut marks on some of the bones, it is likely that the burials were secondary. Floor contexts from niched halls produced high percentages of cups, spoons, and colanders and a higher than usual proportion of decorated wares. Feasting and drinking were important activities in the niched halls. The other material found in extraordinarily high concentrations in these rooms was cal (or lime); this material was often present in amorphous lumps, sometimes in rectangular blocks. We have yet to find a satisfactory explanation for the presence of the cal, but it is noteworthy that it, like human bone, did not occur in the circular galleries on Cerro de las Monjas or in the domestic areas of Cerro del Castillo.

There is a high degree of individuality in the niched halls. Their size and elaborateness vary, and there is also a great deal of differentiation in their orientation—in whether they look outward over the walls or inward to the Castillo, and in whether they seem designed to be "monumental" (i.e., highly visible) or not. These structures are not bounded, not placed in compounds. Most are simply dispersed about the foot of the Castillo. There is no way to move easily from one to another; access between the niched halls seems not to have been a consideration. Two niched halls, Gallery A and the Gallery B complex, are disproportionately large and, in the case of Gallery A, most ostentatiously sited, in direct line with the Castillo Complex. Here surely we see evidence of ranking of lineages and a conscious effort to make this ranking visible.

Figure 14.6. Drawing by Stan Loten of Gallery A, the largest of the niched halls on Cerro del Castillo.

The other option, once one is on Cerro del Castillo, is to proceed into the Castillo Complex proper. The Castillo Complex (see Figure 14.7) has a single restricted entrance that opens onto a large paved Great Plaza flanked by long rectangular galleries. From the Great Plaza, a rather tortuous passage can be made behind a set of niched halls that leads to the Small Plaza, from which access to the circular (actually, spiral) Castillo structure itself is possible.

The Great Plaza measures 50–60 m on a side, and would hold only a part of the 6,000 people that might have been in residence at the site. This is clearly a gathering space; ritual performance is suggested also by the elevation of the surrounding galleries above plaza level. This is clearest along the northern and western margins of the Great Plaza in front of Niched Halls P and M; both structures are elevated on terraces nearly 2 m high, and the offset between the terrace wall and structure wall leaves a stage-like platform facing the Great Plaza. The controlled access and formality of layout underscore the ritual importance of the Great Plaza and adjacent structures.

Access to the Castillo proper was even more controlled and limited. We assume that the Castillo structure was central to the group's religious and political ideology (as is often the case for structures that are central and preeminent at a site), but it is difficult to determine exactly what the Castillo symbolized and how it was intended to be used. The Castillo may

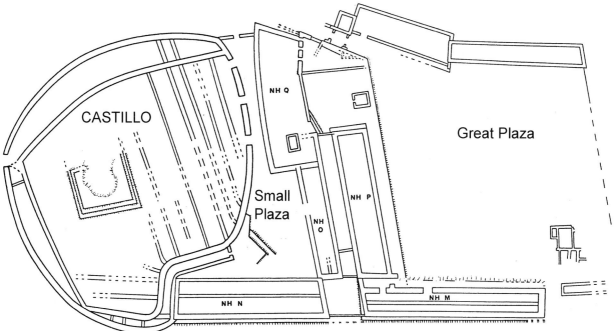

Figure 14.7. Plan of the Castillo complex at Marcahuamachuco.

have been planned to function as a three-dimensional space, but certainly one of the main motivations for its construction must have been the creation of a highly visible monument. The structure is a key feature of the built topography of the plateau visible from a great distance, and it is visually exciting from closer range. Its sheer scale inspires awe; during the Middle Horizon and Late Intermediate period it was the largest human-made feature in the northern sierra. The exterior of the Castillo was a smooth unbroken masonry façade with closely fitted stones expertly placed, unornamented and apparently unplastered.

The interior of the structure, however, was very complex. A series of parallel walls divides the Castillo into long narrow segments; projecting corbel stones on the long walls show these segments were intended to be provided with floors, up to five stories high. The lower floors would have received no light and little air; this is not utilizable space in the ordinary sense.

The Castillo structure was filled in soon after construction. Excavations here were difficult, as massive quantities of fill and fallen stone had to be removed to expose even a small patch of floor. One of two such patches cleared in 1988 had seventeen camelids and a pregnant woman deposited at floor level, but there was no evidence the room was used for any purpose other than the offering. The other segment of floor revealed by deep excavation was sterile.

It is difficult to specify the time at which Castillo was filled in, as the stratigraphy is complex and disturbed by twentieth-century looting. The nature of the fill and the cultural material contained suggests that the lower floors of parts of the structure were filled in very soon after construction, or even as it was built. The Castillo may well have been intended to function as a honeycombed structure like the main temple at Chavín de Huántar, and in fact there are doorways at ground level opening onto the passageway that leads to the Small Plaza. The plan may have been overly ambitious, however; the instability of the internal construction may have required considerable infilling.

Several stone slabs with low-relief and three-dimensional sculpture were found deposited in the fill in the Castillo and in the adjacent niched halls (Topic and Topic 1990: Figures 165 and 166). McCown (1945: Plates 16a, 17b–c) illustrates similar stones collected by Uhle in 1900, and one (McCown 1945: Plate 17a) photographed by Uhle was still on the site in 1989.[4] Some slabs had simple geometric designs, but several fragments had profile feline heads on angular serpent-like bands, very reminiscent of Pashash images (e.g., Grieder 1978: Figure 178). Two large slabs from fill in the Castillo each had a pair of very naturalistic parrots flanking a quadruped figure too badly damaged to identify; again, the birds were very similar to images recorded for the Cabana area (Grieder 1978: Figures 181, 184, 186). In each case the carving was restricted to a single face, which suggests that the blocks may have been incorporated into wall construction. The sacred and symbolic importance of the images is emphasized by their restriction to the Castillo and the immediately adjacent structures.

Despite its internal complexity, the Castillo seems to have been transformed into a masonry-faced mound. Parts of the top may have been visible from below, either from the Great Plaza, the Small Plaza, or other areas of the site. Structures atop the mound that housed sacred images or paraphernalia would have been accessible only to those individuals with the requisite training, pedigree, or experience.

One last point underlines the sacredness of the Castillo, beyond its central location, exclusivity, and sacrifices under the floor. This is the construction technique. Unlike the circular structures on Cerro de las Monjas, the Castillo was not built in sections; there are no vertical wall joints as there are in the circular galleries. Instead, building was continuous and unbroken, and seems to have proceeded in a spiral pattern. This technique was also used in those niched halls that have undergone close examination and underscores the importance of the construction and the desire for an integrated, unbroken building (Loten 2008).

LABOR ORGANIZATION AT MARCAHUAMACHUCO

Despite increasing diversity among archaeologists and anthropologists, there is a strong tendency for researchers to have been socialized within a Western social tradition that places a high value on individualism, regards manual labor as unrewarding, and assumes the inevitability of hierarchy in any endeavor involving more than a few people. Within this conceptual framework, the scale of construction at Marcahuamachuco constitutes unambiguous evidence for the presence of centralized authority and institutionalized coercion. It is very difficult for us to shed a Western framework and assess prehispanic monuments in indigenous terms.

Why build monuments? It pleases the gods. It keeps the world in balance. We honor the earth. We have always built monuments. The elders tell us to. The children need to learn.

Why perform hard labor to build a monument? It pleases the gods. It keeps the world in balance. It is pleasant to work with others. We eat and drink well when we are working together. We are proud of our work. The children need to learn.

Are these answers less valid than those we have traditionally put in the mouths of the people we study? The classic archaeological responses to these questions are phrased in terms of cost, investment, coercion, fear, mystification, and power. But these responses say far more about the modern world than about the prehistoric world.

We would do better to find alternative frameworks within which to evaluate the cultural contexts of Andean monuments. Useful insights into how Andean peoples were organized, motivated, and rewarded for participation in monument construction and maintenance can be gained from observation of the indigenous fiestas and cooperative labor efforts that continue in many parts of the Andes to the present day. These traditional events are strong reminders of the efficacy of the authority exercised by lineage headmen and community elders, and of the power of group consensus and expectation to elicit proper behavior from individuals.

Our interpretation of Marcahuamachuco has certainly been shaped by our observation of the festival of the Virgen de Alta Gracia, a month-long celebration in Huamachuco that brings visitors from as far away as Lima and requires the collaboration of people from all the surrounding countryside (Topic 1994). The various events, rituals, and tasks performed over the course of the fiesta dramatize and make explicit the social structure of the region; the contrasts between men and women, young and old, campesinos and townspeople, powerful and powerless, and the geographic divisions of the basin are highlighted and reaffirmed.

The fiesta period is welcomed by all as a break from routine and as an opportunity to socialize much more widely than normal. Religious fervor can find expression; devotees of different saints and followers of particular spiritual practices compete with one another to show their dedication. A great deal of physical labor is carried out, under the rather tenuous authority of older men. This labor produces tangible physical results of various sorts, but it is only one aspect of the intense interaction, negotiation, and performance that occupies the entire population for the month of August.

The monuments at Marcahuamachuco were probably the result of similar bouts of intensified interaction. The people who built Marcahuamachuco over several centuries were not coerced into laboring by the threat of sanctions or reprisals. The construction was a creative and cooperative process by which the participants defined the parameters of their social, mythic, and physical world.

CONCLUSIONS

I suggest that all of Marcahuamachuco is "monumental," designed to inspire awe in observers. The monuments at Marcahuamachuco were the physical setting for a cycle of ritual activity that took place at several different levels of integration within the group. The physical evidence does not allow us to reconstruct the kinds of ritual carried out at Marcahuamachuco in any detail, although we get tantalizing clues from the first written report on the area (San Pedro 1992 [1560], J. Topic 1992).[5] However the ancient Marcahuamachuco ritual cycle was structured, we can be sure that ritual was integrative, providing an opportunity for the reaffirmation of the traditional ties between individuals and groups within Huamachuco society. The rituals celebrated would also be explanatory, presenting a model of the world as the huamachuquinos understood it; myth, history, geography, and cosmology would be recounted and acted out in various venues, with the impact of the explanation heightened by the physical setting of the site and the break with the normal daily cycle of activities. And the site suggests that the ritual would have been in large part participatory. The site is not laid out like a Greek amphitheater, with clear lines drawn between performers and audience. The spatial organization of structures and open areas at Marcahuamachuco implies the active participation of huamachuquinos in the performance and creation of the rituals that explained their world.

The ritual cycle embodied in the Marcahuamachuco architecture must have been adaptive. Prehistoric Andean societies seem to have been particularly successful in resolving the contradictions that inevitably arise when the needs of individuals and small groups, such as households and lineages, are juxtaposed with the political and economic needs and demands of the institutions that arise and become more complex through time. The strength of Andean society lay in its participatory nature. Andean institutions allowed the participation and collaboration of small groups even when the society as a whole had become very complex. Much decision making was left at the local or lineage level, and this resistance to centralization provided a structural strength that helps to account for the persistence of traditional organization through time.

Acknowledgments

Work was generously funded by the Social Sciences and Humanities Research Council of Canada and by the Trent University Committee on Research, Trent University, Peterborough, Ontario. Permission for the work was granted by the Instituto Nacional de Cultura, Lima. I am most grateful to the many Canadian, Peruvian, American, and other students and volunteers who assisted on the project over the years. In 1986, 1987, and 1989 the Project collaborated with the Huamachuco Architectural Project, directed by Dr. H. Stanley Loten of the School of Architecture, Carleton University, Ottawa.

NOTES

1. Some of this documentation is available in preliminary reports that have been prepared and circulated over the years (e.g., Loten 1987; Topic and Topic 1987) as well as in articles (Topic 1986; Topic and Topic 1990) and theses (Beckwith 1990).

2. Stan Loten (2008) first articulated this important distinction in 1987.

3. The circular galleries are not the only residential areas at the site; the curvilinear galleries that border Cerro del Castillo provided a similar kind of space. The location of some residences outside the walls and others within may be a reflection of dual organization of the lineages constituting the Huamachuco polity.

4. The massive rectangular block is carved to represent a stylized feline face. For many years it was kept (upside down) in a small building on the site that served as a chapel or shrine. Local residents say that candles were burned in the eyes, and offerings were placed in the triangle representing the mouth or nose. The local residents attempted to move the sculpture in 1987, but it slipped off the poles on which it was being carried and injured a man's foot. This was taken to be a bad omen, and the sculpture was abandoned.

5. The Primeros Agustinos account (San Pedro 1992) describes rituals that involved the setting up of a large pole,

sacrifice of cuis (cuyes) [guinea pigs] to the pole, and considerable drinking and dancing. There are many continuities with current practice.

REFERENCES

Beckwith, Laurie
1990   The Function of the Circular Galleries at Marcahuamachuco, Peru. Master's thesis, Department of Anthropology, Trent University, Peterborough, Ontario.

Bourget, Steve
2001   Rituals of Sacrifice: Its Practice at Huaca de la Luna and Its Representation in Moche Iconography. In *Moche Art and Archaeology in Ancient Peru*, edited by Joanne Pillsbury, pp. 89–110. National Gallery of Art, Washington, DC.

Burger, Richard, and Lucy Salazar-Burger
1980   Ritual and Religion at Huaricoto. *Archaeology* 33:26–32.
1991   The Second Season of Investigations at the Initial Period Center of Cardal, Peru. *Journal of Field Archaeology* 18(3):275–296.

Erasmus, Charles
1965   Monument Building: Some Field Experiments. *Southwestern Journal of Anthropology* 21:277–301.

Feldman, Robert A.
1983   From Maritime Chiefdom to Agricultural State in Formative Coastal Peru. In *Civilization in the Ancient Americas: Essays in Honor of Gordon R. Willey*, edited by Richard M. Leventhal and Alan L. Kolata, pp. 289–310. University of New Mexico Press, Albuquerque.

Grieder, Terence
1978   *The Art and Archaeology of Pashash*. University of Texas Press, Austin.

Hastings, Charles M., and Michael E. Moseley
1975   The Adobes of Huaca del Sol and Huaca de la Luna. *American Antiquity* 40:196–203.

Lathrap, Donald W.
1985   Jaws: The Control of Power in the Early Nuclear American Ceremonial Center. In *Early Ceremonial Architecture in the Andes*, edited by Christopher B. Donnan, pp. 241–267. Dumbarton Oaks, Washington, DC.

Leone, Mark P., Parker B. Potter, Jr., and Paul A. Shackel
1987   Toward a Critical Archaeology. *Current Anthropology* 28(3):283–302.

Loten, H. Stanley

1987   *Burial Tower 2 and Fort A, Marcahuamachuco*. Trent University Occasional Papers in Anthropology, no. 3. Trent University, Peterborough, Ontario.

2008   Pre-Incaic Architectural Form and Constructional Technique at Marcahuamachuco, Peru. Unpublished manuscript.

McCown, Theodore

1945   Pre-Incaic Huamachuco: Survey and Excavations in the Region of Huamachuco and Cajabamba. *University of California Publications in American Archaeology and Ethnology*, vol. 29, pp. 223–99. University of California Press, Berkeley and Los Angeles

Moseley, Michael E.

1975   *The Maritime Foundations of Andean Civilization*. Cummings Publishing Co., Menlo Park, CA.

1985   The Exploration and Explanation of Early Monumental Architecture in the Andes. In *Early Ceremonial Architecture in the Andes*, edited by Christopher B. Donnan, pp. 29–57. Dumbarton Oaks, Washington, DC.

Patterson, Thomas C.

1986   The Last Sixty Years: Toward a Social History of Americanist Archaeology in the United States. *American Anthropologist* 88(1):7–26.

Pozorski, Shelia, and Thomas Pozorski

1992   Early Civilization in the Casma Valley, Peru. *Antiquity* 66(253):845–870.

Pozorski, Thomas

1976   *Caballo Muerto: A Complex of Early Ceramic Sites in the Moche Valley, Peru*. Unpublished doctoral dissertation. Department of Anthropology, University of Texas, Austin.

San Pedro, Juan de

1992 [1560] *La persecución del demonio: Crónica de los primeros agustinos en el norte del Perú*. Manuscrito del Archivo de Indias, transcribed by Eric E. Deeds. Algazara, C.A.M.E.I. Málaga, México.

Schaedel, Richard P.

1952   Major Ceremonial and Population Centers in Northern Peru. *The Civilizations of Ancient America: Selected Papers of the XXIXth International Congress of Americanists*, edited by Sol Tax, vol. 1, pp. 232–243.

Shanks, Michael, and Christopher Tilley

1989   Archaeology into the 1990s. *Norwegian Archaeological Review* 22(1):1–54.

Silverman, Helaine

1990   The Early Nasca Pilgrimage Center of Cahuachi and the Nazca Lines: Archaeological and Anthropological Perspectives. In *The Lines of Nazca*, edited by Anthony Aveni, pp. 209–244. American Philosophical Society, Philadelphia.

Squier, E. George

1973 [1877] *Peru: Incidents of Travel and Exploration in the Land of the Incas*. AMS Press, New York.

Topic, John R.

1986   A Sequence of Monumental Architecture from Huamachuco. In *Perspectives on Andean Prehistory and Protohistory*, edited by Daniel H. Sandweiss and D. Peter Kvietok, pp. 63–83. Cornell University Latin American Studies Program, Ithaca, NY.

1991   Huari and Huamachuco. In *Huari Administrative Structure: Prehistoric Monumental Architecture and State Government*, edited by William Isbell and Gordon McEwan, pp. 63–83. Dumbarton Oaks, Washington, DC.

1992   Las huacas de Huamachuco: Precisiones en torno a un imagen indígena de un paisaje andino. In *La persecución del demonio: Crónica de los primeros agustinos en el norte del Perú*, edited by Fray Juan de San Pedro, pp. 41–99. Algazara, C.A.M.A.I., Málaga-México.

1994   El izamiento del gallardete en Huamachuco. In *En el Nombre del Señor: Shamanes, demonios, y curanderos del norte del Perú*, edited by Luis Millones and M. Lemlij, pp. 102–127. SIDEA Ediciones, Biblioteca Peruana de Psicoanálisis, no. 19. Lima.

Topic, John R., and Theresa Lange Topic

1990   Recherches Récents à Huamachuco. In *Inca—Perú: 3000 ans d'histoire*, edited by Sergio Purin, pp. 210–222. Musées Royaux d'Art et d'Histoire, Bruxelles.

1992   The Rise and Decline of Cerro Amaru: An Andean Shrine during the Early Intermediate Period and Middle Horizon. In *Ancient Images, Ancient Thought: The Archaeology of Ideology*, pp. 167–180. Chacmool Conference, University of Calgary.

Topic, Theresa Lange

1982   The Early Intermediate Period and Its Legacy. In *Chan Chan: Andean Desert City*, edited by Michael E. Moseley and Kent C. Day, pp. 255–284. University of New Mexico Press, Albuquerque.

Topic, Theresa Lange, and John R. Topic

1987   *Huamachuco Archaeological Project: Preliminary Report on the 1986 Field Season*. Trent University Occasional Papers in Anthropology, no. 4. Trent University, Peterborough, Ontario, Canada.

Trigger, Bruce

1991   Distinguished Lecture in Archeology: Constraint and
        Freedom. *American Anthropologist* 93(3):551–569.

Uceda, Santiago

2001   Investigations at Huaca de la Luna, Moche Valley:
        An Example of Moche Religious Architecture. In
        Moche Art and Archaeology in Ancient Peru, edited by
        Joanne Pillsbury, pp. 47–68. National Gallery of Art,
        Washington, DC.

Urton, Gary

1990   Andean Social Organization and the Maintenance
        of the Nazca Lines. In *The Lines of Nazca*, edited by
        Anthony F. Aveni, pp. 175–206. American Philo-
        sophical Society, Philadelphia.

Willey, Gordon R.

1948   Functional Analysis of "Horizon Styles" in Peruvian
        Archaeology. In *A Reappraisal of Peruvian Archaeology*,
        edited by Wendell C. Bennett, pp. 8–15. Memoirs
        of the Society for American Archaeology, no. 4. Salt
        Lake City.

CHAPTER 15

WARI POLITICAL ORGANIZATION

THE SOUTHERN PERIPHERY

DONNA J. NASH AND PATRICK RYAN WILLIAMS

ICHAEL MOSELEY'S 1981 DISCOVERY of the
southernmost Wari city at Cerro Baúl opened
a new chapter in the research on the early
Andean highland states. This city, established on a high
mesa in the upper Moquegua drainage around AD 600,
represented a forceful and unique statement of Wari
colonization. Understanding this intrusion—the placement of a colony of Wari loyalists in the Moquegua
Valley—will enable us to understand the nature of the
Wari polity in particular, and the nature of expansive
states in general. Furthermore, the Moquegua colonial
sites are relatively well preserved and good examples of
settlements under direct imperial control.

In this chapter, we describe the political organization
of the Wari colony in the upper Moquegua Valley and
demonstrate how nodes in the sociopolitical hierarchy
were linked in three ways: through shared patterns of
sociopolitical activity, the distribution of luxury goods,
and the circulation of commodities. Previous scholarship examining the Wari capital in Ayacucho and its
provincial installations throughout the Andean sierra has
established links between particular Wari building types
and state administrative practices (e.g., Spickard 1983;
Isbell and McEwan 1991; Schreiber 1992). We build on
these findings to compare administration at several levels
of the political hierarchy and to address two important
questions: How can archaeological remains demonstrate

whether or not the Wari Empire controlled a group of
people? How can we discover the ways that people under
Wari hegemony articulated with the state?

To answer these two questions, we will demonstrate
that identifying the archaeological remains of the Wari
political economy is integral to understanding the
organization and extent of Wari control throughout the
Andes. We present evidence linking patterns of activity
at a Wari provincial center, Cerro Baúl, with those in
smaller settlements, and chart the flow of certain goods
to show the connections between household laborers
and state resources. The material manifestations of
connections between the state and subject populations
were not uniform throughout the empire; however, the
methodology used to make these linkages in the upper
Moquegua drainage can be applied to other regions.

The vast Wari Empire may have extended for more
than 1,000 km of the Andean cordillera. The empire
expanded out of its Ayacucho heartland rather quickly,
establishing control over many areas and pulling
resources to the center from a diverse set of econiches
ranging from the northern highlands to the south coast
of Peru (Figure 15.1). Regional resources and political
complexity varied a great deal from province to province.
Archaeological materials from these different provinces
also exhibit considerable stylistic diversity, which has
generated conflicting inferences about the extent of

Wari control. Some scholars have suggested that Wari was not an empire or a unified political entity (Shady and Ruiz 1979; Topic and Topic 1992, 2000). Others have suggested that the Wari did not control a contiguous territory but rather a mosaic of places, only some of which were under direct control (Schreiber 1992). Many archaeologists agree that the Wari controlled areas where they built provincial complexes, but these scholars hesitate to characterize the kind of relationship the empire had with those groups and regions where no Wari installations are found. Thus, it remains to be seen how the provincial installations operated and how far Wari hegemony extended. We would like to determine the radius of their control.

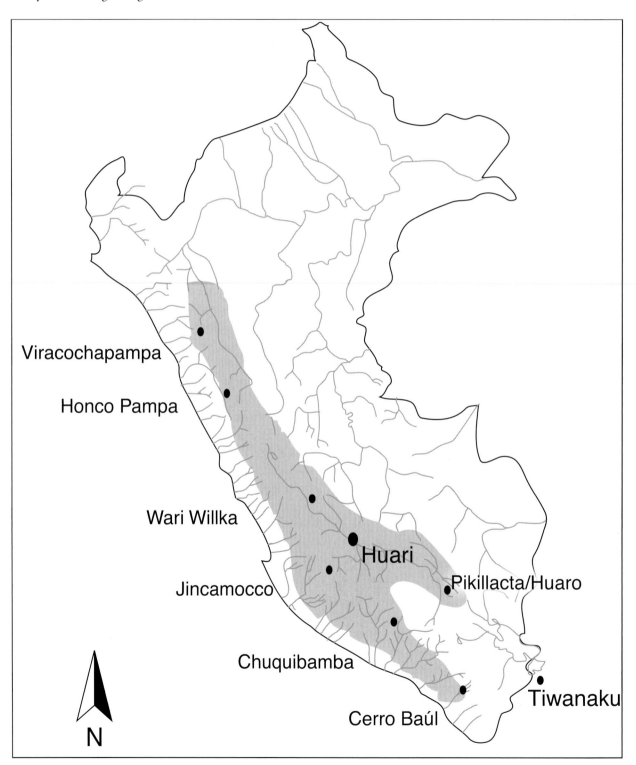

Figure 15.1. Wari influence across Peru.

Provincial administrative centers with standardized components are the most striking and recognizable pan-imperial features. These complexes are in fact what first led to the identification of a pre-Inca sierra empire (Rowe et al. 1956). The notable uniformity of their monumental complexes reflects not only a standardization of measurements (Schreiber 1992) but, more important, a unified set of principles applied to the spatial organization of structures related to state-sponsored activities, most likely reflecting a counterpart or local version of state-imposed institutions (see Nash and Williams 2004). Regardless of the similarities in layout of certain components within provincial centers, no two Wari administrative centers exhibit identical plans (Schreiber 1992; Nash 2002), and the same can be said for the later Inca Empire (Morris 1985; Hyslop 1990). Similarly, artifacts affiliated with the Wari cultural complex, such as decorated ceramic vessels, vary a great deal between provincial centers and have raised doubt about the extent to which these regions were unified under a central administration (see Morris 1982, 1995).

These differences are not surprising and can be linked to several factors. Politically, different kinds of relations must have existed between Wari state officials and regional or local leaders. The preexisting level of social complexity and the size of these polities may have been significant, but equally important was the degree of hostility, cooperation, or relative prestige of regional elites before Wari co-option (see Menzel 1959; Pease 1982; Schreiber 1992; Julien 1993). Wari notions of value and local notions of value may have been at odds as well. Furthermore, Wari concerns with the production and control of status items or the need for certain goods for sacred practice could have determined regional production goals, imperial extraction goals, and the political organization of a particular province (see Levine 1992). Additionally, the organization of specialized local production may have been left intact or transplanted to other areas of the hegemony with similar resources (see Rowe 1982). Preexisting ethnic divisions may have been respected (see Julien 1982; Pease 1982). The character and treatment of each province may have been dictated by the perceived rights or prerogatives of the Wari ruling elite and local elite groups (see Carrasco 1982:30; Alonso 1994:391). The relative importance of maintaining positive relations or the need to defend against border incursions could affect frontier areas, transforming these distant regions of multiethnic overlap into centers of interaction and arenas of culture change and innovation rather than marginal or passive peripheries (see Patterson 1987; Lightfoot and Martinez 1995).

The evidence presented in this chapter is specific to Moquegua, and we recognize that several political, economic, and ideological factors came together to create a unique set of material manifestations representing Wari control in this region. Wari officials in most instances were responding to local institutions, co-opting regional notions of value, and coordinating with indigenous leaders at some level. Combined together, these autochthonous factors may have affected the style of certain luxury goods and the ubiquity of desirable commodities imported into the region through avenues of imperial distribution. Nevertheless, if the Wari controlled a particular region, we would expect that control to be detectable in material remains reflecting links between the capital, the provincial centers, and smaller regional settlements. These material correlates, however, must be carefully identified, and artifacts carrying overt corporate symbols or those emulating classic styles may not be the best with which to document and confirm existing relations of control (Stanish 1989, 1992).

In all regions under Wari control, some kind of sociopolitical interactions were required to connect state administrators to local labor and resources. These activities, in effect, were the source of state power. Reconstructing sociopolitical relations requires a detailed database and the convergence of many lines of information representing the nature of interaction and the suite of activities broadly affiliated with supporting successful relations. Together, all these activities—those related to establishing and negotiating the relative power between groups in a society—can be considered its political economy (see Friedrich 1989).

POLITICAL ECONOMY IN THE ANDES

To answer the specific questions posed earlier in this chapter, we will try to model the political economy. That is not to say that we interpret the relationship between Wari leaders and their followers as purely one of resource extraction. However, in this chapter we are interested in constructing a model of the rather complex web of social relations between Wari provincial officials and subordinate groups. We view the political economy as consisting of the practices and activities performed to establish and negotiate the political order, goods exchanged both as gifts and tribute as part of these relations, and the production and consumption associated with commensal politics, status items, tribute goods, and commodities. The material focus of our analysis is necessary if we want to chart the links between groups in Wari society and use artifacts and their contexts to define patterns of activity and the connections between the producers and consumers within the system.

The concept of political economy is typically associated with capitalist economies and derives largely from a Marxist perspective that looks at the articulations between classes in a complex society (Roseberry 1988). It has been successfully applied to the ancient Andes despite the apparent absence of a market economy (D'Altroy and Earle 1985; Stanish 1992; Kolata 2003).

From the perspective of our research, we hope to uncover changes in the household production of Moquegua Valley groups after they were incorporated into Wari society and its larger economy. Since the Wari colony was an intrusive set of settlements and there is little to no evidence of prior occupation of the upper Moquegua drainage, there is no "before" to which the Wari "after" can be compared. Theoretically, all activities were essentially part of the Wari state's political economy because the colonial settlements were an artificial construct designed by Wari state officials to reproduce the Wari state.

In other state-level societies, the term *political economy* can be used to describe basic productive activities that broadly support the polity and its members (see D'Altroy and Earle 1985; Kolata 2003). All economic potential or productive opportunities are determined by the political organization and the possibilities and constraints produced by the overarching polity (Yoffee 1995). In this chapter, however, we adopt a narrower focus and identify specific spheres of production that were essential to establishing and maintaining political power beyond the basic subsistence needs of colonists and administrators. Additionally, we do not accept the Wallersteinian notion that all changes in the political system are initiated in the core. Ethnographic and archaeological study of the Inca Empire suggests that the central administration may have adopted ideas and resources from conquered polities (Moseley 1985; Rostworowski 1999). We take the view that change in a particular province may stimulate change in the core. Also, changes in the organization of polities on the frontiers or relations with peer polities outside the empire can provide an impetus for transformation (see Lightfoot and Martinez 1995). One of the significant

characteristics of a multiethnic empire is that the parts have their own dialectical trajectories (see Morris 1985), and thus rapid transformations in one province may affect the whole or other provinces in different ways (see Sinopoli 1994).

Thus, setting aside some assumptions that have been subsumed under the term *political economy* (such as world systems theory), we pursue here the idea that the economy is embedded in social relations (Polanyi 1957; Carrasco 1982; Stanish 1992; Janusek 1999). It is important to emphasize that we conceive of productive pursuits, such as the intensification of agricultural production, household production of tribute or exchange goods, workshop production of luxury exports, and other facets of the political economy, as actions in support of the sociopolitical reproduction of individuals, lineages, ethnic enclaves, local polities, and the overarching imperial polity. They are efforts to garner power and influence and are not necessarily engineered to accumulate wealth. Thus, one can acquire political capital to some degree (see Bourdieu 1977) and experience a political profit via a relative increase in prestige, as well as accomplish a successful conversion of foodstuffs into more valuable goods (see Dietler 2001). However, these illusory gains cannot necessarily be stored or hoarded like gold. These status items hold value only as they are displayed and redistributed or exchanged as gifts within the sphere of sociopolitical relations. Perhaps D'Altroy and Earle best explain this particular concept of wealth in the context of the precontact nonmarket Andean economy:

> The wealth was primarily important because of its symbolic use to define and legitimize status distinctions. It validated status positions associated with explicit rights to staple goods from the staple-finance system. The central control of many forms of wealth, as "political currency", translated not into direct access to subsistence goods in the market but into indirect access through control over land and labor. (D'Altroy and Earle 1985:203)

Thus, labor inputs and apparent resource gains in many parts of the ancient Andes cannot easily be interpreted by economic analogy, and it is important to stay away from capitalist notions (e.g., cost, profit, investment); these resource gains or advantages should be interpreted as a form of "political currency" in a dynamic, dialectical, context-relative political system.

MATERIAL ELEMENTS OF THE POLITICAL ECONOMY

The political economy as we have defined it consists of several activities: (1) sociopolitical interactions between individuals and groups, (2) productive activities that are necessary to create the goods exchanged at these gatherings or the food prepared and served at these venues, and (3) the consumption of goods imported to support positive relations between Wari officials and subordinate groups. The Wari occupation in Moquegua was managed through a provincial center built at Cerro Baúl, which was connected to the capital through the flow of status goods and portable commodities. State sponsorship of these political interactions is represented by the use of a similar built environment, the use of Wari status emblems, and state-controlled commodities—especially obsidian. The Wari presence is most evident around the provincial center of Cerro Baúl; however, the size of public facilities implies that much remains to be discovered in the region (Figure 15.2). The full extent of Wari power and control in the south-central Andes remains to be identified by recognizing common elements of the political economy.

The Built Environment. Space is defined by action (Rapoport 1990). In modern practice we apply labels to spaces based on groups of activities or categories of action that take place within different structures of the built environment. Spaces are designed as settings, usually with a particular suite of activities in mind, and can be built in ways that encourage or restrict behavior (Norberg-Schulz 1985). Taken together, the design of a built environment and the artifacts, remains, and traces of activities found within a space provide a good idea of which behaviors were conducted within a structure and how a particular venue may have played a role in the political economy. Understanding the use of space in many contexts reveals clusters of patterned behaviors representative of sociopolitical relations (Paynter 1989; Moore 1996; Nash 2002; Nash and Williams 2005).

Emblems of Status. Status goods can come in many varieties. All are diacritical in that their display, use, or distribution marks a group or individual as prestigious or powerful. In many instances these goods are ornamented with emblems that represent state ideology, religious iconography, or related motifs; some undecorated items, however, are equally valued in ancient economies. For example, certain raw materials hold special value or symbolism because of their color or other attributes; examples are jade and obsidian

in Mesoamerica (Saunders 2001). Also, the source of production or distribution can imbue an object with prestige (Morris 1986; Costin 1993, 1998).

Many of these goods can be identified because of their rarity, quality of production, or high labor input. Undecorated goods are harder to categorize, but by identifying the production locus of particular goods and thus the source of their distribution, researchers may assess the relative value of an object in a political system. In many ancient states, laws were instituted to reserve the use and ownership of certain goods to particular categories of people (Berdan 1987; Peregrine 1991; Costin 1998). Sumptuary laws may also be applied to elements of cuisine or aspects of architectural elaboration, and so we should broaden our definition of status goods to incorporate these important elements in the negotiation and display of power.

Commodities. Commodities are objects that have a use value but that can also be exchanged for other things (Kopytoff 2001). In a nonmarket economy such as existed in the central Andean sierra, exchanges were a significant part of successful strategies. The archaeological record demonstrates that long-distance exchanges were significant to the political economy. Long-term research on obsidian, its sources, and its distribution through time demonstrates that obsidian was mobilized in a unique way during the Middle Horizon (Burger et al. 2000). Research at the Wari capital in Ayacucho demonstrates that obsidian had a special place in the imperial political economy (Stone 1983). The level at which this particular material was mobilized by the Wari suggests that this good, among others, acted as a commodity in Wari society.

WARI CONTEXTS IN MOQUEGUA

For this study, elements of the political economy were teased out of a broad data set through a comparative analysis of household activities at several levels in the sociopolitical hierarchy (see Nash 2002). We describe the most conclusive material correlates of the political economy and relationships between sociopolitical groups; however, many elements of the Wari political economy in the region remain to be defined.

The data are drawn from extensive horizontal excavations on Cerro Baúl and the adjacent Cerro Mejía. Dwellings from small patches of residential terraces have also been sampled. This work has revealed the differences in the basic house structures and three

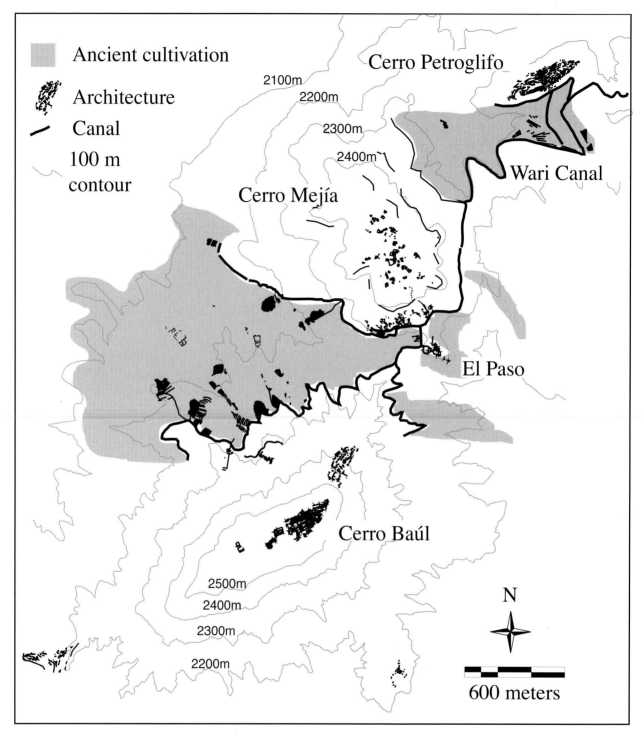

Figure 15.2. The Wari colony in Moquegua.

Table 15.1. Material markers of the Wari political economy.

	Architectural Features/Forms	Portable Objects	Evidence of Wari Control
High-level administration (provincial): Cerro Baúl			
	Monumentality	Luxury/rare goods	Architectural similarity
	Platforms	Symbols of rank	Iconographic similarity
	D-shaped structures	Diverse goods	Centrally distributed commodities
	Storage facilities	Serving pitchers	(obsidian)
	Food/*chicha* preparation area	Bowls and cups	
	Patio/plazas with benches	Feast remains	
Mid-level administration (town or large village): Cerro Mejía			
	Semi-monumentality	Rare goods	Architectural similarity
	Platforms	Symbols of rank	Iconographic similarity
	Patio/plazas with benches	Diverse goods	Centrally distributed commodities
	Storage facilities	Serving pitchers	(obsidian)
	Food/*chicha* preparation area	Bowls and cups	
		Feast remains	
Low-level administration (small village or barrio): Cerro Mejía			
	Remodeling	Diverse goods	Centrally distributed commodities
	Space with curved wall	Serving pitchers	(obsidian)
	Food preparation area	Bowls and cups	
		Feast remains	

levels of administration represented by different scales of sociopolitical relations. Table 15.1 shows the material remains associated with the different levels in the political hierarchy.

At the highest level, Cerro Baúl, the administrative features are obvious and a significant part of the built environment. At the mid-level, the features are less grand but easy to identify. At the lowest level, consisting of managers who labored themselves and supervised their kin or neighbors, administration was recognized only as it stood apart from normal household domestic patterns and exhibited commonalities with features at higher levels of the political economy (Nash 2002). The following sections describe the elements of the political economy at three different levels of state administration and compare these material correlates with a commoner household.

The Provincial Political Economy

Use of Space. On Cerro Baúl, Wari provincial governors used a number of building types to manage people and resources under their control (Figure 15.3). Several of these important political settings lie outside residential complexes. Platforms are prominent architectural features. This is no surprise, insofar as Wari iconography often displays the primary deity standing on a tiered platform. On the western edge of the summit there is a large tiered platform, approximately 20 m². It lies on one side of a rectangular sunken court and across from a larger terraced ovoid mound. These two monuments have

staircases that align with one another and are oriented to the distant snow-capped peak of Picchu Picchu to the north (Williams and Nash 2006). This zone was a place for public ceremony and performance. The size and location of this monument suggest it was reserved for a select group witnessing and performing ceremonial acts.

Platforms are also associated with administrative buildings. Unit 3 is a large enclosure with a rectangular room along the east wall and a cluster of four storage rooms near the west wall (Williams 2001). Limited excavations in the patio suggest there was a wide bench or platform fronting the eastern rectangular room. The room and associated platform may have provided a control point for an administrator in charge of these resources. Unit 9, an elite residential context, also has an elevated rectangular space that can be classified as a platform. It overlooks a bench-lined patio. All these platform constructions symbolize the elevated positions of presiding officials and were visual cues communicating the social order.

The summit of Cerro Baúl has a pair of D-shaped temples, each of which open to the northwest onto a plaza. Lying within walled compounds, both temples are surrounded by clusters of associated rooms. The D-shaped spaces themselves (Unit 5, 10 m, and Unit 10, 11.5 m in diameter) are not significantly large spaces for many people to interact in. The front plaza may have functioned to accommodate individuals at the beginning of an important rite, but they evidently were not permitted to participate in the entire ritual because it took

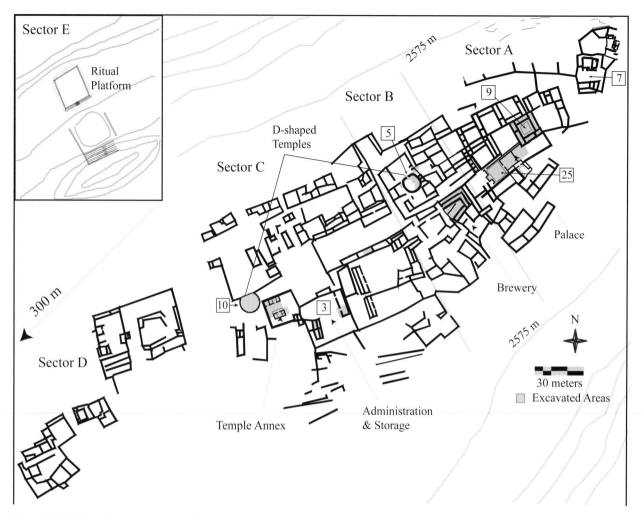

Figure 15.3. Wari settlement on Cerro Baúl.

place in a more restricted setting where few people could witness it. Niches in the walls of the D-shaped structures may have been important for the display of sacred objects or ancestral bundles. Control of ritual reinforced the power hierarchy (see Nash and Williams 2005).

The elite residential sector is divided into several large compounds that contain a variety of spaces; these are composed of at least one Wari patio group (see Isbell 1991 for the description of a typical Wari patio group). In the past few years we have uncovered several structures within one of these monumental residences. Unit 9, an elaborate version of a patio-group residence, has rectangular rooms on three sides and an elevated open area, or platform, to the east. The entire floor of Unit 9 is paved with flagstones. The central patio, approximately 10 m², has a wide bench running along all four sides. The structure was ritually abandoned and contained smashed vessels and varied faunal remains representing a grand feast on the patio floor. Residential

spinning and other activities, represented by spindle whorls and other tools, were apparent in the rectangular rooms; the smallest room, however, was extremely clean and may have served as a residential *huaca*, or ritual space. In comparison with other house contexts in the sample, this entire structure was very clean.

Unit 25, a plaza within the same palatial complex, is 12 m² and has benches along all four sides of the plaza. A broad recessed seating area is centrally located in the west wall. This special niche may have been reserved as a focus for this gathering space, a place of honor for presiding officials or the revered dead. Remains of smashed bowls and serving vessels, including bowl fragments from as far away as Cajamarca (a distance of approximately 1,300 km), suggest this was an important venue for elite gatherings, gifting, and feasting activity. The bulk of the materials are still under analysis; however, all appear to be generally similar to materials recovered from Unit 9.

Units 9 and 25 appear to be two different kinds of places within a single elite residence structured to facilitate gatherings. The interactions in these two spaces may have been qualitatively different in some way. The benches are evidence that the structures were designed for social interaction. Both spaces contain artifacts that have been associated with feasting; however, the materials recovered from these two contexts appear to be elements of a ritual deposition rather than refuse resulting from normal activities conducted in these spaces.

Areas for the preparation of food and chicha do provide evidence that feasting was a significant and regular activity in this palatial complex on Cerro Baúl. Unit 7 is an open rectangular terrace and adjoining patio. This area was used as a specialized zone for the preparation of foodstuffs. This space seems to be part of a larger zone that made meals and feasts for the elites living in the more elaborate structures of the monumental compound, and thus was a facility integral to supporting the political activities hosted in the complex. Since Unit 9 had only one ephemeral hearth (which may or may not have been used for food preparation), such subsidiary facilities would have been crucial to support state-sponsored gatherings with colonial elites or foreign dignitaries (see Moseley et al. 2005).

Emblems of Status. Ceramic vessels exhibiting iconography and more abstract motifs affiliated with the Wari heartland have been unearthed in just a few contexts on Cerro Baúl. These decorated wares are almost always found smashed in ritualized deposits associated with the termination ceremonies of monumental spaces. Some of these vessels exhibit artistic influence from the Tiwanaku style and have been called hybrid vessels (Feldman 1998). Others are clearly affiliated with foreign styles, such as Cajamarca wares and Nazcoid styles; and these were probably imports. Some Wari-style vessels also seem to be imported and reflect the flow of status goods between state officials in the Wari heartland and provincial officials residing on Cerro Baúl.

Locally produced Wari-style vessels rarely exhibit the quality represented by similar local reproductions found elsewhere in the Wari realm. Nevertheless, one particular class of vessels (based on paste and method of manufacture) can be closely linked with elite contexts on Cerro Baúl (Williams et al. 2003). Recent excavations demonstrate that this ware may have been manufactured on the summit within the elite residential compound. Some of these vessels exhibit decoration, but most are high-quality undecorated wares. The distribution of these vessels throughout the Wari colony is difficult to chart because most are undecorated, and we are just beginning to associate that vessel form with context and use. At the present time, bowls, cups, and small serving pitchers are the most frequent vessel types. The potential for using these provincial Wari wares to demonstrate the relationships between settlements is addressed later in the chapter.

Other goods may also tentatively be categorized as status emblems. Textiles are not preserved at Cerro Baúl and surrounding settlements, and this is particularly unfortunate because cloth was the most important medium communicating status in the Inca Empire (Murra 1962; Morris 1995; Costin 1998). Many other types of organic materials that were important markers of wealth also are not preserved. Items that can be categorized as rare include objects for adornment, such as gold. Objects of gold have been found so far in only three places—on Cerro Baúl, at El Paso in a ritual context, and at Cerro Mejía associated with a possible smelting locus. Local sources of gold are present in Moquegua, so it is not surprising that its distribution lies outside exclusive elite contexts.

Blue stone is found in many different contexts of the Wari colony, and was presumably imported from sources well outside the area of Wari hegemony. On Cerro Baúl it was incorporated as a building material in at least one niche of a D-shaped temple, Unit 10. Beads and pendants of this material are associated with residential contexts on Cerro Baúl, and a great deal of production waste is scattered on the eroding slopes just below the specialized food production facility, Unit 7.

Blue stone, some of which resembles lapis lazuli in quality, is outweighed by the abundance of a low-quality, white-speckled sort. It appears that raw material of lower quality may have been widely distributed as flakes so that individual households in the colony could transform them into beads as a form of labor contribution, whereas higher quality raw material was transformed on the summit of Cerro Baúl. Since all primary reduction seems to have taken place on Cerro Baúl, it may be that the raw material of variable quality arrived via the activities of provincial officials in relations of exchange extending outside of the empire.

The manufacture of beads from low-quality blue stone and locally available chrysacolla (which varies from turquoise in appearance to lighter shades of green), onyx, and seashell occurred in most households in our sample. In the instance of locally available material, the raw stone may have been supplied through state channels to households or may have been independently obtained for transformation into a tribute good. Bead making took place in every household on Cerro Mejía (Nash 2002); however, blue stone was not always present. In this instance, a simple ubiquity calculation of the presence of these raw materials based on weights may have provided a skewed picture of relative status between households; however, when the context and type of material are taken into account, it becomes clear that officials on Cerro Baúl were directing the production of beads and finished pendants of various qualities for distribution as part of the provincial political economy, with the highest quality goods reserved for higher levels of imperial interaction.

Such context-based relative comparisons are also important for identifying differences in diet, which were significant between levels in the political hierarchy. Exotic foods, which were prepared and served in elite contexts, acted as diacritical markers of the relative status of hosts in commensal politics (see Dietler 2001; Nash and Williams n.d.). At the provincial center, imported foods from the ocean, high-quality cuts of camelid meat, and the prevalence of cuy contrast sharply with meals elsewhere in the colony. This priority access demonstrates the restricted nature of exchange with distant regions and the symbolic value of cuy, which could be easily fed on scraps but was not present in residential contexts below the summit of Cerro Baúl (Nash 2002; deFrance 2004).

Regular lavish feasts and generosity associated with leadership required an abundance of food and a stockpile of gifts. Storage would have been necessary, and such evidence was present in a variety of contexts. Unit 9 had a storage room partitioned off from Room F. Unit 7 had a bin filled with a chicha ingredient, molle. Unit 3 in the administrative sector had four large storage rooms built with elevated floors supported on wooden beams and a raised threshold. Excavation revealed macrobotanical remains of squash and peanut. Unit 12, a rectangular room in a central monumental zone, was remodeled to serve as three storage facilities, each with a small door. Rooms associated with the D-shaped structures also served storage functions. In most instances, minimal evidence is available to assess the quality of objects stored in these facilities; however, commodities and comestibles were just as significant to the Wari political economy as wealth and prestige goods.

Commodities. Obsidian is abundant in the Wari colonial settlements located in the upper Moquegua drainage. The greatest quantity of obsidian is found on the summit

of Cerro Baúl itself. In most instances, obsidian was formed into large, laurel leaf–shaped points, which can be associated with cooking and other domestic tasks, or smaller triangular bifaces, the majority of which have concave bases but at times exhibit a small tang (Nash 2002). Obsidian cores have not been found; however, small utilized flakes are sometimes recovered. Typically, the only evidence of obsidian reduction is the recovery of small retouch flakes associated with edge sharpening or tiny bits of shatter associated with use.

There are likely other materials that could be described as commodities that were circulating between households during the Middle Horizon among the Moquegua settlements. Thus far we have only been able to categorize obsidian as a good that was unquestionably controlled and distributed through Wari state channels. Future research will focus on identifying other goods that did not necessarily convey status on their users but were nevertheless important as commodities that flowed down through state channels and facilitated the empire's ability to establish reciprocal relations with subordinate groups.

To summarize, excavations have uncovered several spatial venues for sociopolitical interaction on the summit of Cerro Baúl. Two are within a palace complex, Unit 9 and Unit 25, and associated with luxury good production zones and facilities for suprahousehold food preparation. A secular administrative setting, Unit 3, was associated with the control of stored goods. Venues with a more ceremonial function are found in the two D-shaped structures, Units 5 and 10, as well as on the platform on the western edge of the summit. These multiple contexts allowed provincial governors many methods to control and manage labor, resources, and production (see Nash and Williams 2005).

Elite governors on Cerro Baúl had far-flung connections to resources that allowed them to serve the finest meals to their guests using high-quality ceramic wares and to distribute luxury goods made of gold, blue stone, and other precious materials produced within the colony. Through their connection with the Wari heartland, provincial leaders built elaborate monuments that conveyed their power, surrounded themselves with status emblems that displayed their prestige, and had access to luxury goods and commodities that could be exchanged with foreign dignitaries and subordinate leaders to forge relationships of obligation and fealty. Leaders at smaller sites had access to fewer resources, and their management facilities reflect their more limited control (Nash 2002).

At the Level of the Regional Center

Cerro Mejía is adjacent to Cerro Baúl. The sites are connected by the irrigation system. Cerro Mejía is located immediately upslope and to the north on a broad dome-shaped hill (see Figure 15.2). Located on the hill's southern slope, scattered clusters of dwellings are divided by walls into six residential barrios (Figure 15.4). These divisions can be traced down into the agricultural fields. The summit of the hill was also demarcated by large wall segments and accessed by a monumental staircase. This settlement exhibits mid-level administrative facilities on the summit and lower-level administrative facilities located within large residential structures associated with craftsmen in charge of workshops and the leaders of barrios supervising labor efforts focused outside the residential context (Nash 2002).

Use of Space. The summit of Cerro Mejía is organized around a central open space that has two platforms on its eastern edge and a set of smaller lower platforms to the northwest. The associated open space probably required artificial leveling of the hill's summit and is a sizable area, 65 × 75 m. The only two structures that resemble Wari-style architecture are located on either side of the platform complex. Both these structures include platform features.

Unit 145 resembles a patio group with four rectangular rooms opening onto a central trapezoidal patio. This arrangement is not surrounded by an enclosure wall but is attached to a large plaza. The four rectangular rooms are similar in size but were used for different sets of activities. The entire dwelling was designed around facilitating political relations (Figure 15.5).

Room D is on the east side. This elevated space has three stairs that descend to a raised platform. The top stair forms a bench that continues along the length of the room. Two niches in the east wall of Room D can be viewed from the patio because this space has an exceptionally wide opening facing the central space. In the southwest corner of this space there was a storage pit that still contained small flakes of blue stone and chrysacolla. Room D and the central patio space together provided a venue to meet with subordinates.

Room C is a specialized food preparation area. It contained seven hearths of two types and numerous remains of cooking and storage vessels. Four stone-lined hearths to the east of the door are presumed to have been for boiling, a step in the process of making chicha. Three hearths to the west of the door held a dense deposit of ash, with extensive heat alteration to the underlying concave clay matrix. These hearths were filled with a large quantity of discarded camelid

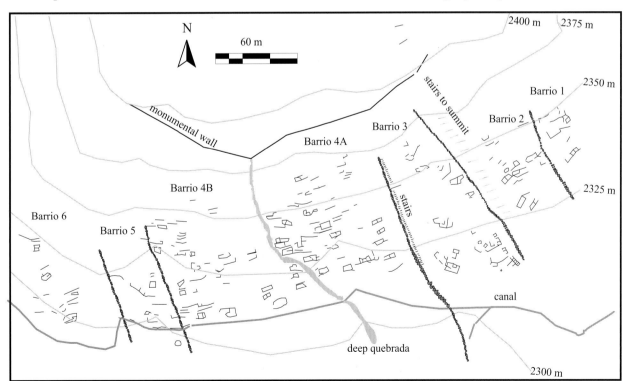

Figure 15.4. Cerro Mejía slope residences.

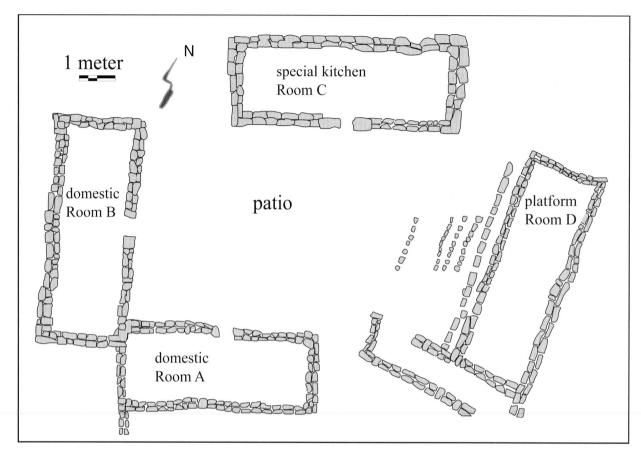

Figure 15.5. Cerro Mejía Unit 145.

long bones. This faunal assemblage is uncharacteristic of food remains in smaller dwellings and indicates that this particular residence had access to a greater quantity of food. This facility had minimal productive debris, which suggests that preliminary preparation of large meals took place elsewhere.

Rooms A and B exhibit qualities of typical residential structures except that they were left cleaner than other household contexts at the site. Regardless of the large cooking facility in Room C, each of these rooms had its own hearth and small associated scatters of productive activity. Room A had a storage pit, which was not typical of other residential contexts on Cerro Mejía. Room B had a low platform that may have been used for sleeping. Unit 145, as a residential structure, was clearly designed to accommodate sociopolitical interaction and to prepare and provide feasts to visitors, subordinates, and perhaps large groups attending events held in the adjacent central platform plaza complex.

Unit 136, the larger elite residence located on the southern side of the platform complex, was also tested in areas to determine if similar facilities were present;

no room, however, was excavated in its entirety. The large compound appears to have incorporated a large plaza, two of the patio group-type structures, and other associated rooms, the whole surrounded by a high stone wall. This structure is the largest on the summit and has been the focus of looting, so that the layout of space is no longer apparent from the surface. None of the rectangular rooms appears to have been elevated above its respective patio; a platform was present, however, and stretched across the eastern side of the large plaza. Test excavations showed that the use of rectangular rooms as quarters was duplicated, and one of these also had a storage pit. Significantly, another rectangular room had an intensive food preparation area, similar to Room C in Unit 145.

Emblems of Status and Commodities. Only a few small, decorated ceramic fragments were recovered during the excavations of the two semi-monumental residences on the summit of Cerro Mejía. Vessels were analyzed based on paste and quality of manufacture. Unit 145 contained vessels of the type associated with elite residences on Cerro Baúl. There also seems to be a distinctive type of pottery associated with Unit 145. Additionally, vessels present in this context were highly variable in form and paste, which suggests that the administrators living in this residence may have engaged in exchange with many subordinate groups or received tribute from a variety of local groups. Details of vessel pastes and their distribution are presented later in the chapter.

Blue stone is present and resembles flakes from the summit of Cerro Baúl. It seems that mid-level administrators may have distributed this and other raw materials to laborers or subordinates for transformation into beads. Obsidian was less abundant in Unit 145 than in Unit 9 on Cerro Baúl; it was, however, present in larger amounts than in commoner dwellings on the slopes of Mejía. The amount present in Unit 145 does not suggest that this unit was the locus of distribution of this good. Perhaps the administrator in the larger, more elaborate residence, Unit 136, would have distributed this resource to subordinates during political relations; however, this structure requires further investigation to understand its place in the political hierarchy. The two administrators may have served complementary roles.

The two mid-level elites on Cerro Mejía probably served as intermediaries between provincial leaders on Cerro Baúl and the populace. They interacted directly with groups of laborers or community representatives. Administrators living on the summit of Cerro Mejía may have had to manage the local agricultural and irrigation system, as well as craft production and construction projects. As such, they would have interacted with administrators on Cerro Baúl and local leaders of small groups. Thus, it is not a surprise that the large dwellings of these leaders resemble those on Cerro Baúl, both in design and in activities, as well as possess some high-quality ceramics and display evidence that the inhabitants had access to camelid meat and the resources to brew their own beer.

The residential areas of the two regional leaders on Cerro Mejía exhibit affinities with the elite residence on Cerro Baúl. The quality of architecture on Mejía is less elaborate. For instance, the entire floor of Unit 9 on Cerro Baúl was paved with flagstones, whereas the same material was reserved only for the elevated room in Unit 145 on Cerro Mejía. In the elite residential compound on Cerro Baúl and in other contexts, there are many facilities for the storage of luxury goods; at Mejía, Unit 145 has only two storage pits. On Cerro Baúl, facilities for the preparation of meals and chicha contained the remains of molle pits and feast remains that included fish, shellfish, and the ribs of camelids on

the floor. On Cerro Mejía in Unit 145, chicha production is present; however, the storage of molle has not been recovered. Abundant camelid bones were found, but the cuts present were not of the same high quality as those found on Cerro Baúl (deFrance 2004). Blue stone at Mejía was found in its raw form, with no evidence of finished goods. In sum, the remains on the summit of Cerro Mejía suggest that the people dwelling there had far less political currency and prestige than those on Cerro Baúl, but the elites at Mejía also had far more access to construction labor, exchange relations, quality foodstuffs, and obsidian than any of the other households on the site of Cerro Mejía.

At the Level of a Social Group

The lowest level of administration has less obvious architectural features and can only be identified through comparisons with other household contexts. The lowest level of the social hierarchy is represented by two different groups: (1) master craftspeople in charge of groups living in clustered dwellings incorporating workshops and (2) supervisors of barrios managing labor contributions focused outside of residential contexts.

Use of Space. Unit 118, located on the summit of Cerro Mejía, does not exhibit a typical patio group organization; it is a large multifamily cluster that consists of two dwellings (Figure 15.6). These houses shared a common wall but do not have internal access between the residences. Each dwelling housed more than a nuclear family (see Nash 2002). There were specialized features and artifacts associated with a workshop of some kind. Apart from common domestic remains and the specialized work areas, one house has a relatively clean room with a rounded back wall, perhaps for the performance of group ritual. The head of this cluster of households seems to have directed this activity and perhaps the group's production.

On the terraced slopes of Cerro Mejía, each barrio has large structures that exhibit specialized spaces that suggest they facilitated activities beyond household production. It seems as if each barrio had a low-level administrator. Unit 4 exhibits characteristics not found in other house structures (Figure 15.7).

Room A has a rectangular enclosed room, which is unusual since other residential structures are more square-shaped. The rectangular shape may reflect a desire to emulate elite space. An unusual amount of charred camelid bone was associated with a large hearth and appears to reflect use and preparation beyond household needs. The large quantity of faunal

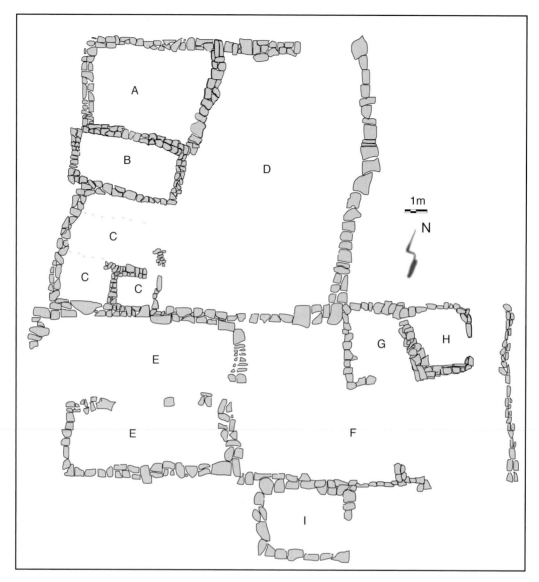

Figure 15.6. Cerro Mejía Unit 118.

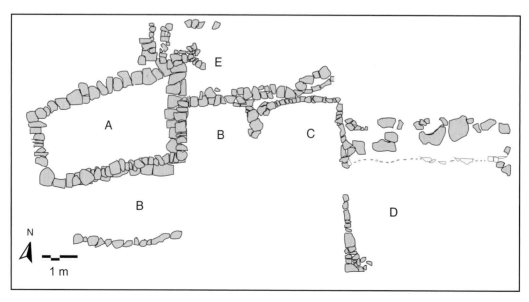

Figure 15.7. Cerro Mejía Unit 4.

remains in this instance signifies greater access to protein resources. Room B, also rectangular, served as an entry room. In this space were remains of serving and consumption vessels. An intermediate space between the enclosed rooms and the patio contained the same. In contrast, a small adjacent alcove with a curved back wall was nearly empty. This feature was added through remodeling, as was Room B. The curved space resembles that in Unit 118 and may have been used for an important group ritual. The patio in Unit 4 was typical. Room E, on a higher terrace level, seems to have been another enclosed room with cooking hearth.

Emblems of Status and Commodities. Both of these large households exhibit spatial venues to support social interaction. Each had a room set aside for receiving visitors and perhaps a household shrine with a curved back wall resembling more elaborate D-shaped structures at the provincial center. These spaces may have been used by a group of households under the direction of a low-level administrator. These architectural elaborations may not have been labor-intensive additions but may have been emblems of the households' relative status among their immediate neighbors.

These households had sufficient facilities to prepare meals for a group of people beyond those dwelling in the residence, as well as more evidence of camelid consumption than their neighbors. These dwellings also contained evidence of exchange or of the receipt of tribute because they exhibited a variety of goods such as bowl forms or biface types. These houses can be linked to interactions with higher levels of the administrative hierarchy through the presence, though in small amounts, of high-quality ceramic wares. Obsidian was abundant in both contexts. Unit 4 may have been an intermediary locus for distributing this commodity to other households in the barrio. Production debris typical of household activities was present in patio spaces, and these households do not seem to have been supplemented by the labor of others to any great degree.

The Houses of Non-administrators on Cerro Mejía

At the foundation of the system there were small, simple houses consisting of an enclosed room and an open patio space possibly bordered by low walls, as well as structures with more than one enclosed room that shared a common patio. Cooking took place in the enclosed room. Enclosed rooms were square and small (Figure 15.8). Most evidence of consumption was found in the patio, along with evidence for other productive activities. Faunal remains were few and consisted of splintered fragments embedded in house floors rather than large elements associated with the hearth.

It is important to note that obsidian was present in every household. In many instances obsidian was recovered only as tiny flakes, resulting from the retouching of bifaces or shatter from their use. Based on relative abundance, it is clear that although every household had access to obsidian, in most instances it was distributed in small quantities, and lithic quarries on Cerro Mejía provided the primary material for most tools (Nash 2002).

Links between Households

Clear links can be made between the administrative residential contexts at the three levels of the political hierarchy. Each structure exhibits space set aside for sociopolitical interactions. The most elaborate contexts are on Cerro Baúl. Contexts for political relations extend beyond the elite residence and are evident in public, administrative, and ritual spaces. At the tertiary center, the archaeological correlates of power relations are similar to but exist at a smaller scale and combine some facilities into one spatial venue when compared with structures at Cerro Baúl. On the summit of Cerro Mejía, public spaces are closely affiliated with elite residences. They are easily identified. In contrast, lower levels of administration were identified only by detailed comparisons of activity areas in the sampled households. Unit 4 did not seem to be an atypical residential context until we compared it with the remains of other dwellings on the terraced slopes of Cerro Mejía. The hearth was abnormally large, and its faunal remains demonstrated differential access to protein resources. Pottery types defined by paste varied more widely in Unit 4 than in other structures, and, most important, space was set aside for interaction.

At all three levels of the political hierarchy, feasting and the exchange of goods were activities key to the provincial political economy. The evidence demonstrates that face-to-face interactions were important. Special ceramic vessels were distributed and used during these political relations, and it seems that elite administrators controlled the production of high-quality vessels important to marking status during sociopolitical gatherings.

In a study of compositional chemistry of Middle Horizon pottery in Moquegua, we demonstrate three distinctive ceramic paste recipes for pottery production in the Moquegua colony. The first is a coarse ware

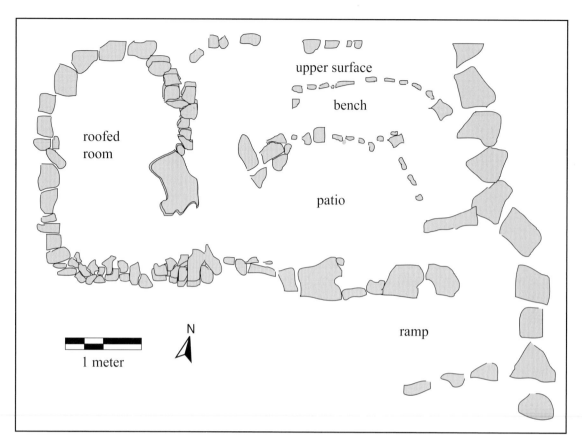

Figure 15.8. Cerro Mejía lower-status house, Unit 5.

with a high degree of biotite temper associated most often with large cooking vessels or *ollas*. The other two groups come in a wide range of forms, but all are associated with serving wares, such as bowls and cups. One of these paste groups is associated most directly with contexts on Cerro Baúl, constituting about three-fourths of the sampled assemblage in an elite feasting context on the summit. The same group is much less represented as one moves to the elite feasting contexts at the regional center of Cerro Mejía and at the homes of local administrators at the same site (20% of each sample respectively). Finally, it is not represented in the sample from the houses of nonadministrators. The second group, consisting of similar vessel forms, has a much broader distribution, especially in intermediate elite and nonelite contexts (Williams et al. 2003).

Obsidian was imported to Moquegua before the Middle Horizon in small amounts, and some fragments have been found in later sites, although based on size some of these obsidian objects may have been collected and reused from Middle Horizon occupation scatters. The sudden influx of obsidian in the Middle Horizon is associated with the Wari presence in this region. Its presence in every household suggests that it was not a status item but rather was widely distributed, perhaps as a good to support a particular kind of production. Obsidian, alternatively, may have been a good of recognized value and was used by the state to maintain reciprocal relations with people supporting the state through tribute or labor services. The sources of this raw material support the idea that the presence of obsidian reflects the flow of goods between the Wari state and the households under its hegemony. Furthermore, the analysis of feasting ceramics suggests that, like obsidian, special ceramics were concentrated in the hands of state elites, who selectively distributed them to regional elites in contexts of commensal politics. Unlike the obsidian, however, these special ceramic vessels did not find their way into the houses of nonadministrators.

CONCLUSIONS

In this chapter we have demonstrated that elements of a polity's political economy can be defined by comparative study of activity areas or the use of space and the distribution, production, and consumption of status emblems and valued commodities. The results of such analyses can provide positive evidence of direct control of local provincial communities. We have purposely restricted our sample to clear examples of direct imperial control. Small settlements in provincial hinterlands may not exhibit monumental features and thus may be difficult to associate with Wari control. This methodology holds great promise for identifying the smallest affiliated communities and providing a fuller picture of the populations supporting provincial centers in different regions.

This methodology can also help identify the political segmentation of larger settlements. The smallest units of administration at Cerro Mejía could be inferred from the barrio walls that divided the site; however, not all such settlements may exhibit such overt partitioning. Excavations of households dating to the Middle Horizon in the Moquegua region can now be compared to the baselines we have established, and we can begin to understand the relationships between small outlying communities and the Wari Empire.

From a broader regional perspective or for investigations based on survey and surface collection, we suggest that the presence of obsidian can be used to trace Wari imperial control. Instrumental neutron activation analysis (INAA) of obsidian from the Wari settlements in Moquegua shows that the highest percentages actually come from sources other than the nearest source, Chivay. In fact, the primary source of obsidian early in the Middle Horizon was the Quispisisa source near Wari itself (Williams et al. 2003). Later in the Middle Horizon, the Alca source in the Cotahuasi Valley was predominant (Burger et al. 2000). Thus, it was likely channeled through the capital and state system. Similarly, other such items may be important in different regions. Links can be made between provincial centers and households in settlements of various sizes through vessel paste resource utilization and even by comparing lithic production technologies.

The size of the gathering areas within the administrative structures on Cerro Mejía and Cerro Baúl suggests a population larger than that present in the surrounding smaller settlements. It is also curious that there is only one tertiary center under Cerro Baúl. Cerro Mejía is not a unique site if we look farther

afield. Corralones is located overlooking the Río Chili on the outskirts of the city of Arequipa, recently excavated by Augusto Cardona. Several of the buildings at Corralones resemble the largest administrative residential structures on the summit of Cerro Mejía (see Cardona 2002:73).

If the sites we have become accustomed to calling provincial centers are truly administrating provinces, it is time to study how these imperial facilities articulated with local populations and connected people with the Wari heartland and with resources from many regions. We need to understand the organization of the supporting populations as they related to different administrative centers (see Mackey, this volume). To understand the Wari Empire we must study all its parts, especially those representing the supporting population.

It is important to begin conceptualizing control beyond valley boundaries, to look for communication routes, and to plot nodes of control between these centers and the Wari heartland. These nodes may be as variable as the provincial centers. The archaeological manifestations of administration on and around Cerro Baúl provide insight into Wari state institutions and the political activities that were used to cull resources and build power in the Wari Empire. We have presented some of the archaeological correlates of the Wari political economy at its different levels in the upper Moquegua Valley and have shown the links between administrative personnel in the provincial administration. Thus we have provided a material foundation and a methodology through which to test models of Wari control and influence and understand the complexities of Wari political relations and the foundation of this early Andean society.

Acknowledgments

The research presented in this chapter would not have been possible without the determination and encouragement of Mike Moseley. Mike initiated research at Cerro Baúl in the 1980s and graciously invited us to take on the daunting task of studying (climbing) this formidable mountain in 1997. The holistic and comparative methodology we try to apply to the Wari colony is of course his, and we hope our research meets the high standards that Mike Moseley has set for those of us who pursue research in Andean archaeology.

Funding for the research summarized in this chapter was provided by the National Science Foundation (grants nos. BCS-9907167 and BCS-0226791), the Heinz Family Foundation, the G. A. Bruno Foundation, the Asociación Contisuyo, the Field Museum, and the Center for Latin American Studies at the University of Florida. We thank Joyce Marcus and Charles Stanish for their editorial comments and their work in pulling this volume together. Any flaws or misinterpretation are our own.

REFERENCES

Alonso, Ana María
1994   The Politics of Space, Time and Substance: State Formation, Nationalism and Ethnicity. *Annual Review of Anthropology* 23:379–405.

Berdan, Frances F.
1987   Cotton in Aztec Mexico: Production, Distribution and Uses. *Mexican Studies* 3(2):235–262.

Bourdieu, Pierre
1977   *Outline of a Theory of Practice*. Translated by Richard Nice. Cambridge University Press, Cambridge.

Burger, Richard, Karen Mohr Chávez, and Sergio Chávez
2000   Through the Glass Darkly: Prehispanic Obsidian Procurement and Exchange in Southern Peru and Northern Bolivia. *Journal of World Prehistory* 14(3):267–362.

Carrasco, Pedro
1982   The Political Economy of the Aztec and Inca States. In *The Inca and Aztec States 1400–1800: Anthropology and History*, edited by George Collier, Renato Rosaldo, and John Wirth, pp. 23-40. Academic Press, New York.

Cardona Rosas, Augusto
2002   *Arqueología de Arequipa de sus albores a los Incas*. CIARQ, Arequipa, Peru.

Costin, Cathy L.
1993   Textiles, Women and Political Economy in Late Prehispanic Peru. *Research in Economic Anthropology* 14:3–28.
1998   Housewives, Chosen Women, Skilled Men: Cloth Production and Social Identity in the Late Prehispanic Andes. In *Craft and Social Identity*, edited by Cathy L. Costin and Rita P. Wright, pp. 123–141. Archaeological Papers of the American Anthropological Association, no. 8, Washington, DC.

D'Altroy, Terence, and Timothy Earle
1985   Staple Finance, Wealth Finance, and Storage in the Inca Political Economy. *Current Anthropology* 26:187–206.

deFrance, Susan
2004   Wari Diet in Moquegua: The Ordinary and the Exotic. Paper presented at the 69th Annual Meeting of the Society for American Archaeology, Montreal.

Dietler, Michael
2001   Theorizing the Feast: Rituals of Consumption, Commensal Politics, and Power in African Contexts. In *Feasts: Archaeological and Ethnographic Perspectives on Food, Politics, and Power*, edited by Michael Dietler and Brian Hayden, pp. 23–64. Smithsonian Institution Press, Washington, DC.

Feldman, Robert
1998   La Ciudadela Wari de Cerro Baúl en Moquegua. In *Moquegua: Los primeros doce mil años*, edited by Karen Wise, pp. 59–65. Museo Contisuyo, Moquegua, Peru.

Friedrich, Paul
1989   Language, Ideology, and Political Economy. *American Anthropologist* 91(2):295–312.

Hyslop, John
1990   *Inca Settlement Planning*. University of Texas Press, Austin.

Isbell, William H.
1991   Huari Administration and the Orthogonal Cellular Horizon. In *Huari Administrative Structure: Prehistoric Monumental Architecture and State Government*, edited by William H. Isbell and Gordon McEwan, pp. 293–316. Dumbarton Oaks, Washington, DC.

Isbell, William H., and Gordon McEwan
1991   A History of Huari Studies and Introduction to Current Interpretations. In *Huari Administrative Structure: Prehistoric Monumental Architecture and State Government*, edited by William H. Isbell and Gordon McEwan, pp. 1–18. Dumbarton Oaks, Washington, DC.

Janusek, John Wayne
1999   Craft and Local Power: Embedded Specializations in Tiwanaku Cities. *Latin American Antiquity* 10(2):107–131.

Julien, Catherine
1982   Inca Decimal Administration in the Lake Titicaca Region. In *The Inca and Aztec States 1400–1800: Anthropology and History*, edited by George Collier, Renato Rosaldo, and John Wirth, pp. 96–112. Academic Press, New York.
1993   Finding a Fit: Archaeology and Ethnohistory of the Incas. In *Provincial Inca: Archaeological and Ethnohistorical Assessment of the Impact of the Inca*

State, edited by Michael Malpass, pp. 234–244. University of Iowa Press, Iowa City.

Kolata, Alan
2003   Tiwanaku Ceremonial Architecture and Urban Organization. In *Tiwanaku and Its Hinterland: Archaeology and Paleoecology of an Andean Civilization*, Volume 2: *Urban and Rural Archaeology*, edited by Alan Kolata, pp. 175–201. Smithsonian Institution Press, Washington, DC.

Kopytoff, Igor
2001   The Cultural Biography of Things: Commoditization as Process. In *The Social Life of Things: Commoditites in Cultural Perspective*, edited by Arjun Appadurai, pp. 64–91. Cambridge University Press, Cambridge.

Levine, Terry
1992   Inca State Storage in Three Highland Regions: A Comparative Study. In *Inca Storage Systems*, edited by Terry Levine, pp. 107–148. University of Oklahoma Press, Norman.

Lightfoot, Kent, and Antoinette Martinez
1995   Frontiers and Boundaries in Archaeological Perspective. *Annual Review of Anthropology* 24:471–492.

Menzel, Dorothy
1959   The Inca Occupation of the South Coast of Peru. *Southwestern Journal of Anthropology* 15(2):125–142.

Moore, Jerry D.
1996   *Architecture and Power in the Ancient Andes: The Archaeology of Public Buildings*. Cambridge University Press, Cambridge.

Morris, Craig
1982   The Infrastructure of Inca Control in the Peruvian Central Highlands. In *The Inca and Aztec States 1400–1800: Anthropology and History*, edited by George Collier, Renato Rosaldo, and John Wirth, pp. 153–171. Academic Press, New York.
1985   From Principles of Ecological Complementarity to the Organization and Administration of Tawantinsuyu. In *Andean Ecology and Civilization*, edited by Shozo Masuda, Izumi Shimada, and Craig Morris, pp. 477–490. University of Tokyo Press, Tokyo.
1986   Storage, Supply, and Redistribution in the Economy of the Inca State. In *Anthropological History of the Andean Polities*, edited by John Murra, Nathan Wachtel, and Jacques Revel, pp. 59–68. Cambridge University Press, Cambridge.
1995   Symbols to Power: Styles and Media in the Inca State. In *Style, Society, and Person: Archaeological and Ethnological Perspectives*, edited by Christopher Carr and Jill Neitzel, pp. 419–433. Plenum Press, New York.

Moseley, Michael. E.
1985   The Exploration and Explanation of Early Monumental Architecture in the Andes. In *Early Ceremonial Architecture in the Andes*, edited by Christopher B. Donnan, pp. 29–58. Dumbarton Oaks, Washington, DC.

Moseley, Michael E., Donna J. Nash, P. R. Williams, Susan de France, Ana Miranda, and Mario Ruales
2005   Burning Down the Brewery: Establishing and Evacuating an Ancient Imperial Colony at Cerro Baúl, Peru. *Proceedings of the National Academy of Sciences* 102(48):17264–17271.

Murra, John V.
1962   Cloth and Its Function in the Inca State. *American Anthropologist* 64:710–728.

Nash, Donna J.
2002   *The Archaeology of Space: Places of Power in the Wari Empire*. Unpublished doctoral dissertation, Department of Anthropology, University of Florida, Gainesville.

Nash, Donna J., and P. Ryan Williams
2005   Architecture and Power: Relations on the Wari–Tiwanaku Frontier. In *The Foundations of Power in the Prehispanic Andes*, edited by Kevin Vaughn, Christina Conlee, and Dennis Ogburn, pp. 151–174. Archaeological Papers of the American Anthropological Association, no. 14.
n.d.   Fine Dining and Fabulous Atmosphere: Feasting Facilities and Political Interaction in the Wari Realm. In *From Subsistence to Social Strategies: New Directions in the Study of Daily Meals and Feasting Events*, edited by Elizabeth Klarich. University of Colorado Press. Forthcoming.

Norberg-Schulz, Christian
1985   *The Concept of Dwelling: On the Way to Figurative Architecture*. Electa Press, New York.

Patterson, Thomas C.
1987   Tribes, Chiefdoms and Kingdoms in the Inca Empire. In *Power Relations and State Formation*, edited by Thomas Patterson and C. Gailey, pp. 117–127. American Anthropological Association, Washington, DC.

Paynter, Robert
1989   The Archaeology of Equality and Inequality. *Annual Review of Anthropology* 18:369–399.

Pease, Franklin
1982   The Formation of Tawantinsuyu: Mechanisms of Colonization and Relationship with Ethnic Groups. In *The Inca and Aztec States 1400–1800: Anthropology and History*, edited by George Collier, Renato

Rosaldo, and John Wirth, pp. 173–198. Academic Press, New York.

Peregrine, Peter
1991   Some Political Aspects of Craft Specialization. *World Archaeology* 23(1):1–11.

Polanyi, Karl
1957   *The Great Transformation: The Political and Economic Origins of Our Time.* Beacon Press, Boston.

Rapoport, Amos
1990   *The Meaning of the Built Environment.* Sage Publications, Beverly Hills, CA.

Roseberry, William
1988   Political Economy. *Annual Review of Anthropology* 17:161–185.

Rostworowski de Diez Canseco, María
1999   *History of the Inca Realm.* Translated by Harry B. Iceland. Cambridge University Press, Cambridge.

Rowe, John
1982   Inca Policies and Institutions Relating to Cultural Unification of the Empire. In *The Inca and Aztec States 1400–1800: Anthropology and History*, edited by George A. Collier, Renato I. Rosaldo, and John D. Wirth, pp. 93–118. Academic Press, New York.

Rowe, John, Donald Collier, and Gordon R. Willey
1956   Reconnaissance Notes on the Site of Huari, near Ayacucho, Peru. *American Antiquity* 16(2):120–137.

Saunders, Nicholas
2001   A Dark Light: Reflections on Obsidian in Mesoamerica. *World Archaeology* 33(2):220–236.

Schreiber, Katharina J.
1992   *Wari Imperialism in Middle Horizon Peru.* Anthropological Papers Museum of Anthropology, University of Michigan, no. 87. University of Michigan Press, Ann Arbor.

Shady, Ruth, and Arturo Ruiz
1979   Evidence for Interzonal Relationships during the Middle Horizon on the North-Central Coast of Peru. *American Antiquity* 44(4):676–684.

Sinopoli, Carla
1994   The Archaeology of Empires. *Annual Review of Anthropology* 23:159–180.

Spickard, Linda
1983   The Development of Huari Administrative Architecture. In *Investigations of the Andean Past*, edited

by Daniel Sandweiss, pp. 136–160. Cornell Latin American Studies Program, Ithaca, NY.

Stanish, Charles
1989   Household Archeology: Testing models of zonal complementarity in the south-central Andes. *American Anthropologist* 91(1):7–24.
1992   *Ancient Andean Political Economy.* University of Texas Press, Austin.

Stone, Jane
1983   *The Socio-Economic Implications of Lithic Evidence from Huari, Peru.* Unpublished doctoral dissertation, Department of Anthropology, State University of New York, Binghamton.

Topic, John R., and Theresa L. Topic
1992   The Rise and Decline of Cerro Amaru: An Andean Shrine during the Early Intermediate Period and the Middle Horizon. In *Ancient Images, Ancient Thought: The Archaeology of Ideology*, edited by A. S. Goldsmith, S. Garvie, D. Selin, and J. Smith, pp. 167–180. University of Calgary Archaeological Association, Calgary, British Columbia, Canada.
2000   Hacia la comprensión del fenómeno Huari: Una perspectiva norteña. In *Huari y Tiwanaku: Modelos vs. evidencia*, pt. 1, edited by Peter Kaulicke and William H. Isbell, pp. 181–217. Boletín de Arqueología PUCP no. 4. Pontificia Universidad Católica del Perú, Lima.

Williams, P. Ryan
2001   Cerro Baúl: A Wari Center on the Tiwanaku Frontier. *Latin American Antiquity* 12(1):67–83.

Williams, P. Ryan, and Donna J. Nash
2006   Sighting the Apu: A GIS Analysis of Wari Imperialism and the Worship of Mountain Peaks. *World Archaeology* 38(3):455–468.

Williams, P. Ryan, Donna J. Nash, Mary Glowacki, Robert Jeff Speakman, Hector Neff, Michael Glascock, Mario Ruales Moreno, and Jamie Clark
2003   Using INAA to Assess Wari Ceramic Production and Exchange on the Tiwanaku Frontier. Paper presented at the 51st International Congress of Americanists, Santiago, Chile.

Yoffee, Norman
1995   Political Economy in Early Mesopotamian States. *Annual Review of Anthropology* 24:281–311.

CHAPTER 16

DIASPORAS WITHIN THE ANCIENT STATE

TIWANAKU AS AYLLUS IN MOTION

PAUL S. GOLDSTEIN

TWENTY YEARS AGO, MICHAEL Moseley outlined the major theoretical and methodological challenges for the study of state expansion in the south-central Andes. Many of the contributors to this book can attest to the special kind of mentorship offered by Moseley. Mike is not a warm and fuzzy hand-holder. Instead, he has an inexhaustible supply of ideas that he generously shares to motivate and inspire those around him. Some pan out. Some don't. But we cannot deny that Mike has a special gift for challenging students, colleagues, and the academic community at large in a phenomenally productive way. This is one tale that started with this kind of challenge-response mentorship. It may have gone in different directions than anticipated, but the process would never have started without that intellectual push from Mike.

In September 1983, Michael Moseley and Robert Feldman hitched a ride in a mining company Cessna and discovered the Omo site, the largest Tiwanaku colonial enclave outside the altiplano. As a graduate student in South America for the first time, I remember them returning to the field house shaking their heads and searching for the appropriate words to describe the size and scale of the place, which had somehow escaped the "windshield survey" up to that day. We later found out Omo was a large, complex Tiwanaku culture settlement

in the Peruvian lowlands. Moseley said something like, "You were the one interested in Tiwanaku, right? Go ahead and find out what it's about." Twenty years later, I am still trying to meet that challenge.

The place where Michael Moseley had suggested I work turned out to provide one of the great case studies of early Andean state expansion, the Tiwanaku colonization of the western slopes of the Andes. By the early 1990s, I had documented a massive colonization of this lowland agricultural valley by highland Tiwanaku colonists in the seventh through eleventh centuries AD. My studies of household archaeology at the Omo sites and subsequent excavations of Omo's Tiwanaku-style temple in 1990 initially favored what I call a "globalist" interpretation of Tiwanaku as a monolithic state "core" that dominated peripheral outliers. My discovery of large, well-organized enclaves of Tiwanaku peoples in distant regions seemed to reinforce this globalist model of Tiwanaku as a proto-imperial polity. Based on the excavation record available by the mid-1990s, the best available explanations for Tiwanaku lowland colonization, one of the earliest episodes of Andean state expansion, seemed to lie in a model of annexation of a periphery under the central direction of a bureaucratic state.

Why had this seemed the most parsimonious explanation for Tiwanaku expansion? A centrally directed, globalist Tiwanaku expansion seemed to make sense largely because of assumptions I derived from comparative studies of archaic states worldwide. Our normative view of the growth of ancient states assumes that increasing complexity and scale are usually accompanied by systemic processes of centralization and the imposition of a hierarchical structure and centralized control of populations, territories, and resources. This is not simply a question of scale but a qualitative distinction, a significant moment of transformation and a punctuation point in the evolution of complex society. States, by definition, rise above chiefly cycling, achieving stability at a higher level of political scale, with enhanced production from subjects and territorial expansion made possible by new institutions of centralized authority (Flannery 1999:5, 15). Territorial expansion is usually a key marker of state institutional consolidation precisely because in most states it necessitates a centralized hierarchy of administrators or governors—a specialized form of government that is qualitatively distinct from chiefdoms. Thus, I reasoned, political authority in an expansive state such as Tiwanaku would be hierarchical, following "a fundamental shift in the regulatory principles and strategies of the central decision-makers" (Spencer 1998:15). It had seemed reasonable to assume that territorially expansive archaic states like Tiwanaku must by definition have had fully centralized forms of government before they ventured into foreign expansion. Many leading Tiwanaku scholars, most of them familiar with the density and vastness of the agrarian settlement systems of its altiplano core, quite reasonably assume "Tiwanaku" to have operated as a unified expansive agent, with centrally coordinated and hierarchically structured rural and political economies at home and abroad (e.g., Kolata 1993, 1997, 2003; Stanish 2002, 2003; Kolata [ed.] 2003). It is also worth noting that altiplano preservation and deep stratigraphy have made it particularly difficult to tease out the fine details of cultural, social, and, I believe, political diversity within the Tiwanaku homeland. But it is precisely this diversity and its spatial expression in regional settlement pattern and household, community, and town plan that is brought into full focus by the arid desert preservation and remarkable horizontal surface exposure of many of the Tiwanaku colonial sites.

In this chapter I outline why Tiwanaku seems to be one of a small number of outlier ancient states that do not always fit our normative generalization with the precision we would like. I further suggest a Tiwanaku state that was successful because it was considerably less

monolithic than its monumental architecture. My new perspective from the Tiwanaku colonies challenges my own earlier globalist view of Tiwanaku expansion by questioning the dominant and leading role of centralized decision making in Tiwanaku expansion. Today, two decades of settlement pattern analysis, excavations, and dates, illustrated with parallels from the ethnographic present, demand a reappraisal of the sociopolitical organization of Tiwanaku colonization in the south-central Andes. I argue that altiplano colonies past and present represent a diaspora and initially came into being as outliers of diverse and discrete corporate social entities rather than as a single state-directed enterprise. Although centralized institutions surely played a role in the expansion of Tiwanaku civilization, their development was contemporary with, not antecedent to, the Tiwanaku diaspora. The enduring diversity within the Tiwanaku colonies tests many of our assumptions about the predominant role of centralization and hierarchy in state expansion and reminds us of the great potential for the significant survival of nonhierarchical social pluralism in ancient states. I would like to think that Mike Moseley might appreciate the challenge, even if not the interpretive content, of this reappraisal.

Potential explanations for a more pluralistic form of territorial expansion in early complex societies may be informed by James Clifford's diaspora model of demographic expansion under modern state societies. According to Clifford, diasporas are

> expatriate minority communities (1) that are dispersed from an original center to at least two peripheral places; (2) that maintain a memory, vision or myth about their original homeland; (3) that believe they are not—and perhaps cannot be—fully accepted by their host country; (4) that see the ancestral home as a place of eventual return, when the time is right; (5) that are committed to the maintenance or restoration of this homeland and (6) of which the group's consciousness and solidarity are "importantly defined" by this continuing relationship with the homeland. (Clifford 1994:304)

Clifford's use of the term *diaspora* thus poses colonization articulated across transnational communities by strong shared identities, expectation of return, and unwillingness, difficulty, or inability to assimilate into host societies. To apply this formulation to archaeological migrations, two distinct approaches are indicated. First, archaeologists may assume that ancient diaspora communities, like those of the present day, often defined themselves in opposition to others. Archaeologically, this may be marked by distinctions in practice, habitus, and activities, and by stylistic as well as spatial segregation from other communities. Second, where there is a convincing case for cultural continuity, constructive analogies may be built for ancient community from the ethnographic record. In the south-central Andean sierra, communities based on shared identity are called *ayllus*.

ANDEAN EXPANSION AS AYLLUS IN DIASPORA

The Andean ayllu provides an example of an ascriptive identity held together by shared conceptions of behavior, history, and common ancestry. Urton defines the ayllu broadly as any "group or unit of social, political, economic, and ritual cohesion and action" (1990:22). Functional definitions emphasize the ayllu's role as either a landholding group (Rowe 1946) or a "kin collective" (Moseley 1992) or a "communal mode of production" (Patterson 1987) for reciprocal exchange and productive labor organization above the level of the nuclear family. Ayllus organize and sponsor ritual events, prepare feasts and drinking bouts, and enact ceremonies that map social relationships, reinforce member affiliation, and reify group solidarity. Members of particular ayllus may revere specific sacred places on the land such as mountains, stone outcrops, lakes, and springs; these sacred places are known as *huacas* in Quechua or *mallkus* in Aymara. Overwhelmingly, however, operational definitions see ayllu membership as primarily determined by literal and fictive descent (Albarracin-Jordan 1996:185; Abercrombie 1998:341; Isbell 1998). In many historic ayllus, the most potent huacas were those related to real or mythic ancestors. Often, as was the case with the Inca royal ayllu (Bauer 1992; Bauer and Stanish 2001) and with ethnographic ayllu communities (e.g., Bastien 1978; Allen 1988; Abercrombie 1998), each ayllu recounts its genesis from specific huacas or mallkus that mark ancestral origin places (Arriaga 1968 [1621]). This association of origin places and ancestor worship with group identity suggests that as a community form, the ayllu is more genealogical than territorial in nature. Ayllus are bounded by history, not borders. This emphasis on kinship, history, and practice in defining ayllu identity is reminiscent of Clifford's discussion of diaspora communities, which are often reified through ethnicity as

"a kin-based identity larger than the family or lineage" (Emberling 1997:303).

Ayllus tend to be segmented into nested hierarchies of subunits, often also called ayllus, at different levels of scale. The symmetry and the nested structure of Andean ayllu systems have led to the generalization of a social structure based on "recursive hierarchy" (Urton 1993). Using the terms "maximal ayllu," "minor ayllu," and "minimal ayllu," Platt has presented the present-day Macha of Potosí, Bolivia, as an example of such a nested system of ayllu identities, with the entire Macha group considered one maximal ayllu, coterminous with ethnic group, a finer level of identification with either of two moiety divisions, a further identity with one of a total of ten minor ayllus, and finally an identity with minimal ayllu or kindred groups (Platt 1986). Similarly recursive hierarchies of identity have been noted for the Lupaqa, Laymi, and K'ulta Aymara, and structural affiliations articulated through these relations often play a part in reciprocal economics and rural migration patterns (Murra 1968; Harris 1986; Saignes 1986; Abercrombie 1998:154–157).

AYLLUS AND DIASPORAS

To respond to a diaspora model of colonization, ancient state colonies must answer to four criteria: residence in peripheral regions, maintained identity with a homeland ethnic group (i.e., the maximal ayllu), structural reproduction of the recursive hierarchy of the homeland in the colonies (i.e., distinctions resembling those of minor and minimal ayllus), and multiethnic coexistence with colonies of other ethnicities.

Expatriate residence of migrant communities must be evident in the form of habitation sites, midden deposits, and associated cemeteries. Settlement evidence should be sufficiently intensive and long term to distinguish a colonial demographic presence from seasonal transhumance or indirect and impermanent forms of contact such as trade, proselytizing, or elite clientage. Diaspora settlements should be of a scale commensurate with the social and ideological reproduction of the expatriate community, minimally enclaves of several hundred households.

As in modern-day diaspora communities, a shared identity among emigrants in a "vertical archipelago" would be marked in the practice of daily life, evident in shared templates of family structure, settlement planning, house construction, domestic features and activities, cuisine, mortuary and ritual traditions, and stylistic choices in everything from pottery and clothing to agricultural techniques. Diasporic identity should be apparent in both style and disposition of a colonial site's entire domestic assemblage, with either imports or locally made artifacts reflecting the maintenance of the tastes and lifestyles of the homeland community. To the extent that this community of identity is endogamous, ethnic identity may also be evident in skeletal biology.

If an ayllu-based nested hierarchy model holds, archipelago colonies should structurally reproduce the homeland's moiety and minimal ayllu units. Within colonial communities, these segments may be evident in spatially discernible residential units that display distinctive material distributions, or stylistic behavior that parallel that of specific social segments in the homeland. These could be evident in microvariations in costume, utensil use, ceremonial or mortuary practice, or other stylistic practices that leave a mark on material culture. Compared with markers for ethnic identity, however, the diacritics for these subdivisions in material culture may be considerably more subtle archaeologically. Intentional cranial deformation, a stylistic behavior that leaves a permanent and unchangeable record on the human body, may be a particularly telltale marker of a descent-based yet socially chosen identity (Buikstra 1995; Hoshower et al. 1995; Blom 1999). Finally, skeletal, dental or molecular biological distance studies of significant samples of individuals may also offer insight into how the genetic component of archaeological ayllus varied over time and across space (Buikstra 1995; Sutter 1996, 2000; Blom et al. 1998; Blom 1999; Lozada 1998; Knudson et al. 2004).

An archaeological test of multiethnicity must provide evidence of contemporary sites of culturally distinct affiliations in close proximity. John Murra himself sketched out this criterion as an archaeological hypothesis:

> I wouldn't be surprised if we find in one single valley settlements of diverse antecedents without any temporal stratification between them. These would simply be peripheral colonies established in the lowlands by cores that were contemporary, but diverse in material culture. (Murra 1972:441)

This means that the enclaves of vertically extended communities in the Andes could have functioned like transparent overlays on a map, sharing regional space without any concept of bounded territories and coexisting with one another but never really interacting.

If Tiwanaku expansion were a multiethnic diaspora (or diasporas), we would thus encounter not one but several contemporary settlement patterns of Tiwanaku subgroups or ethnicities. Conversely, evidence of a bounded, colonialized territory containing only homogeneous settlements of a single affiliation (i.e., a single, spatially bounded community) would tend to contradict the multiethnic coexistence inherent to a diaspora model. Methodologically, therefore, the consideration of multiethnicity requires a research strategy that addresses regional settlement patterns through systematic survey, as well as within-site household and mortuary studies. Both regional and within-site dimensions of community are explored here for our archaeological case, the Tiwanaku colonies of the Moquegua Valley of southern Peru (Figure 16.1).

Over the course of settlement pattern studies in the late 1990s I have come to favor a diasporic perspective on Tiwanaku expansion in the same Moquegua Valley. Detailed settlement pattern data and new dates in this region of intensive Tiwanaku colonization are the major empirical influence that pushed me away from assumptions of centrally directed colonization and toward a diasporic paradigm. Tiwanaku colonization simply looked different from a regional perspective, and far less centralized than it did from my prior single-site view developed from the Omo sites. At the same time, one of the most influential challenges to my old ideas came from present-day Aymara settlers whom we encountered in the course of our survey work. Allow me to relate one of their stories.

DOÑA CECILIA'S TALE

I first met Doña Cecilia Mamani, a highland Aymara homesteader in the Moquegua Valley, in the late 1990s. Her story is typical of a present-day Andean diaspora that may be instructive for our reconstruction of the Tiwanaku migrations of a millennium before. A single mother, she had arrived in Moquegua a decade earlier from the highland Aymara village of Muylaque, bringing two children and a determination to build a better life. During a drought a few years before, her father had passed through Moquegua, perhaps with his herds or to trade. He did not stay, but he noticed a few vacant locations just above the existing canals that he thought could be made green if water could be brought to them. He marked them with stone cairns just in case, because he had many children and only a small farm in Muylaque.

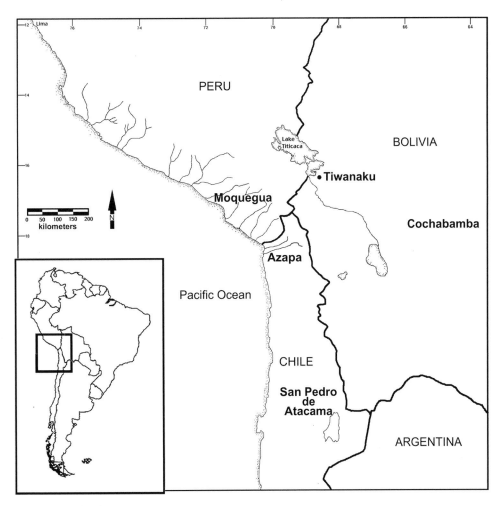

Figure 16.1. The south-central Andes.

Doña Cecilia's father never returned to Moquegua, and, being the eldest daughter, she seldom thought about his stories of opportunities in the lowlands as she married and started a family. It wasn't until her husband left her that she decided to move from her village to Moquegua, becoming one of the first to do so. She began her life in diaspora in a small *chosita*, a woven mat hut that she had built to mark her place on the lands her father had scouted. Supporting herself with the backbreaking work of sorting river stones and gravel for construction, she gradually accrued the capital to legalize her land claim or *denuncia*, obtaining title from the state by proving it viable for farming.[1] With this modest success, she invited her younger siblings and cousins from Muylaque to help her farm, tend herds, and dig and maintain the canal that irrigates the sliver of land that the Mamanis carved out of the desert hillslope (Figure 16.2). Life was still hard, but the lower slopes of Cerro Trapiche were green for

the first time in centuries, and the Mamanis were land-holders in Moquegua. Far from assimilating to their new land, however, the Mamanis still speak of themselves as people of Muylaque, maintaining close contacts with their homeland relatives and frequently traveling there to visit and bring produce.

Hearing countless stories like Doña Cecilia's made me wonder. Clearly, Moquegua's present-day indigenous migration was inextricably linked to enduring ties of community identity and had little to do with the kind of globalist, directed colonization I had described for Tiwanaku a thousand years before. True, unlike the Tiwanaku, today's Aymara diaspora lives within and under the protection of the modern Peruvian state and a global capitalist economy. In Moquegua, the state's massive Pasto Grande canal irrigation project, the creation of a Bolivian-Peruvian free trade zone, and completion of the Ilo-La Paz highway all played some role in

Figure 16.2. Modern agrarian immigrant community constructing canal, Moquegua, 2005.

encouraging migration. However, state policies alone could not explain what was motivating and integrating these communities in motion. The central government's role in inducing migration seemed indirect, unforeseen, and usually unintended. Indeed, the success of the new highland migration has been the bane of Moquegua's Euro-American ruling elite, as the old political balance has been permanently upended. I began to wonder whether any centralized state, past or present, could motivate this kind of popular migration. At the same time, my settlement pattern study was not finding the kind of indications of centralized tribute and hierarchy that I had expected in an annexed Tiwanaku periphery.

TWO AYLLUS IN DIASPORA: THE TIWANAKU COLONIES' SEGMENTARY ORGANIZATION

Tiwanaku's first pioneer settlement in the western valleys of Moquegua and Azapa came about toward the middle of the Bolivian Tiwanaku sequence, probably coinciding with the explosion of population and monumental

construction at the type site (ca. AD 500–725). The earliest dates in Moquegua represent settlements of altiplano people who used Omo-style ceramics (Figure 16.3). Most likely, these first pioneer Tiwanaku colonists were pastoralists, continuing a longer tradition of transhumance by highland camelid herders with migrations to the lowland valleys of increasingly longer distance and greater duration. A degree of pastoral association is plausible for the initial Omo-style Tiwanaku settlements because of their consistent settlement location closer to caravan routes and llama petroglyphs and farther from agricultural areas than other Tiwanaku settlers, and this hypothesis may be supported by the tentlike, ephemeral nature of their domestic architecture. As in the case of Doña Cecilia's family, this kind of occupational distinction was probably not an absolute, but it seems reasonable that the first Tiwanaku migrants would be agropastoral social groups with the greatest mobility.

The most intensive Tiwanaku settlement followed a recently discovered massive flood event that occurred around AD 700. Geomorphological evidence from Moquegua shows this to be an event of cataclysmic

Figure 16.3. Omo-style Tiwanaku kero.

proportions that caused local rainfall, flooding, and remodeling of the local floodplain on a scale not seen again until six centuries later (Magilligan and Goldstein 2001). Like recent El Niño events, this event may also have been an important catalyst to migration as both a "push" and a "pull" to highland migration. Unlike long-term climate change, which might not be perceived by human populations, these short-lived events would have elicited immediate responses to rapid cycles of agricultural instability and competitive dynamics in both the Moquegua lowland and in the altiplano Tiwanaku homeland. In Moquegua, erosion caused by the far more modest 1998 El Niño resulted in the loss of as much as 30% of the richest floodplain lands (Manners et al. 2007). The topsoil losses of the far more severe AD 700 event would have been an agrarian disaster to indigenous populations of Formative "Huaracané" agriculturalists. Without alternative agricultural strategies such as farming upland terraces, creating valley-side canal systems, or reclaiming desert land for agriculture, loss of the mid-valley floodplain may have forced this group to abandon the valley.

At the same time in the altiplano, a powerful El Niño following a period of demographic growth would have caused a severe short-term drought, bringing with it sudden stresses for highland societies. The most mobile populations of highland Tiwanaku would have been the first to react, as herders moved their drought-stricken flocks to lowland regions like Moquegua in unprecedented numbers and for longer periods.

Then as today, the mobilization of migrants with little to lose may have been motivated as much by perceived opportunity as by a desire to escape drought and social stress at home. Although most of the surface water of El Niño floods like those of the AD 700 event would have dissipated rapidly, it is possible that aquifer recharge might have led to the florescence of spring-fed pastures and the creation of new cultivable lands for some period, and that the fluvial modification of landforms by erosion could have changed the location of spring outlets (Figure 16.4). Ironically, even as it led to disaster for the floodplain agricultural systems of the pre-Tiwanaku Huaracané, the AD 700 El Niño could have created new opportunities for pasture and agriculture using different agricultural systems deeper in the desert. Finding these unexploited parts of the lowland valley vacant and lush in the years following the flood, I surmise, altiplano pastoralists became colonists, establishing more permanent settlements and inviting kinfolk to stay for increasingly long periods as farmers. This marks the beginning of the Omo-style occupation.

These first colonists brought with them a full array of traditions and lifeways that marked their strong identity with both the Tiwanaku culture and some of its distinct ethnic subcultures. As their settlements became more permanent, the Omo-style colonists would have brought families and transplanted a Tiwanaku way of life to a foreign region. The settlers would have brought with them conceptions of appropriate domestic architecture and the stuff of everyday life that identified them with their origin communities within the Tiwanaku core region. Tiwanaku redware and blackware serving vessels of the Omo style are indistinguishable from one style of altiplano pottery of Tiwanaku and may well have been imported (Figure 16.5). The distribution of these serving vessels was not limited to the occasional burials of local elites, as it was in the oasis communities of San Pedro de Atacama, or to small enclaves of Tiwanaku traders, as it was in the Azapa Valley of northern Chile (Goldstein 1996). Instead, Omo-style *keros* and pitchers appear throughout the ceramic assemblage of ordinary households in large domestic settlement sites at Omo, Los Cerrillos, and Río Muerto. The colonists used a wide range of specific everyday tools and implements that linked their everyday habitual behaviors to those

Figure 16.4. Spring florescence agricultural claim, Moquegua, 2002.

of their homeland. Even the utilitarian plain pottery that constituted 91% of the ceramics at the Moquegua Tiwanaku sites conformed to highland norms. Although these utensils may have been locally made, their formal and functional identity with altiplano Tiwanaku prototypes confirms that they were made by Tiwanaku-trained craftspeople for the culinary demands and tastes of Tiwanaku consumers. Tiwanaku domestic life, and in this case the domestic lifeway of a specific subgroup within Tiwanaku, was shaped by a powerfully held adherence to a way of doing things—a Tiwanaku sense of habitus. If we accept that cultural identity and social relationships are enacted through the repetitive actions of daily practice, there can be little question that these Tiwanaku colonists were of altiplano origin.

Most major settlement of the Omo style was concentrated in the middle Moquegua Valley in open areas below the modern city of Moquegua, where agriculture can be conducted without artificial terracing (Figure 16.6). Fifteen site components covering a total of 28.7 ha have been associated with the Omo style in the middle Moquegua Valley. Virtually all of the Omo colonial settlement was clustered in large residential sectors at the four major centers of Omo, Chen Chen/Los Cerrillos, Cerro Echenique, and Río Muerto (sites M12, M13, M16, M31, and M70). Visibly segmentary residential space in the Omo-style sites indicates that Tiwanaku colonial society comprised numerous insular communities, each arrayed around its own common plazas for assembly or ritual (Figure 16.7). The Omo-style sites' plaza-centered neighborhoods probably could correspond to minimal ayllus within the Omo-style enclave with specific homeland counterparts, who maintained their spatial separation in residence and ritual to help maintain these distinct identities. Outside of the three town groups, there is a surprising absence of small village sites, and rank size analysis shows no particular hierarchy to the settlement pattern (Goldstein 2005).

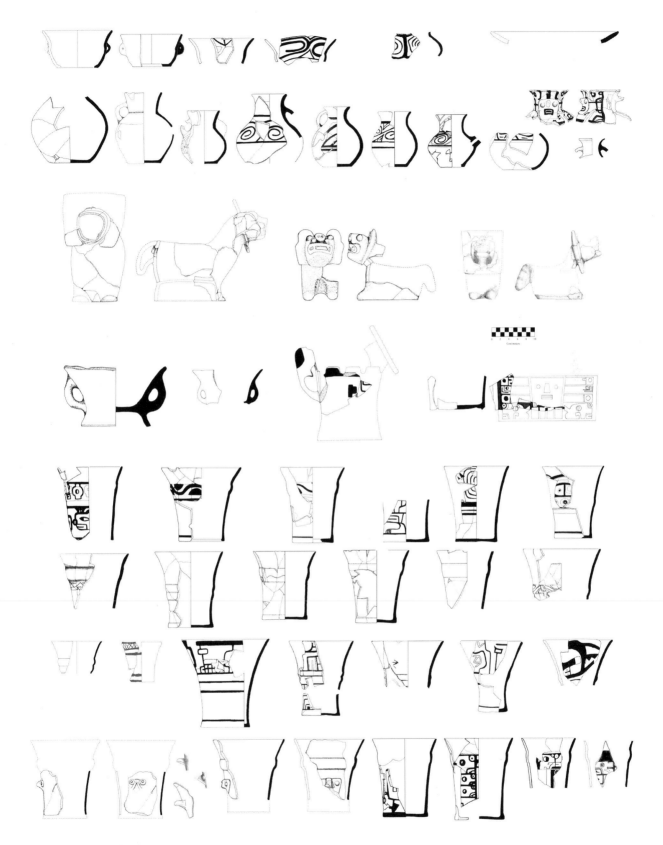

Figure 16.5. Omo-style ceramics.

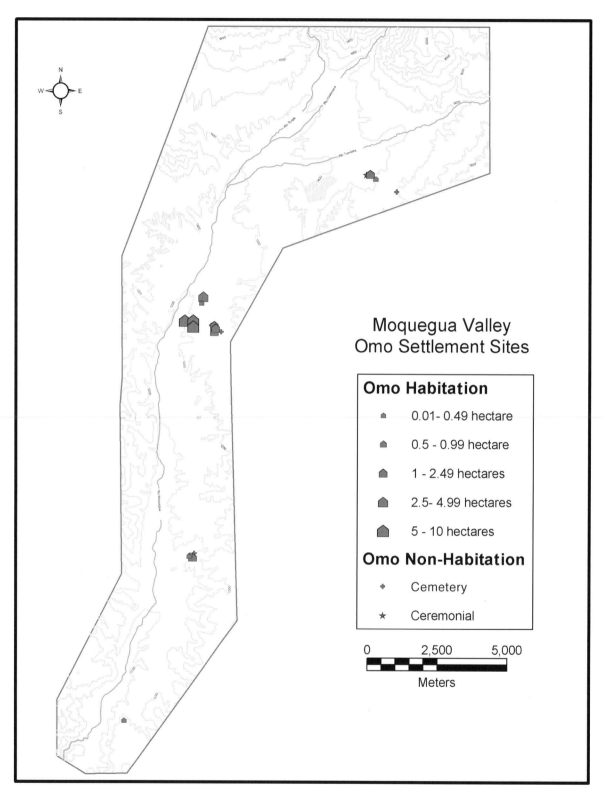

Figure 16.6. Omo-style settlement distribution.

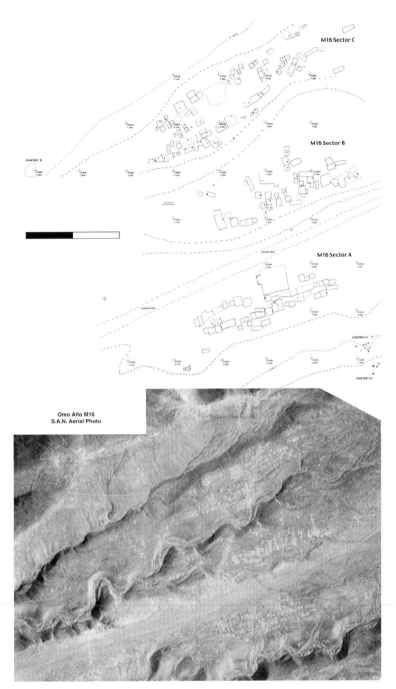

Figure 16.7. Omo-style site plan, Omo M16.

Some time after the initial Omo-style Tiwanaku colonization of Moquegua, a second set of Tiwanaku colonial enclaves appeared. This second wave of migration of Tiwanaku settlers was distinguished by a new style of Tiwanaku material culture known as the Chen Chen style (Figure 16.8). Astoundingly, this separate Chen Chen style migration from the altiplano neither replaced nor mingled with the Omo-style colony but set up shop alongside the Omo-style groups in a distinct and independent settlement pattern in which each site was characterized by lifeways distinct from those of their Omo-style neighbors (Figure 16.9). Thus, Tiwanaku colonization represents not one but two overlapping diasporas.

The Chen Chen style is the most widespread Tiwanaku ceramic substyle in the Osmore drainage and coincides with the most substantial provincial occupation by Tiwanaku colonists anywhere in the Andes. The

Figure 16.8. Chen Chen style ceramics.

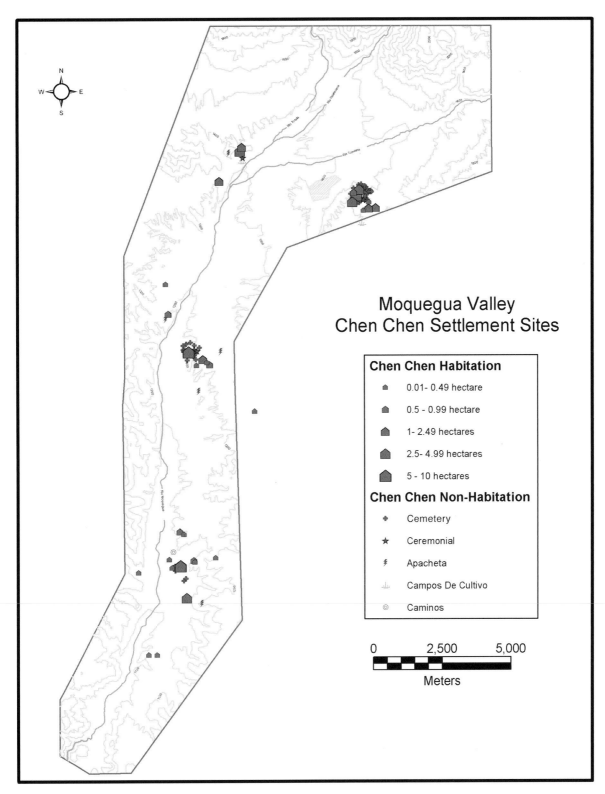

Figure 16.9. Chen Chen-style settlement distribution.

Chen Chen style receives its name from the heavily looted cemeteries at Chen Chen, the first published site of Tiwanaku affiliation in Moquegua (Ishida 1960; Disselhoff 1968). Chen Chen is only one of several large sites in Moquegua that can be identified with an explosive Tiwanaku V expansion. Chen Chen phase settlement covered 54.6 ha in the middle Moquegua Valley, with an additional 10.4 ha of cemeteries. Like the Omo colonial settlements, Chen Chen occupation was clustered at the same three large Tiwanaku site groups of Chen Chen, Omo, and Río Muerto, but segregated in distinct settlement sites within these site groups (M1, M10, M43, M48, and M52), with an additional settlement at Cerro Echenique. The typical Chen Chen village plan included domestic plazas, habitation, storage, processing, and midden areas, with separate cemeteries located around the periphery of the domestic cluster. The Chen Chen-style occupation is unique among the Tiwanaku colonies for the 100-m-long temple mound and sunken court at the Omo M10 site (Goldstein 1993, 2005). The replication of Tiwanaku ceremonial architecture suggests that Omo was a ceremonial or administrative center for the Chen Chen-style enclave in Moquegua, and perhaps for colonists from both colonizing groups. Smaller ceremonial structures have been identified at Chen Chen and Echenique, however, and extensive domestic evidence shows that commensal beer drinking, dedicatory sacrifice of animals and objects, and other Tiwanaku ritual practices were common at the household level as well.

What is remarkable about these two waves of Tiwanaku colonization is the implication that Tiwanaku colonization represents not one but two overlapping diasporas. The enclaves of the Chen Chen-style migration from the altiplano neither replaced nor mingled with the Omo-style colonies but set up shop alongside the Omo-style groups in a distinct and independent settlement pattern. Each Chen Chen-style enclave maintained Tiwanaku lifeways that were distinct from the Tiwanaku lifeways of their Omo-style neighbors. At the three site groups in Moquegua where they coexisted, the Chen Chen-style sites were consistently located to the southwest of their Omo-style neighbors. The Omo temple and other ceremonial structures and locations appear to align along a similar axis. Each village's identification with one of the two great diasporas of Tiwanaku settlement may have been encoded with settlements of each of these two diaspora communities located according to structural norms of oppositional social division across space, perhaps an antecedent to systems like the Inca

ceque system, which functioned both as a cosmology and as a social map for the ayllus of Cusco.

Who were these dual diasporas? If Andean ayllus can be seen as a way in which individuals' social identities are articulated in a recursive hierarchy, the Omo and Chen Chen styles may represent two maximal ayllus within the Tiwanaku confederation that maintained distinctive ethnic identities in diaspora. Kolata, adopting Bouysse-Cassagne's interpretations of ethnic allegiances and identities from ethnohistoric documents, has proposed a complex multiethnic Tiwanaku in the altiplano homeland in which distinct ethnic and linguistic groups aligned into two great maximal moieties of Urco and Umasuyu opposed along a spatial axis formed by Lake Titicaca (Bouysse-Cassagne 1986:207). Kolata argues that these same pluralistic dynamics also were expressed in the division of ritual space within Tiwanaku, a site also known as Taypicala, or "the stone in the middle of the world" (Cobo 1990 [1653]:100; Kolata 1993:101). This vision of a pluralistic Tiwanaku has been expanded upon by Janusek's reading of distinct ethnicities or ayllu-like social groups coresident in altiplano Tiwanaku neighborhoods and their satellite towns as communities of identity within Tiwanaku (Janusek 2002, 2003, 2004).

In desert Moquegua, we can confirm that at least two Tiwanaku maximal ayllus existed because they established two contemporary yet distinct settlement archipelagos. There is not yet enough evidence to connect the binary opposition of Omo and Chen Chen settlement to colonists from any specific locations or origin within the altiplano. Ceramics resembling Moquegua's Chen Chen-style pottery are so ubiquitous throughout the Tiwanaku sphere that they cannot be linked to a particular source. On the other hand, the Omo-style pottery appears to share affinities (notably the frequency of black polished serving ware and certain varieties of vessel shapes) with Tiwanaku ceramics of the Copacabana Peninsula and the lake islands. Notable are the prevalence of polished blackware, the Omo-style kero shape, and the continuous volute motif. This suggests that an earlier, pastoralist wave of colonists may have originated in Tiwanaku communities on the southwestern shore of Lake Titicaca. Similar vessels appearing in Tiwanaku collections from Cochabamba may mark a mirror colony by the same ethnic group on the eastern slopes, yet Omo-style blackware pottery is relatively infrequent at the Tiwanaku type site, indicating that the style was only one of many in use at the cosmopolitan "stone at the center." Future detailed interregional comparisons of household and mortuary patterns, iconography and material culture, ceramic sourcing, and considerations of biological distance and differential nutrition among skeletal populations will be critical to elucidating these cross-cutting affiliations within Tiwanaku.

TIWANAKU COLONISTS AND OTHERS

More research can also help clarify the initial interaction of the Tiwanaku diaspora with indigenous populations. It has been noted that one person's frontier is usually somebody else's homeland (Lightfoot and Martinez 1995:473), and we must start seeing the hitherto invisible people of colonized regions as active participants in their fate. In Cochabamba, Azapa, and San Pedro de Atacama, we see that local people accepted Tiwanaku imports and adopted elements of Tiwanaku material culture (Llagostera 1996; Mujica 1996). Even this moderate degree of cultural interaction implies social and economic relationships between the two populations, perhaps including marriage exchanges to cement alliances. In contrast, in Moquegua we do not find evidence of the indigenous Huaracané people accepting Tiwanaku cultural practices. Tiwanaku artifacts are never found in Huaracané contexts, and no Huaracané artifacts appear in Tiwanaku sites. This discontinuity between the Huaracané domestic tradition and that of the Tiwanaku colonies is borne out by biological distance studies that find little evidence of genetic exchange between the two groups or distinctive practices of cranial deformation (Blom et al. 1998). Putting it together, we can infer that the two populations were not only spatially and culturally distinct but strongly endogamous.

It is possible to interpret the two cultures' lack of interaction in two ways. A globalist scenario might explain the absence of Tiwanaku cultural influences at Huaracané sites by the forced abandonment of the Huaracané villages during the Tiwanaku colonization. A traditional conquest interpretation might assume that the valley's indigenous inhabitants were resettled in new towns where they could be controlled and gradually acculturated as a part of imperial policy. Certainly, this was the case with the Spanish Empire's conquest of much of the Andes, and it is not surprising to see a similar logic applied to settlement changes under the expansion of the great Pre-Columbian civilizations (e.g., D'Altroy 1992, 2001; Schreiber 1992, 1993, 2001).

However, without any trace of Huaracané domestic architecture, practices, or artifacts in the Tiwanaku colonies, this seems unlikely. Huaracané villagers might have been put to the sword, forced to flee, or strategically relocated to some unknown region. Alternately, the great floods of the AD 700 El Niño could have dealt a crushing blow to valley agriculture, wiping out canals and carrying away crops and fertile floodplain soils. Under either interpretation, Huaracané settlement along the fertile valley edge would have been severely disrupted, yet it is hard to envision this entire population simply vanishing with the arrival of Tiwanaku settlers.

A more likely scenario would ascribe the segregation of late Huaracané and Tiwanaku settlement patterns to the deliberate isolation of an Andean diaspora from a culturally distinct host population. This multiethnic coexistence through conscious segregation was possible in part because the Omo-style colonists occupied a different niche both spatially and occupationally. Invariably, the archipelago of Tiwanaku colonies was located in areas outside the Huaracané settlement pattern (Figure 16.10). Entering the valley as pastoralists, the first colonists may have been perceived as noncompetitive by the Huaracané agriculturalists. Whether by cultural preference or by pragmatic design, it is clear that Tiwanaku colonists deliberately avoided the floodplain niche of the Huaracané by clustering their initial settlements near springs and canal-irrigable lands deeper in the desert. The fact that Moquegua Tiwanaku sites were open and unfortified can only be explained by a careful partitioning of valley territory between local populations and Tiwanaku colonists. Only further study directed to dating and understanding the late Huaracané sites can confirm exactly how long this remarkable multiethnic coexistence between colonists and natives survived.

Similarly, we are left with questions of how Tiwanaku colonists interacted with contemporary Wari enclaves in southern Peru. Only 10 km from Chen Chen and the Moquegua Tiwanaku colonies, the Wari center at Cerro Baúl sits atop a sheer-sided mesa that dominates the upper valley. The defensible location of Cerro Baúl, as opposed to the openness of the Tiwanaku settlements, suggests a contrast between military occupation and demographic control. Recently, however, settlement survey has revealed a hinterland of settlements and agricultural fields associated with Wari in the Upper Osmore, while dates from Cerro Baúl indicate a long-term occupation contemporary with Tiwanaku

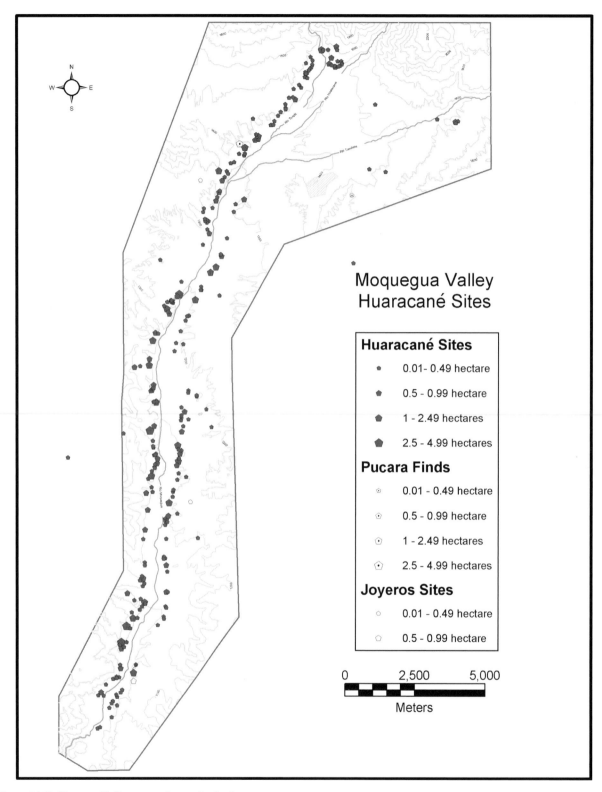

Figure 16.10. Huaracané indigenous settlement distribution.

Figure 16.11. Wari-Huaracané chichería patio group at Cerro Trapiche (foreground), and Tiwanaku settlement at Cerro Echenique (left background). Recent immigrant canals are also visible on the flanks of Trapiche.

(Lumbreras et al. 1982; Watanabe 1990; Feldman 1987; Moseley et al. 1991, 2005; Williams 2001, 2002; Owen and Goldstein 2001; Williams et al. 2001; Williams and Nash 2002). On Tiwanaku turf in the middle Moquegua Valley, a smaller Wari outpost at Cerro Trapiche and the Moquegua Tiwanaku settlement at Cerro Echenique kept watch on each other from hilltops less than 2 km apart (Goldstein et al. in press; Figure 16.11). Yet despite the proximity of the two cultures' enclaves, Wari sherds and obsidian are seldom found in Tiwanaku tombs or household units.

The extraordinary segregation of the Wari and Tiwanaku cultural traditions at different sites in Moquegua indicates that direct interaction of colonists of the two states along their Moquegua frontier was minimal. Considering the long duration of both settlements, this suggests a complex dynamic between conflict and a *modus vivendi* among the descendants of indigenous Huaracané and the Tiwanaku and Wari colonists.

WHAT WAS TIWANAKU?

What kind of state was Tiwanaku? Was it an empire? The answers we choose depend on whether we judge states by their achievements or by the ways in which they achieved them. By most standards, Tiwanaku attained a level of scale and complexity that we usually associate with a powerful state-level society, and perhaps even a proto-empire. The people we call the Tiwanaku created the largest and most cosmopolitan city the Andes had yet seen. They built awe-inspiring pyramids, courts, and palaces and developed industries that produced an immense output of utilitarian and sumptuary goods. To feed their capital city, the Tiwanaku commanded a vast system of intensified agriculture throughout the altiplano core region. Tiwanaku promulgated a set of spiritual beliefs and a corporate art style shared throughout the south-central Andes that helped it unite diverse peoples under its cultural influence. Finally, a far-flung diaspora of Tiwanaku colonists created a network of new towns and ceremonial centers in distant regions.

As I suggested earlier, when we think of the growth of ancient states we often assume that increasing complexity and scale must be preceded by systemic processes of centralization and the imposition of a hierarchical structure on information flow and regulation. Tiwanaku is among a small number of ancient states that do not fit this general pattern. Although some aspects of Tiwanaku are statelike, a surprising amount of political and economic power remained in the hands of corporate groups that may have been very much like the present-day diaspora of ayllus of the Andean highlands. Indeed, when compared with the majority of expansive archaic states, Tiwanaku stands out on several counts.

First, unlike the Inca, whose empire grew through military expansion, there is no iconographic, archaeological, or bioarchaeological evidence that Tiwanaku ever expanded through violent conquest. Inca conquest was backed up by enormous investments in roads, fortresses, garrisons, and military stores, but there is no evidence that Tiwanaku built any military infrastructure for coercive control after consolidation. If Tiwanaku elites exercised military power, they did it in a remarkably subtle fashion, through ideological hegemony rather than physical conquest. Tiwanaku was not a warrior state.

Second, there is only equivocal evidence for kingship and the paramount social classes that would be expected in a fully centralized Tiwanaku social hierarchy. Several buildings at the Tiwanaku site may qualify as residential palaces, but there are simply not enough data to describe any of the elites who lived there as royal, in comparison with the rulers whose palace compounds and monuments are an indispensable part of the ground plans of many early state centers (Flannery 1998). Neither are there Tiwanaku burials comparable in wealth and grandeur to the royal tombs of the Moche, Chimu, or other Andean states, let alone the burial cults of the great civilizations of the Old World. Similarly, there is no oral tradition or textual support for Tiwanaku royal genealogies, nor are there surviving myths of separate origins of Tiwanaku kings and commoners, as might be expected under a fully developed ruling-class ideology. Tiwanaku failed to leave us written inscriptions, and it is likely that Tiwanaku's grandest and potentially "royal" tombs were ransacked long ago. However, the individuals in the high-status tombs that have been studied have been described as priestly rather than secular elites because of their offerings (Wassen 1972; Money 1991). If there truly were kings and high lords of Tiwanaku, we would probably know more about them by now.

Iconographic sources also fail to convey images of unitary secular kingship and social hierarchy in Tiwanaku. Tiwanaku art produced few realistic depictions of narrative scenes and action compared with the identifiable themes that have been so successfully deciphered in Moche art of the northern Andes. Tiwanaku's images are iconic and inscrutable. Nonetheless, it is possible to distinguish real people from gods or mythic ancestors in Middle Horizon iconography, and the distribution of supernatural imagery has been a key tool in assessing the distribution of religious cults (Cook 1992). Portraiture in ceramic vessels and stone monuments also depicts specific human individuals, but their positions and titles are unknown and there is no evidence that they represent a unified cult of royalty. Tiwanaku leaders are seldom, if ever, depicted with weapons, and the Tiwanaku art style does not use a convention of relative size to indicate social rank, as was common in many early-state art styles. Instead, the symbols of leadership displayed in Tiwanaku's great stelae—hallucinogenic snuff tablets, kero chalices, and vestments decorated with totemic animals and supernatural beings—convey more about leaders' ceremonial responsibilities than about their secular power. Even iconographic studies that use the term *king* for Tiwanaku rulers describe a political ideology of pluralism. Berenguer, for example, proposes that the oppositional distribution of kero and snuff tablet icons in Tiwanaku art indicates that Tiwanaku kingship was dualistic, with leaders controlling opposed moieties (Berenguer 1998). If nothing else, the choices of ceremonial objects as symbolic images of power suggest that Tiwanaku rulers commanded ritual rather than physical suzerainty.

Finally, Tiwanaku does not display the requisite features of a hierarchically articulated state political economy. Even in the Tiwanaku core region, many features of the administrative infrastructure that are present in other prehispanic Andean states are missing, and there is little evidence that government institutions exercised direct control over food production or tribute extraction (Bermann 1994:36; Isbell 1997:314). The kinds of centrally planned roads, storage depots, and way stations that characterized Inca administration were relatively underdeveloped in Tiwanaku. Administrative devices like Inca *quipus* (string records) or the clay tokens of protoliterate Mesopotamia that are traditionally associated with state political economies are unknown. Tiwanaku's greatest public buildings had no storerooms or offices for secular economic transactions and were primarily temples designed for worshipful pilgrimage experiences (Conklin 1991; Moore 1996; Protzen and Nair 2000). In terms of urban residential planning, Tiwanaku cannot simply be described as an enormous "company town" of patron elites and dependent attached specialist classes as Alan Kolata proposes (1997:254). Instead, urban specialist groups may have cohered around shared occupational traditions that were reproduced through descent or ethnic affiliation rather than elite patronage (Janusek 1999). There is mounting evidence from Tiwanaku's urban barrios that groups resembling castes or ethnic business networks retained strong corporate identities. Ayllus were the forces to be reckoned with in the Tiwanaku political economy.

Interpretations suggesting less centralization and more local autonomy for the surrounding countryside and towns of the Tiwanaku core region are also gaining support (Albarracin-Jordan 1996; Bermann 1997; McAndrews et al. 1997). This stands in contrast to reconstructions that emphasize highly centralized, state-directed agrarian production (Kolata 1993, 1997, 2003) and regional hierarchy in a tributary political economy (Stanish 2003). Rural agrarian and household crafts production surely increased under Tiwanaku vertical integration, but these changes may have been a relatively superficial overlay on long-standing local patterns (Bermann 1994). Continued local control over land tenure and irrigation management in the countryside also indicates an enduring segmentary structure of largely autonomous local groups within the Tiwanaku state (Albarracin-Jordan 1996; Erickson 1999). At the same time, settlement pattern data for the Tiwanaku colonization of Cochabamba (Higueras 1996, 2001; Anderson et al. 1998), Azapa and San Pedro (Berenguer and Dauelsberg 1989; Rivera 1991; Goldstein 1996; Muñoz 1996), and Moquegua have failed to show a shift to settlement systems indicative of a centralized tributary system.[2] Certainly Tiwanaku's political economy raised sufficient resources to finance the building projects and lifestyles of its core elites. What is troubling is that Tiwanaku did not develop the usual permanent and highly centralized tributary institutions shared by most archaic states (Marcus 1998).

CONCLUSION: ANDEAN DIASPORAS PAST AND PRESENT

The state as a state was not perceived as an administrative or coercive fact as much as the expression of an idea of unity among many diverse peasant localities as actualized in ritual linkages between kings and chiefs (Stein 1985:75).

Despite its achievements, Tiwanaku, like the equally grand states of southern India that Burton Stein describes, "cannot be easily incorporated into traditional models of imperial structure" (Sinopoli and Morrison 1995:85). As in the Chola and Vijayanagara states described by Stein and by Sinopoli and Morrison, Tiwanaku central authority was a ritual suzerainty that coexisted with the persistent autonomy of corporate groups. For the Chola, Stein follows Aidan Southall's terminology in describing these states as segmentary because "the boundaries of political jurisdiction are differently perceived from different points of the system, and a central focus of ritual suzerainty is recognized over a wider area than effective political sovereignty" (Southall 1974:156, 1999). Within the Chola state, these competing interest groups included distinct ethnicities, peasant communities, elite lineages, occupational guilds and castes, and even petty kings. Chola kingship depended on a dizzying array of complex cross-cutting alliances with these local factions. Chola kings had to constantly negotiate their political power with other *rajas*, as is evident in their title of *rajadhiraja* (raja of rajas). What we know of Tiwanaku bespeaks a similarly fluid and ambiguous definition of kingship as a negotiated paramountcy. A Tiwanaku king, if indeed there was such a person, may have enjoyed ritual sovereignty, but may similarly have had to negotiate with autonomous local and corporate groups over questions of labor, tribute, and ceremonial obligations.

Does this leave us no option but to strip Tiwanaku of its statehood? Hardly. Instead, we should celebrate Tiwanaku as an opportunity to explore the outlying alternatives in our evolutionary typology of archaic states, and to accept that comparativist generalization, while a good rule of thumb, is not law. Exceptions make archaeology interesting, and Tiwanaku appears to be one of a small number of states that maintained surprisingly segmentary political structures quite late in the game. Although Tiwanaku civilization lacked many of the institutions and infrastructures of other archaic states, it nonetheless endured for half a millennium and had an enormous influence on the south central Andes.

Was the Tiwanaku state more a state of mind than a political entity? And if the pluralist elements of this loosely confederated state could somehow expand into new territories, can we call these diasporas the origin of Andean empire?

I ran into Cecilia Mamani again near the Trapiche river ford in August 2002, almost exactly three years after our first encounter. I was going to the Cerro Trapiche archaeological site to prepare a proposal for a future season of fieldwork on its Formative, Wari, and Tiwanaku components—some of the most perplexing examples of archaeological multiethnicity in Moquegua. As we crossed the swift-moving water on foot, she pointed out the tiny marker stones her people had placed on the submerged stepping stones, and for once I managed to cross successfully. My colleagues were less fortunate. While the gringos changed their socks, some highland Aymara ladies in traditional *pollera*s attempted the same crossing. Although she seemed to recognize them, Doña Cecilia did not point out the stepping stones, and the ladies shared the gringos' soggy fate. Doña Cecilia and I chatted as we watched with amusement from the other side.

The past three years had not been easy for Doña Cecilia and her extended family, yet overall, the Muylaque colony is thriving. Doña Cecilia's pioneering *chacra* is now one of many Mamani family plots on the slopes below the archaeological site. The kinfolk that followed her in migration had taken land that the valleys' indigenous landholders never would have bothered with and made it verdant with alfalfa, potatoes, and barley. Now she has a small house in town, her children are doing well, and, *gracias a dios*, there was plenty of water this year and the cows are fat.

I shared my latest concern with Doña Cecilia. An enormous 30-m-deep trench had mysteriously bisected the Trapiche archaeological site, literally cutting the mountain in two. I already knew that this was the work of yet another highland Aymara colony, an association of families from the highland town of Pachas. Working weekends and in their spare time, the Pachas group was hand-digging an enormous canal to irrigate deep-desert land that neither the Tiwanaku, the present-day Moqueguanos, nor even the Mamanis of Muylaque would have thought possible. I asked Doña Cecilia about these new "others." Surprisingly, she seemed untroubled by this new invasion, and simply shrugged. "Son de Pachas, no les conocemos, pues no nos importa"—"They are from Pachas, we don't know them, so they mean nothing to us."

After all that archaeology, I may have learned the most important lesson about Andean diasporas from my conversations with Doña Cecilia. Some combination of personal desperation, family ambitions, loyalty, and simple restlessness still drives pioneers like Doña Cecilia from their highland homes to colonize new territories. Many, perhaps most, of these colonists fail. This is an immigrant's tale where success seems to be a matter of luck and family, being in the right place at the right time and bringing kinfolk to work the claim and solidify the clan's holdings. Like the Muylaque enclave, each new colony inevitably comes in contact with colonies of other communities. Multiethnicity has been described as a "language of contention" (Roseberry 1990), and conflict between separate diasporas is not only unavoidable but is critical to maintaining each group's sense of identity. More often than not, however, these multiple diasporas have an uncanny ability to keep to their own and to stay out of each other's way without resorting to the agents of a central state. Thus, Omo-style and Chen Chen-style colonists may have coexisted much as Muylaque and Pachas colonists do today. Even if a hierarchy of Tiwanaku priest-kings or the modern bureaucrats ultimately may be called on to grant titles or oust interlopers, the migrations themselves, and the coexistence among parallel colonies, precede state intervention.

Clearly, state power and hierarchical institutions play a role in these ancient and modern diasporas, but that role is complex and historically contingent. Even under a centralized state in a globalized world, circumstance and history still scatter ayllus across the landscape of the Andes. The Tiwanaku diasporas of AD 1000 and the Aymara diasporas of AD 2000 differ in many ways. Yet in the ways that agrarian communities negotiate identity, kin-organized labor, and multiethnicity to make new lands work, they may be surprisingly similar. Further investigation of this surprising conclusion for the Tiwanaku and modern Aymara diasporas is the kind of challenge that Michael Moseley would appreciate.

NOTES

1. The Mamanis' fields occupy the lower outskirts of the Cerro Trapiche M7 archaeological site. Part of their success in the competitive environment of land claims may result from Doña Cecilia's impressive sense of presence and her negotiating ability with the local Instituto Nacional de Cultura, as well as other state entities.

2. Higueras's consideration of Cochabamba settlement patterns suggests that Tiwanaku-contemporary settlement maintains a "status quo" with no significant reorganization of prior patterns. In contrast, Goldstein finds Moquegua Tiwanaku settlement patterns to be markedly different from Formative antecedents. Nonetheless, while Moquegua Tiwanaku settlement is clustered in several large colonies, the pattern lacks any trace of small scattered hamlets, which would have formed the base of a tributary rural hierarchy.

REFERENCES

Abercrombie, Thomas A.
1998   *Pathways of Memory and Power: Ethnography and History among an Andean People.* University of Wisconsin Press, Madison.

Albarracín-Jordan, Juan
1996   Tiwanaku Settlement Systems: The Integration of Nested Hierarchies in the Lower Tiwanaku Valley. *Latin American Antiquity* 3(3):183–210.

Allen, Catherine J.
1988   *The Hold Life Has: Coca and Cultural Identity in an Andean Community.* Smithsonian Institution Press, Washington, DC.

Anderson, Karen, R. Céspedes, and R. Sanzetenea
1998   Tiwanaku and the Local Effects of Contact: The Late Formative to Middle Horizon Transition in Cochabamba, Bolivia. Paper presented at the 63rd Annual Meeting of the Society of American Archaeology, Seattle, WA.

Arriaga, Pablo José de
1968 [1621]   *The Extirpation of Idolatry in Peru.* Translated by L. Clark Keating. University of Kentucky Press, Lexington.

Bastien, Joseph W.
1978   *Mountain of the Condor: Metaphor and Ritual in an Andean Ayllu.* West Publishing, St. Paul.

Bauer, Brian S.
1992   *The Development of the Inca State.* University of Texas Press, Austin.

Bauer, Brian S., and Charles Stanish
2001   *Ritual and Pilgrimage in the Ancient Andes: The Islands of the Sun and the Moon.* University of Texas Press, Austin.

Berenguer, José
1998   La iconografía del poder en Tiwanaku y su rol en la integración de zonas de frontera. *Boletín, Museo Chileno de Arte Precolombino,* no. 7, pp. 19–37.

Berenguer, José R., and Percy Dauelsberg H.
1989   El Norte Grande en la órbita de Tiwanaku (400 a 1200 d.C). In *Culturas de Chile: Prehistoria desde sus orígenes hasta los albores de la conquista,* edited by J. Hidalgo L., Virgilio Schiappacasse F., Hans Niemeyer F., Carlos Aldunate del Solar, and I. Solimano R., pp. 129–180. Editorial Andrés Bello, Santiago.

Bermann, Marc P.
1994   *Lukurmata: Household Archaeology in Prehispanic Bolivia.* Princeton University Press, Princeton, NJ.
1997   Domestic Life and Vertical Integration in the Tiwanaku Heartland. *Latin American Antiquity* 8(2):93–112.

Blom, Deborah E.
1999   *Tiwanaku and the Moquegua Settlements: A Bioarchaeological Approach.* Unpublished doctoral dissertation, Department of Anthropology, University of Chicago.

Blom, Deborah E., Benedikt Hallgrímsson, Linda Keng, María Cecilia Lozada C., and Jane E. Buikstra
1998   Tiwanaku State Colonization: Bioarchaeological Evidence of Migration in the Moquegua Valley, Peru. *World Archaeology* 30(2):238–261.

Bouysse-Cassagne, Therese
1986   Urco and Uma: Aymara Concepts of Space. In *Anthropological History of Andean Polities,* edited by John V. Murra, Nathan Wachtel, and Jacques Revel, pp. 201–227. Cambridge University Press, Cambridge.

Buikstra, Jane E.
1995   Tombs for the Living . . . or . . . for the Dead: The Osmore Ancestors. In *Tombs for the Living: Andean Mortuary Practices,* edited by Tom D. Dillehay, pp. 229–280. Dumbarton Oaks, Washington, DC.

Clifford, James
1994   Diasporas. *Cultural Anthropology* 9(3):302–338.

Cobo, Bernabé
1990 [1653]   *Inca Religion and Customs.* Translated by Roland Hamilton. University of Texas Press, Austin.

Conklin, William J.
1991   Tiwanaku and Huari: Architectural Comparisons and Interpretations. In *Huari Administrative Structure: Prehistoric Monumental Architecture and State Government,* edited by William H. Isbell and Gordon F. McEwan, pp. 281–292. Dumbarton Oaks, Washington, DC.

Cook, Anita G.
1992   The Stone Ancestors: Idioms of Imperial Attire and Rank among Huari Figurines. *Latin American Antiquity* 3(4):341–364.

D'Altroy, Terence N.
1992   *Provincial Power in the Inka Empire.* Smithsonian Institution Press, Washington, DC.
2001   Politics, Resources and Blood in the Inka Empire. In *Empires: Perspectives from Archaeology and History*, edited by Susan E. Alcock, Terence N. D'Altroy, Kathleen D. Morrison, and Carla M. Sinopoli, pp. 201–226. Cambridge University Press, Cambridge.

Disselhoff, Hans D.
1968   Huari und Tiahuanaco: Grabungen und Funde in Sud-Peru. *Zeitschrift für Ethnologie* 93:207–216.

Emberling, Geoff
1997   Ethnicity in Complex Societies: Archaeological Perspectives. *Journal of Archaeological Research* 15(4):295–344.

Erickson, Clark L.
1999   Neo-environmental Determinism and Agrarian "Collapse" in Andean Prehistory. *Antiquity* 73:634–42.

Feldman, Robert A.
1987   Imperial Expansion in the Andes: Wari Settlements in Moquegua. Field Museum of Natural History. Proposal submitted to the National Science Foundation. Manuscript in possession of author.

Flannery, Kent V.
1998   The Ground Plans of Archaic States. In *Archaic States*, edited by Gary M. Feinman and Joyce Marcus, pp. 15–58. School of American Research Press, Santa Fe.
1999   Process and Agency in Early State Formation. *Cambridge Archaeological Journal* 9(1):3–21.

Goldstein, Paul S.
1993   Tiwanaku Temples and State Expansion: A Tiwanaku Sunken Court Temple in Moquegua, Peru. *Latin American Antiquity* 4(3):22–47.
1996   Tiwanaku Settlement Patterns of the Azapa Valley, Chile: New Data, and the Legacy of Percy Dauelsberg. In *Prehistoria del norte de Chile y del desierto de Atacama: Simposio homenaje a Percy Dauelsberg Hahmann. Diálogo Andino* 14/15:57–73 (special issue).
2005   *Andean Diaspora: The Tiwanaku Colonies and the Origins of Andean Empire.* New World Diasporas Series. University Press of Florida, Gainesville.

Goldstein, Paul S., T. D. Carter, and U. Mathis-Green
In press Colonization and Colonialism: Expansive State Relations and Indigenous Labor on the Tiwanaku-Wari Frontier. *Latin American Antiquity.*

Harris, Olivia
1986   From Asymmetry to Triangle: Symbolic Transformations in Northern Potosi. In *Anthropological History of Andean Polities*, edited by John V. Murra, Nathan Wachtel, and Jacques Revel, pp. 260–280. Cambridge University Press, Cambridge.

Higueras, Alvaro
1996   *Prehispanic Settlement and Land Use in Cochabamba, Bolivia.* Unpublished doctoral dissertation, University of Pittsburgh, Pittsburgh, PA.
2001   El Período Intermedio (Horizonte Medio) en los valles de Cochabamba: Una perspectiva del análisis de asentamientos humanos y uso de tierras. In *Huari y Tiwanaku: Modelos vs. evidencias*, edited by Peter Kaulicke and William Isbell, pp. 623–646. Boletín de Arqueología, Pontificia Universidad Católica del Perú 5.

Hoshower, Lisa M., Jane E. Buikstra, Paul S. Goldstein, and Ann D. Webster
1995   Artificial Cranial Deformation at the Omo M10 Site: A Tiwanaku Complex from the Moquegua Valley, Peru. *Latin American Antiquity* 6(2):145–164.

Isbell, William H.
1997   *Mummies and Mortuary Monuments: A Postprocessual Prehistory of Central Andean Social Organization.* University of Texas Press, Austin.

Ishida, Eiichiro
1960   *Andes: The Report of the University of Tokyo Scientific Expedition to the Andes.* University of Tokyo Press, Tokyo.

Janusek, John W.
1999   Craft and Local Power: Embedded Specialization in Tiwanaku Cities. *Latin American Antiquity* 10(2):107–131.
2002   Out of Many, One: Style and Social Boundaries in Tiwanaku. *Latin American Antiquity* 13(1):35–61.
2003   The Changing Face of Tiwanaku Residential Life: State and Local Identity in an Andean City. In *Tiwanaku and Its Hinterland: Archaeology and Paleoecology of an Andean Civilization*, vol. 2, *Urban and Rural Archaeology*, edited by Alan L. Kolata, pp. 264–295. Smithsonian Institution Press, Washington, DC.
2004   *Identity and Power in the Ancient Andes: Tiwanaku Cities through Time.* Routledge, New York.

Knudson, Kelly J., T. Douglas Price, Jane E. Buikstra, and Deborah E. Blom
2004   The Use of Strontium Isotope Analysis to Investigate Tiwanaku Migration and Mortuary Ritual in Boliva and Peru. *Archaeometry* 46(1):5–18.

Kolata, Alan L.
1993   *The Tiwanaku: Portrait of an Andean Civilization.* Blackwell, Cambridge, MA.
1997   Of Kings and Capitals: Principles of Authority and the Nature of Cities in the Native Andean State. In *The Archaeology of City States: Cross-Cultural Approaches*, edited by Deborah L. Nichols and Thomas H. Charlton, pp. 245–254. Smithsonian Institution Press, Washington, DC.
2003   The Social Production of Tiwanaku: Political Economy and Authority in a Native Andean State. In *Tiwanaku and Its Hinterland: Archaeology and Paleoecology of an Andean Civilization*, vol. 2, *Urban and Rural Archaeology*, edited by Alan L. Kolata, pp. 449–472. Smithsonian Institution Press, Washington, DC.

Kolata, Alan L. (ed.)
2003   *Tiwanaku and Its Hinterland: Archaeology and Paleoecology of an Andean Civilization*, vol. 2, *Urban and Rural Archaeology.* Smithsonian Institution Press, Washington, DC.

Lightfoot, Kent G., and A. Martinez
1995   Frontiers and Boundaries in Archaeological Perspective. *Annual Review of Anthropology* 24:471–492.

Llagostera, Agustín
1996   San Pedro de Atacama: Nodo de complementariedad reticular. In *La integración surandina cinco siglos después*, edited by X. Albó, M. Arratia, J. Hidalgo, Lautaro Núñez, Agustín Llagostera, M. Remy, and B. Revesz, pp. 17–42. Centro de Estudios Regionales Andinos Bartolomé de Las Casas, Cusco; Universidad Católica del Norte, Antofagasta.

Lozada Cerna, María Cecilia
1998   *The Señorío of Chiribaya: A Bio-Archaeological Study in the Osmore Drainage of Southern Peru.* Unpublished doctoral dissertation, Department of Anthropology, University of Chicago.

Lumbreras, Luis, Elías Mujica, and R. Vera
1982   Cerro Baúl: Un enclave Wari en territorio Tiwanaku. *Gaceta Arqueológica Andina* 1:4–5.

Magilligan, Francis J., and Paul S. Goldstein
2001   El Niño Floods and Culture Change: A Late Holocene Flood History for the Río Moquegua, Southern Peru. *Geology* 29(5):431–434.

Manners, Rebecca B., Francis J. Magilligan, and Paul S. Goldstein
2007   Floodplain Development, El Niño, and Cultural Consequences in a Hyperarid Andean Environment. *Annals of the Association of American Geographers* 97(2):229–248.

Marcus, Joyce
1998   The Peaks and Valleys of Ancient States: An Extension of the Dynamic Model. In *Archaic States*, edited by Gary M. Feinman and Joyce Marcus, pp. 59–94. School of American Research Press, Santa Fe, NM.

McAndrews, Timothy, Juan Albarracín-Jordan, and Marc P. Bermann
1997   Regional Settlement Patterns of the Tiwanaku Valley of Bolivia. *Journal of Field Archaeology* 24:67–83.

Money, Mary
1991   El tesoro de San Sebastián: Una tumba importante de la cultura Tiwanaku. *Beiträge zur allgemeinen und vergleichenden Archäologie* 11:189–198.

Moore, Jerry D.
1996   *Architecture and Power in the Ancient Andes: The Architecture of Public Buildings.* Cambridge University Press, Cambridge.

Moseley, Michael E.
1992   *The Incas and Their Ancestors: The Archaeology of Peru.* Thames and Hudson, New York.

Moseley, Michael E., Robert A. Feldman, Paul S. Goldstein, and Luis Watanabe M.
1991   Colonies and Conquest: Tiahuanaco and Huari in Moquegua. In *Huari Administrative Structure: Prehistoric Monumental Architecture and State Government*, edited by William H. Isbell and Gordon F. McEwan, pp. 91–103. Dumbarton Oaks, Washington, DC.

Moseley, Michael E., Donna J. Nash, Patrick Ryan Williams, Susan D. deFrance, Ana Miranda, and Mario Ruales
2005   Burning Down the Brewery: Establishing and Evacuating an Ancient Imperial Colony at Cerro Baúl, Peru. *Proceedings of the National Academy of Sciences of the United States of America* 102(48):17264–17271.

Mujica B., Elías
1996   La integración surandina durante el período Tiwanaku. In *La integración surandina cinco siglos después*, edited by X. Albó, M. Arratia, J. Hidalgo, Lautaro Núñez, Agustín Llagostera, M. Remy, and B. Revesz, pp. 81–116. Centro de Estudios Regionales Andinos Bartolomé de Las Casas, Cusco, and Universidad Católica del Norte, Antofagasta.

Muñoz Ovalle, Iván

1996   Integración y complementaridad en las socie-dades prehispánicas en el extremo norte de Chile: Hipótesis de trabajo. In *La integración surandina cinco siglos después*, edited by X. Albó, M. Arratia, J. Hidalgo, Lautaro Núñez, Agustín Llagostera, M. Remy, and B. Revesz, pp. 117–134. Centro de Estudios Regionales Andinos Bartolomé de Las Casas, Cusco, and Universidad Católica del Norte, Antofagasta.

Murra, John V.

1968   An Aymara Kingdom in 1567. *Ethnohistory* 15: 115–151.

1972   El "control vertical" de un máximo de pisos ecológicos en la economía de las sociedades andinas. In *Visita de la provincia de León de Huánuco en 1562 por Iñigo Ortiz de Zuñiga*, edited by John V. Murra, pp. 427–476. Documentos para la Historia y Etnología de Huánuco y la Selva Central, vol. 2. Universidad Nacional Hermilio Valdizán, Huánuco, Perú.

Owen, Bruce D., and Paul S. Goldstein

2001   Tiwanaku en Moquegua: Interacciones regionales y colapso. In *Huari y Tiwanaku: Modelos vs. evidencias*, pp. 169–188. Boletín de Arqueología, Pontificia Universidad Católica del Perú 5. Lima.

Patterson, Thomas, and Christine W. Gailey

1987   Power Relations and State Formation. In *Power Relations and State Formation*, edited by Thomas Patterson and Christine W. Gailey, pp. 1–27. American Anthropological Association, Washington, DC.

Platt, Tristan

1986   Mirrors and Maize: The Concept of Yanantin among the Macha of Bolivia. In *Anthropological History of Andean Polities*, edited by John Murra, Nathan Wachtel, and Jacques Revel, pp. 228–259. Cambridge University Press, Cambridge.

Protzen, J.-P., and S. E. Nair

2000   On Reconstructing Tiwanaku Architecture. *Journal of the Society of Architectural Historians* 59 (3): 358–371.

Rivera Diaz, Mario A.

1991   The Prehistory of Northern Chile: A Synthesis. *Journal of World Prehistory* 5(1):1–48.

Rowe, John Howland

1946   Inca Culture at the Time of the Spanish Conquest. In *Handbook of South American Indians*, vol. 2, *The Andean Civilizations*, edited by Julian H. Steward, pp. 183–330. Bureau of American Ethnology 143. Washington, DC.

Saignes, Thierry

1986   The Ethnic Groups in the Valley of Larecaja: From Descent to Residence. In *Anthropological History of Andean Polities*, edited by John Murra, Nathan Wachtel, and Jacques Revel, pp. 311–341. Cambridge University Press, Cambridge.

Schreiber, Katharina J.

1992   *Wari Imperialism in Middle Horizon Peru*. Anthropological Papers 87. Museum of Anthropology, University of Michigan, Ann Arbor.

1993   The Inca Occupation of the Province of Andamarca Lucanas. In *Provincial Inca: Archaeological and Ethnohistorical Assessment of the Impact of the Inca State*, edited by Michael Malpass, pp. 77–116. University of Iowa Press, Iowa City.

2001   The Wari Empire of Middle Horizon Peru: The Epistemological Challenge of Documenting an Empire without Documentary Evidence. In *Empires: Perspectives from Archaeology and History*, edited by Susan E. Alcock, Terence N. D'Altroy, Kathleen D. Morrison, and Carla M. Sinopoli, pp. 70–92. Cambridge University Press, Cambridge.

Sinopoli, Carla M., and Kathleen D. Morrison

1995   Dimensions of Imperial Control: The Vijayanagara Capital. *American Anthropologist* 97(1):83–96.

Southall, Aidan

1974   State Formation in Africa. *Annual Review of Anthropology* 3:153–165.

1999   The Segmentary State and the Ritual Phase in Political Economy. In *Beyond Chiefdoms: Pathways to Complexity in Africa*, edited by Susan K. McIntosh, pp. 32–38. Cambridge University Press, New York.

Spencer, Charles S.

1998   A Mathematical Model of Primary State Formation. *Cultural Dynamics* 10(1):5–20.

Stanish, Charles

2002   Tiwanaku Political Economy. In *Andean Archaeology I: Variations in Sociopolitical Organization*, pp. 169–198. Kluwer Academic/Plenum Press, New York.

2003   *Ancient Titicaca: The Evolution of Complex Society in Southern Peru and Northern Bolivia*. University of California Press, Berkeley and Los Angeles.

Stein, Burton

1985   Politics, Peasants and the Deconstruction of Feudalism in Medieval India. *Journal of Peasant Studies* 12:54–86.

Sutter, Richard C.

1996 A Bioarchaeological Perspective on Verticality in the Middle and Lower Moquegua Valley, Peru, during the Late Intermediate Period. Paper presented at the Society for American Archaeology 61st Annual Meeting, New Orleans.

2000 Prehistoric Genetic and Culture Change: A Bioarchaeological Search for Pre-Inka Altiplano Colonies in the Coastal Valleys of Moquegua Valley, Peru, and Azapa, Chile. *Latin American Antiquity* 11(1):43–70.

Urton, Gary

1990 *The History of a Myth: Pacariqtambo and the Origin of the Inkas*. University of Texas Press, Austin.

1993 Moieties and Ceremonialism in the Andes: The Ritual Battles of the Carnival Season in Southern Peru. In *El Mundo Ceremonial Andino*, edited by Luis Millones and Y. Onuki, pp. 117–142. Senri Ethnological Studies, no. 37. National Museum of Ethnology, Osaka, Japan.

Wassen, S. Henry

1972 A Medicine Man's Implements and Plants in a Tiahuanacoid Tomb in Highland Bolivia. *Etnologiska Studier* 32.

Watanabe M., Luis

1990 Cerro Baúl: Un santuario de filiación Wari en Moquegua. In *Trabajos arqueológicos en Moquegua, Perú*, edited by Luis Watanabe M., Michael E. Moseley, and Fernando Cabieses. Programa Contisuyo del Museo Peruano de Ciencias de la Salud y Southern Peru Copper Corporation, Lima.

Williams, Patrick Ryan

2001 Cerro Baúl: A Wari Center on the Tiwanaku Frontier. *Latin American Antiquity* 12(1):67–83.

2002 Rethinking Disaster-Induced Collapse in the Demise of the Andean Highland States: Wari and Tiwanaku. *World Archaeology* 33(3):361–374.

Williams, Patrick Ryan, J. Isla C., and Donna J. Nash

2001 Cerro Baúl: Un enclave Wari en interacción con Tiwanaku. In *Huari y Tiwanaku: Modelos vs. evidencias*, pp. 69–88. Boletín de Arqueología, Pontificia Universidad Católica del Perú 5. Lima.

Williams, Patrick Ryan, and Donna J. Nash

2002 Imperial Interaction in the Andes: Huari and Tiwanaku at Cerro Baúl. In *Andean Archaeology I: Variations in Sociopolitical Organization*, pp. 243–265. Kluwer Academic/Plenum Press, New York.

CHAPTER 17

A WORLD TOUR OF BREWERIES

JOYCE MARCUS

The mouth of a perfectly contented man is filled with beer.
—Egyptian text from ca. 2200 BC

NOTHING COULD BE A more appropriate homage to Michael Moseley than to take him on a world tour of breweries. This tour begins in Upper Egypt, where the archaeological data for beer production and consumption abound, then moves to the ethnographic present Sub-Saharan Africa, where ceremonial beer drinking plays a key social and economic role, and finally arrives in Peru, where we examine evidence for beer production at four prehispanic sites: Huánuco Pampa, Manchán, Cerro Baúl, and Cerro Azul.

ANCIENT EGYPT

In contemporary Western culture, virtually every man or woman has access to beer. In some cultures, however, access could be restricted or even forbidden. Among some ancient societies beer was consumed primarily on special occasions, at public rituals scheduled by elites; in others, beer was widely used to attract, reward, and pay laborers for their work.

In ancient Egypt, for example, laborers for the state were often paid in both bread and beer. One standard wage for an ancient Egyptian worker consisted of ten loaves of bread and a measure of beer that varied between one-third of a jug and two jugs (Kemp 1991:125). In Egyptian hieroglyphic writing,

the determinative (or classificatory sign) associated with beer was the depiction of a specific jug (Figure 17.1). This determinative was used not only in those expressions where one might expect it—"to be drunk" or to have "food and drink"—but also in phrases where we might not expect it, such as "tribute."

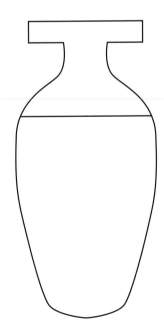

Figure 17.1. Example of the "jug" hieroglyph, a determinative for beer, in ancient Egyptian writing. (Redrawn by K. Clahassey from Kemp 2005:45.)

Egyptian beer, a staple beverage written *ḥnkt* or *ḥqt*, was often placed in tombs so that the deceased could be sustained in the afterlife (Figure 17.2). Wine, too, might be placed in tombs, particularly in those of nobles and rulers. For example, King Scorpion's tomb at Abydos shows the high value placed on beer and wine around 3200 BC (Dreyer 1992; McGovern et al. 1997). Of the twelve rooms that make up the tomb, two (Rooms 3 and 4) contained beer jars and bread molds, while three (Rooms 7, 10, and 12) had as many as 700 wine jars that had been brought from the southern hill country of Jordan/Palestine (Figure 17.3). Forty-seven of the wine jars held grape pips, and several had preserved grapes in them. Eleven vessels yielded sliced figs that had been perforated, strung together, and likely suspended in the wine to add flavor or sweetening. The average capacity of such vessels was 6.5 liters.

Beer was a beverage consumed by both laborers and nobles, and there were several different kinds; the builders of the Fourth Dynasty Giza pyramids could enjoy five varieties. Beer, of course, is much older than that. The earliest known Egyptian breweries date to ca. 3500–3300 BC at Upper Egyptian sites such as Ballas, el-Mahasna, and Hierakonpolis. At Hierakonpolis, archaeologists found vats capable of brewing 1,134 liters. Some of these vats contained a sugary dark residue in which remains of both wheat and barley were found (Geller 1993, 1999). This Upper Egyptian evidence for beer manufacturing is, at present, our oldest for the region.

In Egypt, the art of brewing beer was typically mastered by women, although men could also be involved. Ancient Egyptian women were under the supervision of some kind of chief brewer, such as the high official Kha-bau-Seker, who bore the title "Controller of the Brewing Women" (Murray and Sethe 1937:11; Darby et al. 1977:531).

From scenes painted on Egyptian tomb walls and from wooden models placed in those tombs, we learn much about beer brewing. Because beer and bread shared the same ingredients, we often see brewing and baking being carried out in adjacent scenes in murals or in adjacent rooms in wooden models. Women are shown in prominent roles in both cases. A well-known wooden model found in the tomb of an Eleventh Dynasty high official named Meket-ra shows a brewery in the miniature building's front room and a bakery in the back room (Figure 17.4). In the brewery we see grinding stones, beer jars, dough cakes, and vats for fermentation. In the bakery we see grinding stones,

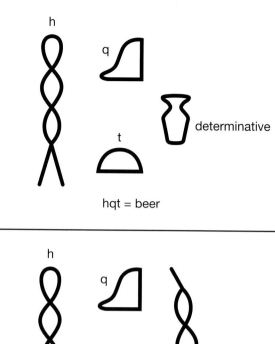

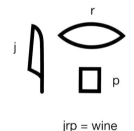

Figure 17.2. Egyptian hieroglyphs for beer (*ḥqt*) and wine (*jrp*). (Adapted by K. Clahassey from Murray and Sethe 1937; Darby et al. 1977; and Davies and Gardiner 1920.)

dough-filled vats, bread-making tables, bread molds to make loaves, and ovens to accommodate the dough-filled molds.

A mural (Figure 17.5) showing both baking and brewing was found in the Twelfth Dynasty tomb of Intef-iker, a vizier at Thebes (Davies and Gardiner 1920). In the upper portion of the mural we see a woman grinding with a handstone (*c*) while another woman (*b*) sieves out coarse elements; still other women (*e, f*) fill the molds with dough, while a man (*d*) tends to the hot bread molds in the oven. In the lower row

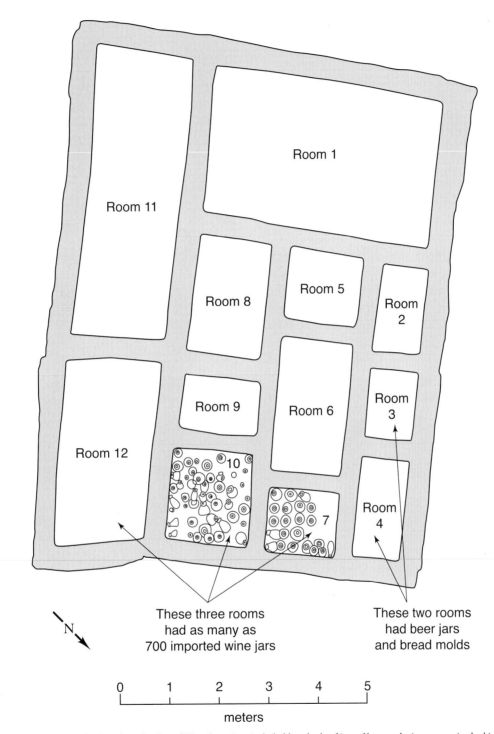

These three rooms
had as many as
700 imported wine jars

These two rooms
had beer jars
and bread molds

N

0   1   2   3   4   5

meters

Figure 17.3. This Egyptian tomb, thought to be that of King Scorpion, included hundreds of jars of beer and wine to sustain the king in his afterlife; Rooms 3 and 4 had locally manufactured jars for beer and bread, while Rooms 12, 10, and 7 contained as many as 700 imported wine jars. (Redrawn by K. Clahassey from McGovern et al. 1997:Figures 4, 5.)

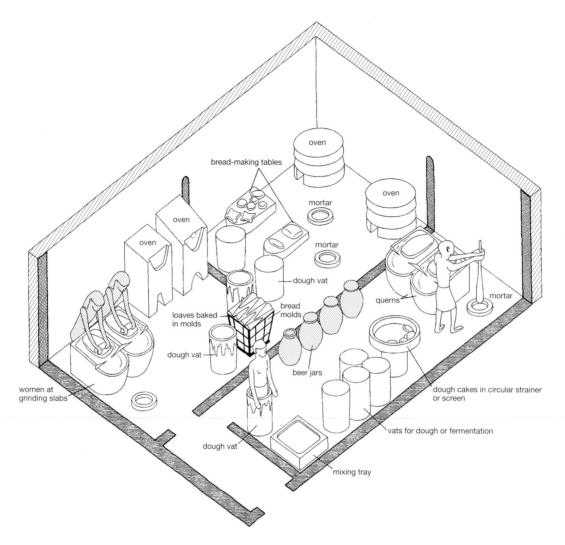

Figure 17.4. This wooden model, with a brewery in the front room and a bakery in the back, shows the close relationship between baking and brewing. This kind of model was placed in the tombs of Egyptian officials, in this case Meket-ra at Thebes, to ensure a steady supply of bread and beer. (Redrawn by K. Clahassey from Winlock 1955:Figures 22–23, 64–65; Kemp 1991:Figure 42.)

we see men who make dough (and perhaps add dates) (*g*), mix dough with water (*h*), decant beer into jars (*i*), then seal the jars (*j*) (Davies and Gardiner 1920:Plates 11 and 12; Kemp 1991:Figure 43).

SUB-SAHARAN AFRICA

Beer making and drinking not only were important to ancient African populations, they continue to be important in the ethnographic present among the Balobedu (Krige 1932), Gamo (Arthur 2003), Mossi and Bisa (Saul 1981), Baganda (Robbins 1979), Samburu (Holtzman 2001), Kofyar (Netting 1964), Tiriki (Sangree 1962), Nyakyusa (Willis 2001), Zulu (Reusch 1998), and Xhosa

(McAllister 2001, 2003, 2004, 2006). In speaking of the Kofyar of Nigeria, Netting (1964:376) says that "occasions which involve the entire community are difficult to imagine apart from beer." He adds that large quantities of beer were drunk (1) when celebrating the harvest, (2) when an admired warrior killed an enemy, or (3) when a man killed dangerous game. Such brave men not only were honored by a beer feast, they also acquired the coveted right to drink from a special fermenting jar for the rest of their lives. In contrast, "the most severe punishment meted out to a man by his community is exclusion from all occasions for beer drinking" (Netting 1964:377). Among the Kofyar, it was the flow of beer that defined behaviors that were socially valued, as well as those that were socially censured.

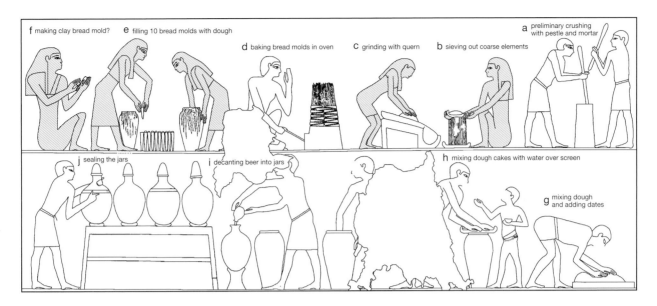

Figure 17.5. This painted scene shows both baking and brewing. Such scenes played the same role as wooden models, ensuring that a steady supply of beer and bread would be available in the afterlife. This painting is from the tomb of Intef-iker, a vizier at Thebes, Egypt. (Redrawn by K. Clahassey from Davies and Gardiner 1920: Plates 11, 12; Kemp 1991:Figure 43.)

Like the ancient Egyptians, twentieth-century Kofyar workers were paid in beer. The tasks of harvesting, gathering thatch, and building corrals "are all occasions on which a beer party can mobilize large work groups without reference to kinship or neighborhood affiliation" (Netting 1964:377). For funeral rites, large quantities of beer were also brewed by relatives of the dead to give to attendees from both patri-kin and matri-kin.

In a similar fashion, cooperative work groups among the Xhosa of South Africa are still rewarded with beer after the work has been completed; even nonworkers attend these events with the expectation of receiving a share (McAllister 2003:195).

LABOR AND BEER IN THE ANDES

In the Andes, chicha or maize beer—also known as *aqa*, *jora*, and *azua*—was an important incentive for men to come to work. In one sixteenth-century document Cristóbal Payco, the leader of the northern Peruvian community of Jequetepeque, explicitly asked the Spaniards for permission to continue to provide chicha to men in return for their work on community projects. He explained,

> the Indians obey their caciques and principales because of that custom that they have of giving them drink . . . if they [caciques and principales] did not give drink to the Indians to work [this land] and to others to plant the

fields of the community to pay tribute, they would not cooperate or come together to do it. (Juan de Betanzos 1551 [1968:60, 72–73])

In Andean society, supplying large amounts of beer was considered an act of generosity even when the relationship between donor and recipient was asymmetrical or hierarchical. Such "generosity" served to mask the fact that the provider was high status, while the recipient was not only low status but obligated to do the work. This attempt to disguise hierarchy as generosity, widespread in ancient Peru (Morris 1982, 1986), was also used in many other parts of the world. For example, Fredrik Barth (1959), in speaking of the Pathans of Swat, Pakistan, describes similar use of "hospitality" to achieve elite goals:

> it might seem . . . that gifts and hospitality would be less important than bribes and payments in supporting claims to authority. As a matter of fact, the reverse is true. Bribes and payments create relationships which render them onerous and hazardous. Gifts and hospitality, on the other hand, are of prime importance in the building up of a political following. . . . A continuous flow of gifts creates needs and fosters dependence, and the threat of its being cut off becomes a powerful disciplinary device. (Barth 1959:77–79)

Abundant documentation shows that Andean leaders who provided liberal quantities of beer attracted sufficient labor to work in their fields (Rowe 1946:292;

Murra 1960, 1980; Rostworowski 1977; Morris 1979, 1982). In fact, studies suggest that many parts of the Andean economy depended on the masking of inequality with hospitality.

In an effort to show the role that chicha played within the Inca economy, Murra (1960) isolated two agricultural systems—one at the local level, emphasizing root crops adapted to the highlands, and one at the state level, emphasizing maize. He showed that state-level political and religious ceremonies as well as agricultural rituals were tied to maize, and that one reason the acquisition of large quantities of maize was considered crucial and prestigious was because maize could be converted into chicha, a beverage of enormous political, social, and economic value.

WHO MADE THE MAIZE BEER?

We saw that women played a prominent role in the making of beer in ancient Egypt, and that seems to have been the case in much of the Andes as well, particularly in the highlands. In the course of administering their empire, the Inca employed a number of strategies, including (1) incorporating some people by peaceful means, such as marriage alliances, (2) incorporating others by not so peaceful means, (3) resettling people, and (4) building new state-controlled installations. Among such state installations were *akllawasi*, or "houses of chosen and chaste women," dedicated to serving the imperial cult by preparing maize beer (Morris and Thompson 1985:28). Rostworowski (1977:241), however, points out that while women were the primary brewers of beer in the highlands, men were often the chicha makers on the coast. She cites a 1621 statement by Pablo José Arriaga that on the coast, men made the chicha, while in the highlands it was the women ("[en] los llanos son hombres y en la sierra son mujeres los que fabrican la chicha" [Arriaga 1968 (1621):106]).

Other Colonial documents show that for some coastal men, chicha making was a profession, not just a part-time activity. One document in the *Archivo General de Indias* says that

> don Pedro Payampoyfel, principal y mandón de los yndios chicheros de este repartimiento, dezimos que nosotros no tenemos otro oficio sino hazer la chicha ques menester para la comida . . . ny tenemos tierras, ny chacaras donde sembrar sino sólo nos substentamos con hacer la dicha chicha y vendella y trocalla en el tianguez, a trueque de maíz y lana y chaquira e otras

cosas, y los yndios labradores no la pueden hazer e no tienen aparejo para ello. (Archivo General de Indias, Justicia 458, folio 2090v)

This statement can be paraphrased as follows: "don Pedro Payampoyfel, lord and leader of the chicha-making Indians of this district, says that we have no other job but making chicha, which is how we obtain food . . . nor do we have lands or fields to plant; rather we subsist only by making chicha and selling it and exchanging it in the market [here he borrows the Aztec word *tianguis*], exchanging beer for maize, wool, shells, and other things; Indian laborers cannot produce it, and do not have the equipment to produce it [beer]."

Drawing on various sixteenth-century documents, María Rostworowski (1977:242) has shown that much of the prestige a coastal lord enjoyed resulted from his generosity, which included his ability to supply his subjects with beer. "When leaving his palace," she says, "a local lord would take with him an entourage of bearers who carried jars of chicha, and wherever the lord's litter would stop, everyone would be provided beer at his expense." When the disapproving Spaniards tried to prevent local lords from providing beer, the latter asked that this custom be continued, at least for such tasks as the communal planting and harvesting of crops and the cleaning of irrigation canals.

THE PERUVIAN BREWERIES

Four archaeological breweries will now be examined to show important differences that exist among them.

Huánuco Pampa, Central Highlands, Peru

Huánuco Pampa was an Inca state installation built on previously unoccupied land (Morris 1979). Like many other state establishments, Huánuco Pampa included *akllawasi*, the buildings where chaste women or *mamakuna* worked for the state by brewing chicha and weaving textiles. Although such akllawasi are known from sixteenth-century documents, Morris and Thompson (1985:28) say that "identifying the actual structures associated with the official religion such as the akllawasi has been one of the most challenging aspects of the study of provincial Inca sites such as Huánuco Pampa." According to Morris and Thompson (1985:91), the only evidence of production at Huánuco Pampa that was "organized on a large scale and probably maintained on a full-time basis is the brewing of *chicha* and the production of textiles." Evidence for

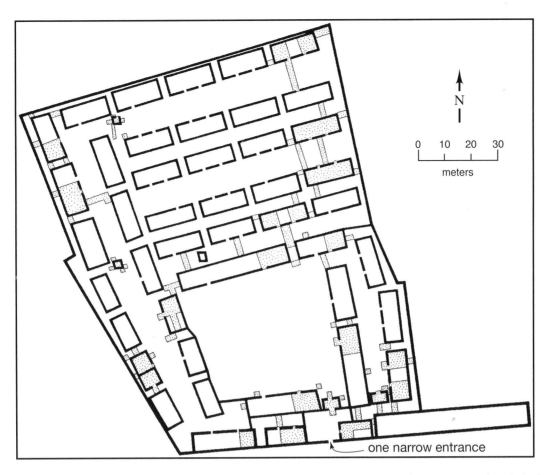

Figure 17.6. This sector of Huánuco Pampa is thought to be where the chosen women or *mamakuna* were living, weaving, and producing beer. This sector produced bone weaving tools, spindle whorls, and thousands of huge ceramic jars for beer. Access to this compound was evidently tightly controlled, since it has only one entrance. (Redrawn by K. Clahassey from Morris and Thompson 1985: Figure 8.)

beer drinking at Huánuco Pampa takes the form of very large concentrations of sherds, all from jars used in various stages of beer production, from soaking the maize to produce malt or *jora*, to boiling the jora, to fermenting (*poqoy*), storing, and dispensing the beer. Morris (1979:28) also recovered the "large rocker flattening stones" that were used to crack open the jora.

Evidence for chicha brewing on a large-scale was concentrated in two sectors of Huánuco Pampa, to the north and to the east of the plaza. The northern sector featured a walled compound with a single tightly controlled entrance on its south side (Figure 17.6). This sector has been interpreted as a place where chaste, chosen women (*mamakuna*) were housed in an akllawasi (Morris 1982:Figure 6.1). Along with large beer jars and other evidence for brewing, Morris found Huánuco Pampa's only concentration of spinning and weaving tools there. Evidently, just as the sixteenth-century documents affirm, "chosen" women at Huánuco Pampa were both brewers and weavers for the Inca state.

The eastern sector included a palace that may have housed the ruler, and adjacent to it a series of twelve long buildings arrayed around two spacious plazas (Figure 17.7). In this area, excavators found evidence of cooking and literally tons of large jars thought to be primarily associated with chicha (Morris 1982:165–166).

These archaeological data from Huánuco Pampa reinforce the sixteenth-century documents in suggesting an Andean reciprocity in which work was rewarded by beer. Reciprocity usually implies symmetry, or equal exchange, but in the Andes such relations often masked asymmetries. Often, the cycle of reciprocal obligations was initiated by royal generosity, with the critical ingredient being chicha (Murra 1960; Rostworowski 1977; Morris 1979, 1986).

Morris (1979:32) demonstrates that chicha was intimately associated with Andean state-level political and religious ceremonies, and that beer-drinking ceremonies were basic to the maintenance of the whole political and economic system. It was not just the fact that

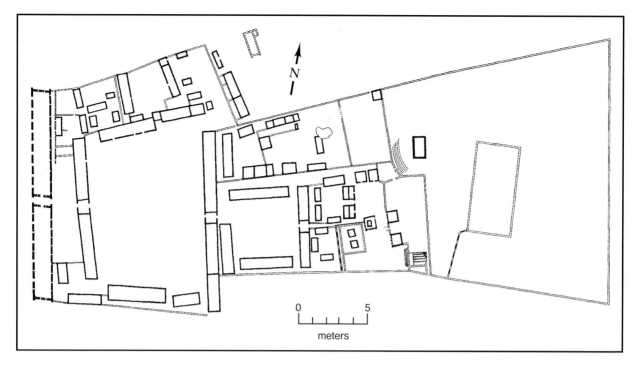

Figure 17.7. This sector of Huánuco Pampa, which possibly served as the palace, yielded evidence of large-scale drinking and feasting. (Redrawn by K. Clahassey from Morris and Thompson 1985:Figure 13.)

millions of liters of chicha were brewed and consumed annually but the way in which beer was dispensed that contributed to Andean leaders' authority. In fact, Morris sees the state's ability to increase beer production as being essential to its political and economic expansion (Morris 1979:32). Over the years more and more land needed to be acquired, and then terraced and planted so that more maize could be harvested.

Manchán, Casma Valley, North Coast of Peru

Manchán was an intrusive settlement, constructed in the Casma Valley of Peru's north coast by the Chimu as the seat of their local administrative authority (Mackey and Klymyshyn 1981; Moore 1981, 1984, 1985, 1989). Excavations at Manchán allowed Moore (1989:685) to answer the question, "How did the Chimu Empire—at least at Manchán—get the chicha it needed?" At Manchán, germinated maize was found with tools and facilities used in chicha making and suggested the following sequence of behavior: the occupants selected maize, removed the kernels from the cobs, soaked the kernels, allowed them to germinate, dried the germinated kernels, then ground or cracked the kernels. This stage resulted in malted maize, or jora. The archaeological correlates of the aforementioned behavior, according to Moore (1989:Tables 1, 2), were maize cobs; large jars for soaking the kernels; patio areas where maize

was allowed to germinate; cloth, matting, or leaves to cover the germinating kernels; the jora itself; and a batán (*maray*) and *chungo* (milling stones similar to a metate and mano) used to grind the jora. The next step in the process was to cook the brew of jora and water, usually for 1–2 days. The archaeological evidence associated with such cooking consisted of hearths, fire-reddened vessels, a stirring stick, and fuel.

The next step in chicha making is separating the desired liquid from its by-products, removing the *alfrecho*, or small fragments of malted maize kernels and their glumes and skins. This can be done by straining the liquid through a basket or cloth, or by allowing the liquid to stand until unwanted items settle to the bottom. The final step (and the most fun) is consuming the beer. The chronicler Bernabé Cobo (1956:242) states that the inhabitants of the north coast drank chicha from *mates* or gourd bowls, rather than from the ceramic or wooden *keros* known from so many highland sites. In line with Cobo's descriptions, abundant mates have been found at coastal sites like Manchán and Cerro Azul (see below).

At Manchán, Moore documents chicha production at the household level, showing that amounts varied from house to house. There is evidence that a cane-walled house at least on one occasion produced 513 liters, a volume that Moore (1989:688) estimates as

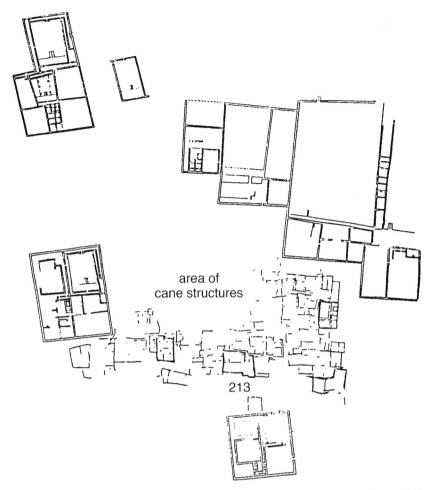

Figure 17.8. Between and around Manchán's adobe compounds, where elite administrators lived, were barrios of cane-walled structures where lower-status people resided. One of these lower-status units was No. 213, which provided abundant evidence of chicha production, including high densities of both jora and chicha dregs (fragments of kernels, glumes, etc.), which suggested to the excavator, Jerry Moore, that this household had produced enough chicha to entertain 171 people. (Redrawn by K. Clahassey from Moore 1989:Figure 2.)

being sufficient to entertain 171 people (Figure 17.8). (At Omo in the Moquegua Valley, Paul Goldstein [2005:209] has also documented chicha manufacturing at the household level.)

Cerro Baúl, Moquegua Valley, Southern Peru

Locally known as the "Masada of the Andes," the fortified archaeological site of Cerro Baúl sits on a spectacular mesa rising 600 m above the Río Torata. Cerro Baúl was a Wari state installation, essentially a group of colonists placed some 600 km south of the capital of Wari itself. Both before and after the Wari period, Cerro Baúl was uninhabited, since the mesa was a very impractical place to live—indeed, all necessities, including water and food, had to be hauled up to the summit with great effort (Moseley et al. 2005:17264). The elite quarters were located on the summit, while lower-status residences occurred on the flanks. Monumental public architecture was constructed on the artificially leveled mesa top. The eventual abandonment of Cerro Baúl was accompanied by elaborate termination ceremonies, including brewing, beer drinking, vessel smashing, and the burning of many buildings on the summit (Feldman 1998; Williams 2001).

Cerro Baúl's evacuation seems to have been a planned event, which probably explains why some buildings were accorded ritual termination or "last rites" that left behind artifacts indicative of the structures' status and nature. One elaborate termination rite took place in the chichería, or brewery, which contained not only its original equipment but also final offerings. Wari colonists left behind abundant symbolically charged artifacts (Williams 2001; Moseley et al. 2005), including *tupu-kuna*, or women's shawl pins, which led the excavators to infer that (just as at Huánuco Pampa) elite women were prominently involved in beer production.

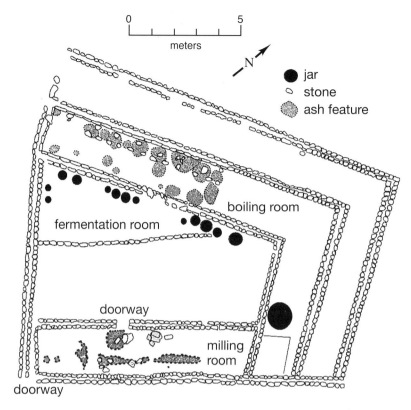

Figure 17.9. Plan of the brewery at Cerro Baúl, Peru, which shows discrete areas for milling, boiling, and fermentation. (Redrawn from Moseley et al. 2005:Figure 5.)

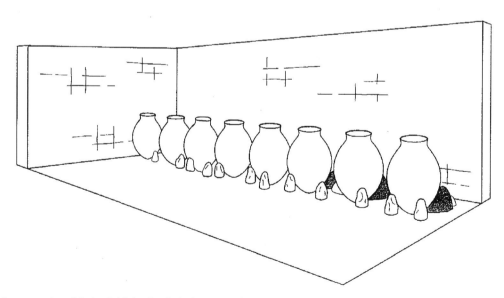

Figure 17.10. Reconstruction of the jars left behind in the boiling room of the brewery at Cerro Baúl, Peru. (Redrawn from Moseley et al. 2005:Figure 6, with the permission of Michael Moseley. Original drawing by Jill Seagard, Field Museum of Natural History, Chicago.)

Trapezoidal in ground plan, the brewery had separate compartments for milling, boiling, and fermentation (Figure 17.9). Its vats could hold up to 150 liters of beer each (Figure 17.10), suggesting a maximum production capacity of approximately 1,800 liters per batch. As the colony of a highland state, Cerro Baúl had keros rather than mates. Individual keros found there could hold at least 12 oz. (0.945 liters), and the largest could hold 64 oz. (3.78 liters). Moseley et al. (2005) suggest that both the quantity and quality of maize beer served at Cerro Baúl varied by social class and rank (as did the food, pottery, and what are interpreted as gifts).

Cerro Azul, Cañete Valley, South-Central Coast of Peru

Cerro Azul, a Late Intermediate fishing community, lies on a bay some 130 km south of Lima, in the lower Cañete Valley (Kroeber 1937; Marcus 1987a, b, 2008). The site sits in a protected saddle between sea cliffs, cobble beach, and an 86-m-high peak. Its most prominent features are ten large residential compounds made of *tapia*, thick walls created by pouring mud between wooden plank molds (Marcus et al. 1999).

One of the large residential compounds, designated Structure D, covered 1,640 m^2 and seems to have been the residence of an elite family and its support staff (Figure 17.11). Divided into a dozen rooms and four to five unroofed work areas, Structure D included living quarters, storage rooms, corridors that controlled access to the interior of the building, and a kitchen area that could have served as a chichería where maize beer was manufactured.

The kitchen/brewery, which covered 110 m^2 of floor space, was designated the North Central Canchón (Figure 17.12). This canchón (or large walled work area) featured two hearth-trenches and numerous large storage vessels set into the floor. Some vessels were so deeply dug in that their shoulders were virtually at floor level; the largest may have been formed and fired in situ. These storage vessels fall into four sizes: the largest could have held almost 2,000 liters, the next in size 700 liters, the next 500 liters, and the smallest roughly 125 liters.

Feature 9 (Figure 17.13) is an example of a vessel that could have held almost 2,000 liters; Feature 16 could have held 700 liters; Feature 15 could have held 500

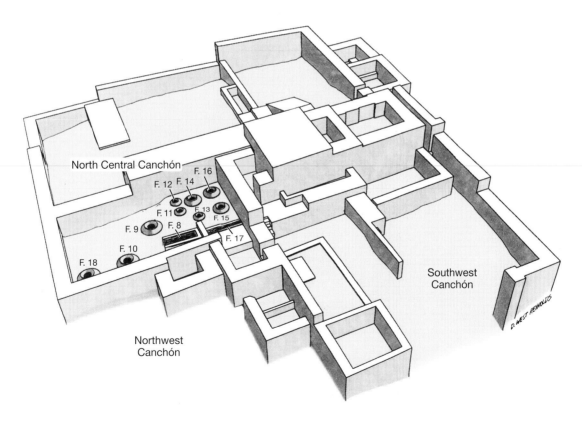

Figure 17.11. Artist's conception of Structure D at Cerro Azul, Peru, showing the North Central Canchón with its hearth-trenches and storage vessels. (Drawing by D. West Reynolds and J. Klausmeyer.)

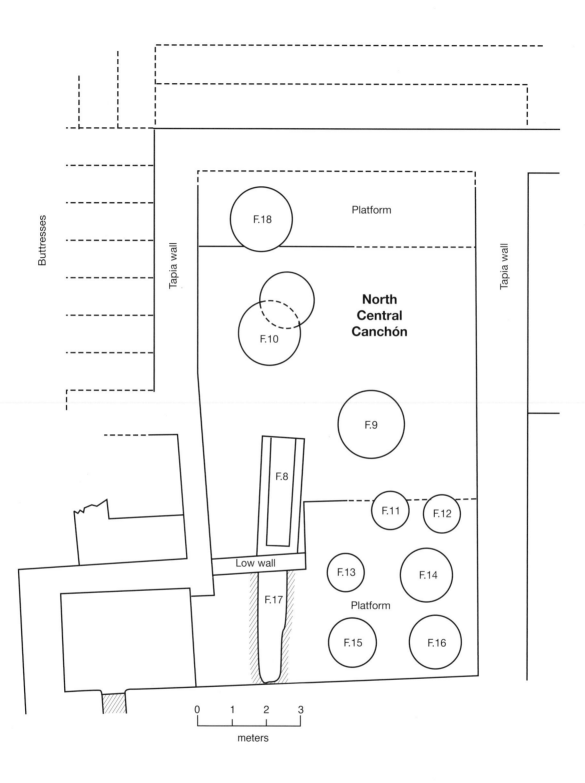

Figure 17.12. Plan of the brewery in Structure D, Cerro Azul, Peru. (Redrafted from Marcus 1987a:Figure 24.)

liters; and Feature 13 could have held 125 liters. We suspect that these four sizes correspond generally to four known Quechua categories, with the largest called *hatun maccma* or *maccma*, the next largest *urpu*, the next *iteco*, and the smallest *puyñu* (Ravines 1978:180).

Had all the vessels in the North Central Canchón been in use simultaneously, their total volume would have been at least 5,000 liters. If, on the other hand, only half of the vessels were filled at one time, their total capacity would have been 2,500 liters, making the Cerro Azul brewery's volume similar to the 1,800-liter capacity of the Cerro Baúl brewery (Moseley et al. 2005:17267). Each vat in the Cerro Baúl brewery had a capacity of roughly 150 liters, corresponding to the smallest of the four vessel sizes set into the floor of the North Central Canchón at Cerro Azul.

We can estimate how many people the Cerro Azul brewery could have served by referring to John Gillin's ethnographic study of the town of Moche. Gillin (1947:46) estimated that each person there probably consumed 3 liters of chicha at a given beer-drinking event. If we apply this figure to Cerro Azul, it suggests that the elite living in Structure D at Cerro Azul could have entertained somewhere between 800 people (if the half-capacity 2,400 liters were produced) and 1,650 people (if the full-capacity 5,000 liters were produced).

We do not know whether Structure D was the only large compound at Cerro Azul producing chicha in volume, or if the other nine large tapia compounds had similar breweries. Potentially, the chicha produced in Structure D could have been used either to entertain elites from other compounds at the same site, or to reward the countless fishermen who filled up the various fish-storage rooms at Cerro Azul (Marcus 1987a, b).

Figure 17.13. The remains of Feature 9, a storage vessel with a capacity of nearly 2,000 liters of chicha, set into the floor of the North Central Canchón, Cerro Azul, Peru. The workman is sweeping a flat beach cobble on which the conical base of the giant vessel rested. (Photograph by J. Marcus.)

Unfortunately, there is no accurate way to determine how many of the storage vessels in Structure D were filled to capacity for a given event. The fact that four different sizes of vessels were present suggests that different events required different quantities of beer.

THREE MODELS FOR CHICHA PRODUCTION

In sum, the sixteenth-century ethnohistoric documents provide us with at least three general models for chicha production. I believe that all three can be documented in the archaeological record.

One model involves aklla or mamakuna, the "chosen women," who were supplied with maize by the state in order to produce maize beer in the akllawasi (Cobo 1956:232–233; Morris 1979:28; Murra 1980:171–172). This model seems to fit the data from both Huánuco Pampa (Morris 1979, 1982) and Cerro Baúl (Williams 2001; Moseley et al. 2005).

A second model involves men who were specialists in producing beer for large-scale elite hospitality (Rostworowski 1977:241). This model may fit the Cerro Azul data, specifically those from the North Central Canchón of Structure D, and it may fit the Ciudadela Tschudi data from Chan Chan (Day 1982:339).

A third model is household production of beer, a part-time activity that could have involved both men and women (Cobo 1956:242). In this case, Moore (1989:689) argues that "there is no reason to expect that the state would be directly involved in either the production of chicha or the maintenance of the residential group." This model may fit the data from Manchán in the Casma Valley and Omo in the Moquegua Valley (Goldstein 2005:209).

With the recovery of more examples of chicherías in the future, we should be able to refine these three models and to determine what is typical of different eras, different regions, and different political and economic systems. At present, our sample is too small to say anything definitive about what the norm was for each era or region.

The study of beer production will continue to provide us with insights about the organization of labor in the Andes. We have ample evidence that when beer drinking was embedded in the language of reciprocity and elites were in charge, we should expect the volume of beer produced and consumed to be large.

The Andean case is likely similar to that described by Barth for the Swat Pathans, who saw lavish hospitality as being of prime importance in creating a political following and fostering economic dependence by subordinates. It was clearly a win-win situation for the Andean elite; they could be seen as "generous" by providing thousands of liters of maize beer, and thus create labor obligations and dependency. The beer-drinking ceremony was a device for making exploitation appear to be an act of generosity, thus making an asymmetrical relation palatable, which was no small feat.

APPENDIX: INTERPRETING THE ARCHAEOLOGICAL REMAINS

As more and more breweries are found, we will need ways to interpret the empirical archaeological data. Relevant here are the African studies that focus on the archaeological signatures of beer production. For example, beer-producing households among the Gamo of Ethiopia have (1) more large vessels; (2) large vessels that show erosion, pitting, and scratches on their interiors and exteriors; (3) large vessels with residue on their interior surfaces that could be subjected to residue analyses; (4) a higher frequency of grinding stones than non-beer-producing households; and (5) a higher frequency of gourds than non-beer-producing households (Arthur 2000, 2003). Since wealthy households produce most of the beer, they own more large vessels. Arthur also shows that the wealthy Gamo can produce more beer because they have a monopoly on landownership, and thus they control access to the grains.

In this appendix we look at some extensive quotations from the ethnohistoric and ethnographic record that may be of use in archaeological interpretation.

Ethnohistoric sources and ethnographies of traditional Andean communities agree on the three basic steps of brewing: preparing the maize, cooking the prepared maize in water, and fermenting the resulting brew. One form of maize preparation involves the germination of kernels. Another involves the conversion of starches into sugars by mixing maize flour with saliva; the saliva provides the enzyme diastase, which triggers chemical activity (Cutler and Cardenas 1947:41).

To begin, we turn to a very early description, that of fray José de Acosta, who in 1590 wrote,

> el vino de maíz que llaman en el Pirú *azua*, y por vocablo de Indias común, *chicha*, se hace de diversos modos. El más fuerte a modo de cerveza, humedeciendo primero el grano de maíz hasta que comienza a brotar, y después cociéndolo con cierto orden, sale

tan recio, que a pocos lances derriba; este llaman en el
Perú *sora*. . . . Otro modo de hacer el azua o chicha, es
mascando el maíz y haciendo levadura de lo que así se
masca, y despues cocido. . . . El modo mas limpio y mas
sano y que menos encalabria, es de maíz tostado: esto
usan los indios más pulidos, y algunos españoles. . . .
(Acosta 1954 [1590]:110)

About 40 years later, fray Antonio Vázquez de Espinosa
said,

El que se haze de mais, que es el trigo de las indias lo
hazen de muchas maneras. La ordinaria llaman *jura* o
asua . . . para hazerla echan el mais en remojo, y despues
lo ponen tapado con alguna estera, y otra cosa, y lo
dexan algunos dias, hasta que todo está nacido, y luego
lo muelen muy bien, y van colando aquella masa con
agua hirviendo, y echan en sus tinajas, botijas, o vasijas
hasta que a hirvido como el vino a cabo de dos dias, y
luego, que a hirvido queda con un picante y lo beben y
usan con el sus borracheras, y hazen sus casas, semen-
teras hacienda cantidad y mingando todo los parientes
y amigos, que es lo mismo que convidarlos al trabajo, y
fiesta, y assi lo uno y lo otro se haze con solemne baile
fiesta y borrachera. . . . (Vázquez de Espinosa 1942
[1629]:397–398)

For an eighteenth-century view of chicha making
on Peru's north coast, we can turn to the paintings of
north coast life published by Martínez de Compañón
y Bujanda (1936). In one painting we see a man and a
woman working together under a ramada to produce
a batch of chicha (Figure 17.14). If this eighteenth-
century north coast scene can be interpreted as evidence
for household production of chicha, this would demonstrate some degree of continuity on the north coast,
since Moore's (1989) excavations at Manchán found
evidence of chicha production at the household level
during the Late Intermediate period (see Figure 17.8).

For more recent descriptions of brewing in traditional
Andean communities, we can turn to archaeologist
Jorge C. Muelle (1945:147–150, 1978), who provides us
with this account of jora preparation in the community
of San Sebastián, Cusco:

En las casas particulares, se prepara jora cada vez que se
intenta elaborar chicha; en las *guiñaperías*, todo el año.
Para este propósito hay *kochas* o pozas en los patios, a la
intemperie, aunque en San Sebastián utilizan frecuent-
emente ollas. Estas pozas son de piedras unidas con cal
y arena; comienza a emplearse también el cemento. . . .
Cada poza contiene por lo regular una fanega de maíz,

Figure 17.14. Scene of chicha preparation on the coast near Trujillo,
Peru, according to Martínez de Compañón y Bujanda (Muelle 1978:245,
Lámina 3).

y mide por lado alrededor de un metro. La razón de
que haya varias *kochas* es su empleo rotativo con el
propósito de tener jora en días consecutivos. Primero,
en una de estas *kochas* se hace remojar el maíz durante
una noche y un día. Los granos se hinchan, entonces
se escurre, operación que se llama *tchúmay*. Después,
se distribuyen a otras pocillas, las cuales deben de estar
muy bien lavadas a fin de prevenir que el *guiñapo* se
malogre; del acomodar los granos extendiéndolos en
el fondo de las *kochas*, para lo cual se utiliza sólo las
manos, se dice *másttay* (extender). Emplean también
las palabras *hásppiy* (arañar). En seguida viene *ppámpay*
o *tápay* (tapar), que consiste en cubrir este maíz con
ichu "nuevo" o con espata de maíz, bien empapados en
agua corriente y sujetos con piedras para que el viento
no los lleve. . . . Se deja el maíz así cubierto por espacio
de ocho días en tiempo ordinario, y por quince en
época de heladas (mayo-agosto); durante ese tiempo se
practica *tchakhchuy*, consistente en regar o rociar con
agua, por las noches, o de día si está nublado, esta jora

en preparación, levantando, enrollando la paja para eso—es lo que se considera mejor riego – o simplemente por encima de ella. En verano se rocía cada tres días; en invierno uno sí y otro nó.

El maíz para hacer *guiñapo* [jora] puede ser cualquier maíz. . . .

Al final de los 8 o 15 días, la persona—hombre o mujer—que prepara la jora suele exclamar al examinarla; "*Olyekha-mushanña* (Están saliendo los brotes)", y procede a recogerla; dos días o tres más, y el *guiñapo* está a punto.

Pero lo frecuente es que se muela el guiñapo en el mismo San Sebastián. Para el efecto, se contrata los servicios de un *kútakh* (moledor), muchacho o viejo que lo machaca en un *maran* [maray], piedra de moler que, para el caso, tiene hasta 1.20 m de largo. . . .

También puede hacerse una segunda molienda con agua y agregando entonces la harina: es propiamente el *péqey*, la primera operación, en seco, es el *amsi*.

En vasijas de barro . . . hacen hervir esta preparación y van removiéndola con un palo. Por supuesto, se necesita tres o cuatro tandas para hacer hervir toda la citada cantidad de jora.

El preparado así hervido vacíase en una canasta con *ichu*, la *isanka*, que hace de coladera y está colocada sobre dos *chakanas* o palos encima de la boca de un *hraki*. El caldo sin fermentar todavía es el *uppi*; en otras partes, pero no en San Sebastián, se llama *tempo* (*timpuy* hervir). Se saca la coladera y se echa al *hraki* una cantidad de *borra* (sedimento espeso de la chicha de varios días) que miden en un *caporal* [a liter and a half]. . . .

Durante una noche, el *uppi* fermenta. Al día siguiente, se vuelve a hacer hervir el *hanchi* (afrecho ["dregs," the small fragments of malted maize kernels] o *guiñapo* [jora] de una pasada) para obtener el *seqe* (líquido de segunda pasada), el cual se agrega a la primera chicha, que para mediodía está a punto de tomarse y se pone por lo tanto a la venta después de despumarse algo. . . .

Es creencia general que los objetos que han intervenido en la elaboración de la chicha no deben salir de la cocina o cuarto donde está se ha preparado porque les da "aire" y se descompone la chicha. . . .

El *akha-wasi* suele tener una mesa y algunas bancas, o silletas, aunque es más frecuente que haya solo poyos

en un ángulo del cuarto que hace de taberna. En otro ángulo está el *hraki* de chicha que atiende la propietaria del establecimiento.

In other words, to recover the whole process archaeologically, one would have to find the vessels in which the kernels were soaked, the grinding stones used to triturate the kernels, the vessels in which the liquid was heated over the fire, the storage containers in which the brew was cooked and fermented, and the mates or keros in which the chicha was served.

At Cerro Baúl's brewery, Moseley et al. (2005) were able to distinguish three different work areas: (1) a milling room where maize was ground, (2) a fermentation room, and (3) a boiling room that had at least seven fire pits (Moseley et al. 2005:17267). Each room clearly had a specific function.

Within the North Central Canchón at Cerro Azul, we found two long, narrow hearth-trenches. These two features could have been used to heat the maize brew, and their length ensured that a whole series of pots could be lined up and set in sequence for cooking (Marcus 1987a:50). Feature 8, the earlier and better made of the two hearths, showed evidence of burning and was filled with white ash (Figures 17.15, 17.16).

The second hearth, Feature 17, was filled with densely packed layers of gray and white ash (Figure 17.17). Feature 17 appeared to have been added to increase the production capacity of the brewery, thereby allowing even more pots to be heated simultaneously. When we excavated Feature 17, it contained basal portions of very large Camacho Reddish Brown cooking vessels, one of which included the residue of jora (sprouted maize kernels) still in it (Marcus 2008:183).

The fuel used in both Features 8 and 17 appeared to consist of whatever discarded wood or cane happened to be available, including *caña brava* (*Gynerium sagittatum*), a broken wooden weaving sword (*kallwa*), and some broken wooden posts that appeared to be willow (*Salix* sp.).

In addition, we found several implements that could have been used to grind the maize. Three *tunaukuna* (handstones for grinding) were found inside Feature 10 (a storage jar); a discarded *maray* or *batán* (grinding slab) was found on the floor of the North Central Canchón; another batán was found in Feature 11 (also a storage jar). We also found a likely "stirring stick" nearby.

In sum, the North Central Canchón included numerous large floor depressions for vessels, some with parts of vessels still in them; two long hearths with ash in them; fuel;

Figure 17.15. Feature 8, a hearth-trench in the North Central Canchón of Structure D, Cerro Azul, Peru, showing the deposit of white ash inside it. (Photograph by J. Marcus.)

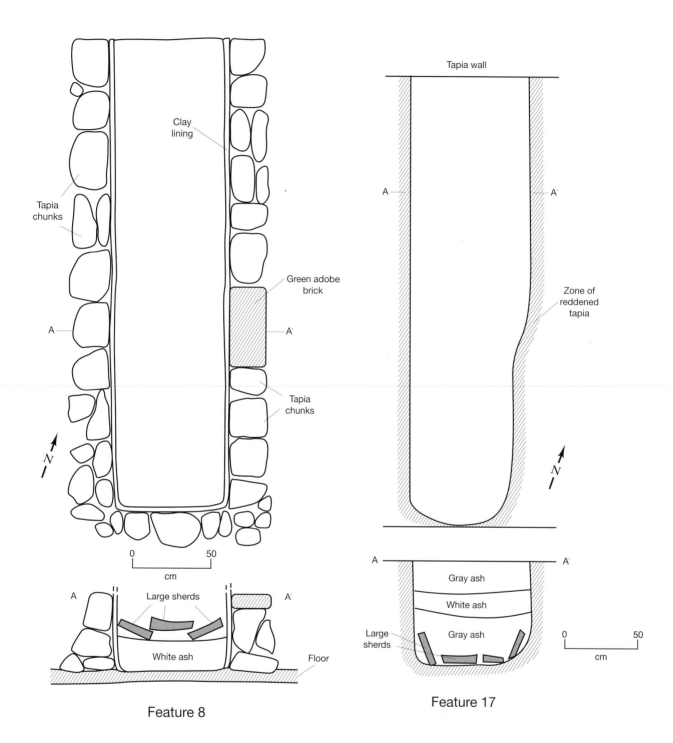

Feature 8

Feature 17

Figure 17.16. Plan and cross-section of Feature 8, a hearth-trench in the North Central Canchón of Structure D, Cerro Azul. The cross-section shows the large sherds above the deposit of white ash.

Figure 17.17. Plan and cross-section of Feature 17, a hearth-trench in the North Central Canchón of Structure D, at Cerro Azul. The cross-section shows the layers of gray and white ash.

grinding stones; and some vessel bases with remains of maize still in them. We are uncertain, however, whether the North Central Canchón was purely a chichería or both a chichería and a kitchen.

If this walled work area operated as both kitchen (*tullpawasi*) and chichería (*akhawasi*), it is possible that both men and women worked in the same room, though perhaps in different activity areas. However, if the canchón was used exclusively for producing beer, and if we apply what we have learned from the sixteenth-century documents (namely, that beer production on the coast was an exclusively male activity), then we may be dealing with a men's work area.

With the data we currently have, one could suggest that women were the likely makers of chicha at both Cerro Baúl and Huánuco Pampa, as Morris and Moseley et al. have suggested. In contrast, men may have been the brewers at Cerro Azul, but our minds remain open on the subject.

Acknowledgments

I thank Mike Moseley for the enthusiastic and tireless support he has provided me from the first day I met him at Harvard.

It is always difficult to put into words the array of feelings we have about professors who are selfless and kind when we most need their patience; Mike was always there to help and to do all the extra things to pave one's path to success. We got to know each other well in a seminar required of all incoming graduate students; he co-taught this class, Method and Theory in American Archaeology, with Gordon R. Willey.

Before class we had many opportunities to talk about our similar experiences at UC Berkeley, where both of us had been before we ended up at Harvard. In fact, we chatted about how both of us had had J. Desmond Clark as our adviser and how he had steered us to Harvard for graduate studies.

When Mike asked me if I had ever taken a co-taught class before, I said, "Yes, indeed; I took Andean prehistory from John Rowe and Dorothy Menzel." Then he smiled and said that he had brought something special to class. "What?" I asked, and Mike responded by saying, "Just wait." Having noted the students' reluctance to talk during class, Mike had the great idea of bringing beer to class; and, as you might guess, that beverage helped a lot, although it sometimes led to a few run-on sentences that never ended! But Mike discovered something the ancient Andean elite also found out—things go better with beer, and attendance improves, too.

The Cerro Azul Project was generously supported by the National Science Foundation (grant no. BS-8301542), and I appreciate not only the funding but the excellent advice offered to me by Charles Redman, John Yellen, and Craig Morris throughout the project.

Permission to excavate Cerro Azul was granted by Peru's Instituto Nacional de Cultura (Credencial no. 102-82-DCIRBM, Credencial no. 041-83-DCIRBM, Credencial no. 018-84-DPCM, Resolución Suprema no. 357-85-ED). I want to thank everyone who participated in the Cerro Azul Project, especially María Rostworowski de Diez Canseco, Ramiro Matos Mendieta, C. Earle Smith, Charles M. Hastings, Kent V. Flannery, John G. Jones, James B. Stoltman, and Sonia Guillén.

Finally, I wish to thank several colleagues for their unflagging enthusiasm and encouragement, especially Michael E. Moseley, Craig Morris, Christopher B. Donnan, Charles Stanish, Robert L. Carneiro, Guillermo Cock, Charles S. Spencer, Elsa M. Redmond, Ramiro Matos, Rogger Ravines, Duccio Bonavia, Jorge Silva, Sonia Guillén, Helaine Silverman, John O'Shea, Jason Yaeger, John Hyslop, R. Alan Covey, Bruce Mannheim, Luis Jaime Castillo, Marc Bermann, Robert D. Drennan, Jeremy A. Sabloff, Geoffrey Braswell, E. Wyllys Andrews, Allison Davis, Howard Tsai, Betty Kottak, Conrad Kottak, Véronique Bélisle, Patrick Ryan Williams, Kenny Sims, Loa Traxler, Robert J. Sharer, and Don and Prudence Rice.

REFERENCES

Acosta, José de
1954 [1590] *Historia natural y moral de las Indias.* In *Obras del P. José de Acosta.* Edited by Francisco Mateos. Biblioteca de Autores Españoles, vol. 73. Ediciones Atlas, Madrid.

Arthur, John W.
2000 *Ceramic Ethnoarchaeology among the Gamo of Southwestern Ethiopia.* Unpublished doctoral dissertation, Department of Anthropology, University of Florida, Gainesville.
2003 Brewing Beer: Status, Wealth, and Ceramic Use Alteration among the Gamo of South-western Ethiopia. *World Archaeology* 34(3):516–528.

Arriaga, Pablo José
1968 [1621] *Extirpación de la idolatría en el Pirú.* In *Crónicas peruanas de interés indígena,* edited by Francisco

Esteve Barba. Biblioteca de Autores Españoles, vol. 209. Ediciones Atlas, Madrid.

Barth, Fredrik
1959   *Political Leadership among Swat Pathans*. Athlone Press, University of London, London.

Betanzos, Juan de
1968 [1551]   *Suma y narración de los Incas*. Biblioteca de Autores Españoles. Ediciones Atlas, Madrid.

Cobo, Bernabé
1956[1653]   *Historia del nuevo mundo*. In *Obras Completas del P. Bernabé Cobo*. Edición de Francisco Mateos. Biblioteca de Autores Españoles, vols. 91 and 92. Ediciones Atlas, Madrid.

Cutler, Hugh C., and Martin Cardenas
1947   Chicha, a Native South American Beer. *Harvard University Botanical Museum Leaflet* 13(3):33–60.

Darby, William J., Paul Ghalioungui, and Louis Grivetti
1977   *Food: The Gift of Osiris*, vol. 2. Academic Press, London.

Davies, Norman de Garis, and Alan H. Gardiner
1920   *The Tomb of Antefoker, Vizier of Senostris I, and of His Wife, Senet*. Allen and Unwin, London.

Day, Kent C.
1982   Storage and Labor Service: A Production and Management Design for the Andean Area. In *Chan Chan: Andean Desert City*, edited by Michael E. Moseley and Kent C. Day, pp. 333–349. University of New Mexico Press, Albuquerque.

Dreyer, Günter
1992   Recent Discoveries at Abydos Cemetery U. In *The Nile Delta in Transition, 4th–3rd Millennium BC*, edited by Edwin C. M. van den Brink, pp. 293–299. Tel Aviv, Israel.

Feldman, Robert
1998   La ciudadela Wari de Cerro Baúl en Moquegua. In *Moquegua: Los primeros doce mil años*, edited by Karen Wise, pp. 59–66. Museo Contisuyo, Moquegua, Peru.

Geller, Jeremy
1993   Bread and Beer in 4th Millennium Egypt. *Food and Foodways: Exploration in the History and Culture of Human Nourishment* 5(3):255–267.

1999   Brewing and Baking. In *Encyclopedia of the Archaeology of Ancient Egypt*, edited by Kathryn A. Bard, pp. 178–179. Routledge, London and New York.

Gillin, John
1947   *Moche: A Peruvian Coastal Community*. Institute of Social Anthropology, Publication no. 3. Smithsonian Institution, Washington, DC.

Goldstein, Paul S.
2005   *Andean Diaspora: The Tiwanaku Colonies and the Origins of South American Empire*. University Press of Florida, Gainesville.

Holtzman, Jon
2001   The Food of Elders, the "Ration" of Women: Brewing, Gender, and Domestic Processes among the Samburu of Northern Kenya. *American Anthropologist* 103(4):1041–1058.

Kemp, Barry J.
1991   *Ancient Egypt: Anatomy of a Civilization*. Routledge, New York.

2005   *Think Like an Egyptian: 100 Hieroglyphs*. Penguin, New York.

Krige, Eileen Jensen
1932   The Social Significance of Beer among the Balobedu. *Bantu Studies* 6:343–357. Johannesburg.

Kroeber, Alfred L.
1937   Archaeological Explorations in Peru, Part IV: Cañete Valley. Field Museum of Natural History, *Anthropology Memoirs*, vol. II, no. 4:220–273. Chicago.

Mackey, Carol, and Alexandra M. Ulana Klymyshyn
1981   Construction and Labor Organization in the Chimu Empire. *Ñawpa Pacha* 19:99–114.

Marcus, Joyce
1987a   *Late Intermediate Occupation at Cerro Azul, Perú: A Preliminary Report*. University of Michigan Museum of Anthropology Technical Report 20. Ann Arbor.

1987b   Prehistoric Fishermen in the Kingdom of Huarco. *American Scientist* 75:393–401.

2008   *Excavations at Cerro Azul, Peru: The Architecture and Pottery*. Cotsen Institute of Archaeology, University of California, Los Angeles.

Marcus, Joyce, Jeffrey D. Sommer, and Christopher P. Glew
1999   Fish and Mammals in the Economy of an Ancient Peruvian Kingdom. *Proceedings of the National Academy of Sciences* 96:6564–6570.

Martínez de Compañón y Bujanda, Baltasar Jaime
1936   *Trujillo del Perú a fines del siglo XVIII*, edited by Jesús Domínguez Bordona. Talleres Gráficos de C. Bermejo, Madrid.

McAllister, Patrick A.
2001   *Building the Homestead: Agriculture, Labour, and Beer in South Africa's Transkei*. Ashgate, Aldershot.

2003   Culture, Practice, and the Semantics of Xhosa Beer-Drinking. *Ethnology* 42(3):187–207.

2004   Domestic Space, Habitus, and Xhosa Ritual Beer-Drinking. *Ethnology* 43(2):117–135.

2006   *Xhosa Beer Drinking Rituals: Power, Practice, and Performance in the South African Rural Periphery.* Carolina Academic Press, Durham, NC.

McGovern, Patrick E., Ulrich Hartung, Virginia R. Badler, Donald L. Glusker, and Lawrence J. Exner
1997   The Beginnings of Winemaking and Viniculture in the Ancient Near East and Egypt. *Expedition* 39(1):3–21.

Moore, Jerry D.
1981   Chimu Socio-economic Organization: Preliminary Data from Manchan, Casma Valley, Peru. *Ñawpa Pacha* 19:115–128.

1984   Political and Economic Integration of the Lower Class: Archaeological Investigations at Manchan, Casma Valley, Peru. Paper presented at the 83rd Annual Meetings of the American Anthropological Association, Denver, CO.

1985   *Household Economics and Political Integration: The Lower Class of the Chimu Empire.* Doctoral dissertation, University Microfilms, Ann Arbor. MI.

1989   Pre-Hispanic Beer in Coastal Peru: Technology and Social Context of Prehistoric Production. *American Anthropologist* 91:682–695.

Morris, Craig
1979   Maize Beer in the Economics, Politics and Religion of the Inca Empire. In *Fermented Food Beverages in Nutrition*, edited by Clifford F. Gastineau, William J. Darby, and Thomas B. Turner, pp. 21–34. Academic Press, New York.

1982   The Infrastructure of Inka Control in the Peruvian Central Highlands. In *The Inca and Aztec States, 1400–1800: Anthropology and History*, edited by George A. Collier, Renato I. Rosaldo, and John D. Wirth, pp. 153–171. Academic Press, New York.

1986   Storage, Supply, and Redistribution in the Economy of the Inka State. In *Anthropological History of Andean Polities*, edited by John V. Murra, Nathan Wachtel, and Jacques Revel, pp. 59–68. Cambridge University Press, New York.

Morris, Craig, and Donald E. Thompson
1985   *Huánuco Pampa: An Inca City and Its Hinterland.* Thames and Hudson, London.

Moseley, Michael E., Donna J. Nash, Patrick Ryan Williams, Susan D. deFrance, Ana Miranda, and Mario Ruales
2005   Burning Down the Brewery: Establishing and Evacuating an Ancient Imperial Colony at Cerro Baúl, Peru. *Proceedings of the National Academy of Sciences* 102 (48):17264–17271.

Muelle, Jorge C.
1945   La chicha en el Distrito de San Sebastián. *Revista del Museo Nacional* 14:144–152.

1978   La chicha en el Distrito de San Sebastián. In *Tecnología andina*, edited by Rogger Ravines, pp. 241–251. Instituto de Estudios Peruanos, Lima.

Murra, John V.
1960   Rite and Crop in the Inca State. In *Culture in History*, edited by Stanley Diamond, pp. 393–407. Columbia University Press, New York.

1980   *The Economic Organization of the Inca State.* JAI Press, Greenwich, CT.

Murray, Margaret Alice, and Kurt Sethe
1937   *Saqqara Mastabas*, vol 2. Bernard Quaritch, London.

Netting, Robert McC.
1964   Beer as a Locus of Value among the West African Kofyar. *American Anthropologist* 66(2):375–384.

Ravines, Rogger
1978   Almacenamiento y alimentación. In *Tecnología andina*, edited by Rogger Ravines, pp. 179–188. Instituto de Estudios Peruanos, Lima.

Reusch, D.
1998   *Imbiza kayibil' ingenambheki*: The Social Life of Pots. In *Ubumba: Aspects of Indigenous Ceramics in KwaZulu-Natal*, edited by B. Bell and I. Calder, pp. 1–40. Tatham Art Gallery, Pietermaritzburg, South Africa.

Robbins, R. H.
1979   Problem-Drinking and the Integration of Alcohol in Rural Buganda. In *Beliefs, Behaviors, and Alcoholic Beverages: A Cross-Cultural Survey*, edited by Mac Marshall, pp. 351–361. University of Michigan Press, Ann Arbor.

Rostworowski de Diez Canseco, María
1977   *Etnía y sociedad: Costa peruana prehispánica.* Historia Andina 4. Instituto de Estudios Peruanos, Lima.

Rowe, John H.
1946   Inca Culture at the Time of the Spanish Conquest. In *Handbook of South American Indians*, vol. 2, edited by Julian H. Steward, pp. 183–330. Smithsonian Institution, Washington, DC.

Sangree, Walter H.
1962   The Social Functions of Beer Drinking in Bantu Tiriki. In *Society, Culture, and Drinking Patterns*, edited by David J. Pittman and Charles R. Snyder, pp. 6–21. John Wiley, New York.

Saul, Mahir
1981   Beer, Sorghum, and Women: Production for the Market in Rural Upper Volta. *Africa* 51(3): 746–764.

Vázquez de Espinosa, Antonio
1942 [1629]   *Compendium and Description of the West Indies.* Translated by Charles Upson Clark. Smithsonian Institution Collection, Washington, DC.

Williams, Patrick Ryan
2001   Cerro Baúl: A Wari Center on the Tiwanaku Frontier. *Latin American Antiquity* 12(1):67–83.

Willis, Justin
2001   "Beer used to belong to older men": Drink and Authority among the Nyakyusa of Tanzania. *Africa* 71(3):373–390.

Winlock, Herbert E.
1955   *Models of Daily Life in Ancient Egypt from the Tomb of Meket-ra at Thebes.* Catalogue, Metropolitan Museum of Art. Harvard University Press, Cambridge, MA.

CHAPTER 18

CHIMU STATECRAFT IN THE PROVINCES

CAROL MACKEY

THE CHIMU WERE ONE of the longest-lasting and largest centralized states in the New World. Their reign continued for more than 450 years, from approximately AD 900/1000 to AD 1460. The consolidation of their heartland, the Moche, Chicama, and Virú valleys, may have taken as long as 250 years (ca. AD 1050–1300 [Keatinge 1974; Pozorski 1987:117]), while the period of expansion was relatively short. During this time of territorial expansion, they extended their empire both to the north and to the south of their capital, Chan Chan, and established three regional centers, Farfán (ca. AD 1300), Manchán (ca. AD 1350), and Túcume (ca. AD 1400) (Keatinge and Conrad 1983; Mackey and Klymyshyn 1990; Heyerdahl et al. 1995) (Figure 18.1). Since a study of a state's regional centers is crucial to understanding its goals, the primary objective of this chapter is to compare the internal organization of the regional centers within their valley context to identify the principles of Chimu statecraft in the provinces.

A state's provincial policies can best be determined by assessing its strategies of expansion and incorporation, both of which may be long-term and complex processes (Schreiber 1992; Sinopoli 2001). A discussion of expansion strategies includes how a territory was acquired (i.e., by military or diplomatic means) and the motivation for establishing control over a new region. The motives for expansion vary and may include political, ideological, or economic reasons (Schreiber 1992). For example, a state's economic control may be manifested in the introduction of, or emphasis on, certain crops, such as maize (Earle et al. 1987).

Incorporation refers to the integration of territory, population, and resources into a state's central political and economic organization (Schreiber 1992). One of the common measures of incorporation into a state's hierarchy is the building of new infrastructure—roads, storage areas, administrative centers—by the conquering state. Archaeologists have used the degree of state investment in new infrastructure, as well as the stylistic canons of the built environment, to indicate the type of governance employed at a newly founded administrative center. When investment is high and the architecture and artifacts mirror those of the conquering capital, then government rule is assumed to have been direct.

A corollary of this concept, posited by Menzel (1959), holds that the infrastructure established by an expanding state often reflects the conquered region's preexisting political organization. Menzel hypothesized that when political organization in a conquered area is sufficiently complex, only minor changes are made to the existing infrastructure, and indirect rule is the norm.

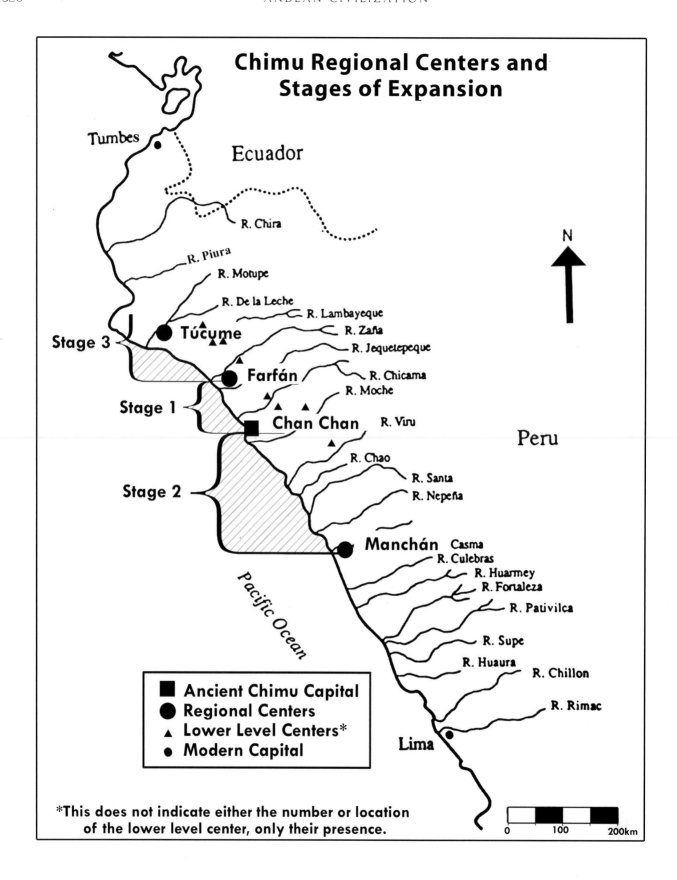

Figure 18.1. Map of the north coast of Peru, showing the Chimu regional centers and the stages of territorial expansion.

However, just the opposite occurs when the preexisting political organization is insufficient to meet the needs of the conquering state. In this case, major infrastructure changes are required, and direct control is imposed. The subject of this chapter, the Chimu, offer an opportunity to explore a variation of Menzel's model, insofar as the Chimu established their regional centers in areas with preexisting complex polities yet made significant changes to the infrastructure at each regional center.

Within their domain, the Chimu demonstrate the typical site-size settlement hierarchy of an early state (Wright and Johnson 1975). Archaeological investigations over the past thirty years, using size and complexity of architecture, have established four ranks of Chimu sites above the village level (Mackey 1987). The first four levels are characterized by monumental adobe administrative architecture that adheres to the architectural canons found at the primary center or capital, Chan Chan in the Moche Valley (Moseley 1975). Thus far, three secondary or regional centers have been identified—Farfán (Jequetepeque Valley), Manchán (Casma Valley), and Túcume (La Leche Valley) (Keatinge and Conrad 1983; Mackey and Klymyshyn 1990; Heyerdahl et al. 1995)—along with a number of lower-level tertiary and quaternary centers, such as the Algarrobal de Moro and Talambo in the Jequetepeque Valley and Quebrada Katuay in the Moche Valley (Keatinge 1974; Keatinge and Conrad 1983; Mackey 1987, 2004). The sites given tertiary or quaternary designations in this chapter were all Chimu built or co-opted and remodeled by the Chimu. Elite residences of local lords are descriptively referred to as lower-level settlements of local lords, since they are outside the four ranks of the Chimu site-size hierarchy.

Below these four administrative ranks, two state-planned villages have been excavated. These villages, Cerro la Virgen in the Moche Valley and Quebrada Santa Cristina in the Casma Valley, lack adobe architecture and instead consist of cane-built (*quincha*) structures. Both villages demonstrate Chimu agricultural policies in that they control large tracts of land (Keatinge 1974; Moseley 1982; Moore 1991). Smaller, nonplanned villages also supplied the staples used at Chan Chan and the regional centers (e.g., S. Pozorski 1982), but they have not been as extensively investigated.

A brief overview of the capital, Chan Chan, is provided first because its architectural canons and social organization are pivotal in assessing the amount of influence exerted by the state in a conquered region.

As in all expanding states, the regional policies of the Chimu were flexible, but certain ones were apparent in all their provincial centers.

THE CHIMU CAPITAL AND THE THREE REGIONAL CENTERS

Chan Chan is located in the lower Moche Valley some 7 km north of the Moche River. Established between AD 900 and 1000, it served as the center of Chimu power until the Incas conquered it around AD 1460. The city's 6 km² core makes it one of the largest prehispanic settlements in South America; in size and complexity, it dwarfs all Chimu provincial settlements. Within 250 years of Chan Chan's founding, the Chimu had consolidated their heartland, which included not only the Moche Valley but also the Virú Valley to the south and the Chicama Valley to the north.

During the five years (1969–1974) of the Chan Chan-Moche Valley Project, the project members developed the basic model of Chimu social organization and administration derived from their investigations of the architecture, settlement patterns, and artifactual remains (Moseley and Mackey 1973; Moseley 1975; Moseley and Day 1982). From these studies four major classes of architecture emerged: (1) large adobe-walled compounds called palaces or *ciudadelas*, (2) smaller adobe-walled compounds, (3) artisans' cane-walled structures, and (4) four adobe mounds or platforms located outside the compounds. The large and small walled compounds were differentiated on the basis of size, building materials, and internal complexity. Based on these data, Klymyshyn (1982) divided the nobility into two classes, each with its own living space. Royalty resided in the large compounds (the palaces or ciudadelas; Figure 18.2) (Day 1982; Kolata 1990; Pillsbury and Leonard 2004), while nonroyalty lived in smaller structures of varying size and complexity that are collectively called elite compounds (Klymyshyn 1982). The elite, in turn, can be divided into subclasses, but in this chapter I use only the terms *royalty* and *elite* (or *nonroyal nobility*).

Chimu royal architecture is distinguished by a complex of related features that include *audiencias*, storerooms, plazas, and above-ground burial platforms. Audiencias are U-shaped multifunctional structures that served mainly as living and working quarters for Chimu nobles (Andrews 1974; Moseley 1975; Kolata 1990; Topic 2003; Pillsbury and Leonard 2004). They are the defining feature of Chimu administrative architecture

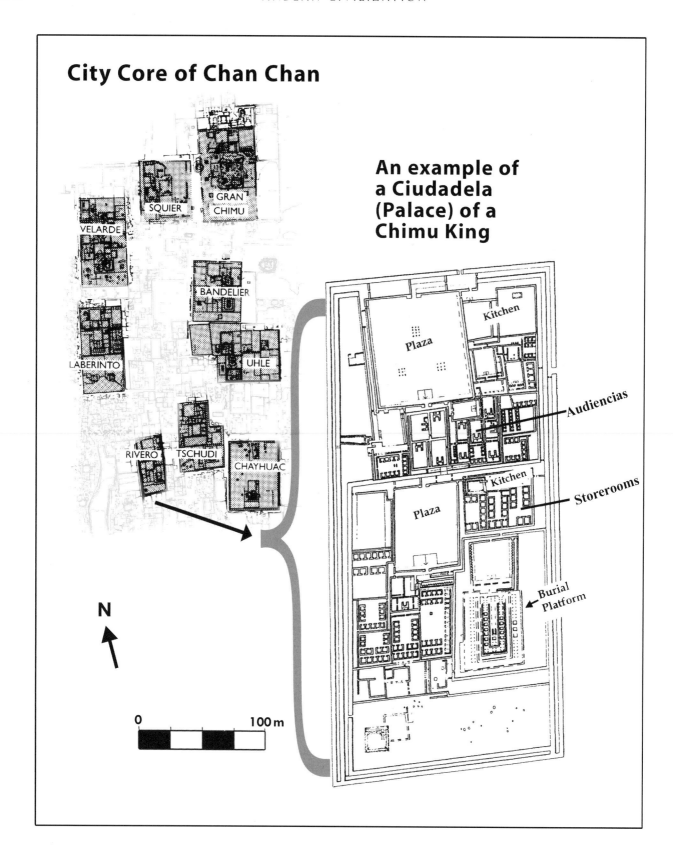

City Core of Chan Chan

An example of a Ciudadela (Palace) of a Chimu King

SQUIER

GRAN CHIMU

VELARDE

BANDELIER

LABERINTO

UHLE

RIVERO TSCHUDI

CHAYHUAC

N

0   100 m

Plaza

Kitchen

Plaza

Kitchen

Audiencias

Storerooms

Burial Platform

Figure 18.2. To the left, a map of the compounds within the core city of Chan Chan. To the right, a detail of the architectural features in a royal compound. After Moseley and Mackey 1974.

since they are found in centers of all ranks throughout the empire (Keatinge 1982; Mackey 1987). Storerooms are contiguous rather than separated, have finished walls and floors, and have high entry thresholds (see Figure 18.2) (Day 1982). There is a quantitative difference between the number of storerooms found in royal palaces and those found in the smaller elite compounds. On average, the royal palaces contained more than 200 storerooms each (Klymyshyn 1987). Elite compounds had only a fraction of the storage found in the palaces, which is one of the indicators of the different functions between them. Palaces secured and accumulated raw materials, staple goods, and luxury items, while elite compounds and regional centers functioned as transshipment points and provided short-term storage (Keatinge and Conrad 1983).

Chan Chan's large plazas mainly functioned as settings for large-scale feasts and ritual celebrations that were part of the reciprocal system noted for other Andean societies (Morris and Thompson 1985; Moore 1996; Uceda 1997). Although best described for the Inca, reciprocity was pivotal to the Chimu political, economic, and social system. This complex network involved trade, the accumulation of goods, state production, and the distribution of highly valued prestige items to individuals within and outside Chan Chan (Moseley 1982).

The fourth architectural element is the burial platform, a key factor in distinguishing between royal and elite mortuary patterns. Only royalty could be interred in above-ground burial platforms. These structures often reached 6 m in height and served as the king's final resting place (Conrad 1982). In addition to their mortuary function, burial platforms also symbolized the ancestors of the royal dynasty and the state's religious and political power. Small cells placed around the central tomb contained the bodies of women who were buried in the platform at the time of the king's death (Pozorski 1971; Conrad 1982). Nonroyalty were not buried in their elite compounds but rather in subterranean tombs located outside the elite compounds (Conrad 1982). As reflected in the architecture of the elite compounds, Chimu nonroyal nobility enjoyed fewer economic, social, and political advantages than royalty. The residences of the nonroyalty were smaller, contained fewer audiencias and storerooms, and had no above-ground burial platforms (Klymyshyn 1982).

At the height of its power, Chan Chan's population included no more than 30,000 inhabitants (Moseley 1975; J. Topic 1990), who mainly lived in cane-walled houses located in and around the city's core. These individuals were not retainers or agriculturists but full-time artisans, who were divided into different ranks (J. Topic 1990). Their primary occupation was to weave fine cloth and produce luxury items of gold, silver, and wood designated for the resident nobility and elites outside the capital (J. Topic 1982, 1990).

In sum, Chan Chan consisted of a hierarchically organized nobility that was served by retainers and a large artisan class (Day 1982). The city's food supply was provided mainly by satellite communities in the Moche Valley (S. Pozorski 1982) and from surrounding valleys (Keatinge and Conrad 1983).

THE REGIONAL CENTERS

After the consolidation of the heartland, the Chimu expanded their territory to the north and south of their capital. During a period of approximately 100 years (ca. AD 1300–1400), the Chimu established regional centers at Farfán, Manchán, and Túcume, in approximately that order. The following discussion focuses on two aspects of consolidation: (1) the preexisting level of political complexity that existed in the conquered regions and (2) the Chimu-constructed facilities.

Farfán: The Jequetepeque Valley
Previous occupation of the Jequetepeque Valley. The Jequetepeque Valley, located some 120 km north of the Moche Valley, was described by Cieza de León as one of the most fertile valleys on the north coast (Cieza 1984 [1551]). Farfán is located in the lower portion of the valley, adjacent to agricultural land and close to the intersection of two ancient routes—the north-south coastal road and the east-west road to the highlands, home of the Cajamarca polity. The site curves around a mountain range dominated by Cerro Faclo, its highest peak, which functioned as the site's lookout and most probably as a geographic marker, since Cerro Faclo is visible from most parts of the lower valley.

Prior to the Chimu conquest, the Jequetepeque Valley was culturally and politically affiliated with the Lambayeque polity, a complex, noncentralized state that wielded its influence over a large area of the north coast from the Chicama to Piura valleys (Shimada 1990, 1995). The heartland of the Lambayeque culture lay to the north in the Leche Valley (Shimada 1990). However, in the Jequetepeque Valley, Pacatnamu, located at the river's mouth, served as the nucleus of Lambayeque power. Although the role of Pacatnamu was primarily ceremonial, as indicated by its more than fifty truncated adobe mounds, it also had residential and administrative functions (Donnan and Cock 1986). A ranked settlement pattern of at least two levels below Pacatnamu is beginning to emerge in the Jequetepeque Valley.

The Lambayeque history in Jequetepeque is significant because a previously unknown Lambayeque occupation was recently discovered at the site of Farfán. Excavations identified an area of 1.5 km that contained the remains of four separated adobe perimeter walls ranging in length from 40 to 100 m, some of which were stratigraphically below Chimu architecture (Mackey and Jáuregui 2002, 2003). The Lambayeque settlement also included two cemeteries and a ceramic workshop (Figure 18.3). The best-preserved compound (called Compound III by Keatinge and Conrad [1983]) is linked stylistically to the architecture of Pacatnamu. Farfán's Compound III contains many of the features found at Pacatnamu, such as "altars," small east-west-facing mounds with ramps at both ends, and *concilios*, or low, U-shaped platforms (Donnan 1986). When Pacatnamu fell to the Chimu army in the fourteenth century, the Chimu did not choose Pacatnamu as their regional headquarters but instead occupied Farfán. None of the four existing Lambayeque compounds at Farfán were reused by the Chimu. Instead, they either razed the Lambayeque structures to their foundations or covered them with fill prior to building on top of them (Mackey and Jáuregui 2004).

The Chimu Occupation of Farfán. Of the six compounds that today comprise the site of Farfán, only Compounds II, IV, and VI[1] (see Figure 18.3) were built by the Chimu; the other structures, based on their construction and brick types, are either earlier or later (Mackey and Jáuregui 2004). The architecture in Compounds II and VI is well preserved, while only a portion of Compound IV remains. The internal features and spatial patterns of the two extant compounds recall the architectural features of Chan Chan's palaces: a plaza, audiencias, storerooms, and burial platforms. Though built only 100 years apart, Compound II, ca. AD 1300, and Compound VI, ca. AD 1400, clearly show a continuation of Chimu architectural canons (Figure 18.4). The feature that links both Compounds II and VI with first-rank royal administrators is the above-ground burial platform—an architectural feature associated only with royalty (Pozorski 1971; Moseley 1975; Conrad 1982). In comparison to Chan Chan, the two Farfán compounds contain fewer audiencias, only two per compound, and fewer than thirty storerooms (Mackey 2006). However,

it appears that the storage space was sufficient to support the administrators and to host state-sponsored rituals and feasts. Evidence of brewing *chicha* (corn beer) included fragments of large jars in the principal patio and areas for brewing chicha outside the perimeter walls. No evidence was found for craft production at Farfán during the Chimu occupation. Neither Farfán's architecture nor its excavated ceramics suggest that the Chimu shared power with local Lambayeque lords at Farfán (Mackey and Jáuregui 2003).

Manchán: The Casma Valley

Previous Occupation of the Casma Valley. The Casma Valley lies some 300 km south of the Moche Valley (see Figure 18.1) and is composed of two river systems, the Casma and the Sechín. Before the Chimu conquest in the fourteenth century, it is postulated that the Casma polity controlled the valley from the large hillside settlement of El Purgatorio. The site includes terraces, cemeteries, small domestic structures, and a number of both freestanding and agglutinated compounds (Tello 1956; Vilcherrez and Vogel 2006). Although both the nature and size of the Casma polity are still being investigated, its influence apparently reached as far north as the Chao Valley (Vogel 2003) and perhaps as far south as Huarmey (Mackey and Klymyshyn 1990; Wilson 1995). Within the Casma and Sechín valleys, prior to Chimu arrival, there may have been a settlement hierarchy of at least two settlement levels below El Purgatorio (Mackey and Klymyshyn 1990). When the Chimu conquered the Casma Valley, they chose land at the valley's southern entrance for the regional center of Manchán.

The Chimu Occupation of Manchán. Manchán is located on the west side of the Casma River, not far from the ancient north-south coastal road and the route to the highlands that terminates near the modern town of Huaráz. Manchán's architecture includes four distinct architectural types: (1) five freestanding Chimu adobe compounds, located mainly in the southern and southwestern portions of the site, (2) four agglutinated adobe compounds in the local Casma style, occupying the northern portion of the site, (3) at least two areas that were built or remodeled during the Inca occupation, and (4) several areas of cane-walled structures that housed part-time artisans, located between the freestanding and agglutinated compounds (Figure 18.5). The individuals who lived in these cane-walled structures produced a variety of goods, including low-grade copper items, fine and utilitarian textiles, and large quantities of chicha (Moore 1981; Mackey and Klymyshyn 1990).

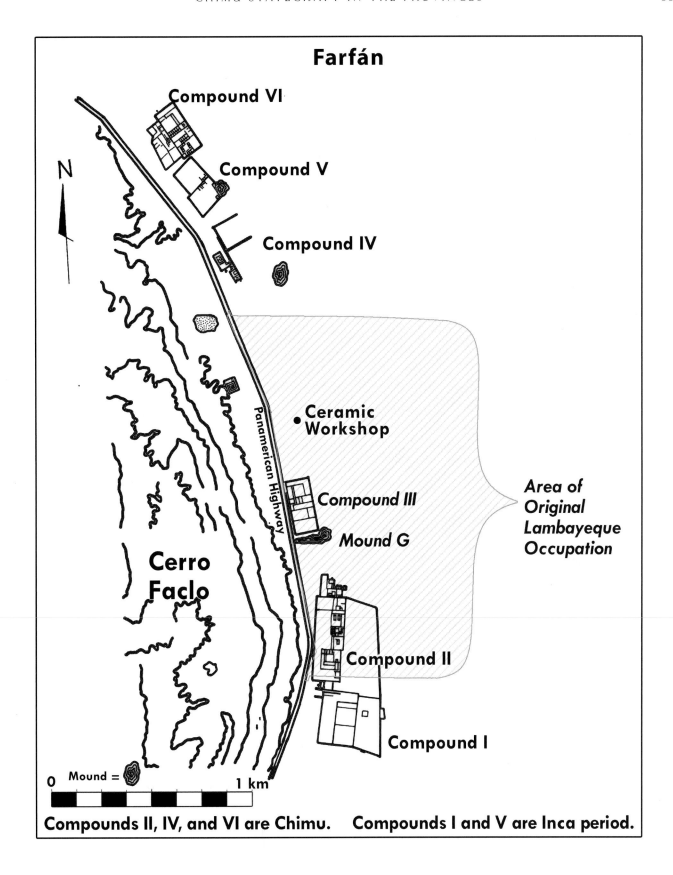

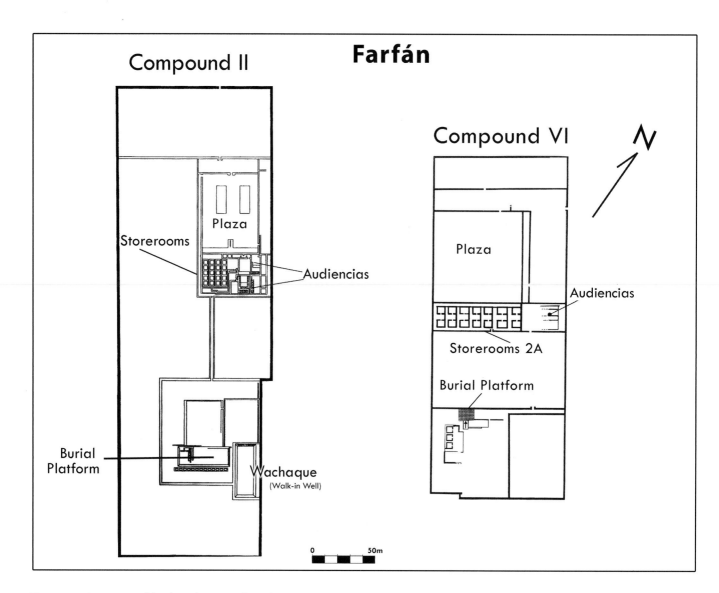

Figure 18.4. Comparison of the plans of Compound II and VI, Farfán.

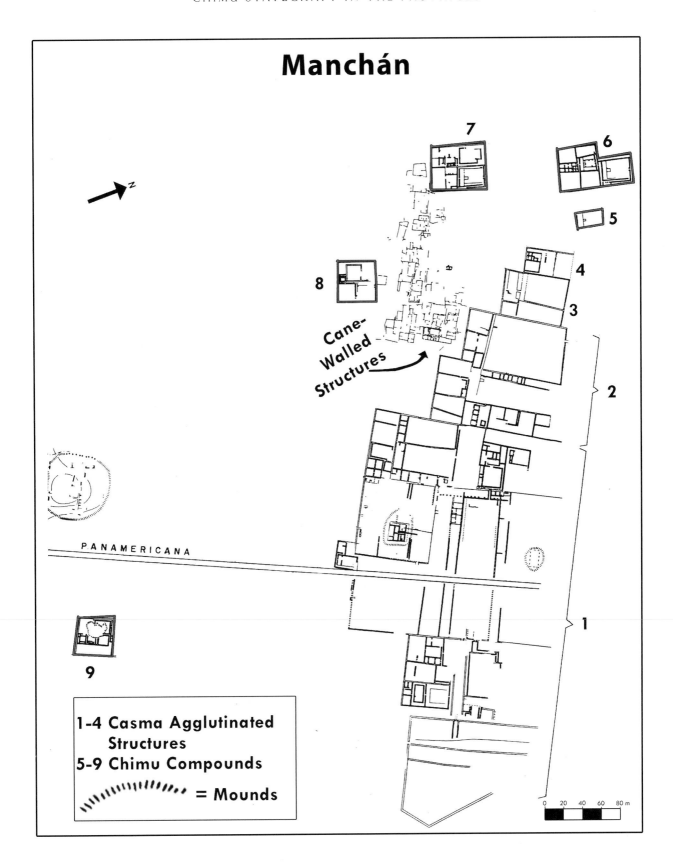

Figure 18.5. Plan of Manchán showing both Chimu and Casma architecture.

The five Chimu constructions are freestanding adobe compounds that served residential and funerary functions (nos. 5, 6, 7, 8, and 9, Figure 18.5). The compounds vary in size, though none is as large as those at Farfán. Compound 6 is built according to Chimu architectural canons and contains two small patios, one of which has wall niches; and two audiencias associated with a group of six storerooms (Figure 18.6). Compounds 5 and 8 may also have served as residences, but poor preservation makes this function uncertain. The evidence that Manchán was staffed by nonroyal administrators includes the small size of the Chimu residential compound(s) and the subterranean rather than above-ground burial structures (Mackey and Klymyshyn 1990).

Contemporaneous with the Chimu compounds were four agglutinated structures that show architectural similarity to the Casma style (see Figure 18.5) (Fung and Williams 1977; Vilcherrez and Vogel 2006). These agglutinated compounds contained patios, generally with low platforms at their southern ends, and residential or storage rooms along the patios' eastern limits (Mackey and Klymyshyn 1990). The largest and most complex of these structures is Compound 1. This compound contains the majority of residential rooms, as well as two small mounds. In its center is a large plaza (ca. 160 × 85 m) that contains sixty-five round adobe columns. This columned patio was not part of the original structure, and evidence of red paint and Late Horizon ceramics indicates that the Inca remodeled this area when they conquered the Chimu.

There is strong evidence that the plazas within the local lord's agglutinated structures were used for ceremonies during the Chimu occupation. The evidence within local compounds (2 and 3; Figure 18.5) includes large Chimu-style *tinajas* (storage vessels) buried up to their rims that contained the dregs of chicha as well as offerings of birds and ground maize wrapped in textiles. The presence of both Chimu and local architecture signals a different political strategy than that employed at Farfán—one that appeared to stress political and economic joint rule (Mackey and Klymyshyn 1990).

Túcume: La Leche and Lambayeque Valleys

Previous Occupation in La Leche Valley. After the Chimu conquest of the Jequetepeque Valley and the construction of Farfán (ca. AD 1300), the northern Lambayeque core area continued to thrive as an independent political entity for 50–100 years. It was only toward the end of the fourteenth century that the Chimu conquered

Túcume, the last capital of the Lambayeque polity, located in La Leche Valley (Heyerdahl et al. 1995). Established around AD 1100, Túcume was located on the coastal plain just south of the Leche River. This immense center covered some 150 ha and was dominated by twenty-six truncated mounds constructed by the Lambayeque (Heyerdahl et al. 1995) (Figure 18.7). To the south of Túcume, in the Lambayeque Valley, survey results indicate a well-developed preexisting political hierarchy as evidenced by at least two settlement levels below Túcume (Tschauner 2001).

The Chimu Occupation of Túcume. Túcume provides the first and so far the only example of a Chimu occupation of a conquered capital (Table 18.1). This is also the first time that the Chimu used preexisting structures, remodeling at least two Lambayeque monumental platforms (Figure 18.7, nos. 1 and 4), while leaving others intact to be used by local Lambayeque lords (Heyerdahl et al. 1995). These new Chimu structures appear to have been built in the Lambayeque rather than the Chimu architectural style (Heyerdahl et al. 1995), since archaeologists did not find Chimu audiencias in any of the remodeled areas at Túcume. However, the Chimu did add one important feature in the southwestern margin of the site: one of the newly built, Chimu compounds, 5c (Figure 18.7, nos. 5a, c), contained an above-ground burial platform. Since this feature is pivotal in distinguishing royalty from nonroyalty at Chan Chan, it is probable that one of Túcume's Chimu administrators was of royal rank. That the Chimu controlled some aspect of production is evidenced by the workshop that manufactured *Spondylus princeps* beads located in Compound 5a (Heyerdahl et al. 1995).

Summary

The Chimu adhered closely to the architectural forms and functions established at Chan Chan and maintained these features both diachronically and geographically. This is especially apparent when we compare the floor plans of the compounds from Chan Chan, Farfán, and Manchán (see Figures 18.2, 18.4, and 18.6). Although stylistic canons of Chimu architecture and ceramics unite these three regional centers, there are major differences among them. In the northern regions, in the Jequetepeque and La Leche/Lambayeque valleys, the Chimu preferred to install members of the royal family as administrators, as shown by the use of above-ground burial platforms at Farfán and Túcume. Only at Manchán did nonroyal nobility rule. In the Jequetepeque and Casma valleys, the Chimu disregarded

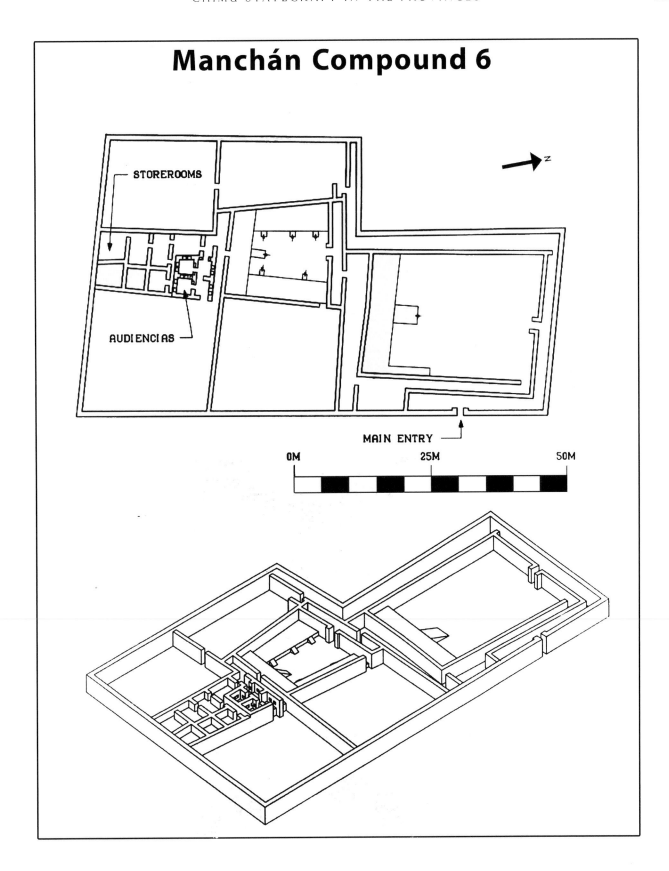

Manchán Compound 6

STOREROOMS

AUDIENCIAS

Z

MAIN ENTRY

0M 25M 50M

Figure 18.6. Chimu Compound 6, Manchán.

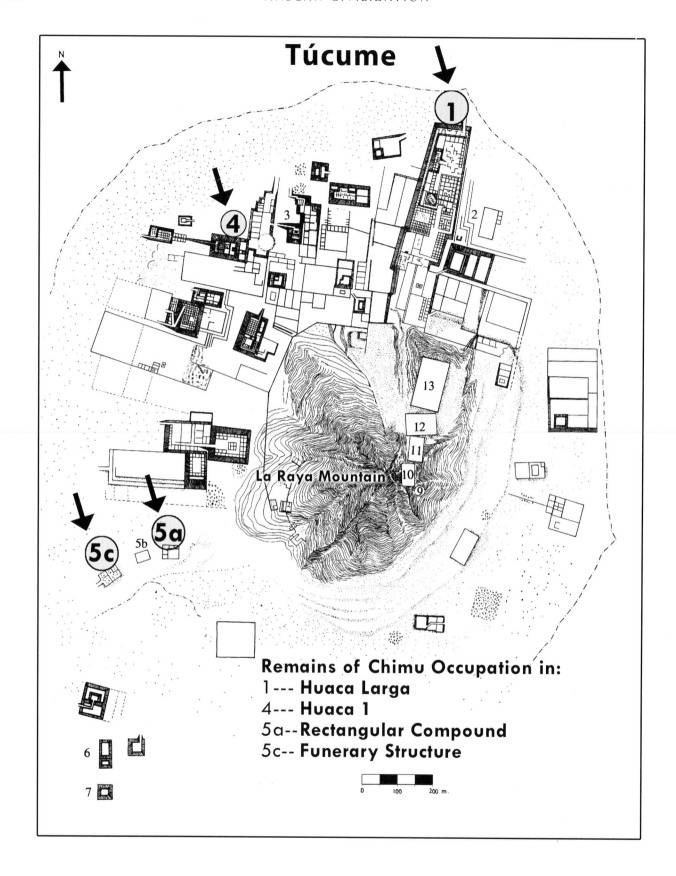

Figure 18.7. Map of Túcume indicating the Chimu occupation. After Heyerdahl et al. 1995.

the preexisting capitals (Pacatnamu and El Purgatorio) and built in other areas within the valley. Only at Túcume did the Chimu occupy the Lambayeque capital and build on or remodel the existing platform mounds. Both Manchán and Túcume witnessed some craft production, and all the centers produced chicha for feasts and celebrations (see Table 18.1).

When the Chimu moved beyond their imperial core, they conquered areas with preexisting complex polities and a well-established infrastructure. According to the model posited by Menzel (1959), we would expect to see few changes in the built environment and indirect political control, since the polities were of sufficient complexity to meet the state's needs. Nevertheless, the Chimu maintained some degree of direct rule in all the regional centers. Although Chimu authority was most evident at Farfán, Chimu political control was also present at regional centers that had joint rule, such as Manchán and Túcume. Variables such as local resistance, a perceived threat to the empire, proximity to transportation routes, or demand for resources could account for the variations in Menzel's model and the imposition of a stronger imperial presence (Menzel 1959; Schreiber 1992). These and other variables are examined in the next section.

THE DYNAMICS OF CONQUEST

Expansion

An empire's territorial expansion involves policy decisions at the highest level of government and reflects the state's underlying objectives for expanding its domain. Expansion is composed of two interrelated aspects. The first focuses on the strategies—military or diplomatic—used in the conquest of a new territory. The manner and means of the conquest influence future relationships with the local population and often the type of rule to be used. Many ancient American empires opted to use diplomatic strategies (D'Altroy 1992); evidence for such negotiated settlements is apparent in the blending of indigenous and imperial styles of architecture or

pottery in many Inca sites (Mackey 2003, 2004; Wernke 2006) or, as in the case of Manchán, coexisting styles. The second aspect relates to the motives for expansion. Conrad (1981, 1982), for instance, suggests that the political concept of "split inheritance" fueled Chimu territorial expansion. In this scenario, each new Chimu king inherited only rulership but not the lands or the revenue from his father, thereby forcing the new monarch to expand into new territories. Direct evidence for why expansion occurred is often difficult to demonstrate, but related data, such as the location of regional centers near crossroads or resources or a clustering of lower-level centers, can provide an indication of an area's importance and perhaps the motivation for conquest.

Nature of the Takeover. The confrontation between the Lambayeque polity and the advancing Chimu Empire is not only illustrated archaeologically but is also supported by an ethnohistorical document. The chronicle of Antonio de la Calancha (1977 [1638]) mentions a Chimu army under the command of General Pacatnamu, who waged a fierce battle to win control of the Jequetepeque Valley from the local polity, which we now know to be the Lambayeque (Conrad 1990). This is the only reference from a seventeenth-century chronicle to a specific valley conquest and a military figure. The conquest of the Jequetepeque Valley in the early 1300s led to the fall of Pacatnamu, the Lambayeque ceremonial/administrative valley capital (Donnan and Cock 1986). The Chimu, however, bypassed Pacatnamu and established their regional settlement at the existing Lambayeque center of Farfán (Mackey and Jáuregui 2003).

At Farfán, the Chimu commemorated their victory by placing Lambayeque burials on top of one of the destroyed Lambayeque compounds before building their Compound II atop this ruined structure. During our investigation of Compound II, subfloor excavations revealed four bodies, all female, lying on top of or next to the destroyed Lambayeque wall foundations (Mackey and Jáuregui 2004). One of these women, Burial 3, had a rough fiber rope around her neck, suggesting

Table 18.1 Chimu regional centers.

Site	Expansion		Consolidation			
	Nature of Conquest		Rank of Administration			
	Coopted	Construction	Burial Platform	Audiencia	Shared Control	Production
Farfán	Terrain	New	Yes	Yes	No	No
Manchán	Unused land	New	No	Yes	Yes	Yes
Túcume	Structures	Remodel/New	Yes	No	Yes	Yes

strangulation (Figure 18.8). They were buried with Lambayeque-style ceramics, and their crania exhibited typical Lambayeque fronto-occipital cranial deformation (Andrew Nelson, pers. comm.).

In contrast, the conquest of the Casma Valley appears to have been negotiated by diplomatic means. The Chimu chose to locate their regional capital in a neutral, previously unoccupied area of the Casma Valley (Mackey and Klymyshyn 1990). The spatial organization of the site shows a clear division between the contemporaneous structures of the local lords and those of the Chimu nobles (see Figure 18.5). The Chimu occupation did not result in a blended architectural style, as previously thought (Mackey and Klymyshyn 1990), since each polity maintained its own cultural identity in architecture and artifacts. The two styles of architecture suggest shared power; however, fineware Chimu vessels replaced the local high-status forms, although Casma Incised utilitarian wares continued to be manufactured (Mackey and Klymyshyn 1990).

At the large Lambayeque center of Túcume, in La Leche Valley, the Chimu co-opted some of the existing monumental platforms. They leveled the structures atop two of the monumental platforms to construct their own elite residences. Further, the platforms the Chimu chose to occupy, Huaca Larga and the adjacent Huaca 1, had been Túcume's iconic landmarks (see Figure 18.7). Constructing new Chimu structures on top of the principal huacas clearly symbolized the imposition of imperial Chimu power and authority. The Chimu, however, did mitigate their intrusion by building in a style that favored local rather than imperial architectural canons. They also allowed elite Túcume lords to continue residing in some of the other platforms, indicating a collaborative strategy reminiscent of Manchán. The ceramics were not a blend of the two traditions. Instead, as at Manchán, Chimu pottery coexisted with the local style (Heyerdahl et al. 1995).

Motivation for the Takeover. There are myriad reasons for the expansion of states into new territories, including political, economic, and ideological considerations. Early states often expanded for economic reasons (D'Altroy 1992; Schreiber 1992), but they were also motivated by ideological concerns (Conrad and Demarest 1984; Bauer and Stanish 2001). Although economics played a major role in Chimu expansion, ethnographic and archaeological evidence favors both ideological and economic concerns. Several of these motives for expansion may help to explain the Chimu focus on the northern portion of their empire.

Ideology appears to be one of the motivators in Chimu expansion to the north of Chan Chan. The northern north coast, and perhaps a portion of modern southern Ecuador, played an important role in Chimu mythology and ideology (Mackey 2001). The legendary founder of the Chimu dynasty, Tacaynamo, was said to have come to the Moche Valley on a balsa raft from the north (Rowe 1948). The myth underscores that he was a foreigner and had to learn the language and culture of the Moche Valley. Mary Helms (1993) suggests that when an event is distant in time and space, a sacred nature is often conferred on the place, event, or individuals. In addition, the resources of the north, metallic ores and *Spondylus princeps*, may have achieved prominence because of their association with this area. The economic as well as the ideological "need" for these resources may have justified Chimu expansion.

The strategic location of the Jequetepeque Valley allowed the Chimu direct access to arsenical copper, silver, and gold (Shimada 1995). The Lambayeque polity at Túcume, to the north of the Jequetepeque Valley, had a long history as an intermediary with Ecuador in the *Spondylus princeps* trade (Heyerdahl et al. 1995; Shimada 1995), a shell that was integral to Chimu funerary rites and an important element in the confection of many prestige items (Conrad 1982; Pillsbury 2004). Although several authors have suggested that the Chimu controlled the *Spondylus princeps* trade (e.g., Moseley 2001), Chimu administration of this valued item may not have occurred until after the conquest of Túcume and may have been a major impetus for the conquest of the last Lambayeque capital.

The Jequetepeque Valley also served as a gateway to the Cajamarca region, home to an important highland polity. During Chimu times, agricultural goods from the Jequetepeque Valley were probably exchanged with the Cajamarca region, just as they were during the Inca period (Cieza 1984 [1551]), for precious metals and camelid fiber (Shimada 1990, 1995). These resources were used by Chimu artisans to produce cloth and works in metal for Chan Chan's burgeoning elite. The luxury goods produced at Chan Chan served as gifts to Chimu nobles as well as conquered elites, ensuring the cooperation of both groups as the empire expanded (Moseley 2001). Cajamarca proved crucial not only for its resources but also later as a political ally against the Inca (Rowe 1948).

The Chimu motivation for the subjugation of the Casma Valley is not as apparent as the conquests north

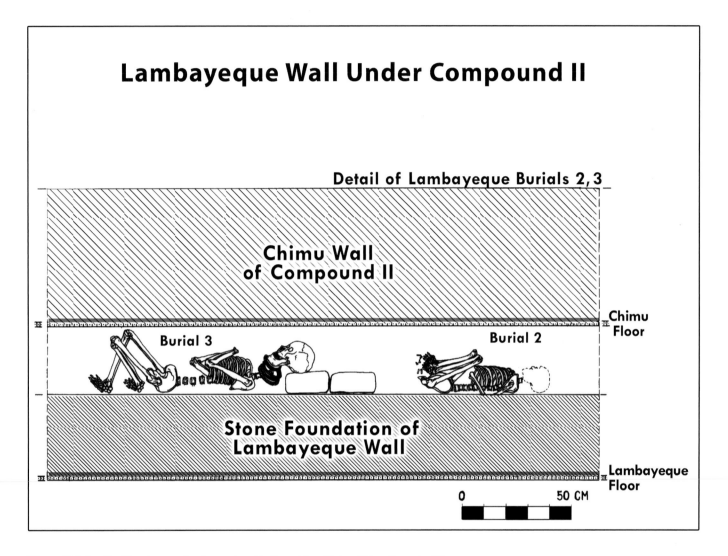

Figure 18.8. Sacrificed Lambayeque females stratigraphically positioned below Chimu Compound II.

of Chan Chan. Although administration at Manchán is seen as a collaborative ruling effort, the Chimu may have viewed the Casma polity as a threat. In addition, the Chimu may have wished to establish alternative routes to the highlands, since the Casma Valley is a gateway to the Callejón de Huaylas and the source of highland resources. Textile production was important at Manchán (Moore 1985), and camelid fibers, excavated in the cane structures that housed Manchán's artisans, may have been exchanged for coastal products. Finally, once Manchán was established as a regional capital, it marked the Chimu's southern frontier and may have been used as a staging area for exploration farther south.

Summary

The Chimu scenarios in the valleys settled by the Chimu cannot be fully confirmed, but the data outlined here reflect our present knowledge. It should be noted, however, that despite new interpretations, an emphasis on the northern portion of its domain offers insights into reasons for expansion into this area and the strong Chimu presence at Farfán and Túcume. Farfán stands apart from the two other regional centers because of its violent takeover and the apparent lack of shared power. The Chimu may have had a long-standing competitive relationship with the Lambayeque polity, and the two may have competed for scarce and valued goods from the Cajamarca region before the Chimu conquest of the Jequetepeque Valley. Additionally, the Chimu may have had to confront the Lambayeque when they consolidated the Chicama Valley as part of their heartland, since there is evidence of a large Lambayeque cemetery at Huaca Cao Viejo in that valley (Gálvez and Briceño 2001; Franco and Gálvez 2005). In contrast, the Chimu appeared to favor a negotiated settlement in the southern regional center of Manchán. Perhaps they viewed the south as less strategic to their plans of expansion, or perhaps the Casma rulers were more willing to negotiate. The data reinforce the argument that resource extraction and control of trade routes fueled Chimu expansion to the north, which in turn was legitimized by the far north's important role in Chimu mythology and ideology.

INCORPORATION OF NEW TERRITORIES INTO THE CHIMU REALM

One of the main concerns of all expanding states is the incorporation of new territories into the state's political and economic organization. Incorporation, like expansion, includes many interrelated aspects and is affected by how a new territory was acquired—through harsh military action or peaceful means. Crucial to the question of political integration is whether state control is direct or indirect. Political control cannot be determined from viewing only the regional centers but must include lower-level settlements, both of Chimu and of the indigenous communities.

Political Control at the Three Provincial Centers

The degree of political control a conquering state imposes on its newly conquered territories is often measured by the similarities to the conqueror's architectural and ceramic styles. By this measure, Farfán deserves to be called the administrative flagship of the Chimu Empire. It was the most architecturally similar to the capital and maintained its adherence to Chimu architectural canons for approximately 150 years, from its establishment in the early 1300s to its conquest by the Incas in AD 1460. Direct rule by Chimu royalty is evident in the inclusion of royal burial platforms in two of Farfán's compounds.

In contrast, Manchán graphically illustrates Chimu shared rule. The absence of an interior above-ground burial platform supports the notion that Manchán's administrators belonged to the nonroyal nobility. Burial facilities were situated within freestanding adobe structures that contained subterranean, prepared tombs (Mackey and Klymyshyn 1990). In terms of political control, the archaeological evidence from Túcume also points to shared rule by the Lambayeque and Chimu lords (Heyerdahl et al. 1995). At least one of Túcume's Chimu governors, however, must have been from royalty based on the presence of an above-ground burial platform.

The role of regional administrators was pivotal to the state's integration policy for several reasons. First, the noble administrators sent from Chan Chan connected the hinterlands to the capital (Keatinge and Conrad 1983; Mackey 2006). They passed on decisions made at the capital to the newly established administrative hierarchy within the valleys and controlled these lower-ranking centers. The administrators at the regional centers were linked by kinship, by noble ancestors, and by the reciprocity system with the ruler at Chan Chan. The regional centers have a small amount of residential space, indicating there was little room for families, retainers, or other retinue, which suggests that the regional administrators probably spent as much time at Chan Chan as they did in the provinces. This view of upper-echelon administrators is supported by the work of Morris and Thompson (1985), who found that high-ranking administrators spent little time at the Inca provincial center of Huánuco Pampa. Second, the provincial administrators were crucial to the asymmetrical reciprocal system, which played a major role in incorporating the outlying territories of the empire (Morris 1998). The administrative centers contained sufficient storage facilities to store commodities such as maize used to brew chicha and had access to animals and other supplies to host large-scale feasts and ceremonies. These ceremonies were one means of introducing ideology, and they may have been one of the important ways that local elites were integrated into the state's administrative hierarchy (Wernke 2006).

Chimu Lower-Level Centers

As part of the state's policies, the Chimu established smaller tertiary- and quaternary-level administrative structures in the valleys surrounding the regional centers. As other scholars have pointed out, the main function of these centers was state control of water and land (Keatinge 1974; Moseley 2001; Hayashida 2006). The Jequetepeque Valley included two Chimu centers that rank below Farfán. The earlier, smaller quaternary center, contemporary with Compound II at Farfán (ca. 1300), was Talambo (Keatinge and Conrad 1983), located at the valley neck overlooking the Jequetepeque River. This small stone compound, with one audiencia but with no storage space or platform, faces the maximum-elevation canal that once carried water from the river northward (Keatinge and Conrad 1983). Algarrobal de Moro, a tertiary center that is contemporary with Compound VI at Farfán (ca. AD 1400), is situated in the northern portion of the valley near a river with an intermittent water supply and close to agricultural fields (Castillo et al. 1997; Mackey 2004). Like Farfán, this center mimics Chimu architectural canons. It has three audiencias and six storerooms but no burial platform, indicating that it housed nonroyal Chimu nobility (Castillo et al. 1997; Mackey 2004).

South of Túcume, in the Lambayeque Valley, the Chimu co-opted or built several centers. Since these sites have not been excavated, it is difficult to place them in the Chimu site-size hierarchy (Mackey 1987) and only possible to state that they rank below the regional center of Túcume. The Chimu co-opted the Lambayeque center of Pátapo, near the important Taymi Canal, and constructed three other structures in highly visible locations on hills along the valley margin. Several of these centers incorporated Chimu architectural features such as baffled doorways and audiencia variants (Tschauner 2001). The ceramics associated with both the Jequetepeque and Lambayeque valleys' tertiary and/or quaternary centers conform mainly to Chimu rather than to local styles.

The Chimu presence was not as evident in the lower-ranking centers in the southern portion of the empire. Some centers within the Sechín and Casma valleys that rank hierarchically below Manchán were originally hypothesized to have been either built or co-opted by the Chimu (Mackey and Klymyshyn 1990). Research has shown that several of these settlements are earlier, such as Laguna II, or later (Chimu-Inca), such as Puerto Pobre (Koschmieder and Vega-Centeno 1996). Until more excavations are carried out, it appears that previous hypotheses regarding tertiary or quaternary administrative centers built or co-opted by the Chimu will remain untested. However, the Chimu did build a state-planned rural village at Quebrada Santa Cristina. Situated at the mouth of the Casma River, this residential settlement, constructed of cane-walled architecture, controlled a vast tract of ridged fields and saltpans designed to reclaim wetlands in the aftermath of a fourteenth-century El Niño event (Moore 1991).

Chimu Relationships with Local-level Lords

It appears that a key element in Chimu provincial policy was to refrain from disrupting the lowest hierarchical levels or the preexisting indigenous local lords, allowing them to remain in place. Insofar as this view is based mainly on the survey and excavation of residences of local lords, further research is needed to assess the impact of the Chimu conquest at the village level to determine its full economic effect. Sapp states (2002) that local Lambayeque lords continued to occupy elite residences such as Cabur in the Jequetepeque Valley. Although Cabur was remodeled in Chimu times, its architecture is mainly Lambayeque in style and did not emulate the dominant Chimu style. The same is true in the Lambayeque Valley, where local elites continued to reside on platform mounds on the valley floor, apparently retaining their traditional positions and responsibility for day-to-day operations in the valley (Tschauner 2001). Within the Casma and Sechín valleys, the survey results imply that the Chimu disrupted neither the valley's preexisting settlement patterns nor control of the local hierarchy (Mackey and Klymyshyn 1990).

Research indicates that indigenous leaders were given positions of responsibility within the Chimu administrative hierarchy by controlling some aspects of production. For example, Tschauner (2001) offers compelling evidence for a locally managed ceramic workshop in the Lambayeque Valley, where potters produced mainly domestic ceramics, some in the late Chimu style. At Cabur, evidence was found within the main compound for the production of objects fashioned from *Spondylus princeps*, as demonstrated by hundreds of pieces of cut shell, perhaps destined to be made into jewelry and beads (Sapp 2002).

Summary

The data presented here illustrate just how complex the notions of direct or indirect control are when applied to the Chimu and their territorial expansion. The terms themselves are heuristic devices meant to show a continuum, and the Chimu case is a good example of the variation along the spectrum. The Chimu example also stands out for two other reasons. First, it shows that Farfán was an anomaly in Chimu regional policies, since the other two regional centers included some degree of power sharing. Second, it shows that direct and indirect rule may occur simultaneously in the same valley. This winning strategy employed by the Chimu gave some degree of autonomy or indirect rule to local lords and did not force assimilation upon them, a strategy also used by the Inca in the Jequetepeque Valley (Mackey 2003). Thus, it appears that a parallel system existed: direct or shared control at the top-ranking centers and a continuation of local rule at the lower levels.

TIME FRAME AND TERRITORIAL LIMITS OF CHIMU EXPANSION AND INCORPORATION

The consolidation of the Chimu heartland—the Moche, Chicama, and Virú valleys—is reported to have occurred within a 250-year period (ca. AD 1050–1300), and conquest to the north and south took place after the heartland was consolidated. Based on recent archaeological investigations, it is possible to reevaluate the Chimu period of expansion in terms of time frame, stages of expansion, and geographic limits. Although the Spanish chronicles suggest two stages for Chimu expansion (Rowe 1948; Keatinge and Conrad 1983; Mackey and Klymyshyn 1990; T. Topic 1990), the archaeological evidence points to at least three (Table 18.2).

Time Frame

According to radiocarbon assays, the Chimu regional center of Farfán was the first to be established, in approximately AD 1300 (see Table 18.2). Although Keatinge and Conrad (1983) posited that Farfán's Compound II was built in AD 1200, several scholars (Donnan and Cock 1986; Sapp 2002) maintain that this occurred at a later time, based on the dates from Pacatnamu that cluster around AD 1310–1340 (C. Donnan, pers. comm.). Wooden spindles excavated with one of the sacrificed bodies atop the destroyed Lambayeque walls, directly under Farfán's Compound II, have been dated between AD 1220 and 1310 (with 2-sigma calibrations), which also supports the later date (see Figure 18.8).

The architectural features of Compound II also support the radiocarbon assays. First, the floor plan and the spatial organization of Compound II resemble the tripartite divisions of the later compounds at Chan Chan (see Figure 18.2). In addition, the morphology of Compound II's audiencias does not conform to the early forms of Kolata's architectural seriation for Chan Chan (Kolata 1990:126–127). Farfán's two audiencias show a blend of features (bins and niches, with bins at the back of the audiencias) that correspond to those found in Laberinto and Grand Chimu, ciudadelas that date between AD 1100 and 1300, rather than to the early types (Figure 18.9).

All of the evidence—radiocarbon assays, architecture, and ceramic morphology—suggests that Manchán was established after Farfán.[2] The Manchán date of AD 1305 ± 75 years shows that it was founded between AD 1230 and 1380. Previously, a date of AD 1300 had been suggested for Manchán (Mackey and Klymyshyn 1990); however, based on a comparison with Farfán, whose Compound VI dates to AD 1400, a later rather than an

Table 18.2. Approximate time line of Chimu conquests.

AD 900/1000–1300	AD 1300/1340	AD 1350–1380	AD 1350/1400
Consolidation of the heartland	Farfán	Manchán	Túcume

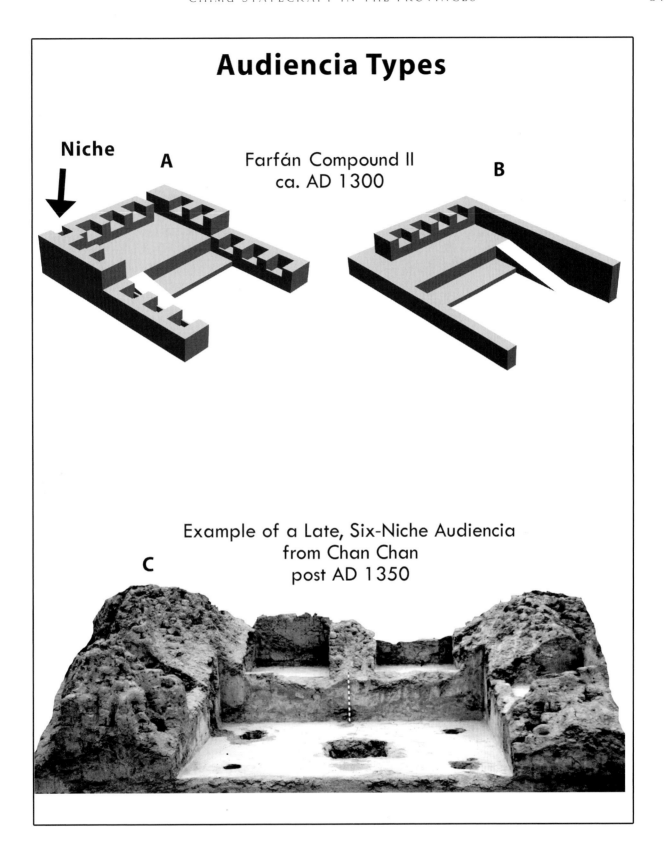

Figure 18.9. Examples of audiencia types from Farfán and Chan Chan.

earlier date is considered more likely. For example, the audiencias at Manchán contain six niches, similar to those found in Chan Chan's late ciudadelas, and this type does not occur earlier than AD 1350 (see Figure 18.9) (Kolata 1990:126–127). Most scholars agree that the conquest of Túcume by the Chimu took place within a fifty-year period that ranges from AD 1350 to 1400 (Donnan 1990; Shimada 1990; T. Topic 1990; Heyerdahl et al. 1995). The lack of audiencias at Túcume makes it impossible to use Kolata's sequence, but Chimu ceramics suggest a date closer to AD 1400 (Topic 1977; Topic and Moseley 1983; see Table 18.2).

The Stages of Conquest and the Extent of the Empire

The Spanish chronicles indicate that the Chimu occupied an area of the north coast that extended from Tumbes in the north to the Chillón Valley in the south. This expanse of more than 1,000 km of the Peruvian coast is further divided into two stages of expansion, each stage covering an area to the north and south of the capital; the first stage is postulated to be two advances of roughly equal distances that extended north to the Zaña and south to the Santa Valley, while the second stage added territory from the Zaña Valley to the Tumbes Valley in the north and from the Santa Valley to the Chillón Valley in the south (Rowe 1948). In rethinking this scheme, there are two major factors to consider. First, present-day archaeological evidence does not support a consolidated Chimu Empire that reached from Tumbes Valley to the Chillón Valley. Klymyshyn and I (1990) suggested that the Chimu consolidated only the area that stretched from La Leche Valley in the north to the Casma Valley in the south. The valleys that lie to the north of La Leche to Tumbes and south of the Casma Valley to the Chillón may have been connected to the Chimu state through trade or marriage alliances and may have been ruled indirectly (Parsons and Hastings 1988; Mackey and Klymyshyn 1990). Future work will determine the validity of this hypothesis and whether Chimu administrative centers existed in areas beyond the limits of consolidation.

A second, related point raises further questions. Although it had been assumed that the Chimu occupied all the contiguous valleys between La Leche and Casma, this has not proved to be the case (Parsons and Hastings 1988; Mackey and Klymyshyn 1990; T. Topic 1990). The Chimu occupied its territory asymmetrically, with a marked emphasis on the northern portion of the realm. To the south of the Chimu heartland, with the possible

exception of the Nepeña Valley (Proulx 1973), there is no evidence of Chimu networks of administrative centers such as those documented to the north of the capital. Although it is not unusual for expanding states to leapfrog across unconquered territory (Sinopoli 1996; Bauer and Covey 2002), how did the Chimu govern the southern portion of the empire, and how did they pass through these valleys to reach Casma? The lack of a Chimu presence in the southern valleys suggests either indirect rule or the approval or assistance of the local lords living in these valleys. Further work on the Casma polity may answer these questions (Vogel 2003).

A final point addresses the number of stages in the Chimu expansion. It would appear at this time that there were at least three major stages of expansion and that these stages were not in symmetrical increments to the north and south of the capital. I argue that the stages follow the chronology of the establishment of the regional centers, extending first to the Jequetepeque Valley, then south to the Casma, and finally north to La Leche Valley.

Summary

Three lines of evidence—architecture, ceramic morphology, and C14 assays—have been used as the basis for a new chronological assessment of the founding of Farfán and Manchán. The evidence points to both of these sites being later than previously thought: Farfán, AD 1300–1340, and Manchán, AD 1350–1380.

Present-day evidence does not support a consolidated Chimu Empire that reached from Tumbes to the Chillón Valley. Instead, a more viable position appears to be an area that ranges from La Leche in the north to the Casma Valley in the south. Further, Chimu power and authority were not evenly distributed within this area, since the majority of settlements were located to the north of Chan Chan. Finally, it appears that there were not two but at least three stages of Chimu expansion.

PRINCIPLES OF CHIMU STATECRAFT

The data presented in this chapter indicate there were both similarities and differences among the regional centers. One of the differences was the rank of the administrators at the centers. For example, the northern centers, Farfán and Túcume, were governed by royal administrators, while Manchán was under the rule of nonroyal officials (Mackey and Klymyshyn 1990;

Mackey 2006). This difference was indicated primarily by the presence or absence of a burial platform. Despite some differences, certain underlying principles of statecraft prevailed at all the regional centers.

The first of these principles was a planned difference in function between the regional and lower-ranked (tertiary and quaternary) Chimu centers. The regional centers had large gathering areas, such as plazas, and sufficient storage space to host rituals and feasts as part of the state-sponsored reciprocal system that was pivotal to the integration of new territories (Morris and Thompson 1985; Wernke 2006). Also, the regional centers were all located near (Farfán and Manchán) or close to (Túcume) major roads, which would have facilitated trade. The lower-ranked centers in the Lambayeque and Jequetepeque valleys all contained audiencias, but not all had storage space. The main function of these centers appears to have been the control of major canals or land (Keatinge 1974; Tschauner 2001).

A second principle of statecraft, and one that influenced the nature of expansion, was the acquisition of valued resources, especially metallic ores and *Spondylus princeps*. These resources, used in the manufacture of luxury items at Chan Chan (Pillsbury 2004), are found to the north of the capital, an area correlated with the highest density of Chimu centers.

A third principle was the use of joint rule, since two of the three regional centers employed this strategy (Mackey and Klymyshyn 1990). Farfán is unique among the three centers in having no evidence of shared power. The political control evident at Farfán may have been an early Chimu strategy, because Farfán was the first center established outside of the heartland. Alternatively, the absence of local lords at Farfán may have been in response to the violent battle that took place between the Chimu and the local Jequetepeque Valley forces (Conrad 1990).

The fourth principle was the use of both direct and indirect rule in the same valley. The regional centers all had some form of direct rule; even those centers that shared power manifested a strong Chimu political component. The state presence was evidenced by Chimu-style architectural features, new construction or remodeling, and state-style ceramics. In the Jequetepeque and Lambayeque valleys the settlements ranked immediately below the regional centers also epitomized direct rule, since they also contained Chimu architectural features and ceramics and were probably staffed by Chimu officials (Mackey 2006).

The corollary to the fourth principle is that at the local level, Chimu policy was nondisruptive, and assimilation of the population did not appear to be a goal. The emphasis at the indigenous level was on indirect rule, providing the local lords and their communities with some degree of continuity and autonomy.

CONCLUSION

Although the Chimu showed flexibility in their provincial planning and strategy, certain underlying principles of statecraft were requisite at all regional centers. At each center, the Chimu altered the infrastructure, either by constructing anew or rebuilding, with the result that state presence was highly visible. The Chimu also conquered areas that had preexisting complex polities. The data presented for the Chimu case suggest a modification of the Menzel model that proposed little change in infrastructure when there was a preexisting complex polity.

Many variables account for the modification of the Menzel model. One of the most likely reasons was a perceived threat to the Chimu state, as demonstrated by the conflict with the Lambayeque forces in the Jequetepeque Valley and was a possibility with the Casma polity. A second factor that might have resulted in the imposition of a stronger Chimu presence in the northern region was the demand for resources important in the manufacturing of luxury goods at Chan Chan. In addition, these high-status goods were pivotal to the continuation of the reciprocity system that provided prestige items to the Chimu nobility and were in turn used to cement relations with local lords.

Recent investigations allow an updating of the chronology, stages, and geographic limits of Chimu expansion, resulting in changes to long-held notions. The data now support a later date for the establishment of both Farfán and Manchán, and the region consolidated by the Chimu now encompasses the valleys from La Leche to Casma, rather than stretching from Tumbes in the north to the Chillón Valley in the south. Finally, rather than the two-stage theory of expansion, it is now more likely that at least three stages of conquest occurred that conform chronologically to the establishment of the regional centers.

Future research may reveal new information about the valleys that have received less attention. Nevertheless, many of the principles of statecraft originally outlined by Moseley (1982) for the Chimu capital, such as centralization of economic goods at Chan Chan, rule through a hierarchical administration, and the importance of the reciprocal system, have been reaffirmed by recent research and have been shown to be operative in the provinces.

Acknowledgments

The data used in this article are the result of many years of research from various archaeological projects. Those that I have had direct association with include The Chan Chan-Moche Valley Project (1969–1974), directed by Michael E. Moseley and Carol Mackey, with research supported by the National Science Foundation and National Geographic Society; The Manchán Project (1981–1984), directed by Carol Mackey and A. Ulana Klymyshyn and also supported by the National Science Foundation and National Geographic Society; and Complejo Arqueológico de San José de Moro (excavation of the Algarrobal de Moro in 1995–1998), directed by Luis Jaime Castillo, Carol Mackey, and Andrew Nelson. The fieldwork on the Chimu portion of the site was sponsored by the Brennan Foundation, California State University, Northridge, and private donations. During the six years of the Proyecto Arqueológico de Farfán (1999–2004) there were two co-directors whom I would like to thank, Enrique Zavaleta (2000) and César Jáuregui (2001–2004). Our project was sponsored by the Brennan Foundation, the John B. Heinz Charitable Trust, Dumbarton Oaks, the National Geographic Society, and private donors. I thank the crews, students, and volunteers whose work made these projects successful.

NOTES

1. Previously it was believed that all six of Farfán's compounds were Chimu built and occupied. Archaeological investigations by the Farfán Project (1999–2004), co-directed by Carol Mackey and César Jáuregui, found that only three were constructed by the Chimu. Of the other extant compounds identified by Keatinge and Conrad (1983), evidence now shows that Compound III is Lambayeque in affiliation, while Compounds I and V were built during the Inca occupation of Farfán.

2. Vogel (2003) states that Cerro la Cruz, in the Chao Valley (south of Virú), a frontier settlement of the Casma polity, was occupied until AD 1300 and there is no Chimu presence prior to that date.

REFERENCES

Andrews, Anthony P.
1974   The U-Shaped Structures at Chan Chan, Peru. *Journal of Field Archaeology* 1:241–264.

Bauer, Brian S., and R. Alan Covey
2002   Process of State Formation in the Inca Heartland (Cuzco, Peru). *American Anthropologist* 104(3): 846–864.

Bauer, Brian S., and Charles Stanish
2001   *Ritual and Pilgrimage in the Ancient Andes*. University of Texas Press, Austin.

Castillo, Luis Jaime, Carol Mackey, and Andrew Nelson
1997   *Informe Preliminar: Campaña 1996 del Proyecto Complejo Arqueológico de Moro*. Instituto Nacional de Cultura, Lima.

Calancha, Antonio de la
1974–1982 [1638]   *Corónica moralizada del Orden de San Augustín en el Perú*. Trascripción, Ignacio Prado Pastor. Crónicas del Perú, 4–9. Universidad Nacional Mayor de San Marcos, Lima.

Cieza de Léon, Pedro de
1984 [1551]   *La crónica del Perú*. Crónicas de América, Historia 16, edited by Manuel Ballesteros Gaibrois. Madrid.

Conrad, Geoffrey W.
1981   Cultural Materialism, Split Inheritance, and the Expansion of Ancient Peruvian Empires. *American Antiquity* 46(1):3–42.

1982   The Burial Platforms of Chan Chan: Some Social and Political Implications. In *Chan Chan: Andean Desert City*, edited by Michael E. Moseley and Kent C. Day, pp. 87–117. University of New Mexico Press, Albuquerque.

1990   Farfán, General Pacatnamu, and the Dynastic History of Chimor. In *The Northern Dynasties: Kingship and Statecraft in Chimor*, edited by Michael E. Moseley and Alana Cordy-Collins, pp. 195–226. Dumbarton Oaks, Washington, DC.

Conrad, Geoffrey W., and Arthur A. Demarest.
1984   *Religion and Empire: The Dynamics of Aztec and Inca Expansionism*. Harvard University Press, Cambridge, MA.

D'Altroy, Terence N.
1992   *Provincial Power in the Inca Empire*. Smithsonian Institution Press, Washington, DC

Day, Kent C.
1982   Ciudadelas: Their Form and Function. In *Chan Chan: Andean Desert City*, edited by Michael E.

Moseley and Kent C. Day, pp. 55–66. University of New Mexico Press, Albuquerque.

Donnan, Christopher B.

1986 The Huaca 1 Complex. In *The Pacatnamu Papers*, vol. 1, edited by Christopher B. Donnan and Guillermo A. Cock, pp. 63–84. Fowler Museum of Cultural History, University of California, Los Angeles.

1990 The Chotuna Friezes and the Chotuna-Dragon Connection. In *The Northern Dynasties: Kingship and Statecraft in Chimor*, edited by Michael E. Moseley and Alana Cordy-Collins, pp. 275–296. Dumbarton Oaks, Washington, DC.

Donnan, Christopher B., and Guillermo A. Cock (eds.)

1986 *The Pacatnamu Papers*, vol. 1. Fowler Museum of Cultural History, University of California, Los Angeles.

Earle, Timothy K., Terence N. D'Altroy, Christine A. Hastorf, Catherine J. Scott, Cathy L. Costin, Glenn S. Russell, and Elsie Sandefur

1987 *Archaeological Field Research in the Upper Mantaro, Peru, 1982–1983: Investigations of Inka Expansion and Exchange.* Monograph 28. Institute of Archaeology, University of California, Los Angeles.

Franco Jordán, Régulo, and César Gálvez Mora

2005 Muerte, identidades y prácticas funerarias post-Mochicas en el Complejo El Brujo, valle de Chicama, costa norte del Perú. *Corriente Arqueológica* 1:79–118.

Fung Pineda, Rosa, and Carlos Williams León

1977 Exploraciones y excavaciones en el valle de Sechín, Casma. *Revista del Museo Nacional* 43:111–155. Lima.

Gálvez Mora, César, and Jesús Briceño Rosario

2001 The Moche in the Chicama Valley. In *Moche Art and Archaeology in Ancient Peru*, edited by Joanne Pillsbury, pp. 141–157. National Gallery of Art, Washington, DC.

Hayashida, Frances M.

2006 The Pampa de Chaparri: Water, Land, and Politics on the North Coast of Peru. *Latin American Antiquity* 17(3):243–263.

Helms, Mary W.

1993 *Craft and the Kingly Ideal.* University of Texas Press, Austin.

Heyerdahl, Thor, Daniel Sandweiss, and Alfredo Narváez

1995 *Pyramids of Túcume: The Quest for Peru's Forgotten City.* Thames and Hudson, New York.

Keatinge, Richard W.

1974 Chimu Rural Administrative Centers in the Moche Valley, Peru. *World Archaeology* 6(1):66–82.

1982 The Chimu Empire in a Regional Perspective: Cultural Antecedents and Continuities. In *Chan Chan: Andean Desert City*, edited by Michael E. Moseley and Kent C. Day, pp. 197–224. University of New Mexico Press, Albuquerque.

Keatinge, Richard W., and Geoffrey W. Conrad

1983 Imperialist Expansion in Peruvian Prehistory: Chimu Administration of a Conquered Territory. *Journal of Field Archaeology* 10(3):255–283.

Klymyshyn, A. Ulana

1982 Elite Compounds in Chan Chan. In *Chan Chan: Andean Desert City*, edited by Michael E. Moseley and Kent C. Day, pp. 119–143. University of New Mexico Press, Albuquerque.

1987 The Development of Chimu Administration in Chan Chann. In *The Origins and Development of the Andean State*, edited by Jonathan Haas, Shelia Pozorski, and Tom Pozorski, pp. 97–110. Cambridge University Press, Cambridge.

Kolata, Alan

1990 The Urban Concept of Chan Chan. In *The Northern Dynasties: Kingship and Statecraft in Chimor*, edited by Michael E. Moseley and Alana Cordy-Collins, pp. 107–144. Dumbarton Oaks, Washington, DC.

Koschmieder, Klaus, and Rafael Vega-Centeno

1996 Puerto Pobre: Centro administrativo Chimu en el valle de Casma. *Revista del Museo de Arqueología, Antropología e Historia* 6:161–201. Facultad de Ciencias Sociales, Universidad Nacional de Trujillo, Trujillo.

Mackey, Carol

1987 Chimu Administration in the Provinces. In *The Origins and Development of the Andean State*, edited by Jonathan Haas, Shelia Pozorski, and Tom Pozorski, pp. 121–129. Cambridge University Press, Cambridge.

2001 Los dioses que perdieron los colmillos. In *Los dioses del antiguo Perú*, vol. 2, edited by Krzysztof Makowski et al., pp. 110–157. Banco de Crédito del Perú, Lima.

2003 La Transformación socioeconómica de Farfán Bajo el gobierno Inca. *Boletín de Arqueología PUCP*, no. 7, edited by Peter Kaulicke, Gary Urton, and Ian Farrington, pp. 321–353. Lima.

2004 La ocupación de dos centros administrativos en el Valle de Jequetepeque: El Algarrobal de Moro y el complejo VI de Fanfán. In *SIAN*, edited by Luis Valle, pp. 75–88. Trujillo.

2006 Elite Residences at Farfán: A Comparison of the Chimu and Inca Occupations. In *Palaces and Power in* the Americas: From Peru to the Northwest Coast, edited by Jessica Joyce Christie and Patricia Joan Sarro, pp. 313–352. University of Texas Press, Austin.

Mackey, Carol, and César Jáuregui
2002   Informe preliminar de Proyecto Arqueológico Farfán. Instituto Nacional de Cultura, Lima.
2003   Informe preliminar de Proyecto Arqueológico Farfán. Instituto Nacional de Cultura, Lima.
2004   Informe preliminar de Proyecto Arqueológico Farfán. Instituto Nacional de Cultura, Lima.

Mackey, Carol, and A. Ulana Klymyshyn
1990   The Southern Frontier of the Chimu Empire. In *The Northern Dynasties: Kingship and Statecraft in Chimor*, edited by Michael Moseley and Alana Cordy-Collins, pp. 195–226. Dumbarton Oaks, Washington, DC.

Menzel, Dorothy
1959   The Inca Occupation of the South Coast of Peru. *Southwestern Journal of Anthropology* 15:125–142.

Moore, Jerry D.
1981   Chimu Socioeconomic Organization: Preliminary Data from Manchán, Casma Valley, Peru. *Ñawpa Pacha* 19:115–128.
1985   *Household Economics and Political Integration: The Lower Class of the Chimu Empire*. Unpublished doctoral dissertation, Department of Anthropology, University of California, Santa Barbara.
1991   Cultural Responses to Environmental Catastrophes: Post-El Niño North Coast of Perú. *Latin American Antiquity* 2(1):27–47.
1996   *Architecture and Power in the Ancient Andes*. Cambridge University Press, Cambridge.

Morris, Craig
1998   Inca Strategies of Incorporation and Governance. In *Archaic States*, edited by Gary M. Feinman and Joyce Marcus, pp. 293–309. School of American Research, Santa Fe.

Morris, Craig, and Donald Thompson
1985   *Huánuco Pampa: An Inca City and Its Hinterland*. Thames and Hudson, New York.

Moseley, Michael E.
1975   Chan Chan: Andean Alternative of the Pre-industrial City. *Science* 187:219–225.
1982   Introduction: Human Exploitation and Organization on the North Andean Coast. In *Chan Chan: Andean Desert City*, edited by Michael E. Moseley and Kent C. Day, pp.1–24. University of New Mexico Press, Albuquerque.
2001   *The Incas and Their Ancestors*. Thames and Hudson, New York.

Moseley, Michael E., and Carol Mackey
1973   Chan Chan, Peru's Ancient City of Kings. *National Geographic* 143:318–345.
1974   *Twenty-four Architectural Plans of Chan Chan*. Peabody Museum Press, Cambridge, MA.

Moseley, Michael E., and Kent C. Day (eds.)
1982   *Chan Chan: Andean Desert City*. University of New Mexico, Albuquerque.

Parsons, Jeffrey R., and Charles M. Hastings
1988   The Late Intermediate Period. In *Peruvian Prehistory*, edited by Richard Keatinge, pp. 190–229. Cambridge University Press, Cambridge.

Pillsbury, Joanne
2004   Luxury Arts and the Lords of Chimor. In *Latin American Collections: Essays in Honour of Ted J. J. Leyenaar*, edited by Edward de Bock, pp. 67–77. Leiden.

Pillsbury, Joanne, and Banks Leonard
2003   Identifying Chimu Palaces: Elite Residential Architecture in the Late Intermediate Period. In *Palaces of the Ancient New World. A Symposium at Dumbarton Oaks, 1998*, edited by Susan Toby Evans and Joanne Pillsbury, pp. 247–298. Dumbarton Oaks, Washington, DC.

Pozorski, Shelia
1982   Subsistence Systems in the Chimu State. In *Chan Chan: Andean Desert City*, edited by Michael E. Moseley and Kent C. Day, pp. 1–24. University of New Mexico Press, Albuquerque.

Pozorski, Thomas
1971   Survey and Excavations of Burial Platforms at Chan Chan, Peru. Bachelor's thesis, Harvard University, Cambridge, MA.
1987   Changing Priorities within the Chimu State: The Role of Irrigation Agriculture. In *The Origins and Development of the Andean State*, edited by Jonathan Haas, Shelia Pozorski, and Thomas Pozorski, pp. 111–120. Cambridge University Press, Cambridge.

Proulx, Donald A.
1973   *Archaeological Investigations in the Nepeña Valley, Peru*. Department of Anthropology, Research Project no. 13. University of Massachusetts, Amherst.

Rowe, John H.
1948   The Kingdom of Chimor. *Acta Americana* 6(1/2): 26–59.

Sapp, William D. III
2002   *The Impact of Imperial Conquest at the Palace of a Local Lord in the Jequetepeque Valley, Northern Peru*. Ph.D. dissertation, Department of Anthropology, University of California, Los Angeles.

Schreiber, Katharina
1992   *Wari Imperialism in Middle Horizon Peru*. Anthropological Papers of the Museum of Anthropology, no. 87. University of Michigan, Ann Arbor.

Shimada, Izumi
1990   Cultural Continuities and Discontinuities on the Northern North Coast of Peru, Middle-Late Horizons. In *The Northern Dynasties: Kingship and Statecraft in Chimor*, edited by M. Moseley and A. Cordy-Collins, pp. 297–392. Dumbarton Oaks, Washington, DC.

1995   *Cultura Sicán: Dios, riqueza y poder en la costa norte del Perú*. Fundación del Banco Continental para el Fomento de la Educación y la Cultura, Lima.

Sinopoli, Carla M.
1996   The Archaeology of Empires. *Annual Review of Anthropology* 23:159–180.

2001   Empires. In *Archaeology at the Millennium*, edited by Gary M. Feinman and T. Douglas Price, pp. 439–471. Kluwer/Plenum, New York.

Tello, Julio C.
1956   *Arqueología del Valle de Casma. Culturas: Chavín, Santa o Huaylas Yunga y Sub-Chimu*. Universidad Nacional Mayor de San Marcos, Lima.

Topic, John
1977   *The Lower Class at Chan Chan: A Qualitative Approach*. Unpublished doctoral dissertation, Department of Anthropology, Harvard University, Cambridge, MA.

1982   Lower-Class Social and Economic Organization at Chan Chan. In *Chan Chan: Andean Desert City*, edited by Michael E. Moseley and Kent C. Day, pp. 145–175. University of New Mexico Press, Albuquerque.

1990   Craft Production in the Kingdom of Chimor. In *The Northern Dynasties: Kingship and Statecraft in Chimor*, edited by Michael E. Moseley and Alana Cordy-Collins, pp. 145–175. Dumbarton Oaks, Washington, DC.

2003   From Stewards to Bureaucrats: Architecture and Information Flow at Chan Chan, Peru. *Latin American Antiquity* 14(3):243–274.

Topic, John, and Michael E. Moseley
1983   Chan Chan: A Case Study of Urban Change in Peru. *Ñawpa Pacha* 21:153–182.

Topic, Theresa L.
1990   Territorial Expansion and the Kingdom of Chimor. In *The Northern Dynasties: Kingship and Statecraft in Chimor*, edited by Michael Moseley and Alana Cordy-Collins, pp. 177–194. Dumbarton Oaks, Washington, DC.

Tschauner, Hartmut
2001   *Socioeconomic and Political Organization in the Late Pre-hispanic Lambayeque Sphere, Northern North Coast of Perú*. Unpublished doctoral dissertation, Department of Anthropology, Harvard University, Cambridge, MA.

Uceda, Santiago
1997   Esculturas en miniatura y una maqueta en madera. In *Investigaciones en la Huaca de la Luna 1995*, edited by Santiago Uceda, Elías Mujica, and Ricardo Morales, pp. 151–176. Universidad Nacional de La Libertad, Trujillo.

Vilcherrez, Percy, and Melissa Vogel
2006   Informe final de Proyecto El Purgatorio, Valle de Casma. Instituto Nacional de Cultura, Lima.

Vogel, Melissa
2003   *Life on the Frontier: Identity and Sociopolitical Change at the Site of Cerro la Cruz, Peru*. Unpublished doctoral dissertation, Department of Anthropology, University of Pennsylvania, Philadelphia.

Wernke, Steven
2006   The Politics of Community and Inka Statecraft in the Colca Valley, Peru. *Latin American Antiquity* 17(2):177–208.

Wilson, David J.
1995   Prehispanic Settlement Patterns in the Casma Valley, North Coast of Peru: Preliminary Results to Date. *Journal of the Steward Anthropological Society* 23(1–2):189–227.

Wright, Henry T., and Gregory A. Johnson
1975   Population, Exchange, and Early State Formation in Southwestern Iran. *American Anthropologist* 77:267–289.

CHAPTER 19

CAMELID HERDERS: THE FORGOTTEN SPECIALISTS IN THE COASTAL SEÑORÍO OF CHIRIBAYA, SOUTHERN PERU

MARÍA CECILIA LOZADA, JANE E. BUIKSTRA,
GORDON RAKITA, AND JANE C. WHEELER

IN HIS SEMINAL WORK, *The Maritime Foundations of Andean Civilization* (1975), Michael E. Moseley proposed that coastal environments supplied sufficient caloric intake to support sedentary populations in prehispanic Peru. Moseley also argued that even with population growth and the complex social organization of large communities, as reflected in the presence of monumental architecture, marine resources offered a stable economic base for their successful adaptation in this coastal environment.

Although widely debated by a number of researchers (e.g., Osborn 1977; Raymond 1981; Wilson 1981), the maritime hypothesis is supported not only by recent archaeological and bioarchaeological studies (Benfer 1990; Sandweiss 1992) but also by the vast ethnohistorical research conducted by the Peruvian ethnohistorian María Rostworowski de Diez Canseco. In contrast to Moseley, who focused on the beginnings of Andean civilization during the preceramic periods on the coast, Rostworowski's research is based on Colonial documents, from which she extracted detailed information about late prehispanic coastal societies. Nevertheless, like Moseley, she concludes that populations relying on marine resources were self-sufficient economically and that the numerous river valleys served as independent foci of cultural development (Rostworowski 1970, 1977, 1989). The work of these two researchers taken together offers a powerful theoretical framework within which we can interpret the dynamic relations among the ecological, political, and social forces that shaped past Andean civilizations.

We can study these dynamic relations by focusing on a complex coastal polity. One of these polities was Chiribaya, a powerful *señorío* on the coast of southern Peru. Chiribaya centralized its power in the Osmore Valley during the Middle Horizon and Late Intermediate period, spanning an estimated 500–600 years (Buikstra et al. 1997). As determined from ceramic decorations and radiocarbon dates, Chiribaya was originally considered to be a cultural and biological extension of Tiwanaku highland colonies established in the middle of the Osmore Valley (Stanish 1992; Owen 1993; Sutter 1997).

Beginning in 1989, two of us (Buikstra and Lozada) conducted a series of excavations in the cemeteries at various Chiribaya sites in the Osmore drainage. One goal was to understand the biological and cultural relationships between Tiwanaku colonists and coastal Chiribaya people (Buikstra 1995). Buikstra and colleagues excavated three major Chiribaya sites: Chiribaya Alta, Yaral, and Chiribaya Baja. Although the coastal site of San Gerónimo was excavated before Buikstra's excavations, data from this fourth site were incorporated into the larger Chiribaya project (Figure 19.1).

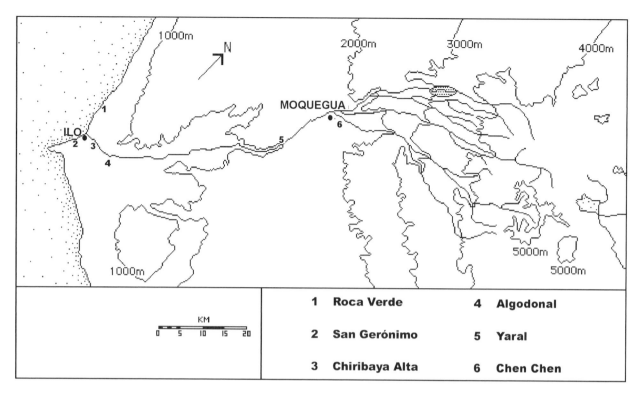

Figure 19.1. Location of sites.

1 **Roca Verde**	4 **Algodonal**
2 **San Gerónimo**	5 **Yaral**
3 **Chiribaya Alta**	6 **Chen Chen**

While analyzing data derived from these mortuary contexts, we realized that the widely used verticality model (e.g., Murra 1964, 1968, 1972, 1975; Brush 1977; Flores Ochoa 1979; Masuda et al. 1985; Mujica 1985; Stanish 1992) failed to explain key features of this coastal Chiribaya society. Specifically, our thirty-four Chiribaya radiocarbon dates demonstrated that Chiribaya had greater time depth, dating back to the Middle Horizon. Instead of first emerging around AD 1000, Chiribaya seemed to date as early as AD 700, making it contemporaneous with Tiwanaku mid-valley colonies (Table 19.1). Furthermore, we found a remarkable degree of economic specialization, and we were able to distinguish marine-based and non-marine-based subsistence activities (Lozada and Buikstra 2002).

Although archaeologists have used certain aspects of the coastal horizontality model developed by Rostworowski, a detailed assessment of her ethnohistorical research had not been undertaken in archaeological contexts until recently. Specifically, Rostworowski identified a series of coastal señoríos prior to the arrival of the Spaniards in the northern and central river valleys of Peru. The Spanish term *señorío* refers to a polity composed of loosely integrated communities of economic specialists such as *labradores* and *pescadores*. These communities were described as biologically and culturally discrete, resulting in the formation of distinct ethnic groups, or *etnías* (Rostworowski 1975).

Through the Chiribaya project, we extensively tested this model using bioarchaeological data. Our research strongly supported the presence of different communities of labradores and pescadores (Lozada and Buikstra 2002). Differences between these two economically specialized groups characterized nearly every category of cultural behavior, including ceramic styles and cranial modification styles, suggesting a fundamental division within Chiribaya society.

One example that illustrates these cultural divisions emerged in the cranial modification patterns. Cranial molding must be undertaken very early in life, from the birth of a child. Indeed, cranial deformation is an irreversible act that was used to show an individual's ascribed corporate membership, which would then accompany the individual throughout the course of his or her life. Inspection of the Chiribaya skulls that were modified indicated that the annular cranial deformation was characteristic of the pescadores, while the fronto-occipital type of skull deformation was practiced by the labradores of Chiribaya (Figures 19.2, 19.3) (Lozada and Buikstra 2002).

Subsequently, Paula Tomczak expanded this study to include paleodietary analysis among the Chiribaya.

Table 19.1 Chiribaya radiocarbon dates.

Date BP	SD	Lab. ID	Site	Abbreviation	Cemetery/ Burial	Context/Assoc.
1020	80	Beta-51068	Algodonal	Alg.	–/–	Tumilaca
870	60	Beta-51066	Algodonal	Alg.	–/–	Post-Algarrobal
800	60	Beta-51067	Algodonal	Alg.	–/–	Post-Algarrobal
1870	50	Beta-51062	Algodonal	Alg.	–/–	Early Algodonal
2000	60	Beta-51063	Algodonal	Alg.	–/–	Early Algodonal
1750	60	Beta-51064	Algodonal	Alg.	–/–	Early Algodonal
870	60	Beta-51059	Algodonal	Alg.	–/–	Ilo-Cabuza
960	60	Beta-51060	Algodonal	Alg.	–/–	Ilo-Cabuza
1040	60	Beta-51061	Algodonal	Alg.	–/–	Ilo-Tumilaca
1050	60	Beta-51065	Algodonal	Alg.	–/–	Ilo-Tumilaca
1140	95	Geochron-18677	Chiribaya Alta	ChA	1/025	None
1040	44	Geochron-18799	Chiribaya Alta	ChA	1/030	None
1190	150	Geochron-18678	Chiribaya Alta	ChA	1/101	None
1205	95	Geochron-18676	Chiribaya Alta	ChA	2/009	Ilo-Osmore
1045	70	Geochron-18679	Chiribaya Alta	ChA	2/263	None
1025	70	Geochron-18680	Chiribaya Alta	ChA	2/270	Algarrobal
1130	70	Geochron-18681	Chiribaya Alta	ChA	3/304	Yaral
1345	70	Geochron-18682	Chiribaya Alta	ChA	3/324	Algarrobal
1070	70	Geochron-18683	Chiribaya Alta	ChA	4/402	San Gerónimo
1110	80	Geochron-18684	Chiribaya Alta	ChA	4/405	San Gerónimo
945	70	Geochron-18685	Chiribaya Alta	ChA	4/419	San Gerónimo
1090	70	Geochron-18686	Chiribaya Alta	ChA	5/503	Ilo-Osmore
1350	70	Geochron-18687	Chiribaya Alta	ChA	5/506	Yaral
1085	80	Geochron-18688	Chiribaya Alta	ChA	5/517	Yaral
1050	90	Geochron-18689	Chiribaya Alta	ChA	6/608	Algarrobal/Ilo-Osmore
805	80	Geochron-18690	Chiribaya Alta	ChA	6/609	Tumilaca
1250	70	Geochron-18692	Chiribaya Alta	ChA	7/702	Algarrobal
1365	80	Geochron-18693	Chiribaya Alta	ChA	7/703	Algarrobal
1200	70	Geochron-18694	Chiribaya Alta	ChA	7/751	Algarrobal
985	75	Geochron-18695	Chiribaya Alta	ChA	8/805	None
935	95	Geochron-18696	Chiribaya Alta	ChA	8/808	None
1200	90	Geochron-18697	Chiribaya Alta	ChA	9/902	Algarrobal
1100	75	Geochron-18698	Chiribaya Alta	ChA	9/904	Algarrobal/Tumilaca
1180	75	Geochron-18662	Chiribaya Baja	ChB	–/113	None
1110	70	Geochron-18664	Chiribaya Baja	ChB	–/124	None
905	70	Geochron-18663	Chiribaya Baja	ChB	–/143	None
850	70	Geochron-18665	Chiribaya Baja	ChB	–/144	None
1010	80	Geochron-18666	San Gerónimo	SG	–/009	San Gerónimo
930	110	Geochron-18669	San Gerónimo	SG	–/141	Yaral
1100	70	Geochron-18673	Yaral	Yar	1/112	Yaral
1000	70	Geochron-18671	Yaral	Yar	1/130	Algarrobal
1085	90	Geochron-18672	Yaral	Yar	1/136	Tumilaca
995	85	Geochron-18674	Yaral	Yar	2/212	None
1290	80	Geochron-18675	Yaral	Yar	2/233	Yaral
840	50	Beta-51071	Loreto Alto	LA	–/–	Ilo-Cabuza
810	60	Beta-51069	Loreto Alto	LA	–/–	Ilo-Tumilaca/Cabuza
990	50	Beta-51070	Loreto Alto	LA	–/–	Ilo-Tumilaca/Cabuza
950	80	Beta-51072	Loreto Alto	LA	–/–	Ilo-Tumilaca/Cabuza
1085	90	ETH-3178	Lukurmata	Luk	–/–	Tiwanaku 5
1180	110	ETH-3179	Lukurmata	Luk	–/–	Tiwanaku 5
990	95	ETH-3180	Lukurmata	Luk	–/–	Tiwanaku 5
1201	96	SMU-1920	Lukurmata	Luk	–/–	Tiwanaku 5
1090	60	SMU-2117	Lukurmata	Luk	–/–	Tiwanaku 5

Table 19.1 (continued)

Date BP	SD	Lab. ID	Site	Abbreviation	Cemetery/ Burial	Context/Assoc.
1000	230	SMU-2165	Lukurmata	Luk	–/–	Tiwanaku 5
730	60	Beta-51073	Loreto Viejo	LV	–/–	Post-Algarrobal
860	60	Beta-51074	Loreto Viejo	LV	–/–	Post-Algarrobal
1460	60	ETH-6306	Tiwanaku	Tiw	–/–	Tiwanaku 4
1390	50	SMU-2468	Tiwanaku	Tiw	–/–	Tiwanaku 4 (Late)
1170	65	ETH-5680	Tiwanaku	Tiw	–/–	Tiwanaku 5
1070	60	SMU-2276	Tiwanaku	Tiw	–/–	Tiwanaku 5
1130	60	SMU-2277	Tiwanaku	Tiw	–/–	Tiwanaku 5
1185	60	SMU-2289	Tiwanaku	Tiw	–/–	Tiwanaku 5
1120	70	SMU-2290	Tiwanaku	Tiw	–/–	Tiwanaku 5
1080	210	SMU-2330	Tiwanaku	Tiw	–/–	Tiwanaku 5
1150	80	SMU-2367	Tiwanaku	Tiw	–/–	Tiwanaku 5
1110	50	SMU-2465	Tiwanaku	Tiw	–/–	Tiwanaku 5
1170	60	SMU-2466	Tiwanaku	Tiw	–/–	Tiwanaku 5
1130	60	SMU-2467	Tiwanaku	Tiw	–/–	Tiwanaku 5
1190	100	SMU-2469	Tiwanaku	Tiw	–/–	Tiwanaku 5
1200	115	SMU-2472	Tiwanaku	Tiw	–/–	Tiwanaku 5
1170	60	SMU-5639	Tiwanaku	Tiw	–/–	Tiwanaku 5
850	70	Geochron-18665	Chiribaya Baja	ChB	-/144	None
1010	80	Geochron-18666	San Gerónimo	SG	-/009	San Gerónimo
930	110	Geochron-18669	San Gerónimo	SG	-/141	Yaral
1100	70	Geochron-18673	Yaral	Yar	1/112	Yaral
1000	70	Geochron-18671	Yaral	Yar	1/130	Algarrobal
1085	90	Geochron-18672	Yaral	Yar	1/136	Tumilaca
995	85	Geochron-18674	Yaral	Yar	2/212	None
1290	80	Geochron-18675	Yaral	Yar	2/233	Yaral
840	50	Beta-51071	Loreto Alto	LA	–/–	Ilo-Cabuza
810	60	Beta-51069	Loreto Alto	LA	–/–	Ilo-Tumilaca/Cabuza
990	50	Beta-51070	Loreto Alto	LA	–/–	Ilo-Tumilaca/Cabuza
950	80	Beta-51072	Loreto Alto	LA	–/–	Ilo-Tumilaca/Cabuza
1085	90	ETH-3178	Lukurmata	Luk	–/–	Tiwanaku 5
1180	110	ETH-3179	Lukurmata	Luk	–/–	Tiwanaku 5
990	95	ETH-3180	Lukurmata	Luk	–/–	Tiwanaku 5
1201	96	SMU-1920	Lukurmata	Luk	–/–	Tiwanaku 5
1090	60	SMU-2117	Lukurmata	Luk	–/–	Tiwanaku 5
1000	230	SMU-2165	Lukurmata	Luk	–/–	Tiwanaku 5
730	60	Beta-51073	Loreto Viejo	LV	–/–	Post-Algarrobal
860	60	Beta-51074	Loreto Viejo	LV	–/–	Post-Algarrobal
1460	60	ETH-6306	Tiwanaku	Tiw	–/–	Tiwanaku 4
1390	50	SMU-2468	Tiwanaku	Tiw	–/–	Tiwanaku 4 (Late)
1170	65	ETH-5680	Tiwanaku	Tiw	–/–	Tiwanaku 5
1070	60	SMU-2276	Tiwanaku	Tiw	–/–	Tiwanaku 5
1130	60	SMU-2277	Tiwanaku	Tiw	–/–	Tiwanaku 5
1185	60	SMU-2289	Tiwanaku	Tiw	–/–	Tiwanaku 5
1120	70	SMU-2290	Tiwanaku	Tiw	–/–	Tiwanaku 5
1080	210	SMU-2330	Tiwanaku	Tiw	–/–	Tiwanaku 5
1150	80	SMU-2367	Tiwanaku	Tiw	–/–	Tiwanaku 5
1110	50	SMU-2465	Tiwanaku	Tiw	–/–	Tiwanaku 5
1170	60	SMU-2466	Tiwanaku	Tiw	–/–	Tiwanaku 5
1130	60	SMU-2467	Tiwanaku	Tiw	–/–	Tiwanaku 5
1190	100	SMU-2469	Tiwanaku	Tiw	–/–	Tiwanaku 5
1200	115	SMU-2472	Tiwanaku	Tiw	–/–	Tiwanaku 5
1170	60	SMU-5639	Tiwanaku	Tiw	–/–	Tiwanaku 5

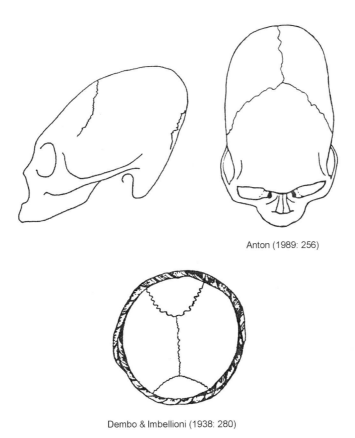

Anton (1989: 256)

Dembo & Imbellioni (1938: 280)

Figure 19.2. Chiribaya annular cranial modification style.

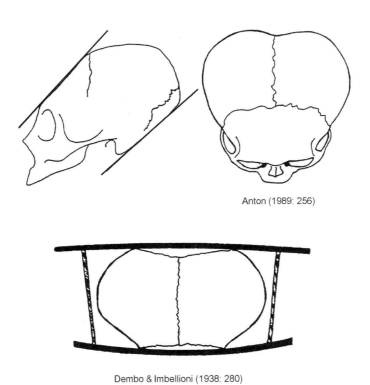

Anton (1989: 256)

Dembo & Imbellioni (1938: 280)

Figure 19.3. Chiribaya fronto-occipital modification style.

Based on carbon and nitrogen isotopes of human bone, she found that food consumption also differed between these two groups. Labradores consumed the greatest amount of terrestrial plants such as grasses, fruits, and tubers, and C4 plants such as maize, while the diet of the pescadores was based primarily on marine resources (Tomczak 2002).

Our genetic distance research showed that Chiribaya biological origins are rooted in earlier coastal traditions (Lozada et al. 1997). This study was based on non-metric cranial traits from skulls recovered in Chiribaya, Tiwanaku, and coastal Formative sites such as Roca Verde in the Osmore drainage. These epigenetic traits, or variations in bone development, have been extremely useful. They are comparable to other methods, such as aDNA, in their ability to estimate genotypic patterning in past populations (Haydon 1993). The two statistical approaches (Manly 1991; Relethford and Harpending 1994) we used in the biological distance analyses provided similar results. As can be seen in Table 19.2 and Figure 19.4, there are genetic differences between Chiribaya and Tiwanaku, while genetically the populations from the Formative coastal site of Roca Verde appear indistinguishable from Chiribaya (Lozada et al. 1997, 2003).

The autochthonous nature of the Chiribaya population on the coast has recently been supported by Knudson, who analyzed the human bone from the same Tiwanaku and Chiribaya sites (Knudson 2004). Knudson's isotopic values for our Chiribaya samples do not cluster with those from mid-valley and highland populations. Instead, those values are similar to those found in the coastal Osmore drainage.

While the testing of Rostworowski's model has been extremely useful to explain key issues regarding Chiribaya, we are also aware that señoríos in the south may have been quite different from those in the northern and central coastal valleys of Peru, as described by Rostworowski. For example, the northern and central coasts have extensive fertile valleys that would have supported large-scale agricultural endeavors. In the south, coastal valleys tend to be narrower, with less arable land. Such differences in both the physical and cultural landscapes may have led to differential access and different priorities in procuring specific subsistence resources. Such differences would likely have left their mark on the socioeconomic composition of southern coastal señoríos.

On the south coast, it is clear that labradores and pescadores were essential to the señorío of Chiribaya; however, it is conceivable that pastoralism, or more specifically the management and exploitation of camelid herds, may have also been of central importance

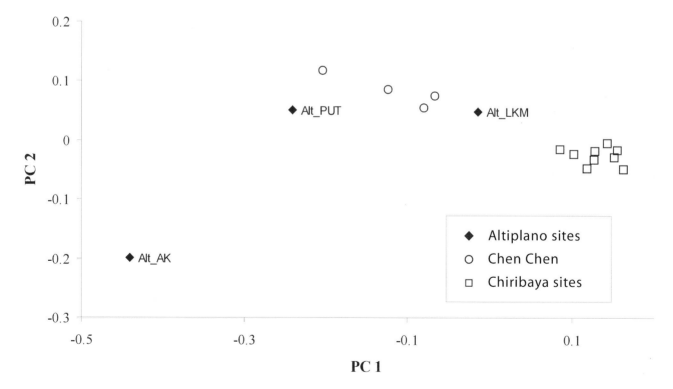

Figure 19.4. Distance matrix, genetic distances method (Relethford and Harpending 1994). Notice the clustering of Chiribaya sites identified by squares, in contrast to mid-valley (Chen Chen) and highland (Akapana, Putina, Lukurmata) Tiwanaku sites represented by circles and diamonds. This pattern reflects the biological separation between Chiribaya and Tiwanaku populations.

Table 19.2 Genetic distance matrix, bootstrap method (Manley 1991).

	Yaral 1	Yaral 2	San Ger.	ChA1	ChA2	ChA3	ChA4	ChA7	Chen Chen	RV
Algodonal	D=0.131 P=0.334	D=0.106 P=0.690	D=0.079 P=0.896	D=0.087 P=0.888	D=0.134 P=0.234	D=0.084 P=0.882	D=0.095 P=0.864	D=0.100 P=0.688	D=0.152 p<0.001	D=0.119 P=0.666
Yaral 1		D=0.102 P=0.868	D=0.098 P=0.780	D=0.115 P=0.672	D=0.128 P=0.510	D=0.119 P=0.524	D=0.088 P=0.962	D=0.120 P=0.566	D=0.203 p<0.001	D=0.153 P=0.346
Yaral 2			D=0.101 P=0.656	D=0.115 P=0.578	D=0.145 P=0.224	D=0.126 P=0.356	D=0.076 P=0.982	D=0.121 P=0.480	D=0.163 p<0.001	D=0.113 P=0.856
San Gerónimo				D=0.103 P=0.470	D=0.105 P=0.610	D=0.102 P=0.390	D=0.089 P=0.884	D=0.094 P=0.684	D=0.155 p<0.001	D=0.134 P=0.332
ChA1					D=0.130 P=0.326	D=0.111 P=0.423	D=0.110 P=0.658	D=0.120 P=0.342	D=0.149 p<0.001	D=0.137 P=0.438
ChA2						D=0.129 P=0.25	D=0.169 P=0.044	D=0.116 P=0.556	D=0.196 p<0.001	D=0.151 P=0.330
ChA3							D=0.119 P=0.478	D=0.138 P=0.090	D=0.149 p<0.001	D=0.103 P=0.846
ChA4								D=0.101 P=0.844	D=0.134 P=0.024	D=0.122 P=0.712
ChA7									D=0.179 p<0.001	D=0.163
Chen Chen										D=0.147 P=0.060

Note: San Ger = San Gerónimo; chA = Chribaya Alta; RV = Roca Verde; D = Distance measurements; P = P-values

in coastal communities in southern Peru. If such a reconstruction is accurate, these practices would have been firmly embedded in the ideological and sociopolitical framework of Chiribaya, and therefore should be apparent through an analysis of mortuary remains.

Camelids played a significant role in Andean societies, as documented by Spanish chroniclers (Cobo 1956 [1653]; Diez de San Miguel 1964 [1567]; Garcilaso de la Vega 1991 [1609]; Polo de Ondegardo 1916 [1559]; Guamán Poma de Ayala 1980 [1614]). Pastoralism and the domestication of animals have been documented in the puna sites of Telarmachay as early as 3500 BC (Wheeler 1984, 1985). Archaeozoological evidence documents the prehispanic use of wild guanaco (*Lama guanicoe)* and vicuña (*Vicugna vicugna*), as well as the domestic llama (*Lama glama)* and alpaca (*Vicugna pacos*) (Wheeler 1995; Kadwell et al. 2001; Gentry et al. 2004; Wheeler et al. 2006) at different sites throughout Peru. As today, camelid products (transport, meat, fiber, etc.) provided an important economic base both at the state and community levels. Furthermore, they are a central fixture in many ritual activities among both highland and coastal societies (Murra 1965; Browman 1974; Flores Ochoa 1977; Pozorski 1979; Shimada and Shimada 1985, 1987; Topic et al. 1987; Flannery et al. 1989; Miller and Burger 1995, 2000; Valdez 2000; Rofes and Wheeler 2003).

We investigated the economic and ritual importance of camelids among the Chiribaya by examining the distribution of faunal remains across Chiribaya cemeteries. Each mortuary site used in this study, including the nine cemeteries of Chiribaya Alta, appears to be associated predominantly either with labradores or with pescadores. We can therefore examine associations between camelid offerings and the occupations of specialists. Furthermore, by examining the correlation between camelid offerings and other variables, such as cranial modification styles and the quantity of grave goods, we aimed to elucidate the symbolic use of camelids in mortuary contexts.

To place these data in context, we first outline aspects of our previous research. San Gerónimo is a site located close to the Pacific Ocean. Individuals recovered from this site are interpreted as the pescadores. In contrast, the mid-valley site of El Yaral was occupied almost exclusively by labradores. As one might expect, Chiribaya Alta, the largest Chiribaya site in the Osmore drainage, displayed a more complex composition. It is located approximately 7 km from the coast and includes at least nine cemeteries. Of these cemeteries, only Cemetery 4 is predominantly occupied by pescadores. Once again, specialists were defined on the basis of mortuary patterns, cranial modification/deformation styles, ceramic types, and dietary reconstruction (Lozada and Buikstra 2002).

Using phenotypic attributes (bone or soft tissue, or both) and dental morphology from twenty-six naturally desiccated animals, Wheeler has identified llamas and alpacas in the Chiribaya domestic contexts of El Yaral, while studies of household refuse carried out by Rofes confirmed that these two animals were the primary source of animal protein in the diet (Wheeler et al. 1995; Rofes 1998; Rofes and Wheeler 2003). Additional studies by Wheeler involved the analysis of sixty-two tombs containing faunal remains from eight cemeteries at Chiribaya Alta (Wheeler 1993). In contrast to El Yaral, the camelid remains at Chiribaya Alta are mostly llamas. (In this chapter, we do not distinguish between llamas and alpacas.)

Our sample comprised 526 burials from San Gerónimo, Chiribaya Alta, and El Yaral. Since looters do not consider camelid remains to be valuable items and thus leave them in situ, we made no distinctions between disturbed and intact contexts. Heads (skulls only or skulls with mandibles) dominated the mortuary assemblages. Less numerous were offerings of limbs and feet. Only seven contexts in Chiribaya Alta contained complete specimens (Wheeler 1993). Because there was no statistically significant patterning to specific body part offerings, no statistical differences between these categories were made (Table 19.3).

Camelid remains were present in all cemeteries, with Chiribaya Alta having the highest percentages overall (Figure 19.5). In contrast, Yaral and San Gerónimo exhibited lower numbers. The presence of camelid remains with the pescadores of San Gerónimo suggests that fishermen also had access to camelids (as did labradores). Although Rostworowski describes the pescadores as a self-sufficient community, they participated in exchange networks, which would have given them access to terrestrial animals and plants, including camelids and agricultural items. In addition, while camelid offerings may suggest the consumption of these animals by pescadores, dietary analyses of San Gerónimo's bones suggest a diet of mainly marine resources (Sandness 1992; Tomczak 2002). Interestingly, relatively few camelids were found in the two cemeteries at El Yaral, a community of labradores.

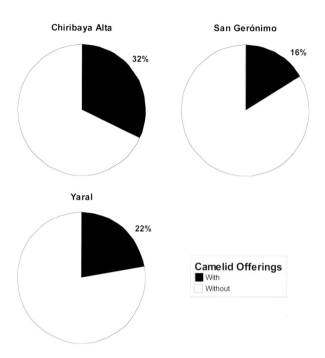

Figure 19.5. Distribution of camelid remains at San Gerónimo, Chiribaya Alta, and Yaral.

To interpret these patterns further, we explored in more detail the frequency of camelid remains in the cemeteries of Chiribaya Alta. As can be seen in Figure 19.6, there is a striking pattern in the distribution of camelid remains throughout cemeteries at Chiribaya Alta. Most of the cemeteries, including the pescadores of Cemetery 4, had similar percentages of burials with camelid remains. In contrast, Cemetery 7, which was associated with elite labradores, was unique in its significantly larger proportion of burials interred with camelid remains.

What would account for such a dramatic difference between Cemetery 7 and the other cemeteries at Chiribaya Alta and other sites? With respect to specific bioarchaeological parameters such as the frequency of cranial modification and total number of grave goods, Cemetery 7 stands apart from other cemeteries. It has

Table 19.3. Association of camelid body parts: Pearson correlation coefficients between the occurrences of various camelid parts.

	Feet	Skulls	Limbs	Mandibles
Skulls	−.126	•	•	•
Limbs	−.066	−.061	•	•
Mandibles	−.086	.361*	−.028	•
Complete Specimen	−.075	−.069	−.016	−.032

* Significant at the 0.01 level

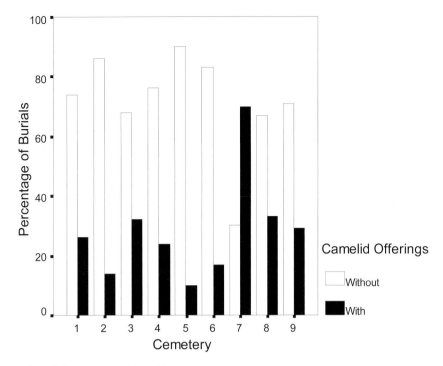

Figure 19.6. Distribution of camelid remains in Chiribaya Alta.

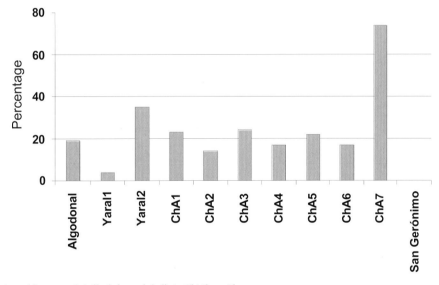

Figure 19.7. Distribution of fronto-occipitally deformed skulls in Chiribaya Alta.

the largest percentage of skulls deformed in the fronto-occipital style, a type of body alteration nearly unique to the labradores (Figure 19.7). Cemetery 7 is also notable for the large number of burial offerings with each interment, far above that found at any other Chiribaya cemetery, and orders of magnitude greater that what is encountered in mortuary contexts at El Yaral.

Scattered ethnohistorical accounts provided by Espinoza Soriano (1975) and Galdos Rodríguez (1977) for the south coast indicate that pastoralists were

usually associated with the labradores (Rostworowski 1981). This is largely supported by our archaeological observations of the Chiribaya. In fact, Rostworowski (1981) hypothesizes that camelid herds and possibly herders were owned by the *curacas* or *principales*. The elites of the labradores would have maintained special access to camelids, and this would have made camelids a valuable symbol of high status in mortuary contexts. As can be seen in Figures 19.6, 19.7, and 19.8, Cemetery 7 stands apart from the other cemeteries in the quantity

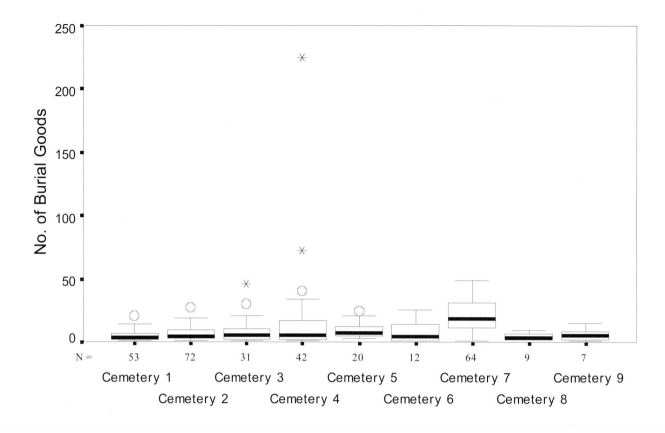

Kruskal-Wallis = 75.981, *df* = 8, *p<.000*

Figure 19.8. Box and whisker plot depicting the average number of burial goods in the Chiribaya Alta cemeteries. Cemetery 7 has the highest number of items per grave.

of grave goods and camelid offerings encountered, as well as in the preponderance of fronto-occipital cranial modification. These bioarchaeological patterns suggest that the individuals buried in Cemetery 7 at Chiribaya Alta constituted a privileged cohort of labradores who had unique access to camelids. Cemetery 7 at Chiribaya Alta has also yielded some of the earliest radiocarbon dates, indicating that social stratification existed early in Chiribaya development, and that elite groups with preferential access to strategic resources were present at the inception of Chiribaya.

As demonstrated by the quantities of camelid bones that cover the surface of the cemeteries of Chiribaya Alta, burial rituals may have included specialized feasting in honor of the deceased. In these festivities, consuming meat from the sacrificed camelids may have been an integral part of the Chiribaya mortuary ritual. The incorporation of only selected portions of the carcass, such as the head and lower limbs in burial

assemblages, suggests that the rest of the animal may have been consumed during such feasts. It is also conceivable that periodic visits to the deceased occurred, as has been documented today among camelid herders in Puno. Aranguren has reported that on a recurrent basis, on November 1, alpacas are sacrificed and placed on top of the tombs. Relatives and friends then proceed to distribute and consume the alpaca in order to "ayudar a comer al muerto" (Aranguren 1975:125).

To place our findings in a comparative archaeological framework, it is useful to examine the presence of camelid remains in other coastal contexts. Colonial documents describing pastoralism among coastal señoríos are quite rare. Archaeologically, however, there is evidence that camelids were important to northern societies prior to the expansion of the Inca and the arrival of the Spaniards. Seminal research by Shimada and Shimada (1985) on the north coast clearly demonstrates that llamas and perhaps alpacas were successfully bred and maintained on the north coast from the early Middle Horizon. In addition, examination of carbon and nitrogen stable isotopes of camelid bones from the central coast of Peru by DeNiro demonstrates that prehistoric camelids spent a considerable portion of their lives on the coast, consuming local plants (DeNiro 1988).

In the lower Osmore drainage, where Chiribaya centralized its power, camelids were an important part of the local fauna and appear to have played a central role in Chiribaya society. Direct evidence of specialized herding practices comes from the detailed work of Wheeler. Her analysis of fibers from a sample of twenty-six alpaca and llama mummies from El Yaral indicates that Chiribaya herders bred animals in order to obtain the finest quality fiber from both llamas and alpacas. Furthermore, she performed a detailed demographic analysis of 140 sacrificial camelids from Chiribaya Alta and concluded that coastal Chiribaya herders followed a strictly controlled breeding program directed toward the production and maintenance of highly selected breeds of fine fiber-producing alpacas and llamas that were preserved at El Yaral. Although modern ethnographic data from the central highlands of Peru show that the sacrifice of camelids is done by beheading the animal (Aranguren 1975), the Chiribaya camelid sacrifices were accomplished by a blunt stroke on the head between the ears (Wheeler 1993).

Further evidence of the importance of camelid breeding among the Chiribaya comes from Rofes's (1998) analysis of faunal remains from the domestic refuse at El Yaral. He found that camelid meat was the principal source of protein in the diet, distantly followed by fish. While the latter food was imported from the coast, the presence of fetal, neonatal, juvenile, and adult llamas and alpacas, along with other evidence, makes it clear that these animals were being reared year-round in the immediate vicinity of the site.

Adding further support to the existence of camelid breeding and herding on the south coast by the Chiribaya herders, Knudson compared camelid bone strontium isotopic values from coastal Chiribaya tombs and mid-valley and highland contexts. She found that Chiribaya camelids were raised locally, not imported from the highlands. In fact, coastal Chiribaya camelid values from Chiribaya Alta were different from Osmore mid-valley locations (Knudson 2004:117), suggesting that Chiribaya herds were living year-round on the coast of Ilo.

Although camelid herding has been recognized for some time among the Chiribaya, it was initially interpreted as evidence of contact with highland communities, and therefore an indication of a vertical mode of economic organization. Jessup (1990a, b), for example, proposed that Chiribaya camelids were present on the coast but were maintained by Chiribaya colonies located in the Osmore sierra, perhaps in the Otora Valley. Ethnohistorical accounts indicate that the richest lomas were concentrated in the areas around Ilo (Cobo 1956 [1653]), and, as proposed by Umire and Miranda (2001), these lomas may have been the principal sources of pastures for the Ilo camelids. Archaeological evidence for corrals used by the Chiribaya herders on the coast of Ilo has also been identified by Umire and Miranda (2001).

In conclusion, Rostworowski finds few ethnohistoric accounts describing camelid herding and management in coastal contexts. Archaeological analysis, however, reveals that pastoralism was a widespread practice along the coast prior to Spanish contact and was an important part of coastal economies.

Pastoralism may have assumed special prominence in southern coastal communities, where arable land was scarce compared with northern and central Peru. In this respect, Rostworowski's model of coastal señoríos, based on ethnohistorical sources, must be applied carefully to archaeological contexts. Although certain principles of this model may be generally applicable, independent archaeological investigations will be required to provide insights concerning each geographic, social, and cultural context. With respect to the Chiribaya, our data indicate that pastoralism was closely associated with labradores and may have been directly controlled by elites from within this community. Camelids served as important symbols for the labradores, especially of the power of their elites in the señorío of Chiribaya.

REFERENCES

Anton, Susan

1989   Intentional Cranial Vault Deformation and Induced Changes of the Cranial Base and Face. *American Journal of Physical Anthropology* 79:253–267

Aranguren Paz, Araníbar

1975   Las creencias y ritos mágico-religiosos de los pastores puneños. *Allpanchis* 8:103–132.

Benfer, Robert

1990   The Preceramic Period Site of Paloma, Peru: Bio-indications of Improving Adaptation to Sedentism. *Latin American Antiquity* 1:284–318.

Browman, David L.
1974   Pastoral Nomadism in the Andes. *Current Anthropology* 15:188–196.

Brush, Stephen B.
1977   *Mountain, Field and Family: The Economy and Human Ecology of an Andean Valley.* University of Pennsylvania Press, Philadelphia.

Buikstra, Jane E.
1995   Tombs for the Living . . . or . . . for the Dead: The Osmore Ancestors. In *Tombs for the Living: Andean Mortuary Practices,* edited by Tom D. Dillehay, pp. 229–280. Dumbarton Oaks Research Library and Collection, Washington, DC.

Buikstra, Jane E., María Cecilia Lozada, Gordon F. M. Rakita, and Paula D. Tomczak
1997   Fechados radiocarbónicos de sitios Chiribaya en la cuenca del río Osmore. Paper presented at the Seminario sobre Arqueología de Ilo, Pontificia Universidad Católica del Perú.

Cobo, Bernabé
1956 [1653]   *Obras del Padre Bernabé Cobo.* Biblioteca de Autores Españoles, vols. 91–92. Madrid.

Dembo, Adolfo, and José Imbellioni
1938   *Deformaciones intencionales del cuerpo humano.* Biblioteca del Americanista Moderno, José Anesi, Buenos Aires.

DeNiro, Michael J.
1988   Marine Food Sources for Prehistoric Coastal Peruvian Camelids: Evidence and Implications. In *Economic Prehistory of the Central Andes,* edited by Elizabeth S. Wing and Jane C. Wheeler. BAR International Series 427. British Archaeological Reports, Oxford.

Diez de San Miguel, Garci
1964 [1567]   *Visita hecha a la provincia de Chucuito por Garci Diez de San Miguel en el año 1567.* Documentos regionales para la etnología y etnohistoria andinas, vol. I. Ediciones de la Casa de la Cultura del Perú. Lima.

Espinoza Soriano, Waldemar
1975   El valle de Jayanca y el reino de los mochica: Siglos XV y XVI. *Boletín del Estudio Francés de Estudios Andinos,* vol. IV-N 3–4. Lima.

Flannery, Kent V., Joyce Marcus, and Robert G. Reynolds
1989   *The Flocks of the Wamani: A Study of Llama Herders on the Punas of Ayacucho, Peru.* Academic Press, San Diego.

Flores Ochoa, Jorge A.
1977   Pastores de alpacas de los Andes. In *Pastores de Puna,* edited by Jorge A. Flores Ochoa, pp. 15–52. Instituto de Estudios Peruanos, Lima.
1979   *Pastoralists of the Andes: The Alpaca Herders of Paratia.* Translated by Ralph Bolton. Institute for the Study of Human Issues, Philadelphia.

Galdos Rodríguez, Guillermo
1977   Visita a Atico y Caravelí (1549). *Revista del Archivo General de la Nación,* nos. 4–5. Lima.

Gentry, Anthea, Juliet Clutton-Brock, and Colin P. Groves
2004   The Naming of Wild Animal Species and Their Domestic Relatives. *Journal of Archaeological Science* 31:645–651.

Guamán Poma de Ayala, F.
1980 [1614]   *El primer nueva coronica y buen gobierno.* Edited by John Murra and Rolena Adorno, translated by J. L. Urioste. Siglo Veintiuno, Mexico.

Haydon, Rex
1993   *Survey of Genetic Variation Among the Chiribaya of the Osmore Drainage Basin, Southern Peru.* Unpublished doctoral dissertation, Department of Anthropology, University of Chicago.

Jessup, David
1990a   *Desarrollos generales en el Intermedio Tardío en el valle de Ilo, Perú.* Informe Interno del Programa Contisuyo, Moquegua.
1990b   Rescate arqueológico en el Museo de Sitio de San Gerónimo, Ilo. In *Trabajos arqueológicos en Moquegua, Perú,* edited by Luis K. Watanabe, Michael E. Moseley, and Fernando Cabieses, vol. 3, pp. 151–165. Programa Contisuyo del Museo Peruano de Ciencias de la Salud, Southern Peru Copper Corporation, Moquegua.

Kadwell, Miranda, Matilde Fernández, Helen F. Stanley, Ricardo Baldi, Jane C. Wheeler, Raul Rosadio, and Michael W. Bruford
2001   Genetic Analysis Reveals the Wild Ancestors of the Llama and Alpaca. *Proceedings of the Royal Society of London B* 268(1485):2575–2584.

Knudson, Kelly J.
2004   *Tiwanaku Residential Mobility in the South Central Andes: Identifying Archaeological Human Migration through Strontium Isotope Analysis.* Unpublished doctoral dissertation. Department of Anthropology, University of Wisconsin, Madison.

Lozada, María Cecilia, and Jane E. Buikstra
2002   *Señorío de Chiribaya en la costa sur del Perú.* Instituto de Estudios Peruanos, Lima.

Lozada, María Cecilia, Deborah E. Blom, Benedickt Hallgrímsson, and Jane E. Buikstra
2003 Interacciones biológicas y culturales entre Tiwanaku y Chiribaya en la cuenca del Osmore, sur del Perú. Paper presented at the 51st International Congress of Americanists, Santiago, Chile.

Lozada, María Cecilia, Deborah E. Blom, Benedickt Hallgrímsson, Jane E. Buikstra, and Sonia Guillén
1997 Patrones microevolutivos en poblaciones arqueológicas en la costa de Osmore, Ilo-Perú. Paper presented at Seminario Sobre Arqueología de Ilo. Pontificia Universidad Católica del Perú, August 23, Lima, Perú.

Manly, Bryan
1991 *Randomization and Monte Carlo Methods in Biology.* Chapman and Hall, London.

Masuda, Shozo, Izumi Shimada, and Craig Morris (eds.)
1985 *Andean Ecology and Civilization: An Interdisciplinary Perspective on Andean Ecological Complementarity.* University of Tokyo, Tokyo.

Miller, George R., and Richard L. Burger
1995 Our Father the Cayman, Our Dinner the Llama: Animal Utilization at Chavín de Huántar, Peru. *American Antiquity* 60:421–458.
2000 Ch'arki at Chavín: Ethnographic Models and Archaeological Data. *American Antiquity* 65:573–576.

Moseley, Michael E.
1975 *The Maritime Foundations of Andean Civilization.* Cummings Publishing Co., Menlo Park, CA.

Mujica, Elías
1985 Altiplano-Coastal Relationships in the South-Central Andes: From Indirect to Direct Complementarity. In *Andean Ecology and Civilization: An Interdisciplinary Perspective on Andean Ecological Complementarity*, edited by Shozo Masuda, Izumi Shimada, and Craig Morris, pp. 103–140. University of Tokyo Press, Tokyo.

Murra, John V.
1964 Una apreciación etnológica de la Visita. In *Visita hecha a la provincia de Chucuito por Garci Diez de San Miguel en el año 1567*, edited by Waldemar Espinoza Soriano, pp. 419–442. Casa de la Cultura del Perú, Lima.
1965 Herds and herders in the Inca state. In *Man, Culture, and Animals: The Role of Animals in Human Ecological Adjustments*, edited by Anthony Leeds and Andrew P. Vayda, pp. 185–216. Publication No. 78, American Association for the Advancement of Science, Washington DC.

1968 An Aymara Kingdom in 1567. *Ethnohistory* 15: 115–151.
1972 El control "vertical" de un máximo de pisos ecológicos en la economía de las sociedades andinas. In *Visita de la provincia de León de Huánuco en 1562*, by Iñigo Ortiz de Zuñiga, pp. 429–476. Universidad Nacional Hermilio Valdizán, Huánuco.
1975 Herds and Herders in the Inca State. In *Man, Culture, and Animals*, edited by Anthony Leeds and Andrew P. Vayda, pp. 185–215. Publication no. 78, American Association for the Advancement of Science, Baltimore.

Osborn, Alan J.
1977 Strandloopers, Mermaids and Other Fairy Tales: Ecological Determinants of Marine Resource Utilization—The Peruvian Case. In *For Theory Building in Archaeology*, edited by Lewis R. Binford, pp.157–205. Academic Press, New York.

Owen, Bruce
1993 *A Model of Multiethnicity: State Collapse, Competition, and Social Complexity from Tiwanaku to Chiribaya in the Osmore Valley, Peru.* Unpublished doctoral dissertation, Department of Anthropology, University of California, Los Angeles.

Polo de Ondegardo, J.
1916 [1559] *Los errores y supersticiones de los Indios, sacadas del tratado y averiguación que hizo el Licenciado Polo.* Colección de Libros y Documentos Referentes a la Historia del Perú, primera serie, 3:1–43. Horacio H. Urteaga and C. A. Romero, editors. Lima.

Pozorski, Shelia
1979 Late Prehistoric Llama Remains from the Moche Valley, Peru. *Annals of the Carnegie Museum* 48:139–170.

Raymond, Scott
1981 The Maritime Foundations of Andean Civilization: A Reconstruction of the Evidence. *American Antiquity* 46:806–821.

Relethford, John H., and Henry C. Harpending
1994 Craniometric Variation, Genetic Theory and Modern Human Origins. *American Journal of Physical Anthropology* 95:249–270.

Rostworowski de Diez Canseco, María
1970 Mercaderes del valle de Chincha en la época prehispánica: Un documento y unos comentarios. *Revista Española de Antropología Americana* 5:135–177.
1975 Pescadores, artesanos y mercaderes costeños en el Perú prehispánico. *Revista del Museo Nacional* 41:311–349.

1977   *Etnía y sociedad: Costa peruana prehispánica.* Instituto de Estudios Peruanos, Lima.

1981   *Recursos naturales renovables y pesca: Siglos XVI y XVII.* Instituto de Estudios Peruanos, Lima.

1989   *Costa peruana prehispánica.* Instituto de Estudios Peruanos, Lima.

Rofes, Juan

1998   *Utilización de recursos faunísticos en El Yaral, asentamiento Chiribaya en la cuenca del Osmore, sierra baja de Moquegua.* Tésis de Licenciado en Arqueología, Pontificia Universidad Católica del Perú. Lima.

Rofes, Juan, and Jane C. Wheeler

2003   Sacrifico de cuyes en los Andes: El caso de El Yaral y una revisión biológica, etnográfica y arqueológica de la especie *Cavia porcellus. Archaeofauna* 12:29-45.

Sandness, Karin L.

1992   Temporal and Spatial Dietary Variability in the Prehistoric Lower and Middle Osmore Drainage: The Carbon and Nitrogen Isotope Evidence. Master's thesis, Department of Anthropology and Geology, University of Nebraska.

Sandweiss, Daniel H.

1992   The Archaeology of Chincha Fishermen: Specialization and Status in Inka Peru. *Bulletin of the Carnegie Museum of Natural History*, no. 29. Pittsburgh.

Shimada, Melody, and Izumi Shimada

1985   Prehistoric Llama Breeding and Herding on the North Coast of Peru. *American Antiquity* 52:836–839.

1987   Comment on the Functions and Husbandry of Alpaca. *American Antiquity* 52:836–839.

Stanish, Charles

1992   *Ancient Andean Political Economy.* University of Texas Press, Austin.

Sutter, Richard C.

1997   *Dental Variation and Biocultural Affinities among Prehistoric Populations from the Coastal Valleys of Moquegua, Peru, and Azapa, Chile.* Unpublished doctoral dissertation, Department of Anthropology, University of Missouri–Columbia.

Tomczak, Paula D.

2002   *Prehistoric Socio-Economic Relations and Population Organization in the Lower Osmore Valley of Southern Peru.* Unpublished doctoral dissertation, University of New Mexico, Albuquerque.

Topic, Theresa L., Thomas H. McGreevy, and John R. Topic

1987   A Comment on the Breeding and Herding of Llamas and Alpacas on the North Coast of Peru. *American Antiquity* 52:832–835.

Umire, Adán, and Ana Miranda

2001   *Chiribaya de Ilo.* Imprenta Eskann, Arequipa, Peru.

Valdez, Lidio

2000   On Charki Consumption in the Ancient Central Andes: A Cautionary Note. *American Antiquity* 65:567–572.

Vega, Garcilaso de la

1991 [1609]   *Comentarios reales de los Incas,* vols.1–2. Fondo de Cultura Económica, Lima.

Wheeler, Jane C.

1984   On the Origin and Early Development of Camelid Pastoralism in the Andes. In *Animals and Archaeology,* edited by Juliet Clutton-Brock and C. Grigson, vol. 3, pp. 395–410. BAR International Series 202. British Archaeological Reports, Oxford.

1985   De la chasse à l'élevage. In *Telarmachay chasseurs et pasteurs préhistoriques des Andes,* edited by Danièle Lavallée, Michele Julien, Jane C. Wheeler, and Claudine Karlin. ADPF, Paris.

1993   Faunal Remains from the Chiribaya Alta Tombs. Report submitted to Jane E. Buikstra. Manuscript in possession of authors.

1995   Evolution and Present Situation of the South American Camelidae. *Biological Journal of the Linnaean Society* 54:271–295.

Wheeler, Jane C., Angus J. F. Russel, and Hilary Redden

1995   Llamas and Alpacas: Pre-conquest Breeds and Post-conquest Hybrids. *Journal of Archaeological Science* 22:833–840.

Wheeler, Jane C., Lounès Chikhi, and Michael W. Bruford

2006   Case Study in Genetics of Animal Domestication: South American Camelids. In *Documenting Domestication: New Genetic and Archaeological Paradigms,* edited by Melinda A. Zeder, Daniel G. Bradley, Eve Emshwiller, and Bruce G. Smith, pp. 329-341. University of California Press, Berkeley and Los Angeles.

Wilson, David J.

1981   Of Maize and Men: A Critique of the Maritime Hypothesis of State Origins on the Coast of Peru. *American Anthropologist* 83(1):93–120.

CHAPTER 20

INCA AGRICULTURAL INTENSIFICATION IN THE IMPERIAL HEARTLAND AND PROVINCES

R. ALAN COVEY

MICHAEL MOSELEY'S RESEARCH ON human ecology along the Peruvian coast has drawn important attention to the relationship between intensive agriculture and the rise and collapse of complex societies (e.g., Moseley 1983).[1] Scholars have noted the maladaptive implications of overreliance on intensive hydraulic agriculture: highly specialized social organization, a religion and an elite ideology tied intimately to surplus production, and an increasing tendency for a growing population to approach carrying capacity—all of which make these systems vulnerable to catastrophic collapse in the long term (Moseley 2000; Williams 2002; see also Rappaport 1979; Read and LeBlanc 2003). Over time, individuals in such systems are less able to respond to unpredictable environmental changes—including, in the Andean region, severe El Niño events, earthquakes, and prolonged droughts—or internal social upheaval.

Although researchers are less than sanguine regarding the long-term prospects of a sustained intensification regime, the expansion of intensive agricultural production still represents a viable risk-reduction strategy in cases where production does not maximize available resources and populations remain relatively small. In this chapter, I consider the positive by-products of agricultural intensification during the coalescence

and expansion of the highland Inca state, as well as the ecological implications of Inca expansion into coastal areas (Figure 20.1). The discussion addresses two important and interrelated themes: (1) Inca state formation and imperial expansion should be considered within a milieu of specific, but contrasting, ecological conditions, and (2) patterns of resource intensification and land tenure outside the imperial heartland varied according to local environmental conditions and extant political complexity. This chapter shows that the Inca actively tailored their strategies to existing practices and localized environmental zones. Case studies from the imperial heartland and a marginal coastal region illustrate differences in administrative strategies, particularly in the degree of Inca elite control over the creation and management of new agricultural resources.

ANDEAN AGRICULTURAL INTENSIFICATION

Before discussing particular cases of Inca agricultural intensification, it is useful to review a few points regarding the social implications of intensive agriculture in the Andes. The development of new agricultural lands, terraced or not, and irrigation systems created new resources that were easier to manage centrally and tended to lend themselves to more complex leadership

365

Figure 20.1. Map of Tawantinsuyu, showing locations discussed in the chapter.

roles. The Huarochirí Manuscript (Salomon and Urioste 1991:62–63) provides a mythological illustration of competition for leadership roles as part of the maintenance and extension of an irrigation canal:

> Pumas, foxes, snakes, and all kinds of birds cleaned and fixed the canal. Pumas, jaguars, and all kinds of animals vied with each other to improve it, saying "Who'll be the leader when we lay out the watercourse?" "Me first! Me first!" exclaimed this one and that one. The fox won, saying, "I'm the chief, the *curaca*, so I'll lead the way first." And so he, the fox, went on ahead.[2]

Concomitant with enhanced leadership opportunities, the improvement of valley-bottom *kichwa* lands in many highland Andean areas promoted forms of political economy and religious organization that were distinct from dry-farming regimes on valley slopes (see Murra 1960).[3] Irrigated terraces at frost-free elevations had the potential to produce impressive surpluses, particularly when maize was cultivated; the maintenance of such a valuable resource lent itself to more centralized

scheduling of irrigation, labor, and ritual activity (see Wittfogel 1957; Bauer 1998; Sherbondy 1993).

In discussing contemporary Andean irrigation systems, Seligmann and Bunker (1993:227) summarize a key observation made by Wittfogel: "the construction and maintenance of an irrigation system requires knowledge that is transmitted from generation to generation, technology to implement that knowledge, and the authority to coordinate a labor force and manage material resources within the specific environment in which it is found." In the Inca period, a strong conceptual linkage existed in the Cusco region between the person of the Inca ruler and the construction of what Wittfogel (1957:23) calls large-scale preparatory (irrigation) and protective (flood control) operations (e.g., AGN Real Audiencia L. 4 C. 26 [1559]; Betanzos 1999 [1551–1557: Bk. 1, Chaps. 13, 43]; Cieza de León 1988 [ca. 1550: Chap. 35]).[4] Based on documentary descriptions, the *sapa Inca* assumed responsibility for defining the scope of intensification projects, providing necessary materials and tools for the work and underwriting festivities to reciprocate labor tribute invested in the project. The logistics of construction were entrusted to lower-order administrators. The ruler named and distributed new terraces and irrigation canals and, as the figure providing knowledge, technology, and authority for the project, retained the lion's share of the new resources for his personal maintenance. For the Inca and earlier Andean civilizations, intensive agriculture provided one means of addressing interannual climatic fluctuations, but large-scale projects required more hierarchical forms of social organization and often resulted in patterns of resource management that preferentially benefited the elite stratum.

STATE FORMATION AND AGRICULTURAL INTENSIFICATION IN THE CUSCO REGION

As Wittfogel (1957:12) has noted, the evolution of a hydraulic order is not inevitable: "It is only above the level of an extractive subsistence economy, beyond the influence of strong centers of rainfall agriculture, and below the level of a property-based industrial civilization that man, reacting specifically to the water-deficient landscape, moves toward a specific hydraulic order of life." New archaeological data from the Cusco region indicate that processes of Inca state formation are likely to have been influenced by the development and expansion of centrally managed irrigation agriculture.

Intensification Potential in the Cusco Region ca. AD 1000

To provide an ecological context for the regional archaeological data, we should begin by considering the landscape of the Cusco region in terms of its potential for intensification at the time of Inca state formation (ca. AD 1200–1300). As other authors have noted (e.g., Gade 1975; Winterhalder 1993), this region is characterized by substantial differences in elevation, temperature, soil quality, and precipitation. Because Inca state agriculture focused on maize—a crop that is cultivated most successfully below about 3400 masl, and where irrigation is possible—a rough approximation of intensification potential may be made by noting locations with large patches of irrigable lands at or below this elevation.[5] River canalization and the construction of terraces and irrigation canals in these zones would allow maize to be cultivated reliably; the year-round availability of irrigation water and the application of guano could make multiple harvests possible and obviate the need for a fallow cycle. Such highly productive, centrally managed resource patches would have contrasted markedly with traditional extensive cultivation practices, which emphasized polycropping, the maintenance of multiple small plots, and regular crop rotation.

The most obvious lands amenable to intensification in the Cusco region are in the Oropesa Basin, the Lucre Basin, and the Huaro area to the southeast of the Cusco Basin, as well as in the Sacred Valley and certain neighboring transverse valleys to the north and northwest of Cusco. The Cusco Basin itself has considerable expanses of valley-bottom lands below the absolute elevation limits for maize cultivation, as well as numerous small side streams that could be canalized for dry-season irrigation. To the south, the Apurimac Valley is too narrow and meandering to provide large planting surfaces. To the southwest and west of Cusco, the Xaquixaguana Valley and Huanoquite region have modest areas where intensive maize production could be pursued (Seligmann and Bunker 1993).

Of these areas with high natural potential for the development of intensive maize agriculture, only the landscapes of the Lucre Basin and Huaro area appear to have been substantially modified prior to AD 1000. Wari colonists settled and transformed these areas after about AD 600, and it is likely that terracing and canal systems were developed at that time, although archaeological studies of the Wari occupation have focused primarily on administrative, domestic, and mortuary contexts, not agricultural production (e.g., McEwan 1987, 1991, 1996; Zapata 1997; Glowacki 2002). Outside the Lucre Basin and Huaro area, the Cusco region does not appear to have been transformed by Wari intensification projects (Covey 2003; Bauer 2004).

Administrative sites in the Wari colonial system were abandoned by around AD 1000, part of a regional settlement transformation in which numerous small polities coalesced. Contrary to the descriptions of some chroniclers, the new polities that developed after AD 1000 exhibited substantial differences in social complexity and political economy (see Bauer and Covey 2002). The Wari installations in the Lucre Basin and Huaro area were abandoned as large villages or towns grew at Chokepukio, Minaspata, and Cotocotuyoc (Dwyer 1971; Glowacki 2002; McEwan et al. 2002). These settlements were all located near the valley floor, in close proximity to maize-producing lands. The Oropesa Basin, lying between the Cusco and Lucre basins, appears to have been almost completely depopulated as valley-bottom villages and productive maize lands were abandoned (Bauer and Covey 2002; Bauer 2004).[6]

In the Cusco Basin itself, settlement after AD 1000 continued to be concentrated on low alluvial terraces immediately above the valley floor. The basin was densely populated in a hierarchical settlement system dominated by the growing urban center at Cusco. Population growth at that time led to the establishment of new settlements in previously unoccupied parts of the basin, as well as the construction of new irrigation canals and agricultural terraces. By contrast, the rich potential of kichwa lands in the nearby Sacred Valley remained unrealized at this time; settlement shifted away from the valley bottom, and the largest settlements were established on high ridgetops at 4000 masl and higher (Covey 2006b).

Ecology and Political Organization after AD 1000

Although future archaeological research will undoubtedly enhance the reconstruction of regional settlement after AD 1000, it appears that the largest sites and most complex polities in the Cusco region occupied areas amenable to intensive maize agriculture (Figure 20.2). The residents of the Lucre Basin and Huaro area appear to have continued to practice maize agriculture, probably by maintaining production infrastructure first developed by their Wari predecessors. This reliance

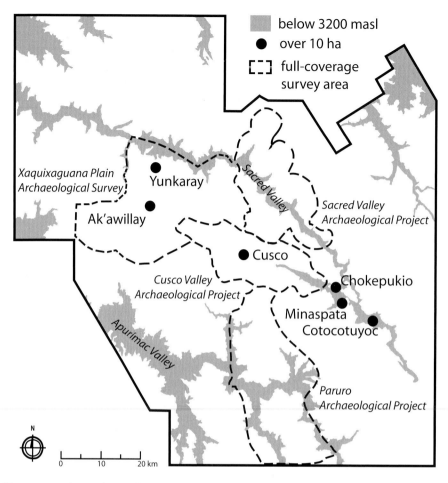

Figure 20.2. Map of Cusco region, showing large Killke period settlements and lands below 3200 masl.

on improved lands sustained complex political and religious hierarchies, but would not have offered great potential for further economic intensification without expanding and acquiring more lands.

Two other large (15–20 ha) settlements have been identified to the northwest of Cusco. Ak'awillay covers roughly 15 ha on a low alluvial terrace just above the valley bottom where maize lands could be cultivated without the development of major irrigation works. At 20 ha, Yunkaray is the largest site in a dense and hierarchical settlement system (with a total occupation area of roughly 120 ha) clustering around terraced and irrigated maize lands just to the south of the Sacred Valley (Covey et al. 2006). By comparison, the growing site of Cusco was situated in a circumscribed basin that still had substantial potential for intensification, was located some 25 km from its nearest large maize-producing rival, and was surrounded by depopulated buffer zones with significant patches of kichwa lands and irrigation water. Cusco itself grew from a large village into a city

after AD 1000, and the settled area of the Cusco Basin at that time was at least twice the size of the settlement system around Yunkaray (Bauer and Covey 2002).

The largest settlements of less complex groups were located at elevations favoring more mosaic economies where herding and dry farming produced reliable harvests but did not provide the kinds of surpluses that could fund territorial expansion. Such groups chose to invest in defensive works, and appear to have pursued strategies to protect the resources they already had, rather than allocate community labor to intensification (see Covey 2006a). In transverse valleys to the north of the Sacred Valley, local groups did not occupy the lower kichwa elevations, in part because conditions of political decentralization made the development of valley-bottom maize lands a risky production strategy. Only a centralized state could integrate the groups living on both sides of the Vilcanota River and then mobilize the labor to reclaim valley-bottom lands for maize agriculture.

Distinguishing between strategies of investing labor in resource retention (defensive works) from agricultural intensification, we can hypothesize that, other things being equal, populations relying on dense, highly patchy resources (intensifiers) grew more quickly than those that pursued more extensive food procurement strategies (Read and LeBlanc 2003:67). Political economies based on intensification regimes were more likely to be centrally administered, and their higher growth rates encouraged expansion over the long term. Expansion into areas lacking intensive agriculture would theoretically involve less intense intergroup conflict, given that dry farming and irrigation agriculture were based on resources that did not overlap substantially. In the Inca case, it appears that population growth and variable climatic conditions acted in tandem to encourage Inca state formation and territorial expansion.

Ecological Aspects of Inca State Formation

Ice core data from the nearby Quelccaya glacier indicate fluctuating but generally more arid conditions between AD 1160 and the onset of the Little Ice Age around AD 1490, and Thompson and colleagues (1985:973) have identified a period of severe, prolonged drought from AD 1250 to 1310. Pollen found in lake cores from the Cusco region also indicates "a sustained period of reduced precipitation and elevated temperatures" after AD 1100 (Chepstow-Lusty et al. 2003:499). Lower levels of rainfall and overall variability in annual precipitation levels would have made irrigation agriculture an appealing production strategy in the second half of the thirteenth century, by which time a centralized state government is known to have developed in the Cusco Basin. The dated expansion of early Inca occupation at the site of Pucara Pantillijlla suggests that the Inca state began to annex and administer new territory to the north of the Vilcanota River by around AD 1300 (Covey 2003, 2006b).

Although additional data are needed, it appears that Inca state formation and early territorial expansion were related to programs of agricultural intensification, which were undertaken in response to population growth and fluctuating precipitation levels. This is not to say that the Inca state formed in response to environmental conditions but rather to observe that political competition and climatic flux from the eleventh century onward provided a competitive advantage to groups that could reliably increase available resources to sustain growing populations. New resources were used to buffer lean years, but also to feed additional laborers and campaigning soldiers, and to underwrite festivals that bound local allies to the Inca elite.

The archaeological evidence indicates that intensification projects enhanced the competitive advantage of the early Inca state, permitting it to incorporate neighboring polities and ultimately promoting a program of imperial expansion. In Cusco, a perceived vulnerability to environmental fluctuations and a rapidly growing urban population would have encouraged the annexation of areas where intensive agriculture could be developed—especially in the Sacred Valley—and the leadership opportunities related to such expansion concentrated resources and authority in the person of the Inca ruler.

Inca Rulers and Intensification Projects

The first intensification projects mentioned in the Spanish chronicles were initiated under rulers who are also credited with the development of other features of centralized state government (Covey 2003). The sixth ruler (Inca Rocca) and his wife (Mama Micay) are said to have built the Chacan irrigation system, and this ruler's Larapa estate in the Cusco Basin has been identified archaeologically as a series of new agricultural terraces, irrigation canals, and villages (Bauer and Covey 2002). Subsequent rulers developed estates on the southern margins of the Sacred Valley, while Inca state administration extended to include groups living in the transverse valleys to the north of the Vilcanota River. The incorporation of both sides of the Sacred Valley permitted the improvement of valley-bottom maize lands, the majority of which were controlled by royal Inca lineages.

ROYAL ESTATES AND THE POLITICAL ECONOMY OF THE INCA IMPERIAL HEARTLAND

The ethnohistoric evidence suggests that the earliest estate construction—the development of new canals, terraces, and villages in the northern part of the Cusco Basin—coincided with the emergence of the Inca state. A few generations of expansion saw the development of royal estates in the Sacred Valley. Estate resources included improved named plots of land that also were associated with residence by members of a ruler's descent group. The site of Pisaq demonstrates a clear tie between estate lands and the ruler and his descendants.

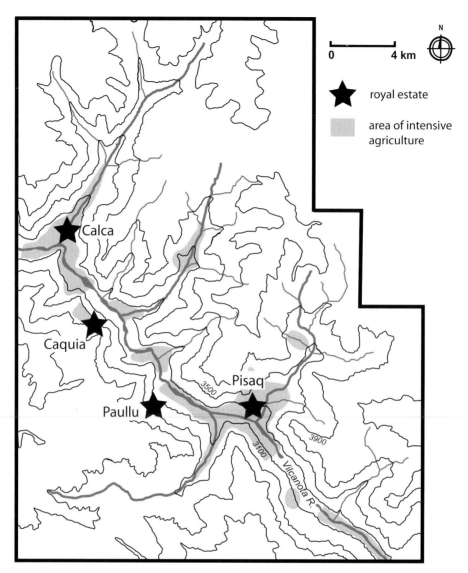

Figure 20.3. Map of Sacred Valley study region, with Inca settlement and areas of agricultural intensification.

Resource and Patronage at Pisaq

The estate of Pachacutic Inca Yupanqui at Pisaq was closely related to the person and lineage of the Inca ruler. Pachacutic allegedly seized the lands of the local Cuyo ethnic group after accusing them of an assassination attempt (Covey 2006b). Accounts of the annihilation of the Cuyo are not supported by archaeological settlement patterns or other Colonial documents, but such discrepancies reflect an Inca conquest ideology that justified the seizure of land and water resources in cases of local treachery or rebellion.

The Inca used labor tribute from conquered groups to canalize the Vilcanota River and construct irrigation canals and agricultural terraces (see Farrington 1983 on

river canalization). The Pisaq estate lands were worked in part by Colla retainers brought to the valley after Inca campaigns in the Titicaca Basin. Colla informants in the Colonial period testified that their forebears had been brought personally to the estate by Pachakutiq (Toledo 1940 [1571]:158–167). As late as 1571, descendants of Pachakutiq's lineage were found living at Pisaq, where there is an impressive complex of Inca architecture still today (Toledo 1940 [1571]:149–158).

The architecture at Pisaq is consistent with domestic and ceremonial use by Inca elites. Access to the different compounds at the site is tightly controlled, and the masonry of the central Intiwatana complex is some of the finest to be found in the Inca heartland.

Looted Inca-style cliff tombs in the canyon below the Q'allaq'asa complex attest to an enduring link between Inca elites and the site. Although the development of agricultural lands at the valley bottom would have resulted in the production of huge agricultural surpluses, the elaborate stone-faced terraces built close to the architectural compounds at Pisaq would have involved a huge labor investment with a much smaller agricultural return. The channeling of water to ceremonial fountains and construction of terraces that can be interpreted as ornamental (i.e., whose construction costs would outweigh their productive potential) is consistent with facilities for elite pleasure and ceremony.

As an estate, Pisaq was linked explicitly to the person of Pachacutic, and some of his descendants occupied the site over a period of a century or more. New valley-bottom lands like these were worked by labor colonists and full-time retainers said to have been conquered and brought to Cusco by the emperor himself. The local Cuyo ethnic group may also have provided labor tribute, and appears to have occupied lands at the margins of the estate. Archaeologically, the enduring association with an Inca lineage is demonstrated by Inca-style tombs and architecture consistent with elite domestic and ceremonial life. The use of innovative architectural forms and the construction of fountains and ornamental terraces are evidence that the site was not merely a bureaucratic outpost.

PROVINCIAL ECOLOGY AND AGRICULTURAL INTENSIFICATION

The ethnohistoric and archaeological evidence suggests an intimate link between Inca rulers and the development of agricultural resources that would help fund expansion projects during their lifetimes and support their lineages after their deaths. The connection between improved lands and a particular ruler is easily discernible in the Cusco region at sites such as Pisaq; in highland provinces and kichwa elevations of coastal valleys, the construction of state farms often had a symbolic imperial patronage, but appears to have been executed to sustain the day-to-day administration of provincial regions (D'Altroy 2002:268–276).

The Ecology of Inca Imperial Expansion

In discussing ecological aspects of Inca state formation and imperial expansion, it is important to note that intensification strategies that were effective in decentralized kichwa areas would be more difficult to impose in many coastal regions, where numerous centralized polities existed in the fifteenth century, and where limited and circumscribed agricultural resources were often already intensified. The Inca were constrained in developing new resources on which a separate central administrative and religious hierarchy could be built. It is not coincidental that coastal regions were incorporated later in the Inca expansion trajectory.

The Tawantinsuyu did eventually make inroads in coastal valleys, often developing roads and waystations in so-called *chawpi yunga* areas (kichwa elevations where intensive maize cultivation was possible), and developing more indirect forms of rule on the coast itself. Such expansion may have been aided by the onset of the Little Ice Age around AD 1500, a period that brought wetter conditions to the Andean region. With more rainfall and higher coastal water tables, the Inca were able to increase production in some coastal areas in a manner consistent with their highland intensification strategies. A closer look at Inca administration in the south-central coastal valleys demonstrates more symbolic connection with the Inca ruler than has been observed for royal estates in the imperial heartland, consistent with the development of many provincial lands to sustain infrastructure rather than elite life.

Imperial Administration in the Titicaca Basin and South-Central Coast

In 1567, Garci Diez de San Miguel interviewed Lupaca elites from the Titicaca Basin regarding patterns of Inca administration. The resulting testimony reveals two different aspects of imperial governance in one provincial region. Pedro Cutinbo, who had served as provincial governor in the early Colonial period, described the labor and wealth that was extracted from the region:

> "he said that sometimes they gave [the Inca ruler] three thousand natives for the war, and other times they gave him all the natives that he requested to build walls and houses and for his service, and children to sacrifice, and maidens who would serve him and the Sun and the Moon and the thunder, and cloth, and they made him many agricultural fields. And they gave him gold and silver that they extracted—the gold from Chuquiabo and the silver from the mines of Porco—and likewise they gave him lead as tribute, and a red pigment called *limpi*, and copper, and feathers, and everything that he cared to ask. As their lord, they gave him many doves and dried meat and ducks from the lake, and they

carried him fish from this lake, in two days from here to Cusco. . . ."[7]

This account contrasts substantially with those of Martín Cari and Martín Cusi, the heads of the upper and lower divisions of the Lupaca province. In response to the same question, these individuals focused more explicitly on the management of staple resources that were kept in storage facilities located in the province (Diez de San Miguel 1964[1567]:22–23, 34). Although staple finance was based on obligations to the sapa Inca, the actual resources were used to maintain local Lupaca elites and to feed and clothe travelers and soldiers passing through the province.

Lupaca elites appear to have organized camelid caravans between the altiplano and lowland production areas where maize, chile peppers, and coca could be cultivated. The evidence from the south-central coastal valleys indicates that lowland agricultural production involved a large number of production areas managed by different local elites in the name of the sapa Inca. Martín Cari named thrity-two locations subject to him as the Hanansaya *kuraka* of Chucuito, including Camata, Moquegua, and Sama. Martín Cusi named forty-five locations subject to the Urinsaya kuraka, including Moquegua, Torata, and Tarata. The available evidence indicates that altiplano elites were responsible for managing *mitmaqkuna* (labor colonists) scattered throughout a region where imperial control was highly variable (Covey 2000). Imperial roads, waystations, storage facilities, and agricultural terracing were developed in parts of the chawpi yunga zone, while the Inca presence on the coast itself was much less visible.

Resource Development at Quebrada Tacahuay

To illustrate the weakness of the link between the south-central coastal valleys and the Inca elite, let us consider the small spring-fed agricultural system found at Quebrada Tacahuay on the Moquegua coast (Figure 20.4). This 30- to 40-ha system comprises thirteen groups of agricultural terraces fed by canals, the longest of which is more than 1.5 km long. Most agricultural lands in this area were developed as small plots located on the quebrada floor or on alluvial terraces as near as possible to water resources. Where present, terraces tend to be of simple construction, with minimal transformation of the natural landscape.

The principal Inca site in Quebrada Tacahuay is TA-37, also referred to as Pueblo Tacahuay (Covey 2000) (Figure 20.5). Located on four domestic terraces close to the largest area of agricultural lands, the site measures 5 ha, at the center of which are the remains of four or more stone structures or enclosures. Inca pottery is present in and around the architectural remains, but simple redwares and provincial Inca designs are much more common than standard imperial polychromes. Only a few fragments of the more than 1,400 sherds analyzed from the site could have come from Cusco, while styles from the Titicaca Basin and northern Chile are much more common.

Several Colonial documents indicate that the imposition of Inca control over the south-central coastal valleys was effected indirectly through altiplano elites, particularly the Lupaca ethnic group. The ethnohistoric record indicates that highland enclaves and colonies were placed throughout the south-central coastal valleys, sometimes in multiethnic communities where local coastal groups were already living. Near the coast, maize and chile pepper were cultivated, and fields were fertilized with guano from nearby islands. Highland elites supervised much of the production, exchange, and transportation of marine and agricultural resources, sending llama caravans from the Titicaca Basin out to the coastal valleys. The authority of these elites rested on traditional kinship obligations, but their power derived from their representation of the sapa Inca, and they were supervised by Inca administrators living in towns in the Titicaca Basin. While coastal settlements were said to have been placed "by the Inca," many aspects of colonization were managed by altiplano elites, who increased their own wealth and power by exploiting the imperial system.

Quebrada Tacahuay offers little evidence of a direct connection with Huayna Capac, the ruler said to have consolidated Inca rule over the region. Even Cariapassa, the highest Lupaca administrator in Inca times, is said to have traveled with the emperor in Ecuador and is unlikely to have visited Quebrada Tacahuay personally or to have benefited substantially from crops grown there (Stirling 1999:174–175). The lands at Quebrada Tacahuay could have supported an imperial waystation or imperial administrators overseeing fishing and guano extraction in the area, but it is unlikely that any resources produced there directly benefited the lineage of the Inca emperor. The architectural remains at the site are consistent with a small Inca enclave or coastal waystation, and it is unlikely that any members of the imperial family lived at or even visited this small peripheral site.

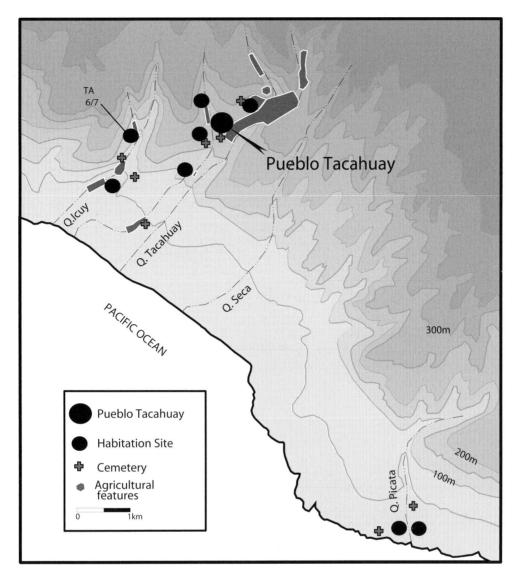

Figure 20.4. Quebrada Tacahuay settlement pattern.

CONCLUSIONS

The evidence from the Cusco region indicates that Inca state formation took place during a prolonged arid period, and that the annexation of Sacred Valley kichwa lands was probably associated with an extended drought. The Inca were ultimately the most successful of many competing polities in the region, owing to both cultural and environmental circumstances. Wari colonization in the Cusco region had introduced new agricultural technologies and patterns of labor tribute, and Inca elites were among a handful of leaders throughout the region with the authority and knowledge to maintain substantial systems of agricultural infrastructure and to organize the construction of new irrigation canals and terraces. The

Cusco Basin had substantial areas where new agricultural lands could be developed, and circumstances of political balkanization after AD 1000 moved populations away from many patches of kichwa lands. Some groups moved to high elevations and pursued extensive agropastoral production strategies, while other populations moved to the Cusco Basin, where the settlement system became more hierarchical and increased resources were required to stave off risks of interannual production variations.

As the Inca state formed, elites came to use labor tribute to develop new agricultural resources, expanding first into areas where such projects would overlap minimally with local economies, but eventually incorporating all political and ethnic groups of the Cusco region. Intensification projects came to be viewed as

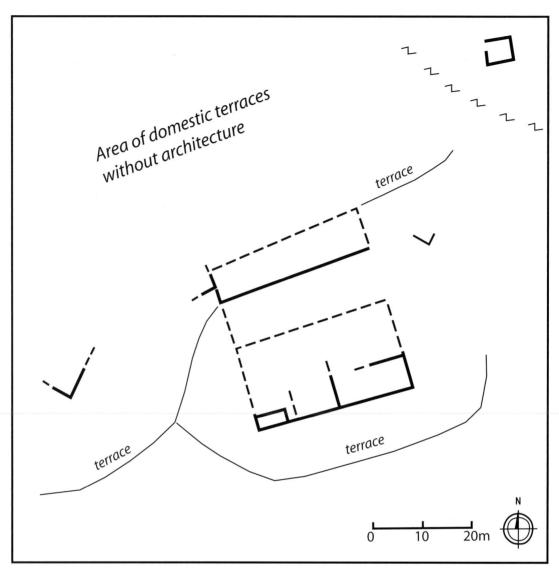

Figure 20.5. TA-37 plan.

possessions of the Inca ruler, and the political economy of the Inca heartland came to be dominated by royal descent groups that controlled substantial estates whose production provided them with sustenance and leisurely living. Whether or not the estate system as we currently understand it represents a sequential investment in developing resources by historical rulers, the strong tie between royal descent groups and estate resources indicates that the long-term effect of agricultural intensification in the imperial heartland was the concentration of highly productive resources under the control of a limited number of lineages and factions. Such patterns hold particularly for kichwa maize lands to the north and east of Cusco, whereas areas to the south and west—which had limited potential for maize

development—appear to lack royal estates and to have been administered differently.

Although royal estate lands were closely linked to the person of the sapa Inca, many provincial regions appear to have been developed only in the ruler's name, and were used to support imperial infrastructure and provincial administration. The largest state farms were constructed in kichwa lands and were administered by local elites under Inca supervision. Inca control of the coast itself was less direct and occurred later, perhaps because the onset of the Little Ice Age increased available water resources and permitted the partial construction of a parallel agricultural economy.

The spring-fed agricultural system at Quebrada Tacahuay lacks the close association with the sapa Inca seen at the royal estate at Pisaq. This system would have produced enough food to support a waystation for caravans traveling to the coast to acquire marine resources or guano for highland fields, but it was unlikely to have provided material support for the lineage of Huayna Capac. The remoteness of Quebrada Tacahuay and the close ties of the south-central coastal valleys to Lupaca elites living in the Titicaca Basin are consistent with the extension of imperial infrastructure to the Pacific coast, and not the development of resources "owned" by a royal descent group.

By looking at the imperial heartland and one marginal provincial area, it has been possible to contrast Inca political economy in the Cusco region with provincial administration. The heartland was dominated by royal descent groups that controlled substantial resources and were increasingly supported by retainer labor. Provincial regions were developed so that they would be more or less self-sustaining in terms of staple production, with Inca elites monitoring wealth extraction and moving populations based on production fluctuations (see D'Altroy and Earle 1985). The conceptualization of Inca state resources evolved over time—from possessions intimately linked to a particular ruler to state resources maintained in the name of "the Inca" as a symbolic overlord. Such changes reveal the importance of resource intensification as a key strategy for risk reduction in the Inca economy, but they also demonstrate the fluidity with which Inca administrative strategies addressed and were affected by local environmental and sociopolitical conditions.

Acknowledgments

The Sacred Valley Archaeological Project was supported by a Fulbright-Hays Fellowship, a Wenner-Gren Foundation Individual Grant, a National Science Foundation Dissertation Improvement Grant (BCS-0135913), and various funds from the University of Michigan, including the Rackham Discretionary Fund, the James B. Griffin Fund, and the Department of Anthropology. Research in Moquegua was made possible by Programa Contisuyo, and I would especially like to thank Mike Moseley, Bruce Owen, Adán Umire, and Susan deFrance. Funding for the Tacahuay research was provided by the University of Michigan Latin American and Caribbean Studies program, and a Collections Study Grant from the American Museum of Natural History allowed me to study the notes and field drawings from Gary Vescelius's research on the far south coast of Peru. Christina Elson and Joyce Marcus read an earlier draft of the manuscript and provided helpful comments.

NOTES

1. Moseley's influence comes not only from his own research but also from his collaborators and former students (e.g., Bawden and Reycraft 2000; Clement and Moseley 1991; Satterlee et al. 2001).

2. The Huarochirí Manuscript provides numerous descriptions of corporate *maintenance* of irrigation resources, but it tends to associate the generative act of intensification with superhuman figures such as Cuni Raya Viracocha and Paria Caca. In this case, the office of *kuraka* or *kamachikuq* is linked with the individual responsible for determining the course of the canal extension.

3. In the Colonial dictionaries, a distinction is made between land that is worked continuously and irrigated (*chacra allpa*) and lands used seasonally, lacking irrigation, or requiring a fallow period (e.g., *cochca allpa, callpa chacra, purum allpa*) (González Holguín 1989 [1608]:65, 297, 679–680).

4. As discussed elsewhere (Covey 2003), the wives of Inca rulers are also credited with such works.

5. Gade (1975) notes that maize agriculture is particularly productive between 2800 and 3200 masl.

6. The walled site of Tipón was established several hundred meters above the valley floor in the Oropesa Basin. The massive site walls enclosed agricultural lands where some maize may have been cultivated, as well as sources of irrigation water (Bauer and Covey 2002).

7. (Diez de San Miguel 1964:30). "[D]ijo que le daban tres mil indios para la guerra algunas veces otras veces le daban todos los indios que querían para hacer paredes y casas y para su servicio y hijos para sacrificar y doncellas para que le sirviesen y para el Sol y la Luna y los truenos y ropa y le hacían muchas chácaras y le daban oro y plata que sacaban el oro de Chuquiabo y la plata de las minas de Porco y asímismo le daban plomo de tributo y un barniz colorado que llaman limpi y cobre y plumas y todo lo que él quería pedir le daban como a su señor y muchas perdices y charque y patos de la laguna y llevaban el pescado de ésta a [sic] laguna en dos días de aquí al Cuzco. . . ."

REFERENCES

Archivo General de la Nación, Real Audiencia, Causas Civiles, Legajo 4 Cuaderno 26 [1559]. Lima, Peru.

Bauer, Brian S.
1998   *The Sacred Landscape of the Inca: The Cuzco Ceque System.* University of Texas Press, Austin.
2004   *Ancient Cuzco: Heartland of the Inca.* University of Texas Press, Austin.

Bauer, Brian S., and R. Alan Covey
2002   Processes of State Formation in the Inca Heart-
        land (Cuzco, Peru). *American Anthropologist* 104(3):
        1–19.

Bawden, Garth, and Richard M. Reycraft (eds.)
2000   *Environmental Disaster and the Archaeology of Human
        Response.* Anthropological Papers of the Maxwell
        Museum of Anthropology, no. 7. Maxwell Museum
        of Anthropology, Albuquerque, NM.

Betanzos, Juan de
1999 [1551–1557] *Suma y narración de los incas.* Universidad
        Nacional de San Antonio Abad del Cusco, Cusco.

Chepstow-Lusty, Alex, Michael R. Frogley, Brian S. Bauer,
        Mark B. Bush, and Alfredo Tupayachi Herrera
2003   A Late Holocene Record of Arid Events from the
        Cuzco Region, Peru. *Journal of Quaternary Science*
        18(6):491–502.

Cieza de León, Pedro de
1988 [ca. 1550]   *El señorío de los Incas*, edited by Manuel
        Ballesteros. Historia 16. Madrid.

Clement, Christopher O., and Michael E. Moseley
1991   Spring-Fed Irrigation System of Carrizal, Peru: A
        Case Study of the Hypothesis of Agrarian Collapse.
        Journal of Field Archaeology 18(4):425–443.

Covey, R. Alan
2000   Inca Administration of the Far South Coast of Peru.
        Latin American Antiquity 11(2):119–138.

2003   A Processual Study of Inca State Formation. *Journal
        of Anthropological Archaeology* 22(4):333–357.

2006a   Intermediate Elites in the Inca Heartland, AD
        1000–1500. In *Intermediate Elites in Pre-Columbian
        States and Empires*, edited by Christina M. Elson and
        R. Alan Covey, pp. 112–135. University of Arizona
        Press, Tucson.

2006b   *How the Incas Built Their Heartland: State Formation
        and the Innovation of Imperial Strategies in the Sacred
        Valley, Peru.* University of Michigan Press, Ann
        Arbor.

Covey, R. Alan, Véronique Bélisle, and Allison R. Davis
2006   Variations in Late Intermediate Period Group
        Interaction in the Cusco Region (Peru). Paper
        presented at the 71st Meeting of the Society for
        American Archaeology, San Juan, PR, April 26–30.

D'Altroy, Terence N.
2002   *The Incas.* Blackwell, New York.

D'Altroy, Terence N., and Timothy K. Earle
1985   Staple Finance, Wealth Finance, and Storage in the
        Inca Political Economy (with Comment and Reply).
        Current Anthropology 25:187–206.

Diez de San Miguel, Garci
1964 [1567]   *Visita hecha a la provincia de Chucuito por Garci
        Diez de San Miguel en el año 1567.* Documentos
        regionales para la etnología y etnohistoria Andina 1.
        Ediciones de la Casa de la Cultura del Perú, Lima.

Dwyer, Edward B.
1971   *The Early Inca Occupation of the Valley of Cuzco, Peru.*
        Unpublished doctoral dissertation, Department of
        Anthropology, University of California, Berkeley.

Farrington, Ian S.
1983   Prehistoric Intensive Agriculture: Preliminary Notes
        on River Canalization in the Sacred Valley of the
        Incas. In *Drained Field Agriculture in Central and
        South America*, edited by J. P. Darch, pp. 221–235.
        BAR International Series 189. British Archaeological
        Reports, Oxford.

Gade, Daniel W.
1975   *Plants, Man and the Land in the Vilcanota Valley of
        Peru.* Dr. W. Junk B.V., The Hague.

Glowacki, Mary
2002   The Huaro Archaeological Site Complex: Rethink-
        ing the Huari Occupation of Cuzco. In *Andean
        Archaeology I: Variations in Sociopolitical Organization*,
        edited by William H. Isbell and Helaine Silverman,
        pp. 267–285. Kluwer Academic/Plenum Publishers,
        New York.

González Holguín, Diego
1989[1608]   *Vocabulario de la lengua general de todo el Perú
        llamada lengua qquichua o del Inca.* Universidad
        Nacional Mayor de San Marcos, Lima.

McEwan, Gordon F.
1987   *The Middle Horizon in the Valley of Cuzco, Peru: The
        Impact of the Wari Occupation of the Lucre Basin.* BAR
        International Series 372. British Archaeological
        Reports, Oxford.

1991   Investigations at the Pikillacta Site: A Provincial
        Huari Center in the Valley of Cuzco. In *Huari
        Administrative Structures: Prehistoric Monumental
        Architecture and State Government*, edited by William
        H. Isbell and Gordon F. McEwan, pp. 93–119.
        Dumbarton Oaks Research Library and Collection,
        Washington, DC.

1996   Archaeological Investigations at Pikillacta, a Wari Site
        in Peru. *Journal of Field Archaeology* 23(2):169–186.

McEwan, Gordon F., Melissa Chatfield, and Arminda
        Gibaja
2002   The Archaeology of Inca Origins: Excavations at
        Chokepukio, Cuzco, Peru. In *Andean Archaeology
        I: Variations in Sociopolitical Organization*, edited
        by William H. Isbell and Helaine Silverman,

pp. 287–301. Kluwer Academic/Plenum Press, New York.

Moseley, Michael E.

1983   The Good Old Days Were Better: Agrarian Collapse and Tectonics. *American Anthropologist* 85(4): 773–799.

2000   Confronting Natural Disaster. In *Environmental Disaster and the Archaeology of Human Response*, edited by Garth Bawden and Richard M. Reycraft, pp. 219–223. Anthropological Papers of the Maxwell Museum of Anthropology, no. 7. Maxwell Museum of Anthropology, Albuquerque, NM.

Murra, John V.

1960   Rite and Crop in the Inca State. In *Culture in History*, edited by Stanley Diamond, pp. 393–407. Columbia University Press, New York..

Rappaport, Roy A.

1979   *Ecology, Meaning, and Religion*. North Atlantic Books, Richmond, CA.

Read, Dwight W., and Steven A LeBlanc

2003   Population Growth, Carrying Capacity, and Conflict (with Comment and Reply). *Current Anthropology* 44(1):59–85.

Salomon, Frank, and George Urioste (eds.)

1991   *The Huarochirí Manuscript: A Testament of Ancient and Colonial Andean Religion*. University of Texas Press, Austin.

Satterlee, Dennis R., Michael E. Moseley, David K. Keefer, and Jorge E. Tapia A.

2001   The Miraflores El Niño Disaster: Convergent Catastrophes and Agrarian Change in Southern Peru. *Andean Past* 6:95–116.

Seligmann, Linda J., and Stephen G. Bunker

1993   An Andean Irrigation System: Ecological Visions and Social Organization. In *Irrigation at High Altitudes: The Social Organization of Water Control Systems in the Andes*, edited by William P. Mitchell and David Guillet, pp. 203–232. Society for Latin American Anthropology Publication Series 12. American Anthropological Association, Washington, DC.

Sherbondy, Jeanette E.

1993   Water and Power: The Role of Irrigation Districts in the Transition from Inca to Spanish Cuzco. In *Irrigation at High Altitudes: The Social Organization of Water Control Systems in the Andes*, edited by William P. Mitchell and David Guillet, pp. 69–97. Society for Latin American Anthropology Publication Series 12. American Anthropological Association, Washington, DC.

Stirling, Stuart

1999   *The Last Conquistador: Mansio Serra de Leguizamón and the Conquest of the Incas*. Sutton Publishing Limited, Phoenix Mill. Stroud, Gloucestershire, England.

Thompson, Lonnie G., E. Mosley-Thompson, J. F. Bolzan, and B. R. Koci

1985   A 1500-Year Record of Tropical Precipitation in Ice Cores from the Quelccaya Ice Cap, Peru. *Science* 229:971–973.

Toledo, Francisco de

1940 [1571]   Información comenzada en el Valle de Yucay . . . Junio 2–Septiembre 6 de 1571. In *Don Francisco de Toledo, supremo organizador del Perú: Su vida, su obra (1515–1582)*, vol. 2, *Sus informaciones sobre los Incas (1570–1572)*, pp. 122–177. Robert Leillier, editor. Espasa-Calpe, Buenos Aires.

Williams, Patrick Ryan

2002   A Re-examination of Disaster-Induced Collapse in the Case of the Andean Highland States: Wari and Tiwanaku. *World Archaeology* 33(3):361–374.

Winterhalder, Bruce

1993   The Ecological Basis of Water Management in the Central Andes: Rainfall and Temperature in Southern Peru. In *Irrigation at High Altitudes: The Social Organization of Water Control Systems in the Andes*, edited by William P. Mitchell and David Guillet, pp. 21–67. Society for Latin American Anthropology Publication Series 12. American Anthropological Association, Washington, DC.

Wittfogel, Karl A.

1957   *Oriental Despotism: A Comparative Study of Total Power*. Yale University Press, New Haven, CT.

Zapata Rodríguez, Julinho

1997   Arquitectura y contextos funerarios Wari en Batan Urqu, Cusco. *Boletín de Arqueología PUCP* 1:165–206.

CHAPTER 21

VOLCANOES, EARTHQUAKES, AND THE SPANISH COLONIAL WINE INDUSTRY OF SOUTHERN PERU

PRUDENCE M. RICE

RECENT ARCHAEOLOGICAL AND HISTORICAL research indicates that earthquakes and volcanic eruptions—particularly the Huaynaputina eruption in 1600—influenced the Colonial wine-based economy of the Moquegua (or Osmore) region of far southern Peru. Study of documentary sources suggests that political agendas may have colored official accounts of the disaster. Overall, Moquegua seemed to have suffered less from the eruption than did the larger center of Arequipa to the north, a conclusion supported by recent volcanological analysis. Eruptions and earthquakes exacerbated existing socioeconomic stresses in the region, and the responses of Colonial settlers to the disasters included the adoption of new patron saints against earthquakes, resettlement of native Andean laborers, and diversified cropping and marketing strategies.

Between 1985 and 1989 I directed the Moquegua Bodegas Project, an archaeological and historical research project focused on the growth and development of the Colonial period viticultural agro-industry in the valley of the Río Osmore in far southern Peru. Two summer field seasons of survey followed by three summers of excavations resulted in the identification of 130 wine hacienda sites in this narrow valley, situated particularly along its rocky margins. Archaeologically, the haciendas could be recognized as such primarily by

the presence of enormous ceramic storage jars (*tinajas*) for wine and brandy or stone-lined *lagares* (vats for crushing grapes) associated with one or more large rectangular adobe storage rooms (*bodegas* proper), usually in ruins. Of these sites, twenty-eight of the best preserved were mapped and shovel-tested, and four of these were more intensively excavated. The findings of this project have been reported in various venues, including theses and dissertations (Smith 1991; van Beck 1991; deFrance 1993; Natt 1997), chapters and articles (Rice 1994, 1995, 1996a–c, 1997, 1998; Rice and Smith 1989; Rice and Van Beck 1993; Smith 1997), numerous presentations at professional meetings, and a book manuscript I am currently preparing.

The purpose of this chapter is not to revisit the strictly archaeological data pertaining to Moquegua's Colonial wine and brandy production but rather to situate this agro-industry within a broader environmental context: specifically, its responses to the frequent and unpredictable earthquakes and volcanic eruptions that plagued the region's Colonial and later history.

The wine and brandy industry of Peru began when the earliest Spanish colonists introduced vines and wines into Andean South America in the mid-sixteenth century. First established around Lima, vineyards spread rapidly southward through the irrigated valleys of the Pacific coast and thrived in the expansive atmosphere of early viceregal prosperity. Wine was in demand both as a beverage and for use in Catholic sacramental rites, but supplies were always critically scarce in the colonies because of the Spanish Crown's mercantilist economic policies. The establishment of viticulture in Colonial Peru was prompted not only by constant shortages but also because the settlers were eager to develop extra sources of income to meet rising taxation and costs of living in the viceroyalty. Wine was a convenient solution to both problems, and the result was an explosive growth of vineyards and wine-making haciendas in the river valleys of the southern Peruvian Pacific coast in the late sixteenth century. One of these was the Moquegua Valley, as the middle region of the Osmore River drainage is known.

MOQUEGUA'S PHYSICAL AND CULTURAL SETTING

Moquegua's wine industry was established in an area that was, in some respects, not too dissimilar in its agricultural potential from the hot, dry Mediterranean region of the southern Spanish homeland. Core components of the traditional Iberian agropastoral economy—sheep, goats, wheat, grapes, olives, and citrus—were easily transferred to Colonial Peru. This transference also facilitated duplication of the Spanish social and economic way of life in the distant colony.

Natural Environment

The environment of the Andean region of South America is characterized by pronounced compression of altitudinal zones and extremes of elevation and climate. The arid to hyperarid Atacama-Peruvian desert of the southern coastal plain is drained by a series of steep, deeply dissected northeast-to-southwest-flowing river courses, with headwaters high in the sierra. These rivers provide ample water for irrigation, and from prehistoric through modern times the mountainsides and valley bottomlands were turned into lush oases, brought into cultivation by means of vast systems of canals and terraces.

The Río Osmore is one of the many abrupt streams traversing the southern Peruvian desert (Figure 21.1), descending approximately 5100 m over a horizontal distance of only about 140 km from its headwaters to the coast. Where the Osmore's three tributaries join, roughly 70 km from the river's mouth, the precipitous descent of the river moderates, forming a broader mid-

valley area—the Moquegua Valley—that became the focus of Colonial period occupation. Lying between 1700 and 1100 m elevation, the 29-km-long Moquegua Valley provides a total area of some 3,200 ha for cultivation, including some of the best soils in southern Peru (ONERN 1976). The town of Moquegua was founded on the southern bank of the Osmore near the confluence of its tributaries, and it was here that Moquegua's wine industry was established.

With respect to climate and weather, Moquegua is pleasant year-round, with moderate temperatures, low humidity, and abundant sunshine. Moquegua experiences temperature variations typical of tropics and deserts, with little seasonal fluctuation but sharp diurnal changes, days being warm to hot and nights often chilly. Given its desert location, Moquegua receives very little precipitation. Rainfall at the coastal city of Arica, Chile, just south of the border with Peru, is approximately 1 mm annually.

Two efforts have been made to reconstruct some general climatic conditions in Andean South America during the Colonial period: a study of ice cores and an analysis of possible El Niño occurrences. Two sample cores from the Quelccaya ice cap (13° 56' S, 70° 50' W), a well-studied glacial deposit located some 200 km northwest of Lake Titicaca on the eastern Andean slope (see Figure 21.1), provide indications of weather in southern Peru during Colonial times (Thompson et al. 1986). Concentrations of particulate matter and changes in oxygen isotopes, among other data, plus analysis of Colonial source materials (Hocquenghem and Ortlieb 1992) suggest alternating periods of wet and dry, and often extremely cold, conditions from AD 1500 to 1720, followed by an extremely dry interval from AD 1720 to 1860.

The El Niño (also called the Southern Oscillation or ENSO event) refers to a warming of Pacific Ocean currents that brings about changed rainfall patterns. In the valleys of the western Andes, ENSO events have been associated with unusually heavy rainfall and flooding in both prehistoric (see Moseley 1987; Moore 1991; Shimada et al. 1991) and historic times (Quinn et al. 1986; Hocquenghem and Ortlieb 1992; Ortlieb 1995). Between the mid-sixteenth century and AD 1900, there were some thirteen ENSO events in the Andes that could be categorized as strong or very strong. Although El Niño events seem to have been felt differently in the Atacama region (southern Peru and northern Chile) as compared with northern Peru and central Chile, some of these resulted in flooding in Moquegua. Chabert and

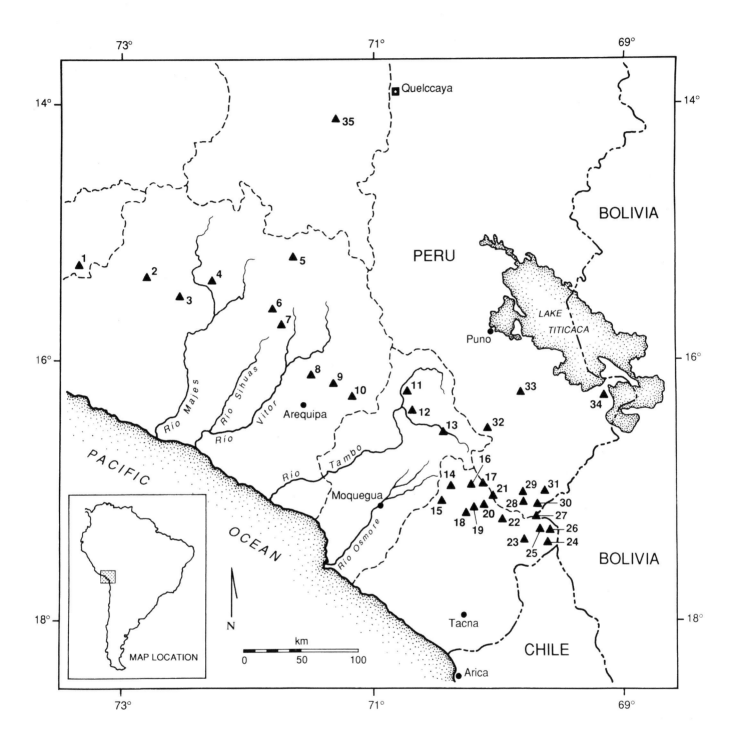

Figure 21.1. The Departments of Arequipa, Moquegua, Tacna, and Puno in southern Peru, showing locations mentioned in text and sites of volcanoes. (After Documental del Perú, 1983, pp. 20–22.) Key: Department of Ayacucho: *1*, Sara Sara. Department of Arequipa: *2*, Solimana; *3*, Coropuna; *4*, Puca Maura (highest volcano in the "valley of volcanoes" in Andagua); *5*, Suquihua; *6*, Sabancaya; *7*, Ampato; *8*, Chachani; *9*, Misti; *10*, Picchu Picchu. Department of Moquegua: *11*, Ubinas; *12*, Huaynaputina; *13*, Ticsane. Department of Tacna: *14*, Tutupaca; *15*, Chuquianante; *16*, Carcave; *17*, Iscailarjanco; *18*, Yucamane; *19*, Calientes; *20*, López Extraña; *21*, Chajina Chico; *22*, Iscampu; *23*, Paucarani; *24*, Condorpico; *25*, Pisarane; *26*, Jucure; *27*, Chila. Department of Puno: *28*, Soravico; *29*, Huancune; *30*, Huancure; *31*, Toccoraque; *32*, Arechua; *33*, Antajave; *34*, Kapia.

Dubosc (1905:26) report that a terrible flood occurred in Moquegua in February 1900 (possibly accompanying an El Niño event; Quinn et al. 1986; see also Ortlieb 1995). This flood destroyed vineyards in Moquegua and uprooted olive trees on the coast, and deposited as much as 1 m of rocky, sandy debris. Similar damage likely accompanied heavy rains and floods in the valley in 1750 (Kuon Cabello 1981:377), 1857, and 1860 (Ortlieb 1995) (Table 21.1).

Cultural and Historical Setting

Social, economic, religious, and administrative affairs in Colonial southern Peru were dominated by Arequipa, 110 km to the northwest, the earliest Spanish city to be founded in the region. There, grapevines were planted almost immediately after European settlement, and productive vineyards were in place on the northern and eastern edges of the city by the mid-1550s (Davies 1984:49; Brown 1986:40). About the same time that vines

Table 21.1. Colonial period and recent earthquakes and volcanic eruptions in southern Peru.

Year	Date, Time, and Event	Magnitude[a] A	B	Estimated Range (km)
1582	January 22, 11:30 a.m.	X		1,000
1582	July 2—Huaynaputina eruption?			
1600	February 19 (Sat.), 11 a.m.–1 p.m. (?)—earthquake and Huaynaputina eruption	IX		600[b]
1604	November 24 (Wed.), 1:30 p.m.	XI	8.7+	1,500
1615				
1618				
1630	November 27			
1655	November 13			
1666	May 20, 3–4 a.m.			
1667	Omate eruption			
1668	April 23			
1687	October 21, 6–7 a.m.	IX	8.0	1,000
1715	August 22, 9–0 p.m.	<VII	7.5	
1725	January 8, 8 a.m.		7.5	
1732	January 23, 7 p.m.			
1769?				
1782?				
1784	May 13, 7:30 a.m.[c]—earthquake and eruption, Misti	XI	8.4	1,000
1787	March 22, 10 a.m.			
1826	—Misti volcano eruption			
1830	August—Misti volcano eruption			
1831	August—earthquake and eruption, Misti			
1833	September 13 (18?)		7.2+	
1865	—Ubinas eruption			
1867	May 28—Ubinas eruption			
1868	August 13, 5:15 p.m.—earthquake and eruption, Misti	XI	9.0	1,300
1869	September—Misti eruption			
1937	—Ubinas lava flow			
1948	May 11			
1956	—Ubinas, moderate pyroclastic eruption, 15 days			
2001	June 23		8.4	

Sources: Cobo 1890 [1653]:215; Vázquez de Espinosa 1948 [ca. 1629]:470, 474; Barriga 1951; Casertano 1963; Kuon Cabello 1981:136–137; Documental del Perú, 1983:22; Dorbath et al. 1990; http://earthquake.usgs.gov/activity/latest/eq_01_06_23.

[a] A, estimate of seismic-moment magnitude, or Mw (from Dorbath et al. 1990). B, Mercalli intensity (from Barriga 1951).
[b] Approximate range of heavy ashfall.
[c] Barriga (1951:323–335) reports an almost daily series of aftershocks lasting through mid-August.

were planted around Arequipa, some of its early settlers began pushing southward in search of additional agricultural lands to cultivate (Davies 1984:134). The Moquegua (Osmore) Valley was an attractive and reasonably close destination for migrants from Arequipa, and the new "Spanish" town of Moquegua maintained intimate ties to that larger center throughout the Colonial period. By 1567, vineyards had been successfully established in Moquegua, and settlers soon were producing wine.

The wine industry of Arequipa and Moquegua flourished as part of Peru's "wine boom" during the late sixteenth century. Not coincidentally, there was at the same time a "mining boom," as these were the decades of peak production in the silver mines of "Alto Peru" (modern Bolivia) (Cole 1985). The largest of the mining towns was Potosí, which grew rapidly to become a populous and wealthy city, and its population of Spaniards, Andeans, and slaves consumed vast quantities of wine produced in the coastal valleys of southern Peru. By the end of the sixteenth century, however, the region's early wine boom had collapsed as a consequence of overproduction, a glutted market, and a steep drop in wine prices.

Despite the "bust" of the wine market, production of grapes and wine continued in the estates of the southern valleys. Haciendas seem to have coped economically in part by diversifying agricultural production, dedicating more land to wheat, introduced sugarcane, and indigenous chili peppers. In the early seventeenth century, *pisco* brandy began to be distilled from grapes on the central Peruvian coast (Huertas 1988) and perhaps also in Moquegua, and emerged as the drink of choice for residents of the coastal cities as well as the mining regions. During most of the eighteenth century the region enjoyed stunning prosperity in an expansive "brandy boom" (Brown 1986; Rice 1996a), but this too had unraveled by the end of the century. It was within this context of booms and busts, and cycles of production of the region's silver mines, that the wine and brandy industry grew to dominate the Colonial economic history of southern Peru in general and the Moquegua Valley in particular.

VOLCANOES AND VOLCANISM IN SOUTHERN PERU

Wine and brandy production not only had to ride out the uncertainties of regional and international economic cycles, it also had to weather natural disasters.

The history of Colonial southern Peru was repeatedly punctuated by devastating earthquakes and volcanic eruptions. Indeed, the entire Andes mountain chain is active tectonically today, and thirty-five volcanoes are known in the southern Peruvian departments of Arequipa, Moquegua, and Tacna. Misti, Chachani, and Pichu Pichu north and east of Arequipa (nos. 8, 9, and 10 on Figure 21.1) are perhaps the most dramatic examples of these primarily andesitic stratovolcanoes, although another eighty-five small cones are noted in the "valley of the volcanoes" in Andagua (no. 4 on Figure 21.1), northwest of Arequipa (Documental del Perú 1983:17–29). The Arequipa-Moquegua region was the only area in the Peruvian Andes to have experienced major volcanism in Colonial and recent times, although it should be noted that the Pichincha volcano far to the north, near Quito, Ecuador, also erupted in the late sixteenth century.

While we can surmise that earthquakes and volcanic eruptions would have played a role in human affairs in prehistoric times too, we lack a good record of their occurrence. Misti volcano near Arequipa is said to have erupted violently in the mid-fifteenth century during the reign of the Inka Yupanqui, destroying the prehistoric community at the base of the volcano and killing its inhabitants. The volcano hurled quantities of ash so high into the air that it fell as much as 150 leagues (ca. 600 km) distant from Arequipa (Kuon Cabello 1981:134).

Although the Colonial period earthquakes were not measured on a quantitative scale as they are today, we know from reports of structural damage that many were quite severe and had catastrophic consequences for the region. Victor Barriga (1951) compiled these reports on Colonial period temblors in Arequipa to estimate their intensity using the Mercalli scale (see also Dorbath et al. 1990 for a review of historical Peruvian earthquakes and scientific estimates of their magnitude). For example, as a result of an earthquake in Arequipa in January 1582, estimated at Mercalli Grade X ("very destructive"), "all the wines and aguardientes of the valleys were destroyed, along with the jars and bodegas. Most of the horses and beasts of burden died, and all that was left were swarms of flies and mice" (Barriga 1951:4; my translation). The most severe damage appears to have been felt north and west of the city (Dorbath et al. 1990:567). Considerable debate ensued in the following months as to whether the city of Arequipa should be moved and rebuilt in a new and less dangerous location (e.g., Barriga 1951:7–9, 20–22). In 1589 the viceroy of Peru ordered that 500 native Andean laborers from settlements within a radius of 25 leagues (100 km) be brought in to help rebuild Arequipa (Barriga 1951:32–34).

In the Department of Moquegua, three volcanoes lie in the upper reaches of the Tambo River, north of the Osmore: Huaynaputina, Ticsane, and Ubinas. Huaynaputina volcano (no. 12 on Figure 21.1), also known variously (and confusingly) as Omate, Ubinas, or Quinistaquillas, lies at lat. 16° 35′ S and long. 70°52′ W. Geographically, it sits ca. 70 km east of Arequipa and 60 km north-northwest of Moquegua, with its "peak" (it lacks a crater) at 4877 m above mean sea level. To the north, near the indigenous community of Ubinas, lies the Ubinas volcano (lat. 16° 36′ S, long. 70° 90′ W), roughly 25 km north of Huaynaputina and 72 km east of Arequipa. Ubinas volcano (no. 11 on Figure 21.1), with a summit at 5,672 m and a crater 1,500 m wide, is not dormant, as it regularly rumbles and emits gases, and it erupted with ashfall as recently as 1969 (http://users.bendnet.com/bjensen/volcano/southamerica/peru-ubinas.html). Ticsane volcano (no. 13 on Figure 21.1) lies ca. 50 km southeast of Huaynaputina. In addition to these volcanoes, the Department of Moquegua is known for geothermal activity, with numerous thermal springs and baths in the upper reaches of the Río Tambo.

Huaynaputina: February 1600

Perhaps the most famous (or infamous) volcanic event in far southern Peru during early Colonial times was the eruption of Huaynaputina volcano on Saturday, February 19, 1600. The best-known accounts of Huaynaputina's eruption—albeit not eyewitness accounts—are those of the carmelite friar Antonio Vázquez de Espinosa (1948 [ca. 1629]:469–473), who wrote in 1629, and Bernabé Cobo (1890 [1653]:203–213), writing nearly twenty-five years later in 1653 (see also de Silva et al. 2000). According to these reports, Huaynaputina's eruption was preceded by three days of earthquakes and was followed by another 200 tremors in the next twenty-four hours. Some of the initial earthquakes heralding the eruption have been estimated as measuring Grade IX ("destructive") on the Mercalli scale (Barriga 1951:53). (Given this accounting, it is odd that these events were not included in Dorbath et al.'s [1990] discussion of major earthquakes in southern Peru.)

The damage from the earthquakes was compounded by destruction caused by the volcano's explosive eruption, which has been called one of the largest eruptions in historic times, comparable to that of Krakatau in 1883 (de Silva and Zielinski 1998). Recent volcanological analyses indicate that the eruption occurred in three stages between February 19 through March 6 (Adams et al. 2001; see also Marino et al. 2002, who identify five phases between February 19 and March 15). The ashfall from the eruption covered an area of at least 300,000 km² (de Silva and Zielinski 1998). Since its 1600 plinian eruption, Huaynaputina has lacked a crater and is not recognizable as a volcano today because it lacks a conical shape.

The cataclysm began at 5:00 p.m., when the volcano started to hurl massive quantities of tephra, ash, cinders, and large rocks into the air (Cobo 1890 [1653]:207). Interestingly, in contemporary descriptions of the disaster these rocks were compared in size to the earthenware vessels used in the region's wine industry, as ranging from fist-sized to the size of dos botijas (two "botijas," small jugs holding ca. 8 liters) or as large as medianas tinajas (medium-sized tinaja, which held ca. 400 liters). Accompanied by terrifying displays of thunder and lightning, heavy ashfall continued off and on for about ten days, darkening the sky so much that there was no daylight (Cobo 1890 [1653]:205). Ash rained heavily in Arequipa, its weight causing the roofs of dwellings to collapse. To the south, ash from the eruption fell on Tarapacá and Antofagasta in Chile, while to the north an ash layer from Huaynaputina has been identified in the Quelccaya ice core (Thompson et al. 1986). The actual depth of the ash deposit in Arequipa is not known with certainty: A soldier quoted by Vázquez de Espinosa (see also Barriga 1951:184) claimed that in Arequipa, the ash blanket was a "vara" (ca. 80 cm) in depth, while official witnesses testifying before the Arequipa cabildo (town council) claimed that the ash layer was a palmo (ca. 18 cm) or more in depth (Barriga 1951:68, 72). For months the ash continued to rain from the sky. The prior of the Convento of San Agustín in Arequipa stated in March 1601 that even then, thirteen months after the February 1600 eruption, the sky remained hazy because of ash still suspended in the air, and witnesses claimed that ash continued to fall through October of that year (Barriga 1951:149). Volcanological and climatological studies indicate that the ash in the air had worldwide effects in lowering temperatures in 1600 and 1601 (de Silva and Zielinski 1998).

Huaynaputina also belched forth huge lava flows, and these, together with the ash, buried small indigenous towns in the sierra and their inhabitants. At least 200 persons died in these pueblos (Cobo 1890 [1653]:209); of the indigenous populace surviving the tragedy, many individuals moved to Moquegua (Kuon Cabello 1981:136). Lava, boulders, and ash dammed the channel of the Río Tambo in various places, forming huge lakes. When the waters broke through, they surged downstream, causing massive washouts, landslides, and other damage to the productive lands on the riverbanks, thus completing the devastation of the landscape (Cobo 1890 [1653]:211–212). Throughout southwestern Peru, the ejecta of the Huaynaputina eruption destroyed field crops, gardens, orchards, olive groves, and vineyards (with mature grapes on them), suffocated livestock and fowl, boiled fish in the rivers, clogged irrigation canals, blocked roads, toppled buildings, and rendered the soil sterile and unproductive (see Davies 1984:95).

Subsequent Earthquakes and Eruptions

Earthquakes are frequent in southern Peru because it is the region where two major tectonic plates, the Nazca and South American, are converging at a rate of 78 mm per year (http://earthquake.usgs.gov/activity/latest/eq_01_06_23). On November 24, 1604, around 1:30 p.m., less than five years after Huaynaputina's eruption, a massive earthquake struck the southern coast. Colonial estimates suggest that it could be felt for some 300 leagues (ca. 1,200–1,500 km), north as far as Lima and inland as far as Cusco (Cobo 1890 [1653]:215–219). In Arequipa the main shock rumbled for many minutes and aftershocks continued for ten to twelve days. Many buildings were destroyed, as were numerous native pueblos outside the city, and forty people were killed. In the interior there were great landslides, and along the coast a series of tsunamis reached 10–15 m in height, completely devastating Arica (Cobo 1890 [1653]:221; Dorbath et al. 1990:560, 571). In Moquegua the damage was no less than in Arequipa, with massive destruction at the wine haciendas and nearby indigenous sierra pueblos lying in ruins (Cobo 1890 [1653]:220). The Richter magnitude of the 1604 earthquake has been estimated between 8 and 9 (Dorbath et al. 1990:571).

Disastrous volcanic eruptions and earthquakes persisted during the seventeenth through nineteenth centuries and into modern times. Some twenty tremors—often described as "large" or "great," and usually accompanied by destructive tsunamis on the coast—occurred in southern and central Peru (see Dorbath et al. 1990:Table 3). These events were frequently accompanied by a "ripple effect" of economic consequences that extended well beyond the immediate physical destruction. For example, an earthquake in 1687 was felt widely from north-central through southern coastal Peru, but its impact on agriculture reverberated much farther to the south. Following the tremor, central Peru's wheat

crop failed, a result of either fine dust remaining in the atmosphere or *roya*, a parasitic fungus that attacks cereals (Barcelli 1982:267). Whatever the cause, this agricultural catastrophe meant that wheat had to be imported into Lima. This then spurred a "wheat rush" in Chile, as producers shifted from pasturage and vineyards to cereals (Wallerstein 1980:152, n. 119). The abandonment of Chilean vineyards—many of which supplied the markets at the Potosí mines—in turn would have favorably affected southern Peru's wine industry, especially that of Moquegua, which lay on the edge of the quake's most severe effects.

Other eruptions and earthquakes include that of the Omate volcano, which is said to have erupted in 1667, while the "Ubinas" volcano had two explosive eruptions in 1865 and 1867 and emitted a lava flow in 1937. Misti volcano, just east of Arequipa, erupted in 1784, 1826, 1830, 1831, 1868, and 1869 (Casertano 1963:1420); the 1784 and 1868 eruptions were accompanied by major earthquakes in the region. Of all the eruptions and earthquakes occurring in southern Peru, the only event of a severity comparable to the 1600 Huaynaputina eruption was the earthquake of August 13, 1868. This temblor occurred near the end of a decades-long decline in Moquegua's economic fortunes, and by the end of the century the wine industry had collapsed. A variety of factors, internal and external, are implicated in this demise, and, not surprisingly, one of them is tectonic activity.

The nineteenth century had begun with a period of cooler and drier weather in the Andes (Thompson et al. 1986) that may have stressed agricultural systems, especially in areas such as Moquegua, where frosts and water shortages were chronic problems. In addition, Peru's viticultural industry was struggling with the collapse of the eighteenth-century brandy boom and competition from cane liquor (*aguardiente de caña*, made from sugarcane). Regional and transnational political affairs, particularly the wars of independence from the Spanish Crown, also disrupted normal commerce. In the late nineteenth century, three additional factors precipitated the collapse of Moquegua's wine industry. One was the outbreak of a multiyear war with Chile, during which Moquegua was invaded four times. Another was an epidemic of phylloxera, which coincided with an outbreak in European vineyards. The third contributing factor was the earthquake of 1868, which resulted in major destruction and economic disruption throughout southern Peru.

Beginning at 5:15 p.m. on August 13, 1868, and lasting five to eight minutes by various reports (Barriga

1951:339–398; Kuon Cabello 1981:123–126; Carpio Muñoz 1990:510–512), the temblor and tsunamis destroyed houses, churches, wineries, and other structures in Arequipa, Moquegua, Arica, and as far south as Iquique in northern Chile. There was great loss of life in Moquegua and elsewhere; 150 people were killed in Arequipa, some, no doubt, as a consequence of the simultaneous eruption of Misti volcano. The Mercalli intensity of the major quake is estimated at Grade XI (Richter at 9.0), and intense aftershock activity continued through the next four months (Barriga 1951:399–402). The 1868 tremor has been compared to the massively destructive 1604 earthquake, both of which propagated two of "the greatest tsunamis ever observed in the Pacific Ocean" (Dorbath et al. 1990:563, 576).

Within the context of such devastation it is interesting to recall a story reported by Cúneo-Vidal (1978:539). This tale, doubtless apocryphal, concerns a "prediction" made by one of the Jesuit fathers of Alto Peru who was departing that country after the king of Spain ordered the Jesuits to leave all the Spanish colonies. This priest, described as a "geologist" of sorts, denounced the deportation in Arica on August 13, 1768, and predicted that within 100 years Arica would be destroyed by an earthquake and tsunami.

More recently in southern Peru, a moderate temblor of about 6.0 occurred in August 1987, during Bodegas Project fieldwork, resulting in minor damage to several Colonial period wine hacienda structures. A far more severe earthquake of magnitude 8.4 occurred on June 23, 2001, with aftershocks above 7.0 (http://earthquake/usgs.gov/activity/latest/eq_01_23_06), resulting in major destruction and loss of life in southern Peru, as well as great damage to the historic bodega structures in Moquegua. It had been noted that "great" earthquakes in southern Peru tended to occur at intervals of 100 years, and the region was well overdue for another disaster (Dorbath et al. 1990:551, 563); perhaps this 2001 quake was the anticipated one. Still unexplored is the possibility of connections between major volcanic eruptions in this area and El Niño events (see, e.g., Handler and Andsager 1990; Walker 1995).

IMPACT OF VOLCANISM ON THE EARLY WINE INDUSTRY: THE 1600 HUAYNAPUTINA ERUPTION

Records in the Arequipa archives provide copious documentation of the extent of the 1600 Huaynaputina disaster in the region (see also de Silva et al. 2000). Two weeks after the start of the Huaynaputina eruption, on March 1, 1600, the *procurador general* (legal representative) of Arequipa, Alonso de Medina, took testimony from eight religious officials from Arequipa and Cusco in preparing a petition requesting help for the city from the king of Spain and the viceroy of Peru. In the style of the time, the testimony of the eight witnesses (Barriga 1951:60–77) is remarkably uniform, indeed almost formulaic, with repeated reference to quasi-biblical measures of forty. For example, eyewitnesses repeatedly referred to the heavy ashfall obscuring the sky and creating night-like darkness that lasted forty hours, and noted that the ashfall destroyed crops and pastures around the city within a distance of 40 leagues (roughly 220 km) (Barriga 1951:62, 64–68, 71, 74–76). Such a radius would extend as far south as Tacna and Arica, east to the Lake Titicaca Basin, and north to the Mages Valley.

Regional recovery from the devastation was slow. Another set of testimony was gathered a year later, on March 26, 1601, by the cabildo of Arequipa for transmittal to the king of Spain. This testimony was intended to inform the king on the state of the city one year after its destruction and consisted of responses to nine "questions," including what was effectively a demand that witnesses affirm that this recent calamity was far more damaging than the 1582 earthquake. In this series of documents, witness after witness (again religious officials) reiterated the environmental devastation and impoverishment of the inhabitants (Barriga 1951:94–119). Father Arce of the Convento La Merced made the desired comparison most succinctly:

> The damage that took place in this city with the earthquake of 20 years ago was only the collapse of houses and buildings, which were reconstructed at little cost. The people of the city continued to enjoy their haciendas after the earthquake was over, and gathered their harvests of wine, wheat, and corn without losing anything more than the buildings of their homes. But what happened with the eruption of this volcano and the continuing rain of ash and sand is most notable in the harm that it has caused, because all the fruits of the land have been lost: vineyards, fields of corn and other grains and vegetables with which the people sustain themselves. Many of these vineyards are completely lost for having been buried by volcanic ash, and others are so damaged that their owners have abandoned them and neither want nor are able to improve them. (Barriga 1951:106; my translation)

Looming large in the witnesses' statements was the damage to the vineyards of the Vitor, Siguas, and Majes valleys "north" (actually west) of Arequipa. Although estimates varied from individual to individual, the destruction was starkly described. Mercedarian Father Arce said, for example, that estates "that used to make 46,000 botijas of wine were able to make only 150 this year, and others 100 and others even less, and there was a vineyard that was expected to yield 2000 botijas of wine and it only yielded 30" (Barriga 1951:105; my translation). Father Diego Pérez of the San Agustín church said that many vineyards never produced grapes; in Vitor where they had expected a yield of 80,000 botijas of wine in 1601, they got only 6,000, and this was expected to be vinegar rather than wine (Barriga 1951:197, 198). Father Domingo Lezo of Cusco noted further that, because of the failure of other crops (especially wheat and corn), food had to be brought in from as far away as Cusco, the Yucay Valley, Cañas y Canches, and other places (Barriga 1951:111).

It is interesting to compare these accounts of economic upheaval in Arequipa with a slightly later description of Moquegua. Friar Antonio Vázquez de Espinosa, originally from Jerez de la Frontera in Spain, traveled through Moquegua in 1618 or 1619 en route from Arequipa to Arica. In his travels he noted not only the many olive groves and vineyards on the coast around Ilo but also the abundance of fruit trees in the middle Osmore Valley, where there were

> quinces, peaches, camuesas, figs and other fruits of Spain and the land, good melons, there are sugar mills and in the lower valley many plots and fields of wheat, corn, garbanzos, beans, and other grains, and a lot of ají, or pepper, which is harvested in this valley . . . and it is well supplied and rich and is a paradise. (Vázquez de Espinosa 1948 [ca. 1629]:476; my translation)

This description was written, it must be remembered, less than two decades after an economic and ecological catastrophe in the region caused by the earthquakes and Huaynaputina eruption in 1600, followed by an even more severe quake in 1604.

The question that arises is how to reconcile Vázquez's statement about Moquegua's bountiful agricultural "paradise" in 1618 with the cataclysmic destruction of fields, canals, and buildings by massive ashfalls and two destructive earthquakes less than two decades earlier. Was Vázquez painting—intentionally or unintentionally—a false picture of Moquegua's verdant landscape? Were Arequipa's official witnesses exaggerating the

destruction? Did Moquegua—although lying physically closer to Huaynaputina than Arequipa—receive less of the ashfall than did Arequipa and its adjacent valleys? How quickly can soils recover from the deposition of massive quantities of volcanic ash? Answers to these questions can be attempted, though most efforts at resolving them are speculative. Here it is appropriate to give further consideration to the nature of the written records, both the official accounts prepared for the king of Spain and the later travelers' descriptions of the region.

First, concerning Vázquez's observations, his motivations are nearly impossible to ascertain from this remove. I know of no specific reason why he might lie or provide a distorted picture of the lands he visited. He could have been struck by some similarities of this viticultural region to the vineyards of his homeland in Jerez and been impressed on that account; at the same time, he may have wished to provide an exciting, glowing travelogue. The remarkable similarity of accounts by Cobo and Vázquez, writing nearly twenty-five years apart, suggests the possibility that Cobo might have based his story on Vázquez's earlier work. On the other hand, it is equally or even more likely that both writers extracted their descriptions from documents in the Arequipa archives (as well as in the Archivo General de las Indias; see Barriga 1951:55–141). Vázquez, however, supplemented his story with an eyewitness account of Huaynaputina's eruption given him by a soldier named Pedro de Vivar (see Barriga 1951:180–184).

Aside from their remarkable similarity, another striking feature of these travelers' accounts is the abundance of detail on the disastrous consequences of this eruption for Arequipa and the utter lack of such reference for Moquegua itself, lying little more than 100 km southeast of Arequipa and populated by families with long-standing ties to that important city. Vázquez (1948 [ca. 1629]:464), for example, commented repeatedly on the quantities of volcanic ash blanketing the landscape around the Majes and Vitor valleys well to the north of Arequipa, and the resultant inhabitability of the terrain. Yet when he reached the Moquegua Valley to the south, there was no mention of ash there, and although he remarked on ash deposits between Moquegua and Locumba, there is no other mention of ash as he traveled farther south. Vázquez ended his itemization of the abundant fruits and vegetables cultivated in the Moquegua Valley by describing the region as a "paradise." Perhaps sufficient rainfall occurred between 1600 and 1618 (see Quinn et al. 1986; see also

Hocquenghem and Ortlieb 1992) to wash through the Moquegua Valley, scouring out the ash and contributing to the lush vegetation.

The official documents prepared in Arequipa at times seem a bit contrived, and the religious officials providing testimony might have wanted to exaggerate the extent of the disaster in order to gain a measure of tax relief from the Crown. Recent geological studies, however, clearly underscore the nearly unimaginable magnitude of the eruption. For their part, the Spanish crown could have viewed the 1600/1604 eruption and earthquakes in southern Peru as a godsend, providing an excuse for terminating the upstart wine industry in the region and the economic threat it posed (Davies 1984:95). But the king of Spain did not formally put an end to it. Instead, royal officials granted the region some tax relief: On August 11, 1601, viceroy Luis de Velasco suspended Arequipa's sales tax (*alcabala*) payments (Barriga 1951:120–122), and this suspension was reiterated and extended after the 1604 quake. (Similar tax relief was again granted after the destruction wrought by the 1687 earthquake.) In addition, as noted, royal officials in Lima sent Andean laborers from Cailloma to help repair the physical damage in Arequipa (Barriga 1951:84, 85, 87). Nonetheless, even as late as 1620 the ash from the Huaynaputina eruption continued to be blamed for diminished production around Arequipa, and the reduced alcabala was extended yet another four years by the viceroy (Barriga 1951:230).

New evidence indicates that substantially less ash did fall in Moquegua than in Arequipa (de Silva et al. 2000; Adams et al. 2001). Prevailing winds in this latitude in February are from the southeast along the Peruvian coast and western slopes of the Andes. Ash from the 1600 Huaynaputina eruption has been found in the Quelccaya ice cap, well to the north of both Moquegua and Arequipa, and even as far away as Greenland (see de Silva and Zielinski 1998). Explosive eruptions such as that of Huaynaputina often are directional with regard to the ejecta, as a consequence of prevailing winds and also the location of the volcano's vents. For example, the various ash and tephra falls from the massive Ilopango (El Salvador) eruption in AD 260 lay mostly to the northwest of the volcano (Hart and Steen-McIntyre 1983:Figures 2-7 to 2-10). In the case of Huaynaputina, the ash fell primarily to the west and northwest, thus giving Arequipa the full brunt of the deposit and largely sparing Moquegua (de Silva and Zielinski 1998).

Bodegas Project excavations in several areas in the Osmore drainage revealed deposits of volcanic ash only10–15 cm thick, presumed to be from the 1600 Huaynaputina eruption. At the site of Torata Alta, a probable *reducción* (Colonial resettlement of the indigenous populations) in the valley of one of the Osmore's tributaries, a sixteenth-century church structure appears to have been toppled by the earthquake and a layer of volcanic ash covers the rubble, abutting the base of the foundation walls (Van Buren et al. 1993:138). In the Moquegua Valley itself, excavations at the Locumbilla wine hacienda site revealed ash on the floor of a sixteenth-century structure, and the structure's entrance had been mortared closed with a seal of stone and clay placed above this ash (see Smith 1991:208–218). In general, however, heavy subsequent (i.e., post-1600) occupation and construction in the Moquegua Valley resulted in removal of most of the ash, and undisturbed archaeological evidence of sixteenth-century settlement activity is typically difficult to locate.

Finally, there is also the question of the time needed for agricultural recovery after ashfalls. Recovery is affected by many variables, including degree of slope of the land and the presence of wind and rain to move ash. In the coastal Andes (e.g., Moquegua) there is virtually no regular rainfall to wash ash and sand down stream channels. Although an ashfall usually can be expected to destroy annual crops (cereals, vegetables, pastures), unless it is exceedingly thick (or weighted with later rainfall), it is unlikely to cause permanent damage to fruit or olive trees, or even vines. Thin ash deposits can actually be beneficial, acting as a blanket or mulch to hold in moisture and contributing nutrients to the soils (see, e.g., Schader and Gumerman 1969). Eyewitness accounts suggest that the Huaynaputina ashfall to the north and west of Arequipa (and of the volcano itself) was a meter or more in thickness, but we lack information on the original depth of the ash in Moquegua to the south.

SUMMARY AND CONCLUSIONS

Several lines of evidence suggest that Moquegua suffered less from the 1600 Huaynaputina eruption than did Arequipa. Although the Moquegua Valley's grapevines lost their fruits and annual crops must have been destroyed, the heaviest ashfall occurred well to the northwest, away from the town, thus sparing the valley's wine hacienda owners more lasting harm. Regardless of the specific effects in one southern city versus another, however, it is clear from the historical and archaeological records that, overall, the tectonic events that plagued Colonial Peru were frequently disastrous for the wine economy. Most consequences of the region's many volcanic eruptions, earthquakes, and tsunamis were obvious and profound: loss of life, collapse of buildings, destruction of irrigation canals, death of livestock, and disruption of agricultural patterns. Sometimes the physical damage caused by the tremors was also followed by disease and pestilence (e.g., after the 1715 quake).

These natural disasters had far-reaching repercussions in the social, economic, and political fabric of the colony. One area of impact was in religious life: The citizens of southern Peruvian cities adopted patron saints against earthquakes, and chapels and religious processions were increasingly dedicated to these saints in the hope of protection from disaster. For example, the Arequipa cabildo very early adopted Santa Marta as a patroness against earthquakes, perhaps as a preemptive action, as they noted that the region is prone to earthquakes. In 1555 they noted that since the saint was adopted, there had been no tremors (http://www.igp.gob.pe/cns/reportes/terrem_testig/terremot_areq_1555.htm).

Santa Marta was not entirely efficacious, however, and the cabildo adopted San Genaro (San Januario) as a new patron against earthquakes after the 1600 eruption (e.g., Barriga 1951:145–147, 152, 153). San Genaro, bishop of Benevento in Naples, Italy, in the early fourth century AD, became the intercessor and protector of the citizenry against the eruptions of Mount Vesuvius: "each year a miracle is performed with his holy blood" and as a result "to this day there have been no more such disasters" (Barriga 1951:145; my translation). Also in Arequipa a chapel was built at the edge of the city, and each year two processions and masses were to be celebrated, one on San Genaro's day (September 19) and one on the anniversary of Huaynaputina's eruption (February 19). By 1601 or perhaps even half a century earlier, Moquegua had adopted Santa Catalina de Alejandría as a patroness against earthquakes. After the 1715 temblor, Moquegua adopted another protectress, Nuestra Señora de Loreto (Kuon Cabello 1981:136).

Another consequence involves relations with the dwindling populations of native Andean peoples in the region. These groups were usually called in from the surrounding countryside to rebuild the cities and canals and contribute to resumption of agricultural and trade activities. Such forced labor pools were organized after the 1582 earthquake (Barriga 1951:10, 32, 35, 37), following the 1600 Huaynaputina eruption and earthquake

(Barriga 1951:84, 85, 87), after the 1604 earthquake (although the still struggling city admitted there was no money to pay them; Barriga 1951:196, 213), and again after the 1687 earthquake, at which time their labor was directed toward rebuilding the cathedral rather than wealthy landowners' homes (Barriga 1951:249). It was frequently noted in cabildo records that the summoned Andeans had fled their home communities (e.g., Barriga 1951:91, 206), although it is not clear whether they left because their homes were destroyed or to avoid the forced labor.

In the short term, one significant economic response to the Huaynaputina eruption was that some of Moquegua's haciendas increased their emphasis on sugarcane. The logic for this is not difficult to comprehend: if deposits of volcanic ash demolished Moquegua's croplands, vineyards might need to be replanted, and new vineyards are usually not profitable for wine making for four to six years. Cane, by contrast, not only could be quickly harvested and turned to profit, but it was a logical alternative in the current market, as sugar was in great demand in the mining communities of Upper Peru (Lynch 1981:236–237).

Another consequence was more far-reaching: The 1600 Huaynaputina disaster has been implicated as a major force in shaping the succeeding course of the Peruvian wine industry. By the end of the sixteenth century, the Peruvian wine boom had ended, the wine market was glutted, and prices were plummeting. It was at this point that Huaynaputina's eruption occurred, which, as noted, decimated production in the valleys surrounding Arequipa. Production fell from 200,000 botijas in 1600 (from the 1599 harvest) to 10,000 in 1601 (Davies 1984:95; Brown 1986:41). The long-term consequence of the early seventeenth-century earthquakes and eruption contributed to the creation of two separate spheres of Colonial wine commerce in Peru. The wine producers of the far south found themselves unable to compete successfully in the broader and wealthier viceregal exporting networks centered on Lima to the north. For this market, the supply curve was instantly tilted in favor of the wine haciendas of Nasca and Ica lying closer to Lima (Davies 1984:91, 97–98). The wine producers of Moquegua and Arequipa, by contrast, were forced to redirect sales of their products toward regional consumers. In the case of Moquegua, production was primarily transported to the highland towns around Lake Titicaca and the mining regions of Alto Peru. This reorientation proved to be permanent, as Moquegua's wine and brandy production was thereafter geared toward a market in the southern highlands. Arequipa, however, lying farther from the Alto Peru markets than Moquegua and farther from the Cusco market than Nasca/Ica—and more heavily damaged by the ashfalls—moved out of wine and its economy diversified earlier, especially toward wool.

Ultimately, on the basis of existing evidence it is difficult to separate questions of hacendados' responses to the late sixteenth-century wine glut, the mining decline, and other socioeconomic stresses, from their responses to the devastating eruption of Huaynaputina volcano in February 1600. Nonetheless, I believe that their primary response (to one or to all of them) was to diversify: particularly planting more sugarcane, but also perhaps more wheat, alfalfa, and orchard crops, which were already grown in the valley. Clearly vineyards continued to be cultivated, and viticulture itself offered some internal diversification, with associated secondary activities such as manufacture of ceramic containers and provision of transport. Economic diversification would have been a useful strategy for the early Spanish colonists for minimizing risk and maximizing gain not only in the unpredictable and volatile economic climate of the times, but also in what was proving to be equally unpredictable: the harsh physical environment of the Andes.

Acknowledgments

I am forever indebted to Mike Moseley for inviting me to join his field project in Moquegua, and to him and Bob Feldman for pointing me toward the fascinating tinajas abandoned in the ruined wine and brandy haciendas of the valley. The Moquegua Bodegas Project was supported in the field by awards from the National Endowment for the Humanities and the National Geographic Society, and I am grateful for that support. Permission for excavations was granted by the Instituto Nacional de Cultura, Lima, Peru. I would like to acknowledge the assistance of Donna Ruhl in the initial surveys, Greg C. Smith in supervising the excavations at Locumbilla, and Mary Van Buren and Peter T. Bürgi for supervising the Torata Alta excavations. My thanks go to Kendall Brown, Shanaka de Silva, and others for sharing with me their perspectives and their data. Figure 21.1 was drawn by Tom Gatlin.

REFERENCES

Adams, N., S. L. de Silva, S. Self, G. Salas, J. Permenter, and
         S. Schubring
2001   Physical Volcanology of the 1600 AD Eruption of
         Huaynaputina. *Bulletin of Volcanology* 62:493–518.

Barcelli, S. A.
1982   *Breve historia económico-social del Perú. Parte II. De la
         economía autónoma a la dependencia colonial.* Editorial
         Jatunruna, Lima.

Barriga, Victor M.
1951   *Los terremotos en Arequipa, 1582–1868.* Documentos
         de los Archivos de Arequipa y de Sevilla, Biblioteca
         "Arequipa," vol. 7. La Colmena, Arequipa.

Brown, Kendall W.
1986   *Bourbons and Brandy: Imperial Reform in Eighteenth-
         Century Arequipa.* University of New Mexico Press,
         Albuquerque.

Carpio Muñoz, J. G.
1990   La inserción de Arequipa en el desarrollo mundial
         del capitalismo (1867–1919). In *Historia general
         de Arequipa,* edited by M. N. Avendaño, G. G.
         Rodríguez, A. Málaga Medina, E. Quiroz Paz Soldan,
         and J. G. Carpio Muñoz, pp. 489–525. Fundación M.
         J. Bustamante de la Fuente, Arequipa.

Casertano, L.
1963   General Characteristics of Active Andean Volcanoes
         and a Summary of Their Activities during Recent
         Centuries. *Bulletin of the Seismological Society of
         America* 53:1415–1433.

Chabert, F., and L. Dubosc
1905   Estudio sobre el viñedo de Moquegua y su recon-
         stitución. *Boletín del Ministerio de Fomento,* año II,
         9:10–83. Tipografía de "El Lucero," Lima.

Cobo, Bernabé
1890 [1653]   *Historia del nuevo mundo,* vol. 1. Sociedad de
         Bibliófilos Andaluces, Seville, Spain.

Cole, J. A.
1985   *The Potosí Mita, 1573–1700: Compulsory Indian Labor
         in the Andes.* Stanford University Press, Stanford,
         CA.

Cúneo-Vidal, R.
1978   *Diccionario histórico-biográfico del sur del Perú,* vol. XI.
         Gráfica Morsom, Lima.

Davies, Keith A.
1984   *Landowners in Colonial Peru.* University of Texas
         Press, Austin.

deFrance, Susan D.
1993   *Ecological Imperialism in the South-Central Andes:
         Faunal Data from Spanish Colonial Settlements in the*

Moquegua and Torata Valleys. Unpublished doctoral dissertation, University of Florida, Gainesville.

de Silva, Shanaka L., J. Alzueta, and G. Salas

2000 The Socioeconomic Consequences of the 1600 AD Eruption of Huaynaputina. In *Volcanic Hazards and Human Antiquity*, edited by Grant Heiken and Floyd McCoy, pp. 15–24. Special Paper 345 of the Geological Society of America.

de Silva, Shanaka L., and G. A. Zielinski

1998 Global Influence of the A.D. 1600 Eruption of Huaynaputina, Peru. *Nature* 393:455–458.

Documental del Perú

1983 Arequipa (15th ed.). *Enciclopedia nacional básica*, vol. 3. Promotora Editorial IOPPE, Lima.

Dorbath, L., A. Cisternas, and C. Dorbath

1990 Assessment of the Size of Large and Great Historical Earthquakes in Peru. *Bulletin of the Seismological Society of America* 80(3):551–576.

Handler, P., and K. Andsager

1990 Volcanic Aerosols, El Niño, and the Southern Oscillation. *International Journal of Climatology* 10(4):413–424.

Hart, W. J. E., and Virginia Steen-McIntyre

1983 Tierra Blanca Joven Tephra from the AD 260 Eruption of Ilopango Caldera. In *Archaeology and Volcanism in Central America: The Zapotitán Valley of El Salvador*, edited by Payson D. Sheets, pp. 14–34. University of Texas Press, Austin.

Hocquenghem, A.-M., and L. Ortlieb

1992 Historical Records of El Niño Events in Peru (XVI–XVIIth Centuries): The Quinn et al. (1987) Chronology Revisited. In *"Paleo ENSO Records" International Symposium, Extended Abstracts*, edited by L. Ortlieb and J. Machar, pp. 143–149. ORSTON-CONCYTEC, Lima.

Huertas Vallejos, Lorenzo

1988 *Producción de vinos y sus derivados en Ica, siglos XVI y XVII.* Lima.

Kuon Cabello, Luis E.

1981 *Retazos de la historia de Moquegua.* Editorial Abril, Lima.

Lynch, J.

1981 *Spain under the Habsburgs*, vol. 2, *Spain and America, 1598–1700*. 2nd ed. New York University Press, New York.

Marino, Jersy, J. C. Thouret, J. Dávila, E. Juvigné, and M. Moscol

2002 Reconstruction and Aftermath of the Catastrophic AD 1600 Huaynaputina Eruption, South Peru.

Available: http://atlas-conferences.com/cgi-bin/abstract/caiq-31.

Moore, Jerry D.

1991 Cultural Responses to Environmental Catastrophes: Post-El Niño Subsistence on the Prehistoric North Coast of Peru. *Latin American Antiquity* 2(1):27–47.

Moseley, Michael E.

1987 Punctuated Equilibrium: Searching for the Ancient Record of El Niño. *Quarterly Review of Archaeology* 8(3):7–10.

Natt, Wendy

1997 Design Structure Analysis of Tin-Enameled Pottery from Pacific South America. Master's thesis, Department of Anthropology, Southern Illinois University, Carbondale.

ONERN

1976 *Inventario, evaluación y uso de los recursos naturales de la costa cuencas de los ríos Moquegua, Locumba, Sama y Caplina.* Oficina Nacional de Evaluación de Recursos Naturales (ONERN), Lima.

Ortlieb, L.

1995 Eventos El Niño y episodios lluviosos en el desierto de Atacama: El registro de los últimos dos siglos. In *Eaux, glaciers & changements climatiques dans les Andes tropicales*, edited by P. Ribstein et al. *Bulletin de L'Institut Français d'Études Andines* 24(3):519–537. IFEA and ORSTOM, Lima.

Quinn, W. H., V. T. Neal, and S. E. Antuñez de Mayolo

1986 *Preliminary Report on El Niño Occurrences over the Past Four and a Half Centuries. Report to the National Science Foundation.* College of Oceanography, Oregon State University, Corvallis.

Rice, Prudence M.

1994 The Kilns of Moquegua, Peru: Technology, Excavations, and Functions. *Journal of Field Archaeology* 21(2):325–344.

1995 Wine and "Local Catholicism" in Colonial Moquegua, Peru. *Colonial Latin American Historical Review* 4(4):369–404.

1996a Wine and Brandy Production in Late Colonial Moquegua, Peru: A Historical and Archaeological Investigation. *Journal of Interdisciplinary History* 27(3):455–479.

1996b The Archaeology of Wine: The Wine and Brandy Haciendas of Moquegua, Peru. *Journal of Field Archaeology* 23(2):187–204.

1996c Peru's Colonial Wine Industry and Its European Background. *Antiquity* 70:785–800.

1997 Tin-Enameled Ceramics of Moquegua, Peru. In *Approaches to the Historical Archaeology of Mexico, Central and South America*, edited by Janine Gasco, G. Smith, and Patricia Fournier-García, pp. 167–175. Cotsen Institute of Archaeology, University of California, Los Angeles.

1998 The Colonial Wineries of Moquegua. Programa Contisuyo. *Illustrated Bilingual Prehistory of the Department of Moquegua*, edited by Michael E. Moseley and Karen Wise. SPCC, Lima.

Rice, Prudence M., and Greg C. Smith

1989 The Spanish Colonial Wine Industry of Moquegua, Peru. *Historical Archaeology* 23(2):41–49.

Rice, Prudence M., and Sara L. Van Beck

1993 The Spanish Colonial Kiln Tradition of Moquegua, Peru. *Historical Archaeology* 27(4):65–81.

Schader, G. G., and George J. Gumerman

1969 Infrared Scanning Images: An Archaeological Application. *Science* 164:712–713.

Shimada, Izumi, C. B. Schaaf, L. G. Thompson, and E. Mosley-Thompson

1991 Cultural Impacts of Severe Droughts in the Prehistoric Andes: Application of a 1,500-Year Ice Core Precipitation Record. *World Archaeology* 22(3):247–270.

Smith, Greg C.

1991 *Heard It through the Grapevine: Andean and European Contributions to Spanish Colonial Culture and Viticulture in Moquegua, Peru*. Unpublished doctoral dissertation, University of Florida, Gainesville.

1997 Andean and European Contributions to Spanish Colonial Culture and Viticulture in Moquegua, Peru. In *Approaches to the Historical Archaeology of Mexico, Central and South America*, edited by Janine Gasco, Greg Charles Smith, and Patricia Fournier-Garcia, pp. 165–172. Monograph 38. Institute of Archaeology, University of California, Los Angeles.

Thompson, Lonnie G., E. Mosley-Thompson, W. Dansgaard, and P. M. Grootes

1986 The Little Ice Age as Recorded in the Stratigraphy of the Tropical Quelccaya Ice Cap. *Science* 234:361–364.

Van Beck, Sara L.

1991 Spanish Colonial Kilns of Moquegua, Peru. Master's thesis, Department of Anthropology, University of Florida, Gainesville.

Van Buren, Mary, Peter T. Bürgi, and Prudence M. Rice

1993 Torata Alta: A Late Highland Settlement in the Osmore Drainage. In *Domestic Architecture, Ethnicity, and Complementarity in the South-Central Andes*, edited by Mark S. Aldenderfer, pp. 136–146. University of Iowa Press, Iowa City.

Vázquez de Espinosa, A.

1948 [ca. 1629] *Compendio y descripción de las indias occidentales*, translated by C. U. Clark. Miscellaneous Collections, vol. 108. Smithsonian Institution, Washington, DC.

Walker, D. A.

1995 More Evidence Indicates Link between El Niños and Seismicity. *Transactions of the American Geophysical Union* 74(4):33.

Wallerstein, Immanuel

1980 *The Modern World-System II. Mercantilism and the Consolidation of the European World-Economy, 1600–1750*. Academic Press, New York.

CHAPTER 22

MICHAEL E. MOSELEY

THE YEARS 1941–1985

JAMES B. RICHARDSON III

MUCH OF THE WORK reported in this book would not have been possible without the theoretical orientation that Michael Edward Moseley brought to interpreting the archaeological record and the infrastructure he developed to undertake large multidisciplinary projects in Peru. My purpose here is not to discuss the significance of the findings presented in the various chapters but to emphasize that if Mike had not turned his attention to the central Andes, our understanding of Andean cultural trajectories would be much different today.

I focus not only on what led Mike to spend his professional career in the Andes but also on the stimuli or "push" factors that prompted him to develop his maritime approach to the interpretation of the rise of complex society in Peru and the multidisciplinary approach he has championed in understanding how Andean societies interacted with their ever-changing landscape. In assessing professional accomplishments over a lifetime, it is apparent that no matter how goal-oriented a person may be, serendipity, unforeseen opportunities, good research design, digging in the right place, and luck play a large role in shaping the career path. Mike set in motion a sea change in approaches to prehistoric Peruvian archaeology, and the means by which he did so show passion and preparation, leavened by serendipity. This chapter looks at the story of his engagement with the discipline over many years.

THE ARCHAEOLOGY HOOK

Mike was born in 1941 in Dayton, Ohio, the only son of Harry and Peggy Moseley. Since his father was a U.S. Army Air Corps medical officer, Mike had the opportunity to experience other cultures at an early age. In 1947 he and his mother were among the first dependents to be sent to Germany after the war. He remembers well his trip on a hospital ship for two weeks across the stormy North Atlantic, where he "puked [his] guts out." This was Mike's first memorable experience with the impact of climate on humans.

Like many archaeologists, Mike became intrigued at a young age by the fact that fossils and arrowheads were lying around to be picked up and studied. This led him, beginning in 1955, to direct or participate in eight archaeological projects before he went to college. Upon the family's return from Germany he lived in Redlands, California, and he became associated with the San Bernardino County Museum. His first experience, when he was thirteen, was directing an expedition to the arid Morongo Valley with a crew of one (Figure 22.1). In reporting on this expedition, the Redlands newspaper said, "Two Redlands Jr. high school students have discovered an interesting hobby of collecting Indian artifacts and are contributing to the collection of the San Bernardino County Museum." Of this experience at El Grieta Cave, Mike observed in his first publication

(Moseley 1955:22), "So once again the little site in the Morongo Valley has contributed a better understanding of the peoples who once lived in and loved the desert which is so much a part of southern California today." He included a description of the geology of the cave area and commented on the arid environment in which the cave was located. This early attention to environment foreshadowed his later professional interests in adaptation to the land, which has made him the leader in the field of interpreting interrelations between humans and their environment. His participation at age sixteen in the Glen Canyon archaeological salvage project in Arizona, where the crews ran the rapids in temperatures above 115° Fahrenheit, instilled in him a further appreciation of the geological context of the sites they were investigating (Figure 22.2) (Nuzzo 2006:4805).[1]

UNIVERSITY TRAINING: REDLANDS THROUGH HARVARD

At age nineteen Mike entered the University of Redlands in California, a strict Baptist university, and stayed for two years, majoring in geology (Figure 22.3). Redlands required compulsory chapel attendance, adding academic credits for missing chapel from those needed to graduate. Needless to say Mike missed chapel frequently. Mike wanted to go to a major university with a strong archaeology program, and learned that he could transfer his two years of credits at Redlands to the University of California, Berkeley. After transferring, he majored in anthropology with a minor in geology. Even at this early stage in his career, he realized that geology could be an asset in his interpretation of the archaeological record.

Finds Interesting Indian Relics

YOUNG ARCHEOLOGIST — Mike Moseley, 13, examines specimen of lizard hooks found in the Morongo Valley where they were used by the Indians a century ago. He is turning them over to the San Bernardino County Historical Society at its meeting in the Asistencia tomorrow.

Two Jr. High Students Discover Indian Artifacts

Figure 22.1. Mike at age thirteen, holding lizard hooks from his work at El Grieta Cave, Morongo Valley, California. (Courtesy of Michael E. Moseley.)

Figure 22.2. Mike at sixteen, leaning on a shovel in the Verde Valley, Arizona. (Courtesy of Michael E. Moseley.)

Figure 22.3. Mike using a plane table at a site in the San Bernardino Mountains, California, when he was a sophomore at the University of Redlands. (Courtesy of Michael E. Moseley.)

Mike's adviser at Berkeley, J. Desmond Clark, sent him to work with F. Clark Howell in Spain at Ambrona in 1963 after he graduated. On that same field crew were Richard Klein, Tom Lynch, and Craig Morris. Clark was also instrumental in Mike's going to Harvard University for graduate study. He considered working either in Africa or South America, but after learning that few students working with Hallam Movius had graduated, he chose South America, with Gordon Willey as his adviser.

At Harvard, Mike took Willey's Maya seminar and wrote a paper on the Maya collapse, which Willey said was not creative enough and gave him a B. In the next seminar, in 1964, Mike decided to shake Willey up by writing a cutting-edge paper on the rise of Peruvian civilization, expressing the theory that the economy was based not on agriculture but on marine resources. In this seventy-page paper, titled "Early Subsistence and Settlement Patterns on the Peruvian Coast," Mike compared and contrasted the Late Preceramic with the Initial period and the Early Horizon. He wrote, "Thus, for the Base (Late Preceramic) societies the overall settlement pattern was one of sedentary communities based upon the exploitation of marine resources. Agriculture entered only in a secondary position" (Moseley 1964:55). This position is now known as the Maritime Foundations of Andean Civilization hypothesis, often abbreviated as MFAC. In the acknowledgments of the third draft of the paper he thanked Edward P. Lanning, Thomas C. Patterson, and John H. Rowe for reading and commenting on it.

He had sent the paper out for review, with a submission to *Ñawpa Pacha* in mind, but John Rowe indicated the data were too scant, making the paper unsuitable for his journal. Willey, however, lauded the paper. This was the first example, among Mike's many key papers, of his "thinking out of the box," in this case by proposing a new, innovative, and at the time a radical theory on the origins of Peruvian civilization. In 1965 he did gain experience in the excavation of coastal shell middens, when he joined Frank Schambach, a fellow Harvard graduate student, and Jim Tuck in the excavations of the Cunningham site on Martha's Vineyard, directed by William A. Ritchie, State Archaeologist of New York (Ritchie 1969:88).

Mike's desire to work in South America came to pass in 1964 when Willey asked Warwick Bray to include Mike in his survey and excavations in the Cauca Valley, Colombia (Bray and Moseley 1971). Willey supported Mike with his Bowditch Chair research funds. On the basis of his Colombian experience, he finalized plans to conduct his dissertation research at the monumental site of San Agustín, with the support of Gerardo Reichel-Dolmatoff. His plans changed when the level of banditry made the San Agustín region too dangerous. Fortunately, Thomas C. Patterson had just taken a position in anthropology at Harvard and provided Mike with an "unforeseen opportunity to work on early coastal sites" in Peru (Moseley 1975:5). Mike said, "I had no intent of pursuing the topic further" (1975:4), but he resurrected his Willey seminar paper and used it as the basis of his National Science Foundation Doctoral Dissertation Grant and a fellowship from the Doherty Foundation. My own case of serendipity occurred one day in 1964 when I was walking down the corridor of Davenport Hall of the University of Illinois. Don Lathrap called out to me: "Hey, Jim, do you want to go to Peru?" At that time I was intending to work in the northeastern United States, but fate drew me to a career in the Andes, just as it had for Mike.

Mike ended up spending fifteen months in 1966–67 excavating sites in the Ancón region where both Ed Lanning and Tom Patterson had also worked (Moseley 1968a, b; Patterson and Moseley 1968). Once, while standing on the ninth-floor balcony of his apartment building in Ancón, Mike noticed fishermen frantically going out to sea and people running inland, and soon he understood why: an earthquake had occurred, and the resulting tsunami hit Ancón and flooded the ground floor of the building and the elevator shaft. Here was another key moment for Mike, showing him the power and significance of natural catastrophes.

Mike completed his doctorate in record time, and in that same year, 1968, he was offered a position in the Department of Anthropology at Harvard (Moseley 1968b).

FROM THE PRECERAMIC TO CITIES

Newly installed in his Harvard office, he spent one of the few summers when he wasn't in the field writing an NSF proposal to investigate the large urban center of Chan Chan. The impetus for turning his attention away from the Preceramic to one of the largest prehispanic urban centers in the Western Hemisphere was that "urbanism was hot in anthropology and I jumped on the urban bandwagon." Of course, the earlier bandwagon of settlement pattern studies, founded by Willey through the Virú Valley Project (Willey 1953, 1956), was now part and parcel of mainline archaeological research. But no one had mapped a major city in the Americas until the Teotihuacan Mapping Project, directed by René Millon between 1962 and 1967. This research, covering a 20-km² urban area, not only addressed the chronology of its development through time but provided a study on how the city was organized (Millon 1992).

Supported by the NSF and other funding sources, the five-year (1969–74) Chan Chan-Moche Valley Project, co-directed with Carol J. Mackey, was the largest Peruvian program of research since the Virú Valley

Figure 22.4. Mike at Cerro Sechín, Casma Valley, in the early 1970s. (Photograph by Patricia Essenpreis.)

Figure 22.5. Mike near Cerro Blanco, Moche Valley, in 1973. (Photograph by James B. Richardson III.)

Project. In those years one could receive funding for archaeological projects without much prior investigation; indeed, Mike spent only two hours at Chan Chan while he was conducting his dissertation research.

Not only was Chan Chan mapped, but also the lower Moche Valley was surveyed to place Chan Chan within its rural support base (Moseley and Day 1982; Moseley and Cordy-Collins 1990) (Figures 22.4, 22.5). In addition, a vigorous program of excavations was undertaken that provided numerous undergraduate and graduate students from Harvard and other colleges and universities the opportunity to pursue research for their bachelor's, master's, and doctoral degrees. The students were supported either through funding from the Chan Chan project or from their own grants, with the project acting as the coordinating organization. Many of the Harvard students he advised in the Chan Chan project are working in the Andes today or elsewhere, archaeologists such as Garth Bawden, Geoffrey W. Conrad, Robert A. Feldman, Kent C. Day, Richard W. Keatinge, Alan L. Kolata, Paul P. Ossa, Theresa Lange Topic, John R. Topic, and Alexandra M. Ulana Klymyshyn.

During the Chan Chan project, Mike did not forsake his Preceramic roots. He continued to tussle with the MFAC hypothesis, and in 1971, on a tour of coastal sites with Gordon Willey, they restudied Áspero and determined that it was a Preceramic temple center, not a Ceramic period site (Moseley and Willey 1973). As a result of the new interpretation of the significance of Áspero, Mike's student Bob Feldman excavated at Áspero in 1973 and 1974 (Feldman 1982). This rekindled Mike's interest in revisiting his Willey seminar paper and dissertation, which resulted in the publication of *The Maritime Foundations of Andean Civilization* in 1975. He noted, "I must stress it took me a decade to gradually shake traditional archaeological preconceptions and come to grips with the blatant implications of the data," that "the earliest coastal villages were based on marine resources" (Moseley 1975:4).

In 1970, when the horrific 7.8 Richter magnitude earthquake hit the north coast, Mike was at Quirihuac Shelter, a Paiján site in the upper Moche Valley, with Paul Ossa and Claude Chauchat. As boulders were rolling around, Mike raced to his motorcycle, which had tipped over and was spilling gas, to ride into Trujillo to see how the laboratory had fared. On the way he had to detour around crevasses in the road and ford streams next to collapsed bridges. It is not surprising that this event further stimulated him to conduct a study of the landscape that Chan Chan, its rural settlements, and

their massive irrigation systems were embedded in. It is with the Chan Chan project that he began to develop his long-term research on the impact of natural catastrophes on prehispanic societies in the Andes.

THINGS THAT GO BUMP IN THE NIGHT

Mike moved to the Field Museum of Natural History, Chicago, in 1973, and in 1976 he began the four-year Programa Riego Antiguo in the Moche Valley. This was also the period that he changed his authorship from M. Edward Moseley to Michael E. Moseley (Mike switched from Mike to Michael Edward and then to M. Edward, before settling on Michael E.). I asked him about this, and he said, "M. Edward Moseley sounded too erudite and had a patrician ring to it, but I am really a cowboy at heart, so the change reflects my fun-loving personality." The establishment of the Programa Riego Antiguo was in response to being a runner-up for Senator William Proxmire's "Golden Fleece" award, given for federal grants for projects that the senator considered had no redeeming value—in this case, studying "the world's biggest mud city"(Nuzzo 2006:4806). This energized Mike to show the political establishment that archaeology is relevant to modern problems. Focusing on Moche and Chimu irrigation systems, he delved into why so much irrigated land had been abandoned in prehispanic times. Was this the consequence of political or social upheavals, or was it due to natural catastrophes that so affect the lives of Peruvians today? Many of his Chan Chan crew also participated in this project. Charles Ortloff, a fluid dynamics expert, also joined the team.

Programa Riego Antiguo launched Mike into yet another research venue, integrating climate change and natural catastrophes into the explanation of abrupt cultural change, so evident in the archaeological record of the Andes. Here, he and his colleagues looked at multiple natural catastrophes, tectonics, El Niño floods, droughts, and dune field migration and their impact on Moche Valley societies through time (Moseley 1978a, 1983a, b; Nials et al. 1979; Moseley and Deeds 1982; Moseley et al. 1983). This focus included his *American Anthropologist* article, "The Good Old Days Were Better: Agrarian Collapse and Tectonics," which, once and for all, demonstrated to a wide audience that landscape alteration through natural processes could not be ignored in interpreting Andean cultural development.

As we know, Mike does not shy away from debates. He, in fact, relishes them, for they prompt additional research by scholars skeptical of his interpretations and those of his collaborators, providing new data that they can use in support of their original conclusions. A case in point is how can irrigation water flow uphill? Thus began the great Chimu Chicama-Moche inter-valley canal debate. Here Mike's team used tectonics in developing an explanation for the tilting of the canal that made the canal inoperable (Ortloff et al. 1982). Their detractors stressed that the canal was abandoned because the Chimu engineers were not skilled enough to undertake such a mammoth construction project and thus were not able to get the canal bed at the right slope to carry water (Pozorski and Pozorski 1982; Farrington 1983). In their rebuttal, Mike and his collaborators provided further data and reaffirmed their conclusion that tectonics, not Chimu engineers, were responsible for the canal's inability to function (Ortloff et al. 1983).

THE SHELL GAME

At the behest of Mike, in 1980 I organized a small team of geologists from the University of Pittsburgh's Geology Department to do a "quick and dirty" research trip in the north coast area to look at Holocene beach ridges and tectonic features north to Talara (Figure 22.6). When geologist Jack Donahue (later the founding editor of *Geoarchaeology*), invertebrate pale-ontologist Bud Rollins, and I arrived in Huanchaco, Mike introduced us to Dan Sandweiss, then a graduate student from Cornell University, who was volunteering with Mike. Mike sent him to the Santa River beach ridges, where he met David Wilson, who mentioned to him there were Preceramic sites along the paleoshore-line. Mike said that Bud and I should go with Dan to Chimbote to see the "funny" shells that Dan had found and that he and Jack would look for tectonic faults interdicting archaeological sites in the Moche Valley. It turned out that Dan was right—these *were* funny shells, and he had recognized them as a warm-water species fronting a cold-water coast, a phenomenon I had dis-covered at the Siches site in 1965. This recognition of warm-water species was certainly a defining moment in Dan's career and just another example of Mike's taking on students and giving them a problem and sending them off to do the research.

Out of this brief investigation came the origins of the El Niño hypothesis and further research on El Niño by me, Dan, and our collaborators (Sandweiss et al. 1983,

Figure 22.6. Left to right, Alfredo Narváez, Michael E. Moseley, Harold B. Rollins, and Jack Donahue at a restaurant near Sullana in 1980. (Photograph by James B. Richardson III.)

1996; Rollins et al. 1986; Richardson and Sandweiss 2008). If Mike had not taken Dan under his wing, this El Niño research would never have seen the light of day, and certainly my research on climate change would have been a shadow of what it became through my collaboration with Dan.

THE LAND OF THE SOUTHWESTERN QUARTER

After the end of the Programa Riego Antiguo, Mike had a new project drop in his lap. In 1980 he received a call at the Field Museum from Robert Pritzker, an owner of the Marmon Corporation, a shareholder in the Southern Peru Copper Corporation. Pritzker asked Mike to come to Ilo to set up a project. When Mike learned that Pritzker was willing to fund the project, he jumped at the chance, and in 1981 he founded Programa Contisuyo, named after the southwestern quarter of the Inca Empire. Programa Contisuyo was designed as an umbrella organization for exploring cultural development in the Moquegua Valley, with the Southern Peru Copper Corporation supplying some funding, logistical support, and housing for a multitude of researchers, many of them former Chan Chan and Programa Riego Antiguo crew members. Many contributors to this book have worked through the Contisuyo program. Like Mike's previous two megaprojects, Programa Contisuyo involved Peruvian archaeologists and students at all levels of the administration and research. This inclusivity has always been a hallmark of Mike's and has brought Peruvian and North American researchers and students together to work on a multifaceted research agenda. Many researchers brought their own funding, and their own students as well. Many of these students continued on to complete their degrees, working on an archaeological problem under the auspices of Contisuyo, including one of the editors of this volume.[2]

As a case in point, in 1982 I received a call from Mike urging me to come to Ilo to investigate the Ring Site. I asked him what the accommodations were like, since I was used to the International Petroleum Company compound in Talara, with its bar and swimming pool, not to mention a beach. Mike assured me that I would be treated as well or better, so off I went. I put together funding, and in 1983 Dan Sandweiss, Bob Feldman, and I did a small exploratory cut in this heavily damaged shell ring, which at the time turned out to have the earliest date for a coastal site in the Americas. We returned

in 1985 and 1987 with larger crews that included geologists (Sandweiss et al. 1989).

Many who have worked or are working today in the Moquegua Valley can cite similar experiences with Mike, who invited their involvement in Programa Contisuyo (known since 1991 as Asociación Contisuyo). Through the program, this region of southern Peru from the coast through the Andes has gone from being *tierra desconocida* to one of the best-studied regions in Peru.

Early in the program, Mike turned his attention to two projects, most notably his continuing research on agrarian collapse, here reflected in the contraction of arable land at spring-fed irrigation systems, such as at Carrizal, due to recurrent El Niño events and ongoing hydrological retrenchment (Clements and Moseley 1989, 1991). His other project was with Bob Feldman on the investigation of the Wari center on top of Cerro Baúl, or the "Masada of the Andes," as Mike referred

Figure 22.7. Mike at Cerro Baúl in 1983. (Photograph by James B. Richardson III.)

to it then (Figure 22.7; Feldman 1989, Moseley et al. 1982). The Wari colonists of the region encountered the Tiwanaku migrants who had come from an empire near Lake Titicaca, migrants who had colonized the region earlier. This encounter was not a clash of empires, for each imperial power occupied different ecological zones and had different economic strategies. This is still the only example from the Middle Horizon of well-documented interaction between the two super-powers. Mike has a knack for catchy paper titles, but my favorite is "Burning Down the Brewery" (Moseley et al. 2005). I am certain that if Mike had been the Wari leader at Cerro Baúl, he would not have allowed a brewery to be destroyed!

He also brought Andean archaeology into the classroom with his 1978 syntheses of the cultural development in this region in *Ancient Native Americans* (Moseley 1978b). This was followed in 1983 with a revision of that article in *Ancient South Americans*, a widely used text that included articles by two of Mike's former students, Bob Feldman and Alan Kolata (Feldman and Moseley 1983; Kolata 1983; and Moseley 1983c). These papers undoubtedly inspired countless students to turn their attention to Peru. Mike's *Incas and Their Ancestors*,

first published in 1992 and revised in 2001, continues to stand as the best source in print today on the subject.

CONCLUSIONS

Since his days at Harvard, Mike has dedicated his research to two major areas, the maritime foundations of Andean civilization and the impact of natural catastrophes and climate change on cultural development in the Andes. Within eighteen years of first arriving in Peru, Mike's work had altered ways of looking at virtually every aspect of Andean prehistory. And at the eighteen-year mark, Mike moved to the University of Florida, to continue teaching and research.

This chapter ends with the year 1985, which saw publication of a 1,500-year record of El Niño floods and droughts based on ice core samples from the Quelccaya ice cap (Thompson et al. 1985). This paper, along with the extensive oceanographic and land-based research on the 1982–83 El Niño (Figure 22.8), spurred an explosion of investigations into the paleoclimate of the Andes by numerous climate researchers, many in collaboration with archaeologists (e.g., Moseley 1987; Rollins et al.

Figure 22.8. From right to left, Robert A. Feldman, Michael E. Moseley, and James B. Richardson III in 1983 near Ilo. Vegetation from 1982–1983 El Niño. (Photograph by Daniel H. Sandweiss.)

1987; Shimada et al. 1991; Moseley et al. 1992; Van Buren 2001). Geological and oceanographic sciences now had important contributions to make with more precise dating of climate perturbations, new geological techniques, and bigger budgets than archaeologists enjoy. Archaeologists quickly began incorporating paleoclimatic, geological, and oceanographic research into their own research efforts. The quick embrace of new findings and techniques was due in large part to the preconditioning of archaeologists who, working with Mike and a few other like-minded individuals, understood that the cultural realm rests on a very unstable landscape, which in the Andes is subjected to more climatic and natural catastrophes than anywhere else on the planet.

The few others referred to above include Ed Lanning, who in a novel thesis posited that progressive desiccation caused the switch from a terrestrial hunting way of life to a maritime way of life (Lanning 1963; Patterson and Lanning 1964). His hypothesis did not pan out, but at that time there were few climate studies that he could turn to for data support or refutation. Lanning was also the first to propose that the Peru Current had changed during the Late Preceramic, bringing with it increased marine resources that resulted in a maritime way of life. Here Ed was partially right, for it has been demonstrated that the Peru Current system did change (Richardson and Sandweiss 2008). At the same time that Mike was at Ancón, I was in Talara conducting my dissertation research, where I found not only early maritime sites but also Pleistocene tar pits and Holocene beach ridges, which soon led me to consider climate change as a major factor in cultural change, and to continue my research on maritime adaptations (Richardson 1973; 1978; Sandweiss, Keefer, and Richardson 1999). It was at this time that I first met Mike, and ever since 1966 we have shared our mutual interests in Andean climate change and natural disasters, usually over a cold beer or two.

For the last ten years or so, Mike has devoted himself mainly to the study of El Niño and tectonic impacts on Peruvian societies, past and present. Mike brought David Keefer of the U.S. Geological Survey to Ilo in 1994, and in 1996, Keefer joined Susan deFrance and Mike in excavating Quebrada Tacahuay, with its early maritime evidence and a record of El Niño floods (Keefer et al. 1998). Keefer has continued to collaborate with Mike on other south coast projects, bringing his geological expertise to bear on reconstructing past climatic and tectonic events (Keefer et al. 2003).

Mike has now returned to his north coast roots with Keefer, where, with Chris Donnan, they identified a mega-Niño that caused the collapse of Dos Cabezas, a major Moche center in the Jequetepeque Valley (Moseley et al. 2008). Most recently Moseley and his colleagues have identified the largest known Peruvian Holocene beach ridge (called Medio Mundo), stretching over 100 km along the Supe coast in Peru. Their study provides evidence for a cycle of natural disasters, dating to circa 3,800 B.P., that resulted in the abandonment of Late Preceramic sites, such as Aspero and Caral, in a 5 valley area of the central coast (Sandweiss et al. 2009).

The MFAC hypothesis is still at the core of mainstream research into the origins of Andean civilization. First proposed in 1964, the hypothesis met with mounting disbelief that a civilization could develop on anything other than an agricultural economic base. In 1992 Mike revisited the MFAC hypothesis, observing that "the value of the MFAC is simply that it helped open up multilinear perspectives on the development of ancient civilization in the Andes and elsewhere" (Moseley 1992a:34). The recent discoveries at Caral by Ruth Shady thrust Mike back into the debate on the priority of marine versus agricultural resources as the foundation for the rise of Peruvian civilization (Shady et al. 2001). Here Mike joined with his former volunteer Dan Sandweiss to again stress that the data from Caral indicate more of a reliance on marine food than on domesticated plants (Sandweiss and Moseley 2001). The MFAC hypothesis continues to promote discussion, the most recent being that of Haas and Creamer (2006), who support the agricultural side of the debate. In 2006 Mike joined with Ruth Shady to return to Áspero in hopes of providing some of the answers concerning the age, evolution, and subsistence strategies of this earliest Peruvian temple center.

If a single person can alter the course of human events, Mike is a prime candidate for the position. His theoretical and empirical research in the Andes has been recognized by his election to the National Academy of Sciences. Luck and serendipity have also played a role. What if in 1965 there had been no bandits shooting up buses and robbing banks in the San Agustín area, and Tom Patterson had not taken a position at Harvard? Had Mike not been diverted to Peru in 1966, our picture of Andean cultural development might be radically different today. As it stands, Peruvian prehistory studies have benefited greatly from Mike's conducting his leading edge research there, as have the large number of students he advised and included in his projects.

Acknowledgments

I thank Patrick Ryan Williams and Charles Stanish for inviting me to be a discussant at the symposium at the 68th Annual Meeting of the Society for American Archaeology on Foundations of South Highland Civilization: Papers in Honor of Michael E. Moseley. The editors of this book, especially Joyce Marcus, did a marvelous job improving this chapter. I also wish to express my deep appreciation to Mike Moseley for his steadfast friendship and his provocative ideas, which have stimulated me in my own research on climate change over the decades. I also thank Mike for helping me delve into his "ancient" history in the writing of this chapter and providing me with his pithy comments on his career.

NOTES

1. See Moseley 1955, 1958, 1962, 1966 for his early papers and Nuzzo 2006 for his field experiences in the Southwest.

2. See Williams in press or the Contisuyo Web site for more information on the history of the program and current projects (http://bruceowen.com/contisuyo/MuseoE.html).

REFERENCES

Bray, Warwick M., and Michael Edward Moseley
1971   An Archaeological Sequence from the Vicinity of Buga, Colombia. *Ñawpa Pacha* 7–8:85–103.

Clement, Christopher O., and Michael E. Moseley
1989   Agricultural Dynamics in the Andes. In *Ecology, Settlement and History in the Osmore Drainage, Peru*, edited by Don S. Rice, Charles Stanish, and Phillip R. Scarr. BAR International Series 545, Part 2:435–456. British Archaeological Reports, Oxford.
1991   The Spring-Fed Irrigation System of Carrizal, Peru: A Case Study of the Hypothesis of Agrarian Collapse. *Journal of Field Archaeology* 18(4):425–443.

Farrington, Ian S.
1983   The Design and Function of the Intervalley Canal: Comments on a Paper by Ortloff, Moseley, and Feldman. *American Antiquity* 48(2):360–375.

Feldman, Robert A.
1982   Preceramic Corporate Architecture: Evidence for the Development of Non-Egalitarian Social Systems in Peru. In *Early Ceremonial Architecture in the Andes*, edited by Christopher B. Donnan, pp. 71–92.

Dumbarton Oaks Research Library and Collection, Washington, DC.
1989   A Speculative Hypothesis of Wari Southern Expansion. In *The Nature of Wari: A Reappraisal of the Middle Horizon in Peru*, edited by R. Czwarno, F. Meddens, and A. Morgan, pp. 72–97. BAR International Series 525. British Archaeological Reports, Oxford.

Feldman, Robert A., and Michael E. Moseley
1983   The Northern Andes. In *Ancient South Americans*, edited by Jesse D. Jennings, pp. 139–178. W. H. Freeman, San Francisco.

Haas, Jonathan, and Winifred Creamer
2006   Crucible of Andean Civilization: The Peruvian Coast from 3000 to 1800 BC. *Current Anthropology* 47(5):745–776.

Keefer, David K., Michael E. Moseley, and Susan D. deFrance
2003   A 38000 Year Record of Floods and Debris Flows in the Ilo Region of Southern Peru and Its Relation to El Niño Events and Great Earthquakes. *Palaeogeography, Palaeoclimatology, Palaeoecology* 194:41–77.

Keefer, David K., Susan deFrance, Michael E. Moseley; James B. Richardson III, Dennis R. Satterlee, and Amy Day-Lewis
1998   Early Maritime Economy and El Niño Events at Quebrada Tacahuay, Peru. *Science* 281:1833–1835.

Kolata, Alan L.
1983   The South Andes. In *Ancient South Americans*, edited by Jesse D. Jennings, pp. 241–286. W. H. Freeman, San Francisco.

Lanning, Edward P.
1963   A Pre-Agricultural Occupation on the Central Coast of Peru. *American Antiquity* 28:360–371.

Millon, René
1992   Teotihuacan Studies: From 1950 to 1990 and Beyond. In *Art, Ideology and the City of Teotihuacan*, edited by Janet C. Berlo, pp. 339–429. Dumbarton Oaks, Washington, DC.

Moseley, Michael E.
1955   El Grieta. *Quarterly of San Bernardino County Museum Association* 3(2):20–22.
1958   Hidden Valley. *Quarterly of San Bernardino County Museum Association* 5(4):5–13.
1962   Field Work at Guapiabit. *Quarterly of San Bernardino County Museum Association* 9(2):16–29.
1964   Early Subsistence and Settlement Patterns on the Peruvian Coast. Gordon R. Willey seminar paper,

Department of Anthropology, Harvard University, Cambridge, MA.

1966　The Discovery and Definition of Basketmaker 1890 to 1914. *Masterkey* 40(4):140–154.

1968a　Early Peruvian Fishhooks: Their Manufacture and Use. *Masterkey* 42(3):104–111.

1968b　*Changing Subsistence Patterns: Late Preceramic Archaeology of the Central Peruvian Coast*. Unpublished doctoral dissertation, Department of Anthropology, Harvard University, Cambridge, MA.

1975　*The Maritime Foundations of Andean Civilization*. Cummings Publishing Co., Menlo Park, CA.

1978a　An Empirical Approach to Prehistoric Agrarian Collapse: The Case of the Moche Valley, Peru. In *Social and Technological Management in Dry Lands: Past and Present, Indigenous and Imposed*, edited by Nancie L. Gonzalez. AAS Selected Symposium Series 10:9–43. Westview Press, Boulder, CO.

1978b　The Evolution of Andean Civilization. In *Ancient Native Americans*, edited by Jesse D. Jennings, pp. 490–541. W. H. Freeman, San Francisco.

1983a　Patterns of Settlement and Preservation in the Virú and Moche Valleys. In *Prehistoric Settlement Patterns: Essays in Honor of Gordon R. Willey*, edited by Evon Z. Vogt and Richard M. Leventhal, pp. 423–442. University of New Mexico Press, Albuquerque; Peabody Museum of Archaeology and Ethnology, Cambridge, MA

1983b　The Good Old Days Were Better: Agrarian Collapse and Tectonics. *American Anthropologist* 85(4):733–799.

1983c　Central Andean Civilization. In *Ancient South Americans*, edited by Jesse D. Jennings, pp. 179–240. W. H. Freeman, San Francisco.

1987　Punctuated Equilibrium: Searching the Ancient Record for El Niño. *Quarterly Review of Archaeology* 8:7–10.

1992a　Maritime Foundations and Multilinear Evolution: Retrospect and Prospect. *Andean Past* 3:5–42.

1992b　*The Incas and Their Ancestors: The Archaeology of Peru*. Thames and Hudson, London.

2001　*The Incas and Their Ancestors: The Archaeology of Peru*, rev. ed. Thames and Hudson, London.

Moseley, Michael E., and Alana Cordy-Collins (eds.)

1990　*The Northern Dynasties: Kingship and Statecraft in Chimor*. Dumbarton Oaks Research Library and Collection, Washington, DC.

Moseley, Michael E., and Kent C. Day (eds.)

1982　*Chan Chan: Andean Desert City*. School of American Research, Santa Fe; University of New Mexico Press, Albuquerque.

Moseley, Michael E., and Eric Deeds

1982　The Land in Front of Chan Chan: Agrarian Expansion, Reform and Collapse in the Moche Valley. In *Chan Chan: Andean Desert City*, edited by Michael E. Moseley and Kent C. Day, pp. 25–53. School of American Research, Santa Fe; University of New Mexico Press, Albuquerque.

Moseley, M. Edward, and Gordon R. Willey

1973　Aspero, Peru: A Reexamination of the Site and Its Implications. *American Antiquity* 38(4):452–468.

Moseley, Michael E., Christopher Donnan, and David K. Keefer

2008　Convergent Catastrophe and the Demise of Dos Cabezas: Environmental Change and Regime Change in Ancient Peru. In *The Art and Archaeology of the Moche: An Ancient Andean Society on the Peruvian North Coast*, edited by Steve Bourget and Kimberly L. Jones, pp. 81–91. University of Texas Press, Austin.

Moseley, Michael E., Robert A. Feldman, and Alfredo Narváez

1983　Principles of Agrarian Collapse in the Cordillera Negra, Peru. *Annals of Carnegie Museum* 52(13): 299–327.

Moseley, Michael E., Robert A. Feldman, and Irene Pritzker

1982　New Light on Peru's Past. *Field Museum of Natural History Bulletin* 53(1):3–11.

Moseley, Michael E., David Wagner, and James B. Richardson III

1992　Space Shuttle Imagery of Recent Catastrophic Change along the Arid Andean Coast. In *Paleoshorelines and Prehistory: An Investigation of Methods*, edited by L. Johnson and L. Straight, pp. 215–235. CRC Press, Boca Raton, FL.

Moseley, Michael E., Donna J. Nash, Patrick Ryan Williams, Susan D. deFrance, Ana Miranda, and Mario Ruales

2005　Burning Down the Brewery: Establishing and Excavating an Ancient Imperial Colony at Cerro Baúl, Peru. *Proceedings of the National Academy of Sciences* 102(48):17264–17271.

Nials, Fred L., Eric Deeds, Michael E. Moseley, Shelia G. Pozorski, Thomas G. Pozorski, and Robert A. Feldman

1979　El Niño: The Catastrophic Flooding of Coastal Peru. *Field Museum of Natural History Bulletin* Part 1, 50(7) 4–14; Part 2, 50(8):4–10.

Nuzzo, Regina

2006   Profile of Michael E. Moseley. *Proceedings of the National Academy of Sciences* 103(13):4805–4807.

Ortloff, Charles R., Michael E. Moseley, and Robert A. Feldman

1982   Hydraulic Engineering Aspects of the Chimu Chicama-Moche Intervalley Canal. *American Antiquity* 47:572–595.

1983   The Chicama-Moche Intervalley Canal: Social Explanations and Physical Paradigms. *American Antiquity* 48:375–389.

Patterson, Thomas C., and Edward P. Lanning

1964   Changing Settlement Patterns on the Central Coast of Peru. *Ñawpa Pacha* 2:113–123.

Patterson, Thomas C., and Michael Edward Moseley

1968   Late Preceramic and Early Ceramic Cultures of the Central Coast of Peru. *Ñawpa Pacha* 1968: 115–134.

Pozorski, Thomas, and Shelia Pozorski

1982   Reassessing the Chicama-Moche Intervalley Canal: Comments on "Hydraulic Engineering Aspects of the Chimu Chicama-Moche Intervalley Canal." *American Antiquity* 47:851–868.

Richardson, James B. III

1973   The Preceramic Sequence and the Pleistocene and Post-Pleistocene Climate in Northwest Peru. In *Variation in Anthropology: Essays in Honor of John McGregor*, edited by Donald Lathrap and Jody Douglas, pp. 73–89. Illinois Archaeological Survey, Urbana.

1978   Early Man on the North Peruvian Coast, Early Maritime Exploitation and Pleistocene and Holocene Environment. In *Early Man in America from a Circum-Pacific Perspective*, edited by Alan L. Bryan, pp. 274–289. Occasional Paper no. 1, Department of Anthropology, University of Alberta.

Richardson, James B. III, and Daniel H. Sandweiss

2008   Climate Change, El Niño and the Rise of Complex Society on the Peruvian Coast during the Middle Holocene. In *El Niño, Catastrophism, and Culture Change in Ancient America*, edited by Daniel H. Sandweiss and Jeffrey Quilter, pp. 59–75. Monograph Series in Pre-Columbian Studies. Dumbarton Oaks, Washington, DC.

Ritchie, William A.

1969   *The Archaeology of Martha's Vineyard*. Natural History Press, Garden City, NY.

Rollins, Harold B., Daniel H. Sandweiss, Ule Brand, and Judy C. Rollins

1987   Growth Increment and Stable Isotope Analysis of Marine Bivalves: Implications for the Geo-archaeological Record of El Niño. *Geoarchaeology* 2(3):181–187.

Rollins, Harold B., James B. Richardson III, and Daniel H. Sandweiss

1986   The Birth of El Niño: Geoarchaeological Evidence and Interpretations. *Geoarchaeology* 1:3–15.

Sandweiss, Daniel H., and Michael E. Moseley

2001   Amplifying Importance of New Research in Peru. *Science* 294:1651–1652.

Sandweiss, Daniel H., Harold B. Rollins, and James B. Richardson III

1983   Landscape Alteration and Prehistoric Human Occupation on the North Coast of Peru. *Annals of Carnegie Museum* 52:277–298.

Sandweiss, Daniel H., David K. Keefer, and James B. Richardson III

1999   First Americans and the Sea. *Discovering Archaeology, Scientific American* 1(1):59–65.

Sandweiss, Daniel H., James B. Richardson III, Elizabeth J. Reitz, Harold B. Rollins, and Kirk A. Maasch

1996   Geoarchaeological Evidence from Peru for a 5000 Years B.P. Onset of El Niño. *Science* 273: 1531–1533.

Sandweiss, Daniel H., James B. Richardson III, Elizabeth Reitz, Jeffrey T. Hsu, and Robert A. Feldman

1989   Early Maritime Adaptations in the Andes: Preliminary Studies at the Ring Site, Peru. In *Ecology, Settlement and History in the Osmore Drainage, Peru*, edited by Don S. Rice, Charles Stanish, and Phillip R. Scarr, pp. 35–84. BAR International Series 545. British Archaeological Reports, Oxford.

Sandweiss, Daniel H., Ruth Shady Solís, Michael E. Moseley, David K. Keefer, and Charles O. Ortloff

2009   Environmental Change and Economic Development in Coastal Peru between 5,800 and 3,600 years ago. *Proceedings of the National Academy of Sciences* 106(5):1359–1363.

Shimada, Izumi, C.B. Schaaf, Lonnie G. Thompson, and Ellen Mosley-Thompson

1991   Cultural Impacts of Severe Droughts in the Prehistoric Andes: Applications of a 1,500-year Ice Core Precipitation Record. *World Archaeology* 22(2):247–270.

Shady Solís, Ruth, Jonathan Haas, and Winifred Creamer

2001   Dating Caral, a Preceramic Site in the Supe Valley on the Central Coast of Peru. *Science* 192:723–726.

Thompson, Lonnie G., Ellen Mosley-Thompson, J. F. Bolzan, and Bruce R. Koci

1985   El Niño-Southern Oscillation Events Recorded in the Stratigraphy of the Tropical Quelccaya Ice Cap. *Science* 203:1240–1243.

Van Buren, Mary

2001   The Archaeology of El Niño Events and Other Natural Disasters. *Journal of Archaeological Method and Theory* 8(2):129–149.

Willey, Gordon R.

1953   *Prehistoric Settlement Patterns in the Virú Valley, Peru*. Bureau of American Ethnology, Bulletin 155. Smithsonian Institution, Washington, DC.

Willey, Gordon R. (ed.)

1956   *Prehistoric Settlement Patterns in the New World*. Viking Fund Publications, no. 23. Wenner-Gren Foundation for Anthropological Research, New York.

Williams, Patrick Ryan

In press   *Ancient Moquegua: Water Politics and Social Formations in the Andean Past*. Cotsen Institute of Archaeology, University of California, Los Angeles.

AUTHORS

Mark S. Aldenderfer
University of Arizona

Garth Bawden
University of New Mexico

Jane E. Buikstra
Arizona State University

Alana Cordy-Collins
University of San Diego

R. Alan Covey
Southern Methodist University

Susan D. deFrance
University of Florida

Christopher Donnan
University of California, Los Angeles

Robert A. Feldman
Independent Scholar

Paul S. Goldstein
University of California, San Diego

María Cecilia Lozada
University of Chicago

Carol Mackey
California State University, Northridge

Joyce Marcus
University of Michigan

Donna J. Nash
Field Museum of Natural History, Chicago

Bruce D. Owen
Sonoma State University

Gordon Rakita
University of North Florida

Richard Reycraft
University of New Mexico

Prudence M. Rice
Southern Illinois University

James B. Richardson III
Carnegie Museum of Natural History
University of Pittsburgh

Daniel H. Sandweiss
University of Maine

Ruth Shady Solís
Universidad Nacional Mayor de San Marcos, Peru

Charles Stanish
University of California, Los Angeles

Richard C. Sutter
Indiana University at Fort Wayne

John R. Topic
Trent University, Peterborough, Ontario

Theresa Lange Topic
Brescia University College at the University of
Western Ontario, London, Ontario

Jane C. Wheeler
CONOPA, Lima, Peru

Patrick Ryan Williams
Field Museum of Natural History, Chicago

INDEX